Praise for *The Sec*

"This is a beautifully written book that introduces and explores the intricacies of the I Ching. Beginning with an exploration of its philosophy and principles, the authors explain how they arise in traditional Eastern medicine and their connections with mathematics, physics, biology, psychology, and virtually every aspect of our existence. If you are interested in understanding an Eastern view of our lives, then this is the book for you."

—**Sheldon Kamienny**, Professor Emeritus of Mathematics
at the University of Southern California

"The authors delve into the complexities of the I Ching, unraveling its profound symbols and principles. The practical applications and real-life examples further enhance readers' understanding and enable the integration of ancient wisdom into our daily experiences. Drawing from diverse fields such as philosophy, mathematics, physics, and psychology, the book demonstrates how these principles resonate with various aspects of our lives, from science and nature to human relationships and personal growth. Prepare to embark on a journey of self-discovery and connection to the universe as you unlock the secrets of the Book of Changes."

—**Professor Sanghoon Lee, MD, PhD, MPH, MBA**, Kyung Hee University College
of Korean Medicine, Director of the International Education Institute of
Korean Medicine, and Vice Director of the WHO Collaborating Centre
at the East-West Medical Research Institute

"In lucid and insightful writing, and by providing many everyday references as well as scientific examples, the authors make the profound principles of I Ching accessible to laypeople, enabling them to understand and connect with its wisdom. The book successfully integrates Eastern and Western thinking by utilizing the principles and wisdom of I Ching. The principles of I Ching underlie all worldly phenomena and, therefore, also underlie traditional Sasang medicine, including pulse diagnosis, acupuncture, herbal treatment, and dietary recommendations for the four main body types. This brilliant and comprehensive treatise is an indispensable tool for deepening our understanding of our life experience."

—**Kenneth L. Subotnik, PhD**, Adjunct Professor, Jane and Terry Semel Institute of
Neuroscience & Human Behavior at UCLA

THE
SECRETS
OF THE
I CHING

ANCIENT WISDOM AND NEW SCIENCE

DR. DAVID S. LEE, MD, OMD, PhD
and
JOSEPH K. KIM, LAc., OMD, PhD

ST. MARTIN'S
ESSENTIALS
NEW YORK

Published in the United States by St. Martin's Essentials, an imprint of St. Martin's Publishing Group

THE SECRETS OF THE I CHING. Copyright © 2023 by David S. Lee and Joseph K. Kim. All rights reserved. Printed in the United States of America. For information, address St. Martin's Publishing Group, 120 Broadway, New York, NY 10271.

www.stmartins.com

Designed by Steven Seighman

The Library of Congress Cataloging-in-Publication Data is available upon request.

ISBN 978-1-250-89647-6 (trade paperback)
ISBN 978-1-250-89648-3 (ebook)

Our books may be purchased in bulk for promotional, educational, or business use. Please contact your local bookseller or the Macmillan Corporate and Premium Sales Department at 1-800-221-7945, extension 5442, or by email at MacmillanSpecialMarkets@macmillan.com.

Originally published in Korea by Inner World Publishing.

First U.S. Edition 2023

10 9 8 7 6 5 4 3 2 1

Contents

Introduction

The complexities of the I Ching begin in the name. Together, the words "I" and "Ching" translate as the "Book of Changes." However, when the terms are studied in depth, we gain a deeper understanding of the meaning of I Ching. "I" (易) implies change. It is made up of two characters: the sun (日) and the moon (月), and like the celestial bodies, "I" implies clarity and change. It means clarity because of the purity and brilliance of the sun and moon. It denotes change because of the transformation of day into night and night into day. Some have said that the word "I" represents a chameleon that changes its color according to its environment. Looking carefully at the character (易), you can see a chameleon's image, which also implies change.

"Ching" (經) intimates strings or threads vertically arranged when weaving cloth. It can also imply the longitudinal lines of a map. The longitude serves as a demarcation of particular regions of the Earth or, by extension, the universe. Though a map is only a rough estimation of a specific area, it indicates our location on Earth or the universe. The I Ching tells of our position in the totality of existence by the same token. By observing the I Ching, we can roughly know the phenomena of nature or the universe. Though there may be many complex theories to explain the forms and wonders of the universe, "Ching" indicates those that connect only the essential principles.

The word "Ching" also implies a road or path. In Chinese, there are three primary characters for the road: Tao (道), Ching (經), and Lu (路). Tao is a big road or path, Ching is a medium-sized road or path, and Lu is a small one. Tao indicates the great road or path that all things in the universe travel. Ching signifies all the paths smaller than Tao but larger than Lu.

According to the I Ching, heaven alludes to the truth (Tao) through symbols or images sent down to earth. We understand the meaning of the vertical lines of the word "Ching" to imply a book that recorded the truth emanating from heaven. "Ching" can also be translated as a bible or holy text. I Ching, therefore, may be translated as the "Bible of Change."

Moreover, "Ching" can be interpreted as "sutra." The Sanskrit word for a holy text, scripture, or bible is "sutra." The English word "suture" stems from the same word. The meaning of "suture" is twofold. In one context, it refers to the material connecting two surfaces, much like the stitches one gets after a severe injury or surgery. Another meaning describes the process of joining separate entities together. Either translation would expand the definition of "Ching" to imply the system or web that is the force binding things together. According to the Eastern view, everything in the universe comprises intimately interconnected patterns, and I Ching's words illuminate this force.

Eastern custom teaches that only a supremely enlightened being or god can write a book called Ching. Regardless of education or expertise, no man or woman can write a Ching or sutra because human beings are limited in their experience and understanding. Only an enlightened being or god has the omniscient perspective necessary to create a sutra. Therefore, the I Ching is considered more sacred than any other book and is regarded as the most critical work in Eastern philosophy.

Any change or modification of the I Ching was a capital crime in the past. The royal court would execute the offender and four genera-

tions of his or her family! The same holds for other Ching, such as the Tao Te Ching, translated as the "Book of Way and Virtue." Though this may seem excessive, it is a good illustration of the importance and purity of the ideas in texts of this nature and the I Ching.

The I Ching is the most profound and challenging to understand among the many Eastern classics. It explains the principles of a changing universe with two symbols: yin (━━ ━━) and yang (━━━━). These two symbols constitute the binary code of the universe. While other classics utilized words, the I Ching used this binary code to express the mysteries of the universe.

The reason for using symbols is that they are more inclusive. The principles of change that apply to all things, even those in remote areas of the universe that are inconceivable to the human mind, cannot be expressed in words. Only in symbolic form can they be represented.

Like a gem buried deep in the ground, the I Ching's meaning is extraordinary, and its acquisition requires significant effort. Because the I Ching is a book about the principles of a changing universe, it was a secret text in the East in ancient times. Only those who recognize the importance of the I Ching and strive to make endless inquiries into its teachings may understand its profound meaning.

Because of the powerful and sacred ways illustrated by the I Ching, enlightened masters did not teach it to people with evil intentions—selfishness, greed, or malice. Misuse of its theories could disrupt the natural order of the universe. The masters were clearly aware of this and took precautions to keep the lessons among those who would use them for self-cultivation and growth rather than harm or destruction. Even today, the most profound truths of the I Ching remain incomprehensible to all but the most cultivated and purified of spirits.

A fairy tale is told in China, called *Journey to the West*,[1] which illustrates the perils of using the powers described in the I Ching. The story tells of a Monkey King who has unlimited superpowers. This monkey, however, is very mischievous. One day a friend of his accidentally drinks some poison and dies. Extremely upset about his friend's death, the Monkey King flies up to heaven and turns back the hands of time to a few moments before his friend's fatal mistake. He then returns to earth and warns the friend not to drink the poison, thus sparing his life.

For this act, the Monkey King was locked up in a prison cell (under a rock) for one thousand years. Then, fortuitously, a Buddhist monk released him on his way to India to receive a Buddhist scripture (sutra). The Monkey King subsequently became his disciple and accompanied him on the long journey involving many mishaps and adventures.

The tale's lesson is that we cannot manipulate the universe's workings for personal gain. While the situation may seem beneficial (in this story, it was the return of the life of the Monkey King's friend), such an action creates chaos in the fabric of the universe. It was this type of event that the masters of the East feared if the I Ching principles unfolded to the masses, especially to the uncultivated.

In the East, the principles of politics, economics, astronomy, and other social and natural sciences all have the yin-yang theory of the I Ching as their foundation. With the introduction of the I Ching into Western society, many people began to study the text. As a result, the ideas encompassed in its pages began to seep into the works of a few eminent Western minds. The following are a few examples:

- Friedrich Hegel, a famous German philosopher, was best known for his dialectical method—thesis, antithesis, and synthesis. His ideas became the foundation for communism. He studied the I Ching under his grandfather, who learned it while serving as a missionary in China. Hegel explicitly states in his autobiography that he got his ideas from the I Ching.
- The great German mathematician and philosopher Gottfried Wilhelm Leibniz created the binary system, the digital foundation of the binary code used by all computers. He did intensive studies on the I Ching. He even wrote a book explaining the parallels between the I Ching and his binary code.
- Albert Einstein is reputed to have studied the I Ching for seven years. His theory of relativity accurately reflects the yin-yang theory's polar nature and mutual transformation, the basis of the I Ching.
- Niels Bohr's theory of complementarity, a pillar of modern quantum physics, also closely

resembles the yin-yang theory or the I Ching. He was so impressed by the I Ching that he put a Tai Chi (or yin-yang) symbol on his coat of arms when he received his knighthood in 1947. Its motto affirms the influence of Eastern philosophy: "Opposites are complementary." He also said, "A great truth is a statement whose opposite is also a great truth."

♦ Carl Jung, the famous psychologist and disciple of Sigmund Freud, is best known for his theories of the archetype and the collective unconscious. He related his concepts to the sixty-four hexagrams of the I Ching. He was so involved in studying the I Ching that he wrote the introduction to Wilhelm's German translation of the I Ching.

Fundamental concepts of I Ching, such as yin and yang, either closely resemble some of the just-mentioned historically noted people's discoveries or directly helped them understand the universe's natural order.

The I Ching is a challenging book to understand for most people. It is equivalent to a college-level textbook. Thus, studying many basic books must precede reading the I Ching. Reading it without taking the proper steps is like presenting an elementary schoolchild with Einstein's theory of relativity to read and understand.

Imagine the I Ching as a calculus book. When a person learns mathematics in school, there is a particular order to study. So a program trying to teach calculus before trigonometry, geometry, algebra, and elementary arithmetic would fail. Likewise, learning the I Ching requires understanding certain fundamental principles, such as Tao, Tai Chi, yin-yang, Sasang, and so forth.

Without the basics, learning the I Ching would be as foolish and futile as studying calculus without knowing how to add or subtract. Moreover, just as knowing the basics of calculus—addition and subtraction—may be applied to many other things besides the study of calculus, we can utilize the understanding of the I Ching basics in many different aspects of our lives.

To fully understand the theories of the I Ching, we must practice the basics and apply them to various situations. The more they can be related to personal experience, the greater the understanding.

Unfortunately, no books currently teach the basics necessary to understand the I Ching. Most books in the United States are little more than translations used for divination. Such a trend is discouraging because the I Ching principles are much more than tools for predicting the future. They explain the changing universe through the expression of symbols rather than the limitation of words.

There are a great variety of philosophical and spiritual ideologies in the West. Although the theories of the I Ching have been integrated into many Western works, the basic concepts are not commonly known. It is, therefore, important for people of the West to initiate themselves in a "primer course" that explains the fundamental notions of the I Ching before undertaking the work itself. This book will help, in such a sense, to simplify the task of understanding the I Ching by applying its theories to various aspects of everyday life: arts, scientific phenomena, human physiology, foods, herbs, and so on. With some effort into studying the concepts defined in this book, the reader will gain insight into the theories of the I Ching and apply this knowledge to social, professional, and daily experiences.

In the East, sutra teaching traditionally begins with reading and rote memorization. Explanations of the writings are typically unavailable, and those that exist are unclear. This lack of clear explanation allows for mistakes and misunderstandings of the meanings of the texts. The student has no choice but to slowly discover the significance of the poetic and enigmatic writings by him- or herself through daily life; the same holds for the I Ching. Words may serve as a guide, but in the end, only experience can truly illuminate its theories.

Despite humanity's remarkable scientific, technological, and social advancement, we are still struggling to answer many of the fundamental questions of our existence. Man has an inherent need to make sense of the universe. Scientific theories attempt to unravel universal uncertainties, successfully discovering and assigning explanations for tangible phenomena. They have not, however, even begun to explore the depths to discover the underlying natural patterns, nor are they equipped to give meaning to things without substance.

The chaos theory acknowledges the changing patterns, but even this recent and advanced theory lacks the tools to give meaning or understanding to their existence. Only the I Ching articulates the answers to these questions by revealing the universal principles that weave through all matter and phenomena.

What You Will Find in This Book

The key to grasping the meaning of the I Ching lies in understanding the interrelatedness of its numbers and symbols. The I Ching is essentially a book about numbers and symbols. Numbers and symbols are universal. Unlike language and words, their meanings are unhindered by time and space. The I Ching utilizes this universality of numbers and symbols to describe all changes in the universe. As outlined in this book, a strong understanding of Eastern principles and concepts is essential for understanding numbers and symbols.

Chapters 1 and 2 describe Tao and Tai Chi, two profoundly essential ideas in studying I Ching. These terms define the universal nature of all things, material and energetic. For many, these concepts are difficult to understand because the nature of what they attempt to portray is elusive. Nevertheless, they are the essential concepts in Eastern philosophy and the I Ching and must be understood. Therefore, throughout chapters 1 and 2, Tao and Tai Chi are presented in their most basic form to be well understood. In addition, scientific and general examples will help relate them to everyday life.

Chapters 3 through 13 introduce two correlative facets of Tao and Tai Chi—the principles of yin and yang, the energetic axes of the universe. These are polar yet complementary forces that affect every aspect of existence. These chapters apply the yin and yang principles to various phenomena in physics, chemistry, sociology, economics, politics, physiology, food, sex, and many other aspects of daily life. These chapters will enable you to apply the theories to your own experiences.

Chapter 14 discusses the trinity principle of the I Ching. This chapter interprets the reason for trinary classifications according to the principles of I Ching. Examples from numerology, the xyz or three-dimensional coordinate system, colors, the human body, DNA, alchemy, and religion elucidate this concept. This chapter also introduces trigrams and hexagrams of I Ching.

Chapter 15 deals with Sasang, the Four Symbols, and Feng Shui, the art of placement that applies Sasang theory to directions. When yin and yang subdivide into four parts, the outcome is Sasang. Feng Shui is the art of arranging all facets of a person's environment to create a harmonious energy flow. There are numerous examples of practical advice for readers to apply to their lives. They include advancing their children's intellect, enhancing their sex lives, improving their business dealings, and learning how to sleep better. Additionally, this chapter outlines the natural patterns of sound, color, orientation, and time, which function according to the Sasang theory.

In chapter 16, humans are classified into four constitutions based on personality, physical characteristics, and frequently occurring illnesses. The chapter also discusses the most effective treatment methods for each body type. This classification is the foundation of Sasang medicine, a form of constitutional medicine created in Korea more than a hundred years ago.

Chapters 17 through 20 discuss another primary theory of Eastern philosophy called the five-element theory. Sasang deals with four elements—wood, fire, metal, and water. In contrast, the five-element system incorporates the earth as the fifth element. Earth is the center that regulates and mediates all changes of the Sasang elements. Yin-yang and five-element theories make up all Eastern philosophy. It is impossible to understand Eastern philosophy without a sufficient understanding of these two theories. These chapters explain the five elements and compare them to the theories of yin-yang and Sasang.

Chapters 21 and 22 discuss the eight trigrams of the I Ching in detail. A trigram is a pattern of three lines, with each line representing yin or yang, symbolizing matter or phenomena on a three-dimensional plane. All events occurring in space and time categorize into three facets. These chapters clarify the individual trigrams' characteristics and their associations with the environment. Furthermore, there is a detailed discussion of Fuxi, or "Earlier Heaven" arrangements of trigrams, and King Wen, or "Later Heaven" arrangements.

The final chapter explains hexagram formations. A hexagram is made by pairing two trigrams, and sixty-four hexagrams explain all matter and phenomena in the universe.

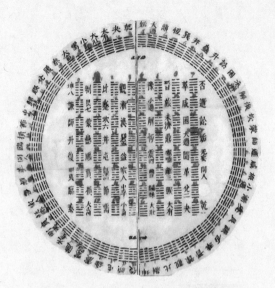

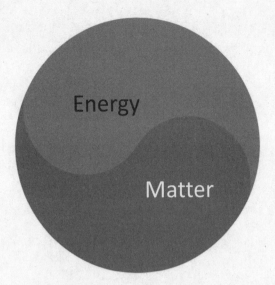

A diagram of 64 I Ching hexagrams sent to Gottfried Wilhelm Leibniz by Joachim Bouvet, a French missionary in China, on April 2, 1703. Leibniz added the Arabic numerals, while Bouvet added the Greek letters.

The Tai Chi Diagram and the Theory of Relativity [E=mc²]. The Tai Chi diagram depicts the very essence of the I Ching, the principles of yin (dark gray) and yang (red). Just as energy transforms into matter and matter into energy, yin and yang constantly transform into one another.

1

Tao

The alternation of yin and yang is called Tao.
—Confucius, I Ching

The Tao that can be called Tao is not the real Tao.
That which can be named is not the genuine name.
—Lao-tzu, Tao Te Ching

道 Tao   德 Virtue

The study of the I Ching begins with the concept of one. One signifies the beginning that is whole and undivided. One can also indicate the end and everything in between. This concept of totality is called Tao, according to the I Ching. The principle of Tao is the foundation of the I Ching and Eastern philosophy. It is the all-encompassing totality and interconnectedness of all things.

Interestingly, number one is used in Korea to translate the word "God." Hananim is the Korean equivalent of the word "God." Hana means "one," and Nim is an honorific title. It translates as "the Supreme One."

Tao, translated as a "way," is the path everything must travel to fulfill its true nature. Tao is the way things are. All differing paths ultimately lead to one pathway called Tao. And the totality of all differing ways is the Tao. According to Eastern philosophical tradition, there is only one path called Tao. Tao is a unique path because it is the source of all phenomena, and all phenomena are but manifestations of Tao.

Tao is of everything; the beginning and

the end; one and all things; the cause and effect; existence and nonexistence; tangible and intangible; concrete and abstract; known and unknown; past, present, and future; space, time, and beyond. Tao is also the guiding principle of all phenomena, yet nothing remains fixed. The only constant in the universe is change. Therefore, the only absolute of Tao is that it is constantly changing.

No matter how small or large, each entity is a manifestation of Tao, as it is complete in and of itself. Macroscopically, we can view the entire universe as a single entity that corresponds to the concept of oneness and Tao. Microscopically, an atom is a single, complete entity corresponding to oneness and Tao. Whether it is the entire universe or a single atom, each is an expression of totality or, in other words, Tao.

Because Tao makes up the totality, it is present everywhere and all the time. Tao is omnipresent and ever present. From the simplest to the most complex entity, Tao is part of all phenomena. But Tao is also the pattern of change and the changing patterns. In short, everything is of the Tao.

Tao is difficult to understand because it is a noun, verb, and adjective. We cannot see, hear, smell, taste, touch, or feel it. Therefore, when we look for Tao, we cannot find it. Because of its elusive nature, it is impossible to describe. As no words can define it, Lao-tzu, the founder of Taoism, wrote, "The Tao that can be called Tao is not the real Tao." By calling it Tao, people hear the word "Tao" and associate it with something other than Tao.

Tao should be easy to grasp because it is

everywhere and part of everything. But we often miss what is right under our noses. In the same way, Tao is elusive because it is so apparent. The following dialogue between Chuang Tzu, the second-leading figure in Taoism next to Lao-tzu, and Master Tong Kuo, a fictional character, illustrates why Tao is so hard to grasp.[1]

Master Tong Kuo asked Chuang Tzu, "Just where is this Tao you are always talking about?"

Chuang Tzu replied, "It's everywhere."

"Come," said Master Tong Kuo, "Can you give me a concrete example?"

"The Tao is in the mole cricket and the ant," Chuang Tzu answered.

"As low as that?" Master Tong Kuo exclaimed.

"The Tao is in the grass and weeds," Chuang Tzu continued.

"But that's even lower!"

"The Tao is in the clay tiles and shards."

"Why is it getting lower and lower?"

"It is in the urine and feces."

Master Tong Kuo was at a loss for words.

"What's the matter?" Chuang Tzu asked with a knowing smile. "Your questions were off the mark from the beginning. You cannot pursue the Tao in any given thing or place. Such is the nature of the great Tao. So when you have Tao in mind, there is no distinction between high or low status. Ants, weeds, clay tiles, and urine and feces are all equal. They all exist because they all follow Tao. Therefore, I say the Tao is everywhere."

Frogs in a Well

If Tao is everywhere, why is it so difficult to realize? Because we live like frogs in a well. We do not and cannot see, hear, taste, feel, and smell beyond the limits of our senses. The human eye can only see the light between the wavelengths of 4,000 to 7,000 angstroms. We cannot see X-rays, Gamma rays, microwaves, or radio waves. Moreover, our ears can only hear sounds between 20 and 20,000 hertz frequencies. Although the sound of the Earth rotating on its axis is said to be enormously loud, we cannot listen to it because its frequency lies beyond our range.

Therefore, our decisions are that of blind men touching an elephant. Microscopes, telescopes, radios, and the like have expanded our sensory fields. Advances in transportation, such as automobiles, airplanes, and rockets, have broadened the scope of our experience. Still, we merely have the experience of traveling to the moon within the observable universe that is ninety-two billion light-years in diameter.

The wavelength of light and the frequency of sound seen and heard by dogs, bees, and snakes differ from those by humans. For these creatures, everything is seen and heard differently than we do. They can detect wavelengths and frequencies that we cannot see or hear. For example, dogs often bark at things that we cannot see, and many animals can sense and feel the coming of earthquakes before their eruptions. Such abilities show that animals can see and listen to other aspects that exist in nature that transcend our narrow perception. If animals knew physics and chemistry, they would derive laws that differ from ours and prove them through experiments. Aliens will see different sounds and lights than we do and apply other laws of physics and chemistry, even though we live in the same universe.

The limits of our senses are like the wall of the well itself. We think that we know everything, but we forget that we are inside the well and overlook uncharted territories beyond the well.

We constantly discover, experiment, prove, and repeat certain laws in natural phenomena. With limited senses, we are only speculating about the true essence of the universe, as if blind men were touching an elephant. Since people are shorter than the elephant, those touching its legs will agree that it is like a pillar. And their findings will become an immutable truth and will be included in textbooks. A blind man climbing a ladder will touch the elephant's head and raise an objection. Other blind men will climb up the ladder to confirm and overturn the shape of the elephant they have known thus far. Discoveries and verifications will eventually reveal the elephant's true nature. However, it would take a long time for the truth to emerge, and Galileo would not have faced the Inquisition.

When will we be able to grasp the reality of the matter we have not seen or heard in the corner of the universe to which we have not yet traveled? This is the reality of the judgment of humans with limited senses. Can we really judge right from wrong without comprehending the whole? We do not know whether or not the correct decision prevailing in our easily accessible world is the wrong judgment prevalent in the world of a moth rushing toward the fire.

We often think we can make decisions for a world we hardly know. We perform and react based on our knowledge, forgetting that many things exist outside our scope of reality. With our limited sense organs, we only see components of Tao but have difficulty seeing the totality.

Although the Tao is everywhere, we are rarely aware of it due to our tunnellike vision. Our tunnel vision obscures our perceptions and perspectives. What we are taught, trained, conditioned, and indoctrinated throughout our lives narrows our views and distracts us from realizing the Tao. For example, in the book *The Little Prince* by Antoine de Saint-Exupéry, the author relates an experience he had as a boy. After seeing a picture of a boa constrictor swallowing an animal, he drew his illustration of a boa constrictor that had eaten an elephant whole. He then took it to many adults and asked them if the image frightened them. They all said they were not afraid and asked why they should be scared by a drawing of a hat. Unfortunately, none of them saw the true essence of the picture due to their limited experiences and perspectives.

In this world, there is no absolute right or wrong. Without the I Ching principle, human judgments of right and wrong have no value. For example, if we consider Earth's history as one whole day (twenty-four hours), humanity would have existed for the time it takes to blink an eye. We live only about one hundred years on Earth, a small planet in a remote corner of the universe that is ninety-two billion light-years in diameter. Thus, we must realize how small we are, and our judgments stem from a narrow perspective. Therefore, our decisions resemble a frog in a well or a moth fluttering into a flame.

There is a saying that a dog of Shu (ancient Chinese state) barks at the sun. The mountains of Shu are high and many, and the sun rises briefly in the sky. The momentary sunrise seems strange to Shu's dog, who barks at it because he thinks it's a thief. This saying describes a person with limited knowledge who talks a lot even though the truth is clear.

There is another reason we cannot see everything in the universe as it is. Our imbalanced emotions impede our understanding of Tao. For example, we experience greed and selfishness. These emotions obscure our vision like dust on a mirror, preventing us from seeing things as they are. Instead, they cause us to selectively see only those things that interest or may benefit us.

Let us say that persons A and B fought. Two people—C and D—were watching it. Let us say C is on A's side, D on B's side, and both are telling the truth. A person who hears C will judge that B is a bad person because he hears only the bad side of B. Likewise, a person who hears D will believe that A is a bad person because he only listens to the bad side of A.

Therefore, an old saying goes that without an impartial mind, one cannot see or hear things as they truly are. The self-limiting perspective will naturally lead to a mistake in judgment. This erroneous judgment determines happiness, an important value in life. Greed and selfishness overshadow and mislead the proper decision needed for true happiness. This mistaken judgment is the origin of all suffering.

The following Eastern anecdote aptly illustrates how our self-limiting view can cause turmoil in life:

There was an old woman with two sons. She cried all the time because of her sons' lots in life. The older son sold umbrellas for a living, while the younger maintained a salt farm. On sunny days, the old lady cried because she worried her older son's umbrella business would be ruined. On rainy days, she wept because she feared her younger son's salt farm would be damaged.

A monk who passed by her one day felt deep sympathy for her. The monk told the older woman to be happy on sunny days because the salt farm will fare well, and to be happy on rainy days since the umbrella business will manage well. So from that day on, the old lady always lived with a cheerful frame of mind.

Leaping Outside of the Well

If our limited perspectives prevent us from realizing the Tao, how do we get past it? How do we see beyond our sight, listen beyond our hearing, and sense beyond our feelings?

We can compare cultivating Tao to wiping a mirror clean. An average person's mirror of the mind is foggy due to greed and a limited standard of judgment. Thus, the Tao does not reflect in the mirror. When the mirror is wiped clean, there is a clear reflection of all things in nature. Only then can Tao be discerned. There are innumerable paths to the Tao; the key is to find the road that encompasses your true nature.

As the Tao is everywhere, it can be realized through any activity, no matter how mundane. For example, a butcher can grasp the Tao if he wholeheartedly devotes himself to his work. By understanding the nature of animals' muscles, ligaments, and bones, a butcher will never need to sharpen his knife. He can cut through the path of least resistance, never dulling or breaking the blade.

A butcher who only trusts in the sharpness of his knife without understanding the Tao will need to sharpen his knife every day. He will cut against the muscles, tendons, and joints. In other words, he will encounter the most resistance because he opposes the natural flow of the universe.

Martial arts, such as tae kwon do (translated as "the way of kicking and punching"), judo ("the way of gentleness"), aikido ("the way of union with the universal energy"), and kendo ("the way of the sword") all end in the suffix "do." "Do" is just another pronunciation of "Tao." It is the same for Eastern cultural arts, such as Dado ("the way/art of the tea ceremony"), Hwado ("the way/art of flower arrangement"), and Seodo ("the way/art of calligraphy").

Although they differ, the ultimate goal of any Eastern art or discipline is the realization of the Tao. But how can flower arranging, fighting, or drinking tea lead one to understand the fundamental principles of the universe?

When we first learn a discipline, we are mere technicians, simply following the necessary steps. Then we transcend this technical knowledge and perform naturally and spontaneously after a while. At this stage, we can completely absorb ourselves in our work. We become "one" with the work or discipline. We can then see a brief glimpse into the Tao. In this state, there is no longer a distinction between an individual and the universe; we become "selfless and egoless." As a result, we discover the potential prevailing in the world and ourselves that we never knew existed. If we continue these experiences, our awareness of the Tao will gradually increase and become "one" with the Tao.

Once we focus our energies on perfecting an art form or other discipline, we slowly polish away the dust of a self-centered perspective, revealing the mirror of the Tao. Through complete devotion to art, discipline, or religion, the realization of Tao is possible.

Symbols of Tao

Many religious texts describe what Tao or enlightenment is and how to achieve Tao by describing particular practice methods and what path to follow. I Ching, however, does not offer specific step-by-step directions to enlightenment. Instead, it expresses the universal truth using symbols or codes, such as trigrams and hexagrams (see chapters 14, 21, 22, and 23).

Accompanying the symbols is a brief, poetic verse that is but one possible interpretation of the symbols' meaning. The trigrams and hexagrams function as symbols that defy specific contextual and literal translation, making the I Ching universally accessible.

With the symbols and codes, the I Ching shows the general principles of Tao. Thus, the book was named "Ching" (a holy text) to represent longitudinal lines or threads that connect all phenomena.

If we consider the Tao to be the analog system of understanding the principles of a changing universe, then the I Ching can be seen as a digital system of understanding. The analog version represents a totality within which all things are associated and connected. The advantage of the analog mode is that it is a more accurate depiction of actual reality.

However, it is impossible to know the entire universe (the whole is unfathomable) because we must traverse every inch of the universe to comprehend it accurately. The digital version represents only general features or an outline of the whole. The whole can be condensed, simplified, and easily inferred from the parts. Nevertheless, unlike the analog mode, we would not know the actual reality.

To condense the entire universe in a single book, and the Tao into a single CD, digital codes known as yin and yang can only be used. So I

Ching uses two digital codes: yin (▬ ▬) and yang (▬▬▬). Leibniz expressed this as "0" and "1." Computers use this binary code for on and off switch signals. We can observe this fundamental principle of yin and yang in the binary code and the resultant digital revolution (see appendix 1 for further information).

Philosophies, Religions, and Tao

The ultimate purpose of the Eastern religion is becoming one with the Tao or the attainment of Tao. Hiking up a mountain is like the path of enlightenment. There are many paths up the mountain. People can select the route near their homes or pick the one they prefer. This is like choosing a particular religion. Climbing to the peak is the struggle to realize an enlightened state.

Once they reach the summit, they can see the world below—the trail of their journey, their homes, and people lost and wandering about as they try to get to the top. The summit is akin to the enlightened state, the realization of Tao. The missionary work is to help or teach an easier and safer path to the people lost in their ways or climbing dangerous ones.

In the East, there are three traditional paths up the mountain to enlightenment or Tao—Buddhism, Confucianism, and Taoism. Though their ways may differ, they are all headed toward the same summit. It is the same enlightenment. Only their methods of cultivation differ.

When Christianity first came to the East, people regarded it as the fourth path, reinterpreting Christianity to reflect their views concerning the Tao. They considered God a personification of the Tao, and Christ a man who realized the Tao and looked upon the Holy Bible as an instruction book that explained the means to enlightenment. They also viewed Jesus Christ in the same light as Buddha (the creator of Buddhism), Confucius (the founder of Confucianism), and Lao-tzu (the founder of Taoism).

When Jesuit missionaries first went to China, many read and studied the I Ching, believing there was a similarity between the teachings of their Bible and this ancient Eastern text. In a letter Leibniz exchanged with Jesuit missionaries, he cites how seventeenth-century Jesuit missionaries tried to persuade Emperor Kang Hsi that the Bible encompasses the natural laws comparable to those found in the I Ching.[2]

The Bible was considered a "Ching" or sutra on par with the I Ching or Tao Te Ching and was named the Sheng Ching, translated as the "Holy Bible." As previously mentioned, "Ching" is written by a person who received a revelation from God or attained enlightenment. They are all sutras about Tao. These religious texts express how to realize the Tao, what the Tao is, and the path humans should follow, as seen by the person who attained the Tao. But I Ching illustrates the pattern of Tao directly through the change of codes or symbols instead of using words.

It is the nature of the Tao to be flexible. And while the I Ching explains the Tao, it does not offer fixed views. However, since words create and limit our perspectives, many religions, such as Buddhism, Confucianism, Taoism, and Christianity, have set dogmas. This belief caused them to splinter into various sects and denominations and created many conflicts, reflecting their adherents' different interpretations of the religious texts.

Taoists, Confucian scholars, and Buddhist monks all study I Ching, transcending the faiths they belong to, because I Ching expresses the Tao with codes or symbols. Thus, not many sects arose among those who followed I Ching. Moreover, according to the theory of I Ching, since truth is always changing, no one waged war by asserting the absoluteness of the truth they discovered in I Ching.

Words cannot hold meaning beyond human experience. Though words can express anything imaginable other than directly experienced, human experience and imagination are very limited. Thus, it is impossible to imagine a pattern of cosmic change that applies even to unknown objects in the remote corner of the universe. Therefore, we humans cannot imagine the Tao named in words.

I Ching does not use words that can mislead by one's limited experience to express the Tao. Instead, it just uses a code called yin and yang. To avoid causing misunderstandings by using the words "yin" and "yang," I Ching uses symbols to express the Tao. In this way, it describes the Tao beyond our living dimension that cannot be seen, touched, or felt.

Lao-tzu used five thousand words in his book Tao Te Ching to explain the existence of the Tao, which exists beyond our senses and is ineffable, and the importance of studying the Tao. But, of course, the actual contents of the Tao cannot be expressed in words, so it does not discuss the actual contents of the Tao. However, in I Ching, the exact unfolding pattern of the Tao is shown using symbols.

Although I Ching shows the unfolding pattern of the Tao, this does not signify a complete articulation of everything about Tao. Just understanding I Ching does not mean attaining the Tao. I Ching only helps to estimate the Tao and convey understanding of the concept of Tao to be able to apply it to real life, but does not provide a complete understanding of the Tao.

When Buddhism first came to China, the I Ching heavily influenced it. As a result, the initial explanation and interpretation of Buddhist scriptures utilized concepts from the I Ching.

Confucius is reputed to have read the I Ching so many times that he broke and repaired the leather bindings of his book three times. Confucius once stated, "If I had discovered the I Ching earlier, I would have read no other book." He recorded his interpretation of the meaning of the I Ching in the famous book *The Confucian Analects,* an essential work for understanding the I Ching. Confucius also wrote an entire commentary on the I Ching called the "Ten Wings."

Tao and Enlightenment

Any religion practiced with sincerity can lead to the realization of Tao. Eastern religions use specific techniques to expand the mind and attain enlightenment. The most common approach involves shedding our delusions. For example, practitioners of Zen Buddhism wrestle with "koans" (paradoxes or puzzles) to simultaneously concentrate their minds and destroy all vestiges of logical, rational, discursive thinking. Their goal is to purify their minds to attain what they term "satori," the realization of Tao. Taoists use meditative and breathing techniques to cultivate their energy. Once their bodies are strong enough, they can communicate and resonate with the powers of the universe.

The "frog in a well" mentality and greed are the true causes of suffering in Eastern religions.

Our judgment criteria are illusions created by limited senses and animal greed to sustain life. Our perception of the universe is a product of our limited senses and desires, so we cannot see the true reality of everything without breaking this illusion.

Taoists maintain that the Tao may only be perceived if one has gone beyond the limitations of the senses and selfish greed and attained "emptiness of the heart." This emptying of the heart implies the extinction of all preconceived notions and judgments, and the mind opened to acceptance. Then objects and phenomena are projected as they truly are, and we can discover the Tao, their common principles, by observing them. Buddhists hold a similar view, evident in the customary use of language. They speak of enlightenment as the realization of Tao, emptiness, or void.

However, the error of judgment and greed cannot be thrown away by trying to do so. Reading I Ching and understanding cosmic change cannot lead to the Tao. An intellectual analysis of the I Ching will not bring enlightenment. No matter how profound, the study of the book cannot change this fact. Nevertheless, the words of the I Ching can serve as a guide to help illuminate the path most suited for discovery. Taoism contends that to attain Tao, we must undergo endless self-cultivation to become free from wrong judgment and greed.

We refer to God as omniscient and omnipotent. Because the Tao is a pattern of cosmic change, one can become omniscient and omnipotent like God through the Tao. Knowing everything about the universe, all is possible.

Traditionally, a person of this standing was called Shen Ren, meaning "Spirit Person" or "Immortal" or even "Human God," and was considered equal to God.

The Universal Nervous System: A Scientific Description of Tao

Throughout the universe, something governs all matter. The human nervous system controls every aspect of its physical and physiological functioning. A similar system exists for the universe, which commands all matter or substance. This "universal nervous system" is the Tao, or God. It ensures that the waters of the oceans connect to the rivers, streams, springs, roots of plants, and even the individual cells of our bodies. It also guides the mind of every individual and the functioning of every cell.

Just as every house receives a supply of electricity, the distal end of God connects to each person's mind. In Christianity, this is the state wherein God is with everyone (1 Corinthians 3:16, "Don't you know that you yourselves are God's temple and that God's spirit dwells in your midst?").

One end of the nervous system materializes into a sperm cell of a man, while another end of the nervous system materializes into an egg cell of a woman. A sperm cell and an egg cell unite into a zygote. According to the principle of change in the I Ching, the zygote repeatedly differentiates into two, four, eight, sixteen, thirty-two, sixty-four, and so forth.

Finally, it becomes all cells in the human body (fig. 1.1).

Though the zygote differentiates and transforms into every human body cell, each cell replicates the zygote with all its characteristics. Cells are guided by an internal regulating system and connect to the body's regulating system via chemicals and nerve-cell impulses. In turn, the body's regulating system links to that of the entire universe through energetic transfer.

There are universal forces that affect our bodies. Some we have discovered, and others remain elusive. We are familiar with the gravitational pull of the Earth, which keeps us from unwanted space travel. The lunar cycles affect the tide and the female body and subtly affect

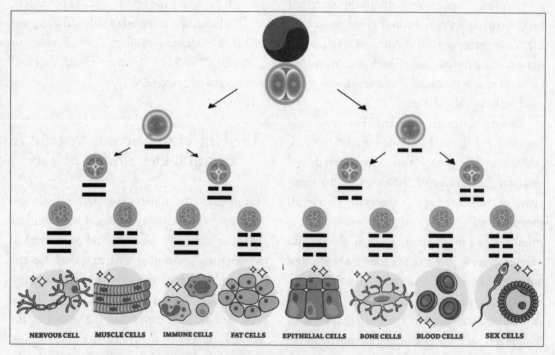

NERVOUS CELL **MUSCLE CELLS** **IMMUNE CELLS** **FAT CELLS** **EPITHELIAL CELLS** **BONE CELLS** **BLOOD CELLS** **SEX CELLS**

Figure 1.1 Differentiation of a Zygote

every living thing. Innumerable waves and fields resonate from the Tao, some communicating with the body's systems, giving it structure and regulating its functions.

A wave is an oscillation that transmits energy from place to place. Energy is not visible, but its effects are. Because the Tao communicates with the body and the body with the cells, the Tao communicates with every bodily cell, forming a single, cohesive system.

When a single element within this system fails to communicate, problems arise. For example, some people have likened cancer cells to the prodigal son of the Christian Bible. The prodigal son took his share of the family inheritance. Instead of using it to support the family unit further, he spent the money frivolously. Once his money had run out, he swallowed his pride and returned home, afraid of what might await him. To his surprise, his family did not reprimand him or attempt to teach him the proper way to act. Instead, his father threw a celebration to welcome him home, bringing him back into his rightful place.

Cancer cells behave in much the same way as the prodigal son. These cells have been severed from the body's regulating system and lack the guidance necessary for proper functioning. As a result, they proliferate and rob the body of elements essential for its existence. For the body to survive, these cells must be excised or, better yet, their communication systems repaired. Cancer will dissipate once its systems reconnect to the body's regulating system.

The restoration method for cancer cells lies in quelling their selfish and purposeless replication and attuning them to the harmonious balance of the body. Similarly, the key to longevity for human beings lies in adjusting the body to the greater harmony of the universe, thereby stopping and possibly even reversing the aging process.

The cultivation of the Tao is known as "studying the reverse order." Human beings develop through the repeated division and replication of a single zygotic cell. Regrettably, the final maturation of this process also results in our death. Taoists believe it is possible to stop or reverse the aging process by cultivating the spirit. With the reversal of this process, it is possible to reach the source of existence and communicate more simply and effectively with the Tao.

When we return to the source and resonate with the nervous system of the universe, we can see every condition, situation, and circumstance around us, like the frog that has leaped outside the well. This return is what "enlightenment" or "Tao realization" means—existing in a state of harmony with the universe. When the nervous system of a microcosmic entity such as a cell or a human being can see the "master plan" of the macrocosmic entity (the whole body, the universe), it will understand its place in the scheme of things.

Cultivating Tao: Eliminating the Imbalance of Yin-Yang

The nervous system of the universe is complete. Its materializing function (yin) and energizing function (yang) take place in a perfect 50:50 balance (Christianity considers the materializing function "good" and energizing function "evil."). The materializing process creates and develops matter by consuming energy. In contrast, the energizing process destroys matter to transform it into energy. Therefore, the universe is everlasting due to the proper balance between the two activities. But no other individual entity has a perfect balance between the two functions.

Among all the entities, human beings are the most balanced, having a slight variance at a ratio of approximately 51:49 of yin to yang. Since there is more yin than yang, there is a selfish desire to accumulate substance rather than consume it. This selfish desire creates sin. Animals have a greater disparity than humans, and plants have more significant differences than animals. Finally, minerals have the most tilt in their yin-and-yang ratio. The following diagram illustrates the imbalance in a coordinate system (fig. 1.2).

The variance of yin and yang determines the nature of each kind of matter, and individually differing actions occur. According to a biblical interpretation, humans also had a perfect balance of yin and yang while living in the Garden of Eden. However, by eating the fruit of the Tree of Knowledge, which had a significant variance of yin and yang, humans developed an imbalance of yin and yang. The cultivation methods of the enlightened sages aim to eliminate or reduce this predetermined variance of yin and yang.

Restoring the balance is done by ingesting

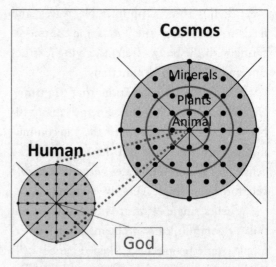

Figure 1.2 Tilt of Yin-Yang. All things in nature have a tilt of yin and yang, which can be diagrammed as dots in the coordinate system. Those closer to the center are more balanced in yin and yang.

substances with the opposite tilt in yin and yang. In addition, reciting mantras (mystical syllables) or incantations (magic spells or charms) can bring about balance in yin and yang. First, the recitation vibrates the body to the frequency harmonized in yin-yang. Then, the harmonized body will resonate with the frequency of the universal nervous system.

As previously mentioned, Zen Buddhists practice solving puzzles called "koans." A sincere effort is needed to solve the riddle, and the mind must focus to an extreme degree. Such an effort and focus is an act of artificially making energizing action to regulate and balance the variance in yin-yang by supplementing the lack of energizing function that comes prenatally.

Taoist meditation maximizes the energizing function that is fundamentally lacking in the body. The practice of quiet and deep breathing with a complete mental focus on the lower abdomen region, called Danjun (elixir field), can maximize the oxygen supply. This practice transforms matter into energy in the "refine the essence and transform it into Qi (vital energy)" process. Next, the mental focus is shifted to the center of the chest and finally to the brain. All the accumulated energy focuses on the brain. This process is called "refine the Qi and transform it into spirit." Ultimately, the human nervous system becomes fully developed to communicate effectively with the universal nervous system. The Taoist sutras conventionally explain this process as follows:

Danjun, located deep in the belly, which corresponds to a woman's womb, is a field where planting and nurturing a red seed (Dan, "elixir") takes place. Focusing one's consciousness on Danjun will create Jing, or essence, which contains all bodily elements. When fully cultivated, Jing transforms into Qi and Shen (spirit). The spirit has one's consciousness, but it is free to transcend time and space when it goes out of the body. Because it transcends time and space, it can travel to wherever it wants in an instant and can see and hear anything anywhere in the universe. The shaman's child ghost, who died young, doesn't know much. But because it is a ghost, it knows the family situation of the person who came to the shaman for divination, simply because of its ability to transcend time and space.

2

Tai Chi

In the I Ching, there is Tai Chi, the primal foundation. This generates the two fundamental forces of yin and yang. Yin and yang give rise to Sasang, and Sasang produces eight trigrams.
—Confucius, I Ching

Tai Chi translates as the "Supreme Ultimate." Simply stated, Tai Chi is a symbolic and pictorial representation of Tao. Because Tao is so elusive and intangible, sages created Tai Chi to express a more concrete embodiment of Tao. Thus, "Tao" and "Tai Chi" are interchangeable terms. The subtle difference is that the I Ching uses Tai Chi, while those training to become enlightened utilize Tao. Since I Ching is a book that expresses Tao in symbols or codes, the Tai Chi symbol contains all principles of I Ching. It exemplifies all that I Ching attempts to explain.

The I Ching states, "Tai Chi generates yin and yang." Yin and yang are the two polar yet complementary qualities that define all things in the universe. Due to this statement, many English books about the I Ching state that Tai Chi is only the principle of the creation of the universe in the beginning. Tai Chi, however, is much more. It is the totality of the universe and its parts. It is the alpha and omega, the beginning and the end.

Because Tai Chi is synonymous with the everlasting Tao, it is ubiquitous and imperishable. It may undergo numerous divisions and transformations, but Tai Chi always remains. For example, water is the same whether it is poured into a single cup or many cups and flows in a single channel or many channels. As Tai Chi divides, it may transform. Still, it carries the original essence, like the body's cells containing the entire genetic code with each division. Thus, as a complete entity, a zygote and a fully developed human are both Tai Chi. Likewise, a seed and a towering oak tree are also Tai Chi.

We can notice the importance of the Tai Chi symbol by the attention many different religions in history have given it. For instance, Taoism and Confucianism revered it as a tool for learning about life and human existence. Taoists used it to teach the changing principles of the universe, and Confucianists applied it to the principles of daily living. Although the classics of Taoism and Confucianism seem to espouse very different ideas, their mutual usage of the Tai Chi symbol shows the oneness in their veneration of the Tao.

The Tai Chi Symbol

In its symbolic form, Tai Chi is beautiful and captivating to see. But historically, China (fig. 2.1) and Korea (fig. 2.2) utilized differing forms of the Tai Chi symbol.

By examining these symbols, we gain some insight into the nature of Tai Chi. Both the Chinese and Korean Tai Chi versions share many traits. Both are circles divided in half by a

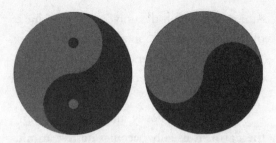

Figure 2.1 Chinese Tai Chi Symbol   **Figure 2.2** Korean Tai Chi Symbol

line shaped like a backward or horizontal letter "S." The circle is symbolic of the nature of Tai Chi. It shows that Tai Chi is all-encompassing. It also symbolizes how everything in the universe is connected—no beginning or end, no break or interruption.

The two halves of the circle represent yin and yang. The separation by the curved line shows that these two qualities transform into one another. The line also illustrates that the division of yin and yang is not rigid but dynamic. The representation of yin and yang in the symbol shows that Tai Chi is not a static entity but a never-ending interplay between these two polar qualities.

We can only perceive Tai Chi through the interactions of yin and yang. Since yin and yang are polar, they occupy one-half of the circle and face each other. The collision of opposite forces creates a spin, like a tornado generated by the clashing of two opposing winds, or a whirlpool produced by the meeting of cold and hot waters, or two antagonistic currents.

Similarly, an electric motor spins due to switching the antagonistic poles of a magnet.

Atoms, Earth, and the universe all spin due to the push and pull of opposing forces in nature. No matter or movement escapes the polar nature of yin and yang as captured in the Tai Chi symbol.

The sun rises slowly and begins to warm the Earth. It usually becomes hottest at midday, then gradually sets and cools down, and night begins. Finally, it usually becomes the coldest at midnight and rises again at dawn. Cold (yin) and hot (yang) alternately exert power in such a way. The I Ching expresses this as "alternation of yin and yang is Tao." This statement implies that the path of all things alternates between yin and yang, or everything changes from yin to yang, and vice versa, in an endlessly repeating cycle.

If we turn the center of the Tai Chi symbol with its center as the axis, we can easily observe the cycle of yin and yang. Yin and yang are joined at the head and tail and take turns waxing and waning. As yang slowly weakens, yin slowly begins to grow in exuberance. Likewise, as yin gradually weakens, yang becomes exuberant. This alternating exuberance represents a minute-by-minute change in the temperature of a day. Additionally, it signifies the change in temperature throughout the year. Thus, the weather is a manifestation of Tai Chi's movements.

On Earth, seasons are caused by changes in the duration of sunshine. Plants, animals, and even minerals transform by this change in daylight hours. In spring, when sunlight increases, plants begin to sprout and grow. Plants grow to their fullest in the summer, when the sunlight is the longest. When daylight diminishes in the fall, the energy used for growth gathers and bears fruit. In winter, sunlight is the shortest; plants store energy in their roots and rest as if lifeless.

In addition, the thermal change in the daily temperature causes a fluctuation in the physiology of plants and animals. In this way, the daily change pattern repeats the yearly change pattern. Thus, the duration of daylight hours of the year is the rise and fall of yin and yang. It is the same for the daily temperature changes. Therefore, nothing else exists but Tai Chi.

The Chinese Tai Chi Symbol

The Chinese Tai Chi symbol is a more dynamic interpretation of nature than the Korean symbol. Both use red (yang) and blue (yin) to represent the interaction between fire and water, the essence of existence. A vertical and backward S-shaped line divides the Chinese Tai Chi symbol. The fire is descending, and the water is ascending, counter to their true natures. The rationale behind this depiction is that fire and water would separate if fire rises and water descends. There would no longer be an interaction or exchange between the two, all movements would halt, and Earth would cease to exist. There must be a dynamic interaction between fire and water for everything to exist in nature. For example, ocean water evaporates and ascends to form clouds while the sun shines down on the Earth so that all organisms may benefit from its warmth.

The dots in the Chinese Tai Chi symbol

represent the concept that each polar quality contains the seeds of its opposite. Placing the dots clearly expresses how yang starts from yin, and vice versa. It is thus more practical than the Korean symbol, which illustrates this notion in a way that the head of the stronger half grows into the tendril of the weaker half.

The Korean Tai Chi Symbol

The Korean Tai Chi symbol is similar to the original Chinese, but the Korean version contains no dots. It also is rotated 90 degrees and inverted. The Korean Tai Chi symbol expresses fire and water as they exist in nature. Since fire tends to rise, its depiction is at the top of the circle. Water naturally flows downward, settling into depressions on Earth to form lakes and seas. Because of this tendency, its depiction is at the bottom. Because water (yin) and fire (yang) are opposites, each fills half of the circle and faces the other.

The horizontal, S-shaped dividing line indicates the relationship between heaven and earth. The upper red half represents heaven, and the lower blue half represents earth. The Korean Tai Chi symbol expresses the perfectly balanced, quiescent state maintained by the interactions of heaven and earth.

The Korean Tai Chi symbol represents the universe's structural aspect, while the Chinese symbol represents its functional aspect. Accordingly, if the Korean emblem is considered yin, the Chinese one is yang in nature.

Although the Chinese and Korean Tai Chi symbols differ, they share the same meaning. This is because they express the principle of the changing universe (Tao) from different points of view.

The Korean Tai Chi symbol, together with four cardinal trigrams of Heaven, Earth, Fire, and Water, is on the national flag of Korea. And it is interesting to note that Carl Sagan, in his landmark book *Cosmos,* stated that the Korean national flag contains cosmological symbols. So he must have understood that the Tai Chi and the trigrams of the I Ching represent the symbols of the cosmos.

Interpreting Tai Chi

There are two methods for interpreting the Tai Chi symbol. The first is called synchronic, or spatial, interpretation. This method views the Tai Chi symbol as a cross section of anything. For example, if Tai Chi symbolizes a person, the two halves can represent the strengths and the weaknesses. On the other hand, if Tai Chi were a coin, the two halves would represent heads and tails. Therefore, Tai Chi symbolizes the dichotomy within any given thing, in which there exists yin and yang and strengths and weaknesses.

Matter and energy are the yin and yang of the universe. The expansive action of the Big Bang (yang), and the contracting action of the black hole (yin), in combination, are Tai Chi. This is Tai Chi on a macrocosmic scale. Tai Chi, however, exists on every level, from the grand to the minute.

Human beings have minds and bodies, and atoms have protons and electrons. Quantum physics has determined that a subatomic particle can behave as a particle (matter) or a wave (energy). Here we see Tai Chi as the smallest known element. Combining these two contrasting behaviors may be conceived as a whole, or Tai Chi. So no matter how great or small something is, Tai Chi is always a whole containing two components—yin and yang.

The second interpretation of the Tai Chi symbol is called the diachronic, or temporal, interpretation. Any point on the circumference of the Tai Chi circle is perceived to be one moment in time. A point moves around the circle, passing cyclically between yin and yang. If it is within the yin portion, it must enter the yang portion sometime later. The cyclical processes that incorporate the past, present, and future are perceived as the whole, or, in other words, Tai Chi.

Through a pattern of repetition, evolution occurs. The units of time are a prime example. Days, months, and years are all Tai Chi. One day is Tai Chi because it is a gradual progression through constantly repeating darkness (yin) and light (yang). The pattern of the changing seasons that happens each year also gives a year the status of Tai Chi. The movement of time results from the alternating expansion and contraction of the universe. Any unit of time that completes a cycle or repeats a pattern may be considered Tai Chi.

The entire process of a zygote differentiating into the more than seventy trillion cells necessary to make up the human body is another diachronic example of Tai Chi. However, it is more linear than the cyclical units of time.

Still another example is the evolution of humanity. If we assume human beings to be the pinnacle of evolution, plants and animals are moments in our past that led to the fulfillment of the human species. From the lowest to the highest creature, the totality of evolution may be considered Tai Chi.

The pattern of evolution is "repeated" in human embryological development. As the human zygote develops, it moves through forms that echo our evolutionary processes. Ernst Haeckel, the nineteenth-century German biologist and philosopher, called this phenomenon "ontogeny recapitulating phylogeny." First, the zygote resembles a fish with a tail and no limbs. Then it resembles an amphibian with legs and a tail. Next, the tail shortens, and the limbs resemble land mammals'. Finally, it takes on the form of a human being. The human zygote is Tai Chi, and the entire animal kingdom is tantamount to a moment in the development of the human zygote. These evolutionary processes also demonstrate how the pattern of a part repeats that of the whole.

The diachronic interpretation allows us to see the transformation of things from yin to yang and back again. Nothing in this universe is constant. Our lives are a pattern of fluctuations, for we experience good and bad times, fortune and misfortune, birth and death. These are all movements around the circle of Tai Chi. Again, this is reflected in the statement "Alternation of yin and yang is Tao." It implies the ceaselessly iterating cycles of yin and yang.

"The Old Man and His Horse" is a famous tale of the East that demonstrates the changes in fortune and misfortune over time. Fortunes (yang) and misfortunes (yin) are yin and yang aspects of one's lifetime (Tai Chi). Other elements include achievements and failures, which can also be considered fortune and misfortune.

The story involves an old man who lived near a country's border. The old man had a horse that ran away one day. When the townspeople found out, they told the man it was a bad omen. Yet, the next day the horse returned with another fine horse. When the townspeople found out, they told the man it was good fortune.

The next day the old man's son tried to break in the new horse. But he was thrown from the horse and broke his leg. When the townspeople found out, they again told the man it was a bad omen.

Soon after, a war broke out with a neighboring country. A military draft mobilized and deployed all young men into the battlefield. However, a broken leg prevented the old man's son from being drafted. It was a terrible battle, and all men who fought died. But through his misfortune, the old man was the most fortunate, as his son's life was spared.

Like Tai Chi, this fable illustrates that there are two sides to every coin (synchronic interpretation) and that every situation will fluctuate (diachronic interpretation). It can change the nature of judgment. It allows us to see people as they are with all their faults and virtues and the positives and negatives of all things. It also allows us to prepare for the worst when things are going well and sustain ourselves with hope when things turn sour.

Tai Chi Is Within Everything

Everything that exists is Tai Chi. Suppose we travel through space and encounter an extraterrestrial that does not resemble anything seen on Earth. We might describe the creature in the following way: "It's huge, and it weighs a lot. It has a red body with three legs, and its head is bigger than its body. It has no hair but three eyes and moves fast."

Would it be possible for this unrecognizable thing to embody Tai Chi? First, to perceive that the creature was large, you would have to have a concept of small. Next, to perceive that the extraterrestrial was heavy, you must have a notion of lightness. Additionally, it must be compared to other colors to perceive its redness. Furthermore, to know that it had three eyes, you would have to understand that the number three was different from other numbers. Moreover, to know that its head was more prominent than its body, you would have to know how to distinguish its head from its body. Finally, to describe it as fast, you must have some notion of slowness.

No matter how alien, the words and concepts used to describe any form or phenomenon come from relating current information to past knowledge and experience. Therefore, we must compare them to their opposites as a part of a whole. In other words, we must link all things to Tai Chi, which includes two polar natures, to be recognized. The largest of the whole would be the entire universe, while that of the smallest would be a subatomic particle.

There must exist an idea of a whole to identify the parts. When you look at the polar characteristics of matter to understand its nature, it has already become Tai Chi. For example, when you say, "That person is a man," it implies that a person is a man, not a woman. Because men and women have opposing natures, the concept of "person" is Tai Chi.

Animals are still another example. The word "animal" means it is not a plant among organisms. Among organisms, animals are active, so they are yang, while plants are yin, as they are relatively inactive. Here, the entirety of the organism with both yin and yàng becomes Tai Chi. When we say organism, we are distinguishing it from nonliving things. Since organisms are yang and inanimate objects are yin, the whole "matter," including these two opposing parts, becomes Tai Chi.

It is wrong to think that only the entire universe is Tai Chi. Any individual entity with the opposite parts of yin and yang can become Tai Chi and function in a similar pattern as Tai Chi. The sages say that the Tao is everywhere in the universe, which means that Tai Chi is everywhere in the universe. Within Tai Chi there is Tai Chi, and within that Tai Chi there is Tai Chi. These subdivisions manifest as the white and black holes of the universe, Earth's water and fire, the human body and mind, protons and electrons of an atom, and wave and particle aspects of elementary particles. The following illustration demonstrates this (fig. 2.3).

Figure 2.3 Fractal Tai Chi

This diagram is the cosmic Tai Chi in its unified (yin) aspect, expressed in terms of yin and yang. It is Tai Chi, where the differentiated yin and yang unify as 16–8–4–2–1.

Illustrated within the Tai Chi diagram's yin and yang parts is a small Tai Chi. Still an even smaller Tai Chi is depicted in the yin and yang of the small Tai Chi, continuing in an infinitely repeating pattern. Modern science calls it the fractal principle, in which parts repeat the pattern of the whole. The term "fractal" was first coined in 1975 by the mathematician Benoit Mandelbrot.

The same fractal pattern exists in terms of time. As previously mentioned, the past and future cycles of time occur due to repeated expansion and contraction of the universe. Seasonal cycles exist within the past and future cycles because of the Earth's revolution around the sun. The day and night cycles occur within a season due to the Earth's rotation around its axis. In this way, both small and large time units embody yin and yang. Since higher and lower time units express yin and yang, Tai Chi is in each unit of time. The fractal Tai Chi figure clearly illustrates this.

We can also use the principle of Tai Chi to explain the human body. Eastern medicine refers to the body as a microcosm, relating the formation of both the body and the universe to the same essential principle, Tai Chi. The universe consists of both matter (yin) and energy (yang); similarly, the human body consists of both form (yin) and energy (yang), structure (yin) and function (yang). We can view the universe as originating from the Big Bang (yang) and reaching an end in the black hole (yin). Human life begins at birth or conception (yang) and will end with death (yin).

All organisms receive energy and nourishment through the mutual interactions of the sun (yang) and water (yin). Similarly, food (yang), the sun's energy concentration through carbon metabolism, and water (yin) influence individual bodily cells.

The universe consists of two elements called yin and yang, and within it are humans and other organisms that consist of yin and yang. And every cell that forms organisms consists of two elements, yin and yang. So the Tai Chi symbol shows us that all phenomena configure from two components—yin and yang, no matter how large or small.

The Tilt of Yin and Yang

A subatomic particle, a cell, an animal, a human being, the Earth, and the entire universe can all be Tai Chi. The reason is that they all function according to the same principles. Their differences lie in the distribution of yin and yang within each one.

According to the I Ching, a tiered system exists regarding the degrees of yin-yang balance. The universe is more balanced than the solar system, which is more balanced than the Earth. Humans are more balanced than animals, and organic matter is more balanced than inorganic matter. This hierarchy continues down to the least balanced entity we have discovered up to this point, the quark.

Eastern astrology represents the animal kingdom with twelve categories according to their variations of yin and yang. The twelve distributions of the zodiac assign twelve different animals. For example, the rat is considered the most yin, with a distribution of approximately 60:40 yin to yang. On the other hand, the horse is the most yang, with a distribution of roughly 60:40 yang to yin. The following diagram illustrates this principle (fig. 2.4). The fluctuations of yin and yang in the smaller Tai Chi symbols represent the variations of yin and yang within Tai Chi.

Individual cells of the body also manifest Tai Chi, the nature of their association displayed by cells with similar yin-yang ratios. Similar cells share similar functions and thus gather to form a particular organ. For example, cells with a greater yang-to-yin ratio assemble to form the heart, the most yang organ. In contrast, cells with a greater yin-to-yang ratio collect to form the kidneys, which are the most yin. Cells with less severe fluctuations unite

Figure 2.4 Tilt of Yin-Yang within Tai Chi of Animals

with their cell type to form the body's other organs. The zygote is considered the most balanced of all the cells in the human body.

Molecules behave in much the same way. The discrepancy of yin to yang within each molecule dictates its nature and functioning. Molecules with similar slants join to form cells, and those cells converge to form organs. Such is the design of the human body.

Tai Chi Among People

Socrates said, "Know thyself." Knowing oneself is the same as knowing one's variance of yin and yang. Buddhism refers to it as "observing one's true nature." Observing one's true nature is the beginning of Tao cultivation. Only by understanding the yin-yang tilt of one's true nature can one return to the original place corresponding to the center.

When applied to human beings, this system can be used as a guideline to illuminate personality characteristics concerning the yin and yang of Tai Chi. These are not, however, absolute terms. The interactions of yin and yang are constantly changing. The I Ching discusses these changes in terms of the relative strengths of yin and yang at any given time.

A deep understanding of the text will lead to a highly accurate prediction of change, similar to calculations made by a computer. Such is the method of divination practiced in the East.

The ratio of yin to yang determines a person's nature and particular tendency and can account for the diversity among people. If all humanity is Tai Chi, the smaller Tai Chi symbols represent the variations in all walks of life that form humankind.

In psychological terms, a person with yin to yang ratio tilted toward, for example, money (yin type) would feel most comfortable in the business world and work to accumulate wealth. Similarly, a person with the opposite slant (yang type) would have a stronger desire to concentrate on academic matters and less attachment to material goods. Those who are more content to deal with life as it comes and enjoy living a day-to-day existence tend to be yin types. They are generally more comfortable with jobs that are not competitive and require more physical labor than mental work. In contrast, those who need to sacrifice life's little pleasures for success are generally happy with highly competitive jobs that require tremendous mental energy. They include business executives and politicians and are usually yang-type personalities.

A further breakdown of this classification system is possible. The degree of variation in the yin-yang ratio among business executives will determine an individual's preference for a top position. For example, an executive with a greater degree of variation (more tilted toward yang) will attempt to become the president of a large company. In contrast, an executive with slightly less variation (less yang) will be content with being either the president of a smaller company or the vice president of a large company. Of course, other factors to consider in every situation include the availability of jobs, the strength of the economy, and so on.

By knowing the yin-yang of everyone, we can infer the variance of a company or a group with several people. Then it is possible to make predictions by calculating and comparing the variation of yin-yang forces among other groups. This knowledge will guide the company or the group in the best course of action to follow.

Let's consider all the people on Earth as a single Tai Chi. The various numbers represent the yin-yang variations in each individual. We can assign numbers to their degree in people. For example, we can set the number 1 to a person with yin-to-yang ratio of 51:49 and the number 2 to a person whose ratio is 51.001:48.999 yin to yang. We can assign 785,467 to a person with a ratio of 56.8:43.2 yin to yang. A person designated with the number 3 and someone with the number 4 will have very similar characteristics and tastes. They will choose similar jobs and lead similar lifestyles. However, there will be a drastic difference between a person assigned the number 2 and a person set to 1,000,800,542. These two people will lead very different lives. Therefore, the number given to each person is their "destiny."

Tai Chi: The Great Neutralizer

Nothing can stay still forever or move forever. Nor can things infinitely move up or down. If these situations were possible, the universe would grow increasingly unstable. So the essence of Tai Chi follows: That which was once still will begin to move, and that which was once moving will begin to still. That which once rose will start to fall, and that which once fell will rise.

By continually changing directions, the universe maintains its structure. However, even the universe must fluctuate. It has constantly been expanding since the Big Bang. But at the end of this process, the principles embodied in Tai Chi indicate that the universe will contract into a black hole. Once in full contraction, the expansion will begin again with another Big Bang. As its movements continually oscillate between expansion and contraction, the universe remains eternal.

On Earth, gravity pulls all things to its center. Then, once everything fully contracts, an explosion, or, in other words, volcanic activity, sends things flying away from the center.

Subsequently, gravity will again pull dispersed matter back to the center, repeating the cycle.

Tai Chi is the force that directs the changes of all movements and activities. It is dynamic neutrality and a state of balance between yin and yang, exerting a neutralizing tendency on everything. We may liken it to centripetal force. For instance, an object on a spinning surface tends to move toward its outer edge, like the ball on a roulette table. Without impediment to its movement, the ball will fly off the edge of the surface. Despite the spin, the centripetal force resists this tendency and keeps objects in their place.

For a spinning surface, friction supplies the centripetal force, whereas gravity supplies it for the spinning Earth. Centripetal force, like Tai Chi, resists all ex-centric (away from the center) tendencies to keep things in place. This resistance keeps all things from losing their relationship with the center and establishes harmony.

Any movement occurring in one direction without changing to the opposite direction will disrupt the harmony and balance and ultimately break down. The function of changing direction back to the center to establish harmony and balance is Tai Chi, the unifying principle of the universe. The following diagram illustrates this process (fig. 2.5).

Science vs. Tai Chi

In a certain sense, the perspectives of Tai Chi and modern science are opposites. Tai Chi fo-

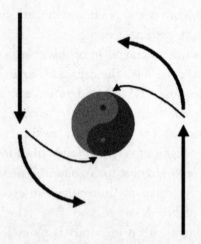

Figure 2.5 Movement of Tai Chi

cuses on the whole, and science on the details. It is impossible to do both at the same time. One cannot see the forest when concentrating on a tree, nor can one focus on one tree while looking at the forest. Although these perspectives have opposing natures, there are benefits to both.

Imagine a town that you have never visited. The scientific exploration process would involve visiting the town and walking its streets. The Tai Chi approach would comprise looking at a map. The scientific method allows for a greater understanding of specific details of the portion of the explored town. There would, however, be places that were not visited and thus not known, and there would be little knowledge of the surroundings. The Tai Chi approach would give a complete picture of the town's layout and the surrounding area, allowing an understanding of how the town "fits into the big picture." However, the details would be lost.

In Chinese, the word "science" is Ke Xue

(科學). Ke (科) means "to analyze or divide," while Xue (學) means "to study." The Eastern understanding of science implies analysis. Scientific knowledge involves a detailed breakdown of things to see their components.

There is no question about the power of invention that science holds. And there are many benefits that society and people have gained because of scientific discoveries. But despite its ability (or perhaps because of it), we must question science's relationship to the harmony and balance of the universe.

The atomic bomb resulted from experimentation with the smallest known particle in the universe. Although the bomb's discovery allowed America to win the war against Japan, it also initiated the Cold War and the imminent possibility of nuclear annihilation. It was almost as though the universe was rebuking humanity for attempting to manipulate nature's forces without analyzing the possible outcomes.

Genetic engineering has developed the capability to clone. Although this is a remarkable development, it raises many important issues. What are the moral and philosophical ramifications of human cloning? Should the power of human production be in the hands of humans? If so, which humans? Although we are not ready to answer any of these questions, science has already given us the power of choice. We are still children regarding these issues, but we play with a real gun.

The development of Viagra has relieved the suffering of male impotence for many. But even this drug has the potential to wreak havoc on the balance of things. Reproduction is a vital function in the universe, an extremely important matter to God. Although death may be the end of an individual entity, to God, there is reproduction, so a part of that entity carries on through reproduction.

Destruction is the beginning of creation, so in the animal world, males sometimes meet their death after sex because their mission has been accomplished and they have become useless. For instance, male praying mantises get eaten by females after sex. There are many other examples in the animal world. The female's task begins after the male injects the sperm into her. When the male is of little use after ejaculation, the male can be provided as a nutrient to the female for future generations after ejaculation. Therefore, male ejaculation involves great sacrifice.

There has been a great deal of research into the effects of sex on athletic performance. According to one study, the performance of male athletes dwindled after sex, but that of females soared. When a male ejaculates, it drains his energy. However, sexual intercourse increases female energy, perhaps in preparation for conception and the nourishment and growth of the next generation.

Nowadays, however, reproduction is often viewed as an unwanted outcome of sex. Because of the advancements in medicine and technology and Earth's overpopulation, people no longer need to have as many children as before. Therefore, the role of sex has transformed from a need to a desire. And as with all pleasurable things, there is a tendency to overindulge.

The male genitalia is like an elongated

balloon. Usually it is flaccid, but with sexual stimulation, it grows erect as blood flows through its tissues, like a balloon filling with air. After ejaculation, an enzyme called phosphodiesterase type 5 (PDE5) prevents blood from flowing into those tissues, preventing further erections. This safety measure ensures that the body has enough time to manufacture more sperm for the subsequent sexual encounter. This enzyme becomes especially active when a person is weak and requires more time for recovery. It is functional, for example, while a man recovers from an illness, suffers from mental or physical fatigue, or when he becomes old. In short, it is present to ensure and protect the body's overall health; it is not a sign of malfunction.

Viagra works by preventing the release of the PDE5 that blocks blood flow to the penis. If a man were impotent due to some underlying weakness, the repeated erections and ejaculations would only further deplete his body. This depletion could show up as weakened immunity, fatigue, or in extreme cases, death. One side effect of Viagra is that it can worsen existing heart conditions. In addition, abuse of Viagra will cause the body to produce low-quality sperm. Any child born out of this situation will not have the same chance at a healthy life as one born from natural circumstances.

Eastern medicine, which embraces the holistic principles of Tao and Tai Chi, does not advise using drugs like Viagra, because their actions deplete the body as a whole. On the other hand, modern science has no qualms about abusing the body, because it doesn't even see the problem. It is too busy analyzing each tree to see the forest.

The Big Picture

Although science is precise and accurate, deriving concrete results with a strong emphasis on the details, its perspective is self-limiting regarding seeing the influence on the whole. Such is its shortcoming as well as its strength. When solving a problem, the I Ching way applies deductive reasoning. It focuses on the attributes of a single line within sixty-four hexagrams. But this process is always unified into Tai Chi, never forgetting to correlate the result to every line within the Tai Chi. It is the principle of the "middle path." It is a way of looking at the totality by paying attention to the overall picture and its parts. Based on this principle, "middle" without excess or deficiency is highly valued in the East.

Koreans revere I Ching and drew Tai Chi on their flag, symbolizing the middle of yin and yang. But Chinese people who esteem "middle" put the Chinese character for "middle (中)" in the name of their country (中國). It implies a country in the center of the world. Still, additionally, it means a country that respects the middle without either excess or deficiency. *Zhongyong* (中用), *The Doctrine of the Mean,* a classic that students must read in a traditional school, is a book at a lower level than I Ching. Still, it is a book that explicitly explains the central principle of Tai Chi, the unification principle as the principle of life.

Hegel, who influenced the theory of communism, learned I Ching from his grandfather, a missionary to China. He advocated the theory of thesis, antithesis, and synthesis. Here, synthesis corresponds to the principle of Tai Chi. Hegel's theory states that an opposite action follows when an action occurs in one direction from a quiescent physical state. Afterward, an intermediate action that unifies the two polar activities transpires. And then the cycle repeats.

Marx reinterpreted this by stating that socially when there is a monarchy, a king suppresses people, and people rebel and overthrow the king and create a democracy or people's government. After that, communism, which has a mixture of both systems' merits, is created. Like Hegel, Marx himself was an expert on the I Ching theory.

It is a natural principle that when men's jackets with wide collars are fashionable for a while, narrow ones look chic. Similarly, wide ones look stylish when narrow ones are in vogue for a certain period. The length of a woman's skirt also lengthens and shortens in this way. This basic theory of I Ching has been in the spotlight in the Hegelian era but did not develop into a deeper theory of I Ching.

The thesis is yang, the antithesis is yin, and the synthesis is Tai Chi. Tai Chi encompasses both yin and yang and implies their unification. It also denotes totality, center, balance, and harmony.

Although it is sometimes necessary to focus on details, they shouldn't obscure your vision of the whole. We can only see the consequences of our actions and live healthier, more productive lives by challenging our limited perspectives.

3

The Basic Principles
of Yin and Yang

Tai Chi generates yin and yang. When Tai Chi moves, it becomes yang;
when it settles, it becomes yin.
—Confucius, I Ching

The principle of yin and yang is the natural order of the universe,
the basis of all things, the mother of all changes, the source of life and death,
and the repository for creating spirit.
—The Yellow Emperor's Inner Classic

Yin and yang are the universal binary language. The binary code is the fundamental language of all computer systems. Similarly, yin and yang are the languages we can use to interpret and understand all the complexities of our lives and the world around us.

Computers store vast amounts of information in minute spaces. They also perform highly sophisticated calculations. Although the power of computers is enormous, their primary language is composed of two characters: 0 and 1. Regardless of size or complexity, you can inevitably break down all input and data translated by computer systems into established series of these two characters. This breakdown allows ease of understanding for anyone familiar with the binary code. It is also the most efficient and coherent method of storing information.

In much the same fashion, an easier understanding of life, nature, and the universe can occur when you are versed in the universal binary language of yin and yang. Regardless of the situation's complexity, all of life's attributes can translate into the language of yin and yang. As a result, you will gain deeper insight into your path and move effortlessly toward your goals.

In short, yin and yang are the code, ruler, gauge, and matrix with which you can convert, measure, calculate, unravel, and interpret all information. Everything is a manifestation of yin and yang, from common to extraordinary, cheap to precious, simple to complex, vulgar to noble, divine to diabolical, concrete to mysterious.

Understanding yin and yang requires a knowledge of the fundamental characteristic pairs and their polarities. The following table shows some of the general characteristics, functions, and directions of yin and yang (table 3.1):

	YIN	YANG
GENERAL CHARACTERISTICS	static	mobile
	darkness	light
	cold	hot
	thick	thin
	turbid	clear
	dense	sparse
	invisible	visible
	rigid	flexible

	YIN	YANG
FUNCTION	passive	active
	suppression	excitation
	regression	progression
	preserve	transform
	completion	initiation
	discontinuous	continuous
	sustaining	changing
	yielding	proceeding
	resting	acting
	nourishing	protecting
	responding	commanding
	decaying	flourishing
	restraint	action

	YIN	YANG
DIRECTION	downward	upward
	internal	external
	centripetal	centrifugal
	front	back
	inside	outside
	north	south
	west	east

Table 3.1 Yin-Yang Characteristics

The following table illustrates other yin-yang pairings relating to various universal phenomena (table 3.2):

	YIN	YANG
UNIVERSAL COMPONENT	substance	energy
QUANTUM MECHANICS	particle	wave
COSMOS	black hole	white hole (Big Bang)
HUMAN BEINGS	body	mind
	Female	Male
MIND	subconscious	conscious
SPIRIT	corporeal soul	ethereal soul
ORGANISMS	plants	animals
CAR	braking system	propelling system
STOCK MARKET	bear	bull
COMPUTER	memory	calculating function

Table 3.2 Yin-Yang and the Universe

Figure 3.1 Fire and Water. Fire symbolizes yang, and water epitomizes yin. The essence of fire is the sun, and the crux of water is the center of the sea. This Tai Chi or Yin-Yang symbol shows it well.

The Six Basic Principles

Yin and yang represent matter and form as well as energy and function. So they are more than fixed, static pairings. The interaction between these two forces brings about all the changes in nature. The six basic principles of yin and yang describe how yin and yang interact. Therefore, the formulation and representation of these relationships give power and meaning to the yin-yang theory. These principles are (1) mutual opposition, (2) mutual dependence, (3) mutual consumption and support, (4) mutual transformation, (5) infinite divisibility, and (6) inversion (form-function relationship).

1. Mutual Opposition

The most basic yin-yang principle, mutual opposition, states that everything in the universe has an opposing counterpart. Whether complex or basic, pure or adulterated, magnificent or minute, everything has a relative opposite. Thus, all phenomena in the universe are either yin or yang. For example, phenomena are either positive or negative, male or female, up or down, open or closed, outside or inside, day or night, acid or alkaline, loved or hated, joyful or sad, and so on.

2. Mutual Dependence

The principle of mutual dependence states that yin and yang depend upon one another. So in addition to having an opposing counterpart, all things also rely upon their opposites. This dependence means that nothing can exist without its opposite, and opposites define everything. For example, there can be no front without a back, no top without a bottom, no inside without an outside. In other yin-yang pairings, the dependence is indirect but no less inescapable. For example, animals (yang) depend on plants (yin) for oxygen, and plants depend on animals for carbon dioxide. Likewise, male and female organisms depend on one another to continue their species.

3. Mutual Consumption and Support

The principle of dependence explains that yin and yang depend upon one another. However, it does not describe *how* yin and yang depend upon and affect each other. The principle of mutual consumption and support elaborates on this relationship by defining the interaction between yin and yang as consumptive yet nurturing.

Yin and yang have a reciprocal relationship. The strength of yin or yang depends on the weakness of its counterpart. When yin grows stronger, yang is consumed and becomes weaker, and vice versa. However, viewed from another perspective, the yin and yang relationship can be supportive. When yin is consumed, yang becomes stronger to fill the void. The same is true of yin when yang is consumed.

An oil lamp provides an accurate illustration of this reciprocal relationship. The oil is the yin aspect of the lamp because its nature is substantial. The flame is yang because movement, heat, and light characterize fire. The flame needs to consume oil to burn. But it will vanish if it exhausts all of the oil, since the oil fuels the flame. In addition, extinguishing the flame will cause a loss of functionality for both the oil and the lamp.

4. Mutual Transformation

Not only do yin and yang define, consume, and support one another, but they also transform into each other. The relationship expresses as one of exchange. When yin reaches its extreme, it transforms into yang. When yang is at its zenith, it transforms into yin. The transformation of yin into yang and yang into yin allows the energetic cycle to continue moving forward.

One example of this principle is Einstein's famous theory, $E=mc^2$. It states that matter (yin) and energy (yang) are different forms of the same thing and can transform into one another. Another example is the discovery by quantum physicists that electrons act as particles (yin) and waves (yang). In 1926 Werner Heisenberg formulated his uncertainty principle, which stated that it is impossible to simultaneously determine these electrons' position and momentum. This phenomenon is the constant transformation of yang into yin, and vice versa. In the infinitely microscopic world of quantum physics, change occurs at such a rapid speed that it is impossible to ascertain a particle's momentum and position simultaneously. This is, in fact, one principle of change mentioned in the I Ching.

In daily life, this principle of change is more gradual. The speed with which this process takes place depends on the number of altered factors. For example, while one electron transforming from a particle into a wave may take an immeasurably short time, day turning into night (yang to yin), and its reciprocal takes twenty-four hours. The waxing and waning of the moon and the changes of the seasons are other examples of this gradual yin-yang transformation.

The principle of transformation is one of conservation. By transforming into each other, yin and yang are recycled and conserved. If yin and yang only consumed each other, they would eventually become depleted. The mutual transformation of yin and yang prevents this from occurring. A dynamic balance is maintained by constantly changing from one to another, often in a cyclical or pendulum-like pattern.

5. Infinite Divisibility

The principle of infinite divisibility states that nothing in the universe is pure yin or yang. Regardless of how yin or yang a phenomenon appears, we can always further break it down into smaller yin and yang components. For example, although daytime is yang, it can be divided into two periods: sunrise to noon and noon to dusk. Sunrise to noon is yang within yang because it is the brightest time of the day. Noon to sunset, when darkness overcomes daylight, is yin within yang. The division of nighttime is similar. Within these divisions are further divisions. Any given hour, minute, or second can be broken down and viewed with its position on the spectrum of darkness and light and assigned more yin or yang properties. We can break down anything until we arrive at the smallest known particle, constantly transforming between yin and yang.

6. Inversion

The inversion principle is the most elaborate and profound principle of the yin-yang theory. Inherent to this principle is the importance of the observer's criteria when assigning yin or yang to things. Like the blind man and the elephant, people interpret situations differently depending on their experiences and perspectives. In the same way, objects and situations have inherently contrasting yin and yang characteristics depending upon the aspect of the object or situation explored and the observer's perspective. This context is what the inversion principle describes, and it does so in three ways, by examining: (1) form and function, (2) alternative position, and (3) essence and manifestation.

FORM AND FUNCTION

One fundamental tenet of the inversion principle is that the form or structure (yin) is inversely related to its function or energy (yang). Depending on the relative perspective of the observer, the same phenomena can appear yin if its structure is analyzed and yang if its function is studied, or vice versa. Following are examples of this contradictory nature of form and function in many different aspects of ordinary life.

Size and Speed

The bigger (more yang) something is, the slower (more yin) its speed tends to be, and the smaller (more yin) something is, the faster (more yang) its speed tends to be.

Let's take a simple example of a bus versus a sports car. The bigger an object, the more yang it is in size. So a bus is more yang than a sports car. However, in terms of speed, the faster an object, the more yang it is. So a sports car is more yang than a bus.

Most of the objects we see around us have a stable form. Therefore, their velocity is easily measured when they move because compared to the subatomic particle they are relatively big (yang with regards to form) and thus slow (yin with regards to function). However, in quan-tum physics, electrons and other particles are extremely small (yin with regards to form) and move at an incredible speed (yang with regards to function). Thus, simultaneous measurement of their position (yin) and momentum (yang) is impossible.

Strength and Density

Density is yin, while strength is yang. The denser an object, the more yin it is. Conversely, the stronger an object, the more yang it is. When analyzing wood and metal from the perspective of density, metal is more yin than wood. However, interpreting these two materials from their relative strength, metal is more yang because it is stronger.

Visibility

In general, things perceptible to the eye are yang, and things that are not visible are yin. In this respect, the body is yang relative to the mind. However, from the perspectives of speed, weight, and density, the mind is much more yang than the body.

The relationship between form and function and the observer's perspective is vital to remember when assigning yin or yang to any object or situation to truly understand the workings of the universe.

ALTERNATIVE POSITION

In addition to form and function, the inversion principle also reveals the yin and yang relationship by comparing various positions, such as upper and lower, front and back, and internal and external.

A famous maxim attributed to Hermes Trismegistus states, "As above, so below; as below, so above." This maxim implies that the same patterns exist on every plane of reality. For example, the human body reflects nature's designs, which reflect universal patterns. Atoms reflect patterns of human cells, which in turn reflect patterns of the human body. Each new level of existence reflects and carries the same information as the next or previous level. The modern fractal theory describes this as "self-similarity." Eastern philosophy acknowledges that the microcosm reflects the macrocosm, and vice versa. This reflection forms a foundation for practices such as reflexology and iridology.

However, applying the inversion principle to this saying, we see how perspective changes the outlook. So let's look at the qualities of softness and hardness and how they manifest in nature.

Watermelons have hard external shells, but inside they are soft. The same is true of cantaloupes, honeydews, and coconuts. On the other hand, peaches are soft on the outside, but inside they have a hard pit, as do apricots, plums, and nectarines. Likewise, fish are soft on the outside but have solid vertebrae inside. However, shellfish, such as oysters, clams, crabs, and lobster, are hard externally but soft inside. We see this in the human body as well. For example, the skull is hard on the outside, but the brain inside is soft. Likewise, the abdomen is soft, but the rigid lumbar spine is inside. These examples show how an object that appears yang externally will be internally yin, and vice versa.

The inversion principle also exists when comparing the upper and lower region of the same thing. Many trees have green leaves (yang) that absorb light from the sun (yang). Underneath, however, are their dark roots (yin) that absorb water and minerals from the earth (yin). Turtles have a hard top shell (yang) but a soft underbelly (yin). Seasons in the Northern and Southern Hemispheres are also inversely related. Summer in the north is winter in the south, and vice versa. In addition, storms in the Northern Hemisphere rotate in a counterclockwise direction, while those in the Southern Hemisphere rotate clockwise.

The inversion principle also manifests when comparing our bodies' front and back sides. According to the yin-yang theory, the front of the body is yin because it is "soft" and more vulnerable than the back (yang), which contains the spine and powerful back muscles. Likewise, the upper body is considered yang compared to the lower body (yin) because it is higher and its movements are less restricted.

Because the nature of yang is expansive and yin is contractive, things that protrude are considered yang, and things that sink inward are yin. For example, the chest and buttocks protrude when looking at the human body, highlighting the inversion principle. In the front of the body (yin region), the chest (upper/yang region) sticks out. But in the back of the body (yang region), an inversion takes place, and the buttocks (lower/yin region) stick out.

These examples are the way nature balances yin and yang.

ESSENCE AND MANIFESTATION

Perhaps essence and manifestation are the most complicated aspect of the inversion principle. It conveys that what is apparent to the naked eye (yin/form/structure) is the opposite of the intrinsic nature (yang/function/energy) of any given thing. This principle is the foundational concept giving rise to statements such as "putting on a facade," "wearing a mask," and "don't judge a book by its cover." They convey a profound universal truth.

Water, for example, appears soft and malleable and conforms to any container it enters. It is, however, the catalyst for any hardening process. Consider cement or clay. Both will remain in the form of powder until mixed with water. Life, too, requires the presence of water. Scientists search the universe for water to indicate the potential of other life-forms. Water is essential because, even though it initially appears to soften things, it causes them to gather and solidify (yin). Only through such yin actions can a birth take place. Water provides the contractive (yin) force necessary for a birth (yang) or an explosion (yang) to take place eventually. This contractive force is the intrinsic nature of water—soft on the outside and hard on the inside. Metal is just the opposite. While it appears solid, any metal put into a fire will melt into liquid. So while metal seems to be a hard substance, its true nature is soft.

People are much the same. While a person may appear hard on the outside, those people generally cover up a very soft internal personality. Conversely, people who appear weak by nature may carry a great deal of strength inside.

The inversion principle emphasizes the observer's perspective when assigning yin and yang qualities to any object or situation. It reminds us that different perspectives produce different conclusions. When added to the other five principles, it completes the theory of yin and yang, giving us the guidelines necessary to better understand the complexities of our lives, nature, and the universe.

4

Yin and Yang of Human Beings

Nothing on Earth is perfectly balanced in yin and yang. Still, humans are the most balanced of all God's creatures, followed in decreasing order by all other animals, plants, and minerals. On an individual level, each person has a unique variance of yin and yang, resulting in different physical and mental characteristics. On the whole, however, people share more similarities than differences. According to the Human Genome Project and other recent studies, fundamentally, people are approximately 99.98 percent similar to one another and only 0.02 percent different. The degrees of yin-yang variance also fall into this 0.02 percent, making the difference slight yet significant.

Yin Person, Yang Person

All people are born with a fundamental tilt of yin and yang. Divided into two groups, those who possess more yin than yang would be yin people, and those who have more yang than yin would be yang people. Of course, the ratio of yin and yang varies from person to person.

Nevertheless, all yin people share common qualities associated with a preponderance of yin, and all yang people share common attributes associated with a prevalence of yang.

God embodies the perfect balance of yin and yang and therefore suffers no illnesses and lives eternally. On the other hand, human beings struggle through life trying to maintain health because of their yin-yang variances. Regardless of what condition a person experiences, it is usually due to a fundamental imbalance of yin and yang. Yang persons have insufficient yin and an excess of yang. Yin persons have deficient yang and a surplus of yin.

It is possible to counter these imbalances through diet and lifestyle. However, it is not feasible for a yang person to transform into a yin person, or vice versa. This is one limitation of being human.

YIN PEOPLE

Yin gathers and materializes energy into substance. The external energetic activity of yin, however, appears weak. The physical and physiological characteristics of yin persons result from these factors. Yin persons have greater bone mass and more flesh, and their physiological activities (such as blood circulation) are slower. As a result, they tend to be physically slow, cold, and psychologically more passive and indecisive than yang people.

Yin people exude elegance and calm. They are stable and tranquil, especially in the seated position. They speak prudently and cautiously, trying to hide their weaknesses and not make mistakes, particularly with people they meet for the first time. However, their tendencies are often misinterpreted as coldheartedness or indecision because they overthink. Yin persons dislike extreme situations. So they try to remain passive, finding comfort in their present condition. At the same time, they continually compare themselves to others because of their insecurities. Therefore, they feel anxious and apprehensive when they advance ahead of the group.

Physically, yin persons tend to have big hips and narrow shoulders. Their weight is either average or heavy, and they are generally big-boned. Their movements tend to be slow, and their hands and feet are cold. They dislike cold weather, so they usually close the windows and set their thermostats to higher temperatures at home. Ordinarily, yin persons like to drink warm water and eat hot soup. They also like warm colors, such as red, orange, or yellow, to balance their "cold" constitutions.

Eastern medical practitioners thoroughly analyze numerous physical features to fully understand a person's yin-yang nature. Observation provides insight into the cause and proper treatment of various illnesses for each patient. Three primary areas of diagnosis are the patient's complexion, specific properties of the tongue—including color and coating—and the pulse. An Eastern medical diagnosis of a yin person would most likely reveal a pale complexion, a pale tongue without vitality, and a weak pulse, indicating low blood pressure.

YANG PEOPLE

Yang dissolves substances and transforms them into energy. Thus yang persons have less mass, manifesting in thin bones and slim stature. The energetic action in their bodies is intense, so their physiological activity is vigorous. As a result, they tend to have warmer bodies and swift physical movements.

Yang people have the opposite characteristics of yin people. Yang people have fast and light movements. They seem unsettled in the seated position, like a wobbling top about to fall, which is difficult to see because they rarely sit still. Instead, they are constantly on the go and move swiftly from place to place.

Yang people are decisive. They feel frustrated around people whose judgments or movements are slow. They have enormous dreams and goals, so they are continually dissatisfied with their present situation and may change jobs frequently. Yang persons generally like to lead people and dislike having others meddle in their affairs. They simply do not want any obstructions on the path to their goals. Yang people would not hesitate to go up to total strangers and tell them what they think. They are also not shy about their weaknesses and have no problem revealing their

YIN PEOPLE	YANG PEOPLE
appear calm	appear active
pale complexion	reddish complexion
pale tongue	reddish tongue
deep and weak pulse	superficial and stronger pulse
weaker sound to the pulse beat when checking the blood pressure	stronger sound to the pulse beat when checking the blood pressure
narrow shoulders and wide hips	broad shoulders and narrow hips
colder hands	warmer hands
tends to set thermostat higher	tends to set thermostat lower
likes hot water in average weather	likes cold water in average weather
likes soup	likes salad
prefers warmer colors, e.g., red and yellow	prefers cooler colors, e.g., blue and green
walks slowly	walks fast
makes decisions slowly	makes decisions quickly
satisfied easily	difficult to satisfy
introverted	extroverted
dislikes meeting new people	likes to meet new people

Table 4.1 Yin People, Yang People

innermost selves to others. They are sympathetic and tolerant of mistakes made by others because they frequently make mistakes.

Physically, yang persons tend to have stronger, broader shoulders and smaller, weaker hips. They generally have thinner bones and are thin despite eating a lot. Yang persons have warm hands and feet and cannot tolerate hot weather. They generally like to keep their windows at home open and set their thermostats at low temperatures. Yang persons prefer cold water and typically want to order raw salads rather than hot soups at restaurants. They like cooling colors, such as blue and indigo, instead of warmer colors. An Eastern medical examination of a yang person would reveal a reddish complexion, a red tongue, and a strong pulse, indicating higher blood pressure.

TREATMENT FOR YIN PEOPLE AND YANG PEOPLE

Yin persons can prevent and treat disease by eating more yang foods (see chapter 7, "Yin and Yang of Food and Diet"). They also need to develop a more broad-minded and positive attitude toward life. They should also exercise more with a greater emphasis on rapid movements.

Yang persons can supplement their shortage of yin by eating more yin foods. They should also try to be realistic about life, discarding idle fantasies and grounding flighty emotions. Yang persons can also supplement their yin through meditation, because it settles and quiets both the body and mind.

Yin and Yang of Personalities

The personalities of yin and yang people coincide with several established personality theories, including the Type A and Type B personality theory developed by Dr. Meyer Friedman and Dr. Ray H. Rosenman in the 1960s. According to Friedman and Rosenman, Type A personalities are goal-driven, deadline-setting workaholics. They are competitive multitaskers whose sole focus is on the outcome rather than the process. They are sensitive and confrontational and speak and move quickly and frequently. Conversely, Type B personalities are more relaxed and easygoing. They tend to enjoy the process and simply take things in stride. They focus on the present moment and work methodically. They prioritize and delegate responsibilities. Needless to say, yang persons correspond to the Type A personality, while yin persons correspond to the Type B personality.

The Type A–Type B model is a theory created to research and explain the link between personality and heart disease. However, this theory is incomplete compared to the yin-yang model because it ignores physical traits and focuses only on overt personality characteristics. Accordingly, it proved to be a largely invalid indicator of heart disease.

Carl Jung developed another personality theory that coincides with the yin-yang theory. Jung defined people as either introverted or extroverted and explained that these were congenital instinctive traits.

The energetic tendencies of extroverts extend outward, so their identity is dependent upon feedback from the external world and other people. They are energetic, social, and outgoing people who feel comfortable meeting new people and facing creative challenges. On the other hand, they are aggressive, impulsive doers, movers, and shakers who act first and think later. They focus more on the quantity or breadth of life experience than quality and depth.

The energetic tendencies of introverts extend inward, so they are more likely to focus on and appreciate their inner process. Introverts tend to be reflective and quiet and prefer solitude. They often feel uncomfortable in new situations or meeting new people, so they choose more intimate social situations. Introverts are idealists who dislike change. They consider all angles before acting and focus more on the quality and depth of life experience rather than the quantity or breadth.

Extroverts are yang, and introverts are yin. However, because people possess both yin and yang traits, elements of the opposing personality find their way to the surface in certain situations.

Yin and Yang of Human Physiology

A dynamic interplay between yin and yang is at the heart of the body's physiological functions. These two forces that support and define one another also mutually transform. The yin or substantive aspect of the body transforming into the yang or energetic facet is known as "energizing." This is what occurs when matter converts into energy.

The reciprocal process, energy (yang) converting into matter (yin), is known as "materialization." In the body, the end product of materialization is cellular formation, while the end product of the body's energizing function is muscle movement and glandular secretion. The constant interplay of these two functions is what we call life.

Stimulating the five senses can activate the materialization and energizing processes. External stimuli, being either yin or yang in nature, are translated by the brain in regard to their relative strength and tilt of yin or yang. For example, the color red (fire/heat) is a yang stimulus, while the color blue (cold/water) is a yin stimulus. High-pitched, high-frequency sounds are yang, and low-pitched, low-frequency sounds are yin. Fragrant smells are yang, and foul smells are yin. Flavors that are sweet, pungent, or salty are yang, whereas bitter, sour, or astringent flavors are yin. Pleasant, warm, or pleasing pressure sensations are yang, while rough, burning, stabbing, needle-like, abnormal sensations are all yin. Once the brain receives the stimuli, it analyzes the input and activates the appropriate energizing or materializing physiological action by sending orders to various body parts through the nervous and hormonal systems.

When the body requires more energy (yang), a command goes out to the sympathetic nervous system. This increases the secretion of hormones such as epinephrine, cortisone, thyroxine, and testosterone. At the same time, the liver initiates the process of glycolysis. In glycolysis, glycogen (a by-product of sugar) stored in the liver is converted into glucose and then supplied to muscle cells via the blood. Once in the muscle cells, glucose is transformed into its simplified state, called acetyl coenzyme A (acetyl CoA). Acetyl CoA then enters the TCA cycle (citric acid cycle, or tricarboxylic acid cycle, or Krebs cycle) to create adenosine triphosphate (ATP), a rarified form of energy. ATP then stimulates muscular activity.

When the body needs more cells (yin), a command goes out to the parasympathetic nervous system. This increases insulin, growth hormone, parathyroid hormone, estrogen, progesterone, and melatonin secretions. Parasympathetic stimulation also stops the TCA cycle and stimulates glycogenesis. These processes create the fats and proteins necessary for cellular formation. The following diagram (fig. 4.1) illustrates the energizing and materialization processes.

During the day, when it is bright and noisy (yang), the materializing function is almost at a

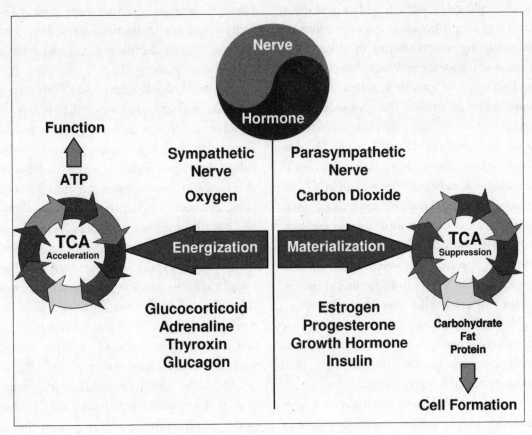

Figure 4.1 Yin and Yang of Human Physiology

complete standstill, while the energizing process is in full swing. Stimulation of the sympathetic nerves and secretion of cortisone occurs, and muscles become active. The organs above the diaphragm (a yang region) become excited. As a result, there is an increase in heart rate, blood pressure, lung capacity, and breathing rate. Glycogen breakdown increases so that the distribution of glucose and oxygen to every cell can occur. Inside the cells, the TCA cycle is hard at work creating ATP. Because of this energizing function, people are generally better suited to perform physical activities during the day.

At night (yin), when it is dark and quiet, the energizing function quiets down, and the materializing process creeps into action. Stimulation of the parasympathetic nervous system and secretion of growth hormone and melatonin occur. As a result, there is a reduction in muscle movement and a decrease in heart rate, lung function, and blood pressure. Accordingly, asthma attacks and neuralgic pain due to poor blood circulation worsen at night. Glycogenesis occurs, and the TCA cycle slows down. Acetyl CoA is used to form protein and fats, which afterward creates cells. New cells replace old ones, people gain weight, and children grow taller. This gives truth to the old Eastern adage "To grow taller, you must sleep a lot." Additionally, parasympathetic nerves regulate the reproductive system, so men get erections without external stimulation at night, and women's sexual desires increase.

The energizing and materialization processes are also sensitive to seasonal and climate changes. Yang seasons (spring and summer) activate energizing actions, so people tend to lose weight. Conversely, the materializing action is stronger during the yin seasons (autumn and winter), so people tend to gain weight. Habitants of northern polar regions (yin), where the materializing action is stronger, tend to have larger bodies. In contrast, those of the southern, tropical areas (yang), where the energizing action is stronger, tend to have smaller bodies.

Yin and Yang of the Life Cycle

Some of the most advanced theories of quantum physics state that matter broken down into its most minute component is nothing more than vibrating energy. Hence, the entire universe consists of only empty space. This theory coincides with the famous Buddhist statement "Color is emptiness, and emptiness is color." Emptiness implies a vacuum or void, while color implies perceptible things with form or shape. When you translate this into yin and yang, comparing perceptible and imperceptible, color is yang, and emptiness is yin. Yin is implicit. It is anything that has not yet revealed itself. Yang is explicit and anything that has already manifested. The human body comes from emptiness, becomes form, and then returns to emptiness. From yin, it becomes yang and then returns to yin, or, in other words, ashes to ashes and dust to dust.

According to traditional Eastern medicine, it is often said that infants are "bodies of pure yang" (although nothing exists that is pure yang). This is because infants have rapid pulses, their bodies are shiny, and they give off a lot of heat—all yang traits. Human life begins as inorganic matter (yin) and progresses to its peak of yang at birth. As people age, they gradually move toward yin again. At approximately forty years of age, the phenomenon of materialization is distinctly noticeable. It becomes more pronounced with each advancing year. When people die, they return to yin, to an inorganic state. From this perspective, sad though it may be, human beings begin dying the moment they are born.

CHILDREN AND ELDERS

Comparing the dispositions of children and seniors clearly illustrates the differences between yin and yang. Children are very active, while seniors move much less frequently and more slowly. Children babble with little regard for what they say, while older adults generally speak more slowly and thoughtfully. In addition, children are usually more comfortable in cold weather. They are not as averse to eating cold foods as the elderly. Because children have a lot of yang, they are lacking in yin.

On the other hand, older adults have plenty of yin, so their yang lacks. Because of these attributes, Eastern medicine often bases its children's diagnoses on syndromes from insufficient yin. Older adults, meanwhile, are diagnosed based on syndromes that result from a lack of yang. Therefore, Eastern medicine advises children to eat foods and herbs rich in yin, and older adults to eat foods and herbs rich in yang.

YIN AND YANG OF A MIDLIFE CRISIS

At forty, men's and women's transformation toward yin and away from the "pure yang" into which they were born becomes profound. It results in significant mental and physical changes. This is commonly known as a midlife crisis, primarily caused by hormonal changes.

Testosterone is responsible for masculine traits. When its levels are high, men are more yang in nature. They are louder, more boastful, and more active. They can also be more broad-minded and thus more tolerant. The heightened yang energy is comparable to having more firepower, giving its owner more courage. Yang energy expands outward, affecting other people, situations, and conditions. Yin energy tends to contract inward and withdraw, leading to a narrower focus.

After forty, as male hormonal secretions dwindle, men become more practical and narrow-minded. Their yin (contracting) energy grows, and their yang (expanding) energy dissipates. As a result, men's yin characteristics become more prominent. They begin to question the power that yang had over their lives. Seemingly insignificant things bother them, and suddenly they become concerned with issues that never bothered them before. Their ideas of taking over the world transform into simply seeing it from a more relaxed perspective. Rather than being active participants, they become passive observers from the sidelines.

Feminine traits (yin) are primarily due to the secretion of female hormones, such as estrogen and progesterone. After forty, there is a reduction in the secretion of female hormones, and women's yang characteristics become more prominent. They become more broad-minded and socially active, focusing more on activities outside the family. The drop in female yin hormones facilitates their yang energy, hence, they become more yang, or active.

During a midlife crisis, as men's masculinity and women's femininity decline, they may develop feelings of emptiness or depression. One way for men and women to endure this crisis is to understand the reason for their changing states (and those of their partner or spouse) using the theory of yin and yang as a guide.

These changes are part of the natural cycle of life. However, the state of adulthood is one of relative stability compared to childhood or adolescence. So when hormonal changes occur later in life, it is often difficult to cope with the sudden change. The best way to weather the storm is to maintain perspective and attempt to restore balance by supplementing the waning yin or yang energy.

Eastern medicine considers hormonal changes to be a decline of Jing, or essence. This is the substance from which all the body's energy derives (see additional discussion on Jing in chapters 5 and 14). Therefore, Eastern medicine recommends diet and lifestyle modifications to help build Jing. Additional recommendations include taking supplements and herbal remedies and performing exercises targeting hormonal health and spiritual clarity.

Later chapters discuss many of these solutions. In addition, doctors and acupuncturists trained in Eastern medicine are good sources of information and guidance. Acupuncture has been shown to help balance hormones and maintain health. Many Eastern herbal formulas are available to restore balance to the system.

Mental and spiritual cultivations through meditation, prayer, and mind-body exercises, such as Tai Chi, Qigong, and yoga, are very important to help balance yin and yang energies. They also promote the intuition and awareness necessary to maintain a broader perspective of life's natural cycles.

Easterners and Westerners

Another way to illustrate the yin-yang variations among people is to look at the differences between Easterners and Westerners. Although generalizations are ultimately stereotypical, there is always some element of truth to them. Remember that when we say "an Easterner is like this" or "a Westerner is like that," we do not mean that all Easterners or Westerners fit the stereotype. We are simply pointing out general tendencies.

If we look at physical activity, we find that, on the whole, Westerners tend to be more active (yang) than Easterners. As a result, their facial expressions change frequently, and their movements tend to be rapid. On the other hand, Easterners tend to have slower, more subtle ways of expressing themselves and slower physical activities because they tend to be more yin.

The difference between the two is demonstrated in their expressions when others treat them unkindly: Westerners will grimace, frown, and generally appear upset, whereas Easterners will tend to mask their expressions. Remember, yin persons possess a more significant materializing function that causes a reduction in energy consumption. This, in turn, slows down physiological functioning, such as that of facial expressions.

In Korean, Jum Jahn Ta is translated as "gentle." Its literal translation is "not young." The East holds great respect for elders (yin). So Easterners tend to increase their age when asked how old they are. In the West, things are just the opposite: people always want to be perceived as younger (more yang). They dislike being thought of as "old" and frequently assign a negative connotation to it. There is an incredible amount of money spent on cosmetic surgeries and beauty products in America every year. People fear becoming old because of the social stigma attached to the aging process. Youth implies activity (yang), while age implies slowing down (yin).

Statistics show that Westerners' heads are roughly one-eighth the size of their bodies. On the other hand, Easterners tend to have heads nearly one-seventh the size of their bodies. According to Eastern physiognomy,[1] a person with a smaller head in proportion to the body tends to think more practically and, as a result, tends to make decisions and execute ideas quickly. On the other hand, a person with a larger head proportion tends to be idealistic, indecisive, and less likely to implement ideas. Additionally, the form-function principle states that smaller things move faster. Thus, Westerners have a more yang-type brain functioning, and Easterners have a more yin-type brain functioning.

There are always exceptions, but we can also see these yin-yang characteristics in the everyday activities of these two groups of people. Westerners use saws designed to cut wood only while pushing. Eastern saws, in contrast, are designed to cut only during the pulling stroke. Westerners typically sweep the dust away from their bodies when they sweep the floor. Easterners tend to sweep the dust toward their bodies. These seemingly insignificant habits have a simple rationale: since Westerners are yang, their pushing force is more developed. They are, therefore, more comfortable pushing things away from their bodies. The opposite is true of Easterners. Since they are yin, their pulling force is more developed. They are, therefore, more likely to pull things toward their bodies.

The pushing-pulling contrast is also evident in social behaviors. Westerners tend to be more extroverted and sociable ("pushing out of their shells"). In contrast, Easterners tend to be more introverted and timid ("pulling into their shells"). When a person is bashful, there is a tendency to contract the body as energy gathers inward.

When eating soup, Easterners usually tilt the bowl toward their bodies (yin) and spoon the soup toward their bodies. In contrast, Westerners may tend to tilt the bowl away from their bodies and initially spoon soup away (yang) before bringing it back to their mouths. The utensils used while eating also demonstrates a yin-yang contrast. Generally, Westerners use knives and forks to eat their meals. These utensils are dissimilar to one another and thus independent and solitary pieces. They are also typically made of metal and are more yang in nature. Easterners generally use chopsticks that are only effective in pairs, often made of bamboo or wood, and do not cut or penetrate the food. These qualities are yin in nature.

Because Westerners are generally more yang than Easterners, they have a lot of heat in their bodies. Therefore, they are more comfortable in a cooler environment. When Easterners (with relatively less heat) go into an air-conditioned room where Westerners congregate in the summertime, they tend to feel very cold. Often Easterners who work with Westerners must wear sweaters while working indoors in the summer. A lot of heat implies that the substance rapidly changes into energy, a yang phenomenon.

There are many more examples of this yin-yang dichotomy. For instance, when calling someone to them, Easterners will make a hand motion with their palms down (yin), whereas Westerners will make the same hand motion with their palms up (yang). It may sound funny, but Easterners usually call their dogs with a palm up. Another example is when ringing a large bell. Easterners will hit it with a wooden pole from the outside (exterior to the interior: yin motion). Westerners usually strike it from the inside with a clapper (interior to the exterior: yang motion).

One of the most noticeable differences between these two groups is the places where people choose to sit. Most people sit on a chair in the West, whether at home, out dining, or at work. But in the East, though customs have changed quite a bit due to Western influence, most people sit with a cushion on the floor. Sitting on a chair is more yang due to its proximity to the heavens (yang), while sitting on the floor is more yin due to its proximity to the ground (yin). This difference may be due to the traditional dominance of the Heavenly Father or God (yang) figure in Western culture, while Eastern cultures revere Mother Nature (yin).

While Westerners have usually worn black (yin) to funerals, traditional Eastern mourning clothes have been white (yang). In the East, death is considered a return to the source. Life and death are seen as two sides of the same coin or as a circular path with the soul being reincarnated or transmigrated repeatedly. White is considered the color of life and enlightenment. It is the base from which all other colors emerge, like a blank canvas before any great work of art. Thus, from this life with its vast array of colors, at death, a person returns to the source to be able to start life anew.

Nowadays, people often wear black at funerals in the East and the West. Darkness and death have always been yin qualities associated with black. Black matches the solemn atmosphere (yin) of the funeral.

Conclusion

Yin and yang allow us a vantage point from which we can clearly see what distinguishes one person from another. They provide a platform to differentiate ourselves from others based on our innate attributes, psychological tendencies, physical differences, and personal leanings. They also function as a personal guide to the human condition, giving us insight into what we can do to establish balance within ourselves and harmony in our relationships. Yin and yang allow us to appreciate the intricacies and delicate balance of the human race without judgment or prejudice. They remind us that our differences exist so that we may live with more understanding.

5

Yin and Yang of Sex

Without a doubt, sex is one of the essential parts of our lives. It can impact our lives positively or negatively—mentally, emotionally, and physically. By applying the yin-yang theory to sex, we can better understand it to enhance our lives. One crucial way the yin-yang theory looks at sex is from the perspective of the energetic exchange that occurs during the act. This perspective implies that sexual activity can objectively strengthen or weaken a person. It can either give a person vibrant health and longevity or poor health and premature death. Before looking at sex, it is crucial to understand the inherent sexual differences between men and women in terms of yin and yang.

Yin and Yang of Men and Women

What makes men and women different—genetics, hormones, social influences? While these play essential roles, applying the yin-yang theory to gender differences reveals a more general distinction.

Relatively speaking, men are yang, and women are yin. Yang is an ascending, outward-moving, expansive energy, reflected in the physical and psychological characteristics men embody. Yin is a descending, inward-moving, contracting force, reflected in women's physical and emotional manifestations.

Physically, men typically have more well-developed upper bodies and shoulders, while women generally have more developed lower bodies and hips. Men also tend to be physically larger, stronger, and faster and have more body hair—all yang traits. Since men are more yang, they also burn more energy, generate more body heat, and perspire more than women while performing the same amount of work.[1]

Women tend to be physically smaller, slower, and weaker than men, with less body hair. However, women can procreate life and tend to live longer than men. Their longevity results from their superior ability to conserve energy and delay the breakdown or degeneration of their bodies.[2] In addition, as they store more fat cells (yin) in their bodies, they also usually have softer skin. These are all yin traits.

Psychologically and behaviorally, men tend to be more aggressive and reckless (yang), while women tend to be more cautious, patient, and polite (yin). Men are often more extroverted, competitive, dogmatic, self-righteous, and resolute, while women may be more introverted, passive, cooperative, gentle, docile, empathetic, caring, and indecisive. Men tend to rely on logic and reason, while women tend to find it easier to rely on intuition and emo-

tions. Men may be louder and display their emotions more readily, while women may be quieter and more apt to hide their feelings. Nevertheless, in our society, the sentiments expressed by men are more yang in nature, like anger and pride.

In contrast, women are usually quite comfortable showing more yin emotions, such as acceptance, sadness, or even jealousy. As extreme yin always turns into yang, women are more talkative and sentimental than men. The psychological differences between men and women mentioned in John Gray's book *Men Are from Mars, Women Are from Venus* are clear manifestations of yin and yang characteristics.

The following yin-yang diagram illustrates men's and women's physical and psychological differences (fig. 5.1).

Figure 5.1 Yin and Yang of Men and Women

This diagram represents the relative size of the head to the reproductive area of the body. The male symbol emphasizes the upper (head) region (the rounded aspect), while the female symbol emphasizes the lower (uterine) area. Eastern traditions assign psychological attributes to these physical differences. An Eastern saying goes, "Men think with their heads, and women think with their uteruses." It means that men are more rational and logical (yang), whereas women have greater intuitive (yin) abilities.

The yin and yang distinctions between men and women also come into play when looking at the genital shapes and the nature of sexual intercourse. Men's genitals protrude outward, while women's genitals are more "contracted" into the body. When sexually aroused, men get an erection. Expansion is yang in nature, and an erection of the male genitals is considered the epitome of yang expression. For men, obtaining an erection is a relatively rapid process, as is attaining orgasm and the subsequent diminished desire for additional sexual activity. As yang is swift, these actions are consistent with men's yang nature. Men's reduced desire for sex after ejaculation is due to the principle of extreme yang converting into yin. Women tend to be slower to achieve excitation, followed by longer orgasms and slower settling. Slow changes are yin.

During sex, men often enjoy vigorous motion, while women receive pleasure from slower, more fluid movements. Women frequently move in response to their partners, making them more yin. Additionally, women often close their eyes during sex to enhance the feeling of pleasure. With their eyes closed, their focus is more internal and thus more yin. Women are known to be more vocal during sex than men. When women become very sexually aroused, yin is in the extreme. Following the principle of mutual transformation, when yin is in the extreme, it converts into yang, and the yang energy rises to the throat to escape as cries of passion.

It is interesting to note that an intimate relationship exists between sounds made during sex and the energy of the internal organs. Eastern medical theory states that the kidneys are the most yin organs in the body because they are dark in color and sit low in the abdomen. The kidneys are also in charge of all sexual activity. Moaning is the most yin sound a person can make. It is low and comes from deep within. During sex, when the activity of the kidneys is at its zenith, people moan.

On the other hand, the heart is the most yang organ because it is high in the body and red. Its primary functions are regulating mental activities, emotions, and blood circulation. The sound related to the heart is laughter. Laughter is the most yang sound as it is high-pitched and generally comes from the chest. When the heart is healthy and happy, laughter occurs.

The relationship between the heart and the kidneys is an interplay between yin and yang. Although the kidneys govern sex, the heart plays a vital role in controlling the mind, emotions, and blood circulation to the sex organs. When the body is balanced, the heart and the kidneys are in harmony. This will lead to abundant sexual energy and pleasurable sexual experiences.

The Infinitely Divisible (Wo)man

Although men are ultimately more yang and women more yin, the relationship between yin and yang always adheres to the six basic principles (discussed in chapter 3).

YIN AND YANG OF SEX • 59

The principles of infinite divisibility and inversion state that nothing is ever purely yang or yin. This includes the attributes of men and women. Men possess specific physical characteristics that are yin when compared to women. For example, men's chests are generally flatter (more yin) than women's. They also have thicker skin, and their voices typically resonate at a lower frequency.

Another way we see infinite divisibility at work is by characterizing men and women as wholly more yin or more yang. Women (yin) can classify as yin women or yang women (women with more yang attributes and tendencies). Men (yang) can also be subdivided into yang men or yin men, depending on their natures.

There are several ways to determine the yin or yang nature of men and women, strictly by their physical appearance. For example, dark colors indicate yin energy because they are more "inactive" and "quiet." Thus, darker skin and hair are more yin qualities.

Thick and elastic lips are considered yin. Lips are part of the lowest (yin) orifice and sense organ of the face and are considered yin. Their thickness indicates an abundance of yin energy in the yin region of the face.

The eyes are yang because they are the brightest, most active, and the highest sense organ on the face. They reveal the state of yang energy in the body. People with strong yang energy tend to have reflective, brilliant, penetrating eyes compared to those with less yang (or greater yin) energy, who tend to have "sleepy" eyes.

According to Western stereotypes, women with blond hair are typically considered sexy. However, this stereotype may not be true when applying the yin-yang theory to hair color. The head is the highest point on the body and is where yang reaches its extreme. Following the principle of mutual transformation, once yang reaches its extreme, it transforms into yin. So, anything that grows from this region—hair—is considered yin. Bald persons, therefore, have a yang nature and are considered more aggressive or reckless. The hairs on the armpits or genitals are even more yin as they are hard and dark.

According to the yin-yang theory, as the nature of yin is dark, the darker a person's hair color, the more yin (and thus sexy) the person. The more yin there is, the more developed the genitalia. The greater the yin, the more pleasure derived and immersed in sex, and the longer one's sexual arousal. The lighter the hair color, the more yang the person has. So blond-haired women are more easily aroused and active but quickly cool down.

The following table indicates the general yin and yang distinctions of various parts of our bodies (table 5.1).

The following are descriptions and examples of (1) yin woman, (2) yang woman, (3) yin man, and (4) yang man.

1. THE CLASSIC YIN WOMAN
- HAIR: brown or black
- EYES: sleepy and seductive
- LIPS: thick
- SKIN: dark and soft
- HIPS: wide

	YIN	YANG
Shoulders	narrow	wide
Hips	wide	narrow
Abdomen	protruding	flat
Head hair	dark, thick	light, thin
Body Hair	less	more
Skin	dark	light
Head size	larger	smaller
Lips	thick	thin
Eyes	sleepy	penetrating, sparkling

Table 5.1 Yin-Yang of Physical Characteristics

- PERSONALITY: quiet, refined, soft-spoken, secretive, seductive
- EXAMPLES: Marilyn Monroe, Gina Lollobrigida, Sophia Loren, Catherine Zeta-Jones, Angelina Jolie, Penélope Cruz, Cleopatra

2. THE CLASSIC YANG WOMAN

- HAIR: blond or red
- EYES: sharp, reflective, sparkling
- LIPS: thin
- SKIN: fair/light-colored and delicate
- HIPS: narrow
- SHOULDERS: relatively wide
- PERSONALITY: outgoing, cheerful, bright, talkative, social, tomboy-like
- EXAMPLES: Madonna, Jennifer Aniston, Gwen Stefani, Pamela Anderson, Jessica Simpson, Sarah Jessica Parker

3. THE CLASSIC YIN MAN

- HAIR: thick, dark
- EYES: sleepy
- LIPS: thick
- SKIN: dark or rough
- HIPS: fairly large (for a man)
- SHOULDERS: relatively narrow
- ABDOMEN: protruding lower abdomen (yin region)
- PERSONALITY: somewhat dull and tactless
- EXAMPLES: Antonio Banderas, George Clooney, Robert Downey Jr., Russell Crowe, Johnny Depp

4. THE CLASSIC YANG MAN

- HEAD: relatively smaller
- HAIR: thin or bald
- EYES: sharp, reflective
- LIPS: thin
- SKIN: fair
- HIPS: small
- SHOULDERS: wide
- PERSONALITY: quick to take action, sensitive, rash, reckless, or foolhardy
- EXAMPLES: Brad Pitt, Arnold Schwarzenegger, Dolph Lundgren, Fabio, Clint Eastwood, Sting

Source Qi and Grain Qi

Eastern medical doctrines refer to the body's energies as Qi (pronounced "chee"). Qi initiates, activates, catalyzes, and supports every thought, action, emotion, and bodily function. There are several different types of Qi involved in these activities.

Among them are food energy called Grain Qi and the energy originating from birth, known as Source Qi (the yang state of Jing). This energy is consumed during sex. The Source Qi is like a car's battery, continuously charged by the Grain Qi but eventually running out. A car battery can be replaced, but a person will die when the Source Qi is exhausted.

The Source Qi functions as all energy needed before a person is born, and the Grain Qi is made. The Source Qi controls the production of Grain Qi even after it is made. If the human body needs a lot of Grain Qi, an appetite is increased to produce it quickly; if the body does not need much Grain Qi, appetite is decreased, and its production is slowed down. If the body is overweight with a lot of fat accumulation, it suppresses the appetite. If the body is emaciated, it causes an appetite to increase, so more food is taken in. However, if the Source Qi is deficient, such functions cannot occur. As a result, overweight individuals have difficulty coping with hunger, leading them to overeat to satisfy their appetite. The thin person, in contrast, doesn't know whether he or she is hungry and works continuously until they collapse from a lack of energy.

Among the Grain Qi, the yang aspect, known as Wei or Protective Qi, mainly circulates on the body's exterior. It triggers an inflammatory reaction to drive out harmful bacteria or viruses entering the body. The Source Qi follows the Protective Qi during such an action, receiving reports and giving orders. If the Source Qi is insufficient, the Protective Qi attacks and causes inflammation, even though the substance is not harmful, causing allergic rhinitis, asthma, and dermatitis. In addition, unable to distinguish whether a substance is friendly or foe, Protective Qi mistake the necessary bodily cells as bacteria and attack them, causing diabetes, lupus, or rheumatoid arthritis. In diabetes, the attack is made on the beta cells of the islets of Langerhans, which produce insulin. All connective tissues in the body are attacked in lupus, and in rheumatoid arthritis, the connective tissues around the joints are attacked. The Source Qi balances the yin-yang physiological functions of the body. In physiology, this is called homeostasis. Similar to a house's thermostat, it functions to raise the temperature when the weather is cold and lower it when it's hot.

The Source Qi adjusts the thermostat's needle according to the bodily time clock based on the programmed DNA and surrounding environment. Then the yin and yang alternately function, and the physiological function of a lifetime occurs. If there is a lack of the Source Qi, the balance of yin-yang function breaks down and disease occurs. As the Source Qi is gradually consumed, it eventually disappears, and in old age, suffering from many diseases occurs before death. Some people get sick at an early age because they received less Source Qi when they are born, and it is easier to get sick in old age when the Source Qi is lacking. The quantity of the Source Qi is the "life" or "destiny" of a person.

A long and healthy life depends on the preservation of the Source Qi. Since this energy is received at birth as a terminal of the cosmic nervous system, its safeguarding and sufficient charging can cause an awakening of the nerves, resulting in enlightenment and a healthy and long life. Therefore, Taoist cultivation art, which researches enlightenment and immortality, makes an in-depth study of it.

Huangdi, the Yellow Emperor (2711–2599 BCE) of the legendary era, is responsible for transmitting the Tao to China and is considered a deity. He is the king of the immortals and the father of Chinese civilization. He is known to have compiled the Eastern medical bible, *The Yellow Emperor's Inner Classic,* and the sex bible, *The Plain Girl.*[3] These are books about the Tao of medicine and sex written from the perspective of I Ching. In addition to these books, the Taoist self-cultivation practice of Danjun breathing, meditation, and sex also treats Source Qi like a treasure.

Meditation is also a way to calm the body and mind to replenish the Source Qi that rises from the extreme of the yin. People who do not meditate will gradually consume their energy, but those who meditate are supplemented by meditation to some extent. But eventually all of the Source Qi is depleted. If you succeed in meditation and become enlightened, you can

return to the origin of Source Qi and live like a god, but very few have succeeded in this endeavor.

Yin-Yang Dynamics of Sex

The I Ching states that the interplay of two opposing forces created the universe: *expansion,* embodied by the Big Bang (yang), and *contraction,* exemplified by the black hole (yin). The same is true for human beings. When men and women are separated, yin and yang are divided. Through intercourse, invocation of the same expansion and contraction forces transpire, creating a universe (Tai Chi). The following diagram (fig. 5.2) portrays the Tai Chi of a man and a woman with two numbers. In the I Ching, the number 6 represents yin, and the number 9 represents yang. The number 6 also symbolizes the earth, while 9 denotes heaven. As 6 and 9 join, earth and heaven unite to become Tai Chi, or totality.

Figure 5.2 Tai Chi of a Man and a Woman

During intercourse, the yang elements manifest expansive energy, such as increased heart and respiratory rates and an elevated state of excitement. When men reach orgasm, the expansion process reverses with the ejaculation of semen, a yin substance. At the same time, the woman's uterus contracts and absorbs the semen along with the energy surrounding the semen. If an egg fertilizes, a new universe is created approximately 270 days later with the birth of a baby.

The interplay of yin and yang during sex highlights the significance of the energetic exchange. For this reason, men and women need to understand the dangers of engaging in frequent sexual activity with an improper partner and the benefits of sex with a partner who is an energetic match.

A great deal of energy exchange occurs between two people engaging in sexual activity. Orgasms release Source Qi from the body. The release and absorption of Source Qi can make a person stronger or weaker depending on their partner.

Yin women take longer to warm up and attain orgasm, and their climaxes last longer. Because the nature of women is predominantly yin, yin women are particularly adept at absorbing energy; they also tend to be particularly attractive in a dark and seductive way. Yin also represents reproductive capabilities, so strong yin women tend to carry their pregnancies well and have strong children.

Yang men are predominantly yang and are easily aroused, quickly attain orgasm, and readily release significant quantities of their Source Qi. Yang-natured men who frequently engage in sexual activities with yin-natured women would risk their health. As the man discharges his Source Qi, the yin woman would be able to absorb her partner's energy. Because of her strong absorptive force, she would reclaim most of her own. So, as she grows more vital

from this relationship, he grows weaker. Ultimately, his immune system may weaken, and he could become susceptible to catching colds or developing allergies.

Sex manuals in the East expound on the importance of identifying a strong yin woman. A woman of this nature is known as "a woman beautiful enough to cause the downfall of a country" because she could extract the Source Qi of any ruler who fell under her spell. This is akin to the story of Helen of Troy or Cleopatra, who dismantled able-bodied rulers with their womanly ways.

The strong yin man would not suffer much loss of Source Qi even if he were to have sex with a strong yin woman. Upon ejaculation, he would release less Source Qi (because of the strong absorptive power of yin) and reabsorb some of the Source Qi released.

Men born with strong yin energy can absorb the Source Qi of women. If this type of man frequently has sex with a woman with strong yang energy, there is the danger that she may lose a lot of her Source Qi and become ill. She could become thin and emaciated, with dark circles under her eyes and an increased tendency for illness.

Like a strong yang man, a strong yang woman will get sexually excited and orgasm quickly, scattering her Source Qi, unable to reabsorb it. This type of woman would benefit by meditating and eating foods like seafood and taking herbs, such as Rehmannia root, that nourish the body's yin energy (see chapter 7 on diet).

On the other hand, the strong yin man

should take herbs that tonify yang, such as ginseng, and make an effort to ejaculate faster. This way, he can release and return the Source Qi that he absorbs from his partner.

A strong yang man should attempt to cultivate his yin energy through meditation and ingesting yin-nourishing herbs and foods. Meanwhile, the strong yin woman should ingest herbs that are yang in nature. She should also exercise to strengthen her yang energy. This way, she will experience quicker and more frequent orgasms, releasing a portion of the Source Qi she accumulated.

Fortunately, the yang man has an appropriate partner in the strong yang woman. This woman shares the same characteristics as the strong yang man. She has fair skin, relatively wide shoulders, thin hair, sharp eyes, narrow hips, swiftness, and sensitivity. She, like her counterpart, will attain orgasm quickly. However, she will not be able to absorb most of the Source Qi released by the man; thus, a portion of it will return to him. Therefore, when a strong yang man has sex with a strong yang woman, he will feel that his orgasm is relatively slow and will release less of his Source Qi.

Health, Longevity, and Enlightenment

The cultivation of Source Qi is the path to health, longevity, and enlightenment. In the past, wealthy men of the East (primarily nobles and businessmen) bought concubines to maintain their health and increase their longevity. The household steward, well-versed in the principle of yin and yang, would make the purchase. First he would examine the prospective woman's physiognomy and translate it into yin and yang. Then, if she were a strong yang woman who could readily release her Source Qi, she was purchased.

Some women use sex to "recharge their batteries." It is easier for women to do so because they are naturally yin and have the inborn capacity to absorb Source Qi. After all, copulation and fertilization require that women "absorb" the male Source Qi (sperm) into their uterus. Although they may be well over forty, they maintain the beauty and skin of much younger women by frequently having sex with young men. Since younger men are more yang, they quickly release their Source Qi for these women to absorb.

There exist in the East masters who have learned to move their Source Qi at will through training, meditation, and ingesting herbs. These masters, trained in the art of supplementing their Source Qi through sex, will generally attempt to attract women with strong yang energy. These men bring women to orgasm quickly to absorb the released Source Qi. Once they absorb their partner's Source Qi, they quickly leave to meditate and transform their newly acquired energy into their own Source Qi. Unfortunately, intentionally stealing another person's Source Qi is both troublesome and unethical and thereby hinders reaching enlightenment.

Koong Hap

To prevent an imbalance of yin or yang in a relationship, couples in Korea have a "Koong Hap" done before marriage. Koong Hap is a prediction of marital harmony performed by a fortune teller with an in-depth understanding of yin-yang principles. "Koong" refers to the uterus or the reproductive organs, and "Hap" implies the act of checking the fit, or suitability, of two things. Thus, Koong Hap suggests checking whether or not a couple's reproductive organs are compatible.

Traditionally, it was not possible to know whether a couple would be able to have orgasms at the same time before marriage. Therefore, Koong Hap would check the horoscopes of both partners for compatibility. One aspect of Koong Hap involves looking at the body shape of each partner. If the upper body is relatively more developed, that person is yang, and vice versa. Through this simple observation, one can determine whether both members of the couple shared the same energy (yin or yang) or not. If the yin and yang of a couple were in complete opposition, the results were not favorable and the couple was deemed incompatible.

Therefore, knowing the Koong Hap before marriage was an essential precautionary measure. Preventing illness and premature death due to loss of Source Qi during sex was its purpose. Of course, there is much more premarital sex in modern times, during which two partners can determine their sexual compatibility.

Nevertheless, the more astrological aspects of Koong Hap are still widely practiced, perhaps to maintain cultural tradition.

Southern Man, Northern Woman

In Korea, there is a saying: "southern man and northern woman." It implies men from southern regions and women from northern regions are more masculine and feminine, respectively, than men and women from other regions. Because southern regions have more sunlight, they are brighter and thus infused with more yang energy, resulting in the people living there being more yang. People living in southern climates are more active, open-minded, and romantic. As men are naturally yang, southern men are considered the epitome of masculine yang energy.

On the other hand, northern regions have less sunlight and thus less yang energy. Therefore, in comparison to southern regions, northern regions are yin. The relative abundance of yin energy makes the people living there more yin. Thus, people of northern climates are more passive, introspective, and less social. As women are yin, northern women are viewed as particularly yin or feminine.

Based on this yin-yang perspective, southern men are more active, social, and generally more popular with women. Meanwhile, northern women tend to be more quiet, passive, gentle, shy, and feminine, implicitly attracting the attention of men. Although this concept might seem radical, some observations that we usually take for granted in the West support it.

For instance, on an international scale, cultural icons of romance in the Western world are often from southern climates. Don Juan and Giacomo Casanova are "Latin lovers" from Spain and Italy. In contrast, it is hard to conceive of an "Arctic lover." The cold northern climates call images of snow and ice to mind rather than burning passion.

The nature of yin and yang, which men and women possess, is the primary determining factor in sexual attraction or repulsion. People with similar characteristics are often attracted to one another, while those who are strongly dissimilar would not want to be near one another. While it is true that "opposites attract," this only happens when the differences are slight. Men and women who are exceedingly different would be unable to circumvent those opposing characteristics to develop harmony in their relationship.

6

Yin and Yang of the Brain

In her remarkable personal account, Jill Bolte Taylor, a brain scientist and researcher, tells what it is like to survive a massive stroke of the brain's left hemisphere.[1] According to Taylor, her left hemisphere repeatedly went "offline" during the stroke. As a result, she oscillated between possessing the left hemisphere's cognitive awareness and abilities and moving into an uncharted realm where she could not distinguish herself from surrounding objects or communicate in an understandable language. Her extraor-dinary experience boldly illustrates that the two hemispheres of the human brain control separate functions of human activity.

Taylor's insight into the brain's inner workings aptly demonstrates how everything in the universe, including the human brain, comprises two opposing forces. By recognizing the yin and yang aspects of various brain parts, we better understand the brain's complexities.

The Two Hemispheres of the Brain

The left hemisphere is considered yang since it is in charge of language and calculations and because the speed at which this hemisphere processes information is relatively fast. The left hemisphere is also in charge of logic, reason, analysis, and digital interpretations. Its strength is in synthesizing objective data. Linear, rational thought and objective reasoning are yang because they are more rapid, concrete, and direct processes.

The right hemisphere is yin because it is in charge of artistic talents and intuition, which occur at a slower rate. Creativity may appear spontaneous, but intuition and inspiration require considerable self-actualization. It is a lengthy process, and true works of art involve great deliberation, study, and planning before they materialize. The right hemisphere also controls the brain's analog processing and symbolic interpretations. Therefore, subjectivity, intuition, and nonlinear thoughts are yin processes.

Following is a chart of the yin-yang distinctions of the brain (table 6.1).

The yin and yang distinctions between the two hemispheres illustrate the brain's opposing forces. However, in a well-functioning brain, the two hemispheres communicate through the corpus callosum, demonstrating the mutual dependence of yin and yang.

Forebrain—Hindbrain

Yin-yang theory considers dynamic activity and evolutionarily advanced functions to be yang. Therefore, when the brain splits into its front and rear components, the front half is considered yang and the back half is considered yin (table 6.2). The front of the brain contains the motor cortex, which

LEFT HEMISPHERE (YANG)	RIGHT HEMISPHERE (YIN)
mathematics	art
language	symbols
science	music
logic	emotion
reason	intuition
analytical	holistic
digital	analog
information	inference
concrete/objective	associative/subjective
linear	geometrical

Table 6.1 Yin and Yang of Brain Hemispheres

Yang	Yin
anterior cortex	posterior cortex
motor movement	sensory reception
cerebrum	cerebellum

Table 6.2 Yin and Yang Regions of the Brain

controls physical activities (yang). It also includes the brain's newer (yang) part, the cerebrum, in charge of more evolved functions (yang), such as reasoning and judgment.

The hindbrain is in charge of sensory reception, a yin activity, because it is the act of *gathering* information. Following the principle of mutual consumption and support, this sensory reception (yin) is stronger when all muscular activity (yang) has ceased. The hindbrain also contains the cerebellum, the evolutionarily older (yin) part of the brain that is responsible for more primitive (yin) functions, such as reflex and balance (fig. 6.1). These functions are yin because they are more innate and physical.

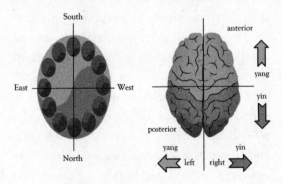

Figure 6.1 Yin and Yang Regions of the Brain

Memory and Sensation

The brain is in charge of both memory and sensation. Technically, memory is the storing of information. Because it is a gathering or contracting action, memory is considered a yin process. The hippocampus, which stores memories, is located in a yin region of the brain in the deep folds of the temporal lobe.

Applying the principle of infinite divisibility to memory gives us a more accurate picture of this process. There are two distinct types of memory: short-term and long-term. As the name implies, short-term memory (also called "active memory") is transient (yang). It holds small amounts of information for short periods and is rapidly accessed—all yang characteristics. On the other hand, long-term memories are retrieved more slowly (yin), and the brain holds large quantities of these memories for long periods. In addition, structural (yin) changes to neural pathways occur to store this information. For all of these reasons, long-term memory is considered yin.

A homunculus is a map of the sensory zones of the human body imposed onto the brain (fig. 6.2). This map conforms to the principles of yin and yang. The face and hands are located in the upper body and are more mobile (yang). Their sensory zones are in the outermost regions of the brain (yang). The legs and sexual organs are situated in the lower body and are less mobile (yin). Their sensory zone folds into the brain (yin) at the upper right corner of the map (central sulcus). The internal organs, which are more yin than the arms and legs, also fold inward (yin) at the lower left corner of the map (lateral sulcus).

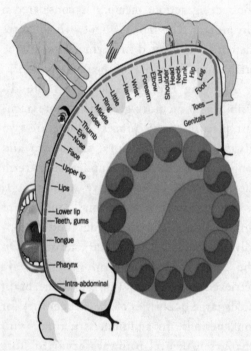

Figure 6.2 Homunculus

Yin and Yang of Sense Organs

One of the major tasks of the brain is sensory perception. Our senses give flavor and color to life and protect us from harm. Yin and yang characteristics distinguish these sense organs.

It is possible to analyze the yin and yang of sense organs on the face (eyes, ears, nose, and mouth) by examining their position, function, movement, and workload. When viewed at their location, the eyes and ears are yang organs because they are on the upper part of the face. Additionally, they receive information as sound waves and light frequencies, both energetic (yang) stimuli. The nose and mouth sit lower on the face (yin) and receive input in the form of molecules and substances (yin).

It's possible to break these stimuli down further. Since light moves more rapidly than sound waves, it is more yang. The molecules of odors are larger and move more slowly than light or sound but are smaller than substances required to stimulate taste. Therefore, in terms of speed and weight, light is the most yang, followed in decreasing order by sound, odors, and flavors.

The eyes and mouth are more active (yang) than the nose and ears in movement. The eyes constantly blink, and the mouth opens and closes during many activities, such as eating, speaking, and breathing. On the other hand, the nose and ears infrequently move, if at all. Regarding workload, however, the inversion principle comes into play. Because the eyes and mouth can open and close, there is a significant amount of time, while sleeping, for example, when they are at rest and do not take in any stimuli. This makes them more yin. On the other hand, the nose and ears are always open and do not have a mechanism with which they can escape stimuli, making them more yang in this sense.

The Polar Nature of Vision and Hearing

People rely on their vision more than their hearing in most situations in today's society. Ironically, the sensory information we get from our ears is superior to that which we receive from our eyes. The ears can sense vibrations much farther away (yang) and much more dispersed (yang) than visual information that the eyes can receive. For instance, ears can hear sounds from all angles, whereas eyes can only see what is (mostly) in front of them. From inside a room without windows, ears can still hear sounds from outdoors, while eyes cannot see what is beyond the walls. Therefore, the ears are more yang than the eyes in terms of sensory abilities.

The ears are also in a yang position, since they are posterior to the eyes. The yin-yang theory states that the back is yang, and the front is yin. So the eyes are the most yang based on their highest position on the face. Remember that yin and yang can change with differing perspectives, allowing another way to view positions.

However, we can see that vision and hearing have opposing natures regarding bodily movement. People crane their necks to get a better look when trying to see better. This requires that the body become more active (yang). When attempting to hear unfamiliar sounds, people drop their heads and still their physical movements to pay closer attention (yin).

Conclusion

Like everything in nature, every part of our bodies has a yin and yang aspect. The brain, the most complex of all physical forms, is no exception and comprises both yin and yang. Likewise, sense organs, extensions of the brain, also have yin and yang aspects. Yin and yang complement and support each other to create and sustain all things. Similarly, the two hemispheres of the brain and all the sense organs, whether yin or yang, must cooperate to help us better perceive, recognize, and comprehend various things.

Yin and Yang of Food and Diet

Arguably, the most important thing we can do daily to balance our bodies' yin and yang energies is to maintain a healthy diet. Along with the air (yang) we breathe, food (yin) gives us the energy to maintain, repair, build our bodies, and function daily. But what is a healthy and balanced diet?

A healthy diet starts with foods beneficial to our bodies, which balance our yin and yang energetic tendencies. The basis for the yin-yang category of foods includes the food source, taste, temperature, smell/odor, and their actions on the body once digested. Once we determine the nature of food, we can decide if it will support or harm our health and we can make informed decisions about what is truly a healthy diet.

Looking at the Source

Considering the source of food is one way to determine its nature. The yin-yang continuum of food sources is illustrated here (fig. 7.1). Animals are yang in nature, while plants are more yin. This is because animals are yang due to their active, dynamic dispositions, while plants are yin due to their passive natures. However, these statements hold true only when animals and plants are alive. According to the inversion principle, yin and yang change depending on whether the animal is alive or dead. Thus, meat is yin compared to fruits and vegetables regarding nutrition and digestion.

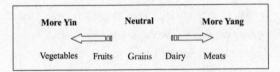

Figure 7.1 Yin-Yang Spectrum
of the Basic Food Groups

Nutritionwise, foods from animal sources are higher in nutrients (yin) than food derived from plant sources. Among plant sources, grains contain more nutrients, and are thus more yin, than fruits and vegetables.

The yin and yang of various foods can also be determined by how the body processes the foods. Foods that are difficult or impossible to digest completely are molecularly sluggish, meaning that the foods' molecular components are slow and difficult to break down in the digestive process. For example, fats and oils are molecularly slow and difficult to digest.

Likewise, fiber is indigestible because its molecular interactions are extremely slow. Following this line of reasoning, we see that the more fat, oil, or fiber a food contains, the more yin it is. In addition, foods the body cannot fully process tend to have a slightly offensive and

bitter (yin) taste hidden within. On the other hand, foods that digest easily, such as spices, have highly active molecules that help facilitate digestion. Therefore, pungent and sweet foods digest much more quickly than those with a bitter or sour taste. For this reason, fruits are more yang than vegetables because they are sweeter.

Again, the food source and the digestion of the food have a reciprocal relationship stemming from the inversion principle. Foods that are more yang in nature are more yin regarding their digestion, and vice versa. For example, meat products (yin, otherwise yang when they are live animals), primarily composed of fats and proteins, take longer (more yin) to digest than fruits and vegetables, mostly composed of natural sugars, fiber, and water. Because they take longer to break down, they require more water and energy for digestion. In addition, the energy the body ultimately receives from this digestive process is slower to arrive (yin) and more prolonged (yin) once it begins.

On the other hand, yang-natured foods are broken down quickly, require little energy or water to digest, and give the body quick energy. In addition, the sugars and water contained in yang-natured foods aid in the digestion of yin-natured food. Thus, people crave sweets, coffee, or tea after eating a heavy meal.

Taste and Craving

Taste is crucial when determining which foods are beneficial and which are harmful.

The body's deficient nutritional elements often influence the type of taste it craves. For example, children and teenagers prefer hamburgers and processed sweets to carrots and cabbage. The reason for this is that their bodies' rapid growth and development need large quantities of both immediate and sustained energy. Meat offers sustained nutrition (yin energy), while the sugar found in sweets feeds children's rapidly changing internal environment (yang energy).

The elderly crave meat and sugar less often. That is not to say that elders don't enjoy steaks and ice cream. Instead, their internal systems have less need for the nutrients derived from these foods. Taste makes people automatically select what is necessary for their bodies and differs from person to person and from time to time.

Eastern medicine has been researching the effects of tastes for thousands of years, understanding that taste plays a vital role in determining the medicinal characteristics and physiological effects of foods and herbs. Just as Western medicine analyzes the chemical composition of a drug to determine its function, Eastern medicine analyzes tastes to assess the impact of food or herbal medicines.

Taste results from the individual yin-yang variance that synthesizes a substance's entire development and composition. Unlike Western pharmaceuticals, foods and herbs are ingested entirely, and Eastern traditions consider them medicinal if they cause significant physiological changes in the body. Substances with a yin-and-yang balance similar to the human body and that cause few bodily changes are considered foods.

One thing to note is that every element in food has an independent effect on the body. Because of the multitude of food components, modern chemistry cannot analyze the total effect of any food. Instead, Western science would need to break down the elements to a quantum physical level and study their relationships to determine the body's responses to various foods.

In Eastern medicine, there are five basic tastes: pungent, sweet, sour, bitter, and salty. Their classification into yin or yang depends on their effects on the body. For instance, spicy, sweet, or salty foods will induce yang actions in the body, while those that are sour or bitter will induce yin actions. A balanced meal includes all five flavors.

PUNGENT

Pungent foods are yang because they disperse energy and activate the body's yang functions and internal processes. They stimulate the digestive system by increasing the production of saliva and juices and augmenting peristalsis, the muscular contractions that move food through the digestive tract. They also invigorate mental function and other physiological activities. For example, when we eat hot peppers or wasabi, we feel stimulated and more awake and aware. We may start to sweat, and our breathing may become more rapid. We also may feel like drinking a big glass of cold water—our system's attempt to neutralize the fire (yang) with water (yin).

Hot peppers (chili, jalapeño, habanero) are the epitome of pungent foods. Other examples include garlic, ginger, onion, cinnamon, black pepper, clove, nutmeg, turmeric, fennel, and mustard. The pungent taste is the predominant flavor of these foods and thus their major categorization. Nevertheless, all foods contain several flavors, giving each food its unique taste and medicinal action.

Sweet

Sweetness, in Eastern medicine, is defined as anything sweeter than water and is the distinguishing factor between foods and nonfoods or medicines. All foods, grains, meats, fruits, and even bitter vegetables have some element of sweetness stemming from their carbohydrate component, which supplies energy and nourishment to the body.

According to Eastern medicine, the sweet taste is considered the most balanced flavor because it moderates and harmonizes internal actions, is easily assimilated, and benefits digestion. It nourishes (yin) while supplying energy (yang) to the body. Sweet foods such as honey, malt syrup, and sugarcane moisten dryness. Their medicinal uses include easing dry cough and constipation.

Honey, considered the sweetest food, has many medicinal effects and is traditionally used to combat stomach spasms. The yin-yang theory states that the body's energy is in a continuous cycle of contraction and expansion. Pain occurs when energy remains in a contracted (yin) state. Because the sweet taste is balanced, it can ameliorate any extreme of yin or yang. Drinking honey mixed with warm water during stomach spasms will dissipate pain like melting ice with hot water.

Honey's action on the body is different than that of processed sugar. Sugar loses many of its natural qualities and nutrients during the refining process. Honey is eaten in its unadulterated state and has far more medicinal effects and fewer harmful properties. It also contains enzymes that benefit the digestive system, and its sugars are more easily broken down and assimilated than those in processed sugar.

The level of sweetness determines the overall yin-yang classification of sweet foods. Although sweet is the most balanced taste, it is a fundamental energy source and incites yang actions in the body. Because of this, mildly sweet foods are mildly yang, and primarily sweet foods are more yang.

Sour

Sour is yin and a contracting flavor. It promotes the inward drawing of energy and fluids, slows the body's physiological activities and respiration, decreases blood pressure, and cools the body. Because of sour's accumulating effect, Eastern medicine recommends using sour herbs for symptoms like coughing or diarrhea, which cause energy or fluids to pathologically leave the body.

When the body's functions have sped up and energy is spent after exercise, sour drinks like lemonade taste great. This is because the sour taste slows down and constricts energy to help the body return to a balanced state. Children tend to like sour foods, such as pickles and Sour Patch Kids, because the yin energy of the food balances their yang nature. The sour taste actually aids in materializing substances for growth, regeneration, and the production of new cells. This is also the reason why older adults do not like sour foods. They have less production of new cells and so have less need to gather the energy for the materialization of substances.

BITTER

Bitter is also yin. It descends (yin) and cools (yin) the body's energy. Diseases that are yang in nature are due to excessive heat in the body and manifest with a high fever and rapid pulse. Western medicinal substances prescribed for these illnesses, such as quinine, corticosteroids, and antibiotics, are incredibly bitter and curb the excessive yang activity with their yin effects. Likewise, herbs that clear heat, reduce inflammation, and detoxify are also bitter. However, herbs have fewer and less-severe side effects since the whole plant is used, not just its parts, as in Western pharmaceuticals.

The properties of the bitter taste (cool and descending) can also promote bowel movements. Most purgatives, substances that vigorously stimulate bowel movements, are bitter.

Extremely bitter substances elicit a strong adverse physical reaction in the body. This protective mechanism shields us from ingesting things that could strongly slow or stop our life energy, such as poisons or toxins.

SALTY

Salt and water have opposing natures. But, just as yin and yang attract, water and salt are also drawn together. For example, old water (seawater) is salty because over time the water chemically attracts enough salt to change its composition. Likewise, the body requires salt to retain water. Therefore, sodium and chloride, the elemental components of salt, are essential in maintaining the proper physiological functioning of the body.

Water is the substance most representative of yin. Salt, its opposite, is the quintessential yang substance. Water washes and erodes all things into the ocean and absorbs and conceals them. Salt, the crystallization of seawater, is volatile. When fried, salt explodes. In the past, nitrate (a salty taste) and salt were the main ingredients in explosives. Nitroglycerin (a nitrate) dilates the blood vessels of the coronary artery during attacks of angina (pain in the chest resulting from a lack of blood to the heart). Sildenafil citrate (brand name Viagra), first studied as an alternative to nitroglycerin in the treatment of angina, was fortuitously found to expand the blood vessels of male genitals. It thus became the now-famous drug for impotence.

For these reasons, salt produces yang actions in the body, such as increasing blood circulation and raising blood pressure. In addition, it can help dissolve hard masses or soften hard lumps and is used medicinally for hard lymph nodes or hard stool. Because of its yang action, salt can also improve the digestion of meats, grains, and legumes.

Artificial Flavors

One exception to the principles governing taste is found in the pharmacologically active ingredients extracted from plants and artificially synthesized. The actual flavors of artificial condiments, such as MSG and saccharin, are masked, and their influences on the body differ entirely from their tastes.

For instance, MSG is a sodium salt of glutamic acid, which stimulates receptors in the taste buds specific for meat. Therefore, ingesting MSG causes the body to perceive that it has consumed a great deal of meat and reacts accordingly, releasing digestive enzymes and preparing for the influx of fuel. Unfortunately, activating these physiological processes without the nutritional base to support the metabolic processes causes some side effects in MSG-sensitive individuals. They include chest pain, headaches, heartburn, facial pressure, and excessive sweating.

Saccharin is an artificial sweetener three hundred to five hundred times sweeter than sugar. Saccharin stimulates taste buds that fool the body into perceiving that it has just ingested large quantities of sugar. As with MSG, the body begins metabolic processes, including the release of insulin, in response to the perceived influx of calories with no nutritional base to support the operations.

Since saccharin's invention, there has been much controversy about the health risks of artificial sweeteners. For years the FDA tried unsuccessfully to ban saccharin. Many scientific studies show that stimulation of the taste buds by artificial sweeteners induces increased insulin production, which can be very damaging to the body. To better understand the potential harm, let's analyze this process using the principles of yin and yang.

When a sugar (yang) enters the body, there is a surge of energy while the sugar remains in the bloodstream. However, blood sugar levels must remain balanced, so the body produces insulin to transform and store the sugar. The transformation and storage of sugar are yin actions that slow the body's metabolism.

When a person eats or drinks saccharin products, the body produces massive amounts of insulin in response. The body, however, lacks the nutritional base to support the influx of insulin. This can result in an insulin reaction (extremely low blood sugar) with signs and symptoms such as hunger, sweating, and trembling. In addition, if the body's cells remain hungry over time, the structure of the cellular DNA may change to stay alive, resulting in a fundamental change in the cells, which may become cancerous.

Temperature/Nature/Energy

The "temperature" of a food is another essential factor in determining the food's yin and yang characteristics. According to Eastern medicine, there are four basic food temperatures: hot, warm, cool, and cold. Hot or warm foods are yang, and cold or cool foods are yin. Temperature indicates the reaction the food causes in the body, whether it comes from the freezer or the stove. For instance, eating watermelon and cucumbers or drinking beer will elicit a cold sensation. In contrast, eating chili peppers or cinnamon or drinking hard liquor evokes a hot feeling.

Warm or hot (yang) foods speed up the metabolism, aid digestion, improve blood circulation, promote sweating, and increase energy levels and mental alertness. Conversely, cold or cool (yin) foods slow the metabolism; calm the nerves; reduce inflammation, fever, and thirst; eliminate toxins; and treat constipation and various skin conditions.

Generally, foods from animal sources tend to be warmer, and those from plant sources tend to be colder. Meats are usually warm, and seafood is typically cool. Spices are hot (yang), while fruits and vegetables usually are cooler (yin).

Smell/Odor

Smells are divided into yin and yang. Smells that people are attracted to are considered yang, while unpleasant, offensive odors are considered yin. Generally, yang fragrances stimulate the nerves, while yin odors depress the nervous system's response. In other words, yang fragrances tend to support physiological activities, whereas yin odors suppress them. Thus, yang fragrances can facilitate digestion, eliminate gas, and stop nausea. They can also promote sweating, disinfect germs, and even eliminate parasites. Yin odors, in contrast, can calm the mind and emotions, as yin odors concentrate human energy in the lower region. In small amounts they can rejuvenate, or in large quantities they can resuscitate. Thus, they can be used to revive from fainting, coma, and collapse. This is the principle of extreme yin generating yang.

Meat

BEEF

Cows are gentle in nature. A cow has the same qualities as a loving mother. Eastern traditions teach that the vibrational frequency of the sound that cows make is identical to the central frequency of the universe. Yoga practitioners chant the mantra "Om," which is similar to the "moo" of cows when seeking balance, by resonating their bodies with the sound of the universe. In this way, their yin and yang become balanced as they become "one" with the universe in perfect harmony. These qualities indicate that the cow is an animal with a very harmonious yin and yang.

The energetic composition of beef is very similar to that of the human body, though it is slightly more yin. Because of this similarity, the human body savors the taste of beef. And because its yin-yang energy is well-balanced, beef can be eaten by almost anyone without disrupting the body's natural energetic flow.

The large body and slow and droning movements of cows indicate their yin nature, but they have horns that depict yang energy reviving. Thus, their yin is on the verge of transforming into yang. The season that relates to the cow is the period halfway through the transformation from winter to spring, when yang energy is beginning to awaken. Thus, the stored and dormant energy during the winter is starting to activate and be consumed. The Eastern zodiac cycle illustrates this by placing the cow in the north-northeast position. The significance of this is that, energetically, beef has the power to convert matter into energy.

Though not scientifically validated, we can presume that obese people who want to eat meat should eat beef since it has the power to transform substances into energy. Those who eat only beef and no other food will not store fat from its nutrients. Beef will instead consume fat stored in the body, similar to a high protein–low carbohydrate diet. However, this is not a balanced or healthy way to lose weight. The purpose of this example is to illustrate the energetic properties of beef.

Pork

Pigs are fleshy and plump and are known for their gentle, relaxed, and carefree nature. In addition, pigs reside low to the ground, are relatively inactive, and many are dark in color. These are all yin traits, making pigs the most yin land animal (yang), so their energetic characteristic is yin within yang.

Because of the strong yin nature of pigs, pork is considered highly nourishing. It readily adds weight to the body and stabilizes overactive metabolisms. Hyperactive children with low body weights would benefit from eating pork. It can help calm their dynamic nature and allow them to concentrate and focus.

Pork's yin nature also nourishes the reproductive organs in the body's yin region. Additionally, because pork is meat and retains that strong yang function, the combination of its yin and yang actions gives pork the ability to increase virility.

Poultry

Birds are more yang than other animals because they can fly; thus, the meat we derive from birds is more yang than any other meat source. Although chickens usually do not fly, they are birds and share many similar characteristics. Their tendency not to fly makes them more yin. However, chickens can be incredibly aggressive (yang), and their movements may be rapid (yang). Therefore, chicken meat activates yang functions in the body.

Though wild ducks can fly, most domesticated ducks cannot. Thus, domestic ducks are more yin in nature. Ducks, in general, are considered yin birds (yin within yang) because they live near water and have disproportionately large hips. The hip region is the body area with the least distribution of blood vessels and is therefore considered languid. Inactivity is yin in nature, as is the lower half of the body. Thus, the energy derived from duck meat tends to sink as its nutrients make their way to the reproductive organs. For this reason, eating duck (yin) with white wine (yang) is a great aphrodisiac.

Seafood

Fish move akin to their nature: although they can move quickly, they generally move slowly. They use their bodies (trunks) for propulsion more than their fins, which function similarly to arms, wings, and legs in land and air animals. As the trunk is more yin than arms and legs, fish are considered animals with well-developed yin. They also live in lakes' and oceans' cold and dark water (yin). Freshwater fish are more yin than saltwater fish since there is no salt (yang) surrounding them. They are less compressed by the forces of water due to the smaller bodies of water in which they live.

Although fish are yin, they are of a higher order than most other foods from the sea. They are vertebrates and are different from other, more primitive, marine animals such as squid and octopus, and shellfish like clams, shrimp, and lobster. These more primitive organisms are more yin in nature than fish. They contain a good deal of cholesterol, a fatlike yin substance that provides the building material for cell membranes and can accumulate in our arterial walls. Because their nature inclines toward yin, they do not contain the yang energy required to move the blood and prevent cholesterol buildup. Fish, on the other hand, are more balanced. Studies have shown that certain types of fish, such as salmon, herring,

mackerel, and sardines, contain high omega-3 essential fatty acids. As a result, they can lower the body's saturated fat and cholesterol levels, which is a yang action of fish.

Sea cucumbers live in the ocean (yin) and are dark and creepy (yin). The sea cucumber is called the "ginseng of the sea" in China and Korea. Like ginseng, the sea cucumber is a potent aphrodisiac. Its appearance also resembles the male genitals. The Doctrine of Signatures states that "like attracts like," or, in other words, things that are similar in appearance can give and take energy from each other. Thus, sea cucumbers, with their resemblance to male genitals, are considered to have the ability to strengthen the male sexual organs.

Dairy Products

Milk

Milk is perhaps the most balanced food. It contains a well-rounded combination of energy and nutrients necessary for the growth and activity of children. Historically milk has been used for various disorders, such as fatigue, underweight conditions, upset stomach, difficulty swallowing, diabetes, and constipation. It is also useful as a blood tonic.

Of the various types of milk, goat's milk is the most yang, cow's milk is the most yin, and human's milk is the most balanced. Anything fed to an infant must be well-balanced. Cows nurse for a much shorter time and grow much faster than humans. This is partially due to the immense growth potential in cow's milk. Cow's milk is highly yin for the human system. Because of this, many people have an allergy to the sugar (lactose) and the protein (casein) in milk and dairy products. Food allergies indicate the unbalanced nature of that particular food.

Soured milk products, such as buttermilk, kefir, yogurt, cheese, and cottage cheese, are pre-digested by the bacterial action of the souring process. They are, therefore, more easily digested (yang) in the body. Yogurt is the most yang and cheese is the most yin of these products.

Eggs

Eggs and milk are both well-balanced. However, milk is more yin, while eggs are more yang. Milk from the breast, situated in the upper body, provides an image of providing water to animals. An egg reminds us of a fluttering chick breaking out of a hard shell with a strong contraction. If the action of milk is downward, the activity of the egg is upward. The yang of eggs applies only to the portion we eat, the white and yolk. The white is more yang between these two portions, and the yolk is more yin. The egg white is in the outer portion and is less dense. The yolk is more central, denser, and contains most of the cholesterol and nutrients we derive from eggs. It is also the nutritional source for a developing chicken.

When an egg is fertilized, a germinal disc (yang within yin), a tiny white spot on the yolk, grows into an embryo (Tai Chi). On the whole, eggs are more nutritious than milk. They are more balanced because they contain relatively equal amounts of yin and yang, just like an atom, a zygote, the universe, or Tai Chi.

Nuts

Nuts are fundamentally oily seeds surrounded by thick shells. Shells gather and consolidate energy (yin). The nuts inside are relatively more yang because they have the potential to sprout and disperse their energy. The thicker the shell, the stronger its yin action and the stronger the yang action (penetrating force) of the nut inside (fig. 7.2).

Figure 7.2 Penetrating Force of a Seed

Nuts such as peanuts, walnuts, chestnuts, pine nuts, hazelnuts, pecans, and pistachios invigorate blood circulation in the superficial regions of the body, accelerate metabolism, and lower cholesterol.

All nuts have a thin brown lining between the nut and the shell with astringent (puckering) and bitter tastes. The astringent and bitter tastes and the brown (dark) color are yin. This thin lining also contains large amounts of tannin, a chemical that can stop bleeding and diarrhea. Its yin properties can benefit people who suffer from chronic coughing, diarrhea, or bleeding. The lining can also be boiled and taken as tea. Yang-natured people who are thin, restless, and have excellent circulation should eat nuts with this thin lining. This can prevent conditions of yin deficiency due to yang excess.

Grains

Determining grains' yin-yang nature is a relatively arduous task today. This is because food preparation has advanced so that the removal of whole husks from grains and slicing off their outer layers takes place before they reach the store. This type of food processing makes the original tastes of grains challenging to determine. Only when the husks of the grains are intact can their flavors truly be discerned. But by looking at the fundamental nature of grains, it is possible to determine their yin-yang characteristics.

Barley, wheat, buckwheat, and oats are relatively yin grains, whereas rice, sweet rice, and sorghum are relatively yang. Yin grains are more difficult to digest than yang grains. Thus, people with weak digestive systems experience gas when they eat them. Oatmeal, for instance, is suitable for constipation because it does not digest completely and serves as bulk.

RICE

Rice is a yang food that supplies the body with significant amounts of yang energy. There are, however, wide varieties of rice that supplement the body's energy differently. Rice processing occurs by trimming the outer layers to varying degrees. Removing the layers makes the rice whiter, more easily digestible, and more yang in nature. Brown rice retains its bran and germ layer and is, therefore, more difficult to digest. Because of this, the energy we derive from eating brown rice is more balanced in yin (bran) and yang (inner rice).

Long-grain rice is more easily digestible than short-grain or glutinous rice. Although they are both white, their shapes are different. Yin-yang theory maintains that round objects are more yin, as they condense or gather energy. In contrast, long objects are yang, as their energy extends to the outside. According to these principles, long-grain rice is more yang than short-grain or glutinous rice.

Like seeds, whole grains have a well-balanced distribution of yin and yang. However, seeds and grains lose their ability to support and initiate life if there is a significant discrepancy between yin and yang. For example, suppose we eliminate the outside of the food (yin) and only eat the inside portion (yang). In that case, the nature of that food becomes too tilted in one direction, causing harm to our bodies. Therefore, overeating white or polished rice or white flour without other foods to balance their side effects can lead to problems. We will discuss this later in the "Diet and Disease" section.

WHEAT

Wheat grows well in cooler climates such as that of Northern Europe. Because of this, it is more yin in nature than rice, which grows well in warmer temperatures, such as in Southeast Asia. Wheat is also slightly more bitter (yin) than rice. There are many reasons why a person becomes overweight. Because of its yin characteristics, wheat as a staple of one's diet is a reason why a person tends to become overweight.

The yin nature of wheat can treat various illnesses from excessive yang. For example, the mind is yang compared to the body. Therefore, the mind likes to remain calm (yin). People constitutionally tilted toward yang or under great stress have more yang energy in their bodies. So it is more difficult for them to remain calm. These people can easily develop heart palpitations, insomnia, and irritability. Eating wheat and wheat products can help alleviate these symptoms. The outer layer of wheat is more yin than the inner layer, so eating whole wheat would be more beneficial for people who suffer from these conditions.

Premenstrual syndrome (PMS) among women develops due to dysfunction in the body's reproductive system—a yin region. Eating wheat can help strengthen and invigorate the system and alleviate PMS symptoms. However, since wheat is a food, not a medicine, its yin action is mild. Therefore, long-term consumption is necessary for its effectiveness.

Oats

Oats are not as sweet as rice and contain a more bitter flavor (yin). They are a rough grain and have many tasteless fibers. These fibers are considered yin in nature because their structure is tightly knit, making them difficult to digest. Because oats do not entirely digest, they are effective for relieving constipation. Fibers, located on the outside, like a shell or peel, are yin because they protect and compress the inner contents. Oats' yin nature is effective against diabetes or heart disease caused by the overconsumption of refined sugar (yang) or refined meat (yang). Oats help mend the imbalance of the modern diet oversupplied with yang energy.

Barley

Barley is yin in nature. It is cool and the most difficult grain to digest. Eating barley will make a person's stomach stay full for a more extended time. It also prevents constipation because it contains a lot of fiber. These characteristics clearly point to its yin nature.

Corn

Mature corn is a more primitive (yin) plant than the other grains. The plant has a larger body (yin), more rounded leaves (yin), and corn silk (yin) growing through the top of the ear. Because of these features, young, fresh corn resembles yin-natured vegetables more closely than the other grains. It is on the border between grains and vegetables. Therefore, corn is a good side dish to meat because it contains yin characteristics similar to vegetables and will establish harmony with meat's yang qualities.

Corn, dried in the sunlight, becomes very hard (yin) due to its intense consolidating energy. However, when heat (yang) is applied to a specific corn known as *Zea mays everta*, it explodes to become popcorn. Corn's ability to secure its dual nature stems from its internal balance. Maintaining this balance occurs through the strong yin energy derived from the outer aspect of the corn kernel and the strong yang energy of the clearly visible germ that resides inside. This germ is what explodes outward and sprouts through the hull (pericarp) of corn kernel, and so is a quintessential yang substance.

In Eastern medicine, the kidneys are considered yin, but they also contain the body's innate yin and yang energetic stores. Corn has a similar construct energetically and in its shape, therefore, it acts on the kidneys. The strong yin nature of corn's hull has a diuretic effect on the body. The more yin corn silk is an even stronger diuretic. Because of these actions, corn can treat such diseases as urinary difficulty or hypertension due to excessive yang and kidney stones. Additionally, the minerals (yin) derived from corn, such as iron, potassium, and magnesium, can be acquired in greater amounts by eating young corn, which has less starch (yang).

Fruits

Fruits are primarily sweet (yang) with varying degrees of tartness (yin). Their sweetness provides energy to the body, and their sour flavor activates gathering energy in the body. Their high water content (yin) also serves to supply the body with water.

Lemons

Lemons are much more sour than sweet. They elicit a strong contracting action in the body. Excess consumption of lemons may damage our natural balance. This is why we cannot tolerate more than a few drops of lemon juice at a time.

Lemons are also highly fragrant. Powerful scents indicate vigorous molecular activity. The smell of fish is yin because it suppresses digestive functioning. A few drops of lemon juice on fish will neutralize the yin odor and improve the body's ability to digest the fish. Another positive effect of lemon's strong fragrant smell is its antiseptic and antimicrobial action. As a result, it can treat dysentery and parasitic infestations.

The gathering property of the sour taste of lemons combines well with the dispersing action of alcohol—vodka in particular. Lemon juice can calm down palpitations and nausea from excessive intoxication. It has a calming, sobering effect and can soothe the stomach.

Limes

Limes have a similar taste and similar functions to lemons. They are cooling and clear summer heat, promote bodily fluids to relieve thirst, regulate the stomach, and prevent miscarriages. Both lemons and limes are highly beneficial to pregnant women.

When a woman becomes pregnant, her blood volume increases by 20 to 30 percent. This results in increased cardiac output and more pressure on the vessel walls. When yang becomes extreme, energy moves outward, leaving the inside empty and malnourished. As a result, the stomach becomes weak, and women often cannot eat early in pregnancy. In the first term of pregnancy, they may experience nausea and vomiting because of the sudden change in their blood volume. These symptoms gradually disappear as their bodies adapt.

Nausea and vomiting tend to worsen in the morning when the body's yang energy is activated and blood volume and circulation increase. That is why it is called "morning sickness." For the same reason, a person's pulse is stronger when first waking up than when yang energy is weaker later in the day. Carbonated water mixed with lime is excellent for calming the symptoms of morning sickness. It is suitable for pregnant women to drink as much of this concoction as possible at least three times a day for several days until the symptoms subside. They should also smell lemons as often as they can. As with aromatherapy, they will stimulate the olfactory system and affect the brain center that controls digestion. Fragrant smell acts positively on human physiology and stimulates digestion. In contrast, rotten odor weakens the digestive system and makes one vomit.

Like lemons, some alcoholic beverages, such as gin and tonic, use limes. They are also served with drinks such as tequila and Mexican beer. Their purpose is to prevent vomiting that may occur with alcoholic drinks. As a result, alcohol intake can be increased as well.

A word of caution: Those who suffer from excess stomach acid or ulcers must be very careful with lemons and limes due to their high acid content.

Oranges

Oranges have similar actions to lemons. They are, however, sweeter, less sour, and thus more yang. Orange peels added to beef dishes create a highly desirable taste because the peels supplement the shortage of yang digestive energy in beef. In Eastern medicine, dried orange peels are combined with other herbs to treat digestive problems and illnesses resulting from the excessive intake of alcohol.

Apples

Apples grow in cool climates. They have a sour taste and a cool temperature, so they belong to the category of yin fruits. Due to their yin nature, apples can help the body produce fluids, moisten dryness, and clear lung heat. Thus, they can treat thirst, cough, and dry mouth and neutralize the toxic effects of cigarettes.

Apples also have a sweet taste that affects the digestive system. Therefore, they can help treat indigestion, loss of appetite, and diarrhea. Regardless of their medicinal value, apples are typically difficult to digest due to their yin nature. Cooking them reduces their yin nature, sweetens their taste, and makes them easier to digest. There are many cooked or baked apple products, like applesauce and apple pie. Among the varieties of apples, Fuji apples are sweeter and less sour than other types of apples and are the most easily digested. In general, people with weak digestive systems should not eat many apples or should eat them cooked or at least remove the peel.

PEARS

Pears contain a lot of water and fiber. The more fiber a fruit contains, the stronger its yin nature. Asian pears have more water and larger fiber particles within their pulp than other pears; thus, they are more yin. Pears can strengthen the respiratory system and stop chronic coughing. The lungs and respiratory system are considered yin within yang. They are located above the diaphragm (yang) but have the yin function of absorbing oxygen. People who suffer from a chronic cough lack gathering energy of yin and damaged yang energy. An Eastern remedy for this illness is well-cooked pears with honey (yang). Cooked pears are also suitable for residual coughing after the common cold or flu.

PEACHES

Peaches have a sharp tip and a lot of hair, or "fuzz." These features indicate that they have stronger dispersing or yang energy than other fruits. When yin people suffer from poor digestion, they should eat peaches. If the sour taste is unappealing, they can eat canned peaches, which have been fully ripened and soaked in sweeteners. Canned peaches are excellent for helping convalescent patients recover their energy. Eastern medicine uses peach seeds to eliminate stagnant blood because they help promote blood circulation. In the East, peaches chase spirits away, according to a folk belief. Therefore, they are not placed on the table at ancestral memorial services alongside other foods. The reason is that the yang nature of peaches

expels the yin-natured spirits who are being honored.

GRAPES

Grapes grow on vines. Vines grow inward and have a pulling nature, so they coil onto things near them and pull those things inward. Grapevines are plants with stems, leaves, and fruit curled tightly together. Grapes are cold in nature, and the leaves of grapevines are sour. All of these traits give grapes a very yin nature. The darker the grape, the more yin it is. Grapes are excellent for people of fiery character caused by a surplus of dispersing (yang) energy and a lack of gathering (yin) energy, with weak knees and low backs. The knees and low back are in the yin regions of the body and are vulnerable to weakness in people who lack yin. The yin/gathering nature of grapes can assist these people in balancing their yin and yang energies.

CHERRIES AND KIWIS

Cherries and kiwis are two other examples of fruits that gather energy. Therefore, yang-natured people (such as those described earlier) should regularly eat cherries, kiwis, and grapes to prevent and treat yang-natured diseases.

KOREAN MELONS

Korean melons also grow on vines. They have a bitter taste near their stems but do not have strong gathering action as they contain almost no sour taste. Nevertheless, they do have yin-nourishing actions due to their cool nature and the abundance of moisture they contain. Still, because of their strong yin nature, if yin-natured people overeat Korean melon, they would most likely get a stomach ache and diarrhea.

WATERMELON

Though watermelon has a cold temperature (yin) which can cool the body, it also has a strong dispersing action (yang) because a thick peel encases it. Like thick-shelled nuts, the thick-peeled watermelon disperses energy. In addition, it is red, the color of fire, and crisp. This crispness indicates that it has vigorous molecular activity, a yang trait. Because of this, watermelon is beneficial to the heart and assists it by improving blood circulation. Urine output increases as more blood moves through the kidneys. Therefore, watermelons are great for obese people who suffer from a slow metabolism and have heart disease, high blood pressure, or diabetes.

CUCUMBERS

In general, foods that grow on vines typically have a strong yin nature because of the gathering action of the vine. Vines depend on other structures to support them: they cannot stand on their own, nor do they grow straight upward. These are all yin qualities. Cucumbers grow on vines but do not have an intense gathering action because they are not very sour. Their yin action derives from their sometimes slightly bitter taste, their cooling and descend-

ing nature, and abundance of moisture. Cucumbers can help stop thirst and promote urination. They also detoxify and cool the blood. When applied externally, cucumbers can cool inflammation and treat burns.

TOMATOES

Tomatoes are the reddest (yang) and most salty (yang) fruit. Thus, they can help facilitate digestion and stimulate the appetite. Because of these functions, tomatoes are cooked and made into ketchup. Meats are the most challenging food to digest. Thus, putting ketchup on meat helps digestion. Higher-quality meats such as steak are more yang, and processed meats such as hamburgers are more yin because they contain tendons, ligaments, and fat. Therefore, the yang in ketchup helps with the digestion of hamburgers. Ketchup also helps balance the yin of potatoes and thus goes well with french fries.

Vegetables

Vegetables, in general, are more yin than meat or fruits. So they have a harmonious effect when combined with various meat and fish dishes. Their harmonizing actions include improving digestion, reducing odor, and detoxifying.

RADISHES

Radishes are edible roots that have a sweet and pungent taste. Roots gather energy from the ground and raise it upward (yang). The pungent taste (yang) of radishes stimulates the digestive functions of the stomach. Therefore, people with weak digestive systems can benefit tremendously from eating radishes.

Wasabi and horseradish are stronger, more yang forms of radish since they are incredibly spicy (yang). Wasabi alone or a combination of horseradish and mustard made into a paste complements raw fish. Fish are yin in nature, and sashimi (raw, uncooked fish) is very yin. Sashimi by itself can injure the body because of its strong yin nature. Therefore, eating wasabi with its pungent, yang taste counters the strong yin nature of raw fish.

CARROTS

Carrots are orange in color and grow in the shape of a narrow, upside-down triangle. Both of these attributes symbolize yang. Orange is very similar to red, representing yang in the Tai Chi symbol. The upside-down triangle with its point on the bottom is symbolic of the upward-spreading nature of fire. In addition, the carrot leaves are narrow and spread out in several directions. This is yang, relative to the broad leaves of other plants.

In humans, the eyes correspond to the element fire because they are the brightest part of the body. Carrots can improve the eyes' functioning. Night blindness is the first symptom of eye weakness, and carrots are especially beneficial for this ailment. The reason is that the yang of carrots can overcome the yin of the night.

According to the Doctrine of Signatures, like treats like. In the body, the liver has the shape of an upside-down triangle and is a yang organ. Carrots, similarly shaped, can strengthen the liver. Carrots also contain a lot of fibers that correspond to the skin, tendons, and fascia of the human body. Thus, in Eastern medicine, they are used to treat skin disorders and relieve the fatigue of the motor system.

POTATOES

Potatoes are an extremely yin vegetable. They have broad, soft leaves (yin) and can have an unpleasant bitter taste (yin). Potatoes with dark blue or purple skins (yin colors) and the eyes of germinated potatoes contain a toxin called solanine (a yin toxin). Solanine can cause poisoning, with symptoms including vomiting, abdominal pain, diarrhea, headaches, and even mental disorders. The tongue senses the solanine's bitter taste to warn against its ingestion that will harm the body. Because of their yin nature, potatoes taste better when cooked or combined with yang foods. For example, baking potatoes will add some yang. However, there is a greater increase in yang when potatoes become french fries. The process of frying (yang) in oil (essentially a lump of yang) and then adding salt (yang) achieves that.

As potatoes are yin, they can treat the conditions of a person with a yang constitution. For example, those who suffer from excess secretion of stomach acid and intestinal ulcers can treat it by drinking potato juice every morning. In addition, potatoes can heal inflammatory conditions such as burns.

GARLIC

Garlic is highly yang in nature. It has a strong smell and a mixture of pungent and sweet tastes. Thus, its characteristics enable it to affect the digestive system strongly. It is also known to have an antiseptic and anticancer effect.

Cancer cells are generally more rigid than the surrounding cells, and so they are yin. Through its strong yang action, garlic can kill bacteria and intestinal worms and help prevent certain types of cancer. In addition, it can improve the body's metabolism and blood circulation, and it warms the body. Therefore, garlic may be helpful for yin-natured people who tend to be cold (body, hands, and feet), have poor circulation and digestion, and suffer from low energy.

Here is an interesting side note. The nature of Dracula and all other vampires is extremely yin. They are soulless creatures that only thrive at night and live in dark, damp places. Garlic is an extremely yang substance that can neutralize strong yin substances. That is why folktales tell of vampires threatened by garlic.

GINGER

Ginger, like garlic, is yang in nature. It is warm with a very spicy and mildly sweet taste. Its warmth is highly beneficial for the digestive system. It is one of the best foods for stopping vomiting. It is similar to garlic because it can kill bacteria and has anticancer properties. It reduces the smell of fish (yin) and can detoxify seafood poisoning (yin). It can induce mild sweating and is used to eliminate the common cold (yin). Like garlic, ginger is best for those who are yin in nature.

Slightly spoiled meat will have an offensive smell that suppresses digestive functioning. Eating it can damage the body. Garlic and ginger have an antibacterial effect and, used in large amounts, can combat bacteria that have begun to grow in the meat. Bacteria and germs generally like to grow in dark, damp places, indicating their propensity toward yin. When you use a substance that is yang in nature to neutralize the effect, the bacteria can no longer flourish.

LETTUCE

Lettuce has broad leaves, mostly water, a slightly bitter taste, and a cool temperature—all yin characteristics. Vegetables are more yin than other foods, and lettuce is even more yin. The extreme yin of lettuce can be a tranquilizer to treat problems due to an excess of yang, such as insomnia, anxiety, and restlessness. Most of the lettuce found in America is modified to eliminate the bitter taste. Thus, it has lost some of its yin functions. Yin-natured foods can strengthen the function of the kidneys, large intestine, and women's reproductive system, which all belong to yin. They are, therefore, effective for treating edema, urinary difficulty, constipation, yeast infections, and hemorrhoids.

Alcoholic Beverages

All alcoholic beverages are yang. The more alcohol in the drink (higher proof), the more yang it is. Alcohol is volatile. Volatility means that the molecular movement is very active and the substance is very yang. It speeds up blood circulation, quickening the pulse and turning the face red because of its rapid molecular activity. Western medicine, however, considers alcohol a depressant. After the initial stimulation, alcohol depresses the central nervous system, because when yang reaches its extreme, it converts into yin.

Alcoholic beverages have a pungent taste that stimulates the secretion of digestive juices and increases peristalsis. When taken with food, especially meat, alcohol behaves like spices and aids in digestion. While the effects of other yang-type foods may be relatively slow, the effects of alcohol appear quickly. Alcohol absorbs through the stomach lining into the bloodstream. Drinking distilled spirits with nothing in the stomach to buffer them can disintegrate the stomach lining. Therefore, they are better with foods like cheese or meat than taken on an empty stomach. Drinking white liquor on an empty stomach is the quickest way to get an ulcer. But nothing beats it as an aid in digesting meat.

BEER

Beer is the most yin alcoholic beverage. One reason is that it derives from barley malt. As previously stated, barley is a very yin grain. It grows in cooler weather and sprouts during winter—the most yin season. Beer also contains hops fermented with barley to give beer its bitter flavor. Hops are bitter (yin) and have a sedating effect (yin).

Because beer contains alcohol, it has a brief stimulating effect—yang—followed by the depressant effect derived from the yin actions of hops and barley. So some people use beer to substitute for sleeping pills, as it relaxes the body and mind.

WINE

Although many grapes are sweet, some also contain sour and astringent properties, which belong to yin and function to gather and consolidate energy.

Alcohol accelerates energy transformation and temporarily strengthens the body. This is why people tend to lose their inhibitions when they are drunk. Wine is more yang than beer but more yin than spirits (distilled liquor). Darker colors are more yin, and brighter colors are more yang. Because of their hues, white wine is more yang than blushed wine, which is more yang than red wine. Although red is the color of fire, red wine has a descending, gathering nature and a calming effect from dark grapes. White wine and, to a lesser extent, blush wine are lighter and have ascending action. They go right to the head, making a person feel giddy. The yang nature of white wine complements the yin nature of fish, and the yin nature of red wine balances the yang energies of beef.

Yin foods such as pork, oysters, sea cucumbers, duck, tortoise, and eel supply nutrients to the reproductive organs. These nutrients, however, take a while to reach their destinations. Drinking white wine, such as the famous wine of China called Maotai (120 proof), together with any of these yin foods, will hasten the activation of the body's sexual energies, like throwing gasoline on a fire. In addition, many of these foods are cooked with spices to enhance their aphrodisiac qualities.

Vodka

Vodka is strongly yang. Its energy rises straight to the head. No better liquor exists for people living in cold regions and those whose physiological activities easily stagnate. Because it is extremely yang, the body tends to reject the taste. Mixing it with lemon or lime can sedate its nature. People with too much yang energy will be at greater risk of damaging their system if they consume excessive amounts of alcohol, especially vodka.

Whiskey

Whiskey is darker than vodka because it is made in oak barrels that have been smoked. Its color indicates that it is more yin than vodka. The longer whiskey is kept in the dark cellar (yin), the more balanced its yin and yang will be and the better it will taste. Whiskey is distilled from fermented grain mash (yin) and has many yin characteristics. Its energy can descend to the genital region (a yin region) and stimulate sexual desire by the yang action of alcohol. Thus, a small amount of whiskey may be useful as an aphrodisiac.

Sodas/Soft Drinks

Soft drinks supply the body with water (yin) and sugar (yang). This yin-yang balance makes them taste excellent, so almost everyone enjoys drinking them. Because they provide water and quick energy, we crave sodas more after exercise, when we have sweated and are fatigued. With intense training, our energy becomes concentrated in the external regions of our bodies, namely our arms and legs, which are yang. At the same time, the function of our digestive system (yin) declines. Sodas' carbonation gives them a sharp, biting taste, which is yang, stimulating digestion. It is also the reason soda tastes better than simple sugar water.

Cola

Adding kola-nut extracts to carbonated water makes cola. Kola nut is a seed that belongs to the cacao family. As previously mentioned, nuts have a strong dispersing energy (yang) because hard shells (yin) surround them. Caffeine is one of the main ingredients that enhances this function of the kola nut. The yin function of the kola nut oil (yin) normally antagonizes this yang function. However, when producing cola or chocolate, we remove the oil while processing kola and cacao beans. Therefore, the dispersing energy is enhanced.

Further contributing to cola's yang action are its carbonation and phosphoric and citric acids. Other ingredients commonly added to colas, such as cinnamon, vanilla, and nutmeg, also have strong yang natures. Moreover, cola contains strong aromatic fragrance (yang) oils, such as orange, lime, or lemon fruit peel. Thus, all in all, these ingredients give cola a very potent yang action.

Cola's strong yang action can dissolve or transform the body's fats (yin) into energy. This fat-dissolving function makes the cola taste good after eating greasy meat. But drinking too much cola on an empty stomach can literally melt the inner lining of the stomach or duodenum, causing ulcers. In addition to melting fat, cola's strong yang action can damage bone (yin) structure. This effect is easily demonstrated by holding cola in the mouth for a while, then grinding the upper and lower teeth together. As a result, the teeth's surfaces will feel rough and worn.

Although cola is yang in nature, it possesses yin qualities that serve to balance it out. Cola is dark due to its caramel coloring, with a slightly sour and astringent taste. These yin characteristics constrain the yang action of cola and prevent it from being toxic to our bodies. Without them, cola would not be fit for human consumption.

Dr Pepper

Although Dr Pepper appears similar in color to colas, it has a reddish hue, indicating its yang nature. It also has a very pungent and spicy taste and can therefore facilitate digestive functioning. Dr Pepper is the best choice for people with weak digestive systems who dislike adding ice to soda.

Ginger Ale, 7UP, Sprite

Ginger Ale, 7UP, and Sprite all have a lemon-lime flavor. As previously mentioned, lemons and limes calm the digestive system to treat symptoms such as nausea and vomiting. Theoretically, these three sodas can settle the stomach. However, ginger ale is the most effective of the three because it contains ginger—a famous digestive tonic with a yang nature. The traditional uses for ginger ale include easing motion sickness and stomach upset, stopping coughs, and soothing sore throats. All of these actions of ginger ale coincide with the usage of ginger in traditional Eastern medicine, which commonly uses it as a cold remedy. It is the most yang of the three lemon-lime sodas because it contains ginger.

Root Beer

Traditionally brewed root beer is entirely different from other soft drinks. It is a tonic or elixir made by fermenting herbs such as juniper berry, sassafras root, and ginger with yeast. Root beer is a drink that replenishes consumed energy, but it is also a medicine that can strengthen the stomach and lungs. However, since root beer has a high concentration of nutrients, it has a slightly nauseating taste, which can somewhat burden digestion. Thus the fragrance of wintergreen has been added to help facilitate digestion.

Juniper berry is yin in nature since it is a fruit that gathers energy into matter. Fragrant herbs such as sassafras, ginger, and wintergreen are yang as they have dynamic molecular activity. Root beer can ultimately strengthen various body functions, but it cannot instantly quench thirst or stimulate digestion like other soft drinks.

From the perspective of the digestive system, root beer is the most yin, cola is second, clear sodas are next, and Dr Pepper is the most yang. Unfortunately, constant soft drink consumption will ultimately weaken the digestive system. Their cold temperature saps the yang energy, weakening the digestive fire. In addition, carbonated water can overwork the digestive system, causing gas, bloating, abdominal pain, and diarrhea, exacerbated by the caffeine in some soft drinks.

Diet and Disease

According to Eastern medicine, disease results from an imbalance of yin and yang in the body. Therefore, to restore health, a proper diagnosis of the yin and yang imbalance must first be made, after which specific dietary and lifestyle guidelines are recommended to restore balance.

Ideally, foods and herbs should be taken entirely, because the whole food or plant is more balanced than any component. For example, the interior of a kernel of rice, a seed, or a nut is considered yang because it contains stored energy ready to penetrate outward and sprout. The exterior is yin because it holds energy inside. If individual components of foods are isolated and consumed, they may create disturbances in the system, and disease may

develop. Ingesting whole foods and herbs will provide a natural nutritional and energetic balance. Unfortunately, modern society processes and refines foods so that their original natures are all but lost.

Human activity must also be balanced in yin and yang. To acquire energy (yin action), energy must be used up and consumed (yang action). Today, most people have little need to exert any energy when obtaining food from a store or restaurant. Therefore, calories are more easily accumulated than burned up.

Diabetes and hypertension are two examples of diseases common to yin-natured people who overeat and accumulate (yin) a surplus of nutrients without burning them up (yang). Diabetes results from the body's inability to make or process insulin. There are two types of diabetes: one is thought to be genetic (type 1 insulin-dependent diabetes), and the other is closely linked to diet and exercise (type 2). Type 2 diabetes is more than four times as common as type 1 diabetes.

When blood sugar levels increase, insulin is released into the bloodstream. The presence of insulin allows sugar to move from the blood into the body's cells. Insulin is, therefore, a yin hormone because of its gathering nature. Exercise activates the body's cells and burns up carbohydrates, which are complex sugars. Thus, it is easier for insulin to transport the remaining glucose into the body's cells after exercise.

Diabetes was rare during the days of hunting and gathering, because obtaining food required physical exertion. People had to hunt for days to obtain even a small piece of meat.

Hunting brings about a heightened state of awareness and improves the functioning of the body's systems. Additionally, people used to work long hours in fields to harvest grain. After harvesting grains, they removed hulls and manually pounded the grain with a mortar and pestle. Since people worked off all their calories, this led to proper insulin secretion. So to prevent diabetes, it is essential to avoid highly refined foods (yang) and to get enough exercise.

High blood pressure is another disease common to yin people, because they tend to gather energy and transform it into substances, such as cholesterol and arterial plaque. High blood pressure is a direct result of clogged blood vessels. These clogged vessels cause a drop in the blood supply to tissue cells. The cells signal to the brain that they are not receiving the nutrients they need, and, in response, the brain commands the heart to beat faster to increase the blood supply to the cells. The heart responds, but the narrowed blood vessels impede circulation and cause pressure to build up (high blood pressure). If this cycle continues, the coronary artery, which supplies blood to the heart, will also accumulate cholesterol. When the heart tries to pump blood under these conditions, it easily fatigues, eventually leading to angina or heart failure.

Yin-natured people tend to conserve and store fat and cholesterol instead of dissolving them and transforming them into energy. As a result, their blood vessels become congested, putting undue pressure on blood vessel walls.

Their metabolic actions also tend to be slower, contributing to the buildup.

NUTS AND CHOLESTEROL

Nuts sprout by penetrating through thick shells. Their penetrating force (yang) is powerful. This force can pierce the cholesterol-clogged (yin) blood vessels. The accumulated fats and cholesterol (yin) in the blood transform into energy (yang), and cholesterol levels drop. As a result, the cholesterol sticking to blood vessel walls (particularly the coronary arteries) dislodges and dissolves. Angina disappears as the coronary artery opens up, and heart attacks are prevented. Vegetable oils found in nuts are unsaturated fatty acids and can transform the saturated fatty acids attached to arterial walls.

Several studies have documented the cholesterol-lowering effects of walnuts. For example, one study presented at the Third International Congress on Vegetarian Nutrition in 1997 at Loma Linda University School of Medicine in California was "Nut Consumption, Cardiovascular Disease Prevention and Longevity" by Joan Sabaté, a professor and chair of nutrition at Loma Linda University School of Public Health.

In this study conducted with approximately thirty-one thousand Seventh-day Adventists in California, researchers found a significant reduction in the risk of myocardial infarction (heart attack) and death from ischemic heart disease (insufficient blood supply to the heart) with increased nut consumption.

NATURAL SUBSTANCES VS. PHARMACEUTICAL DRUGS

Ingesting natural substances (foods and herbs) has a much less volatile effect on the body than a chemically altered substance does. Western pharmaceutical drugs are isolated components, many of which are artificially synthesized substances typically found in whole plants. They significantly change the body's state of yin and yang. However, pharmaceutical drugs do not nourish a deficiency of the body, which would give the body a chance to regulate itself. In addition, the isolated components in these drugs are unrestrained by other elements naturally found in plants. Thus, they create a deficiency due to their imbalanced yin-yang nature. The strong effects of Western drugs create a turbid internal environment. The body responds to this disruption of yin and yang by exhibiting unpleasant physical symptoms known as side effects.

Feed Your Needs

Human beings are tilted. Although they are the most centered of all organisms on Earth, each person possesses specific characteristics that are more yin or more yang. The combination of these characteristics defines the person. For example, physiological processes are generally weaker in people with a lot of yin. This most strongly affects their digestive systems. Thus, they tend to have more difficulty digesting meat, and their digestive systems are better suited to break down foods from plant sources than animal products. Yin-natured people also tend to prefer sweet and pungent foods, which speed up the metabolism. As previously mentioned, sweet foods are yang because they are the energy sources for physiological activity. Spicy foods are yang because they speed up the secretion of digestive juices and promote blood circulation.

Yang-natured people have a faster metabolism and a robust digestive system. As a result, they generally have less difficulty digesting meat. These people also prefer bitter and sour foods that slow down their metabolisms. Bitter foods are yin because they tend to be cooler and have a descending action. In contrast, sour foods gather energy inward and slow down blood circulation.

Categorizing groups is also possible according to yin and yang. These are generalizations, and there is always yin within yang and yang within yin. For example, vegetarians are thought to be more yin than meat eaters because of the nature of the foods they eat. Fruits, vegetables, and grains are more yin than meat products. Consuming these foods can make people more yin and put less stress on their stomach functions.

Easterners are considered more yin compared to Westerners. Generally, Eastern people eat more vegetarian dishes, while Western people eat more meat. Meat dishes are not standard fare in the Eastern diet; they are reserved for special occasions. Eastern meat dishes are also prepared to facilitate digestion with marinades and spices, while Western meats are marinated less often.

Carbohydrates, proteins, and fats can also be classified into yin and yang. Fats are the most yin, and carbohydrates are the most yang. Calories represent the amount of energy derived from a particular food. In every gram, fats have nine kilocalories, or kcals (units of heat). This implies that fats contain a higher concentration of energy. Things that are more concentrated are molecularly slower and thus more yin. Proteins have four kcals per gram and are more yang than fats but more yin than carbohydrates. Although carbohydrates contain a similar number of calories (3.9 kcals per gram), they provide a more easily accessible form of energy and are thus more yang.

When there is a severe threat to your health due to an insufficient supply of essential nutrients, you will crave certain foods, whether or not they are present in your environment. When there is less of a need, cravings will only develop when you see or smell food that can adequately serve the deficiencies of your system. Therefore, visiting a buffet restaurant that stocks a wide variety of foods is beneficial. Getting to an exotic buffet that stocks foods you would not ordinarily see would be much better. At the buffet, you should see and smell the foods and try to select the ones that appeal to you. If something tastes good to you, your body is probably lacking in the elements it contains. Eat each food until it does not taste good anymore. When you lose your craving or taste for food, your body has ingested a sufficient amount of the essential elements found in that food. Eat-

ing more would be harmful to you. You should go through the line more than once, seeing and smelling the food to find the ones that appeal to you. This way, you can ensure that your body gets its fill of all the necessary nutrients.

Cooking According to Yin and Yang

The yin-yang spectrum for cooking preparation is as follows: The more fire that comes into contact with food, the more yang the cooking method. Broiling is the most yang, then dry roasting and grilling (unless the chef torches the food). Frying is the next yang method, followed by baking, sautéing, and steaming. Foods that are eaten raw (fresh is most yin; dried is less yin) are the most yin or coolest in temperature, as they do not come into contact with heat.

Meats eaten without salt or spices are more challenging to digest. The body borrows the yang action of salt or spices to digest meat thoroughly. Salt tenderizes meat by breaking down its muscle fibers. Spices are molecularly dynamic and very fragrant. They facilitate digestion by increasing the secretion of digestive juices and promoting peristalsis.

Salt is essential for the flesh to function as part of a living animal. As a part of a live animal, it receives its salt supply through blood vessels. When carnivores kill their prey, a good pool of blood (and salt) is still pulsing through the animal's muscles. Humans, however, eat processed meat with the blood drained and the salt supply radically reduced.

Aside from salt and spices, cooking plays a significant role in digestion. For example, a rare steak is more yin to digest than one well done. Therefore, the more you cook meat, the easier it is to digest. This is why yin people, who tend to have weaker digestive functioning, generally prefer marinated, seasoned, and more cooked meat than do yang individuals.

Many Chinese dishes are cooked over an intense fire using a wok. The shape of the wok enhances the strength of the fire. Flames ignite inside the wok and kill the yin bacteria as a disinfectant. The aroma produced by this cooking method serves a function similar to adding spices to the food, as it stimulates the digestive system. Other cultures ignite alcohol over food for the same reason. This method of cooking is effective if done correctly. If not, undercooked food will taste horrible, while burned food will taste bitter.

Chinese meat dishes generally contain nuts (cashews, peanuts, etc.), which are more yang in digestion than meat. As previously mentioned, nuts contain a high amount of unsaturated fatty acids and help increase HDLs (high-density lipoproteins, known as "good cholesterol"). In addition, these substances can remove the yin LDLs (low-density lipoproteins, known as "bad cholesterol") from arterial walls (a yang action). Therefore, nuts taste good with meat dishes high in saturated fat that promote LDLs.

Dishes containing the same ingredients may taste good in one restaurant and not in another. The difference lies in the preparation of the foods, the proportions of the ingredients, and the cooking methods. All of these factors bring about different physiological reactions in each individual.

Conclusion

Many factors are associated with diet and food, from a food's source to its taste, temperature, smell, and cooking method. Evaluating all of these components through the principles of yin and yang will help clarify the properties of foods and help us predetermine their effects on our bodies. Foods are not good or bad (except for junk food), and you must consider their impact on the body and their combination with other foods in a balanced diet.

There are two requisites to improving one's health with food. The first is to understand who you are in terms of yin and yang, and the second is to know the yin and yang impact of various foods. Armed with such knowledge, you can accurately balance yourself with an assortment of foods suited to your yin or yang. Then you will be on your way to optimal and radiant health.

8

Yin and Yang of Politics

In this world, no decision is ever all good or all wrong. The merits of one choice may be seen as shortcomings when viewed from another perspective. This truth is the inversion principle at play and the nature of politics in the United States.

The US government is primarily a bipartisan system reflecting the interplay between yin and yang. This system allows political issues to be viewed from multiple perspectives, often with very different interpretations. We see this constantly as Democratic policies are favored by the more liberal-minded, and Republican policies are favored by conservatives. However, while this is a simplistic view of a complicated system, the reality of political divisions is clearly seen when explained using the theory of yin and yang.

"Liberal" is not necessarily synonymous with a Democratic outlook, and "conservative" is not always synonymous with being Republican. There are conservative Democrats and liberal Republicans. This is the principle of yin within yang and yang within yin. If Democrats are yang, liberal Democrats are yang within yang, and conservative Democrats are yin within yang. Similarly, conservative Republicans are yin within yin, while liberal Republicans are yang within yin. The various demands of the times determine whether the government itself will tilt toward yin or yang, conservative or liberal, Republican or Democratic.

The Democratic and Republican Parties' policies are bent on maintaining a balance. The Democratic Party is known to be pro-choice. Ultimately, this allows death (yin) to occur. On the other hand, the party is fundamentally against the death penalty, ensuring life (yang). The Republican view is just the opposite. The party is known to be pro-life (yang), which warrants more people, but is in favor of the death penalty (yin).

Regarding taxes and monetary distribution, Democrats are known to be more liberal-minded (yang). However, they are generally the party responsible for tax increases and greater government regulations. These are yin actions because higher taxes centralize the distribution of wealth, while more governmental regulations restrict the activities of people in society. The taxes, however, are then put into programs attempting to equalize the distribution of wealth. This is a yang action because it is an outward and progressive form of government. Republicans are known to be more conservative (yin). They generally favor lowering taxes and having fewer governmental regulations (yang). However, this may allow the allocation of money to remain stratified and centralized (yin).

The US Government

The US government is separated into three branches: the executive branch, which enforces the laws; the legislative branch, which creates the laws; and the judicial branch, which maintains the laws. These different levels were devised to prevent absolute rule by any single branch of government. In terms of the I Ching, the three branches maintain the harmony of yin and yang.

The executive branch has many workers and layers, from the president of the United States to the police. For example, the president can veto laws passed by the legislative branch. This gives one person a great deal of power (yang). In addition, this branch of government is charged with enforcing the laws through police regulation. It is the most yang aspect of the government.

The judicial branch is an interpretive body. Decisions handed down by juries and local, state, and federal courts are based on laws that have already been established. For example, the Supreme Court's rulings are guided by the Constitution. Such restrictions are extremely yin in nature. Because this level of government does not create laws, its true power lies in interpreting laws for all citizens, including the president, to follow.

The legislative branch represents the people

and has both yin and yang characteristics. Every member of this branch and society must adhere to the nation's laws. There are strict regulatory mechanisms by which laws can be passed and the people's voices heard. These mechanisms are considered yin. On the other hand, the legislative branch has the power to impeach the president and the Supreme Court justices. It thus maintains ultimate authority over both the executive and judicial branches. It also can create laws. In addition, even if the president were to veto a law, it could still be passed by the legislative branch. These activities are yang in nature. Because of its dual yin-yang nature, the legislative branch is the most balanced among the three branches and is considered Tai Chi.

Capitalism vs. Communism

Despite the wide variety of government and economic systems, capitalism and communism (socialism) are two major contrasting systems when viewed through the lens of yin-yang theory. Capitalism recognizes private ownership of property and goods. Under this system, regulating individual economic activity becomes increasingly difficult because it is very dynamic, individualistic, and diffuse. This aspect of capitalism is yang. Communism suppresses individual economic activity, and economic regulations aim to benefit the whole. These activities are directed inward toward a single center and are yin.

The world's governments classically fol-low the principles of yin and yang. The yin-yang principle of transformation is evident in the current movement of communist governments, such as Russia and the People's Republic of China, toward the ideals of private property and the strength of capitalism. The reverse is occurring in the capitalistic United States. Big business conglomerates merge to form larger, unified entities with concentrated interests. When action diversifies greatly, there is a tendency to restructure. In addition, when guidelines are too stringent, there is a tendency to disperse. The capitalism and communism of the Cold War era no longer exist. Their influences move toward one another, so they become difficult to distinguish.

Morality and Politics

Political affiliation is a personal and often sensitive subject. Nevertheless, politics guides people's lives and is entwined with many other areas of life, including religion, economics, family, morality, and so on. One of the most public examples of politics meeting personal decisions came to light during the impeachment of President Clinton. Clinton's actions, however, can be better understood when analyzed using the principles of yin-yang theory.

In the East, male genitals are referred to as a "yang substance," meaning they are infused with a great deal of yang energy. The ignition of sexual desires is referred to as the "movement of yang energy." At the time of his indiscretion, Clinton was relatively young and had much power. Youth implies activity, a yang quality, and the power of this nature is also yang. On the other hand, morals and ethics are principles that bind and impede the flow of instinctive urges and are therefore considered yin. Yang-natured people naturally dislike yin impediments. In addition, when yang energy moves in a person who already has intense yang energy, moral yin cannot restrain it and is easily overcome. Therefore, such an individual is less likely to heed morality. Though he may exercise caution for fear of reprisal, he nevertheless will proceed with his affairs.

Clinton's indiscretions are an indication of his exceedingly yang-type personality. It can be viewed that while his actions in the Oval Office were morally reproachable, his yang nature was nationally beneficial.

Economics, like politics, is intimately tied to morality and ethics. A state of economic depression is yin, while economic growth is yang. Therefore, it is best to have a yang-natured person as president to activate or revitalize a depressed economy (yin). Only a yang-natured individual can overcome sluggish yin and revive the economy. An excessive yin person who is overly concerned with morals could never accomplish this. George Bush Sr., who was greatly worried about his moral appearance, could not restore the country to economic health. In contrast, President Clinton, who tested America's ethical standards, managed to get the country's economy back on track. According to these principles, the economy would see more significant gains under a liberal administration (though not necessarily Democratic) and would tend to be depressed under a conservative rule.

Fortunately for President Clinton, there is a connection between having liberal morals and inciting a strong economy. Americans seem to place greater value on economic revival than on the indiscretions of their president. Clinton's impeachment proceedings might have run a different course if this were not the case. Most people will forgive (or at least ignore) indiscretions while their bank accounts grow. During economic prosperity periods, people are more likely to commit immoral acts as they look for exciting and unusual ways to spend their newfound wealth. Recall, for example, the prosperity of the "Roaring Twenties" and its correspondingly high crime rates.

Eventually, however, yang will transform into yin. The I Ching states, "Extreme yang produces yin, and extreme yin produces yang." Abundant economic life generates activity, and excessive activity (yang) is bound to transgress even the most sacred restraint (yin). When this happens, social problems crop up until they finally reach the forefront of public consciousness. Once the excitement of economic revival is replaced by stability and comfort, people's minds return to issues of morality. The resurgence of morality generally slows activity, and economic decline begins again.

There are indicators of stages of yin-yang development in nature and society. For example, a popular saying in the stock market is that the state of the economy can be known by the hemline of skirts at any given time. More specifically, the rise of hemlines indicates economic revival, and the popularity of long dresses signifies economic depression. This may seem outrageous, but the connection becomes apparent by applying the principles of yin and yang. Economic revival (yang) is accompanied by more freedom and activity, while economic depression (yin) means more restraint and emphasis on morality. Indicators, such as skirt length, are referred to as "images" in the I Ching.

Politicians could significantly improve their governing abilities if they analyzed these images and used them to determine whether the current of the times was flowing toward yin or yang. It is also crucial for them to understand whether their own nature belongs to yin or yang and to cultivate their weaknesses. In ancient Eastern politics, those who did not understand yin-yang and the I Ching were considered children in the political world, incapable of governing effectively. Theories of the I Ching were also studied and utilized by more modern political thinkers, such as Chairman Mao and Karl Marx.

9

Yin and Yang of the Economy

The material (yin) and energetic (yang) aspects of the economy are rooted in the interchange and exchange of money (yin) and labor (yang). Money is considered yin because it is tangible, stored energy. Labor or work is yang because it involves the activity of the body or mind. Like everything else in the universe, the material (yin) and energetic (yang) aspects of the economy constantly transform into one another. Work and labor (yang) are converted into money (yin) when people receive financial compensation. Money can then convert into work and labor when used to pay people for their efforts. Viewed in this way, we see that work is the energy and money is the substance of the economy. Work transforming into money and back into work is similar to yin transforming into yang and back to yin.

The body stores surplus energy as fat. When needed, fats transform into carbohydrates, which may then convert into ATP (the energy unit of the body) to contract muscles (or do work). Similarly, surplus energy from labor is converted into money and stored in the bank (or other safe locations). When needed, money is used, and there is energy transfer.

One of the most basic principles of economics is the law of supply and demand. When there is a need for a product or service (demand), a person able to fill the need (supply) should reap the benefits of their labor, and the greater the need, the greater the benefit. Demand is considered yin. It calls for the reception of goods, whereas supply is yang because it involves the sending out of goods. When there is more supply (yang) than demand (yin), prices go down; when there is more demand (yin) than supply (yang), prices go up. An excess of either yin or yang will create its opposite. An excessive supply (yang) will make prices drop (yin), and increased demand (yin) will generate higher prices (yang). Falling prices are considered yin because they contract, whereas rising prices are yang because they expand or inflate.

Some people work all their lives and do not accumulate wealth, while others may inherit significant sums of money and never have to work. A young person who inherits money obviously did not have to work very hard to acquire wealth. The inheritance, however, did not develop by itself. At some point, an effort was made to amass wealth. Once the effort is in a yin form, it is easily transferred from one person to another.

Another factor that comes into play is the psychological and social stresses accompanying money intake. Illegal, high-risk work tends to be more highly paid than a similar legal occupation. Dealing with drugs, for example, is a highly stressful and dangerous job. The social and legal restrictions on selling drugs give higher value to the product because more effort is required to make and distribute or smuggle the drugs than would be necessary if the drugs were legal. In addition, the social stresses that fall on the people involved in the process contribute to the perceived worth of the drugs.

Making easy money by selling drugs does not mean the person did not do much work. Instead, dealers are given large lump payments for their emotional and potentially physical suffering. Dealers must endure significant stress or tension to avoid being caught. Illegal or dangerous work takes a tremendous toll physically, mentally, and emotionally in a short time, compared to legal jobs, which can also be highly stressful but not to the degree that illegal activities are. In addition, the large payment was in exchange for throwing away the dealers' self-esteem, for they suffered personal shame and public disgrace, as well as insult and slandering from others. Eventually, they can end up in jail or be killed. Thus their money was not easily earned.

Another stressful occupation is prostitution. Here, the shame and disgrace sex workers suffer is much greater than what they would incur from other jobs. At first glance, it appears that sex workers make much money for very little work. However, a sex worker's shame may be several hundred times more than she would feel if her job involved cleaning dishes or a bathroom. The more fortitude required to succeed in an occupation and the more abuse (actual or potential) a person may endure due to "professional hazards," the more money can be made in a short period.

Doctors and lawyers are paid more money

per hour than plumbers or electricians because the number of hours of training and education doctors and lawyers undergo is higher than the training requirements for plumbers and electricians. When all of the factors are considered, the wage disparity is easier to understand, thus reducing the need to be envious of how others earn money. The money (yin) one makes is directly proportional to the degree of effort and suffering one endures while working (yang). For example, business executives may earn more money than their employees. However, they must take on much greater responsibility, thereby using (yang) or expending (yang) a tremendous amount of mental energy.

The rules of yin and yang also apply to money acquired by chance, such as from the lotteries or Las Vegas slot machines. In these situations, there is the possibility of winning a large sum of money instantly, and everyone is given, more or less, the same odds of winning. If you toss a coin a thousand times, the chance of landing on heads or tails is equal every time. Fortune and misfortune in a person's life are similarly dispensed.

Most people consider it a misfortune not to have a lot of money. They feel depressed because they do not seem to be making enough money in proportion to their amount of work. Having a proper yin-yang perspective can reduce the suffering of these people. People do not earn enough money because they may not work hard enough. People must work hard physically and constantly manage the direction of their businesses. They need to mentally prepare for changes that may arise in the future. The ability to predict the future of one's business is based on extensive knowledge that can only be gained by investing a great deal of effort and learning lessons through trial and error. People must read books, ask experts, and experience failure to learn from their mistakes instead of blaming their misfortune on economic tides.

Success does not necessarily equal wealth. However, economically successful people work physically or mentally hard to convert their work into money, irrespective of their luck. In prosperous times they work hard and save their earnings instead of spending irresponsibly. They continue to work hard in bad times, using setbacks as learning experiences to improve their future performance.

Applying Yin-Yang to the Stock Market

Suppose you are a fund manager in the stock market. Your primary concern is the rise and fall of stock prices. Yang is a surge in prices, and yin is a downturn. Determining the time at which these may occur is Tai Chi. This diagram represents the trend of prices (fig. 9.1). A through B denotes the rise in prices after a fall. Points B through C represent the time when prices are rising. C through D represents the fall in prices after a period of increase. And D through E is when prices are bottoming out.

The factors affecting stock market prices

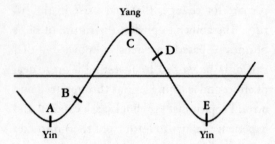

Figure 9.1 Yin-Yang of the Stock Market

can be divided into yin and yang. Factors that raise the prices are yang, and those that lower prices are yin. Those can be further broken down into immediate results and long-term results. For instance, something that raises the prices in the market immediately is yang compared to something with slower development. In this example, the rise in stock prices (yang) is Tai Chi, and the speed of the effect on the market is broken down into yin and yang. This can be applied to yin as well. The result is a spectrum of yin and yang to help determine when might be a good time to invest. Once these trends are defined, the prices of the changing market can be compared to the changing patterns of I Ching, and you may be able to predict the changes in the stock market.

10

Yin and Yang of Perspective

Differences in perspectives and perceptions are the root of many conflicts and misunderstandings. Confucius said, "If you do not have it in your mind, you will not see or hear it." Every visual object, sound, smell, taste, and feeling we perceive, we relate to our past experiences to interpret and understand the sensation. If we hear a sound we have never heard before, we must investigate its origin to conceptualize where it is coming from. The same is true of thoughts and ideation. If a person is not aware of the existence of something, he or she cannot conceive of it. For example, we did not know there was a possibility of damaging the atmosphere's ozone layer until we knew there was an ozone layer.

Anything viewed with a yang expectation will appear more yin. Conversely, anything considered with a yin expectation will seem more yang. The scandal surrounding President Clinton's term in office is an example of people in high places with high expectations from the public. People in high positions have a greater distance to fall. The mistakes made by those who are most respected are greatly amplified. This is in sharp contrast to events that surround the lives of those who do not hold public office.

Doctors, lawyers, and judges all have the honorific character of "teacher" at the end of their titles in Korea. At the same time, the people who hold these jobs are sometimes referred to as "licensed thieves." When we expect the world from people (yang), anything they do wrong will appear like a crime (yin). This is because we have high expectations from famous people. Thus, even a minor offense is blown out of proportion. On the other hand, when we have fewer expectations from people (yin), their actions can seem great (yang). This is an example of how yang constantly changes into yin, and yin into yang, in the material world and reasoning.

It all boils down to expectations—or, more specifically, perspectives. Most of us have been educated on the so-called "truths" determined by scholars and scientists. We believe that we live on Earth, a small part of the solar system, a minute portion of the Milky Way, and still an infinitesimal fragment of the infinite universe. We classify ourselves as "organisms" when considering the duality between organic and inorganic matter. We classify ourselves as "animals" when considering the duality between plants and animals. Among the group "animal," we consider ourselves part of the subset "mammal," and so on.

From our egocentric perspectives, we believe that we can observe the natural world with clarity, but we are unaware of the filter of our preconceived notions. For example, we stand before a fire and think how strong the flames are, forgetting that the fire is not so hot in relation to the sun. In this way, we lose perspective, allowing our daily problems to encompass our thoughts. As a result, we are not looking at the bigger picture.

A Perspective on Medicines of East and West

Easterners created Eastern medicine, and though it differs radically from Western medicine, it has the same human body as its subject. Neither view is more correct than the other; they are simply different interpretations of the same structures and functioning.

The ancient sages who founded Eastern medicine drew the internal organs in an abstract, idealistic manner and spoke of the physiology of the organs differently. They were not "wrong" or "inaccurate." Rather, they emphasized a different aspect of the organs. Eastern doctors were obviously acquainted with the internal organs. They conducted cadaver and animal dissections. Nevertheless, they drew and spoke of the organs' structures and physiology differently because they operated from a different mode of thinking or reasoning. Their innate perspectives were derived from different experiences, teachings, and observational points of view.

Seeing the Big Picture

Experiments conducted within the realm of the scientific method purport to be free of interpretation. However, subjectivity exists whenever a human being is involved in either administrating or analyzing data. Perhaps this is the final experiment leading to the conclusion of a book that the experimenter has taken ten years to complete. The experiment results determine whether or not the work will be published. The findings most definitely will adhere to the hypothesis of the experiment. There is also a great competition to establish funding for experimentation, and the results can be interpreted in more than one way, depending on the desired outcome. This is not to say that pure scientific research is not without merit. We must keep in mind the human element in every situation. As in daily life, the observational viewpoint varies significantly in scientific research. The psychological state of the observer greatly determines what information is absorbed and how that information is interpreted.

The reasoning of the yin-yang theory allows an investigation to occur from the observer's viewpoint while maintaining the whole's perspective. It does, however, leave room for bias in its calculations. For example, someone well-versed in yin-yang reasoning would claim that fire is intense only after carefully comparing everything in nature or the universe to fire. This system of analysis would be as follows: within the universe, in our solar system, on Earth, among organisms, between fire (yang) and water (yin)—fire is hotter (yang). The degree of fire's strength can also be classified according to the principle of infinite divisibility of the yin-yang equation. There is yin within

yang and yang within yin. Using this comparison method, the strength of the fire is put into perspective.

Analog and Digital Analysis

The reasoning process of yin-yang theory is, in one respect, identical to the process a computer uses to recognize data. A computer "thinks" in digital mode rather than in analog. Analog is a method of interpreting data by comparison. An analog clockface has hands rather than simply displaying numbers. By looking at an analog clock, we can see how the seconds, minutes, and hours relate to one another. A digital clock's face tells the precise time but does not show how one moment relates to the five before or the ten after. Analog indicators function by comparison and proportional relationships. It is not enough to know the stock's price when buying stocks. A good investor would want an analog comparison of the stock's cost for reference.

Both analog and digital methods of analysis have their strengths and weaknesses. While analog allows for comparison, digital can be more exact. The digital mode is superior in clarifying random and confusing situations into a logical order, but it does not give a complete and holistic view of things. The yin and yang mode of reasoning allows a person to switch from analog to digital, and vice versa. This means that it enables both inductive and deductive reasoning.

This is the beauty of yin and yang. It gives a

holistic view that illuminates the relationships between things, and at the same time, it provides an analytical and detailed view of any situation. Yin and yang together show the whole picture and close-ups of each part. This method of reasoning can help eliminate the observer's preconceived notions and allow a complete understanding of all things in nature.

The following are diagrams of an analog Tai Chi and a digital Tai Chi (fig. 10.1). In the analog Tai Chi, the boundaries between each color are unclear and seem to blend together.

However, there is a clear and distinct boundary distinguishing the two representative colors of yin and yang in digital Tai Chi.

Figure 10.1 Analog and Digital Tai Chi

11

Yin and Yang of Music

Music is a universal language that can genuinely gather and unite people. This is echoed in the famous phrase "The family that sings together stays together." It embodies the principles of yin and yang more clearly than anything else because music can be a source of joy, pleasure, and healing (all yang qualities) as well as of sorrow, fear, sickness, and terror (all yin qualities). Music can bring about peace and tranquility as well as confusion and chaos. It is considered by many to be the most profound form of expression humans create. Can you think of a television show, radio program, commercial, movie, or Broadway show that does not have music?

We hear music everywhere, whether during the holiday season, at an inauguration, graduation, or commencement, or simply at a party. In nature, we hear the chirping of birds or cicadas, the rustling of leaves, and the sounds of a stream or river. Life would be exceptionally dull, monotonous, and boring without the melodic variations between passion and peace or excitement and tranquility. In fact, nothing in this universe would exist without music. Music is life itself, and without it, no life can exist.

Influence of Music

Sounds affect people's minds. Music with a high pitch and fast tempo can excite people, while music with a low pitch and slow tempo can mellow them. Beautiful music can develop by attuning sound frequency, tone, and rhythm to the I Ching theory. This can be accomplished by alternating sounds with a high pitch and fast tempo with those with a low pitch and slow tempo or by combining sounds with a low pitch and fast tempo with those with a high pitch and slow tempo. It is noise when there is no order to the pitch (high/low) or beat (fast/slow).

Human physiology resonates according to the principles of the universe. Noise impedes the natural processes of human physiology and is, therefore, harmful. Thus, people are naturally repelled by this type of noise. Listening to beautiful music, however, harmoniously promotes positive human physiology. Therefore, people are naturally attracted to this type of music and will pay high admission prices to hear it performed live. Beautiful sounds that have a similar frequency to human physiology are the sounds of life (yang) because they facilitate physiological processes. On the other hand, noise is the sound of death (yin) because it impedes healthy human physiological processes.

The direct influence of music is shown by its impact on plant life. People are familiar with talking to and playing music for plants to help them grow. Numerous reports exist about plants' accelerated growth when showered with beautiful music.[1] However, if you play noise and try to grow plants, they will not grow well; flowers may not blossom, and trees may have difficulty bearing fruit. Though smog might contribute to making trees wither on a busy city street, the noise from the traffic is also a significant factor.

There have also been numerous studies regarding the development and intelligence of children related to musical influence. There have been reports of higher IQs in children born to women who played baroque music for them while they were in the womb. A recent report from China states that listening to Mozart may increase the IQ levels of children who are less than six years old. Aside from increasing children's IQ levels, Mozart's music has also increased the milk flow of cows in Brittany, France, and quelled drug trafficking in Edmonton, Canada.[2]

Music Therapy

Creating music influenced by a thorough study of how sounds affect the human body and mind would be like developing a new drug to treat specific ailments. For example, treating psychological disorders and certain organic diseases would be possible. "Music therapy" already exists in the East and West. Many CDs address specific problems, such as headaches, pain, and depression.

There are two ways in which music can induce healing. The first is by vibrating the eardrum to stimulate the brain. When music vibrates the eardrum, sound changes into electrical signals transmitted to the brain. The brain interprets the signals and creates sensations or emotions that cause bodily reactions through the nervous and endocrine systems. The second way music can affect the body is by resonating directly with molecules or cells to stimulate physiological processes.

Diseases arise out of an imbalance of yin and yang. The purpose of human physiological processes is to maintain a dynamic balance. Yin and yang fluctuate up and down within specific parameters: sometimes yin is greater than yang, and other times yang is greater than yin. While these two elements are in constant flux, disease occurs when there is a continued excess of yin without the recovery of yang or vice versa.

Music with a yin nature can activate the yin functions of the human body. For example, yang-type diseases are due to the excessive excitation of sympathetic nerves. Here, a person is emotionally excited or has a fever, headache, a fast pulse, and high blood pressure. Stimulating the yin functions will excite parasympathetic nerves and balance yin and yang to treat these diseases. Likewise, yang-type music can be applied to treat yin-type diseases in which a person has a cold body, pain, coldness in the abdomen, a slow pulse, and low blood pressure. When a person listens to yang-natured music when yang is not recovering or yin-natured music when yin is not recuperating, yin and yang will return to a balanced state and healing will occur.

In Korea, healing is done with musical instruments in several ways. For example, people suffering from stomach ailments, such as indigestion, stomachaches, or bowel problems, such as constipation or Crohn's disease, are treated with the sounds of drums. Drums are hollow and covered with animal skin. This is similar to the constitution of the bowels. Therefore, the sounds of drums resonate with the whole abdominal cavity, bringing it back to a balanced state.

Headaches are treated by playing a small gong, a percussion instrument made of metal. The sounds a gong makes resonate with the brain's cells, causing them to reverberate in a synchronized fashion. This action helps eliminate headaches and aids people in focusing or concentrating. Korean archers, renowned for their accuracy and who have consistently won gold medals in the Olympics and other international competitions, are well known for practicing for their events surrounded by loud gong sounds.

These are examples of treating specific ailments with music. But there are other things music can do. For instance, diseases of society can be treated by playing music balanced in yin-yang to harmonize and settle people's minds. Can a person develop thoughts of stealing while listening to sacred music majestically played with a pipe organ in a cathedral? When you watch a movie and something is about to happen, music with an unbalanced tone and rhythm plays in the background. This causes people to become unsettled and anxious. There is an abrupt change in the high and low tones and a sudden change in the tempo. The balance of yin and yang is broken explicitly to elicit feelings of anxiety, fear, confusion, and chaos. Try turning down the sound on a scary movie and feel how your apprehensions fade. If this type of unbalanced music becomes popular, society may become disordered and fall into confusion. But if yin-yang–balanced music becomes popular, society can become stable and orderly.

The Sounds of Society

The dynamic nature of American society is reflected in its popular music. Today's popular music resonates with a greater yang frequency, adding to the momentum of society. If we were to analyze all of the music currently played in American culture in terms of pitch and tone, we would probably find a 60:40 ratio of yang to yin music because of the predominance of rap music. Many young people like gangster rap, which has a strong beat. It is a yang form of music that resonates with young people who naturally are yang. However, because rap music is so yang, it can overstimulate the yang functioning of the body and lead to an imbalance.

Nevertheless, some of the most popular rap music has a relative yin-and-yang balance. These songs usually begin with a strong sense of tension (yang) that resembles a battlefield, and then a female voice (yin) appears. Therefore, despite a push toward the extreme, an opposing force always attempts to restore the yin and yang's relative harmony. This is the homeostatic mechanism of Tai Chi.

We can gain insight into someone's personality by understanding the nature of the music the person chooses to listen to. This may seem an obvious point, but once we better understand the nature of yin and yang, knowledge of what may stimulate a person can lead to a greater understanding of many other aspects of that person. For example, many older adults are likelier to listen to classical or country music. Classical music is yin-yang balanced music, whereas country music is generally yin-type. These two forms of music relate well to the yin nature of mature age. People with strong religious convictions tend to enjoy religious music, which is often yin. This, too, is a reflection of people's physiological and psychological states. Moreover, by listening to the music of a specific period or region, we can understand the conditions and trends of that society.

Yin and Yang of Instruments

The lower the pitch an instrument produces, the more yin it is; the higher the pitch, the more yang. The tuba is the most yin among wind instruments, and the piccolo is the most yang. Among stringed instruments, the double bass is the most yin, and the violin is the most yang. Percussion instruments have a wide variety of sounds. Among them, the bass drum sounds are the most yin, and those of the triangle are the most yang. The piano may be considered a percussion instrument because it creates sounds by percussing tight strings. It has the most balanced yin and yang characteristics of any instrument. It is said that the sound produced by playing the central key of a piano has the same tone as the cry of a newborn baby.

The tone of an instrument determines its yin or yang classification, and within each instrument, there may be further divisions of yin and yang depending on the notes played. When instruments combine to play a structured mixture of high and low tones and long and short rhythms, they create harmonious sounds. This is an example of the divisions of yin and yang within everything. Just as all things with different yin and yang tilts gather together to compose the universe, cells with diverse yin and yang tilts form a human being. So rhythms and tones with the variance of yin and yang can also gather to make balanced orchestral music.

The Power of Music

Napoleon's army is said to have gone to battle with marching music. This music helped raise fortitude and a fighting spirit to the highest degree. It helped set the right tone so that fear and hesitation melted away from the minds and bodies of his men. Playing music during battle was a technique used frequently in the East. Armies of the East were led to attack with a drum sound and to retreat with the gong sound. They sometimes used instruments with a high-pitched timbre to confuse and bring chaos to their enemies.

The influence of yin and yang music on a society and its people is quite strong. Masters of the East who understood this principle heavily emphasized the study of music. Yulryeo, reflections on music as interpreted by the I Ching, is considered the highest form of study and meditation in the East. In modern terms, Yulryeo is the study of vibrational waves and frequencies. The classics of the East are studied in a particular order, with Yulryeo as the final chapter.

With a good understanding of Yulryeo's principles, synchronizing the frequency of the mind, body, and spirit with the Tao is possible through the frequency of the music. This is what happens in chanting. It is also the nature of the power of authority that music can have. People's minds can be influenced by resonation. Recall the last time you unexpectedly heard a song from your childhood. Music has the power to elicit strong feelings and emotions. It can influence the psychological aspects of the human mind as well as the physical aspects of the human body. It can be used to harm as well as to heal.

The powerful influence of music can be seen not only on a personal level but also through the existence and continuity of an entire state or nation. For example, a Hwangjong, or "Golden Bell," is immediately made when a new dynasty comes into power in the East. A Hwangjong is a bell that produces the most balanced tone in music, like the central key of the piano. All musicians tune their instruments to the Hwangjong. During ancient times in the East, the Hwangjong was made to produce a perfectly balanced sound with 50:50 proportions of yin and yang. If the pitch tilted to either yin or yang, even slightly, the country was considered unbalanced, leading to chaos and the dynasty's downfall.

The Pied Piper is another famous tale that resonates with the same yin-yang principles. The power of the piper's flute was in tune with the balanced pitch of the Golden Bell. Rats, animals, and children would follow him because of the flute's perfect pitch. They would not have been drawn to the sound if it were not in tune. The Hwangjong of ancient dynasties is like the flute of the Pied Piper.

I Ching was written during the Zhou dynasty (1066–221 BCE). At that time, music served as a means of government, so Yulryeo, an interpretation of music according to I Ching theory, and Hwangjong, were very important. For example, giant bells were excavated from the tomb of Zheng, one of the vassal states of the Zhou dynasty (fig. 11.1). When restored to their original state, the bells consisted of three tiers, like the trigram of I Ching. The number of bells was the same as sixty-four hexagrams.

A careful observation of the patterns engraved on the bells during the Zhou dynasty will show that they are in the shape of trigrams and Tai Chi (fig. 11.2). It demonstrates a profound relationship between the Hwangjong and I Ching during the Zhou dynasty.

The same bells of Zheng are still in use in traditional Korean music. Still, their size has been downscaled and simplified, as much as the profound meaning of Yulryeo and Hwangjong has diminished.

Figure 11.2 Zhou Dynasty Bell, Tokyo National Museum, Tokyo, Japan

As the center of all waves, Hwangjong became the standard for measuring all things made of waves. For example, volume was measured by the number of grains that went into the Hwangjong, and the measuring rulers were created based on the bell's length. So among the ancient rulers of Korea (fig. 11.3), there was one called Hwangjong Cheok, or the Hwangjong ruler (fig. 11.4).

Figure 11.1 Bells of Zheng

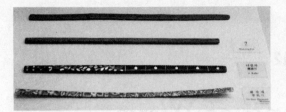

Figure 11.3 (above) Traditional Korean Rulers. National Folk Museum of Korea, Seoul, Korea

Figure 11.4 (right) Hwangjong Ruler, a Rectangular Brass Ruler Carried by the Secret Royal Inspector, National Palace Museum of Korea, Seoul, Korea

12

Yin and Yang of Wave

Everything in the universe is composed of matter with visible forms and energy without visible forms. Regardless of how small matter is split, it is always divided into two parts—matter and energy. Matter can be measured by its mass, while energy can be known by its wave pattern.

Just as yin transforms into yang and yang into yin, matter (yin) changes into energy (yang), and vice versa. Matter has an energizing tendency, while energy has a materializing tendency. When matter transforms into energy, it appears as a wave. Not only are the compositions of all things in the universe made up of two components, yin and yang, but so are their movements. The movements manifest by alternating a strong and weak energy emission in a wave pattern (fig. 12.1).

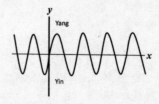

Figure 12.1 Movements of All Things in the Universe

Ultimately, a wave is an alternating occurrence of yin and yang. When the x coordinate, representing time, is added to the y coordinate, which expresses the strength (yang) and weakness (yin) of energy, the wave can be described in such a graph. All things that have movement have such a waveform. For instance, the Earth rotates on its axis and revolves around the sun. It fluctuates between yin and yang of day and night by rotating on its axis according to the time. It alternately repeats winter and summer according to time flow by revolving around the sun.

All human beings live, and their pulses change, according to an iteration of yin and yang. The pulse speeds up during the daytime and the summer, which belongs to yang. In contrast, the pulse slows down during the night and the winter, which belongs to yin. When the changes of yin and yang in these three aspects are shown in a diagram, it appears as follows (fig.12.2):

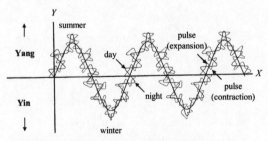

Figure 12.2 Changes in the Pulse According to the Seasons

As yin-yang exists within yin and yang in the composition of the whole creation, there is yin-yang within yin and yang in their movements. This is clearly shown in the diagram.

All matter is expressed by the yin-yang variance. Likewise, the wave represents the yin-yang of energy flow according to the yin-yang variance. Therefore, the constituent components, the substantial aspect of everything in the universe, and the wave, the energetic aspect, can be classified according to yin-yang variance.

Waves are classified according to the number of yin and yang changes that occur within a second. The greater the number of changes, the more yin the wave is, while the fewer changes indicate a yang wave. This is due to classifying the yin and yang of energy and not of matter. Since the viewpoint has turned 180 degrees, the standard of yin and yang changes. This is the inversion principle. When classifying constituent components that are still, the faster movements imply yang. Yet when categorizing dynamic energies, the quicker motion indicates yin. Therefore, the energy of a wave with a higher frequency becomes yin, while a lower frequency wave becomes yang.

Since everything in the universe has substantial and energetic elements, human beings can recognize them through material or energetic aspects. For example, individual objects have a particular sound or color, and sounds and colors can be identified as energetic waves. Those waves of energy beyond the measuring range of our senses, such as ultrasound, infrared, gamma rays, and X-rays, which do not appear as sound or color, can still be recognized by measuring instruments.

The waves, recognized as sound or color, are measured by the sense organs, such as ears or eyes, and then analyzed by the human brain. Those waves beyond the measuring range of sense organs, so that measuring instruments must be used to recognize them, can be analyzed through computers, which correspond to the human brain, to identify their particular characteristics. If the yin-yang of a wave based on the computer's analytical standards is applied, then the information of yin and yang of that matter can be known. This implies that the precise nature of matter can be understood by measuring the wave of matter through the measuring instrument that contains a program for analyzing yin and yang.

13

Yin and Yang of the Universe

Yin	Yang
matter	energy
proton	electron
particle	wave
Qi (energy)	Li (organizing principle)
long wave	short wave
black hole	white hole

Table 13.1 Yin and Yang of the Universe

The universe is composed of matter and energy, yin and yang. Yin relates to the tangible, perceptible, substantive aspect, or the ability to hold form, while yang is the intangible, imperceptible, energetic aspect, or the ability to enact change. Energy moves matter; matter produces energy.

Another way of looking at yin and yang is that yin is the physical body, while yang is the mind or mental functioning. This division is evident when we look at human beings. The body is a substance in humans, and the mind is energy. The mind controls and regulates the body, while the body houses and nourishes the mind. All organisms have minds that govern the body. However, when we look at the mind for what it truly is, a compilation of energetic guiding principles, we understand that even inorganic substances have primitive minds.

Let's look at a piece of granite. Granite is composed of mica, feldspar, and quartz. If we further break down quartz, we are left with one silicon atom and two oxygen atoms. A silicon atom (like all atoms) consists of a nucleus (a "solid" substance) and electrons (orbiting particles of energy).

According to the theory of yin and yang, the solid nucleus is yin and the external active electrons are yang. In addition, we know that yin and yang can be subdivided into smaller and smaller aspects. Therefore, regardless of how small subatomic particles may be, they can always be further divided. Following this reasoning, whenever there is a substance (yin), there must also be an energetic component (yang). So whenever there is a body (yin), there must also be a mind (yang).

Looking back at our example, the substantive aspect of the granite is the "body," and the energetic aspect is its "mind." This mind allows the granite to interact with and respond to external stimuli, such as gravity and electromagnetic and nuclear forces.

Energy and Matter

If an atom is the size of a football field, its nucleus is the size of a tennis ball. Although a rock appears solid, it is composed of atoms that contain mostly empty space. This is why shortwave radiation, like X-rays, can penetrate solid matter. If we split the nucleus of an atom, we would find elementary subatomic particles (yin) that are nothing more than oscillating fields of energy (yang). We can see them because they oscillate at such a high rate that they appear to be solid particles, much like a spinning pinwheel seems solid (fig. 13.1).

Einstein proved in his theory of relativity ($E=mc^2$), that energy constantly changes into matter and matter into energy—yin to yang

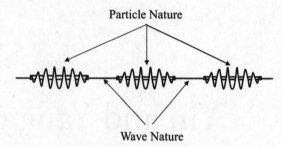

Figure 13.1 Wave and Particle

and back again (the fourth principle of yin and yang). If we were to perceive things as they truly exist, nothing would be solid and nothing would be stationary. For example, if the elementary particles that form all substances are nothing more than vibrating energy, there is no real difference between energy and matter.

Everything in the universe is made up of a single substance called Qi (vital energy), like the water that forms springs, streams, rivers, and oceans. Differences in things are caused by "vital energy" taking on various shapes according to time flow, similar to ocean waves responding to tidal and climate changes. Influenced by external forces, such as the sun's energy, electromagnetic waves, gravity, cosmic rays, and so on, this energetic medium momentarily holds a form. However, it can take any shape as determined by the nature of the relationship of its component particles to their surrounding forces.

Qi (Vital Energy) and Li (Organizing Principle)

Eastern scholars who study I Ching called the vibrational energy "Qi" and the organizing principle "Li." The combination of Qi and Li creates all things in the universe. If you consider Qi as water, then Li is the container. If Li is a mug, then the Qi will conform to the shape of a mug. If Li is a bottle, then the Qi will conform to the shape of a bottle. At the quantum level, Li is the force of attraction that binds energy into particles and particles into matter. Qi is the particles that succumb to the attraction.

Buddhism states, "All that exists is the same as that which does not exist." A substance with color that can be observed is the same as that which does not have any form. Likewise, that which does not have any form is the same as a substance with color and can be seen. These statements imply that since all types of matter, with their various colors and shapes, are ultimately energy vibrations, they do not indeed have forms. Conversely, imperceptible energy vibrations exist within the vast emptiness of space without color or shape.

Eastern scholars' studies into the true nature of the universe were as intense and profound as current studies into the nature of subatomic particles conducted by quantum physicists. The difference lies in the methodology. Quantum physics is actually on the road to proving what theorists of the East have known for eons. Confucian scholars attempted to study yin and yang in a rational, "scientific" manner. Taoists and Buddhist monks, however, tried to discover the true nature of the universe through intuition and meditation.

Quantum physics explains that subatomic particles have the dual nature of being both a particle and a wave. The wave characteristic is yang, and the particle nature is yin. The famous "double slit" experiment in particle physics demonstrated that a particle of light can integrate information about its surroundings and act according to that information. In the investigation, light passes through a piece of paper with two slits onto a screen. The light spreads out evenly when the experiment is performed with only one slit exposed. When both slits are exposed, it lands in alternating light and dark intervals because of interference patterns (a different rule of physics). This experiment became famous because when it was done using only a single photon (a light particle), the results were the same even though there was no interference. The photons appeared to "know" where they were expected to go and reacted to their surroundings. This implies a degree of consciousness, even at the most elemental level. Yin-yang theory explains that there is always a yin aspect and a yang aspect, matter, and energy, regardless of the phenomenon.

Mind and Body: Manifestation of Yin and Yang

So far, we have discussed why subatomic particles have both a mind and a body. Considering that everything, animate and inanimate, is composed of these little "thinking" things, everything in the universe has both a mind and a body. The difference is the complexity or simplicity of the controlling mind. Organisms have complicated and well-developed minds, whereas inanimate objects have minds that are simple and more primitive. Regardless of the complexity, however, every mind communicates with the universe's mind. This is similar to how all Earth's surface water connects with the boundless sea, and how the energy from a power plant is transmitted to the night-light in a child's room.

"Thinking" subatomic particles gather to form atoms. Atoms combine to form molecules, and molecules form cells. Cells unite to form tissues in the human body, and these tissues create our organs. All of these structures are composed of subatomic particles. Thus, the functioning of all our organs and body systems depends on the unification of their mental aspect. This unified mind is connected to the brain through nerves. The substantial facet of each tissue joins the physical body through the structures of the body's systems, such as the circulatory, digestive, reproductive, and nervous systems. What we consider to be our mind is actually an integration of the mental aspects of the individual constituent components. Our

body is an integrated system of these components' substantial and physical facets.

The mental and physical aspects of animals, plants, and minerals combine to make up the Earth. Likewise, the psychological and physical components of individual stars combine to make up the mind and body of the whole universe. And the mind of the universe is Tao or Tai Chi.

Black Holes vs. White Holes

The universe's movement is a perpetual succession of birth or production (yang) and death or destruction (yin). The quasar or white hole (yang) generates birth, and the black hole (yin) is responsible for the death. The manifestation of the white hole is the Big Bang, and that of the black hole is the absorption of everything, even light.

At the end of the black hole is the white

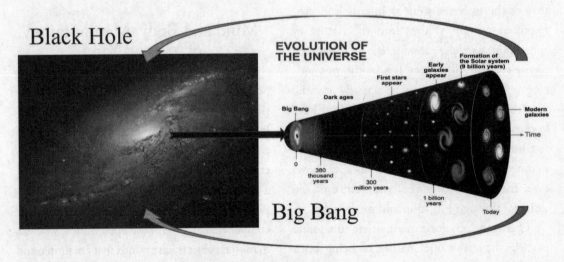

Figure 13.2 Black and White Holes

hole. Stars that have been sucked into the black hole contract and ultimately explode out the other end from the white hole. This action is known as the Big Bang. All substances that expand because of this explosion lose speed gradually and get sucked back into the black hole. These substances contract and explode out again, and thus the cycle continues. We can illustrate this process (fig. 13.2).

The following diagram is a simplified drawing of the black and white holes (fig. 13.3).

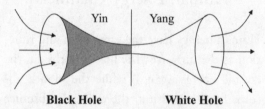

Figure 13.3 Black and White Holes Enlarged

As matter gets sucked into the black hole, it makes a spiraling motion. This is similar to a ball bearing's spiral movement dropped into a funnel or water in a drain. So, likewise, when matter explodes out of or ejects from the white hole, it also makes a spiraling motion. This motion is the causative force behind the rotation and revolution of stars and galaxies.

The black hole is the ultimate yin associated with a negative charge. The white hole is the utmost yang related to a positive charge. These positive and negative charges are reflected in the Earth's north and south magnetic poles (fig. 13.4). Its electromagnetic field is shaped like the model of the universe formed by the black and white holes.

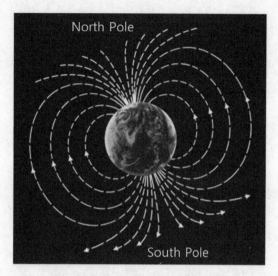

Figure 13.4 Earth's Magnetic Field

The principles governing black and white holes and the yin and yang of the universe can also be applied to ordinary, everyday substances. For instance, we can measure the voltage of an egg at the ends of its major axes, which indicates an egg's positive (expanding) and negative (contracting) force (fig. 13.5).

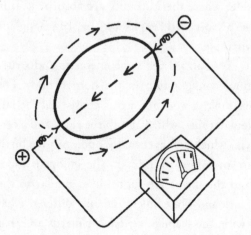

Figure 13.5 Magnetic Field of an Egg

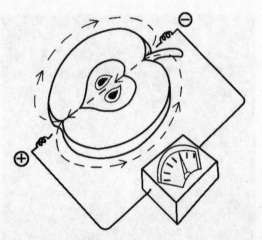

Figure 13.6 Magnetic Field of an Apple

tubes in the uterus. But, there is only one original black hole in the universe.

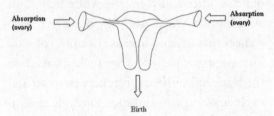

Figure 13.7 Black and White Holes of the Uterus

If you look carefully at various fruits, such as apples, you will find positive and negative poles in each one. Looking at the shape of an apple, it appears that the absorption of the apple's energy occurs toward its stem. This energy then spreads out toward the opposite end of the apple (fig. 13.6). It aligns and arranges the substances that compose the apple, determining its shape. The seeds of the apple sprout from the opposite side, where the nutrients are absorbed. This is the so-called "explosion" or "Big Bang" of an apple.

We can see the same energetic and structural configuration in the human body. For example, a woman's uterus consists of the fallopian tubes, which absorb the eggs, and a cervix, which will eventually open to give birth to an infant (fig. 13.7). The fallopian tubes and the uterus are funnel-like, similar to the black and white holes. The only difference between the shape of a woman's uterus and that of the universe is that there are two fallopian

Human Energy Channels

Human beings have the same form and function as the universe. The nose absorbs air, the cosmic energy (yang), while the mouth absorbs food and drink, the celestial substance (yin). Cosmic energy and substances transform into the vital energy (Qi) required by the body. The yin actions of the body manifest as the body's excretions (urine, feces, semen, etc.). These substances can nourish the planet and aid in the process of birth and renewal. The yang actions of the body manifest as Qi, which circulates in channels and nourishes the body and mind.

The body has six yin channels (or meridians, along which acupuncture points are located) and six yang channels. In addition, two special channels—the Ren, or conception channel, and the Du, or governing channel—control the yin and yang of the body. Because the body reflects the orientation of the universe, the Ren and Du channels flow in the same direction as the flow of stars during

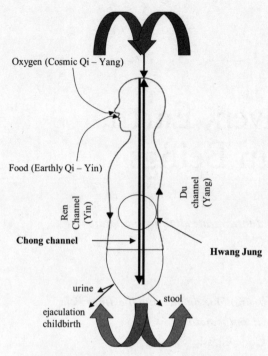

Oxygen (Cosmic Qi – Yang)

Food (Earthly Qi – Yin)

Ren Channel (Yin)

Chong channel

Du channel (Yang)

Hwang Jung

urine

ejaculation childbirth

stool

Figure 13.8 Human Energy Channels

a Big Bang. In addition, there is another unique channel called the Chong, or penetrating channel, which flows along the central axis of the human body. This channel is the same as the central axis of the universe (fig. 13.8).

In the center of the Chong channel is a mysterious place called Hwang Jung, literally translated as the "Golden Courtyard." This is believed to be the origin of life and death in a person. Human beings are programmed to flow from birth toward death. Hwang Jung can change the direction of this flow. The universe's genesis began with the white hole, and its destruction will start at the mouth of the black hole. The interface between the black hole and the white hole is the Hwang Jung.

Trinity: Heaven, Earth, and Human Beings

One begets two, two produce three, and three create all things in nature.
—Tao Te Ching

*One is the beginning; out of the Void, One begins. One divides into the Three Poles,
but its foundation remains boundless.*
—The Celestial Code Classic

The purpose of the discussion of Tao, Tai Chi, and yin-yang in the previous chapters was to illustrate the importance of these concepts in studying the I Ching. Tao and Tai Chi represent a totality based on the number 1. On the other hand, yin and yang, which stem from Tao and Tai Chi, are based on the number 2, or the binary system. However, Tao and Tai Chi manifest not only as the number 2 (yin-yang) but also reveal themselves as the number 3.

What Is Three? I Ching Is the Union of Numbers 2 and 3

I Ching theory explains that for anything to manifest in the present dimension, it must have both yin and yang components. Numbers, the fundamental principle of all manifestations, also have yin and yang aspects. A yin number always escorts every yang number, because yang numbers are too vibrant and unstable to manifest in form without being accompanied by yin numbers.

If not paired with yin, yang energy would be transient on every level—physical, mental, and spiritual. Conversely, yin numbers must have yang numbers to move and change. Yin and yang coexist in an utterly dependent relationship. Numbers have the same relationship to yin and yang because they signify the universe's workings.

Numbers 1 and 2 must be recognized and understood before expressing number 3. Number 1 is representative of Tai Chi. It exists inside all numbers as the perfect balance of yin and yang.

When any number is multiplied or divided by 1, that number remains the same. However, adding or subtracting 1 from any number changes it to a number reciprocal in yin and yang ($3 + 1 = 4$ and $4 - 1 = 3$). Number 1 can either keep a number in a neutral state or transform yin to yang or yang to yin. This capability is also the way of Tai Chi.

The number 1 includes all phenomena: the universe, stars, planets, people, animals, amoebae, and so on. Containing the balanced properties of yin and yang, 1 signifies unification and harmony. The number 3 also comprises a balance of yin and yang and shares the same profound meanings of unification and harmony. These two numbers most closely resemble the center or balancing point.

While number 1 defines the universe, the numbers 2 and 3 are the first yin and the first yang numbers, respectively. After 1, 2 and 3

are the next in line, representing yin and yang. The combination of 2 and 3 can form all other numbers as well, as illustrated here:

$$2 \times 2 = 4$$
$$2 + 3 = 5$$
$$2 \times 3 = 6$$
$$(2 \times 2) + 3 = 7$$
$$2 \times 2 \times 2 = 8$$
$$3 \times 3 = 9$$
$$(2 \times 2) + (3 \times 2) = 10$$
Etc.

Eastern numerology connects the number 1 with heaven. The first yin number is 2 and is related to the earth. 1 and 2 gave rise to 3, formed by the union of the energies of heaven and earth. Therefore, 3 represents humanity in particular and everything in nature. While 1 (heaven) can exist by itself, 2 (earth) requires 1 to support it, and 3 (humans) could not have come into being without both 1 and 2.

The number 3 has the same energetic and creative capabilities as the eastern direction, springtime, and dawn. Dawn rises from the east with the sun. The direction and the time of day are akin to springtime, the beginning of a new year. These three things have even distributions of yin and yang energies. The springtime is both cold (yin) and hot (yang), while dawn has both the darkness of night (yin) and the brightness of the day (yang). The east is between the extremes found in the north (yin) and the south (yang).

The I Ching understands the importance

and the power of the numbers 2 and 3. Therefore, its system of hexagrams is the manipulation and integration of 2 and 3 or, in other words, the binary and the trinary systems (classifications based on the number 2 and the number 3, respectively).

The binary system, representing even (yin) number changes, is better suited to express form (yin). In contrast, based on the number 3 (yang), the trinary system is better suited to represent function (yang). These contrasting attributes are due to the restless nature of odd numbers and the more settled nature of even numbers.

For any event or action to occur or progress, there must be an initial motion (yang), return (yin), and mediator or neutralizer (Tai Chi) that converts the different processes into their opposites to form a single unit, phase, or segment. That is why 3 or its multiples express all functions (movements) of the universe.

Einstein had a seven-year obsession with the I Ching. He praised it as "a great mathematical explanation of the universe."

Many tales support the accuracy of the art of Sangsuhak. One tells of a master who had spent many years teaching his son the computations and intricacies of this mathematical art form. One day the master decided to test his son and asked him to calculate the number of dates growing on the tree in their garden. The son set about to do his calculations. First, he determined the number (with a matching hexagram) corresponding to the nature of their tree. He then figured out the number (hexagram) corresponding to the direction that the tree faced. Finally, he determined the number (hexagram) related to the present time.

After deducing these numbers, the son performed his calculations with an abacus, concluding that there were 2,884 dates on the tree. The father, with his computations, came up with 2,885. Because there was a discrepancy of 1, the master ordered his servants to pluck all the dates from the tree and count them. The count came out to 2,884 plus 1 date half-eaten by bugs. Thus, both the son and the father were correct.

Sangsuhak: A Study of Symbol and Numbers

Sangsuhak is a traditional Eastern study that interprets the I Ching with mathematical terms. Sang is translated as a symbol or image, Su as a number, and Hak as "to study." Sangsuhak attributes numbers to the structure and function of everything in nature. Mathematically manipulating these numbers can determine any phenomenon's past, present, and future.

Trigrams and Hexagrams

Tai Chi is 1. It is the undifferentiated totality. When Tai Chi divided, it became 2, the forces of yin and yang. Yin and yang each split to become the forces of Sasang, translated as the Four Symbols (see chapter 15). The division of Sasang led to the creation of the eight trigrams, and the further subdivision of the eight trigrams established the sixty-four hexagrams of the I Ching.

Looking at this system of separation and

division, it would seem that the I Ching is based solely on a binary system, a system of classification based on the number 2. However, as previously mentioned, the I Ching includes the numbers 2 and 3 in its interpretation of the universe. Thus, its principle is based on both the binary and trinary systems.

The I Ching uses symbolic codes to convey the nature of all things. The hexagrams are six lines arranged in a particular order to represent specific parts of nature. The hexagrams are the principal symbolic codes of the I Ching, designed by placing two trigrams ($2 \times 3 = 6$), one on top of the other. The lines of the hexagrams have two possible natures. They can be either yin (a broken line) or yang (a solid line).

The trigrams consist of three lines, each with two possible natures. Therefore, there are eight possible trigrams, 2^3 or $(2 \times 2 \times 2) = 8$. The hexagrams, being a combination of any two of these eight trigrams, therefore have sixty-four possibilities, 8^2 or $(8 \times 8 = 64)$. The following diagram (fig. 14.1) illustrates how a single hexagram breaks down into its parts.

Eastern philosophy is an extension of the lessons of the I Ching. The trigrams are organized so that the upper line represents heaven, the middle line represents humanity, and the lower line represents earth.

Sam-Taegeuk: A Symbol of Trinity

The traditional Tai Chi symbol depicts yin and yang, or the binary nature of the universe.

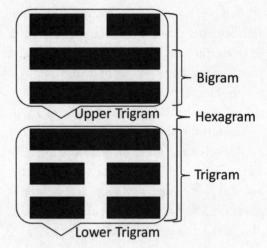

Figure 14.1 Formation of a Hexagram

Because it does not explicitly demonstrate the number 3, an alternative Tai Chi symbol in Korea called Sam-Taegeuk (fig. 14.2A) segments Tai Chi into three parts. Sam implies the number 3, and Taegeuk means "Tai Chi." Next to Sam-Taegeuk is the Dharma wheel (fig. 14.2B), commonly seen in Indian and Tibetan temples. It is a symbol that further differentiates Sam-Taegeuk into Sasang (chapter 15) and eight trigrams (chapter 21). Both Sam-Taegeuk and the Dharma wheel are symbols representing the same Tao.

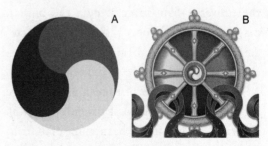

Figure 14.2A Sam-Taegeuk
Figure 14.2B Dharma Wheel

Red is yang and implies heaven. Blue is yin and describes the earth. Yellow was added to represent the meeting and harmony of yin and yang and is used to portray humanity.

The famous Buddhist saying "One universe created by the mind" speaks literally of a universe created by the mind where nothing exists outside what the mind or brain can perceive and understand. Things exist when we exist and disappear when we disappear. Nothing is of value unless we are active participants in it. This notion has scientific validity.

It can be seen in the placebo effect and in theories that describe the universe as a holographic image created and interpreted by the mind. Additionally, there are findings in quantum physics that show the significance of the observer on the position or velocity of subatomic particles. These findings indicate that particles react differently when observed than when no one is watching. Such reactions may also be true of the universe.

The I Ching dictates that human beings are the most vital element in the universe because their composition of yin and yang is more balanced than any other entity. Human beings, therefore, are considered the center of the universe. Sam-Taegeuk puts the human perspective in its proper place. The sages created Sam-Taegeuk and Tai Chi symbols to better understand the universe and ourselves.

In various quarters of Korean palaces, there are paintings of Sam-Taegeuk patterns (fig. 14.3). Their purpose is to instill the meaning of the trinity into the hearts of a king or his subjects. On the throne, the picture reflects the importance of Sam-Taegeuk. There are drawings of the sun and moon, or yin and yang, in the sky. Five peaks represent the five elements on the Earth, and the king is in the center. The king corresponds to 3, the center of yin and yang. Beneath the throne is the king's subjects and the people. The meaning of this painting is to govern people by carefully examining the laws of heaven and earth.

Figure 14.3 A Throne of a King, Gyeongbokgung Palace, Seoul, Korea

Space, Time, and Color

All things in the universe have three fundamental properties: space (direction), time, and color. We understand that human beings exist in three-dimensional space. Most structures made by human beings use 45-, 60-, 90-, 120-, or 180-degree angles. These numbers are also multiples of 3.

Mathematically, a three-coordinate system called the x, y, and z axes represents three-dimensional space. Each axis extends to infinity in two directions, from negative to positive.

Therefore, the combination of these *three* (the axes) and the *two* directions of each axis describes space. The following diagram illustrates this idea (fig. 14.4):

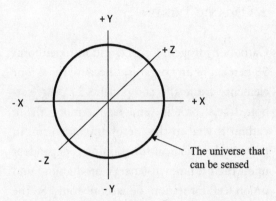

Figure 14.4 Coordinates of Cognitive Space

The number 3 is essential in the perception of space, but it is also vital to our perception of time. We experience and discuss time in three segments: past, present, and future. The present time is an ever-changing axis that balances the past with the future. Many masters of the East emphasize the importance of "staying present" as a way to happiness and enlightenment. To accomplish this, I Ching teaches people to be flexible to change because the present never stays the same.

Coincidentally, one year is twelve months, each roughly thirty days long, while a single day consists of twenty-four hours. Each hour, in turn, is sixty minutes, and one minute is sixty seconds. All are multiples of three.

The trigrams of the I Ching allow us to qualitatively observe any moment in time. They give us a sense of our place in the scheme of things. Each line of a trigram expresses heaven, humans, and earth, as well as the past, present, and future.

The numbers 2 and 3 are theoretically sufficient to express any situation or matter in our three-dimensional world. Therefore, the I Ching communicates in hexagrams, consisting of the number 2 (two trigrams) and the number 3 (the number of lines in a trigram). Two trigrams are essential to represent the two sides of any given situation: what can be seen or tangible right now (substantial/yin) and what is not apparent or imperceptible at the moment (energy/yang).

Now that we see the trinity principle at play in space and time, let's shed some light on the subject of color. There are two sets of three primary colors. One comprises reflective colors of red, yellow, and blue. (These are also the colors of Sam-Taegeuk symbol mentioned earlier).

Certain combinations of these colors will create various other colors, such as purple (red and blue), orange (red and yellow), and green (blue and yellow). A combination of all three reflective colors makes the color black.

The other set consists of the generating colors: red, green, and blue. Combining these three colors creates the color white. Together the two groups provide a multitude of colors in nature.

Trinity of the Universe

In addition to the three fundamental properties of space, time, and color, many other qualities and functions in the universe manifest in sets of three. For instance, everything in the universe rotates in a circular or elliptical pattern, following the flow of the number 3. A circle has 360 degrees, a multiple of 3. The factor pi used to compute the circumference of a circle is 3.14 and can be rounded to 3. In addition to having three composite parts (proton, neutron, and electron), the atom has electrons that orbit the nucleus, which rotates. Similarly, the Earth spins on its axis while orbiting the sun. In turn, the sun orbits around the center of the Milky Way galaxy, itself in a state of revolution.

1. THREE STATES OF EXISTENCE

In the universe, things exist as either a solid (yin), liquid (between yin and yang), or vapor (yang). For example, when water is heated, it evaporates and becomes a gas, or vapor. In its neutral state, water is a liquid; when water is frozen, it becomes solid.

Caterpillars begin as larvae, which is a fluid-like existence. They then transform into physically inactive pupae, like solid ice. Finally, when the time is ripe for birth, the pupae transform into butterflies and float away like vapor.

Whether in the mother's womb or in an egg, land mammals and birds are compared to the solid state because relatively little movement occurs compared to the amount of activity the body partakes in after birth. The fetuses remain suspended and confined in their fluid surroundings in the womb or in the egg. Once freed from their capsules, they embody the liquid state, growing and changing rapidly and fluidly. In death, their bodies disintegrate like vapor into the air.

2. ORGANIC TRINITY

Carbon, hydrogen, oxygen, and nitrogen form 98 percent of any organism because these four elements create the components of cells (carbohydrates, protein, and fats). Among them, carbon is vital to the life of any organism, in that all physiological functioning is dependent upon the breakdown (energy production) and union (cell formation) of carbon atoms. So the presence of carbon atoms differentiates animate life from inanimate objects in our realm of the universe.

When carbons unite, it is usually six carbons that form a single group. The resulting shape of their formation is a hexagonal structure. Thus, organic substances that are essential in creating organisms have hexagonal structures. For instance, sex hormones and adrenocortical hormones have hexagonal structures.

Benzene (C_6H_6) and toluene (C_7H_8) are aromatic chemical compounds derived from petroleum and coal tar, the fossil remains of prehistoric animals and plants. While the number of carbon and hydrogen atoms varies, both have hexagonal structures diagrammed as six-membered rings (figs. 14.5 and 14.6). Thus, coal and petroleum products, such as plastic, paraffin wax, and fiber (textile), also have hexagonal structures. It is the same for various other chemicals, like dyes, pesticides, and drugs essential in our daily lives.

Benzene C_6H_6

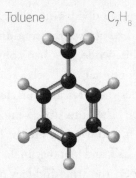

Figure 14.5 Benzene

Toluene C_7H_8

Figure 14.6 Toluene

Again, we see the principle of three at the molecular level with cells consisting of carbohydrates, proteins, and fats, and in the hexagonal structure of the carbon molecules formed by the cooperation of three and two.

Carbon is the most critical element in organisms. In terms of molecules, however, water is the most vital. Among the various types of water, one type is called hexagonal water (fig. 14.7). This type of water has the most pleasing taste due to its freshness and moderate temperature. It has a hexagonal structure formed by three molecules. The water in the fluid of healthy organisms also has a hexagonal structure. Thus, hexagonal water tastes better because our bodies need it. Therefore, we will be healthier by drinking large quantities of it.

Figure 14.7 Hexagonal Water

Carbon and water are proofs that demonstrate how the formation by the number 3 or a multiple of 3 (6) is most appropriate for the structures of matter that construct life. Other examples of hexagonally structured molecules in nature include beehives, turtle shells, quartz crystals, and snow crystals (fig. 14.8).

Figure 14.8 A Turtle's Shell

The number 2 symbolizes the Earth. Life cannot exist without the elements found in Earth's belly. Therefore, the number 2 must be present for the fundamental structures of life to take shape. But the number 3 is equally essential for life, as it supplies the energy and movement to the substance of yin.

3. ATOMIC TRINITY

We can observe the trinity principle at the molecular and atomic levels. An atom consists of protons, electrons, and neutrons. In terms of its electromagnetic charge and mass, a proton has a positive (yang) charge and greater mass (about two thousand times the mass of the electron). In contrast, an electron has a negative charge (yin) and a smaller mass. The neutron has roughly the same mass as the proton but holds no charge and thus functions as the mediator of yin and yang or Tai Chi.

However, the inversion principle occurs between the movement and position of the proton and electron. An electron orbits the nucleus, consisting of proton and neutron held together by the nuclear force. As a result, it is more unrestricted in motion, jumping from atom to atom. Thus it is yang in nature. On the other hand, the proton is yin because of its central position and heavier weight than the electron. The neutron, meanwhile, is harmonized in yin-yang because it has no charge and moderates both the proton and the electron. However, in terms of sheer speed, the proton and neutron inside the nucleus have stupendous velocities of about forty thousand miles per second, making them yang compared to the electrons orbiting the nucleus at a relatively slow rate of six hundred miles per second.

Bodily Trinity

Trinity also can be found in the human form. Humans, the lords of all creation, most closely resemble the universe compared to any living or nonliving entity on Earth. The human body has three sections: the head, torso, and legs. Each segment subdivides into three.

The head comprises the cranium, maxilla, and mandible, while the torso consists of the thoracic, abdominal, and pelvic cavities. The spine includes the cervical, thoracic, and lumbar vertebrae. The arms divide into the upper arm, forearm, and hand, while the legs consist of the thigh, calf, and foot (fig. 14.9). The fingers and toes repeat the arms-and-legs pattern and divide into three segments.

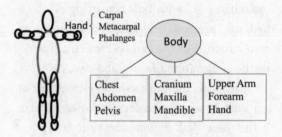

Figure 14.9 Trinity of a Body

The result would be two mirrored, symmetrical halves when the body divides sagittally (split down the middle from top to bottom).

This is because humans have two eyes, two nostrils, two ears, two arms, and two legs. Even the single parts of the body, such as the mouth and throat, are symmetrical. Let's look closely at a hexagram of the I Ching. Notice that it actually mirrors the human body (fig. 14.10). This gives some insight into why the principles of the I Ching are the most accurate devices for explaining all phenomena of the universe.

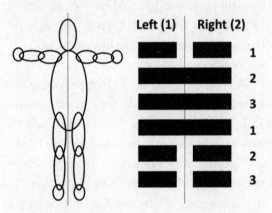

Figure 14.10 Trinity of a Body and a Hexagram

In addition to the body's outer structure, the trinity principle occurs in internal anatomy and physiology. For example, according to neuroscientist Paul D. MacLean's triune brain model, the human brain can be divided into three distinct segments, each representing a different stage of evolution.[1] The first or oldest part of the brain is called the R-complex, or reptile brain, engaging in a crucial role in instinctual behaviors for survival and reproduction, such as aggression, dominance, ritualization, and territoriality. The second is the limbic system, or mammal brain, associated with complex emotions and decisions, such as bonding, empathiz-

ing with others, and safeguarding the group. The last segment is the neocortex, the primate brain, which supervises complex brain functions—reasoning, planning, problem-solving, perception, and verbal language.

The control system of human beings consists of three parts: the nervous system (yang), the endocrine system (yin), and the hypothalamus (balance between yin and yang). The hypothalamus is part of the brain, yet it secretes releasing factors. These are hormonal precursors that allow the endocrine system to do its job. Thus it has the dual nature of belonging to both the nervous and endocrine systems.

The nervous system, too, consists of three segments: the brain, central nerves, and peripheral nerves. Meanwhile, the endocrine system secretes three chemicals: releasing factors from the hypothalamus, such as the corticosteroid releasing factor; stimulating hormones from the pituitary, such as adrenocorticotropic hormone; and target hormones from various other endocrine glands, such as corticosteroid hormone from the adrenal cortex.

The trinity principle can also be observed in some endocrine glands themselves. The pancreas, for example, secretes three hormones. The first is insulin, which carries sugar (glucose) out of the bloodstream and into the body's cells. The second pancreatic hormone is called glucagon. It brings sugar back into the bloodstream. The third pancreatic hormone is called somatostatin. It regulates the other two hormones. An I Ching interpretation would label insulin as yin, glucagon as yang, and somatostatin as the mediator of yin and yang.

There are many more anatomical examples of the trinity in the human body: three types of blood cells (red, white, and platelet), three types of muscle tissue (skeletal, smooth, and cardiac), three layers of skin (epidermis, dermis, and subcutaneous tissue), and three types of salivary glands in the mouth (the parotid, sublingual, and submandibular glands).

There appear to be four skin colors that populate the planet: black, white, red, and yellow. Skin color, however, depends upon the proportion of only three substances that color (pigment) the skin: melanin, which gives rise to the dark brown to black color; hemoglobin, which gives rise to the red color; and fats, which gives rise to the yellow color. These three pigments are found in every color of skin in various proportions.

The dominance of any pigment results in a particular skin color. For instance, if melanin is dominant, the person will have darker skin. If hemoglobin is dominant, the skin will have a red color. Yellow skin has a more significant amount of fat pigment, while white skin lacks all three. So while there is a distinction in skin colors, they all share the same three components.

Genomic Trinity

Western science states that our appearances and physiology differ because of the variances in individual genetic structures. For example, chromosomal genes determine protein structure, resulting in different cell structures, hormones, and enzymes regulating cell functions. Differences in these components give rise to the varieties in human shape and physiology.

DNA is a complex molecule composed of thousands of units called nucleotides. Each nucleotide has three components: (1) sugar, (2) phosphoric acid, and (3) a base. The bases are adenine, guanine, cytosine, and thymine. Adenine and guanine are purines of nine atoms (3×3, a yang number), while cytosine and thymine are pyrimidines of six atoms (3×2, a yin number). This is a clear illustration of the trinity principle in the formation of nucleotides and bases.

A codon is a strand of DNA providing the genetic information (code) for a specific amino acid. The four bases are paired in two combinations: adenine with thymine (uracil in RNA) and guanine with cytosine. A single pairing of nucleotides is like a single letter of the alphabet in the language of genetics. Codons form by a sequence of three pairs of bases. If a base pairing is like a single letter, then a codon is like a word in the genetic text. The sequence of codons determines the sequence of a single specific amino acid, and the sequence of amino acids determines the structure of the resultant protein.

For example, if a codon is AGC (which pairs with UCG), it results in amino acid arginine. If it is CGA (which pairs with GCU), it is called serine. Proteins, in turn, generate the various types of cells in the body.

Our investigation into genetics shows a remarkable similarity between DNA and the I Ching's trigrams and hexagrams. A single pair of bases is essentially a single pairing of yin and yang. A single codon (three bases) is a trinity relationship and is the fundamental unit in genetics. When we compare a strand of DNA with a trigram, we can see similarities in how numbers 2 and 3 encapsulate to store information (fig. 14.11).

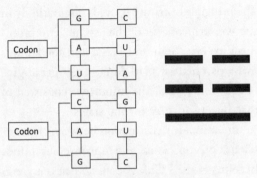

Figure 14.11 DNA and a Trigram

Codons are composed of three nucleotide pairs, and each nucleotide exists in one of four possible forms. There are 4^3 ($4 \times 4 \times 4$) or sixty-four possible codons. This is the same method I Ching uses to construct the sixty-four hexagrams. Essentially, the I Ching compels us to see that the universe exists within every individual and, in fact, in every living cell. It is a discovery that bears remarkable similarity to Western science's discovery of DNA.

The Three Treasures

According to Eastern philosophical and medical tradition, the Three Treasures reside within our bodies: essence, Qi, and spirit (fig. 14.12). Essence designates the state just before energy's transformation into substance. It is strongly re-

lated to sexual energy; sexual prowess is called Jing Li, or essence power, and a sperm cell is called Jingzi, or essence seed. Qi indicates the dynamic, active energy resulting from essence's complete transformation. Spirit refers to the purest portion of the Qi that regulates our bodies.

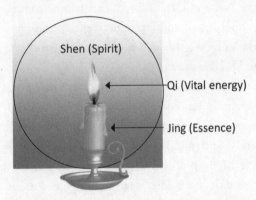

Figure 14.12 Essence, Qi, and Spirit. The candle-light clearly demonstrates their relationship.

Essence goes through a yang transformation (diffuses) to become Qi. Qi also goes through further stages of yang transformation to become spirit. In turn, spirit goes through a yin transformation (gathers or concentrates) to become Qi; and Qi goes through further stages of yin transformation to become essence again. If you consider the physical body yin, then essence, Qi, and spirit, all deemed energy, are yang.

This yang may divide into three: essence is yin within yang, Qi is the middle or balance of yin and yang, and spirit is yang within yang. In the East, the mind is called Jing-Shen, or essence-spirit. This is because Easterners believe that the mind is composed of a more-or-less substantial aspect (Jing) and an energetic aspect (Shen). Eastern medical texts call the brain a "warehouse of consciousness," from which spiritual enlightenment (wisdom) is said to arise. The brain is also called the "sea of marrow." As marrow forms from essence, the brain is made of essence. It is stored and activated between the kidneys in the Mingmen, or the "Gate of Life." Eastern medicine attributes proper sexual and reproductive functioning to the kidneys. This is how essence influences reproductive prowess.

Essence is the root of the body's energy. If the body has enough essence, it follows that enough Qi and spirit will develop to keep the body and mind healthy. Although spirit is the highest cultivation of the body's energy, one must have adequate essence to mature it. In other words, one needs to gather as much essence as possible so that the spirit may evolve into higher states and communicate with the spirit of heaven or universe.

Chapter 7 mentioned that food dishes that increase sexual energy boost the body's essence. Therefore, having a lot of essence indicates sexual prowess. When there is plenty of essence, the amount of Qi proportionately increases so that one does not feel fatigued and can work continuously with a high degree of enthusiasm. It also follows that the amount and strength of spirit will increase.

When there is plenty of essence, the brain functions optimally and the mind becomes clear. According to Eastern medical theory, the prevention and treatment of Alzheimer's disease lie in taking in foods or herbs that create an abundance of essence in the body. A wealth of essence will extend one's life span, and enlightenment will become achievable.

Psychological Trinity

The principle of trinity unfolds fascinatingly in the Western concept of the psyche. Two prominent experts, Sigmund Freud and the famous Swiss psychiatrist Carl Jung, drew paradigms of the workings of the mind that consisted of three layers or three mental states.

Freud made a distinction between the conscious, preconscious, and unconscious mind. In terms of the I Ching, consciousness is yang, as it is an explicit state of awareness. On the other hand, the unconscious is hidden, and its workings are mysterious. It therefore belongs to yin. The preconscious, meanwhile, can be considered Tai Chi because it acts as a mediator enabling the unconscious to communicate with the conscious.

A more popular and far-reaching paradigm of the mind is the realm of the famous psychological entities—the id, ego, and superego, according to Freud. These systems also function at various levels of consciousness. The id, the oldest and most primal of the three, is the original self and a primary energy source. The entire psyche is fueled by this instinctual, unconscious reservoir of impulses, which includes libido. It is, in essence, the yang of self.

If the id is yang, the ego is Tai Chi because it is the mediator of yin (superego) and yang (id) within Freud's psychic system. The ego, representing the conscious self, regulates id impulses.

Based on reason and the reality principle, the ego arrests or postpones id's urges until an appropriate circumstance arises for discharge.

Basically, the superego is a moral conscience, a mental censor for the ego, gauging actions according to the values the parent and society instilled in the individual. Therefore, the superego can be considered the yin of the psyche.

Carl Jung, a one-time disciple and colleague of Freud's, reduced the psyche into three levels that differed from Freud's classifications. He termed the levels consciousness, personal unconscious, and collective unconscious. Consciousness, represented in a pyramid, is a small piece at the top. The larger personal unconscious lies beneath consciousness, and the collective unconscious, the majority of the pyramid, is found at the bottom (fig. 14.13).[2]

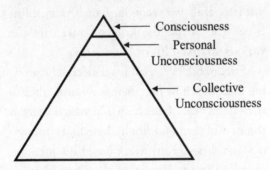

Figure 14.13 Structure of the Psyche

Consciousness, the working mind, is the field of inner and outer awareness, with the ego as the individual's focal attention. The personal unconscious is the psyche level infiltrated with images, behaviors, and memories from an individual's life experiences. They are subliminal, rejected, ignored, or repressed from the conscious mind. Lastly, the collective unconscious is an immense storehouse of universally accessible information, transcending boundaries of time or space. It contains the whole existence of life, including tribal and cultural memories of humanity.

Jung is known to have had a great interest in the I Ching. He studied it intensely and even wrote the foreword to Wilhelm's translation of the ancient text. His I Ching study significantly impacted his theory of the psychological structure of the mind. Most likely he applied the design of the three-tiered trigram to his theoretical system.

Decisive Trinity

In many popular American spectator sports, a coin is tossed at the beginning of the game to determine who will get the initial advantage. With only two options, heads or tails, there is a clear winner and loser with no possibility of a tie, which is an efficient decision-making method. However, it is a decision that sees black and white and no gray.

The coin toss is a method that fits well with the temperament of Westerners. Such an analytical, linear, logical conceptual framework has established a brilliant material civilization, as evidenced by the wealth of countries like the United States. In terms of the I Ching, this method distinguishes yin and yang.

In the East, people use the "rock-paper-scissors" decision-making method instead of coins. A fist with two fingers spread out makes scissors, a completely closed fist creates rock, and an open hand makes paper. The scissors can defeat paper by cutting it but loses to the rock, which smashes it. The rock can win over scissors but loses to the paper, which wraps it. The paper can win over the rock yet loses to scissors.

If both persons display the same gesture, it is a tie, and they simply make the same or another motion on the new count of three. This method of determining a winner allows for yin, yang, and the balance of the two (a tie). So it fits well with Eastern thought by finding meaning in the third, or the median, option rather than an either-or approach. Thus, Easterners were able to develop a spiritual civilization based on the principle of the "middle path," or "golden mean."

An additional decision-making tool is a die. Dice are said to have originated from China. A die has six sides ($2 \times 3 = 6$) and offers many more winning and losing possibilities than a coin or the rock-paper-scissors game. Dice are most similar to the hexagrams of the I Ching as each one comprises six elements and is a divination tool. The movement of the universe, as seen from the Earth, consists of three segments, or phases (multiple of 3). So a die, made up of the six numbers, like an I Ching hexagram, is the most appropriate tool for divination and making the right decisions.

Political Trinity

Previously, we discussed the bipartisan form of the US government and its three branches. Here we again see the manifestation of the trinity principle. The executive branch, which enforces the law, is yang, and the judicial branch, which maintains and interprets the law, is yin. Meanwhile, the legislative branch is Tai Chi, having aspects of both yin and yang. For example, it can pass laws and holds the power to impeach anyone in either branch, thereby having control over both.

Additionally, we can see the trinity principle in each of the three branches. For instance, the prosecution can be considered yang in a court of law within the judicial branch, as it initiates actions to prosecute those who break the law. But on the other hand, the defense is yin, as it tries to defend and prove innocence. Meanwhile, the judge stays in the middle, listens to both sides, yin and yang, and makes a final decision. So the judge is the mediator of yin and yang.

In an Eastern monarchy, there is the king or queen, and beneath that ruler are generally three ministers. There is the prime, or chief, minister and two secondary, or deputy, ministers who advise the king or queen on the various affairs of his or her country.

Friedrich Hegel used his dialectical reasoning to express how first there is tyranny (thesis); then democracy (antithesis), in which there is the rule of law; and finally hereditary monarchy (synthesis). Karl Marx based his ideas on Hegel's theory. He stated that first there is monarchy (thesis), which is yin; then democracy (antithesis), which is yang; and finally communism (synthesis), which is Tai Chi.

Although communism appears to have a balance of yin and yang, it is incomplete. This is because human beings must have more freedom (yang) in their lives than restriction (yin) and should not be artificially hindered. So communism actually has too much yin in its

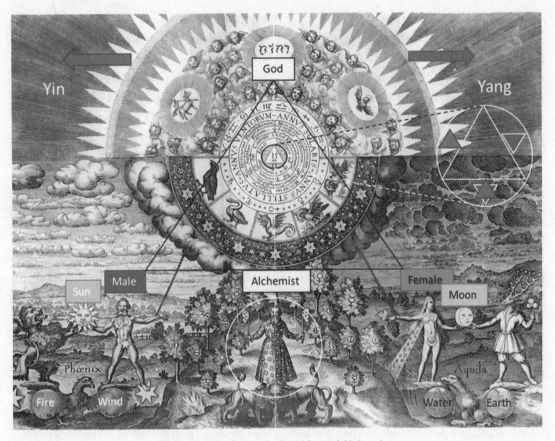

Figure 14.14 Cosmological View of Alchemists

system to be thoroughly practical for humanity. And just as Tai Chi is constantly evolving, the synthesis also evolves into a new thesis, which then creates its antithesis by necessity, from which comes a synthesis to harmonize the two in a constantly iterating cycle of change.

Trinity of Alchemy

In the book *Museum Hermeticum,* published in 1625 in Frankfurt, Germany, a drawing ex-

presses the cosmological view of the alchemists (fig. 14.14). This drawing is divided into two halves, the left side representing the day (yang) and the right side representing the night (yin). In addition, the top and bottom split into heaven (yang) and earth (yin).

In the center of the yang side, a man holds the sun (yang) in one hand, while on the yin side, a woman has the moon (yin) in one hand. On the left, a ferocious lion (yang) also holds the sun, and a phoenix (yang) supports both the lion and the man. On the right, a docile deer (yin) helps to hold the moon, and an eagle (yin) supports the deer and the woman. Finally, an alchemist stands on top of a lion that has one head and two bodies, between the man and woman. The alchemist's divided body indicates a balanced person in yin and yang. Together, the man, the woman, and the alchemist symbolize the number 3 or the trinity of the earth.

The masters of the East attempted to correct their yin-yang imbalances by ingesting elixirs and practicing breathing and meditation. Looking at this drawing, it is inevitable that the alchemists, who demonstrated their awareness of yin and yang, attempted to harmonize them. Once the masters or alchemists establish a balance of yin and yang, they become omnipotent and omniscient, like God. God is omnipotent and omniscient and sits in the position of yin-yang harmony in the center of heaven.

In the center of heaven, Hebrew characters refer to God, and two symbols on the right and left shine like God. God and these two symbols represent the trinity. Surrounding them are angels that emit light. They, too, are divided into yin and yang, and although their variance of yin-yang is not significant, they nevertheless have a discrepancy (angels are yang; Satan is yin).

Surrounding humans are plants, animals, and minerals. The symbols written on the trees that surround the alchemist represent minerals used in alchemy. Around the foot of the alchemist are water and fire, symbolizing the yin and yang of the earth. Next to the water and fire are earth, water, fire, and wind, which illustrate Sasang, the Four Symbols, according to

the I Ching (see chapter 15). Earth and water are on the yin side, while fire and wind are on the yang side. They fit well into the differentiation pattern of yin and yang. (Note: triangular lines have been added to show their relationship with the sun and moon in a trinity pattern.)

The principles of alchemy are represented in concentric circles in the area between the alchemist's head and the spiritual domain. In the innermost circle, there are five triangles. A large triangle representing yin, yang, and the harmony of yin-yang sits in the center. On its sides are an upside-down triangle representing yang with unsettled and dynamic nature, and an upright triangle representing yin with settled and passive/static nature. The middle (bottom) is a figure consisting of two overlapped triangles. This figure symbolizes gold (equivalent to elixirs of Taoism) harmonized in yin and yang.

This drawing incredibly depicts the cosmological view of the I Ching. It is possible to draw an inference from the picture. The Eastern masters who created elixirs with the I Ching principles, and the Western alchemists who made gold followed the same path of self-cultivation. The predecessor of modern science is alchemy, and the predecessor of alchemy may have been the I Ching.

Trinity of Pyramids

One of the most explicit representations of the trinity principle is in the Great Pyramids of Egypt. When observed externally, a pyramid consists of four triangles and one rectangle. If the pyramid is cut horizontally, its cross section is a rectangle. If it is cut vertically with the inclusion of the tip, it becomes a triangle. A rectangle is a figure that expresses the number 2, while a triangle is a figure that defines the number 3. Although a rectangle can convey the number 4 with its four sides, it fundamentally represents the number 2, as 4 arises from multiples of 2.

Horizontally, pyramids represent the number 2, but vertically they represent the number 3. Thus, they symbolize yin (2) and yang (3). So within them, pyramids contain the critical elements of the universe, yin and yang. We can even say that pyramids horizontally express the binary structure representing yin and yang and vertically illustrate the configuration of the trigrams and hexagrams, with a multiple of 3 forming their lines in a three-dimensional model.

Essentially, the pyramids symbolize the fundamental pattern of the structure of the entire universe. The pyramid's tip embodies the one God, or Tao, that integrates and regulates the underlying matrix. It represents the unifying point of all manifestations.

Philosophical and Religious Trinity

The principle of trinity clearly manifests in the philosophy of Hegel. A form of reasoning exists called the "dialectic process," wherein two people argue separate points and eventually reach a conclusion. Throughout the history of philosophy, this process has served to reveal the truth or reality of life. Hegel was fond of this process and incorporated the trinity principle into his philosophical framework. Dialectical reasoning is the core of Hegelian logic.

According to Hegel, conflict resolution was the only way human thought progressed. The resolution was only possible through presenting a thesis, its contradiction of an antithesis, and the resulting synthesis of ideas. Once the two sides joined as one synthesis, the dialectic process would begin again. This three-part philosophical principle relates to the trinity principle almost precisely.

The thesis is yang. It is what is known or thought to be true. The antithesis is yin because it creates conflict and begins the process of argument and interaction. The synthesis is Tai Chi because it is the outcome of the interaction of two opposing sides. It is the center, with components of both arguments (yin and yang) in its form. The end product of this form of dialect was, Hegel believed, the absolute truth of life.

We can observe the principle of trinity, or triune, in many religions worldwide. For example, in Catholicism, a person begins prayer with the cross sign, reciting the words "in the name of the Father, the Son, and the Holy Ghost." At the same time, the person draws a cross with the right hand, beginning with a vertical line (yang) from the head to the abdomen, followed by a horizontal line (yin) from shoulder to shoulder. Then both hands join in prayer in front of the heart, signifying the center (Tai Chi) formed by the two invisible intersecting lines.

At this time, the head corresponds to the Father in heaven. The abdomen corresponds to Christ and all things on Earth, including human beings. Both shoulders are the Holy Ghost, which connects human beings and God. Finally, the center of the cross is the location of the heart, where the Trinity gathers in a union.

The drawing of a cross involves three stages. The first stage is touching the four regions (head, abdomen, and shoulders); this corresponds to the Sasang bigrams (see chapter 15) of I Ching's principle of differentiation. The second stage is joining both hands in prayer, which corresponds to number 2 (yin-yang). And the third stage is bowing the head with the hands still in prayer, corresponding to number 1 (Tai Chi).

The bigrams and trigrams formed with the numbers 2 and 3 are symbols representing the structure or function of the universe. Other cultures or civilizations symbolize them with triangles (Star of David) or three-dimensional pyramids. The motion of making a cross with the hand expresses the fundamental structure of all things in the universe, resembling these symbols. It implies that everything unifies as one under God.

The following picture (fig. 14.15) is a mural at the Rila Monastery in Bulgaria. The triangle behind the head of God represents the Trinity. The bird under God expresses the Holy Spirit and acts as an intermediary between man and God. The human with the halo under the bird represents Jesus. The triangle embodies the three as one.

Figure 14.15 Rila Monastery, Bulgaria

The I Ching is a book recording the principle of change for all things in the universe. Catholicism is a religion that refers to a God who leads all change in the universe. Because it is so, they have come to share some similarities with other religions. For instance, in Buddhism, service to Buddha is done with the hands together in a prayer position. The left hand (yin) and right hand (yang) join to create a harmony of yin and yang as a worship offering to Buddha, who coincidentally epitomizes the balance of yin and yang.

The triad figures of the Buddhas frequently seen on the shrines in Buddhist temples indicate that Buddhism attaches great importance to the number 3 (fig. 14.16). The central figure is Shakyamuni Buddha, the founder of Buddhism. The figure on the right is Samantabhadra, the bodhisattva (Buddha-to-be) of kindness or happiness. The statue on the left is Manjushri, the bodhisattva of wisdom and intellect.

Figure 14.16 Triad Buddha, Geumsansa Temple, Wanju, Korea

According to Buddhist precepts, there are three spheres, or planes, where living beings stay. The first is the immaterial, or formless, plane of existence, where pure spirits live without a material body. The second, where ethereal beings without sensuous desire live, is the material plane of existence. The third is the plane of desire, where gross material beings live. This is where animals and human beings live.

Another way the trinity principle manifests in Buddhism is in the doctrine of three bodies of Buddha, called trikaya. They are the physical and mental bodies and a cosmic law called Dharma, equivalent to Tao. These bodies play a central role in the Buddhist doctrine of the process of salvation.

Tantric Buddhism also speaks of three bodies in slightly differing ways—mind, speech, and body. In actual spiritual practice, the mind is related to visualization, the speech to mantra (a mystical syllable or phrase) recitation, and the body to the mudras, or hand gestures. The practice of all three creates and changes the body's energy to help one move through his or her issues and into higher states of consciousness or enlightenment.

Tantric Buddhism focuses more on training based on incantations than other forms of Buddhism do. Because of this emphasis, they place speech between mind and body, as the focus of cultivation. Also, in Tantric Buddhism, the polarity of yin and yang is often depicted with sexual symbols in the form of active male and passive female deities. The two polarities come together as one in the dynamic unity of Tai Chi in the process of eternal bliss or enlightenment through their ecstatic sexual embraces, resulting in a trinity.

In addition to the number 3, many Eastern and Western religions frequently use trinity and hexagonal patterns to express the universe and God. The following three pictures illustrate varying trinity patterns. The first (fig. 14.17) is the architectural design of the main entrance to the Matthias Church in Budapest, Hungary. It shows trinity symbols in a hexagonal format.

The other two pictures (figs. 14.18 and 14.19) are the doorframes at Geumsansa Temple and Songgwangsa Temple, respectively, in Korea. Again, there is a pattern of the universe on each of them. A single part has the structural pattern of the whole. The triangle of parts repeats the whole triangle pattern, while the circle of parts repeats the whole circle pattern. If you closely observe the triangles, there is a Star of David. Whether a Catholic church or a Buddhist temple, the craftsmen who fashioned these patterns must have shared a common thought pattern.

Figure 14.17 Matthias Church, Budapest, Hungary

Figure 14.18 (left) Geumsansa Temple, Wanju, Korea

Figure 14.19 (right) Songgwangsa Temple, Suncheon, Korea

Shinto is the traditional religion of Japan and is replete with the trinity principle. Shinto worshippers clap their hands twice before clasping them in prayer, making three total movements. Lit candles are in three units, and incense burners have three legs. In addition, many aspects of the Shinto shrine demonstrate the principle of three.

The entrance to the Shinto shrines is a Torii gate composed of three horizontal lines, formed by two horizontal beams and the ground (fig. 14.20). The three lines represent heaven, earth, and humanity. Again, this implies the universe's formation by the primary numbers 1, 2, and 3. The two vertical beams (yin and yang) support the horizontal beams so that the gate creates the Chinese character for heaven (天). This gate is similar to a Hongsalmun, a red arrow gate, which serves as a gate for entering sacred places such as shrines, tombs, and academies in Korea (fig. 14.21).

Figure 14.20 A Torii Gate, Kehi Shrine, Tsuruga, Japan

Figure 14.21 A Hongsalmun (a red arrow gate) at a Confucian temple and school, Pyeongtaek, Korea

As in most Shinto shrines, there is also a stone lantern (fig. 14.22) in a pyramid shape with a square base (earth/ground), a light lit at the tip (God/heaven), and four standing triangles (human). There are three entrances (fig. 14.23) to the altar (one large and two smaller doors, one on each side). In the same way, the altar consists of three rooms.

bolizes the spirit (Tao). It is a trinity symbol composed of three small circles within a larger circle (figs. 14.24 and 14.25). The three circles appear to be spinning and have tails like comets. The embossed brass figure better expresses Sam-Taegeuk (the Korean trinity symbol) in three dimensions.

Figure 14.24 Trinity Symbol, Usa Shrine, Usa, Japan

Figure 14.22 Stone Lantern, Kibitsu Shrine, Okayama, Japan

Figure 14.23 Entrances to the Shinto Altar, Usa Shrine, Usa, Japan

Figure 14.25 Trinity Symbol on a Drum, National Museum of Japanese History, Sakura City, Japan

The central room of the shrine contains an altar; in front of it is an ornament that sym-

The Shinto palace houses three precious artifacts utilized in the emperor's coronation ceremony: a copper mirror, a sword, and a curved jade jewel (fig. 14.26). The copper mirror symbolizes the universe, sun, or God; the sword symbolizes man (yang); and the jade symbolizes woman (yin). Together they represent the trinity of God, or Tai Chi, yin, and yang.

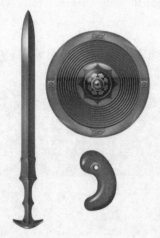

Figure 14.26 Three Treasures

A sacred shrine in Korea known as Jongmyo, or "ancestral temple of the royal family," enshrines the ancestral tablets of successive generations of kings of the Joseon dynasty (1392–1910) and holds memorial services for them. It can be considered the predecessor to the Shinto palaces of Japan. Inside, many trinary structures exist, including Sam-Taegeuk, which symbolizes God and the universe (figs. 14.27 and 14.28).

The main entrance to the Matthias Church in Budapest, Hungary, (fig. 14.29) is quite interesting in that Korea, Japan, and Hungary all use Sam-Taegeuk, or the trinity symbol.

Perhaps no religion or philosophy emphasizes the importance of the number 3 more than Taoism. Taoism is the teaching

Figure 14.27 Sam-Taegeuk at the Entrance to Jongmyo, the Ancestral Temple of the Royal Family, Seoul, Korea

Figure 14.28 Jongmyo is a masterpiece of architecture that has fascinated world-renowned architects. Some called it the Parthenon of Asia.

of Dangun,[3] including the Cheonbugyeong, the Celestial Code Classic (see appendix 3 for further information), which started in Korea's Samsinsan (Three Spiritual Mountain) and blossomed in China. It is clear that Taoism

Figure 14.29 Matthias Church, Budapest, Hungary

begins and ends with 3, like the Celestial Code Classic.

Chapter 1 of Tao Te Ching, the most popular and one of the three most revered texts of Taoism, states, "One begets two, two produce three, and three create all things in nature." It implies that the number 3 is the foundation from which all things emerge. A number appearing in Taoism's writings is generally 3 or multiples of 3. They all have the foundation in I Ching's principle of three.

For example, the previously mentioned three forms of energy known as the Three Treasures—Jing (essence or generative energy), Qi (vital energy), and Shen (spirit or spiritual energy)—are perhaps the most critical concepts in the practice of the internal alchemy of Taoism.

In Taoist internal alchemy, practitioners attempt to regulate, cultivate, and refine these energies inside their bodies through breathing, correct postures, quiet movements, imagery, and meditations. Three bodily areas called Danjun (elixir field) store these energies. There are three Danjuns situated between the eyebrows (upper Danjun, also known as

the celestial realm), near the heart (middle Danjun, or the terrestrial realm), and a few inches below the navel (lower Danjun, or water realm). In addition to physical and mental health, the ultimate goal for practitioners of internal alchemy is to attain immortality and enlightenment.

Besides these energies, there are concepts of three guardian deities, known as the Three Primal Ones, who protect the body from illness. They are said to reside in the three Danjuns. In contrast to these guardian deities, three "monsters," or "poisons," live in the cavities at the three gates along the spine. The monsters control the gates that regulate the energetic activities of the Danjuns. Then there are concepts of nine (3 × 3) "worms" that live in the nine cavities along the spine at various acupuncture points. These monsters and worms bring about illnesses in the body and mind. The Taoist practitioners of internal alchemy aim to keep these monsters and worms in check, eliminate them, and cultivate the Three Treasures to achieve health, longevity, and ultimately immortality.

Also, Taoism's cosmological view divides the heavenly and earthly worlds into nine (3 × 3) divisions. It speaks of the Ninth Heaven, the highest celestial world, and the Ninth Earth, the lowest (hell) of the earthly world. In internal alchemy, they refer to the upper and lower Danjuns, respectively.

The six-channel theory, consisting of three yin and three yang channels in acupuncture and Eastern medicine, derives from the Taoist concept of three, which comes from the I Ching.

When visiting China you will find that a

gate with three doors, such as the one shown in the following figure, most likely indicates a Taoist monastery or a place related to Taoism (fig. 14.30).

Figure 14.30 The front gate of a Taoist temple in Taishan, a sacred mountain, Shandong Province, eastern China. This mountain is the birthplace of Chinese Taoism.

Confucianism, along with Taoism and Buddhism, is one of the three major religions from the Far East. It has the "three fundamental principles and the five moral disciplines in human relations." The three fundamental principles delineate the three most critical ethical issues emphasized in Confucianism. They involve three essential human relationships: sovereign and subject, father and son, and husband and wife.

The principle states that there should be righteousness between sovereign and subject, affection between parent and child, and differential duties between husband and wife. The relationship between the ruler and subject and parent and child is vertical, while that of husband and wife is horizontal. Of the vertical connections, that of sovereign and subject is yang, as it takes place outside of the home, while that of parent and child is yin, as it is a domestic affair. Since the relationship between husband and wife takes place horizontally, it takes place at a different level. Thus, it is the middle of yin and yang.

In Confucianism, there is an important concept called Jungyong, meaning "middle path" or "golden mean." It is the central moral virtue. To acquire Jungyong, one must know the two extremes of any situation or circumstance. The two poles correspond to the yin and yang of Tai Chi, while Jungyong implies the center of yin and yang.

Jungyong, however, does not mean an absolute middle. Instead, it involves selecting the middle path after considering both extremes. Things generally occur somewhere in the middle of two expectations. The most healthy and prosperous way lies on the central line in any situation.

For instance, the sale of goods takes place halfway between the price wanted by the seller and the desired price of the buyer. This means that the sale takes place at a third price. In addition, diseases of the human body occur when there is hyper- or hypo-functioning of an organ or system. Successful treatment centers the wayward energy to restore balance and functioning. And in governing a nation, a king can only be efficacious when he selects the Jungyong between two parties. One is the people's party, which wants development and growth while sacrificing the kingdom's stability, and the other party is that which wants stability while forfeiting development and growth.

Those with excessively extroverted personalities can quickly accomplish things at work but just as easily make mistakes. In contrast, those with overly introverted tendencies make fewer mistakes but are slower in progress. Thus it is most desirable to handle a workload according to its nature and a "middle," or balanced, personality. This is what acquiring or maintaining Jungyong indicates. Since Jungyong contains both yin and yang, it must have three elements—yin, yang, and Tai Chi.

Confucianism also involves three virtues: wisdom, benevolence, and courage. These virtues are acquired through the following six arts (a multiple of three): calligraphy, ceremony, charioteering, archery, mathematics, and music. In addition, Confucianism emphasizes the trinity concept of heaven, human, and earth, as depicted in Sam-Taegeuk symbol (fig. 14.31).

The trinity principle also appears in Hinduism, a religion of India. There exists the Supreme Trinity of Brahman, Shiva, and Vishnu. The soul, or inner essence, of all phenomena is Brahman. Thus, Brahman exists in both living and nonliving things. Brahman is the creator (yang), preserver, or transformer (between yin and yang), and reabsorber (yin) of everything. Therefore, Brahman is also Tai Chi, the ultimate matrix of the universe.

Like yin and yang, the polar energies from Tai Chi, Brahman also manifests as Shiva and Vishnu. Vishnu is often regarded as the manifestation of the preservative aspect of the Supreme, while Shiva is of the destructive function. Thus, Vishnu can be considered as yang, and Shiva as yin.

Figure 14.31 Gyeongbokgung Palace, Seoul, Korea. There are trinity patterns at the bottom of stairs and door posts, showing that the knowledge of Sam-Taegeuk is the foundation of academics.

Another way trinity appears in Hinduism is through Shiva, Vishnu, and Shakti, currently the three most highly revered divinities in India. Although Shiva represents the destructive aspect, he is also known as the cosmic dancer and god of creation. In this way, Shiva represents the yang energy of the universe. Shakti, the Divine Mother and Shiva's wife, represents the feminine power of the universe as an archetypal goddess and, thus, yin. Therefore, Shiva is the yang energy of the universe, Shakti is the yin energy, and Vishnu is Tai Chi because he upholds universal harmony and divine order in the world.

A mandala, known as a kolam, can be found

in the entrance to Hindu households (fig. 14.32). It clearly shows the fractal pattern of the Star of David. The next picture shows I Ching's trigram drawn on an elephant statue in a Kapaleeswarar Hindu temple in Chennai, India (fig. 14.33). The top, middle, and bottom horizontal lines represent heaven, earth, and humanity. The central dot represents unity, like the vertex of a pyramid. It is like a seed or egg containing an entity's complete information.

Figure 14.32 Kolam, a Traditional Design, Chennai, India

Figure 14.33 A Trigram on Elephant Statue, Kapaleeswarar Hindu Temple, Chennai, India

The Star of David, the symbol of Judaism, also demonstrates the principle of the trinity (fig. 14.34). It also symbolizes God with its hexagonal pattern. The star is created by over-lapping an upright triangle (yang) and an upside-down triangle (yin), manifesting Tai Chi. Each triangle in and of itself embodies the trinity. The tip is Tai Chi, while the remaining corners represent yin and yang. It could also correspond to heaven, where the other two corners symbolize earth and human beings.

Figure 14.34 Star of David in the National Flag of Israel

The Kabbalah, the teachings of esoteric Jewish mysticism, provides a means of approaching God directly and includes the principle of creation and its process involving ten divine emanations, called *sefirot*. Each of the sefirot is associated with a certain number and symbol. In the Tree of Life, which depicts the ten sefirot, groupings were done in threes in the triangular formation, as illustrated in the following diagram (fig. 14.35). For instance, Keter (crown, God), Hokhmah (wisdom/paternity), and Binah (understanding/maternity) sit on the top of the Tree of Life in a triangular formation. Beneath them are Hesed (love), Gevurah (power/righteousness), and Tiferet (beauty, the mediator between love

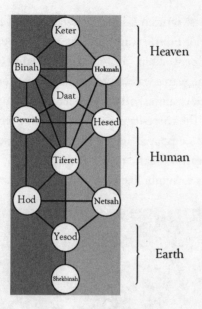

Figure 14.35 The Tree of Life

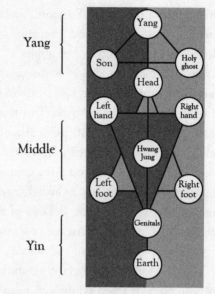

Figure 14.36 I Ching Interpretation of the Tree of Life

and righteousness). Further beneath them are Netsah (eternity), Hod (splendor), and Yesod (foundation/genital), with Shekhinah (kingdom/presence) centered at the bottom.

The Tree of Life is a diagram depicting the Kabbalah's creation principle. In terms of Eastern philosophy and the I Ching, it is a diagram expressing Tao. Since the I Ching is a diagrammatic representation of the principles of creation, the Kabbalah is easily explained through the I Ching's trinity principle. Thus, the interpretation of the Tree of Life is possible through the I Ching principle, as in the following diagram (fig. 14.36). The illustration depicted on on the left has an eleventh sefirot called Daat, a pseudo-sefirot representing knowledge and reflecting Keter at a lower level.

The importance of the number 3 is difficult to overestimate. If the number 2 represents the polar relationship of yin and yang, the number 3 represents their unification. If number 2 brings discord or conflict, number 3 will conjure harmony. The number 3 contains yang and yin (1 and 2, respectively), so it can be considered the critical number representing totality. The number 3 also represents creation or generation. It is produced from yin-yang polarity, similar to the birth of an organism from the male and female.

Many religions incorporate the number 3 into various aspects of their beliefs and practices in significant ways. Concerning religious imagery and prayer, 3 is a symbolic number, as it is the number of the universe and the number of God. It symbolizes a fusion of fragmentation, a harmony of discord, and the true nature of the universe and its creator.

There are many additional examples of the trinity as manifested worldwide. For example, a famous passage tomb, Newgrange, in Ireland, is older than the pyramids of Egypt. This monument dates back to circa 3200 BCE. Although no one knows who constructed it, its design allows rays of the rising sun to touch the ground at the center of the tomb for approximately twenty minutes on the winter solstice. Because of this, many archaeologists believe that the people who built the tomb were culturally advanced. The large stones that form the base of the mound bear many beautifully designed symbols. Among the engravings are many concentric spirals in groups of three that resemble Sam-Taegeuk, or the trinity Tai Chi symbol (fig. 14.37).

Figure 14.37 Entrance to the Passage Tomb Newgrange, Ireland

Many relics of China's Yin dynasty (also known as Shang dynasty), the legendary period from the sixteenth to the eleventh century BCE, have been excavated recently from the city of Anyang (the ancient capital of the Yin dynasty located in northern Henan province) at the basin of the Yellow River. Among them, archaeologists found oracle bones that contained

the first written Chinese characters and many superior bronze wares utilized for religious sacrifice or worship (fig.14.38). The quality of the bronze wares was unprecedented in history. In addition, almost all of them have three support legs. The three-legged support is relatively unstable compared to the four-legged base. Yet the reason for the nearly exclusive use of three legs is to symbolize God and the universe.

Figure 14.38 Bronze Wares, Shandong Museum, City of Jinan, Shandong, China

The next picture is the Mycenaean sword of Agamemnon, from the sixteenth century BCE (fig. 14.39). There are spiral decorations from its base to its tip. It is Sam-Taegeuk fractal pattern in which the three concentric spiral patterns make up the whole in all directions. It is on display at the National Archaeological Museum in Athens, Greece.

Also displayed are gold roundels found near Agamemnon's tomb in Greece, dated around

Figure 14.39 Mycenaean Sword of Agamemnon, National Archaeological Museum, Athens, Greece

1600 BCE (fig. 14.40). They are dress ornaments representing constellations. Embossed decorations of concentric circles are fractal shapes spreading out from the vertex like a pyramid. This signifies the three-dimensionality of the up, down, left, right, front, and rear. It is a trinity.

dynasty (fig. 14.42). The five elements is a more differentiated form of Sam-Taegeuk.

The last image (fig. 14.43) is pottery from 1700 BCE exhibited at the Archaeological Museum of Fira, Santorini, Greece. On it is a clear depiction of a Japanese-style Sam-Taegeuk.

Figure 14.40 Gold Roundels, National Archaeological Museum, Athens, Greece

The next image is a Japanese earthenware showing the pattern of Sam-Taegeuk dating back some three thousand years (fig. 14.41). The image following it depicts the five-element Tai Chi symbol on a bronze utensil of the Zhou

Figure 14.42 Zhou Dynasty Utensil, Tokyo National Museum, Tokyo, Japan

Figure 14.41 Japanese Earthenware, Tokyo National Museum, Tokyo, Japan

Figure 14.43 Archaeological Museum of Fira, Santorini, Greece

15

Sasang—The Four Symbols

The nature of matter or phenomena clarifies as it breaks down into pieces. These resulting pieces are easier to understand and manage because they are less complex. However, perceiving interrelationships between the fragments is more challenging unless we define the whole.

Sasang, or the Four Symbols, is a subdivision of yin and yang. When yin divides into two aspects, one part is more yang, while the other is more yin. The more yin part (yin within yin) is called Taiyin (greater yin), and the more yang part (yang within yin) is called Shaoyin (lesser yin). The division of yang is similar, producing yang within yang, called Taiyang (greater yang), and yin within yang, called Shaoyang (lesser yang).

Both Shaoyin and Taiyin belong to yin. But since "Shao" implies "lesser" and "Tai" implies "greater," Shaoyin has a lesser amount of yin (more yang), while Taiyin has a more significant amount of yin (less yang). The same is true for Shaoyang and Taiyang. Together, these four subdivisions of yin and yang—Taiyin, Shaoyin, Taiyang, and Shaoyang—are called Sasang.

Since Sasang is a subdivision of yin and yang, it is, thus, Tai Chi. So these elements are only understood through their relationship to one another and to the whole. Eastern philosophy and medicine attempt to understand things as a whole: all parts are interrelated and defined by one another.

On the other hand, Western science excels at compartmentalizing and subdividing, figuring out the nature of individual entities accurately, and efficiently applying and utilizing it in our daily lives. However, its problem lies in finding a correlation between each entity. In other words, it cannot tie cosmological phenomena to the elementary particle world or how they both relate to the wonders around us.

Eastern philosophy does identify these interrelationships to some extent, as it sees the big picture. But it is not precise, since it does not compartmentalize and divide as much as Western science does. Herein lies the difference between science and Eastern philosophy.

Unfortunately, Western science and medicine break things down to such an extent that the complete picture is lost. This situation is similar to the problem that faced the nursery rhyme character Humpty Dumpty. Humpty's fall allowed people to see his makeup in greater detail (albumin, yolk, countless eggshell shards). Still, it also made it impossible to "put Humpty together again."

The loss of a complete picture is precisely why the I Ching limits its subdivisions to the sixty-four hexagrams and applies a single unifying principle to each. Sixty-four is the highest number of divisions humans can remember and handle holistically without losing the relationship between the individual aspects. Further division would only result in a loss of the sense of the whole.

Dividing something according to yin and yang is like measuring it with a ruler scaled in inches. On the other hand, splitting something, according to Sasang, is like measuring it with a ruler scaled in half inches. Sasang "measurement" gives a more accurate description of the nature of a thing. However, the smaller the subdivisions become, the more difficult it is to grasp or sense the relationship of one thing to another.

Suppose you measure something with a more detailed ruler. In that case, you have to memorize the length to the nearest decimal point, and you will have difficulty sensing how long it is. This means you cannot compare it to the size of everything you know, and it does not relate to what you know.

Characteristics of Sasang

To divide all things in nature into Sasang, we must first understand the nature of each aspect of Sasang. Just as the combination of yin and yang creates Tai Chi, so does the grouping of Sasang.

TAIYANG

Taiyang corresponds to the spring season. During springtime, the energy stored throughout winter begins to reactivate. Grass, trees, and other plants use their stored energy in seeds or roots to sprout. Animals that hibernated or brumated during the winter, including the bear and the snake, awake at this time. Such is a perfect image of Taiyang energy, the beginning of dynamic activities. Humans follow the same patterns as plants and animals. Our minds and bodies become increasingly active after being dulled by the confinement and darkness of the long winter months. Desires rekindle and awareness broadens.

The phenomenon of the spring season is comparable to a water fountain springing forth from the ground or a metal spring expanding after being compressed. The I Ching expresses it with the following Taiyang symbol (fig. 15.1):

Figure 15.1 Taiyang

Like a seed sprouting, the springtime activation is within the energy gathered by the plant and crystallized. It is the manifestation of the entire process that preceded it. A steel spring's rebounding contains its compression force—the greater the compression, the greater the reaction. Similarly, springs of water hold the energy of rainfall.

Accordingly, the I Ching uses symbols instead of words. Words are more restricted in their interpretations and frequently serve only to remind readers of isolated instances and provide limited perspectives. The adage expresses "a picture is worth a thousand words." The expression of yin and yang as symbols au-

tomatically brings about an awareness of the web of interrelationships. When one recognizes yin, it is only understood in its relationship to yang, and vice versa, allowing for a holistic and comprehensive view. An awareness of the "spring" energy (yang) of Taiyang, for example, is only possible with an understanding of the energy of accumulation and compression (yin) that essentially had to take place first.

The time of day associated with Taiyang is daybreak. Dawn is the time for waking from night's sojourn. It is a transitional period when the night is in the process of changing into the day. Therefore, this period retains the characteristics of both yin and yang.

Two major divisions of the body's nervous system are sympathetic and parasympathetic. The sympathetic nervous system is in charge of the body in action. In contrast, the parasympathetic nervous system controls the body's relaxation and growth functions. The parasympathetic nervous system is most active at night, so energy can readily transform into matter. Growth hormone stimulating the body's cells, particularly bones, is maximally secreted at midnight.

Meanwhile, there is a minimal secretion of corticosteroid hormone, which accelerates carbohydrate metabolism to make energy. Instead, its secretion is increased at daybreak to help produce the energy necessary for daily activities. Dawn is therefore the time of day in which the body begins to use the energy gathered through the night and the time for restarting daily (yang) activities.

SHAOYANG

Shaoyang corresponds to summer. Though Taiyang is a much stronger internal force, its energy remains at a minimal level of activity and remains restrained like Pandora's Box. However, the most active utilization of the energy stored during winter is summer (Shaoyang). Therefore, the properties of Shaoyang express the characteristics of summer—dynamic, hot, large, exuberant, and colorful.

Seemingly small spring buds retain tremendous amounts of potential energy, developing into leaves and flowers in the summer months. Whereas the yang energy of Taiyang is a laser beam, direct and powerful, the yang energy of Shaoyang is warm, active, and dispersed like the light from a fire. While dynamic and thriving, the yang energy of summer is already on the decline.

Animals and people are increasingly active during the summer. Therefore, metabolic functioning increases and greater consumption of energy occurs. As a result, physical and mental activities heighten as well. Although the best way to avoid summer heat is to stay indoors in a well–air-conditioned room, people prefer to travel outdoors to plains, mountains, and oceans.

The hours corresponding to Shaoyang are around noon, when the sun is brightest. During this time, trees are most active in metabolizing carbon dioxide. The tempo of activity for all animals, including humans, is at its pinnacle. Human mental activity is at its peak, and the brain functions of memory and concentration

are at their best. It is also when the body feels hunger and needs its energy replenished.

Summer, the peak of energy consumption, marks the beginning of energy transforming into matter. The principle of mutual transformation states, "When yang reaches its extreme, it converts into yin." Therefore, Shaoyang's symbolic representation of summer is the yang line positioned on top, or outside, with a yin line on the bottom, or inside (fig. 15.2).

Figure 15.2 Shaoyang

This symbol represents the active yang functioning (energy consumption) at the top, or outside. At the same time, the bottom, or inside, is empty, and yin functioning (materialization) takes place.

As summer comes to an end, autumn begins. Similarly, rain begins to fall once hot weather is extreme. Human behavior follows the same pattern. Summer is the time for spending, while earning belongs to the autumn months, and saving coincides with winter. People tend to spend more money on clothes, cars, vacations, and entertainment during summer. However, once funds are low, they become more resolute about earning and saving.

TAIYIN

The characteristics of Taiyin (fig. 15.3) are exactly opposite to those of Taiyang. While

Taiyang is the beginning of matter transforming into energy, Taiyin is the beginning of energy transforming into a substance. It is associated with autumn, when the energy used during summer is gathered back in and made into substance. During autumn, grass and plants begin to wither, while leaves change color and fall because they no longer receive energy. Instead, a part of the trees' energy solidifies as fruit, and the rest becomes stored in the roots.

Figure 15.3 Taiyin

The summary of the functional aspect of a tree's energy is as follows: In spring, it concentrates in the bud and stem and ascends straight up. In summer, it spreads outward toward the leaves and branches. In autumn, the gathering of energy back toward the trunk takes place, with the leaves dropping to the ground. Finally, in winter, the energy descends to the roots (fig. 15.4).

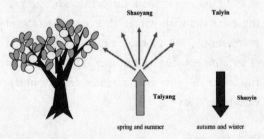

Figure 15.4 Functional Energetic Direction of a Tree

Taiyin corresponds to the time of day surrounding sunset. It is the period of rest after the busy activities of the day. It is also when energy consumption ceases and energy conservation occurs to prepare for tomorrow's activities. Finally, it is an intermediary stage when the day changes into night and when the energies of yin and yang coexist.

Corticosteroid hormones secrete in smaller amounts, and a person becomes tired. After sunset, the sympathetic nervous system relinquishes its control over the body's physical activities and releases acetylcholine, stimulating the digestive system and constricting the pupils. Known as the chemical opposite of adrenaline, acetylcholine also slows the heartbeat. The pupils constrict, the eyes close, and the digestive organs become more active, refining ingested nutritive substances. These phenomena occur because energy is transforming into matter.

Shaoyin

Shaoyin corresponds to winter. The energy, gathered and transformed into substance in autumn, is stored during winter for spring usage. The process of further refining and compressing the energy to the point just before exploding is Shaoyin.

Fruits and seeds, basically lumps of energy, fall to the ground and are buried. Then the cold winter weather compresses them even more by freezing them. Meanwhile, the life activity of the tree is concentrated mostly in the roots. In other words, the tree's energy becomes stored in the roots.

Winter is the time when animals move and eat less. Bears, snakes, and frogs hibernate or brumate to store energy. Similarly, people are less likely to begin new projects and wait for spring. Such is also the season for the holidays. Red poinsettias and decorative lights brighten up the inside and outside of homes, a subconscious effort to supplement yang energy when yin is exuberant.

Energetic activities peak in the summer because yang energy is most potent. On the other hand, yin energy is strongest in winter and materializing activities peak. Here we see the principle of mutual transformation take place again. The extreme of yin (the winter solstice) gives birth to yang to generate the spring activities and bring back to life the energy that previously transformed into substance.

However, winter is merely the beginning of a movement. It begins from the interior but is hardly noticeable from the outside. Therefore, the Shaoyin symbol in the I Ching is a yin line on the exterior, or upper, region with a yang line on the interior, or lower, part (fig. 15.5). It symbolizes the state of yang coming back to life.

Figure 15.5 Shaoyin

Winter nights that have been getting longer begin to pivot at the solstice and progressively get shorter. This is the Shaoyin function. The times of day corresponding to Shaoyin are the three hours before and after midnight. During this time, animals enter a deep, inactive sleep with almost no energy consumption in their limbs.

In children, the strength of energy transformation into substance is so active that they literally grow taller. The growth hormone production is at its peak, and the corticosteroid hormone involved in energy production is at its lowest. As night advances, egg and sperm production become increasingly active, while parasympathetic stimulation results in sexual excitation.

A deeper understanding of each Sasang function occurs only by comparing its peculiarities against others. For example, the gathering function of autumn should be compared to the generating function of spring. Likewise, extreme energy consumption and initiation of the materializing process of summer should be compared to the extreme materializing process and the beginning of energizing function of the winter.

The analogy of a water fountain can also lead to a better understanding of the functions' interrelationships. The water stored inside is the stored energy of winter. As it first spouts from the tip of a fountain, it symbolizes springtime energy. The strong spurting, rising, and spreading of water toward the sky denotes summer energy. The loss of strength in rising and subsequent falling and gathering of the water into the pool is autumnal energy (fig. 15.6).

The Interrelationships Between Sasang Symbols

While the divisions of the seasons are considered Sasang, the combined seasonal changes of

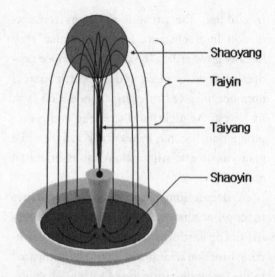

Figure 15.6 Sasang of a Fountain

a single year are Tai Chi. There are two basic ways to view the order of the seasons based on the form-function principle, beginning with spring. The cycle based on the form or quantitative aspect is Taiyang (spring) → Shaoyang (summer) → Taiyin (autumn) → Shaoyin (winter). In contrast, the cycle based on the function or energetic aspect is Shaoyang → Taiyang → Shaoyin → Taiyin.

The formative aspect, for example, of spring, is that there is a greater quantity of yang (Taiyang/greater yang) than in any other season. This is because more substances can become yang during the spring. However, by the form-function principle, more substance indicates slower functioning. Therefore, the function of spring is not in a fully dynamic state. Accordingly, the functional aspect of spring is Shaoyang, or lesser yang.

However, there is quantitatively less yang

during summer, as much of the yang used to fuel the exuberant activities becomes depleted. Thus, concerning form, summer is Shaoyang. Since a smaller amount of form means quicker (or more) function, summer is Taiyang regarding function because its energy is the most dynamic and active. The order for the yin aspects, Taiyin and Shaoyin, may be understood similarly.

Just as spring, summer, autumn, and winter form one cycle, Taiyang, Shaoyang, Taiyin, and Shaoyin form one cycle. We can draw a diagram of these cycles corresponding to the path of Earth's revolution around the sun (fig. 15.7).

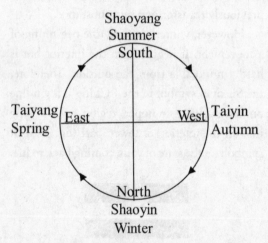

Figure 15.7 Form or Structural Aspect of Sasang

The diagram shows the principle of Sasang in the same way that the Tai Chi symbol represents the principles of yin and yang. The circle expresses the continuous cycles of Sasang. It also describes how the sun rises from the horizon (Taiyang), reaches its zenith in the sky

(Shaoyang), sets below the horizon (Taiyin), and disappears at night (Shaoyin).

In the diagram, the horizontal and vertical lines represent the polar relations between Taiyang, Taiyin, Shaoyang, and Shaoyin. The horizontal line represents left and right, and the vertical line represents above and below. The Shaoyang is in the upper position, the Shaoyin in the lower. The Taiyang is on the left, and the Taiyin is on the right. Shaoyang and Shaoyin communicate vertically (above and below), while Taiyang and Taiyin communicate horizontally (left and right).

The significance of these relationships as horizontal or vertical is that Taiyang and Taiyin exchange energy, while Shaoyang and Shaoyin exchange energy. Therefore, when you think about Sasang, it is crucial to consider the pre- and post-relationships of a cycle and the polar relation along the same axis.

Just as yin and yang transform into opposites, Sasang also does so. This could follow a cyclic order to the next one, or one on the same axis in a polar relationship. For example, Shaoyang can transform into Taiyin in a cyclic order, or to Shaoyin in a vertical axis relation, or go in an opposite direction.

The circulation of Sasang movements can also be drawn as a wave (fig. 15.8). The rising phase from below to above the reference point is Taiyang. The stage going up, reaching its zenith, and coming back down is Shaoyang. The phase going from above the reference point to below is Taiyin. Lastly, the step dropping to its lowest point and then rising again is Shaoyin.

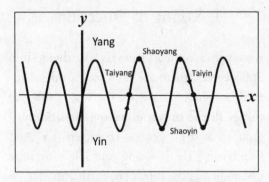

Figure 15.8 Wave Cycle of Sasang

Another example to demonstrate the polar nature of each Sasang function to its opposite is that things belonging to Taiyang have hot exteriors but cold interiors. However, those that are Taiyin have cold exteriors and hot interiors. Meanwhile, Shaoyang has hot upper and cold lower regions, whereas Shaoyin has cold upper and hot lower areas (fig. 15.9).

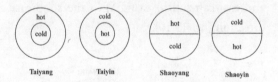

Figure 15.9 Polar Nature of Sasang

Sasang Classification of All Things in Nature

We have described the essential characteristics of Sasang. Based on their differing characteristics, everything in nature classifies into Sasang. Following is a Sasang classification of many things in life (table 15.1):

1. Sasang of Directions

Although a compass's points can divide into 360 degrees, there are only four cardinal directions. Similarly, despite the vast number of things in the universe, Sasang classifies four groups based on general characteristics. And in following the yin-yang principle of infinite divisibility, as the directions further dissect, so too can each form of Sasang be further broken down into yin and yang aspects.

For example, Taiyang has elements that are more yang or yin. When further divided, we arrive at Sasang within Taiyang. Within the yang aspect of Taiyang, there are Taiyang and Shaoyang. Within the yin aspect, there are Taiyin and Shaoyin. This is similar to the division of the directions, in which there is east-east-north (east EN) in the northeast direction and east-east-south (east ES) in the southeast direction (fig. 15.10).

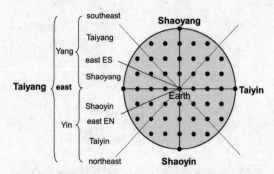

Figure 15.10 Sasang within Taiyang: The closer to the south things are, the more yang they are and the closer to the north, the more yin they are. This diagram demonstrates that there are classifications of yin-yang within Taiyang, and yin-yang within yin and yin-yang within yang.

FENG SHUI, OR THE ART OF PLACEMENT

Feng Shui, or the art of placement, is quite popular nowadays. There is a worldwide interest in Feng Shui, and bookstores in the United States, for example, are flooded with Feng Shui books. Feng Shui is literally "wind" and "water," which are the two things in nature that best exemplify the movement of energy. Thus, Feng Shui is a way of arranging our environment so that nature's energy can flow in the best possible manner. This in turn changes or influences our "energy," or "luck," resulting in health, prosperity, and longevity. Each Sasang is related to a direction that emits particular energy. Therefore, to fully understand Feng Shui, one must study the energetics of Sasang before studying its more esoteric aspects.

EAST: TAIYANG

The similarities exist between the energetic forces of Taiyang and the limitless energy force of the sun. The reason is that the Chinese characters for the word "sun" (太陽) are the same as for "Taiyang." Coincidentally, the direction associated with Taiyang is the east, also the direction that gives birth to sunrise.

In the ancient times of Eastern cultures, the princes' palaces sat on the east side of the imperial palaces. One aspect of Feng Shui states that because children belong to Taiyang, it is wise to place their rooms on the east side of a house. Children act in unison with the sun, going to bed early and rising early.

Establishing a child's room on the eastern side of a house ensures the reception of Taiyang

	Taiyang	Shaoyang	Taiyin	Shaoyin
Seasons	spring, spring equinox	summer, summer solstice	autumn, autumn equinox	winter, winter solstice
Functions	birth	growth	gathering	storing
Direction	east	south	west	north
Position	left	upper	right	lower
Basic elements (four elements)	wind	fire	earth	water
Computer	input unit (keyboard)	arithmetic unit (CPU)	output unit (printer)	storing unit (memory/hard drive)
Daytime	morning	midday	evening	midnight
Sense organ	ear	eye	nose	mouth
Physiological function	nerve function	circulatory function	digestive function	reproductive function
Mental state	optimism	mania	pessimism	depression
Economy	recovery	boom	recession	crisis/panic
Stock market	bull market	ceiling	bear market	floor
Politics	neo-communism	capitalism	neo-capitalism	communism
Aging cycle	childhood	young adulthood	middle age	old age
Chemistry	weak acid	acid	weak alkaline	alkaline
Physics	sound	light	smell	taste
Four universal forces	electromagnetic force	weak nuclear force	gravity	strong nuclear force
Energy source	wind	solar	crude oil (petroleum)	water
Geometry	Δ	▽	O	•
Color	green	red	yellow	black
Animal kingdom	amphibians	birds	mammals	fishes
Plant kingdom	grasses	trees	big trees	mushrooms
Sports	baseball	basketball	soccer	golf
Emotions	anger	joy	sadness	pleasure

Table 15.1 Sasang Classification

energy. For example, suppose a child is lazy and would rather sit on the couch and watch TV than play outside. Then his parents should attempt to move his room to the east side and incorporate other tools to manipulate his room's energies. This type of child has a surplus of Taiyin energy, which does not consume energy but materializes. If this child stays in a western room, his laziness will become even more pronounced.

People who have recently started a business would also benefit from having their rooms situated in the east to help them rise earlier in the morning and get a jump on the day.

For clarification, the most critical factor in working with Feng Shui's energetics is a room's physical location. For example, the eastern room sits on the eastern side of a house, the west on the western side, and so on. Since energy enters a room through the doors and windows, the second relative feature of Feng Shui is their placement in a home as well. Doors and windows may not always correspond to the position of the rooms of a house; an eastern room may have a door that opens to the west, for example. Therefore, the most significant factor is the room's location, followed by the placement of the doors and then the windows.

SOUTH: SHAOYANG

Shaoyang is associated with the southern direction, as the south receives the most sunlight in the Northern Hemisphere and is the most yang location. In addition, the south is a tropical region of abundant forests and thriving animals on Earth. It is also the place of dynamic interaction between the sun (yang) and rain (yin). For these reasons, for a business to thrive, an office should face the south, its entrance and windows directed the same way. The same also applies to a person working out of the home. This way, the Shaoyang energy of the south can permeate the room, allowing dynamic activity for the business to succeed. Southern rooms are also beneficial for shy, introverted persons as well.

The world's great metropolises (e.g., Hong Kong, Los Angeles, and New York) are places of dynamic business activities. They are generally situated where an enormous mountain range is to the north and a wide flatland area is to the south. This type of land configuration corresponds to Shaoyang and is full of vitality. Therefore, traditionally in the East, royal palaces faced the south, as did the king's throne, in an attempt to ensure a prosperous country. Arrangements of the city's buildings should also face south since its energetic movement is sizable and fast.

In human societies, money is energy, and in big cities, it circulates in large amounts. Therefore, stores and shops facing the north have a poor chance of succeeding. They would have a better opportunity if their entrances faced the south and windows were added onto the southern side of the building.

If that is not possible, lamplight could illuminate the place and give off a more vibrant, energetic flow. In addition, a good heating system to raise the room temperature, and bright colors for the furniture and walls would give businesses more Shaoyang energy. Finally, flowers and plants belong to Shaoyang and can help elevate the depressed or sunken energy of the north. Therefore, as many plants and flowers with sharp, pointy leaves as possible should be brought into places of business.

West: Taiyin

The west belongs to Taiyin. The sun sets in the west, ending the day and the beginning of the night. It is a place where activity transforms to rest. Therefore, it is the best location for the bedrooms of older adults so that they may stay in harmony with their body's natural rhythms. Since it is an excellent place to rest quietly, a person who works late and wants deep sleep should sleep in the west. It is also beneficial for people who have insomnia. If no rooms are facing the west, positioning the head in that direction would be the next best thing.

On the contrary, people who tend to be lazy and always oversleep should avoid using western rooms. Similarly, men with impotence and low sexual vitality should not use a western room. Since the sun rises in the east and sets in the west, an erection summons Taiyang energy from the east. Erections occurring early in the morning are due to Taiyang energy. As this energy shifts to the west, it withers. Therefore, men who are quickly excited but have a problem with premature ejaculation due to hypersensitivity should stay in a western room to slow their energy.

Dieters, however, must avoid sleeping in a western room since the energetics of Taiyin are accumulating and slow. This hinders progress toward converting the substance into energy and instigates materialization. As a result, food will not burn or convert into energy. Instead, it will settle as body fat due to energy converting into a substance. For the same reason, gym owners should not set their gyms on the city's west side or have a west entrance. The west is the place of rest from the movement. Thus, there will be a reduced desire to exercise for the people there, resulting in reduced membership.

Overactive persons typically have difficulty gaining weight regardless of how much they eat, are impatient, and have trouble completing tasks. In this situation, the energizing function is outplaying the materializing process. Yang's dynamic action does not have yin's gathering action to balance it out. So although a person may be very busy and active, there is no outcome or fruition commensurate to the energy expended. Therefore, they would significantly benefit from using the western room as a bedroom or workroom.

The west is where the materializing function that rests from movement and secures internal stability rises. So people will gain weight there and become more even-tempered, practical, and prudent. Since utility presides over emotion in this direction, they will break away from romance and fantasy. Regardless of how others perceive them, they will carry out their tasks, whatever they may be, to the end if they can make a profit. Most living rooms and bedrooms of people who have made a lot of money from small businesses sit on the west side.

Restless children with difficulty concentrating and remaining calm should be given a western room. After a few months, the energy of this room should help quiet the child and allow him or her to be more contemplative and thoughtful. A sense of adult-like dignity will be noticeable in the child's conduct and reasoning. Similarly, a child with a high IQ who does not fare well in school for lack of effort will become a better student after using the western room.

The west, where activity stops and reflections on past deeds occur, also corresponds to the latter stages of the aging cycle. Since Taiyin energies make a person sit quietly and think, it also corresponds to middle age, when a person reminisces about the past.

NORTH: SHAOYIN

The north is where Shaoyin energy predominates; the Northern Hemisphere has the least daylight compared to the south. The maximum amount of yin energy accumulates here, bringing activity to a halt and making it less active and slower. The yang energy in Shaoyin is not apparent outside but is stored and poised on the verge of action.

A couple's bedroom is better off facing the north since it is the quietest and darkest, making deep sleep more likely and comfortable. Although a western room is better for people who have trouble falling asleep, a northern room is better suited for those who can fall asleep quickly but wake up at night. This is because the west creates yin, which permits a person to fall asleep. But the north is the direction that greatly amplifies yin to allow continuous sleep.

Shaoyin-natured people are generally shy and meticulous. They tend to contemplate too

deeply and have digestive problems. This type of person should avoid using a room facing north. Shaoyin people can also easily fall into a depression, and the energy of the north will only exacerbate their situation. Adding yin to a person already yin-natured is like turning the person into complete yin, which can cause severe stagnation. Since there is less sunshine and the nature of winter is very yin, depression in Shaoyin is generally worse. Those of Shaoyin nature would greatly benefit from moving their bedroom to the south side of the house or placing a large mirror in their bedroom with a bright light reflecting on it to make artificial sunlight.

A room facing north is excellent for cheerful and talkative children in the company of friends who like to play outdoors. However, children who become sleepy and have difficulty studying should have a study room facing the south. Having Shaoyin children use a southern room will help increase their metabolic functioning, improve digestion, and increase energy. They will also have increased blood circulation to the brain, which will help them stay awake longer. However, because these children have Shaoyin characteristics, their physiological activities become even slower in a north-facing room.

The east externalizes yang energy to begin physical activities. However, the true beginning of yang energy is in the north. The lower yang line of the Shaoyin symbol (⚏) of the I Ching demonstrates this principle. The yang energy is drawn from the lowest part of our bodies. Desires that develop from this part of the body are usually sexual. Therefore, using a northern room as a bedroom is suitable for inducing deep sleep and is also beneficial for developing sexual desires. Couples should have an active sexual life, and the best place to incite dynamic sexual activity is in a northern-set bedroom.

Most people prefer to keep their sexual business private. Although sex can be performed as actively as any sport, it is publicly not accepted as a spectator sport. There is good reason for the sexual organs to be tucked deep in the human body and for privacy to be preferred when having sex. Sex is an activity that is yang within yin.

In general, all activities must be disclosed to be evaluated as good, and in modern times, everything must be disclosed to be accepted as ethical. But why does revealing sexual life constitute the only unethical act?

Sexual intercourse is an activity for creating new life. To make the seed of a new life, which possesses a 50:50 balance of yin and yang, it must go through one complete cycle of yin and yang. By transitioning through the yang (Taiyang and Shaoyang) and yin (Taiyin and Shaoyin) phases and completing the process of transformation into a substance (the end of the yin process), a healthy seed of life is born.

However, if a yang-type activity progresses to a midpoint without completing the yin process, the seed will not ripen. Thus, effort must be made to create the maximum yin environment. Only then can the seed of new life be complete (matured). After being complete, yang activity begins to sow the seed.

For men, parasympathetic nerves activate when the environment becomes yin, and the energy descends and gathers in the body's lower region. Then, as the pressure builds from the accumulated energy, it tries to find an exit. This is sexual desire.

When sexual desire is activated, the male genitals in the yin region (groin) point upward to begin yang activity (erection). Likewise, women's nipples in the yang region (chest) point upward to begin yang activity. In women, yang action in the yang region has already started, though the female genitals located in the yin region have not yet arrived at the climax of yin. Therefore, water (vaginal secretion), symbolic of yin, begins to flow.

Women reach climax more slowly than men do because women are yin in nature and, therefore, slower in bodily action. The climax in women comes when yin reaches its extreme and transforms into yang. Thus, the environment must be yin, dark and hidden, and breathing can be slowed down to help yin attain its extreme. This is why sexual activity should be as discreet as possible and the bedroom kept in the northern part of the house, where more yin energy exists.

How to Enliven Your Sexual Life

In a house where the husband or wife commits adultery, we will frequently note that the bedroom is on the southern or eastern side. A bedroom facing south or east indicates a hindrance in the sexual life of a couple because these directions are where yang energy is vigorous. Therefore, the husband and wife cannot derive satisfaction from their sexual life with one another and will instead look for sexual activity elsewhere. Doing so secretly (yin) satisfies their sexual needs.

For men, a new woman holds an air of mystery. This is because whatever a person does not know well is yin, and what they know is yang because it is exposed. Therefore, since a woman that a man does not know well is very yin, he will feel great sexual desire. However, as the number of sexual encounters increases, the mystery surrounding the woman disappears. She becomes yang and loses her ability to feed the man's desires.

The yin energy given off by humans is weaker than that given by the northern direction. If a couple's bedroom were to face the north, even if one of the partners fools around, he or she would soon come home. Such a bedroom would increase sexual desires in either partner, making the other partner more desirable and allowing immense sexual pleasure.

Sexual life is like the study of quantum physics. The deeper you delve into it, the less you know. The bedroom should be on the north side of the house to attain Shaoyin energy to rekindle dampened love between a couple. If this is not practical, darken the bedroom walls and hang dark curtains on the windows. Also, dim the lights and add plants with broad leaves and small red flowers to raise sexual desire. The bed should have a thick, soft, and comfortable mattress, while the furniture should be of a classic style. Sexual activity must always be fresh and new, like a gift covered with layers of wrapping paper. You must not immediately reveal your true self. Instead, make it a rule to constantly surprise your partner and always retain an air of mystery.

Women should use classic perfumes, such as those introduced years ago. Perfume quickly stimulates the primal part of the brain called the "limbic system" to activate animal instincts (the hypothalamus, the center of sexual desire, is part of this system). Classical perfumes have similar odors to that of female animals in heat. For example, many classical perfumes imitate the smell of the glands of musk deer.

Perfumes introduced in recent times awaken the brain with their yang odor. This causes energy to concentrate on the upper part of the body, resulting in decreased sexual desire. Similarly, soaps, toothpaste, and other substances with menthol-like odors cause a reduction in sexual desire as well.

Try to vary the perfumes you wear and observe your husband's or boyfriend's reactions. Select a few varieties that cause a strong response and keep those for your private use. If you find a perfume that caused the first sexual impulse in your man when he was young, you will have a "slave of love" for life. For more sexual desire and potency, eat dark-colored, yin-type foods as mentioned in chapter 7, "Yin and Yang of Food and Diet."

2. Sasang of Light and Color

We have previously mentioned that everything in the universe differentiates into three components: time, direction, and color. Each element contains Tai Chi, yin-yang, trinity, and Sasang. We have discussed these topics at length, so our discussion here focuses on Sasang.

The Sasang of time, on a small scale, is morning, midday, evening, and midnight. It is spring, summer, autumn, and winter on a larger scale. The Sasang of direction is north, south, east, and west. The Sasang of colors is blue/green, red, yellow, and white/black (fig. 15.11). Eastern philosophy makes a minimal distinction between the colors blue and green. Black and white colors can be considered as one color since their difference is whether or not black color exists.

Although innumerable colors exist, they are all created by synthesizing these four colors. When we combine them, we can make any color. For example, when the three generating colors of red, blue, and green are combined, it results in white. When the three reflective colors of red, yellow, and blue combine, black results. From these colors, you can create seven colors of the rainbow.

Figure 15.11 Sasang Symbol

Green/Blue

Green is the color of Taiyang and the color of spring. It is the expansion of energy when new life sprouts forth from plants, trees, and flowers. The buds, grasses, mountains, and plains

renew their lives and become green. Because of their association, green things are Taiyang in nature.

The most crucial feature of springtime is growth. Taiyang is also growth; therefore, green indicates growth in progress. Green represents the transformation from substance to energy. When a person looks at something green, the same effect occurs in the body. Bodily energy expands, and a person's spirit and mood elevate, becoming generous with a smile.

Blue is the color of water and the sky. Ocean water is blue because the long wavelengths of light, such as red, orange, and yellow, are absorbed, while the short wavelength of blue is scattered. The sky is blue because sunlight becomes widely scattered by gases and particles in the atmosphere; blue light is scattered more than others due to its shorter waves. The sky and water of the Earth are powerful and immense, clearly representing the nature of Taiyang. So looking at the vast expanse of sky or water, too, brings about the same feelings as the color green.

Red

Red belongs to Shaoyang. It is the color that appears during the peak of energy consumption. That which has dynamic energy consumption is fire. Its color is generally red. The heat of the summer, the "season of fire," can be expressed as red.

Red substances have an intense, energetic nature of Shaoyang. Blood is red and is the internal environment in which the body's most vigorous activities occur. Red also has great luminescence as its energy disperses. Women, in general, are more appreciative of receiving flowers because of their yin nature and, hence, the need for yang energy to balance their yin. The representative color of flowers is red, and red roses represent the fire of passion. Although red is the most closely associated with Shaoyang, all bright colors have a similar effect on the body. Sun, fire, flower, blood, heart, and so on—all are red, as their energy consumption and movement are dynamic. Red excites and shocks the body and mind to get the energy moving.

Shaoyang is the time when yang is moving toward its end, and yin is beginning. It is the starting point of a gradual slowing down of activity. Fires not continuously fed will burn out in no time. Once the sun reaches its height of intensity, it remains there for a brief moment before beginning its decline in the sky. Flowers also reach their pinnacle of activity and begin to wither and die within days. Leaves drop after changing into their autumnal hues. The soaring stock price corresponds to Shaoyang, which is likely to fall sharply. Therefore, the rising stock price is displayed in red on the stock chart.

People, plants, animals, water fountains, the stock market—everything has a height of existence from which it begins to fall. Red is the color representing the transformation from a state of activity to the start of a decline.

YELLOW

Yellow belongs to Taiyin. It is the color that occurs when the activities that consume energy are reorganized into a substance. Yellow is the color of fruition. When grains are ripe, they appear yellow. As fruits ripen, their hues change from green to yellow. Once substances show a yellow color, their energy has transformed into substance. Yellow fruits are foods that have stored energy. Pumpkins, especially, are primarily yellow-orange and represent the materialization of energy. The sight of a yellowish pumpkin fills your heart and makes you feel happy.

In the United States, there is a holiday called Halloween. October 31 is when it starts to get chilly. This day is said to be when the souls of the dead return. Children carve pumpkins with ghostly faces to decorate their houses with lanterns, and at night the children go to neighborhood homes in spooky costumes to get candy. As Halloween approaches, kids love buying pumpkins. Children are active by consuming energy during the day or summer. But they gather energy during the night or winter to increase the number of cells and their height. To multiply cells and grow taller, they need food in the form of stored energy. A yellowish pumpkin is a food with well-stored energy, and the candy is a food with well-kept energy as sugar. So Halloween is the custom of supplementing the nutrients easily lacking in autumn and winter to grow taller with supplementary foods such as pumpkin pie, pumpkin soup, and candy.

There is no Halloween in Korea, but there is a day in winter when children steal and eat food. It is not a crime to enter someone's house and steal food on that day. Instead, it is the thoughtful attempt by ancestors to supplement the nutrients easily lacking for growth during the winter.

The basic theory of I Ching must have been transmitted to the West via the Silk Road and through Greece. According to I Ching's theory, the Taoist masters made the elixir for immortality. Their counterpart is alchemists in the West who may have created Halloween. The Western masters who wore black clothes as a symbol of creation and made elixirs by Western logical thinking were most likely degraded to the image of witches or magicians in the West. Nevertheless, its trace seems to remain on Halloween.

BLACK

Black is the color of Shaoyin. It is the color of winter, when the activities that consume energy stop, and storage of substances occurs until springtime. Trees turn black when burned. Coal is black, as is petroleum oil. Black represents a halted state of energetic activity on the exterior while the interior contains enormous stored energy.

In nature, the night brings about a significant decrease in action, while vigorous activity still takes place on the interior of plants and animals. What is happening is that stored energy is boiling briskly inside to give us enough strength to rise in the morning or spring. Black indicates intrinsic energy preparing for activity even though activity is at a standstill.

Black color represents all colors between white and black according to their activity. Therefore, the more black color there is, the weaker the activity, and the more white color there is, the stronger the activity. The amount of black a color blends with can also indicate its strength of action. For example, if green mixes with black, it appears dull. Therefore, Taiyang activity is weak in this color. On the other hand, if green combines with less black color, it seems bright and has more dynamic Taiyang activity.

As stated before, dark things are good for strong sexual vitality. Since their yin surface is hard, the breakdown and assimilation speed is slow, storing a great quantity of energy. Slow to activate, the deeply stored energy mainly acts on the sexual energy that kicks up at night in the lower part of the body. Dark-colored foods, such as sea cucumbers, oysters, pork, black beans, black sesame seeds, brown rice, shark, eel, mussels, and so on, are all good for sexual vitality.

Similarly, people with dark skin tones or dark hair are often sexually strong. The speed at which their sexual desire starts is slow, but they enjoy sexual activity that lasts for more extended periods. The black stallion is famous for being a symbol of stamina.

All things that exist in this universe have their peculiar colors. When you divide an object's color into Sasang, you can better understand its nature.

3. Sasang of Sounds

The most common rhythm used in music is the 4/4 beat. That means there are four counts for every measure. In a choir, there are four predominant vocal groups. In the high range are the sopranos (Taiyang) and the altos (Shaoyang), while the lower range consists of the tenors/baritones (Taiyin) and the basses (Shaoyin). Together, these voices create harmonies with balanced yin-and-yang ratios, so the sounds are pleasing to the ear. As a result, the music resonates with the harmonious sound of the universe.

Among the folk music of Korea, Samulnori, or "four instrument play," is performed by four people with four different percussion instruments (fig. 15.12). One instrument, called a Book, is a drum made of leather. Another instrument is the Janggo, an hourglass-shaped drum made of leather. These two drums produce yin sounds. In addition to the Book and Janggo, two brass percussion instruments are called the Jing, a large gong, and the Kwaenggwari, a small gong. These two instruments produce yang sounds.

traditional percussion quartet

Kwaenggwari   Jing   Book   Janggo
Taiyang   Shaoyang   Taiyin   Shaoyin

Figure 15.12 Sasang of the Four Instruments (Samulnori)

Each of the instruments corresponds to one of the four Sasang energetics. Of the yin in-

struments, the Book creates a lower sound. It is yin within yin and belongs to Taiyin. The Janggo has a higher sound. It is yang within yin and belongs to Shaoyin. Meanwhile, the Kwaenggwari, because it is smaller, creates high-pitched sounds. It is yang within yang and belongs to Taiyang. Lastly, the Jing gong makes lower-pitched sounds. It is yin within yang and belongs to Shaoyang.

We can divide the human body into four sections. The head cavity is Taiyang, the chest cavity is Shaoyang, the abdominal cavity is Taiyin, and the pelvic cavity is Shaoyin. The four instruments have specific effects on each of these sections, their frequencies resonating with the four primary cavities of the body. For example, the Kwaenggwari is known to stimulate the head cavity strongly. The playing of Jing sends a tingling sensation through the chest cavity. The Book causes the abdomen to palpitate, and the Janggo vibrates the bladder.

When there is an Asian traditional percussion contest, people are moved by the huge drums of Japan and admire the various percussion instruments from India. However, people who haven't seen Samulnori are disappointed by the shabbiness of the instruments. Samulnori has no sheet music, and the drummer beats them at will to the excitement of the time. Perhaps because the tones resonate well with people's bodies, the body and mind of the listeners writhe in sync with the sound of the music. When the performance is over, people from all countries stand up and give thunderous applause.

Players of the four instruments say that diseases can heal with vibrations. When patients with chronic headaches sit in a room and listen to the Kwaenggwari for a short time, their headaches are said to disappear. Digestive problems, including chronic abdominal pain, can be treated similarly using the Book.

From an Eastern medical standpoint, these treatments make logical sense. Since most headaches are due to improper blood circulation to the brain and poor metabolism, the sound of the Kwaenggwari is beneficial in treating this type of problem. When the sound of the Kwaenggwari resonates with the cranial cavity, the brain vibrates and blood circulation to the head improves. When blood travels to the head more easily, overall metabolism also improves.

Treatment of digestive problems works similarly, using sounds from the Book which resonate with the abdominal cavity and the stomach, small and large intestines, liver, pancreas, and spleen. As with the cranial cavity, these organs also vibrate in correspondence to the sound of the Book. In so doing, blood circulation to this body part improves digestive functions.

Samulnori is called Nongak, which implies "traditional music performed by farmers." One farmer said that instead of spraying pesticides on his paddy field, he played the Kwaenggwari daily. He then compared the yield with a paddy field sprayed with pesticides. The comparison showed that the yield of the rice paddy where he played the gong was similar to that of the rice paddy sprayed with pesticides. Music has the same effect as the pesticide. Insects could not withstand the sound of the Kwaenggwari, which differed from their resonant frequency, and either died or disappeared.

In Buddhism, there are also "four instruments." Buddhism tries to edify all life through the vibration of sound. The drum named Bupgo comprises leather covering a wooden frame (Fig. 15.13). It thus makes a sound that resonates with both animals and plants. Shaoyang is the energy of spring when life springs up. Therefore, the drum that creates Shaoyang vibration promotes the life of animals and plants. Here, due to the change in the context, the inversion principle comes into place. So the drum is now categorized as Shaoyang instead of Taiyin.

Figure 15.13 Bupgo, Magoksa Buddhist Temple, Gongju, Korea

The iron plate shown on the following page is called the Woonpan (fig. 15.14). Its sharp sound vibrates the air. It is the energy of the Taiyang, like the summer. With its sound, flying creatures prosper. The bell called Beomjong makes a soft, settling sound (fig. 15.15). It has the effect of stabilizing the brain of a constantly busy person. Like the energy of autumn, it brings life activity into fruition and repose. The energy of Taiyin brings about a re-laxed feeling and weight gain. This particular bell is a replica of the fifteen-hundred-year-old Emile Bell in Songdeoksa Buddhist Temple. It has the best design and sound quality in Korea, where advanced iron smelting technology has existed for centuries. A sense of ease and deep relaxation comes with its sound.

The last of the four instruments, called the Mokuh, is made by carving wood from the inside (fig. 15.16). It produces a dull bass sound, and this low tone makes life in the water beneath the ground thrive. It is the energy of Shaoyin, which prepares for the next life while resting.

Figure 15.14 Woonpan, Keumsansa Buddhist Temple, Wanju, Korea

Figure 15.16 Mokuh, Keumsansa Buddhist Temple, Wanju, Korea

Figure 15.15 Beomjong, Kyungju Bell Pavilion, Kyungju, Korea

4. Sasang of Art

In Korea, traditional schools known as Hyang-gyo focus primarily on educating children about the I Ching. These schools' unique characteristics are the large drawings of the Tai Chi symbol on their front gate (figs. 15.17 and 15.18). There are also college-level schools called Seowon (fig. 15.19). Aside from academic classes, these schools' art classes focus on the Sagunja, the "four gentlemen plants." Sagunja consists of the plum (symbolic of spring), the orchid (symbolic of summer), the chrysanthemum (symbolic of autumn), and the bamboo (symbolic of winter) (fig. 15.20).

Figure 15.17 Kwangju, Korea

Figure 15.18 Kansung, Kangwondo, Korea

Figure 15.19 Pil-am Seowon, Jangseong,
Jeollabuk-do, Korea

Figure 15.20 Sa Keun Ja—4 Drawings

The plum endures the fierce cold of winter and is the first to bloom magnificently. It symbolizes Taiyang, which uses the energy stored during the winter for the flowering and new growth of spring. The leaves of the orchid spread out in all directions like water from a fountain, representing Shaoyang energy. The orchid symbolizes plants flourishing in the summer by consuming energy. Chrysanthemum is not flashy in color but gives a cool and abundant feeling. It is a symbol of Taiyin that fittingly expresses its nature of bringing forth fruition by organizing the splendor of summer. Lastly, bamboo's ability to extend straight without bending, even in the cold of winter, pertains to Shaoyin. Its ability to stand tall is due to the strength of its roots. During winter, it embraces energy inside and waits for the new life of springtime to arrive.

The children who attend these traditional schools learn to meticulously observe the nature of these four plants and are considered good painters if they can lucidly express their characteristics in drawings. What they learned in these classes will be kept as a hobby for the rest of their lives. Such teaching and this hobby provides a method to facilitate mastering the nature of the Sasang.

5. Sasang of Fundamental Components (Four Elements) of the Universe

Ancient Greeks and Indians saw the fundamental components of the universe as the four elements of earth, water, fire, and wind. In Sasang, wind belongs to Taiyang, fire belongs to Shaoyang, earth belongs to Taiyin, and water belongs to Shaoyin. All things on Earth are nourished by water, grown and developed by fire, and moved by wind. The earth element establishes all its forms. This may seem like a primitive view of nature. However, if we translate these ancient elements into scientific terminology, we can find profound meaning in them. If the people who initially established the elements were reborn in modern times and received education in science, they would state the following: "Wind is an activation of energy, earth is substance, fire is the zenith of energizing function, and water is the zenith of the materializing function." Thought of in these terms, the primitive view of nature becomes scientific.

Humans breathe (wind), drink water, receive sunlight (fire), and eat fruits, seeds, and animals born from the earth. Therefore, the components that form our bodies are wind, water, fire, and earth.

Plants, in turn, absorb inorganic matter (earth), such as minerals and water. They also absorb carbon dioxide from the air (wind), receive sunlight (fire) to undertake photosynthesis, and bear fruits and seeds. Therefore, the elements that form plants are earth, water, wind, and fire.

Mountains fundamentally consist of earth, or soil. Water moistens them and creates caves and valleys. They are warmed by the sunlight and cooled by nightfall. When they are cooled, rocks crack and are blown by the wind, causing changes in their shapes. Therefore, mountains also comprise earth, water, fire, and wind. As you can see from these examples, these elements compose everything in nature.

To break down nature into four classifications, the earth is Taiyin, water is Shaoyin, fire is Shaoyang, and the wind is Taiyang. In dividing them into two categories, we find that they are energy (yang) and substance (yin). Since energy and substance are not two but one, they are Tai Chi. So ultimately, the four-element theory, which forms the main component of Greek and Indian natural philosophy, can be interpreted using the theory of I Ching.

The element representing the Taiyang is wind, wherein the activation of energy begins; the element representing the Shaoyang is fire with abundant energy; and the element signifying the Taiyin is the earth conveying matter. The element denoting Shaoyin is water, which cools the activities of other substances but has infinite energy within.

The four elements make a continuous cycle

in which wind feeds the fire that results in ashes, which becomes earth. Earth contains water within, while water creates wind through evaporation. These forms follow this cycle: Taiyang → Shaoyang → Taiyin → Shaoyin.

Wind (Taiyang) and earth (Taiyin) have an antagonistic relationship. The wind can tear down the earth, while the earth can stop the wind from moving. Fire (Shaoyang) and water (Shaoyin) also have an antagonistic relationship. Fire causes water to transform into steam, while water can put the fire out. Indeed, there is a great deal of similarity between the four-element theory and the Sasang theory (fig. 15.21).

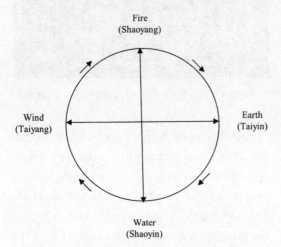

Figure 15.21 Four Elements and Sasang

SASANG AND THE GENETIC CODE

Science explains the differences in human beings by the variations in their arrangement of organic bases, which compile each individual's genetic code. The differences between humans and animals are also due to the disparities in this arrangement of organic bases composing their DNA, which forms the chromosomes of human cells. The four organic bases have individual characteristics and, when arranged differently, create the infinite possibilities of life-forms. Ultimately, they determine human destiny because they are responsible for predisposition to illness, sex, physical frame, brain chemistry, and so on.

According to their natures, the four bases—adenine, guanine, cytosine, and thymine—can be assigned to Sasang. Just as Sasang differentiates from yin and yang, the four bases belong to two parent organic compounds, purine and pyrimidine. Adenine and guanine are purines, while cytosine and thymine are pyrimidines. These are further divided into yin and yang depending on their natures. The purines have nine (a yang number) atoms in their structure. Thus, adenine and guanine are yang in nature. The pyrimidines have six (a yin number) atoms, so cytosine and thymine are yin in nature.

Of the Sasang components, Taiyang has the most potent energy, as it is the greater yang, while Taiyin has the most mass, as it is the greater yin. Adenine is the major component of ATP (adenosine triphosphate), the fundamental energy unit in cellular metabolism. Thus Taiyang corresponds to adenine, while its complementary pair Taiyin corresponds to thymine. This is because adenine permanently bonds with thymine in the DNA bonding of bases.

So the Shaoyang corresponds to guanine, and Shaoyin corresponds to cytosine. Again, the Shaoyang and Shaoyin are complementary, just as guanine bonds with cytosine. Nevertheless, they are also Tai Chi, having the common feature of organic bases.

SASANG AND SWASTIKA

Sasang Tai Chi symbol represents a division of the regular Tai Chi symbol. The swastika (later adopted by the Nazis) is a simplified representation of the Sasang symbol. In essence, they both represent the four elements of nature and their circular movements.

Pythagoras said that the left side (arm) of the swastika points to the earth while the right arm points to the sky. The left and right sides, and heaven and earth, imply yin-yang and Sasang. The swastika on early Neolithic pottery (sixth millennium BCE) shown here is one of the oldest swastikas in the world (fig. 15.22). The ancients used it to symbolize the sun or the sky as an emblem. Perhaps the

ancients looked at the galaxy and drew the swastika to illustrate it (fig. 15.23). Suppose the Tai Chi or the swastika is a product of scientific civilizations before the last Ice Age on Earth. In that case, it is likely that the galaxy was observed through an astronomical telescope and then drawn.

Figure 15.23 Swastika-Shaped Spiral Galaxy

Besides ubiquitously symbolizing peace, harmony, good luck, fertility, and well-being, the swastika is also widely known as the symbol of creation. For example, in the I Ching, Hado and Nakseo, two enigmatic drawings, represent the sun, sky, and creation (see chapter 17, "The Five-Element Theory"). So there is an intimate relationship between them.

By observing the centers of the concentric spirals in the following Cycladic "frying pan" dating back to 2800–2700 BCE (fig. 15.24), we can notice that the heads of both the yin and yang of Tai Chi wrap around each other. It has the shape of a small Tai Chi. It concretely expresses the movement of Tai Chi

Figure 15.22 Early Neolithic Pottery (6th Millennium BCE), Sofia Archaeological Museum, Bulgaria

spreading from the center to the periphery. It illustrates the delicate movement of Tai Chi in the center, gradually exerting a more substantial influence on its surroundings. Each bigram of Sasang is composed of yin and yang; thus, it is Tai Chi. Four concentric spirals with different positions and directions depict Sasang Tai Chi.

Figure 15.25 Archaeological Museum of Fira, Santorini, Greece

Figure 15.24 Cycladic "Frying Pan," National Archaeological Museum of Athens, Greece

We can observe many more appearances of the Sasang symbol around the world: a simple symbol of Sasang Tai Chi on ancient pottery, dating back to the eighth to seventh century BCE (fig. 15.25); on the end of an old Korean roof tile (fig. 15.26); on the center decoration of a shield (fig. 15.27); and on the shield of a Viking (fig. 15.28).

Figure 15.26 National Museum of Korea

Figure 15.27 National Museum of Korea

Figure 15.28

16

Sasang Medicine

Dr. Je-ma Lee revolutionized traditional Eastern medicine by creating Sasang medicine approximately one hundred years ago. Sasang medicine is a constitutional medicine that determines a person's body type based on physical and mental characteristics. Then specific treatments are applied based on this determination.

Traditional Eastern medicine classifies the signs and symptoms of a disease by what is known as "syndrome differentiation," or "pattern identification." In contrast, Sasang medicine focuses first on differentiating a person's constitution, or body type, before considering syndrome differentiation. Accordingly, traditional Eastern medicine is called "syndrome medicine," and Sasang medicine is called "constitutional medicine."

Western medical divisions of disease causes can differentiate both medicines. Western medicine separates pathological causes into hereditary factors and environmental factors. According to this mode of thought, traditional Eastern medicine primarily deals with environmental factors, while Sasang medicine emphasizes genetic factors.

Sasang medicine is theoretically consistent with the principles of the I Ching. Clinically, it has the advantage of preventing illnesses by correcting the imbalances within each body type before their onset. It is a unique medicine of Korea, which depicts Tai Chi and the four trigrams on the national flag and on the gates of traditional schools.

The Cosmological View of Sasang Medicine

The cosmological view of Sasang medicine is identical to that found in the I Ching. The cosmological view of the I Ching will be reiterated here for those who do not yet understand its meaning. The essential concept is that all things in nature possess variations of yin and yang (fig. 16.1).

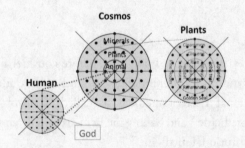

Figure 16.1 Tilt of Yin-Yang. All things in nature have a tilt of yin and yang, which can be diagrammed as dots in the coordinate system. Human diseases, which are disharmony of yin-yang, can be remedied by yin-yang variances of myriad things in nature.

As stated, life has less variation between yin and yang in analyzing things in nature.

Although this degree varies among animals, they always contain more yang than yin. Chinese restaurants often display Zodiac charts in which you can see the twelve animals of the Chinese horoscope. Among these twelve animals, the horse has the highest degree of yang (and less yin), whereas the rat has the lowest degree of yang (and the most yin).

On the other hand, plants retain more yin than yang. This is because, while animals move actively, plants do not. Plants, like animals, also have variable ratios of how much more yin than yang they contain. For example, ginseng, an herb that invigorates metabolism, has a relatively lower amount of yin than moss, which grows in cold, damp regions.

Humans have the most negligible variation in yin and yang compared to animals and plants. Therefore, among all things in nature, organisms have less variation in yin and yang than minerals, while animals have less variation in yin and yang than plants. In fact, humans are relatively close to a 50:50 ratio, allowing us to maintain a near-perfect harmony and balance of yin and yang.

Among myriad things in nature, minerals have the most significant variation, some having a tremendous amount of yin and a small amount of yang. In contrast, other minerals have a considerable amount of yang and little yin. For example, sulfur, which can readily turn into fire, is significantly more yang than yin among the minerals. In contrast, mercury, which is very heavy and cold, is substantially more yin than yang.

Since life is essentially a "balancing act,"

any sustained extreme of yin or yang destroys it. Therefore, like minerals, those with extreme variations in yin and yang cannot support life. Living organisms, by nature, must have a lesser variation in yin and yang than minerals, or else they would be unable to sustain life. However, just because something has no life does not imply it possesses zero yang (mind).

In the principle of yin and yang, nothing exists that has 100 percent yin or 100 percent yang. Therefore, there is only variance between yin and yang; all matter contains yin and yang. As long as there are yin and yang, no matter how small in quantity, consciousness or "intelligence" exists to recognize its surroundings, think, and make a decision.

For example, no matter how small you cut a magnet, the resultant pieces maintain the north and south poles and can orient to the magnetic field. Likewise, no matter how small you break a substance down (e.g., into subatomic particles), it still possesses a dual nature as a particle and a wave. This proves that there is no pure yin or yang.

As was previously mentioned in chapter 13, "Yin and Yang of the Universe," the famous "double slit" experiment in particle physics shot photons through a single slit and a pair of slits. The experiment demonstrated that when the photons were shot one at a time with both slits open, they refracted, selected, and knew where to go instantaneously. As a result, they found their way into the light areas. Furthermore, they avoided the dark regions, creating alternating light and dark bands. If a photon does not have a mind of its own, as Dr. Stephen Hawking mentions in his book *A Brief History of Time,* a single electron "must be passing through *both* slits at the same time!"[1]

From this experiment, it is possible to draw several conclusions. One is that photons can "choose a path" by processing information about their surroundings and are "intelligent." Another is that nothing is purely yin or yang, even at this infinitesimally minute level. This is a particle (mass)–wave (energy) duality in quantum physics. At every level, once again, yin and yang occur together.

What is called *evolution* by some biologists is nothing more than the progression of a substance from a greater to lesser variation of yin-yang. In other words, from extremes of yin-yang to yin-yang balance. In the evolutionary process, minerals became plants, plants became animals, animals became humans, and humans became sages. Therefore, people who have greatly cultivated themselves are sages who act and think like gods.

In Sasang medicine, a perfectly harmonized person in yin and yang is called a sage or enlightened being and is considered a god. God is a perfect harmonization of yin and yang, completely unbiased, without greed or desire for particular things. Partiality or prejudice only appears in beings of yin and yang imbalance. This imbalance creates desires, which generate sin, suffering, and sickness. With this in mind, God suffers no diseases and can live forever.

Although humans have fewer variations than other animals, they still maintain imbalances in yin and yang. Just as a warped record album wobbles on a record player, human beings live their lives to an imperfect tune. Ultimately, the variation of yin and yang in humans is inherited.

As originally conceived, humans were to embody a 50:50 ratio of yin and yang, much like God. However, according to the Christian Bible, Adam and Eve violated God's command by eating the fruit of knowledge instead of the perfectly balanced foods in the Garden of Eden. This, in turn, gave rise to the distinction between yin and yang and all of our subsequent woes. If the author of the Bible had read the I Ching, they would have understood this concept of the yin-and-yang variation.

Because human beings do not embody the perfect balance of yin and yang, regardless of how healthy a person may be, they are still predisposed to certain diseases. Although a standard Western medical exam might not reveal any abnormalities, it does not eliminate the possibility of illness. Western medical exams cannot accurately measure the tilt of yin and yang within a person. Therefore, they cannot predict ailments that may arise in the future, nor can they perceive diseases that may exist at a subclinical level.

Even if a person has a significant imbalance of yin and yang (e.g., a 40:60 ratio), Western medical examinations will show nothing if the disease does not clearly manifest. For example, it can take approximately five years for a single cell of certain types of cancer to develop and ten years for the tumors to grow one centimeter, big enough to be detected by an MRI's measuring unit of one cubic centimeter. This implies that some cancer diagnoses can only be made after fifteen years of continued imbalance in yin and yang. By the time a single cancer cell is detected, tens or hundreds of cancer cells may have already metastasized to other places in the body through the blood or lymph vessels.

Absolute health can only result through the determination and adjustment of the body's fundamental yin and yang imbalance. The diagnostic methods of Sasang medicine can illuminate this path to health. According to Sasang medicine, people who constitutionally have more yin than yang are called yin-type persons. Those who have more yang than yin are called yang-type persons. Yin persons who gradually accumulate yin are Tae-eumin, while those whose yin starts to decrease after initially having a large quantity are called Soeumin. Yang persons who tend to increase their yang progressively are Taeyangin, while those whose yang starts to diminish after having an initially large amount are Soyangin.

Homeostasis occurs when there is a harmony of yin and yang. But a disease occurs when yin and yang deviate from homeostasis. Sasang medicine takes full advantage of the different energetic tilts of things in nature. For example, suppose a virus with a 40:60 variance of yin to yang invades and upsets the body's homeostasis. Then Sasang medicine can restore balance by offering medicine or food with the opposite (60:40) variance. It is possible to cure diseases with almost any substance because all things in nature have uniquely differing tilts of yin and yang. Foods have slight variations in yin and yang and do not cause dramatic changes in physiology.

Nevertheless, eating them according to your body type is still important. The reason is that the ingredients we use as food (plants and animals) have a more significant imbalance of yin and yang than the human body. For example, yang foods taken in large quantities over time can bring yin persons to balance as effectively as any medicine. However, to harmonize yin and yang in the shortest amount of time possible, remedies of a mineral origin are taken, as they have a more significant tilt in yin and yang.

The difference in the nature or attributes of plants, animals, and minerals is relatively easy to distinguish in comparing Eastern herbal medicines with Western pharmacological drugs. This is because Eastern herbal remedies are typically made from animal and plant sources and must be ingested in large amounts to make an impact. In contrast, Western drugs, composed primarily of minerals, have an immediate effect with just a minute dosage (a few milligrams).

There is no real distinction between foods, medicines, and toxic substances in traditional Eastern medicine because they all exist along a continuum. Substances with a slight tilt in yin and yang (such that they do not significantly change the yin and yang of humans when eaten daily) are considered food. Substances that have a more significant tilt in yin and yang, causing greater changes in the disparity of yin and yang within humans, are considered medicines. Lastly, substances that have an ex-treme tilt in yin and yang are enough to tilt the yin and yang of humans into irreparable imbalance. As a result, they are toxins or poisons capable of killing quickly.

Grains may serve as a staple in everyone's diet since they have the least amount of yin and yang tilt among all plants. As rice has a Shaoyang nature, it can supplement the lack of yang in Soeumins. Wheat's Taiyang nature may supplement the lack of yang in Taeeumins. Barley has a Shaoyin nature and can enhance the deficient yin of Soyangins. Buckwheat has a Taiyin nature, so it can supplement the lack of yin in Taeyangins.

Foods are not the only means of treatment used in Sasang medicine. Various types of stimulation have a yin and yang tilt as well. For example, different sounds can regulate the imbalances of each body type. So may light, smell, tactile sensations, temperature, seasons, and the four emotions of joy, anger, sadness, and pleasure. In truth, all matter or phenomena that we can and cannot conceive have a tilt of yin and yang. They can be applied to regulate a person's constitutional imbalances.

The External Appearance of Sasang Body Types

Traditional Eastern medicine is the study of syndromes. It uses the patient's subjective and objective temperature, the pulse's strength, and the speed of pathological changes, among other things, to determine the nature of the abnormality in the physiology of the internal organs. On the other hand, Sasang medicine is a constitutional medicine. It emphasizes a person's physical build and the functional strengths of two paired internal organs, which we will discuss later.

There is a good reason for the difference in emphasis. First, structure generally gives insight into functional tendencies. Secondly, understanding the innate aspects of a human being requires the consideration of the fundamental attributes of a person that don't change quickly, such as a person's physical frame. Conversely, the strength and weakness of physiological functions, such as pulse, and the rapid change in disease symptoms are unsuitable for constitutional discernment, which is the original makeup.

In considering the human body as Tai Chi (totality), the Sasang distribution is as follows: the head is Taiyang, the chest is Shaoyang, the abdomen is Taiyin, and the pelvis is Shaoyin. The shape of a head is like a bud sprouting from the body. Due to its location in the highest part of the body, it is considered yang. But it is hard since Taiyang is yang that has not yet fully blossomed. The shoulders and arms extend out from the chest, giving it the shape of a funnel, trumpet, or branching tree, spreading yang energy upward and outward. The chest region is also always hot. For these reasons, the chest belongs to Shaoyang. The abdomen is round and holds a large amount of fat (stored energy). It can be compared to the exuberant fruits of autumn and belongs to Taiyin. The pelvis is the region surrounded by the cold buttocks and is the attachment site of the legs (yin appendages). It calls to mind the image

of tree roots storing wintertime energy and belonging to Shaoyin. See the following diagram (fig. 16.2).

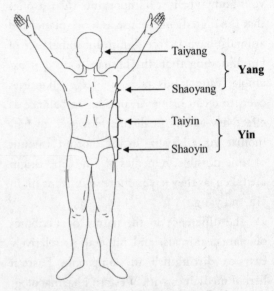

Figure 16.2 Sasang of Human Body

Taeyangins

The outstanding characteristic of the Taeyangin body type is the large head, a sign that a Taeyangin's brain and spinal cord are well developed (fig. 16.3). Thus, in general, Taeyangins are very smart. There are quite a few brilliant and creative heroes and geniuses among the Taeyangins, including Napoleon, Lenin, Picasso, and Van Gogh. However, excessive brain development carries the possibility of degeneration (by the principle, "extreme yang converts into yin"). Following a surge in stocks, the market crashes naturally. It is said that the difference between genius and fool is paper thin. So

Taeyangin can often be found in patients who suffer from mental disorders, cerebral palsy, or Down syndrome, which all result from brain or spinal-cord abnormalities.

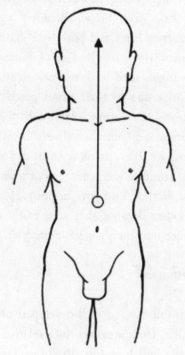

Figure 16.3 Taeyangin

An alien's depiction often includes a big head, slim trunk, and weak, skinny legs. It is similar to the body composition of Taeyangins. Coincidentally, in the future, once machines can perform all manual labor, this is what the human form may come to resemble. Man's arms and legs will become weak and atrophied from lack of use. Meanwhile, the head, the only body part frequently used, will grow more prominent because it houses the brain.

When yang becomes strong, yin becomes weak. According to genetics and Eastern medicine, the brain, spinal cord, bones, sexual organs, and legs belong to the same system. The energy of Taeyangins tends to concentrate in the organs of the upper region (resulting in their brilliant minds), making the organs in the lower area generally deficient. This results in weak reproductive organs. Thus, Taeyangin women frequently have infertility, and Taeyangin men suffer from impotence. Taeyangins also have typically weak bones and legs (yin), so their legs may become paralyzed when they get sick. The abdomen and waist, which belong to Taiyin, are also vulnerable. Thus, Taeyangins usually have thin waists and easily develop problems in their lower backs.

Although the constitution is not precisely inherited, constitutional transmission is highly correlated. Taeyangins are estimated to be about three to four in ten thousand, making them the rarest among the constitutions.

Soyangins

The most prominent part of Soyangins is their wide chests and broad, highly placed shoulders (fig. 16.4). Their torso has the shape of an upside-down triangle, while their hips, which are the Shaoyin region and the opposite of the Shaoyang region, are small. The Road Runner cartoon character depicts the Soyangin body type. It has a lot of muscle mass concentrated in its chest and shoulders, but almost none in its hips, except for its powerful legs. Chickens possess a Shaoyang nature and make excellent tonics for Soeumins.

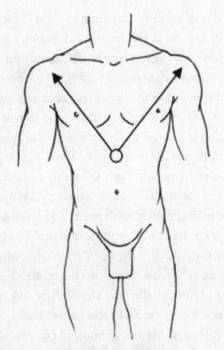

Figure 16.4 Soyangin

The chest, a well-developed region in Soyangins, contains the heart and lungs. So those of this constitution generally have good blood circulation and a healthy supply of nutrients. They also have strong metabolisms, which make their movements very active. So they are like people who drink alcoholic beverages. Soyangins have loud voices and love to talk about themselves, believing that they are the cream of the crop and that there is nothing they cannot do. They are also quite reassuring, for they always positively interpret things.

Soyangins spend a lot of time on their appearance. They are veritable social butterflies, cheerfully flitting from friend to friend. They possess a strong sense of righteousness and place a high value on honor. However, since

their yin energy is weak, they cannot see things through to the conclusion and tend to neglect matters concerning their health or family.

Do you remember Elvis Presley or the Fonz (from *Happy Days*)? Both had the Soyangin body shape, with broad shoulders and relatively narrow hips, and both lived flashy, dramatic lives with a relative lack of domesticity.

Soyangins tend to have weak reproductive capabilities due to their small pelvises (part of the Shaoyin region). Although premature ejaculation is a common ailment in Soyangin men, unlike Taeyangins, men and women of this constitution are generally not infertile. In general, both Taeyangins and Soyangins have thin bodies because they can easily convert substance into energy (a yang process).

TAE-EUMINS

Tae-eumins have a well-developed abdomen and waist. These areas are thick relative to their shoulders and hips (fig. 16.5). So Tae-eumin

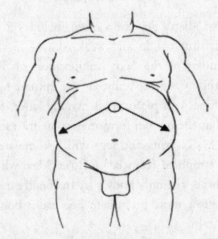

Figure 16.5 Tae-eumin

bodies do not have an hourglass shape, even when they do not have a potbelly.

Taiyin is associated with strong materializing energetics. Therefore, the Tae-eumin constitution has a predisposition for obesity. Generally, an obese person can be considered Tae-eumin, except for those who can lose weight quickly by regulating their diet. Because Tae-eumins have a strong materializing energy, even when they are not obese, they always have a big trunk and thick bones. Overall, Tae-eumins tend to be tall, weigh a lot, and have large eyes, noses, ears, and mouths.

The energy of Tae-eumins centers around their abdomen and waist, leading to a well-developed digestive system. As a result, Tae-eumins are excessively greedy regarding food and get very hungry after a bit of work. Although they overindulge when eating, they tend to digest things well.

Tae-eumins have weak hearts and lungs, as their chest region, which belongs to yang, is relatively undeveloped. Thus, they commonly suffer problems related to blood circulation and oxygen supply. Since their blood circulation and oxygen supply tend to be inadequate, nutrients do not convert readily into energy and instead accumulate as fat in their bodies.

Physically, Tae-eumins are the most yin of the four body types and have the most developed bodies. Although their heads (Taiyang region) are smaller in relation to their bodies, Tae-eumins are generally fleshy and more physically developed than people of any other constitution. So their heads appear to be relatively large. Concerning thinking, they tend to lack creativity but have quick, discerning abilities when it comes to profit and loss. Nevertheless, Tae-eumins generally try not to use their heads too often. They think only when necessary, like making money, making themselves comfortable, or supporting their families. They tend not to use their heads for "impractical," idealistic matters, such as art, creativity, impressing others, and the like. Generally, Tae-eumin thought patterns are very practical and materialistic. They primarily focus on acquiring money, as it is the energy of human society. However, Tae-eumins can become very poor because of their inherent tendency toward laziness of both body and mind.

Externally, Tae-eumins tend to accumulate property or money, but internally, they accumulate fat by reducing their energy consumption. Thus, for Tae-eumins, the function of materialization takes place both internally and externally. Many Tae-eumins are rich and powerful: Aristotle Onassis, Donald Trump, Lee Iacocca, and so on. President Clinton is also a Tae-eumin, although he may have lost some dignity due to his indiscretions with Monica Lewinsky, another Tae-eumin. Nevertheless, it is undeniable that the country's economy is much wealthier because of his efforts.

There are many Tae-eumins among opera singers, for example, Luciano Pavarotti and Plácido Domingo. Tae-eumins make excellent opera singers, not because of their romanticism or creativity, but because they can produce powerful, beautiful sounds from their large, resonant trunks. Some Tae-eumin comic characters include Bluto (from the *Popeye* series), Fred Flintstone, and Yogi Bear.

Soeumins

Soeumins have a well-developed pelvis and hips. Whether they are standing or sitting, they appear remarkably stable. Their shoulders and chests, in the Shaoyang region, are relatively narrow, and their hips look big. The torsos of Soeumins resemble upright triangles (fig. 16.6). Anyone who is not particularly overweight but has enormous hips and thick legs may be considered to have a Soeumin body type. Shaoyin is associated with the winter, so Soeumins lack yang energy. They generally enjoy eating spicy foods and chicken, a Shaoyang animal, in an attempt to supplement the yang.

All athletes, regardless of their sports, need strong legs. Good footwork is necessary, even in boxing. A boxer's punch is only effective if the strength of the legs supports it. Many Soeumins excel in sports because they have strong legs. However, sports that require strong shoulders and upper bodies, like swimming or gymnastics, put Soeumins at a disadvantage. These sports are more appropriate for Soyangins.

Soeumins take on many of the characteristics of winter. They are generally quiet, love sexual activity, and produce strong children. The reproductive system contained within the pelvic cavity is the Shaoyin region, so Soeumins typically have healthy reproductive systems. Traditionally in Korea, one of the first things parents considered when selecting a bride for their sons was the size and flexibility of the girl's hips. She was chosen if the hips were large and flexible, for she could bear strong children with her superior reproductive capability.

The Personalities and Behaviors of Each Body Type

It is challenging to discern people's constitutions simply by asking them about their personalities, since their opinions of themselves can be somewhat biased: too lenient, or too harsh.

For example, people might perceive themselves as rash, impatient, or frivolous because they have made a few mistakes in the past. On this basis, you cannot view them as Soyangin. On the other hand, it is common for

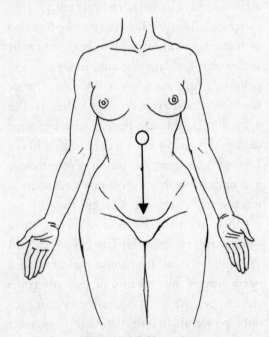

Figure 16.6 Soeumin

people to view themselves as indecisive, since not everyone is capable of making decisive decisions. But, again, you cannot jump to the conclusion that this person is a Soeumin. Similarly, having suffered losses because they couldn't hide their inner feelings, people think they are good at revealing them. In that case, it is wrong to conclude that the person is of a Soyangin constitution.

As you can see, it is more productive to attempt to discern constitutional types through physical characteristics rather than personality structures because people tend to have illusions about themselves while their true natures remain untold. It is difficult at first, but with a thorough understanding of the individual Sasang characteristics and continued practice, the constitution can be known through the person's physical shape and behavior without asking questions.

TAEYANGINS

Taeyangins have characteristics that resemble springtime. They have plenty of energy in reserve, like budding sprouts, and can powerfully push that energy out. In other words, they are full of vitality and confidence. Like the springtime energy, which only rises and does not stay beneath the ground, they only know how to move forward. Taeyangins are courageous, optimistic, masculine, and thoroughly unconcerned about what other people think. They are self-righteous and know no regrets.

As their energy only moves toward one-sided consumption, Taeyangins are obsessively

single-minded. This enables them to make decisions forthwith. This, combined with their excellent minds, make them ideal leaders. The resolute decision-makers Hitler, Lenin, and Napoleon were Taeyangins. People tend to follow Taeyangins implicitly because they are so bright, seemingly clear-headed, and decisive. Unfortunately, other body types do not fare as well as leaders. Soeumins are too indecisive and hesitant, while Soyangins tend to change their statements and intentions whenever they run low on energy or encounter obstacles. Tae-eumins are overly prudent and slow to adapt to changes.

As Taeyangins are single-minded, they develop one-sided characters, capable of plowing forward but incapable of reflection or introspection. While this leads to success in most endeavors, it can cause them to fail miserably. Although their intelligence and overflowing vitality overcome most obstacles, some cannot, and Taeyangins lack the reflection necessary to tell the difference. Witness Hitler's attack on Russia, resulting in a war on two fronts, or Napoleon's devastating winter campaign against that same country. Insurmountable obstacles also have a deleterious effect on the health of Taeyangins. They make them extremely angry, like gunpowder set off in a small, enclosed space; any extreme anger results in a deterioration in their health.

Taeyangins have an urgent nature and are always in a hurry. This allows them to finish their work quickly but makes them unceasingly restless and impatient, especially when things don't go as smoothly or swiftly as they'd like. Therefore, Taeyangins need to learn a little from Tae-eumins. Tae-eumins have a "take-it-easy" attitude toward life. When they get stuck in pursuing their goals, they take a break. They do not seriously think about how to get over the next hurdle. Instead, they indulge themselves in recreational activities to refresh themselves. If you are sure you are a Taeyangin with an urgent nature, you should pay careful attention to the Tae-eumins around you. If you can learn from them and emulate their strengths, you will not get sick or commit yourself to terrible mistakes. If you combine a few Tae-eumin qualities with your inherent diligence, you will be able to succeed in all your endeavors and live the remainder of your life in abundance and comfort.

SOYANGINS

Soyangins have the characteristics of exuberant summer energy. They resemble drunk people, constantly cheerful, loud, and in high spirits. Additionally, they are invariably optimistic and always think things will turn out all right.

Like the bright summer sun, Soyangins enjoy shining in the eyes of others. They make grand displays of their abilities and exaggerate and embellish their stories when describing events. Soyangins consider the concealment of emotions to be a disgrace.

Part of this philosophy of full disclosure involves telling people whenever they make a mistake. Soyangins never hesitate to point such things out, nor are they reluctant to point out their idea of viable solutions. They also frankly and immediately acknowledge their own mistakes. Since Soyangins are bright as midday, they dislike hiding things.

When learning something new, Soyangins think they fully understand it after spending just a few moments in study. This is because they are unwilling to take the time to sit down and absorb anything completely. Instead, they are constantly on the lookout for new projects. Yet once they find a new project, they immediately quit it and look for something else. This restless, roaming behavior is because Soyangins possess the nature of fire. Like fire, they ignite swiftly and passionately and just as swiftly burn themselves out. Just as fire is always restlessly spreading to new fuel, Soyangins are unable to stay in one place. As a result, they cannot observe the "step-by-step" of a process and can only know the world through the blur of hurried glances.

Since they learn things quickly but roughly, they appear to know everything but do not know anything in great detail. Thus, at work they may be able to get by for a while with broad generalizations. But they get stuck whenever anything deeper, more detailed, or specific is required (any topic they did not pay adequate attention to). When they encounter such an impasse or an insurmountable obstacle, for that matter, the energy within them becomes obstructed. When they are unable to find a solution due to their rash temperament, their anger arises to attempt to penetrate through it. At these times, Soyangins can fly into sudden rages.

For Soyangins to be able to work at something persistently, it must constantly be new and exciting. But, unfortunately, jobs of this sort are rare. Moreover, since Soyangins always adopt a "know-it-all" attitude toward work, they quickly lose interest and are liable to face many obstacles. So they move on to something more interesting. Thus, a vicious cycle ensues. An Eastern saying, "A dragon's head with a snake's tail," aptly portrays this aspect of the Soyangin personality.

Although Soyangins are very helpful to others, they tend to neglect their family affairs. Although others may praise them and call them good and kindhearted people, their wives and children consider them insubstantial, empty, and false since they only pay attention to the affairs of others, neglecting the concerns of their own families. In this, Soyangin people are like the summer. Again, in the summertime, the energy of all things is exuberant on their exterior but lacking on the inside.

This "externally strong, internally empty" aspect of Soyangins manifests itself in other ways. For example, while Soyangins may wear brand-name clothing and drive fancy cars, this flashy exterior may conceal a lack of enough money to pay the rent or no money in the bank.

Soyangins always have anxious minds. In Soyangins, as yang is in its most exuberant state, yin begins to develop. As energy consumption is at its extreme, it begins to materialize. As this energy contracts, it leaves an empty feeling in Soyangins, resulting in ever-present anxiety. When confronted by this inexplicable anxiety, Soyangins easily give up on any work they have started. This is true even when they are earnestly helping other people out. Because So-

yangins give up on such projects and renege on their promises, they get complaints from others, even though they think they have suffered significant losses helping others.

Both Soyangins and Taeyangins have urgent temperaments. Taeyangins can overcome most difficulties when they arise due to their penetrative, propulsive power of springtime. Soyangins, however, simply give up halfway when faced with obstacles. This is because they have already consumed most of their energy and have nothing left to back them up in the ensuing struggle. Again, since yang is in its extreme state in Soyangins, it has already begun to transform into yin. The braking, suppressive force of anxiety interrupts the propulsive drive of their urgency, halting them dead in their tracks (like a parking brake applied to an accelerating car).

Although both Taeyangins and Soyangins have short tempers, there is much difference in the frequency of their anger. Taeyangins do not lose their temper over trivial matters but explode when faced with insurmountable obstacles. Soyangins, on the other hand, frequently lose their temper over trivial issues, dissipating their energy like the summer sun and prematurely giving up on the project or work that's troubling them.

TAE-EUMINS

Tae-eumins resemble the autumn season. In autumn, energy is gathered inward and transformed into a substance so that fruition may occur. Tae-eumins have inward, reserved,

THE SECRETS OF THE I CHING

prudent personalities like the autumn energetics. Their words and actions are always considered, like carefully grown autumn harvests. And, through steady, cumulative efforts, they eventually seek to reap the benefits of their harvests.

Tae-eumins place the utmost importance upon the "harvest," which is the security and comfort of themselves and their families. So they do not participate in any affair that endangers or jeopardizes its full fruition. Therefore, they are incredibly doubtful and fearful of any variables or changes that might affect their work in progress. They also have little interest in "idealistic" ventures, such as helping in the affairs of their country or assisting others in need. Instead, they prefer to look at people and issues strictly in terms of profit and loss. These characteristics indicate their propensity toward results, like nature's function to attain autumn fruition.

Tae-eumins are secretive. They dislike it when others find out their actual plans or intentions. They also dislike it when others discern their true feelings. This extensive concealment is purely to safeguard their accumulated harvest of knowledge and wealth. Hiding things, after all, is nature's way of gathering energy. Those who carry a lot of keys (implying that they have a lot of things that are "locked up") are generally Tae-eumins.

Tae-eumins don't get excited very easily. Nor do they move very much unless they absolutely must. This is because Tae-eumins try to conserve energy to complete the process of materialization that they embody. As a result, many Tae-eumins

take greater pleasure lying on the couch watching TV and eating potato chips than traveling and adventuring around the world.

In addition to this propensity for immobility (both physically and emotionally) is a somewhat dull sensibility. Tae-eumins do not react to stimuli unless they are extreme. Stimuli that might frighten Soyangins are usually no big deal to Tae-eumins. In situations where other constitutions might be in a panic, Tae-eumins can often maintain themselves with equanimity, eating their meals calmly and sleeping soundly. They can enjoy themselves in recreational activities, even in the middle of a battlefield!

Tae-eumins are born businesspeople for many reasons. First, Tae-eumins do not allow themselves to get carried away with emotions. Thus, even when they feel good about something, they don't become overjoyed, and even when disliking something, they don't hate it. The capacity to avoid extremes of emotion allows Tae-eumins to keep a practical, levelheaded view of things necessary for good business. For example, as they never get angry over the impudent actions of their customers, they are appreciated by their patrons as stable and secure individuals.

Tae-eumins are also extremely patient. They can wait situations out until they are in their favor. On the other hand, other body types tend to be relatively rash, trying to close their business deals as quickly as possible, often to their disadvantage. Yet another reason why Tae-eumins make natural businesspeople is their inscrutability. As stated previously, Tae-eumins do not by nature display their inner selves. Thus, their competitors can never figure out what they are doing.

According to the I Ching, all good things have a shadow, and all bad things contain a redeeming light. Tae-eumins may seem foolhardy as they do not move fast with the flow of time and appear to take a loss. But by patiently waiting, they know there will come a time when the tide will turn. These characteristics and behaviors of Tae-eumins make them successful in various fields.

No matter how good a substance is, it will rot if retained. For example, the accumulation of wealth is desirable; however, the accumulation of fat (stored energy) within the abdomen and other body parts is not. This fat can form plaque that lines the walls of blood vessels, impeding circulation and metabolism and resulting in severe conditions like heart disease, stroke, hypertension, and diabetes.

To become healthy, Tae-eumins should learn to emulate some of the characteristics of Taeyangins and Soyangins. They should strive to convert the accumulated substances of their bodies back into energy and use that energy to activate their sluggish metabolism. Their metabolism should then be able to eliminate the accrued wastes burdening their systems smoothly. Emotionally, Tae-eumins should stimulate a feeling of urgency within themselves. They should occasionally stir themselves up into anger or allow themselves to get a bit frightened or shocked now and then. Cultivating these emotions within themselves will help them to invigorate their physiologies.

SOEUMINS

Soeumins take on several of the characteristics of winter. In the wintertime, energy is stored and conserved. But, on the inside, pressure builds as energy struggles to push upward and outward against powerful compressive forces. This is true of seeds, for example, and homes in which people confine themselves through the winter. Soeumins take on this energetic quality and thus have shy, depressed personalities.

Soeumins seem gentle, possessing the softness of the water that represents Shaoyin qualities. However, this water cannot freely flow because it freezes and stagnates in the cold winter air. Thus, Soeumins are generally inflexible in thought and obstinate in character. Frequently employers fail to see this aspect within their Soeumin workers simply because Soeumins follow orders obediently, without expressing their opinions. The reason for this is not that Soeumins lack opinions but that they store them inside. Soeumins are actually the most stubborn-minded of the four constitutions. Ordinarily, they will listen to what others say. Still, once they determine that what others say is wrong, they will staunchly hold to their position, no matter how much subsequent evidence others might provide to the contrary.

People tend to think more in the winter or at night (Shaoyin times). Thus, Soeumins are overly pensive. Weighed down by so many thoughts, they are unable to make decisions. Also, they are meticulous, calculating gains and losses down to the very penny and considering every task's bright and dark aspects. Therefore, they are hesitant to begin new projects and slow at working on projects that have already started. As a result, they lack the Soyangins' urgency needed to leap into things.

Like Taeyangins, once Soeumins believe their work is correct, they close their minds and do not think about anything else. They hang on to their beliefs as though their lives depended upon them. Despite this stubborn faith, however, Soeumins are unable to act quickly. Again, their contemplative nature causes them to consider their actions' positive and negative aspects, slowing their resolve, like a car running through molasses.

When Soeumins get emotionally hurt, it stays with them a long time. This is because yin changes slower than yang. Thus, although it may take some time to offend a Soeumin, it is difficult for them to forgive or forget once it happens. As a result, Soeumins usually do not talk with their spouses for a long time after a fight. In contrast, offended Soyangins cuss at others until it seems they want to kill them. Then, shortly afterward, they turn 180 degrees and become sympathetic. This is one of the most explicit differences between the temperaments of these two types.

Soeumins like to judge the rights and wrongs of other people's actions and behaviors. The same is true for Soyangins. This is because (if you refer to the Sasang symbols) there are both yin and yang in these body types. Thus, both Soeumins and Soyangins are concerned about distinguishing between the yin and yang in others. This makes them both meddle in affairs that do not concern them. However, the method of meddling differs according to the amount of yin and yang in the body type. Soyangins, for example, point out the faults of others directly and immediately, whereas Soeumins discern the weaknesses of others when they are not around (in other words, they talk behind their backs).

If you consider Soyangins as optimistic and active, then Soeumins must be pessimistic and passive. Whereas Soyangins are always thinking about the positive side of life, Soeumins consistently ponder the negative side. To use the cliché, when the cup is half full, Soyangins would simply relish that there is still half a cup of water, whereas Soeumins would lament that there is only half a cup.

Each constitution has its own advantages and disadvantages, so there is no good or bad constitution. It is not true that a certain food cures all ailments and laughter cures all ailments. Foods that are good for Soyangin are bad for Soeumin, and laughter is good for Tae-eumin or Soeumin but bad for Soyangin.

Physiology and Pathology of Each Body Type

As we stated earlier, the shape of a person's body gives insight into the person's constitutional type. Body shape is significant because it is determined by the size and strength of the various internal organs. Thus it allows us to comprehend these organs, which establish the characteristics of a person's physiology and personality.

The torso contains four significant organs: the liver, lungs, spleen (which includes the pancreas), and kidneys. Although the heart is vital for survival, Sasang medicine considers it more of a mechanical pump than an actual Zang (visceral) organ. The heart is a perfect balance of yin and yang because of its central position amid the other four organs. However, its characteristic balance does not help determine individual constitutions, as it does not give insight into energetic variations.

Traditional Eastern medicine associates the liver with the wood element, which shares the characteristics of the spring. The lungs are associated with the metal element and autumn. The spleen (which includes the pancreas) is related to the earth element and the transitional period between the seasons. The kidneys are associated with the water element and winter. Lastly, the heart is associated with the fire element and summer (these elements will be explained in greater detail in the next chapter).

The functions of the Zang organs are described metaphorically as governmental posts needed to successfully run a country, such as the Ministry of Internal Affairs, the Ministry of Foreign Affairs, the Ministry of National Defense, the Department of Transportation, and so on. Therefore, the entire country is jeopardized if any post fails in its duties. Similarly, if any Zang organ does not function properly, the individual's health is at risk.

Sasang medicine interprets the internal organs in a slightly different manner. As previously stated, traditional Eastern medicine associates the spleen with earth, and the heart with fire. Sasang medicine reverses these relationships. The spleen (and pancreas) is responsible for glucose production and regulating the digestive system. Food is literally the "fuel that fires" our physiology; it takes "digestive fire" for digestion and assimilation. For this reason, Sasang assigns the spleen to the fire element and relates it to the summer season. Meanwhile, since the heart is the most balanced organ in terms of yin and yang, Sasang relates it to the earth, also considered the most stable and balanced element.

Another difference between traditional Eastern medicine and Sasang medicine lies in the functional organization of the Zang organs. Traditional Eastern medicine views the organs as government posts, each with its field of duty. On the contrary, Sasang medicine holds that the body's physiological functioning depends on a delicate balance between paired complementary organs. Although it is perhaps a simpler system, it nevertheless provides several unique and powerful insights into the nature of the human body.

The liver and lungs form one complementary pair, while the spleen and kidneys form another. The liver is in charge of storing and consuming glucose, the body's primary energy source. Therefore, it would make sense that the liver would be associated with Taiyin and the autumn's strong accumulative harvesting energies. Still, it is associated with Taiyang and the spring. The shape of the liver is an upside-down triangle, which implies that energy is dispersing. This makes the liver an "explosive" organ, strongly related to the emotion of anger.

The lungs control respiration (the gaseous exchange of oxygen and carbon dioxide) and oxygen circulation throughout the body. They have an intense dispersing energy. Yet, like the liver, they are not associated with the aspect of Sasang we'd expect them to be. Instead, the lungs are associated with Taiyin. The lungs cover the other organs like an umbrella and move energy down toward the liver, making the accumulative tendencies of Taiyin possible. In this sense, the lungs are considered compressive and appropriately Taiyin.

The spleen (pancreas) controls all digestive functions and sources much of the body's energy. Because Shaoyang is associated with exuberant, consumptive fire, it makes sense that the spleen is associated with its energy. Finally, the kidneys determine whether to eliminate or reabsorb substances. Therefore, they are primarily responsible for storing substances in the body and are associated with Shaoyin and the winter. As long as the liver, lungs, spleen, and kidneys function in earnest, the body maintains its health.

According to Dr. Je-ma Lee, Taeyangins have large lungs and small livers, whereas Tae-eumins have large livers and small lungs. In other words, Dr. Lee said that the peculiarity in the physical frames and mental characteristics of Taeyangins and Tae-eumins is based upon the relative sizes of their livers and lungs.

But wait a minute! Didn't we just say that the liver is Taiyang and the lungs are Taiyin? If this is true, why did Dr. Lee say that Tae-yangins have small livers and Taiyins have small lungs? To respond to this, we must look at the principle of form and function. Recall that in the yin-yang theory, when something has a small form, it tends to have a quick (or strong) function, and vice versa. The enlarged size of the lungs in Taeyangin resulted from the lungs' attempt to gather the overwhelmingly strong energizing action of the liver when they were initially being formed. Thus, when we say that the distinctive quality of Taeyangins is their large lungs and small livers, this implies that the lungs' function is weak, while that of the liver is strong.

In other words, Taeyangins have a strong "spring" energy due to the powerful propulsive force of their livers and a weak capacity for storing energy as a substance due to the deficient gathering function of their lungs. On the other hand, Tae-eumins are precisely the opposite. Their large livers and small lungs imply that they have weak livers (explosive, "spring" energy) and strong lungs (accumulating, harvesting energy) (fig. 16.7).

Also, according to Dr. Je-ma Lee, Soyangins have large spleens (or pancreases) and small kidneys, and Soeumins have large kidneys and small spleens (or pancreases). In this situation, the large spleen and small kidneys of Soyangin types correlate with a strong spleen and weak kidney function, and the small spleen and large kidneys of Soeumins correlate with a weak spleen and a strong kidney function. Why is this so? Doesn't the principle of form and function also apply in this case?

The principle of form and function applies

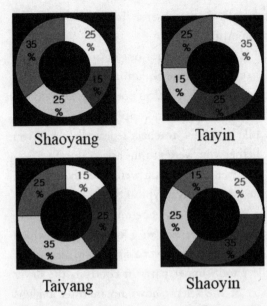

Figure 16.7 Sasang Proportions in Percentage

in the case to the liver and lungs and not to the spleen and kidneys because the former are organs involved in transitional processes and periods (the beginnings of yang and yin). But on the other hand, the latter pair of organs involve the extreme or exuberance of yin or yang. Therefore, the "mixture" in the transitional periods results in the inversion of the liver and lungs' form and function. But the extreme of Shaoyang and Shaoyin results in the congruence between the spleen and kidneys' form and function.

FOUR SENSE ORGANS

A person's characteristics are revealed in the most distinctive features of his or her face. It is a common tradition in the East and West to assess someone's character by observing that

person's face. In general, the sizes of the eyes, nose, mouth, and ears determine the overall facial impression, and judgments are made about a person's character. The nature of the whole is determined by observing the harmony of individually differing constituent elements. The I Ching describes this method as knowing Tai Chi (the totality) through understanding Sasang (the four primary sense organs of the face). In physics, this methodology involves knowing the characteristics of energy (the personality) by looking at the substantive attributes (the different parts of the face).

The ears belong to Taiyang, the eyes belong to Shaoyang, the nose to Taiyin, and the mouth to Shaoyin. We can understand the Sasang attributes of the sensory organs by examining the yin-yang attributes of the stimulants of the organs. The eyes and ears are yang because of their location on the upper part of the face. They receive energy in the form of sound and light frequencies.

But the nose and mouth are yin because their location is on the lower part of a face. They receive molecules of substance as well as whole substances. Of the yang stimuli, light has a more vigorous activity and moves at a more rapid speed. It enters the eyes, belonging to Shaoyang. Sound has a slower yang activity than light and enters the ears, which belong to Taiyang. Smell has a weak yin activity since it results from the movement of molecules of matter and enters the nose, which belongs to Taiyin. Food is lumps of matter, which have the most yin activity and enter the mouth, which belongs to Shaoyin. The I Ching principle considers these facets the "mutual correspondence between similar matter." Or, like the simple adage, we might say, "Birds of a feather flock together."

Taeyangins have superior hearing abilities. Children with exceptional hearing, able to listen to sounds inaudible to others, are generally considered Taeyangin. You can often see these type of children stop or still their bodies to listen to these imperceptible noises. Because of their superior hearing, Taeyangins tend to have excellent musical abilities. Musicians who were Taeyangin include Beethoven and Debussy. The sensory information drawn from the ears is superior to what the brain can receive through the eyes. Although people are much more visual in today's culture, the ears can sense vibrations farther away and far more dispersed than the eyes can pick up. This action allows Taeyangins to generally be more knowledgeable, creative, and gifted than others.

The most yang part of the body is the face, and the most yang part of the face is the eyes, "the windows to the soul." They send out information about the whole body. Thus, it is essential to look at the eyes when determining a person's body type.

Soyangins have well-developed eyesight. Their eyes sparkle and seem to penetrate whatever is in their path. In fact, sometimes, it can seem as though their eyes generate heat because they are so intense. Soyangins have rapid eye movements and can take in their surroundings quickly. For example, they tend to remember things that whiz by them in a split second while riding in a car. Although they take in a great deal of information at a glance, they generally do not observe things carefully or for a long time.

If the light shines out of Soyangins' eyes, it's the opposite for Soeumins, whose eyes seem to soak up the light. So Soeumins' eyes do not have much luster and appear rather sleepy. If, while in school, teachers repeatedly asked you whether you were falling asleep during a lecture, even though you were intently listening, you are probably a typical Soeumin.

Women of the Soeumin body type frequently have *sanpaku,* a condition in which the upper eyelids cover a significant amount of the pupil's upper part. In contrast, the lower part of the sclera shows up in three regions around the pupil (left, right, and below). As a result, these women appear to be staring into the deepest parts of themselves and are frequently considered very sexy.

Subconsciously, the eyes gaze at a person's region of interest. Soyangins are interested in the outside world, a yang region. Therefore, their eyes shine outwardly with a sharp gaze. In contrast, Soeumins are more interested in their internal environment, feelings, and emotions. They have vigorous kidneys and strong reproductive systems situated deep within the yin part of the body. Therefore, their eyes tend to fix on those regions.

Taeyangins have a dynamic activity of yang internally, but their yang energy does not shine outwardly as much as it does from Soyangins. The Taeyangin gaze is not as bright as a Soyangin's. Rather, it is penetrating and confident. Taiyin energy is predominantly gathering or compressive. Their eyes tend to be bleary, blurry, dull, or fearful. Courage arises when energy "springs up" due to a strong spring function. Fear arises whenever energy gathers inward. Have you ever seen a frightened cow's wide-eyed, slow, blinking gaze? These are the eyes of Tae-eumins.

Vision and hearing have opposing natures. For example, people crane their necks to get a better look when trying to see better. This requires that the body becomes more active (yang). On the other hand, when attempting to hear unfamiliar sounds, people drop their heads and still their physical movements to pay closer attention (yin). Research done at the University of California at Irvine demonstrates this polar relationship. Both authors have participated in the relationship between acupuncture and brain stimulation using a functional MRI (magnetic resonance imaging). The research involved stimulating a person's body using various stimuli and scanning the brain with functional MRI to determine the part activated by the stimuli. The results indicated that the auditory cortex was suppressed when the visual cortex was activated, and vice versa.

Eastern physiognomy describes the nose as a place to check the state of a person's wealth. Those with large and wide-tipped noses with wide, firm nostrils tend to possess wealth. This shape indicates that the function of gathering and materializing is strong. Many Tae-eumins thus have this type of nose. Soyangins, however, who generally consume energy, tend to have pointy noses. Even if Soyangins earn a lot of money, they usually do not have accumu-lated wealth due to their extravagant spending (dispersing/yang function). The nose is thick and sticks out of the face due to an abundant substance supply and thus belongs to Taiyin.

The mouth, a region where substances enter the body, is seen as yin. Sound, light, and molecules enter the ears, eyes, and nose (respectively) frequently. Still, the substances that enter the mouth are much larger (yin). Therefore, Soeumins tend to have thicker and larger lips, whereas Soyangins tend to have thinner and smaller lips.

Four Organ Systems

Following the yin-yang principle of "infinite divisibility," the four Sasang organ classifications divide into subgroups that perform specialized functions. They belong to one of the four groups determined by their shapes and functional nature. The lungs, small intestine, head, neck, ear, and Shen (spirit) belong to Taiyang. The pancreas, stomach, chest, shoulders, eye, and Qi (vital energy) correspond to Shaoyang. Taiyin contains the liver, gall bladder, waist, abdomen, nose, and blood. And the kidneys, bladder, pelvis, hip, genitals, and Jing (essence) relate to Shaoyin (fig. 16.8).

The human body arises from a single cell divided repeatedly, carrying the genetic information of the whole with every separation. Each cell has and develops slightly different characteristics as it reaches its independence. Cells with similar characteristics form specific organs and body parts, like people with particular talents joining to form a ballet company

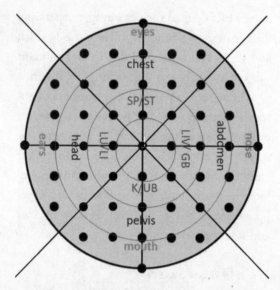

Figure 16.8 Sasang of Organ Systems

or soccer team. Although there are numerous cells and organs in the body, they can be broadly classified into four categories. These four groups manage human physiology and can be classified into Sasang by distinguishing their yin-yang attributes.

Taeyangins have large lungs and small livers, so they tend to have big heads, the domain of the lungs, and thick necks. In contrast, their waists, the realm of the liver, are usually thin. Tae-eumins, who have large livers and small lungs, often have thick waists, small heads, and thin necks compared to their bodies. Soyangins, who have large spleens/pancreases and small kidneys, often have large chests and shoulders, the domain of the pancreas, and small hips, the region of the kidneys. Soeumins, who have large kidneys and a small pancreas, are often precisely the opposite.

The digestive tract connects the mouth and

anus. The throat and esophagus belong to Taiyin, the stomach belongs to Shaoyang, the small intestine belongs to Taiyang, and the large intestine and anus belong to Shaoyin. The throat and esophagus must bring substances into the body from outside, so they belong to Taiyin. The stomach is hot and dynamically active because it must break down food and thus belongs to Shaoyang. The small intestine assimilates glucose, amino acids, and fatty acids for the body's energy source. This is similar to the function of springtime pulling energy out of substances stored all winter.

For this reason, the small intestine belongs to Taiyang. On the other hand, the large intestine and anus absorb water from the dregs and eliminate waste, which eventually becomes stored in the ground. This is similar to the action of winter, and so they belong to Shaoyin.

Taeyangins have weak functioning of the throat and esophagus. As a result, they may have trouble eating and vomit easily. In extreme cases, they can develop cancer of the esophagus. Soyangins have a weak function of the large intestine and anus, resulting in poor elimination, so they chronically suffer from constipation. Tae-eumins have a weak function in the small intestine and can develop diseases in which cells cannot properly absorb glucose, such as diabetes. They also have a reduced ability to break down cholesterol, accumulating in the blood vessels and becoming plaque, eventually leading to arteriosclerosis. Soeumins have weak stomachs and trouble digesting food. So they are always complaining about their digestion.

Four Forms of Qi (Vital Energies)

Four major forces guide the universe that science acknowledges. They are electromagnetic, gravitational, strong nuclear, and weak nuclear forces. The electromagnetic force corresponds to Taiyang energy as it instantly spreads outward in all directions. The gravitational force affects the entire universe and holds everything in place in an inward (centripetal) direction. Thus it corresponds to the Taiyin energy. The strong nuclear force binds protons and neutrons together in the nucleus of an atom. Therefore, it corresponds to Shaoyin energy. Finally, the weak nuclear force responsible for nuclei decay (and thus radioactivity) corresponds to the Shaoyang energy. Since the body is a microcosm reflecting the universe or the macrocosm, four energies function in the body, distinguished by the domain they act upon and the nature of their activity. They are Shen (spirit), Qi (vital energy), blood, and Jing (essence).

The Shen (spirit) implies mental, conscious activity. It belongs to Taiyang because it develops from Jing, which corresponds to the winter. Although Shen functions in the brain, the lungs ultimately supervise it. This is why brain cells are among the first cells to die when there is a lack of oxygen. This leads to the dissipation of Shen.

Qi is first produced from the breakdown of food. Here, Qi implies the energy within glucose, the energy produced by its breakdown and stored in ATP. Since Qi comes from food, it belongs to Shaoyang, and the pancreas controls it.

Blood also contains a significant number of nutrients produced from the breakdown of food. Therefore, it, too, can be considered a form of energy. Qi is considered yang since its movements are more rapid, whereas blood is slower, hence yin. Blood, mainly stored in the liver, the Taiyin region, belongs to Taiyin. The liver supervises blood's actions.

Though Jing or essence is a state of energy, it is an energy that can immediately convert into a substance. It is the most yin energy and is held in the state immediately preceding the development of a sperm or an egg. If the Jing does not become a sperm or egg, it will transform into neurons and aid in performing mental activities. This implies that Jing produces spirit. Because Jing is the most yin form of energy, it belongs to Shaoyin, and the kidneys regulate it. Like water, ice, and vapor, the energetic states of spirit, Qi, blood, and Jing are originally the same. They are merely manifestations of different functional states of energy. Therefore, Jing can turn into spirit at any time, and Qi can turn into blood at any time or vice versa (fig. 16.9).

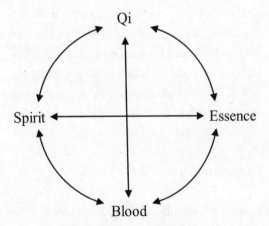

Figure 16.9 Four Energies and Their Relationships

Depending on the situation, one state can turn into any of the other three states. The relationship between the organs and the energies is as follows:

* The lungs function through spirit.
* The spleen operates through Qi.
* The liver functions through blood.
* The kidneys operate through essence.

Taeyangins have an abundance of spirit, so they tend to be the brightest and most creative. Soyangins have an abundance of Qi and so are cheerful and outgoing. They are also romantic, active, and have rapid behaviors and physical movements. Tae-eumins have plenty of blood and so they are well-nourished. As a result, they have thick bones and strong bodies. Finally, Soeumins have plenty of essence, so they have strong sexual energy and bear strong children.

In a negative sense, Taeyangins lack blood, so their bodies are smaller, thinner, and weaker. Soyangins lack Jing and are weak in sexual vitality. Soyangin women often have difficulty conceiving and may give birth to a weak child. Tae-eumins are lacking in Shen. They tend to be less creative and lack artistic qualities. Soeumins lack Qi and are predisposed to depression and overcontemplation. They are passive, with slow movements, and they lack versatility.

EMOTIONS AND SASANG TYPES

Eastern philosophy and Sasang medicine acknowledge the four basic emotions of joy, anger, sadness, and pleasure. All other emotions are said to arise from a combination of these four. Anger rises in an attempt to penetrate a blockage of energy. Joy arises when energy is properly spreading throughout the body. Sadness occurs when energy is gathering inward. And pleasure is the outcome of energy that is stored well.

Anger is the emotion that corresponds to the energy of spring. It tries to penetrate through the outside layer (matter). It belongs to Taiyang and arises from the liver. Joy is like the energy of the summer, which spreads out vigorously. It belongs to Shaoyang and occurs when the pancreas has vigorous activity. Sadness is an emotion that is like the energy of autumn, which gathers inward. It is the emotion that comes from watching the falling of the leaves. It belongs to Taiyin and occurs when the function of the lungs is active. Pleasure is an emotion that comes from knowing there is plenty of food stored for the winter. It also arises from sleeping or resting comfortably or having sex with someone you are in love with. Therefore, it corresponds to Shaoyin.

The liver is invigorated when there is neither too much nor too little sadness. However, excessive anger can damage Taeyangins' livers and weaken their lungs. Since getting angry damages their health, they must learn to embrace others with compassionate minds.

The pancreas is invigorated with a moderate amount of joy. However, extreme joy will overstrain the pancreatic function of the Shaoyang, damaging it and weakening the kidneys. It may seem that all diseases will disappear if we laugh and have fun, but the energy is overconsumed, and the kidneys and their sphere of influence are damaged. Injuries to the bones, bone marrow, and genital organs all occur at the same time. The reason is that "middle path" was not obtained. Therefore, it is important to meditate quietly and develop the storing function of the kidneys.

The lungs are invigorated when there is neither too much nor too little sadness. However, for Tae-eumins, undue sadness will overstimulate their lung function, damaging them and weakening their liver function. So Tae-eumins with excessive sadness must be wary. When they feel sad without any reason, it may indicate a great liver deterioration, so they should take medicine that will protect the liver's function and should participate in fun activities.

Finally, the kidney function is invigorated with a moderate amount of pleasure. Still, too much pleasure will burden the kidney function, damaging it and weakening the pancreatic function. Therefore, Soeumins should be cautious of too much pleasure, especially having too much sex.

In *The Doctrine of the Mean*, one of the Four Books[2] of Confucianism, it is said that the state wherein emotions of joy, anger, sadness, and pleasure have arisen in the heart but have not been expressed is called "middle." This is the state of emotions that is neither deficient nor excessive and is good for the body and mind.

STATE OF IMBALANCE (PATHOLOGY OF EACH BODY TYPE)

Taiyang energy ascends rather than descends. Thus this constitutional type frequently has difficulty eliminating waste. Thus, when Taeyangins have good bowel movements and ease in urination, they are in good health.

Soyangins have a fiery nature that dries the water in their bodies, causing them to get constipated easily. Therefore, the ease and frequency of their bowel movements can determine the state of a Soyangin's health.

Tae-eumins fall ill because their energy only gathers inward and does not disperse. If a Taeeumin tends to sweat easily, it is proof that their energy is dispersing well and they are in good health. In fact, Tae-eumins feel refreshed after profuse sweating. With sweating, waste products are eliminated, while cholesterol accumulated in the blood vessels gets washed out. Tae-eumins usually sweat more than the other body types. So if they are not sweating adequately, it is due to excessive energy gathering. They may soon fall into serious illnesses like hypertension, heart disease, and diabetes and even suffer a stroke.

Soeumins only store energy and do not want to use it. They constantly have digestive problems because of an insufficient energy supply to their stomach. For good digestion to occur, the stomach needs sufficient energy to activate the secretion of digestive juices. When a Soeumin's digestion is good, it is proof that he or she is healthy.

The Soyangin physiology corresponds to summer, whereas Soeumin relates to winter. Soyangins love to drink ice water, while Soeumins request "no ice" when they order a soft drink. If Soeumins can drink ice water well, it is proof that there is sufficient energy in their stomachs. Nevertheless, they should not make their bodies cold.

Soeumins do not sweat easily. However, their energy cannot spread to the skin when they become weak physically. Thus, sweat pores are not regulated and develop excessive spontaneous sweating. When they sweat like this, it indicates that they do not have energy in the body. At this time, their speaking voice becomes feeble.

Those who sweat after a sauna bath and feel heavy and fatigued are Soeumins. Soeumins lack energy due to their inherently weak digestive systems, causing improper digestion and assimilation. In Tae-eumins, there is plenty of energy, but since their energy does not circulate well, they tend to feel heavy, as if there is no energy within them. When Tae-eumins take sauna baths, they usually feel light and cheerful when they step out. This is because sweating through exercise or sauna invigorates energy circulation.

However, stimulating energy circulation through exercise and sauna bathing actually implies energy depletion. This means you are not supplying energy from the outside. Thus, Soeumins, naturally weak in energy, will suffer a further energy shortage, causing them to feel fatigued and exhausted from sweating.

Tae-eumin and Soeumin types both have excessive descending physiological action in their bodies. So both of these types of people easily have diarrhea. Tae-eumins gather substances and accumulate them. This then transforms into waste products, which in turn creates various illnesses. Therefore, it is a good sign of health for Tae-eumins to eliminate waste products through sweating, urination, or bowel movements. Soeumins are originally weak in energy, without surplus waste products

to eliminate, like Tae-eumins have. Therefore, for Soeumins, frequent sweating, urination, and bowel movements cause their energy to dissipate simultaneously. When a person feels tired after sweating or having diarrhea, they are most likely a Soeumin. If instead, the person feels better, they are probably a Tae-eumin.

The Method of Health Cultivation for Each Body Type

The I Ching describes health as the perfect balance of yin and yang. This can only be achieved by reducing the tilt of inborn yin-yang. There are three ways to harmonize yin and yang. First is mental cultivation, to regulate one's temperament or hereditary disposition. The second is ingesting foods or medicine to supplement the deficiencies or weaknesses of yin and yang. Lastly, by regulating the stimulation of the five types of stimuli that enter the body from the outside: light, sound, smell, taste, and bodily sensation.

CULTIVATING YOUR MIND

Receiving treatment after an illness strikes is the worst method for cultivating health. Preventing disease by maintaining a regimen of healthful practice is a much more effective method for bringing the body into balance. Eating foods that match the body's constitutional deficiencies can achieve such balance. More important, regulating the temperament can accomplish balance. There are four desires that each body type needs to be wary of above all else. Taeyangins must be cautious of rudeness and debauchery (self-indulgence). Soyangins should look out for ostentation and extravagance. Tae-eumins need to stay clear of greed, and Soeumins should avoid indolence.

Taeyangins lack planning and moderation due to their excessive liver function that emits energy. This will bring about a state of rudeness and debauchery. The more Taeyangins engage in this mental state, the more their energy is released and the weaker the gathering function of the lungs becomes. If Taeyangins stay vigilant of their mental state, the overly strong radiating energy will slow down, and the yin-yang of their physiological function will remain in harmony.

Soyangins must always stay cautious of self-display and extravagance. These mental states arise when energy disperses outward. Therefore, this body type should instead concentrate on remaining plain and simple. When Soyangins place value on these qualities, energy will gather and transform into matter so that they can build a stronger foundation for themselves.

Tae-eumins must rid themselves of greed. Greed is a psychological state that occurs when energy gathers and accumulates as a substance. They must realize that the world is not just for them. Keeping wealth all to oneself can be likened to accruing cancer cells in one bodily region. Because cancer cells are also cells of the body, there may be some use. However, there is total neglect of the body's allocation rules when one region of the body becomes overly greedy and only gathers cells into that region.

It is essential to have some fat, stored glucose, in the body to properly function. However, diseases such as hypertension, heart disease, and stroke occur when the body is greedy. Greed grows from a lack of experience and knowledge. Tae-eumins need to get out and experience life rather than remain sedentary. They need to open their eyes and minds to new information and stimulate the body and mind directly. Any stimulation will help their physiology run more smoothly and use stored energy. So Tae-eumins must remember that reducing greed in general, and not only for food, is the most effective way to burn fat.

Soeumins tend to be easily satisfied. They feel vindicated when they win a small battle. Soeumin types must guard against being satisfied over trivial matters and becoming lazy. Satisfaction and laziness occur when there is no longer consumption of energy. If Soeumin types become satisfied with their way of thinking and what they have, they can become obstinate and have problems harmonizing with others. Being satisfied with trivial things will cause the body and mind to become "frozen." When the body becomes frozen, indigestion will develop due to a lack of energy, and the hands and feet will become cold. The body will also always feel cold. When the mind becomes frozen, Soeumins become narrow-minded and unable to get along with people. In addition, no matter how hard they work, their efforts may be futile because of their mistake in judgment due to a narrow perspective. Therefore, Soeumins must open up their hearts and develop a broader perspective to avoid becoming obstinate.

Regulating personality traits is very difficult.

It is also challenging to distinguish the strengths and weaknesses of one's personality. The famous saying by Socrates, "Know thyself," is the same as knowing the tilt of your own yin and yang. When the yin propensity is placed on the *x* coordinate, and the yang propensity is on the *y* coordinate, every person's peculiar characteristics can easily be determined as the *x, y* coordinates of a single point.

Correction of weaknesses in personality and disposition can only occur through ceaseless self-cultivation. When this happens, yin and yang will harmonize, and their cross point will move toward (0, 0), the intersection of the *x* and *y* coordinates. At this point, a person will reach enlightenment. Following is a diagram of this process (fig. 16.10).

It is fascinating to note the ancient ideograph of the Yin dynasty for the word "different" (fig. 16.11). It is an appearance of a flabbergasted person about to cover his face. At the time of the creation of the I Ching, a human head was compared to heaven (universe), and in this figure, the shape of the head appears as Sasang Tai Chi or Sasang coordinates. The head, which represents the universe, is described as Sasang Tai Chi or a coordinate since differences between everything comprising the universe are due to their degree of variance in yin and yang. The ideograph demonstrates how recognizing the differences between objects involves finding the variance of yin and yang in each matter and indicating it with the hands pointed toward the Sasang coordinates.

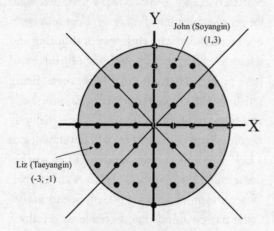

Figure 16.10 Coordinates of Sasang disposition: The disposition coordinates that fall within the circle are healthy. For example, in the case of a Soyangin, when the mental state of vanity/ostentation is severe, then the coordinate value of the disposition becomes larger, and disease will develop. The closer a Soyangin's coordinate value is toward (0, 0), the better the health.

Figure 16.11 Ancient and Modern Ideographs of the Word "Different"

Understanding the nature of yin-yang and Sasang will bring about an understanding of each person's individual strengths and weaknesses. It is difficult to distinguish the constitution of successful people in this world only by analyzing their personality characteristics. Such people are successful because they have corrected their inherent weaknesses.

On the other hand, many people are not successful even though they are adamant in their self-cultivation attempts. These people are not successful because they misinterpret their weaknesses and do not understand in which direction they should make adjustments. Therefore, learning and applying the principle of yin-yang and Sasang would allow these people to see the fruits of their efforts.

Distinguishing your constitution is difficult because people are naturally biased, retaining illusions about what and who they are. When you are drawing conclusions about the constitution of others, your constitution will always be much more apparent. Eventually, through practice and more profound knowledge of yin-yang and Sasang, you will be able to clarify other people's true natures, leading you to a greater understanding of your own. You can determine your strengths and weaknesses when you can accurately see yourself.

If you are Soeumin, you should find a Soyangin to spend time with and use him or her as your teacher. If you frequently try to imitate the Soyangin characteristics to cultivate yourself, your tilt of yin-yang will decrease. Then you will become successful and be able to maintain good health. If you are a Taeyangin, you must find a Tae-eumin and take that person on as a teacher.

The weaknesses of Tae-eumin become the strengths of Taeyangin, and vice versa. For instance, Tae-eumins need to learn Taeyangin's urgency, while Taeyangins, in contrast, need to study Tae-eumin's prudence. Constitutions are not transformable. You are born with a particular body type and will die with the same one. Attempting to change specific attributes of your personality will simply bring about a more balanced state closer to the central $(0, 0)$ in the x, y coordinates.

MENTAL DISORDERS AND SASANG MEDICINE

Depression is a clinically significant psychological disease. It occurs more frequently in the yin body types—Soeumin and Tae-eumin. Constriction of energy causes depression. The Western pharmaceuticals used to treat depression work to prolong the effects of internally produced chemicals, such as endorphins or epinephrine. They have the same effect as cocaine or heroin, causing the illusion of having a great deal of energy. However, their effects only last as long as the time it takes for the liver's detoxification process to render them harmless.

Depression disappears when there is a vigorous supply of energy. Thus, Soeumins can treat their depression by hanging out with Soyangin friends and going out to talk for a while. However, if this is difficult to do, they should eat foods or take health supplements that strengthen their yang energy.

Manic disorders occur more frequently in yang body types—Soyangin and Taeyangin. This disease occurs when there is a surplus of energy and a person cannot consolidate it. If a Soyangin can learn to be satisfied with the little things, like Soeumins tend to do, their ostentatious tendencies will not progress into megalomania (expansive delusions), nor will they progress into a manic disorder.

Bipolar is a condition with alternating occurrences of mania and depression. This disorder is seen more frequently in Tae-eumins and Tae-yangins because these body types have strong functions of guiding the transformation from yin to yang (Taeyangin) or yang to yin (Tae-eumin). It is the same for schizophrenia. Paranoia is a yin disorder and often occurs in the stubborn yin constitutions, Soeumin and Tae-eumin.

Foods and Herbal Medicine for Each Body Type

TAEYANGIN FOODS AND HERBAL MEDICINES

Taeyangins generally have a lot of heat due to their exuberant yang. Therefore, meats, which have much more yang energy than vegetables, are not suitable for Taeyangins. Neither are spicy foods, as they will only make Taeyangins' already vibrant energy even more vigorous. Raw salads and fish (sushi) are preferable to cooked foods for this constitution. Taeyangins should be cautious of sweet foods and practice incorporating more sour foods into their diets. Sweet foods belong to yang and become a source of energy, while sour foods gather energy. Overall, sour and bland foods are good for Taeyangins, whereas sweet or greasy foods are not. Fruits

and vegetables are healthier than grains and meats.

The following are some of the best foods for the Taeyangin constitution. These foods, if eaten regularly, can help balance the constitution.

BUCKWHEAT

The best grain for Taeyangin consumption is buckwheat as it does not contain much starch and thus is not a significant energy source. It also has a slightly puckering taste that gathers energy. In Korea, buckwheat noodles in cold soup are a popular dish during the summer, as they can cool the summer heat.

FISH

As mentioned previously, raw fish is much better than cooked meat as a source of protein. Fish receive a lot of yin from the water they live in. Eaten raw, they can significantly strengthen the weak yin in Taeyangins.

GRAPES AND ACTINIDIA FRUIT (HARDY KIWI)

It is a known fact that sour tastes gather energy. Grapes and hardy kiwi both have sour flavors and are grown from vines, which have strong gathering energy since they need to pull in and find support in other plants, as their ascending springtime energy is weak. The seeds of grapes also have a puckering taste. Taeyangins like to eat grapes since they lack such gathering energy. Among famous Taeyangins, Napoleon was known to have enjoyed wine greatly and drank large quantities daily. However, he preferred cheap wines as they still maintained a rather sour taste.

Chinese Quince, Pine Needles, and Acanthopanacis (Also Known As Eleuthero)

Chinese quince is a fruit whose hard texture resembles a piece of wood, indicating a strong yin nature. However, it also has a sour taste. Pine needles, too, have a sour taste. Those sharp and pointy substances are similar to the head or body hairs, therefore having the propensity to go out to a body surface. Nevertheless, the sour and puckering tastes they contain assist in the gathering function of the skin. Overall, trees that live throughout the four seasons and whose leaves do not fall off during winter are more yin in nature than other trees because their transformation is slower. Therefore, they can supplement the yin lacking in Taeyangins.

Chinese quince and Acanthopanacis are frequently used as herbal medicines, as both help strengthen the weak low back and legs of the Taeyangin constitution. Acanthopanacis, which grows in Siberia (called Siberian ginseng), has a similar effect as ginseng. Though not concretely proven, some still use it to substitute for ginseng. Acanthopanacis is an herb that nourishes the shortage of yin in Taeyangins, whereas ginseng is an herb that nourishes the lack of yang in Soeumins. The difference in their effects is enormous. Though Acanthopanacis has some effect on Soyangin, it is not an herb that can be used irrespective of body

type. So those who are not of Taeyangin body type should not try to take them.

Soyangin Foods and Herbal Medicines

Soyangins resemble the characteristics of summer. Therefore, cool foods are good for them, including raw foods such as salads, fruits, and greens, rather than cooked foods. Darker foods such as oysters, sea cucumbers, blackberries, and black sesame seeds are exceptionally healthy for the Soyangin diet since darkness indicates yin nature. Such foods will supplement the weak yin of their constitution. Because the energizing function is strong in Soyangins, they tend to be thin. Thus, meats with plenty of fat, such as pork or duck, are a good tonic for them. Foods that are slightly bitter or greasy and have thick textures are also suitable for Soyangins to consume.

Moreover, foods with cool, refreshing sensations, like mint, also have beneficial effects. However, for Soyangins, eating sweet foods is like pouring oil onto their exuberant fire (yang energy). Therefore, sweet foods should be ingested at a minimum since they contain sugar that immediately turns into energy and heat.

Pork

Soyangins have a high expenditure of energy. So meats with a high fat content make the best tonics for this type. Soyangins are generally thin since the function of materializing is weak in their bodies. Therefore, meat that especially has highly concentrated energy is better for them, pork being the best for this constitution.

BARLEY

Barley can strongly withstand cold weather as it can penetrate through the snow and sprout. Early sprouting of barley shows that it has finished its strong function of storing substance early. For many, barley does not digest well and creates a lot of gas. Due to their strong digestive systems, Soyangins will experience neither. Instead, barley will slow down the function of the pancreas so that the overall physiological pace of the Soyangins will also slow down, benefiting their health.

MUNG BEANS

Mung beans are an excellent food for Soyangins. They are Shaoyin due to their cold nature. Physiological energy tends to accelerate and rise and thus develop heat in the Soyangin constitution, allowing this type to easily get constipated. Mung beans assist in countering these tendencies. Eating them invigorates the function of the large intestines and promotes bowel movements.

VEGETABLES

Though most vegetables are good for Soyangins, cucumbers, lettuce, and burdocks are especially suitable. A bitter taste occurs when a substance is burned, as energy no longer exists and activity has been stopped. The lettuce and cucumber are Shaoyin plants that have the energy of winter. Lettuce retains a slightly bitter taste, while the wild cucumber also has a bitter aftertaste. Meanwhile, the roots of the burdock plant are very long. Long roots contain energy that has been deeply stored in the ground. The energy that goes deep into the soil is excellent for Soyangins, whose energy keeps rising upward. This vegetable causes diarrhea when too much of it has been eaten, benefiting the Soyangin constitution that commonly suffers from constipation.

FRUITS

Among fruits, strawberries, pineapples, and Korean melons are especially good for the Soyangin constitution. Strawberry plants have more fruits and seeds (yin: autumn and winter) than leaves and stems (yang: spring and summer). Therefore, they are more yin in nature. Pineapples give a very cooling sensation when eaten, while the energy gathered in the center creates the opposite energetics of their sharp, spreading leaves. Therefore, they are fruits with a Shaoyin nature to counter Shaoyang energy. Korean melon is a yellow-colored melon that has a similar nature to the cucumber. It is very cooling and produces essential bodily fluids. Among other melons, sweet-tasting cantaloupes and honeydews are Taiyang fruits better suited for Tae-eumins.

SEAFOOD

The best seafood for Soyangins includes oysters, sea cucumbers, sea squirts, tortoises, and turtles. Oysters have a gray color with dark edges and a lot of cholesterol. Since the cholesterol does not dissolve well, it has yin characteristics. Sea cucumbers and sea squirts are primitive animals.

These primitive animals belong to yin, as they are slow in change and action. Because they belong in the water, they coincidentally belong to Shaoyin. Sea cucumbers are especially dark (a yin color), while sea squirts are bitter (a yin taste), balancing the Shaoyang energetics.

WINE AND BEER

Wines are yang in nature. Like fire, they stimulate the metabolism. Since they are yang, they are not beneficial to yang persons. Beer, however, is suitable for the Shaoyang because of two ingredients—barley and hops. Western herbology uses hops as a replacement for sleeping pills. A substance that causes drowsiness indicates a strong function of stopping activity—precisely what hops do. When you drink beer, its alcohol component acts first. Initially, yang effects, such as a red face, hot bodily feeling, and vigorous physiological activity, occur. Soon afterward, the yin effect of barley and hops kicks in and causes sleepiness. However, beer's excess coldness and descending nature can cause diarrhea if you drink too much of it at once.

TAE-EUMIN FOODS AND HERBAL MEDICINES

The right foods for Tae-eumins nourish their yang while strengthening the function of the heart and lungs to invigorate blood circulation.

WHEAT

Wheat, with its cooling nature, is excellent for Tae-eumins because they develop internal heat and dryness due to the excessive gathering function and the weakness in circulation. It also has a calming effect on the minds of Tae-eumins, as they can easily develop fear and palpitation when out of balance.

SEEDS AND NUTS

Seeds enclosed in hard shells contain an enormous spring force that resists the strong gathering function of their shells. In other words, seeds have the effect of powerfully dispersing energy. Remember, the Taiyang energy can penetrate and sprout through the thick ground. Therefore, all varieties of nuts are excellent for Tae-eumins, such as walnuts, pine nuts, peanuts, almonds, chestnuts, and ginkgo nuts. Other seeds surrounded by a hard shell, such as Job's tears, and beans, are also good. In addition, since nuts and seeds contain vegetable oils made of unsaturated fatty acids, they can clean up the arteries of the Tae-eumin, overly accumulated with animal cholesterol.

BEEF

As Tae-eumins are overly greedy toward foods and have good digestion on par with Soyangins, they tend to eat a lot of meat. However, meats are generally unsuitable for this body constitution if they contain a lot of animal fats. Beef and deer meat are good for Tae-eumins, though removing beef from their diets may make more sense as it adds additional animal fats to a system already overloaded with fats. However, beef has the medicinal effect of stimulating metabolism to dissolve those animal fats. To understand this, you must first observe a cow.

Cows are slow in movement and have large bodies and horns. Being large physically can be compared to the unlimited energy stored in the ground during winter. Horns that protrude from their large heads have the same energy as new sprouts that penetrate outward in the spring. For this reason, cows can be considered animals with Taiyang energy. Therefore, eating beef invigorates the liver's function of regulating spring energy while offsetting the lungs' gathering function, which is overly active in Tae-eumins. In addition, the liver's energizing function will break down both the fats from beef and the accumulated fats. Many Koreans enjoy eating cooked cow's head, an excellent method for taking in Taiyang energy.

DEER HORN AND BEAR GALLBLADDER

Deer horn is the best medicine for strengthening the weak liver function in Tae-eumins. Deer are highly sensitive animals, easily frightened due to a strong liver function that quickly propels energy. This energy ascends and penetrates the head to create their horns. Among animals, deer are the most yang in nature, their heads the most yang part of their bodies. The most yang of this part is the velvet that springs forth in the springtime. However, the ossified bones, which the velvet turns into during autumn, are ineffective. Therefore, if Tae-eumins, who accumulate all energy into substance in their bodies, take deer horn, they would become just as sensitive as deer. Not only would their metabolisms speed up, but the cholesterol and fats accumulated within

their blood vessels would also break down and transform into energy.

Another medicine beneficial to the Tae-eumin constitution is the bear gallbladder. (Authors' note: We do not recommend that you go out and try to buy bear gallbladder, as it is an illegal substance. We are just presenting the concept behind how it works).

Bears are Taiyin animals. Due to the strong gathering function, they have reduced energy going to the musculoskeletal system and body surface. But their energy disperses even less to those regions during winter, when all of nature's energy is stored inward. So they must hibernate throughout winter.

The function of the liver is to wake up and ignite the bear's energy. Bile mediates this function of the liver. Coincidentally, the bear gallbladder strengthens the liver function in Tae-eumins as well. So when a person ingests a bear gallbladder, liver functions improve. This allows nutrients that are transformed into waste matter and act as toxins inside the blood vessels, such as cholesterol, to be converted into energy and detoxified. Unfortunately, though bear gallbladder is a wonderful medicine, you cannot improve the constitution with just a single dose.

FRUITS

Fruits good for Tae-eumins include pears, ume plums, plums, prunes, and apricots. The trees of these fruits are of similar families, sharing the "urgent" nature of blossoming flowers before the growth of leaves in the summer. They are trees with a dynamic springtime nature, therefore containing a lot of Taiyang energy. Since the fruits of these trees maintain seeds, they, too, have a strong Taiyang nature to supplement the liver function of Tae-eumins.

YAM

Yam is the root of a vine belonging to a genus of herbs called *Dioscorea*, which is therapeutic for Tae-eumins. Since the stem of its vine lacks spring energy and cannot grow straight up, it crawls on the ground instead. Its root has a strong function that tries to send the stem straight up. Because this is so, the root induces the liver's functions. Eating yam, however, has a much weaker medicinal effect compared to *Dioscorea opposita* (wild yam), the species used in Eastern medicine.

MA HUANG

This herb featured on TV, radio, in newspapers, and in magazines that deal with health and weight loss is the main ingredient in many popular weight-loss formulas. But unfortunately, it also happens to be the main ingredient in fen-phen, which has given heart problems to its users in recent times.

Ma huang is a pungent and warm herb. It is an herb that probably has the most vigorous dispersing action. Therefore, it is commonly used as a cold medicine, as it has the strongest diaphoretic, or sweat-producing, action of any known herb. Ephedrine is the main component of this herb. When observed, ma huang is like a thin twig with a hollow in the middle. This hollowness indicates that the energy is strongly dispersing outwardly. During the winter, you can also notice that snow around ma huang melts due to its hot and dispersing nature. Therefore, it is one of the best herbs for Tae-eumins. Nevertheless, those with a lot of body heat should not use it. It can quicken their heart rate and bring on problems such as palpitations, restlessness, insomnia, and hypertension.

SOEUMIN FOODS AND HERBAL MEDICINES

Soeumins are lacking in energy. Therefore, people with this constitution should take sweet foods or sweet herbal medicines, as those can readily turn into energy. Because Soeumin types have weak stomachs, no matter how good a medicine or supplement is, it can harm rather than help them if it is undigested. On the whole, easily digested foods or slightly pungent foods that stimulate digestion are beneficial. Additionally, fragrant foods with an active molecular activity are suitable for the Soeumin constitution.

GRAINS

For Soeumins, rice is the best grain, as rice is sweet and does not contain other tastes. With its warm nature, it also digests the best and strengthens the digestive system.

FRUITS

As far as fruits are concerned, many tropical fruits with a warm nature are good. They include mangoes, coconuts, peaches, Chinese dates, oranges, and ripe (not sour) Mandarin oranges. Although oranges and Mandarin oranges retain a slightly sour taste (a yin taste), they are still basically sweet and fragrant enough to facilitate digestion. Accordingly, Eastern medicine uses orange peels to aid digestion. Therefore, for the Soeumins, orange juice made with peels intact is better than eating an orange without peels.

MEAT

Though meats are good for Soeumins, as they are warming, they can sometimes be damaging for them due to the difficulty in digesting them. Therefore, pork is not recommended among meats, as it is the most difficult to digest. On the other hand, chickens are excellent, as they digest well, along with lamb, which has a sweet taste and warm temperature.

FISH

Although fish generally have a yin nature due to the influence of water, anchovies and yellow corvinas are very yang-natured. Anchovies are small and have quick movements. When you catch an anchovy and take it out of the water, the way it jumps up and down is similar to Shaoyang movements. In Korea, yellow corvinas are given to convalescent patients with weak digestion. These fish digest well, and they also strengthen the digestive system. In other words, they invigorate the stomach function.

SNAKES, EELS, AND LOACHES

Snakes, eels, and mudfish benefit the Soeumin person. As they are all dark-colored, creepy an-

imals, they possess a yin nature. However, they are also animals that dig holes to live in, implying their strong penetrating action. These animals are yang within yin, invigorating the yang energy within the kidneys and supplying yang energy to the pancreas. Scientifically speaking, these animals will most likely produce adrenal cortex hormones.

It was previously mentioned that kidneys have a winter action in Eastern medicine. The seeds produced through the act of winter of the previous generation, the essence of humans, are kept, and new ones are made and stored for the next generation. The essence contains both the original yin and the original yang. The original yang is necessary for the further production of the essence. The adrenal cortex controls the original yang, while the kidneys supervise the original yin.

Soeumins have an overly active yin function of the kidneys, which overwhelms the weak yang function of the pancreas. Therefore, to balance the Soeumin constitution, foods that can supplement the yang of the pancreas need to be consumed more often. But, more important, Soeumins need to eat foods that increase the original yang of the kidneys, since the yang of the pancreas depends on the original yang of the kidneys. Such foods include snakes, eels, and loaches (mudfish), which are yang within yin.

Foods that contain the original yang are also able to strengthen sexual vitality. Although Soeumins generally have good sexual stamina, their energy sometimes has trouble getting started. We can compare this to having whole ammunition stored in a ware-house but no desire to fight, or having a full gas tank but a weak or broken starter. Snakes, eels, and loaches are suitable for those who derive long-lasting pleasure during sex but have a problem initially feeling the urge for sex. It is better to eat these foods together with strong liquor, which will act as gunpowder, dynamically activating the yang energy.

VEGETABLES

Among vegetables, radishes, cabbages, onions, green onions, and garlic are suitable for the Soeumin constitution. Radishes and cabbages have sweet and pungent flavors, indicating that they have plenty of sugar, a source of instant energy, while the spicy taste facilitates digestion. Onions and green onions both also have powerful smells, indicating vigorous molecular activity for digestive stimulation. Since these vegetables can digest meat well, meat dishes taste better during meals that include these vegetables.

Onions, green onions, and garlic belong to the same allium family, having bulbous roots that sprout in all directions from the center and retain pungent tastes and strong smells. In the previous chapter, the "Sasang of Art" section mentioned that among the plum, orchid, chrysanthemum, and bamboo, the orchid retains the Shaoyang nature. Like the onion, green onion, and garlic, the orchid sprouts from a bulb, and its sharp leaves spread out in all directions. Orchids, however, cannot be used as food, since their leaves and roots are almost without water,

and the sweet taste needed by the body is not present.

In contrast, onions, green onions, and garlic are foods that contain water and essential nutrients. Since they have strong smells and pungent tastes that stimulate digestion, they are used similarly to spices. Among the three, garlic has the most vigorous yang nature. Therefore, it has been in the limelight recently as a health supplement. Theoretically, garlic supplements the yang lacking in the body. With the strong yang, its juices can kill molds that are yin in nature and microorganisms such as bacteria and viruses.

Since garlic is a food with strong yang energy, it can invigorate the yang in humans. Eating garlic activates bodily energy to speed metabolism and increase energy. As all bodily functions invigorate, the immune system becomes stronger to prevent disease, and the body's ability to recuperate speeds up.

Koreans love garlic so much that there is even a mythological story about garlic. No matter what type of dish they eat, Koreans always have garlic. Almost no Korean dish goes without garlic in it. For example, kimchi, a popular Korean side dish, comprises three-quarters Chinese cabbage and one-quarter garlic. Korean people consider any food eaten without kimchi a snack.

Many Japanese lived in Korea during the Japanese colonial era (1910–1945). When dysentery was widespread, many people died because no antibiotics were available. But, surprisingly, most people who died were Japanese. Once doctors discovered the antibacterial effect of the garlic, they explained the reason: because Koreans ate kimchi every day, the garlic worked to kill the bacteria that tried to invade their intestines.

Garlic is also perfect for sexual vitality. Try eating garlic and meat for one week and compare the effects to that of Viagra. They may stimulate your sexual impulses more and better prolong and sustain your erection than Viagra does. For this reason, garlic is one of the forbidden foods for Buddhist monks living in a temple, so as not to interfere with their training.

If you eat plenty of garlic, your erection in the morning will be better. In the case of men, women who pass by them will look more beautiful. In fact, whether or not women around them look prettier than in ordinary times is the yardstick of sexual vitality that they can measure on their own.

Yang-natured spices stimulate digestion. As previously mentioned, the main problem with meat is its digestability. Although both stimulate the digestion of meat, garlic is better for digesting beef, whereas ginger is good for pork. Both vegetables share the similarities of having pungent tastes and strong fragrances that give them their yang nature and the excellent ability to digest foods.

The fragrance of garlic spreads farther away than that of ginger, while its bulb has sharp leaves that extend from the center. This constitutes spring energy stored in the seed covered in a hard shell during the winter, penetrating outward. Since garlic has this Taiyang nature, it matches well with beef, which is also Taiyang in nature.

In contrast, the fragrance of ginger does not spread far and it does not have a round bulb. However, it has a stem, broader leaves, and a hotter taste than garlic. Thus, it has a yang nature in a more advanced stage, constituting the energy of summer when there is vigorous, energetic activity. With this Shaoyang nature, ginger offsets the extreme yin of pork, which belongs to Shaoyin. Therefore, combining beef and garlic, with their same Taiyang nature, and pork with ginger, which are opposites of Shaoyin and Shaoyang, might not make sense. Still, you should not forget the inversion principle discussed in chapter 3, "The Basic Principles of Yin and Yang." According to this principle, the application of yin-yang becomes the opposite, since Taiyang-Taiyin and Shaoyang-Shaoyin are polar.

Though garlic is good for Soeumins, it is also suitable for Tae-eumins as it contains both Taiyang and Shaoyang energetic natures. No matter how good the effect of garlic is, it is only suitable for Tae-eumins and Soeumins, but not Taeyangins and Soyangins. Garlic can harm yang types because it adds additional yang to those whose constitutions are already overflowing with yang.

To become healthy, you should always think about what your body is craving in the present state. You must pay attention to eating foods that can supplement the nutrients that are lacking in your body at the current time. In a healthy state, no matter how good the food is theoretically, it is not suitable if your body is not craving it. Therefore, you should select and eat the foods appropriate for your body type and try to avoid foods that do not match your body type. For example, if you are Tae-eumin, you should eat more nuts with a Taiyang nature and avoid grapes, kiwis, and cherries with Taiyin natures. If you are Soyangin, you should eat more pork and barley with Shaoyin energetics and avoid chicken and ginger, which have Shaoyang natures. Foods that are good for Taeyangins are harmful to Tae-eumins, just as foods beneficial for Soyangins are harmful to Soeumins, and vice versa. Please refer to the following chart for the foods that match your body type (table 16.1).

	Taeyangin	Soyangin	Tae-eumin	Soeumin
Grains	buckwheat	barley	wheat	rice
Meat	none	pork, duck, eggs	beef, deer	chicken, turkey, lamb
Seafood	sushi, clams	oysters, sea cucumbers, sea squirts, tortoises, turtles	brown seaweed, kelp, laver, cod, hairtail	anchovies, yellow corvinas, snakes, eels, mudfishes
Legumes and nuts	none	adzuki beans, mung beans	soybeans, peanuts, all varieties of nuts	sesame seeds
Vegetables	all vegetables (especially those in salads) except spices	cucumbers, lettuce, burdock, hops, celery, eggplant, potatoes	bean sprouts, cauliflower, broccoli, mushrooms, yams, radishes, water parsley, napa cabbage, garlic	cabbage, carrots, tomatoes, radishes, onions, green onions, garlic, ginger
Fruits	grapes, kiwis, cherries, Chinese quinces	strawberries, raspberries, blueberries, blackberries, boysenberries, pineapples, Korean melons, bananas, avocados	pears, plums, ume plums, prunes, apricots, cantaloupes, honeydew melons, watermelons, pumpkins	oranges, Mandarin oranges, peaches, apples, mangoes, Chinese dates, hawthorn berries
Other	wine, quince tea	raspberry wine, green tea, beer	beer, coffee	distilled liquor (kaoliang, soju), citron tea

Table 16.1 Dietary Guidelines for Four Body Types

17

The Five-Element Theory

木 Wood 火 Fire 土 Earth 金 Metal 水 Water

Ancient Inscriptions of Five Elements

Yin-Yang, Sasang, and the Five Elements

The entirety of Eastern philosophy is composed of the yin-yang and five-element theories. The I Ching, however, does not mention the five elements. Instead, it explains changing phenomena with the yin-yang principle, the binary system (2–4–8–64). Therefore, the five-element theory gives an alternative method of interpretation that allows for even more significant comprehension of the I Ching principles.

Both theories measure and define phenomena. Although their measurement modes are different, the objects they measure are the same. The five-element theory simply gives a more detailed and specific interpretation. For example, if we compare both theories to rulers, then the scale of yin-yang would be in inches. In contrast, the five-element theory would be in centimeters. Since the five-element ruler divides into more parts, it can express a more detailed view of the various aspects of the same thing. Another yin-yang ruler with a more detailed scale is called the Sasang ruler and closely resembles the five-element ruler (fig. 17.1).

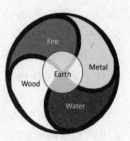

Figure 17.2 Yin-Yang of Universe

Figure 17.3 Five Elements of the Universe

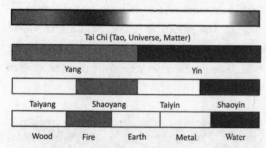

Figure 17.1 Tai Chi, Yin-Yang, Sasang, and Five-Element Rulers

The I Ching describes the entire universe and its changing pattern with yin and yang, Sasang, and the eight trigrams. On the other hand, the five-element theory explains them using five symbols: wood, fire, earth, metal, and water. Thus, the five-element theory divides the universe into five equal parts. The following diagrams express the universe from the yin-yang perspective of I Ching and the five elements (figs. 17.2 and 17.3).

Just as a measurement in centimeters can convert into inches, the five elements can convert into yin and yang. For example, wood and fire are yang, while metal and water are yin. The earth element corresponds to the center between yin and yang. In the Sasang classification, wood corresponds to Taiyang, fire corresponds to Shaoyang, metal corresponds to Taiyin, and water corresponds to Shaoyin.

Though Sasang and the five-element theories share similarities, neither can be excluded. The primary difference between the two is the addition of earth into the five-element theory. Earth is an expression of the dynamic relationship between yin and yang. Earth is within Sasang, but since Sasang is concerned with the formative or structural aspects of things, this dynamic expression is unmanifested. "Sang" in the word "Sasang" means "image" or "symbol," and "Xing" from "Wuxing" (five elements) means "movement." Thus, Sasang relates to the shape or structure of matter, while the five-element theory involves its function.

Both theories are interrelated. For example, a function can be implied by assessing an object's shape. In doing so, it is more appropriate to apply the Sasang theory to the properties of a form. Conversely, by knowing the function of an object, the shape can be inferred. Therefore, to properly grasp the function of an object, it is better to use the viewpoint of the five elements. This is why yin-yang and five-element theories coexist in Eastern philosophy.

When we are discussing one of the four aspects of Sasang, the emphasis must be on the totality of the Sasang. It is this totality of the Sasang that corresponds to the earth element. The earth element, which represents the state of yin-yang harmony of the whole, perpetually exists. It is just not clearly explained or manifested. So, again, the principle of all things in nature can be expressed only with the yin-yang theory. However, if the five-element theory is also understood, the function of all things in nature can be easily and speedily understood.

The Nature of the Five Elements

We have seen the importance of the five-element theory and its relations to the yin-yang and Sasang theories of the I Ching. Let's now discuss the individual attributes of each element and their relationship to each other. Each element has many correspondences, including color, sound, smell, emotion, and taste properties.

There is also a relationship between the individual elements and the internal organs based on their bodily functions, colors, and shapes. Furthermore, each internal organ has an external tissue to which it is connected. These external aspects reflect the health of the internal organ, thus illuminating problems of the elements that are out of balance.

WOOD

Wood represents birth. It is the beginning of new life and the force of Taiyang, transforming from a state of substance into one of dynamic energy. Thus it is spring, the beginning of a new year, and all activities in nature. In terms of direction, it corresponds to the east, where the sun rises. In nature, plants and trees epitomize the wood element (fig. 17.4). The nature of wood is to grow, and growth is movement. Therefore, all things that begin with movements also belong to the wood element. The organ that corresponds to wood is the liver, and its external counterpart is the eyes. The green color and sour taste belong to wood.

Figure 17.4

FIRE

Fire is bright, hot, moves quickly, and disappears easily (fig. 17.5). It has no definable shape. It is the force of Shaoyang that represents the energetics of summer. Wood and fire elements belong to yang, but wood represents yang's beginning, while fire is the zenith of yang. The south, a place of the greatest amount of sunlight, corresponds to the fire element in terms of direction. Among internal organs, the heart is considered the hottest organ. Thus it is associated with the fire element. On the face, the tongue, the most sizzling sense organ, belongs to fire. Among colors, red belongs to the fire element. In terms of taste, the bitter taste occurring from burnt things belongs to the fire element.

Figure 17.6

Figure 17.5

METAL

Metal is heavy, cold, solid, and stable (fig. 17.6). All those things in nature with these attributes belong to the metal element. As these attributes are yin, the metal element belongs to yin. It is the nature of metal to begin the transformation from energy into substance. The gathering force of Taiyin is the settling and declining of life. It is also the energetics of fruition and falling leaves in autumn and the sun's setting in the west. The internal organ that corresponds to metal is the lungs, and their external counterpart is the nose. The color white belongs to metal. In terms of taste, pungent corresponds to the metal element.

WATER

Water attributes are easier to understand when considering an ocean rather than a cup of water (fig. 17.7). Ocean water is cold and dark with enormous potential energy. It can sink and store anything. These attributes belong to yin, so water belongs to yin. Both the metal and water elements belong to yin. However, metal corresponds to the Taiyin, the beginning of yin. In contrast, water corresponds to the Shaoyin, the yin's zenith. Shaoyin also epitomizes the storing and cold energy of winter, the water element.

The fire and water elements have a polar relationship. Fire is the peak of the energetic activity, while water is the peak of materialization. The north, the coldest and darkest direction, corresponds to the water element. Among internal organs, the kidneys correspond to this element since they are dark and situated in the deepest part of the body. On the face, the ears belong to the water element because they are located at the head's rear and

Figure 17.7

are funnel-shaped to absorb sound. The black color and salty taste correspond to the water element.

EARTH

The meaning of the earth element is crucial because it is an addition to Sasang. Earth is a complicated element because of its multifaceted nature (fig. 17.8). The earth element comprises a mixture of components from the other four elements. There are components of wood, fire (volcanoes, magma), metal, and water con-

Figure 17.8

tained within the earth. In addition, it includes cold, hot, light, heavy, dark, and bright things. As a result of having both yin and yang, the nature of earth is the most balanced in yin and yang, more so than any other element. Therefore, all those things containing the intermediate nature of yin and yang belong to the earth element.

The entire universe, the Earth, and human beings are all harmonized in yin and yang. Therefore, they all belong to the earth element. Within Tai Chi, there is a balance of yin and yang. Thus Tai Chi as a whole corresponds to the earth element. Although the sky is yang and the ground is yin, all organisms situated between them are influenced by both and belong to the earth element.

Putting water on a fire extinguishes it. Striking a tree with an iron axe can kill it. But no matter what comes close to the earth, it does not reject it. The strength of earth is a virtue. In Confucianism, embracing everything is considered a virtue and is regarded as the greatest quality a human being should possess.

Many Confucian classics ultimately extol this virtue and emphasize how it should be kept in people's hearts. Also in Confucianism, the golden mean (moderation) is suggested as an action to be followed by human beings, which corresponds to the earth element. Neither too much (yang) nor too little (yin) is the golden mean. Unfortunately, commonly read Confucian classics do not provide detailed explanations of the I Ching's trigrams or hexagrams and the yin-yang and five elements. They also do not utilize these codes to explain ethics. Nevertheless, understanding the true meaning of Confucian classics is impossible without knowing I Ching and yin-yang and the five-element theories.

Tao, Tai Chi, and the earth element make up the nature of God, who, in turn, governs all things in the universe with impartiality. In maintaining this impartial balance, there exists death and sickness. In other words, good and evil coexist because both are necessary to maintain balance. Similarly, a mother's love is associated with the earth element in being unconditional. Coincidentally in the West, the earth is often compared to a mother, as in Mother Nature.

The earth element ensures that the other four elements stay in balance. If wood is overactive, it is transformed into fire; if fire is overactive, it is converted into metal; overactive metal is changed into water; and so on. Overactivity in one element is due to a weakness in its opposite element's functioning. Thus, the opposite element must be invigorated to bring it into balance. For example, if wood is overly strong, then metal, its opposite, is weak. Metal must therefore be strengthened to suppress wood's functioning.

The earth element oversees maintaining the harmony of seasonal cycles. The turning points between the seasons belong to the earth. When the growth function of spring is too strong, earth soothes and coaxes it into summer. When the energy-consuming function of summer becomes too strong, earth changes summer into autumn to begin the process of storing the captured energy as a substance. When enough energy is gathered by autumn, earth changes it into winter, which functions to store energy. Once activities come to a complete halt, earth gushes forth with the energy needed to incite spring again.

If life were to function linearly, it would disappear almost at once. The function of the earth element, then, is that of a centripetal force, changing linear movement into a circular movement for life to recycle continually. Atoms, molecules, the Earth, the solar system, and the entire universe continue in a perpetual circular motion due to the functioning of the earth element.

Yet if there is only movement without rest, things will disintegrate and disappear. And if there is only rest without movement, there is death. The earth element sets things that are resting (yin) into motion (yang), and makes things that are moving (yang) rest (yin). It gently pulls what is going forward (yang) backward (yin), and subtly causes that which is going backward (yin) to go forward (yang). The earth element causes everything to circulate or rotate endlessly; therefore, the earth element is the force of life itself.

Since the earth element must regulate the other four elements, it can best function as a regulatory mechanism if it lies in the center. If wood is on the left, fire is on top, metal is on the right, and water is on the bottom, then earth is in the center. Directionally, wood relates to the east, fire to the south, metal to the west, and water to the north. Earth, again, is found at the center. These relationships can be diagrammed as follows (fig. 17.9).

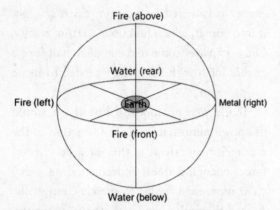

Figure 17.9 Directions and Five Elements

Ancient Eastern governing systems had the king at the center of the kingdom. Above the king was heaven (the principle of the universe or God), whose will the king followed. On the king's left was his prime minister, while on the right was his secondary minister, both men providing advice and support. Beneath the king were his subjects. In such a political system, the king was the earth element.

The most physically active parts of the human body are the four extremities. The arms and hands are yang, and the legs and feet are yin. Since most people are right-handed, the left hand is seen as having less natural movements and is, therefore, yin within yang. The right hand, which moves more freely, becomes yang within yang. The right leg is also less restricted, and thus yang within yin. The left leg, which is more limited, becomes yin within yin.

Put another way, the left hand is associated with wood and the right hand with fire. The right leg corresponds to metal, and the left leg to water. The brain, which governs the four

limbs, is the earth element. Seen from the exterior, as illustrated in the following diagram (fig. 17.10), the head becomes the earth element. The head becomes the center when looking at a person walking from the top.

Although the head is the center of physical movement, the abdomen becomes the center of nutrient supply. Thus, a human body contains two earth elements according to differing perspectives. We can break down every aspect of the body in such a manner.

For example, on the hand, the thumb represents the mother and belongs to the earth element. This is because the thumb can freely make contact with the other fingers, like the earth element that harmonizes and integrates

Figure 17.10 The Abdomen Is the Center.

all other elements and has an intimate cooperating function. In contrast, the rest of the digits have difficulty contacting fingers other than those right next to them.

The internal organ corresponding to the earth is the pancreas, situated in the body's center. This organ secretes a variety of digestive enzymes and insulin. Insulin controls sugar metabolism, the source of the body's energy. The pancreas's external counterpart is the mouth. Among colors, yellow belongs to the earth. Regarding tastes, sweet belongs to the earth element.

The Five Elements of Color

There are three primary colors, as previously mentioned in chapter 14 on the trinity principle. Green, red, and blue are the three generative colors, while blue, red, and yellow are the three reflective colors. A mixture of three generative colors results in white color, while that of three reflective colors is black color. White and black colors can also contrast each of the original colors. White color appears when the contrast is bright (high), and black occurs when the contrast is dark (low). Combinations of these colors create all the colors in nature.

The colors corresponding to each stage (force) are as follows:

- Trinity: red—yang; blue—yin; yellow—moderator
- Sasang: green—Taiyang; red—Shaoyang; yellow—Taiyin; black—Shaoyin

- The five elements: green—wood; red—fire; yellow—earth; white—metal; black—water

The natures of various colors were described in detail in chapter 15, "Sasang." We will reiterate some information to relate them to the five-element theory.

GREEN

The color of the wood element is green. Grasses, plants, buds, and leaves all rapidly proliferate. They are nature's green and the expression of the wood element's strength.

In Eastern philosophy, the term used for green is "Qing." However, this term also connotes blue. Therefore, it would be most appropriate to think of blue and green (bluish-green, like cyan) whenever there is a mention of the term "green." Green is the representative color of springtime. As it begins yang activity, green belongs to the wood element in the five-element theory.

When we look at green, we get a thought or feeling to go outside and begin working. Such a nature of green serves as a metaphor for a tree's springtime awakening to sprout after a long winter sleep. The green color happens to be the color of trees. When we look at the green color of mountains and plains, we think about our youth's dreams and dynamic activity. The green light in a traffic signal tells us to go because green gives us feelings to begin moving. We instinctively know that the objects with green color perform the function of the wood element of the springtime.

RED

In Eastern philosophy, the red color can imply a wide variety of things, such as the redness of fire, sun, blood, and flowers. No matter what it is, there is heat when there is a dynamic activity. When there is heat, it turns into the red color. So red is the color that appears when a substance is at its peak of yang energy, or when the yang is in its zenith and belongs to fire among the five elements.

We can say that there is a vigorous, energetic activity within things with a red color. We can say that the sun is the reddest and has the most significant energetic activity among things around us. The blood in the heart is the reddest and has the fastest activity in our bodies. Among plant sources, red chili peppers are red; when a person eats one, sweating and blood circulation become invigorated. Experiments have confirmed that when people are under the influence of red floodlights, they become excited, and their body temperatures rise.

WHITE

The color white appears when there is only reflection without absorption of the full spectrum of colors. It emerges immediately before the energetic activity comes to a halt. All things with white color will soon stop the energetic activity and begin to contract. The hair of older adults turns white because their bodies are now beginning to cease activity.

When we look at the white color, we think about the mountains and plains covered in snow and feel the tranquility and solitude. We also sense cleanliness and purity. These are emotions that are felt when there is a stoppage of all activities.

White mainly serves as a background color, extends widely, and does not reveal itself. The nature of white color corresponds to the nature of the metal element that stops vigorous activity and promotes rest. The white color is also the bright color of the metal. Therefore, we can instinctively know that the objects with white color have the function of metal, which is the function of autumn.

On a wedding day, the bride wears a white dress. This indicates how she will now stop the frivolous or imprudent lifestyle (activities of wood, fire element) and marry (function of metal element) and may produce a baby (function of water) to become a mother.

BLACK

Black color implies the dark of the night or charcoal. It occurs when the activity consuming energy comes to a halt. It is the color that appears when yin is at its extreme and belongs to water in the five-element theory. We can say that those things with black color have slower activity than those with other colors. Due to its yin nature, it can absorb things. This is why charcoal can absorb many types of substances. Charcoal goes into water purifiers and absorbs impure substances, so it has the effect of purifying the water. When the light is made dark, people become calm and sleepy. So if you want to rest your body and mind, you must dim the lighting and make the color of the walls and furniture darker.

When we look at the color black, we bring up images of darkness and death and become fearful. Black is the color of death and brings energetic activity to a complete stop. People become afraid of the color black because it appears when an action opposite to the life of human beings occurs. Black cats, bats, and dark clothes of the devil or Dracula cause fear because objects with black color stop the energetic activity and take away life. Since the color of death is black, we often wear black when we attend funerals.

The most exuberant energetic activity in plants takes place when flowers are blossoming. So all flowers have bright colors. There are no flowers that have completely black color, as black represents the halting of energetic activity.

Kidneys have the darkest color among our bodies' five Zang (solid) organs. The function of kidneys is to filter impure substances. During one's lifetime, the period of old age is when the activity is slowest. That is why the skin of the elderly may be darker in comparison to children's.

Yellow

The color of earth is yellow. Yellow is the color of ripening; grainfields are often yellow at harvesttime, and so are some lush ripened fruits. Yellow represents harmony, stability, and abundance. It is the general color of the earth (soil) and the color of gold, which symbolizes permanence and affluence.

Gazing at the yellow color brings peace to mind, like looking at our mothers when we were young, or the Earth's vastness. Gold is the most precious among rare metals because it provides the same feeling.

Yellow is the earth element's color, and so it is the most balanced. Therefore, kings wear golden crowns and use golden ornamentation, because yellow, the color of the center, is the color of objects that govern the energy of all four directions.

All objects with a yellow color belong to the earth element, and so they harmonize and resolve the conflict between objects tilted toward yin or yang or toward the natures of wood, fire, metal, or water. For instance, yellow mediates and harmonizes the green of spring and summer with the white (frost or snow) of autumn and winter. It also mediates and harmonizes the darkness (black) of night and the light (red) of the day. In other words, things of earth nature balance all other elements.

Again, when we see yellow, we think of a field that has turned yellow when the rice is ripe, and of abundance, stability, and harmony. So we value things with yellow color and try to approach them. Generally, those with yellow color have a fragrant smell and sweet taste. It would be the central tone on the musical scale if it made a sound. However, some yellow things have a foul odor and bitter taste. This is the reason why people try to avoid feces. Although they have a yellow color, it does not have all the attributes of the earth element. Because yellow contains all of the wood, fire, metal, and water elements, the functional

234 • THE SECRETS OF THE I CHING

characteristics of a yellow object that we feel instinctively are not strong.

We have learned the relationship between the colors and the five elements. Each color represents the energetic nature of the five elements, and every substance in this universe manifests in one or more colors. There is, however, a deeper connotation to colors in the overall scheme of things.

Science teaches that everything humans can see with the naked eye has a particular color that is part of the rainbow made by the refraction of sunlight. A Buddhist expression aptly describes the relationship between the colors of nature and the true nature of things. Among the eighty thousand sutras in Buddhism, one called the Heart Sutra is considered the single most crucial sutra. It contains the phrase "Color is emptiness and emptiness is color," which is the core of Buddhist teachings.

Although the rainbow has seven colors, when light breaks down, there are only three colors that combine to form the additional four. These, as previously stated, are the primary colors of red, blue, and yellow. There are two natures of light. One is reflective, and the other is generative. Reflective light is the light we see when sunlight hits off of an object. We see the color not in the object but as a reflection absorbed through the eyes.

Generative light is the light source, like a laser or sunlight, which is the light's actual color. When the three reflective colors of red, blue, and yellow combine, black appears. When the three generative light colors of red,

blue, and green unite, the outcome is white. Black occurs when all light is absorbed. White is the reflection of all light. Thus, it is black (yin) when there is no light and white (yang) when there are significant amounts of light.

Meanwhile, the three reflective colors occur when there is a medium-light intensity. From the perspective of human beings as the center, the universe comprises such a light system. From a human perspective, white sunlight is above, while plants, animals, and minerals are in the center, created from a mixture of the three reflective colors plus white and black. Deep in the ground is the black color.

Everything in the universe has its unique color based on combining the five elemental colors. And everything has its peculiar characteristics and functions, understood by analyzing its colors based on the five-element theory. Therefore, we can determine the five fundamental natures in all things by understanding the functions of the five essential colors.

Rainbow-Striped Garments for Children

Korean children frequently wear clothing with colorful striped sleeves (fig. 17.11). The colors of the sleeves are similar to the seven colors of the rainbow. It is not exactly known when children began wearing rainbow-striped clothing. Still, it seems that the Korean ancestors wanted to naturally teach the children the principles of the I Ching by having them wear these clothes. The clothes teach the principles of change of the five fundamental colors, including the additional color of white, the base of the cloth, and the black color that appears when the clothing becomes dirty. Due to their bright yang nature, the three reflective colors appeal more to children (yang) than to adults (yin). Not only do the children wear striped-color clothing, but they frequently play with multicolored tops.

Figure 17.11 Traditional Korean Children's Clothing

Spinning Tops

Everything in the universe is in a constant spin. The Earth rotates on its axis, carrying all of its inhabitants. It revolves around the sun, together with the moon and all other planets that make up our solar system. The sun is also in constant motion, moving our solar system in rotation with others. The universe itself is in a spin, possibly moving with other universes.

On a microcosmic level, the atom's electrons and nucleus spin. Even the molecules spin, so long as they don't collide with one another. Microcosm and macrocosm mirror one another, spinning, moving, growing, and destroying.

All objects that are spinning have circular shapes. The Earth is round, and so are the stars and suns. A spinning top symbolizes an atom, the Earth, and the universe. In Korea, children play with these spinning tops, which they paint with multiple colors (fig. 17.12). The tops teach the children about the motion of the universe. Spinning the multicolored top is like spinning a small universe or the Earth that contains various things.

Figure 17.12 Children's Tops

If the I Ching expresses the universe through the symbols of yin and yang, the top expresses the universe through its color and shape. A top consists of a piece of metal (yin) at the center and wood (yang) surrounding the metal. When the top spins, there are two forces at play. One is the centrifugal force, which causes the wood to move or spin outward. The other is the centripetal force that makes the piece of metal move or rotate inward. Like these two contrasting forces, wood and metal have opposing natures (metal controls wood). As proof, when the colored top spins, the color becomes darker toward the center or down the spinning top.

If the top is a hemisphere, the colorful equator (the flat surface on top) can immediately change to resemble the black tip of the southern pole (the piece of metal in the center at the bottom). Thus, the top also expresses the Buddhist principle of "Color is emptiness and emptiness is color."

The differences we perceive in nature are dependent upon our point of view. All things in nature with different colors and shapes are identical substances that appear temporarily dissimilar depending on the angle of view. Therefore, the spinning top ultimately teaches us that the universe is of one piece and that friends and enemies are of one body.

Like the two sides of a coin, myriad colors of the universe are merely yang cross sections arising from the dark spot (yin, black hole) at the center of the circular movement of the top's lowest point. According to the viewpoint, they can become a black spot (bottom) or a world of tumultuous colors (top). With its various colors currently looked at, the world is only a cross section of space at a certain time, while yin is transforming into yang and yang into yin. It is just a slow video that lasts tens or hundreds of years.

By a child's hand, the top repeatedly spins and stops. Moment after moment, the locations of the colors change directions. While the top is spinning, blue and yellow combine to form green, yellow and red combine to form orange, and red and blue to form purple. Again, all the colors combine to create innumerable colors and ultimately concentrate back into the black. Looking at the changing colors of the top is like looking at the creation of the universe.

People who know of the dark and solemn atmosphere inside a Buddhist temple become surprised at the brilliant decoration of its exterior (figs. 17.13 and 17.14). This, too, like the spinning top, gives a lesson on the principle of "Color is emptiness and emptiness is color." It does so by harmonizing the solemnness of Buddha, who achieved enlightenment of the "emptiness" within, and the brilliant exterior decoration.

Figure 17.13 Exterior Ceiling of a Buddhist Temple, Geumsansa, Wanju, Korea

Figure 17.14 Exterior Ceiling of a Buddhist Temple, Jeondeungsa, Incheon, Korea

Sounds and the Five Elements

All things that move create sounds. For example, atoms vibrate at a tremendous rate and move like waves. But they give off sounds beyond the range of human hearing. Similarly, the Earth rotates rapidly, creating a sound humans cannot hear. However, when gauged by various measuring instruments, the sound reveals itself in the form of a wave.

Our perceptions of sound, color, smell, and taste are not much different. Each sound is distinguished by its wave and frequency, as are the diverse colors. The fragrance of a rose is at a certain frequency, just as the smell of fish is at another. Even various tastes are distinguished because they differ in frequencies as well.

The smallest unit of matter is a quark, and a quark has two aspects: a particle and a wave. Therefore, all matter in existence appears as a wave, which is measurable. According to the five-element theory, we can classify all things as waves of five types.

The sounds that fall into the human audible frequency range belong to the earth element. When a wave falls into the range of 20 to 20,000 hertz, it vibrates the eardrum, allowing humans to hear the sound. Under certain conditions, ultrasound can chase pests like rats and mosquitoes away because these frequencies beyond human hearing range have a significant tilt of yin and yang. Sounds of this nature can threaten the lives of organisms able to hear them. Waves with lower than audible frequencies correspond to yin, whereas waves with higher frequencies pertain to yang.

We can further divide even sounds within the audible range. Just as there are yin and yang within yin and yang, there are wood, fire, earth, metal, and water elements within the earth element. Sounds made by humans or animals correspond to the earth element. The sound of thunder or an earthquake, on the other hand, because it wakes nature and causes change to take place, belongs to the wood element. The rain sounds, the flowing of streams, and ocean waves all belong to the water element. The unmistakable sound that occurs from metal clashing (i.e., cymbals) belongs to the metal element. The sounds of a car accelerating, the scream of a fire engine, a machine running, and a volcano eruption all belong to the fire element.

Furthermore, the sounds of humans and animals can also divide into five elements. The human voice belongs to the earth element, which is the most harmonized in yin-yang. Of the human sounds, singing also belongs to the earth element, whereas the sound of shouting belongs to wood. Exuberant use of energy makes a person happy, and laughing occurs spontaneously. Therefore, laughter belongs to fire. Crying, on the other hand, belongs to the metal element. It is a sound intermittently made when energy is confined, because the use of energy is almost impossible. Crying comes out as the shoulders, which belong to the fire element, droop.

There are two types of moaning. One is a sound made when a person is sick or dying, and the other is the sound of pleasure during sex. Moaning corresponds to the water element, which can divide into yin and yang. The yin aspect of the water element is the period from the beginning of its function to its peak. The yang aspect is from its peak to when it converts into the wood element. Moaning due to illness belongs to the yin part of the water element, as it is the sound made when energy is about to be cut off. Moaning during sex, in contrast, pertains to the yang part of the water element. Here, water's function of contracting energy into matter has reached its zenith, and the energy revives again.

Each sound can further divide. The sound of singing, for example, can be divided into five musical scales. Traditional Korean music consists of five octaves, each with five scales. Each scale also contains the five elements.

The note that belongs to the earth element is called "Goong" ("G" or "so" on the Western scale); the note belonging to the fire element is called "Chi" ("D" or "re"). The note that corresponds to the metal element is "Sang" ("A" or "la"); that which belongs to the water element is "Woo" ("E" or "mi"). Finally, the note that belongs to the wood element is "Gak" ("C" or "do").

Goong is symbolic of a palace located in the center, the position of the earth element. It is the abode of the king who regulates and governs. It is also the sound made by a baby calling for its mother.

The diatonic scale of Western music, which uses seven notes (those above as well as ti and fa), combines two additional half notes with the five notes used in the pentatonic scale of Eastern music. The diatonic scale may be more convenient for the performance of manufactured music. In contrast, the pentatonic scale may be more suitable for expressing the music created by nature and gauging the principle of all things in nature.

Smell and the Five Elements

A smell results from molecules detaching from a substance and directly stimulating the olfactory nerves in the nose. Each substance has a distinctive smell, making it easy to identify. Although certain substances seem not to have a scent, the reality is that their scent lies beyond the capabilities of the human senses. This is evident in the way that animals pick up odors that humans cannot.

As in sound, smell, too, has five fundamental types. These five smells combine in various ways to create all scents. For example, the fragrance of ripe fruit or flowers belongs to the earth element. Substances with such pleasant smells can often be eaten and thus benefit human lives. These organic compounds have a harmonious balance of yin and yang. Compounds with an extreme tilt toward yin or yang will cause harm to the human body and correspondingly have a foul smell.

A burning smell belongs to the fire element. It is sickening to smell the burning of rubber or plastic, but the smell of meat slightly burning is pleasant to most people. The reason is that raw meat has a high concentration of nutrients that are hard to digest and assimilate. The slightly burnt smell of cooked meat is pleasant because, through cooking, it becomes easier to digest. Because bread digests more quickly than meat, the smell of burning bread (not baked) is not as pleasant as meat, and that of vegetables is even less so.

Eastern medicine slightly burns the herbs utilized to facilitate digestion. In particular, if an herb has an excessively yin nature (e.g., cold, heavy), which can hinder digestion, it is slightly burned before use. For example, licorice is baked in honey to help facilitate its digestion. However, this is not necessary for substances that are naturally easy to digest.

Eastern medicine describes the action of the stomach as "churning and ripening" to break down food. It is necessary to add heat to the stomach to perform this function. Suppose the heat has already been added to the food, as indicated by its burnt smell. Then it is tastier and more easily digested. In contrast, if a substance has a burnt smell without being burned, we can assume that it possesses the exuberant activity of the fire element.

A rotten smell belongs to the water element. Rotting occurs at death when activity stops. Eating or smelling a substance with a putrid odor slows the body's activity. Thus, if a person or an animal is sick and has a high fever, constipation, and excess sweating, substances with a putrid smell can be taken as medicine to cool the body. The reason for this is quite simple. When the physiological function is not in balance, correction is a must. Eating rotten food (water element) will control the fire and restore balance for a state that tilts toward the fire element.

A goatish smell is a smell of animals with hair or feathers, like a veterinary hospital. This smell belongs to the wood element. Though it does not have as exuberant an energetic activity as fire, it often occurs in animals that all have some dynamic, energetic activity.

A fishy smell belongs to the metal element and is the smell of raw meat or fish. The smell also occurs when energetic activity begins to slow down. For example, it occurs just before the rotting of a dead animal. It is also the smell of animals that live in the water. These animals are considered yang within the water and are closer to the metal element. Substances with a fishy smell are in a state in which energetic activity is slowing down, and the function of materialization is taking place.

The Five Elements of Taste

The sense of taste plays a vital role in distinguishing the nature of matter. In particular, taste is indispensable for finding out the effects of foods or herbs. Since foods and herbs are organic compounds, it would not be possible to determine their effects by analyzing their components. It is laughable to say that a certain herb will have a specific action because it contains a particular ingredient. This would be like visiting New York City at night and seeing many homeless people, then saying that the United States is a place where only homeless people live.

If a substance in an organism has a certain one-directional nature, another substance within the organism must exist with the exact opposite nature. This is the only way an organism can survive without dying. In fact, the main difference between organic and inorganic matter is that in organic matter, yin and yang form a harmonious balance so that a one-directional action does not occur.

The components that form a single herb each have their unique taste. The mixture of these tastes creates a composite taste. Consider what happens when a color picture printed with a computer printer is enlarged. Different-colored, individual dots (pixels) form an image (fig. 17.15). These dots are only one of five colors and are round in shape. Together they depict a particular form and color scheme. The same holds true for tastes.

You cannot say these pictures are Marilyn Monroe. Medicinal effect of a single herbal component cannot be the effect of the whole herb.

Figure 17.15 The picture on the right is not Marilyn Monroe—it is made up of a bunch of smaller individual pictures. The medicinal effect of a single herbal component cannot be the effect of the whole herb.

Let's suppose that ginseng has sixty-four components that compare to the pixels of a computer picture. Each component has an individual taste. Those tastes gather to make the single composite taste of ginseng. Only by understanding which of the five elements that the combined taste belongs to can the full effect of ginseng be known.

However, it would be wrong to select only one or two of ginseng's components and assume that their tastes and corresponding effects parallel the whole of ginseng. It would be like observing only one or two pixels' colors and saying those colors create the entire computer image.

Unlike water, herbs are a composite of many substances. Thus, it is impossible to assume the effect of herbs based on chemical analysis unless the nature of each substance is entirely discovered and understood. Only holistic analysis based on taste makes it possible to measure the effect of herbs. Therefore, the five-element classification of colors, smells, and tastes are necessary to best analyze the effect of herbs.

If possible, nuclear magnetic resonance (NMR) spectroscopy[1] can be mobilized to figure out the wave pattern of each atomic unit and the pattern of the overall composite of waves formed by those units. Then, analyzing them according to the five-element theory will make it possible to determine the effect of each herb more precisely.

The relationship between each taste and the five elements is as follows:

- A sour taste belongs to the wood element.
- A bitter taste belongs to the fire element.
- A pungent taste belongs to the metal element.
- A salty taste belongs to the water element.
- A sweet taste belongs to the earth element.

The unripe fruit on a tree tastes sour, so the taste of the wood element is said to be sour. Burnt substances taste bitter, so the taste of the fire element is said to be bitter. Placed on the tongue, a piece of metal has a biting taste, thus, the taste of the metal element is considered pungent. The ocean, the most significant body of water, tastes salty. The taste of the water element, therefore, is considered salty.

On the other hand, the taste of the earth element is sweet. Grains, which best represent substances that arise from the earth, are sweet. Although it is unlike the sweet taste of sugar, even yellow soil has a slightly sweet taste, which is why the earth has a sweet taste.

Because of the inversion principle, all tastes perform the actions of their opposite elements when they enter the body. In other words:

- A sour taste (wood element) gathers energy (a function of the metal element).
- A pungent taste (metal element) activates energy (a function of the wood element).
- A bitter taste (fire element) hinders energetic activity (a function of the water element).
- A salty taste (water element) brings energetic activity to its zenith (a function of the fire element).

The only exception to this involves the sweet taste of the earth element. Sweet has the function of augmenting and boosting and moderating energy. Like the earth element itself, sweet tastes have a harmonizing effect when they enter the body.

For further information on tastes, please refer to the yin-yang of foods (chapter 7) and the five elements of herbs (chapter 20).

The following table classifies common objects and functions according to the five-element theory (table 17.1).

The Principles of the Five Elements

All elements are intimately related to each other in one of two ways. They either support one another or they restrain each other. The supporting relationship is known as the Generating Cycle, and the restraining relationship is called the Controlling Cycle (fig. 17.16). For example, according to the yin-yang theory, how yin produces yang and yang gives rise to yin corresponds to the Generating Cycle. In contrast, the opposition in yin and yang's polar natures belongs to the Controlling Cycle.

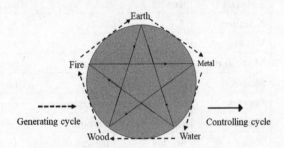

Figure 17.16 Generating and Controlling Cycles

THE GENERATING CYCLE

Wood generates fire, fire generates earth, earth generates metal, metal generates water, and water generates wood, thus completing a cycle.

Elements	Wood	Fire	Earth	Metal	Water
Seasons	spring	summer	late summer and transition of seasons	autumn	winter
Directions	east	south	center	west	north
	left	front	center	right	rear
	left	top	center	right	bottom
Functions	generating	growing	transforming	gathering	storing
	ascending	dispersing	harmonizing	collecting	descending
Weather	wind	heat	dampness	dryness	cold
Viscera	liver	heart	spleen/pancreas	lung	kidney
Bowels	gall bladder	small intestine	stomach	large intestine	urinary bladder
Sense organs	eyes	tongue	mouth	nose	ears
Tissues	tendons	blood vessels	muscles and flesh	skin and body hair	bones, bone marrow
Senses	vision	taste	touch	smell	hearing
Emotions	anger	joy	contemplation	grief	fear
Taste	sour	bitter	sweet	pungent	salty
Color	green	red	yellow	white	black
Sounds	shouting	laughing	singing	crying	moaning
Smell	goatish	burnt	fragrant	fishy	rotten
Bodily fluids	tears	sweat	slobber	snot	spittle
Animals	reptiles	birds	mammals	shelled animals	fishes
Numbers	3, 8	2, 7	5, 10	4, 9	1, 6
Vowels	e	i	a	o	u
Musical note	gak (do)	chi (re)	goong (so)	sang (la)	woo (mi)
Shape	△	▽	O	▫	•
Fingers	middle finger	index finger	thumb	ring finger	pinky finger
Musical tone	alto	soprano	tenor	baritone	bass
Tree	branch	flowers and leaves	stem	fruit	roots
Human body	left hand	right hand	head	right foot	left foot

Table 17. 1 Five-Element Classification

This cycle expresses the process of change among the five elements. The five elements represent a changing process. When the elements in generating relationships are next to each other, they are in a supportive relationship comparable to the mother-son relationship.

Wood, for example, provides fuel for the fire, which, when extinguished, creates ash. The ash then becomes the earth. The reason why ash makes a good fertilizer is that they are both of a similar nature. When the earth hardens, it becomes stone, which contains metal. When metal melts, it flows like water, as the ice melts into water. In addition, in the physical world, water is always found where there is metal ore. Finally, wood grows by absorbing water, and the cycle begins again.

The five elements are merely symbols representing substances and phenomena that form the earth. Thus the element wood does not only represent the wood in trees. It also embodies the total group of all things in nature, with wood attributes or substances signifying its functions.

In transforming substance into energy, wood can be easily understood by thinking of it as the beginning stage of energy created from the substance, and the manifestation of that process. On the other hand, metal represents the beginning stage of a substance formed by gathering energy, and the embodiment of that process.

Here is an example of how the Generating Cycle works. When the liver, which belongs to the wood element, is diseased, blood congestion in the liver can result in congestive heart failure. This is wood (liver disease) generating fire (heart disease).

Let's look at another example. When too many trees are growing in a certain region, a forest fire can easily start due to the high oxygen concentration in the area. The fire is needed to create more carbon dioxide; it burns the trees to balance the quantities of the two gases. This is a natural phenomenon of wood producing fire.

The earth element mediates wood's generation of fire. When one of the elements becomes excessive, the earth transforms it into another element to maintain an overall balance.

Wood and fire have a mother-son relationship. The wood element is the mother, and the fire element is the son. The mother tries to help her son first by consuming nutrients that would go to her body so that she can create her son. Then she gives of herself 100 percent to raise this child. She then disappears around the time the child is ready to become independent. Such a relationship is the Generating Cycle.

THE CONTROLLING CYCLE

The forces of nature help or restrict and hinder one another. The relationship between the five elements also follows this course. The interaction of yin and yang, which at times attract or reject each other, demonstrates this principle. We've seen how certain elements can produce other elements; now, let's look at how they can control one another.

In the five-element theory, water restrains fire, earth restrains water, wood restrains earth, metal restrains wood, and fire restrains metal. This is one complete Controlling Cycle.

The Generating Cycle incites things to go forward (in the direction of yang or production). In contrast, the Controlling Cycle initiates things to go backward (in the direction of yin or destruction). Through the functioning of both cycles, every movement in the universe is in a state of oscillation. The Generating Cycle pushes everything out from the center, creating a centrifugal force. On the other hand, the Controlling Cycle pulls everything back in, creating a centripetal force. In terms of human life, the centrifugal force is the desire to go off to faraway places when one is young. The centripetal force is the desire to return home when one is old.

The circular movement of all things in nature occurs due to the Generating and Controlling Cycles. On a microcosmic level, an electron orbits around the nucleus in an atom, making tiny yet rapid circular movements. The nucleus itself has orbiting particles, which also make circular movements. Molecules that have orbiting atoms make circular movements themselves. Cells made up of such molecules would undoubtedly also move in a circular motion if there were no surrounding obstacles.

On a larger scale, animals make circular movements around their sleeping sites. In addition, when the animals are about to die, they return to an area near their birthplaces if they can.

When we are looking at circular movement from a 90-degree angle, it seems to oscillate or vibrate. When this movement is not observable

to the naked eye, as in atoms or molecules, there is a high probability that the circular movements also look like oscillations (alternating motions). According to time, the effects of this vibration move outward, like ripples on water. A diagram of this interaction will look like a sine wave (fig. 17.17). Ultimately, it is nothing more than the unfolding of circular movements across time. Such is the essence of yin-yang, Sasang, and the five elements.

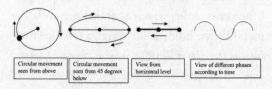

Figure 17.17 Circular Movements

Circular movement can arise from the total of the Generating Cycle and the Controlling Cycle vectors, as illustrated in the following diagram (fig. 17.18).

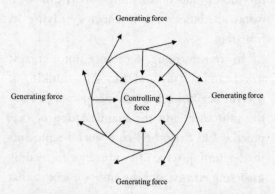

Figure 17.18 Generating and Controlling Cycles

If only a Generating Cycle existed without a Controlling Cycle, the movement would only occur in one direction, and everything would ultimately disappear. This is because the relationship between the two cycles is necessary for the circular motion to occur. Thus, the Generating and Controlling Cycles occur for the perpetual existence of the universe through the repetition of circular movements; this promotes constant regeneration. Without both cycles, there would be no life or death.

The Generating and Controlling Cycles are themselves yin and yang. The Generating Cycle is yang, and the Controlling Cycle is yin. The earth element supervises and mediates their movements. Here, earth's purpose is to create continuous, perpetual motion, the basis for the harmony of yin and yang.

The following are some examples of this harmony. Some trees that grow by absorbing water can only grow straight when trimmed by a metal instrument (pruning). The fire that occurs by burning wood can burn for a long time when restrained by water. For example, a damp log will take longer to burn than a dry one. The fertile earth that results from ashes is not swept away by a flood if the roots of trees are firmly grounded in it. Metal, produced by a transformation of the earth, has value only when refined and shaped by fire. Water can flow without becoming stale only when regulated by the earth (as in high and low embankments).

Typically, we think of things that control as harming (doing evil to) the controlled things. However, though often considered undesirable, control may be beneficial (doing good) from a holistic perspective. Misfortune, for example, as a manifestation of control, can be thought of and used as something to train and cultivate a person. If a person can positively deal with it in such a way, there will come a time when the circular motion will head upward (in the positive direction). Therefore, the person can gain peace of mind even amid misfortune.

Hado and Nakseo: Two Maps of the Universe

The history of the I Ching is shrouded in myth and mystery. Legend has it that Emperor Fuxi, generally regarded as the founder of China, saw a dragon-horse come out of the Yellow River some five thousand years ago. On the back of this beast were fifty-five dots that formed a star-shaped marking. After studying this diagram, Fuxi understood the master plan of the universe and mapped the dots, now called Hado, or the Yellow River Map (fig. 17.19). He discovered the laws of creation and development of the universe within the placement of the fifty-five dots. He realized the intrinsic principle of the universe and how everything undergoes such limitless variation that the human mind cannot comprehend the complexities.

From this map, Fuxi designed his version of the placement of the eight trigrams of the I Ching, known as the Earlier Heaven sequence of the eight trigrams (see chapter 22 for details). The Hado is the blueprint for the I Ching and the universe. Other than creating the I Ching, Emperor Fuxi is also credited with teaching the people of China the necessary skills to survive and thrive in the country. He taught them to fish, trap, cook, write, and chart the heavenly and earthly cycles. He is known as the First Mythical Emperor of China.

About one thousand years after the discovery of Hado, a portion of China was experiencing a flood. Emperor Yu of the Xia dynasty (ca. 2070–ca. 1600 BCE) was down by the River Lo, trying to find a way to control the raging water. Out of the river came a turtle carrying mysterious markings on its back. Emperor Yu recognized the importance of these markings. From them, he generated Nakseo, or the River Lo Map (fig. 17.20). The principles inherent in the map gave Emperor Yu the insight necessary to control the flood. It also served as the basis for creating the Later Heaven arrangement of trigrams by King Wen, the founder of the Zhou dynasty. In contrast to the Hado, Nakseo describes the principle of the Controlling Cycle, or the destructive forces of the universe, balancing the generating energetics of the Hado.

Although these maps do not explicitly state any of the principles drawn from them, their symbols and numerological significance hold the information necessary to understand what guides the universe.

It is easy to question how such simple drawings could so clearly express the principles of change in the universe. Therefore, it is also easy to disregard them. However, upon closer inspection and with the help of knowledgeable teachers, one learns that there are several volumes' worth of information one can write on the deep meanings of these drawings. Nevertheless, for

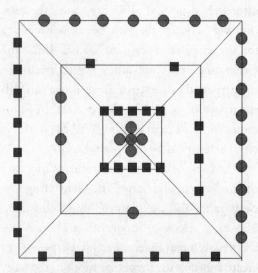

Figure 17.19 Hado (Yellow River Map)

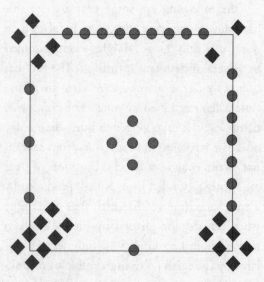

Figure 17.20 Nakseo (River Lo Map)

this book, we will try to simplify those meanings.

To understand the drawings, it is necessary to first learn about the numbers' yin-yang and five-element assignments. Odd numbers are not stable and they express movement; therefore, they are yang in nature and are drawn using light colors. Even numbers, on the other hand, are stable and they express immobility; therefore, these are yin in nature and are drawn using dark colors.

Hado (The Yellow River Map)

Numbers 1 and 6, assigned to the northern direction at the bottom of the drawing, represent the water element. Numbers 2 and 7 represent the fire element and are attached to the southern direction at the top. Numbers 3 and 8 represent the wood element; these are assigned to the eastern direction, the left side. Numbers 4 and 9, allocated to the western direction on the right side, represent the metal element. Finally, positioned at the center, 5 and 10 represent the earth element.

Different energies come from each of the four directions. The energy of water comes from the north, the energy of fire comes from the south, the energy of wood comes from the east, and the energy of metal comes from the west. The earth's balanced energy comes from the center. The exterior of these energies exists as a form or shape. So the inside numbers, representing energy or function, pair up with outside numbers, signifying form or shape. Each energy-form pair is then attached to its corresponding direction.

The numbers from 1 to 5 are generating numbers representing energy and are placed on the inside. Positioned on the outside, the numbers 6 to 10 are completing numbers and

denote form. The yin-yang pairing of corresponding numbers indicates the inversion (form-function) principle. As mentioned, this principle states that yang-natured energy has a yin-natured form. In contrast, yin-natured energy has a yang-natured form.

The quiet and dark energy of the north is represented by number 1. The energy of its opposite, the south, is represented by number 2. The energy of the east, created by the interaction of 1 and 2, is represented by the number 3. The energy of its opposite, the west, is represented by the number 4. The center, which has the energy of all four directions, is represented by the number 5. The number 6, made by adding 1 to 5, is again placed in the north. The number 7, formed by adding 2 to 5, is placed in the south. The number 8, placed in the east, is made by adding the number 3 to the number 5. The number 9, made by adding 4 to 5, is placed in the west. Finally, 10 is formed by adding 5 to 5 and is assigned to the center.

According to Hado, the numbers 1 and 2 oppose each other, as do 3 and 4. This represents the polar nature of the yin-yang relationship between them. The numbers 3 (yang) and 8 (yin) pair up in the east, while 4 (yin) and 9 (yang) pair up in the west. Such pairing describes the polar relationship between yin-yang pairs for every element in each direction.

These opposing relationships, in turn, explain the Controlling Cycles such as water controlling fire, or metal controlling wood. They also explain the generating relationship, which follows a circle in the direction of sunrise (clockwise). Furthermore, it describes how yin becomes yang, and yang transforms into yin, or mutual transformation.

The total of the numbers assigned to the yang directions of east and south is 20. It consists of 15 on the outside and 5 on the inside. The total of the numbers assigned to the yin directions of west and north is also 20. Again, this consists of 15 on the outside and 5 on the inside. This expresses the balance between yin and yang. Though the natures and quantities of wood, fire, metal, and water differ, these numbers ultimately imply that wood and fire (yang) have a balanced relationship with metal and water (yin).

In the center are the numbers 5 and 10, showing how the earth element is the most balanced in yin and yang through its position and the numbers. For example, the total generating number for wood and fire is 5, and their total completing number is 15. Likewise, the total generating number for metal and water is 5, and their completing number is 15. Thus, the sum of the completing numbers derives from adding 10 to the total of the generating numbers.

The five representative substances that form the universe each have different shapes according to their formation from the variance of yin and yang. The completing number, which assigns form and structure, portrays this. They also have different natures or energies shown by the generating number, which sets the function. However, since each entity comprises yin and yang, it is Tai Chi. And the sum of all things yin in nature is identical to that of all things yang, thus forming Tai Chi. This shows

that the universe is in a state of complete balance. It also shows that the entire universe can be looked at through the model of the earth element, the central axis, as it supervises the equilibrium of the whole universe.

NAKSEO (THE RIVER LO MAP)

Nakseo has the same numbers as Hado but in a different configuration. This difference is essential for what Nakseo implies. In Hado, each pair of numbers settles to an interior or exterior position in the four cardinal directions and the center. However, in Nakseo, yin and yang numbers are not assigned interior-exterior positions. Instead, only the yang numbers sit in the four cardinal directions.

In contrast, the yin numbers are situated between the cardinal directions. When looked at clockwise, the yin numbers precede yang numbers, implying that yang arises from yin. Yin and yang also circulate alternately. Hado turns in the order of the Generating Cycle; Nakseo flows in the order of the Controlling Cycle. If Hado represents a form that occupies space, Nakseo signifies energy that changes over time.

In Hado, northern numbers form antagonistic relationships with the south, situated on the opposite side. In Nakseo, however, the same adjacent numbers in Hado are assigned to the opposite side. For example, in Hado, 1 and 9 were juxtaposed, but in Nakseo, they face each other; In Hado, 2 and 8 were juxtaposed, but in Nakseo, they oppose each other (fig. 17.21).

In Hado, elements wood, fire, metal, and water are assigned according to the order of the

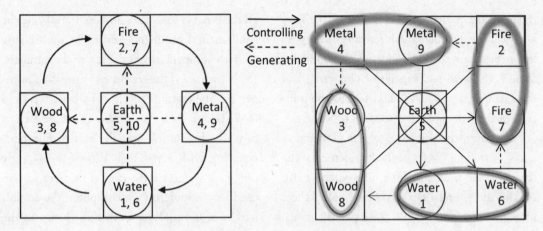

Figure 17.21 Hado (left) and Nakseo (right)

Generating Cycle in a clockwise direction. On the other hand, in Nakseo, the elements are set in a counterclockwise direction according to the Controlling Cycle.

In Hado, the yang elements of wood and fire are adjacent. Also, the yin elements of metal and water are adjacent. But in Nakseo, they oppose each other, and the total of the numbers that face each other is 10, forming unification moment by moment (fig. 17.22).

The earth element is situated in the center, as the number 5 is the midpoint of the number 10. This implies that the earth presides over the harmony of yin-yang movement from the center. The sum of the numbers from the yang movement of wood and fire is 20. The sum of numbers from the yin movement of metal and water is 20. They form an opposing, yet balanced, relationship. But unlike in Hado, wood and fire are not adjacent in Nakseo. The same goes for metal and water. Instead, they face each other in opposing relationships.

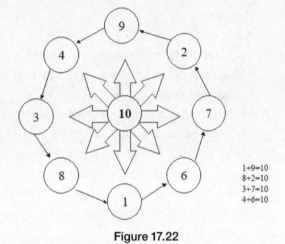

Figure 17.22

THE MUTUAL RELATIONSHIP BETWEEN HADO AND NAKSEO

The numbers in the four cardinal directions in Hado are the foundation of the principles of Sasang and the five elements. The numbers located in the eight directions in Nakseo are the foundation of the eight trigrams and the nine palaces.[2] Hado and Nakseo demonstrate the principle in each number from 1 to 10. They also expresse the polar and intertransforming relationships between yin and yang. Additionally, there is the triad relationship of yin, yang, and the earth element (Tai Chi), as well as the principle of the four cardinal directions of Sasang.

Moreover, the principles of the Generating and Controlling Cycles of the five elements, the tenets of hexagrams, and the nine palaces exist. Finally, the interrelationships between all of these principles lie hidden within these two diagrams. The Hado and Nakseo drawings thus express everything from the simplicity of yin and yang to the complexity of myriad things in the universe.

To recap:

- Hado explains forms that occupy space, whereas Nakseo explains the function or energy that changes over time.
- Hado expresses a state of stillness, whereas Nakseo expresses a dynamic state.
- Hado contains principles of yin, whereas Nakseo contains principles of yang.
- Hado explains the Generating Cycle, whereas Nakseo explains the Controlling Cycle.

With this background, let's now apply the principles of the five elements to everyday life.

Human Physiology and the Five Elements

It is essential to understand why human physiology is based on the five elements rather than Sasang. Just as three primary colors give rise to all the other colors, the numbers 1 and 2 are the fundamental numbers. Adding or multiplying the two numbers creates the rest of the numbers.

Number 1 is the epitome of yang, and number 2 is the epitome of yin. In a binary system (1–2–1–2–1–2–1–2), number 2 can be seen as both the beginning and the end of numbers, equating with zero (1–0–1–0–1–0–1–0). By doing so, we create the digital number system used by computers. In a computer, the combination of 0 and 1 represents all things in the universe. Computers can translate all things in the universe as barcodes of ones and zeros to read, memorize, and calculate.

Numbers 1 and 2 are all-inclusive. It is, therefore, challenging to subdivide the nature of matter with just these two numbers. On the other hand, the numbers 3 and 4 allow a more precise division and practical usage in the I Ching. They are the second order of odd (yang) and even (yin) numbers. The trigrams of the I Ching and the pyramids of ancient Egypt illustrate how these two numbers can express all things in nature.

The trigrams symbolize a universe that has two ways of changing—yin and yang—drawn with three lines representing the three coordinates of x, y, and z. Each line of the trigram corresponds to one of the coordinates. The pyramid symbolizes a universe in harmony through the coexistence and mutual dependence of the triangle (yang) and the square (yin) that compose its structure.

In the I Ching, there are both yin and yang within yin and yang, thereby expressing the universe's infinite divisibility and holographic principles (fig. 17.23). If a pyramid is sliced

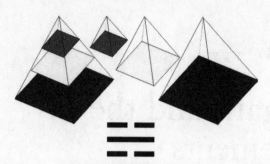

Figure 17.23

Figure 17.24 Triad Buddha and Four-facet Buddhas

horizontally from the top, one gets consecutively larger pyramids as the slices move down. No matter how small, each pyramid expresses the universe in its entirety, demonstrating how a square or a triangle ultimately arises from a single point (the tip corresponding to the number 1).

In a pyramid, the square (yin) that lies flat is stable and expresses yin, which has no movement. In contrast, the triangle (yang), which stands in a diagonal position, is unstable and represents yang, with constant movement.

The theory of I Ching is well embedded in Korean Buddhism. Triad Buddha and Four-facet Buddhas can be found in Namsan (south mountain), located at Gyeongju, the capital of the ancient kingdom of Korea, Shilla (57 BCE–935 CE) (fig. 17.24). There is a good representation of 3 and 4.

Yin numbers (2, 4) more accurately express form or shape (yin), whereas yang numbers (1, 3, 5) are more helpful in representing function (yang). Thus, Sasang is better at discovering the functional strengths and weaknesses between the paired internal organs a person is born with. But the five elements are better for expressing the current physiological functions of the organs and their mutual relationships. Therefore, *The Yellow Emperor's Inner Classic*, the bible of Eastern medicine, explained ever-changing physiology, pathology, pharmacology, and diagnosis using five elements instead of Sasang.

18

The Five Organs and the Five Elements

A substance with form can change into energy at any time. Energy unites to become a form, so closely observing the shape can make its function known. Likewise, taking a closer look at the function created by energy can provide insight into the form.

In Eastern medicine, the human body is a microcosm, as it has the basic elements of the whole, like a pyramid. The universe is composed of five groups of substances belonging to wood, fire, earth, metal, and water and functions according to the principles of the five elements. Likewise, the human body is composed

of the same five groups of substances belonging to the five elements. Its physiology also occurs according to the principle of the five elements. The abdominal and thoracic cavities are in the center of the human body. Organs inside them represent the five elements.

The heart, which pumps red blood throughout the body, is like the sun, the great fire on Earth, and belongs to the fire of summer. Like summer, it is responsible for invigorating the energizing activities of the body.

The kidneys have the darkest color among the organs in the body cavity. They sit at the bottom of the deepest part of the body, and their function is to make urine, corresponding to water. So they belong to the water element that corresponds to winter. Like winter, they are responsible for facilitating the materialization activities in the human body.

The color attributed to the lungs is white, and sitting at the top, they cover the chest cavity like the lid of a kettle. Like the lid of a kettle, they collect steam, which is active energy, and turn it into the water and drop it down. The action of converting energy into matter is the function of the metal element, which corresponds to autumn. So the lungs belong to the metal element.

The liver sits between the kidneys and the heart. Its color is purple, but the body's interior is all red due to the color of blood. By subtracting red from purple, the color of the wood element, blue, remains. The liver has an inverted triangle shape in the form of a fire. So it looks like it will transfer the energy stored in the kidneys to the heart. Since the liver converts glycogen to glucose, stored in the form of a substance, it has the function of springtime, which changes substances into energy. So the liver belongs to the wood element.

The spleen in Eastern medicine is actually the pancreas. It sits in the middle, with the heart at the top, the kidney below, and the liver to the left. So it belongs to the central earth element. It secretes insulin to regulate sugar metabolism, essential for maintaining life. Glucose supply to the remaining cells of four organs is very important. Insulin plays an important role in their glucose supply as it has the most important function of carrying glucose into the cells. The spleen is yellow and located in the center. It has a regulating function, so it belongs to the earth element.

The Generating Cycles of the Five Organs

The physiological activities of the body exist for two reasons. One is to preserve existence, and the other is to create the potential for reproduction. The heart is the organ in charge of maintaining life, and the kidneys are in charge of preparing for the next generation. Because the heart belongs to the fire element and the kidneys to the water element, Eastern medicine defines the physiology of the human body as an interplay between fire and water. In fact, the I Ching describes the entire movement of the universe as the "mutual communication between fire and water."

The heart is in charge of all the blood and blood vessel activities. The heart's control of the blood and functioning allows the body's physiological activities to occur. Some of these activities are ingesting an energy source (food), the breakdown and refining of the energy source, its distribution to individual cells, and the energy usage within the cells. This supervision by the heart involves the function of transforming polymers (compounds such as protein, fats, and starches) into monomers (molecules such as amino acids, fatty acids, and glucose). These monomers then transform into the energy that manages the body's physiological activities.

In contrast, the kidneys' supervising action involves changing energy into monomers and monomers into polymers to create new cells. (Please refer to chapter 4, "Yin and Yang of Human Beings," for further information.)

Essentially, the heart transforms matter into energy, and the kidneys transform energy into matter. In Eastern medicine, these processes are referred to as "Qi transformation" and "materialization," respectively. Although the heart governs Qi transformation, the other four organs assist in this function.

The spleen (pancreas) has a dual function and assists in Qi transformation and materialization. It belongs to the earth element, so it is the most balanced organ in yin and yang. Its Qi transformation function involves the secretion of digestive juices to break down food. Its materializing function consists of the secretion of insulin and glucagon, which help regulate the body's sugar metabolism and contribute to the building up of the cells.

Energy is essential to stay alive. While the heart supervises the energy distribution through the body, the source of this energy is the liver's breakdown of fats, proteins, and carbohydrates. The liver supports the process of glycolysis, which transforms glycogen, the stored form of carbohydrates, into glucose. Once sugar is in the form of glucose, it moves into the bloodstream. At this point, the heart can supervise the distribution of glucose. According to the five-element theory, this process is wood generating fire.

The breakdown function of the liver is only possible when the kidneys filter unnecessary waste products from the blood and supply pure fats, proteins, and glucose to the liver. The adrenal glands, situated atop the kidneys, also belong to the water element. The adrenals secrete two hormones called corticosteroid and adrenaline. These two hormones must be supplied together to the liver for the liver's dynamic breakdown function to occur. This is the process of water generating wood.

One of the essential aspects of Qi transformation is the ingestion, breakdown, and absorption of food. The pancreas supervises this function. A person feels hunger when there is a substantial secretion of pancreatic juices as well as the secretion of glucagon that generates carbohydrate metabolism. When a person eats food, the pancreas secretes enzymes to create glucose, which then enters the bloodstream. The heart must carry this glucose in the bloodstream and supply it to every cell, assisting the pancreas. Such a process is known as fire producing earth.

The final process of Qi transformation is transporting glucose across the cell membrane and infusing oxygen into the cell to transform the glucose into energy. The pancreas secretes insulin to facilitate the glucose entering the cell, and the lungs supply oxygen, which finally creates energy. Here, the pancreas assists the function of the lungs, a process called earth generating metal.

The lungs and kidneys are yin organs, so their function in Qi transformation is not as significant as their role in the materializing process, which creates new life. In Eastern medicine, the adrenal glands that belong to the kidneys are called the Gate of Life. According to this perspective, the Gate of Life is where the creation of life takes place.

The kidneys supervise the materializing actions in the body. These actions include transforming energy into matter, storing that matter to be utilized when needed, and creating new cells to replace old cells to maintain current life. But most important, creating reproductive cells is the ultimate purpose of the materializing function. The kidneys store substances with the assistance of the lungs. The lungs are in charge of exchanging gases between the body and the environment. They also regulate the proportions of oxygen and carbon dioxide that enter the bloodstream.

Qi transformation occurs when the supply of oxygen (yang) to the body increases and the amount of carbon dioxide (yin) decreases. In contrast, the materializing function occurs when there is an increase in the supply of carbon dioxide (yin) and a decrease in the oxygen (yang) supply.

The lungs are the only organs that can be regulated voluntarily and give people a way to control their Qi transformation and materialization functions. When breathing is rapid and shallow, the oxygen supply increases, giving rise to the Qi transforming function. With dynamic physiological activity, swift energy consumption occurs, and as a result, the life span shortens.

Conversely, when breathing is slow and deep, there is a reduction in oxygen supply, giving rise to the materializing action. With the decrease in physiological activities, energy accumulates so that there is an increase in the production of new cells, including reproductive cells. New tissue forms in the body when the new cells outnumber dying cells. In contrast, aging occurs when the dying cells outnumber new cells.

Slow, deep abdominal breathing can reverse the natural aging process. Adding meditation to this breathing process will not only slow the physiological processes but will also slow the thought processes. This will open the door to inspiration and the Universal Mind rather than strictly relying on the human mind, the "frog in a well" mentality mentioned in chapter 1. Through such a process of transcendence, one will eventually realize enlightenment. Eastern masters, experts in the I Ching, present this method as a means of health cultivation and antiaging and a way to be reborn and realize enlightenment.

Some scientific studies provide evidence of the ability to slow the aging process. For example, in one experiment, a man lived in a cave without sunlight for several months. The experiment's results proved that living in a cave can slow aging. When a person is living in a yin-type environment (no sunlight), breathing slows, as do the body's physiological functions, so the ratio of new cell production increases. Thus, the proportion of new cells produced is greater than that of the old cells that die.

Another example is an experiment examining the number of eggs a hen can produce. In the chicken yard, hens with a low rate of laying eggs are placed in a dark setting for several weeks and given a minimum amount of food. The hens' egg production increased under these conditions. Again, it is the same principle of creating a yin environment to enhance reproductive cell synthesis. In the same vein, gray mullets develop a white membrane over their eyes to obscure their vision during their spawning season. These examples show how reducing thought and stimulation through abdominal breathing and meditation may lead one to the fountain of youth.

Although the kidneys ultimately make reproductive cells, the lungs transform energy into matter to begin the process of materialization, creating the fundamental substance for the reproductive cells. In terms of the five elements, this is metal generating water.

The kidneys oversee storing the energy made by the lung function, mainly as fat near the digestive organs in the abdomen or muscles or as glycogen in the liver. The adrenal glands' function is to develop new cells, including the reproductive cells, eventually replacing the old cells in each bodily region using these substances. Steroidal hormone, a sex hormone, generally mediates this function, playing the role of a catalyst. The liver's generating (wood) energy helps create these hormones. With cholesterol as the raw material, the hormones develop from the adrenals, testicles, and ovaries, all belonging to the kidney system.

The Controlling Cycle of the Five Organs

The lungs regulate the function of the liver. The liver's most important function is the creation of ATP (adenosine triphosphate). ATP is the co-enzyme that stores and releases the energy used in cellular processes through the TCA cycle (Krebs cycle) and the electron transport channels. When the oxygen supply from the lungs is inadequate for the TCA cycle and the electron transport channel to function properly, only a minute amount of ATP is produced. This is the phenomenon of metal controlling wood in the five-element theory.

The heart regulates the function of the lungs. The lungs' process of exchanging gases primarily depends upon the quantity of blood in the capillaries of the alveoli. If the blood supply is adequate, the lungs can actively fulfill their function of sending oxygen to the whole body. If the blood supply is inadequate, a healthy exchange of gases cannot occur, and lungs cannot execute their function. This is the principle of fire controlling metal.

The heart is the most significant organ (of the five organs) because death is imminent if its function stops. Just as the sun supplies energy to Earth, the heart also supplies energy to the various regions of the body.

The five-element principle states that water regulates fire. In fact, the kidneys regulate the heart's activity in two ways. First, the kidneys secrete ACE (a vasoconstrictor), causing the blood vessels to contract, thereby inhibiting the heart's action. Secondly, the kidneys regulate electrolytes such as sodium, potassium, and calcium, which are essential to the heart's muscle activity.

The adrenal glands oversee the yang functions of the water element, while the kidneys control the yin. The adrenal glands secrete adrenaline and aldosterone, accelerating the heartbeat. They also increase the sodium levels in the blood, raising blood pressure.

The pancreas regulates the function of the kidneys. It secretes insulin and supervises the glucose entering the cells, which depends on its exchange with sodium. The excretion of urine from the kidneys depends on the quantity of sodium in the body. A high sodium concentration can lead to edema and high blood pressure due to the lack of discharge of urine from the kidneys. Therefore, the function of the kidneys is regulated by sodium, which is regulated by the pancreas. This is the phenomenon of earth controlling water.

In Eastern medicine, the herb that epitomizes the nature of the earth is licorice root. In traditional Eastern medicine, a known side effect of licorice is edema. Overeating licorice (natural, not candy) will weaken kidney function, and swelling will occur. This is a recently discovered phenomenon inferred several thousand years ago by applying the five-element theory (the principle of earth controlling water).

The liver regulates the function of the pancreas. The pancreas oversees regulating the glucose supply to the cells by producing glucagon (yang) and insulin (yin). But it can only complete its task when the liver transforms stored glycogen, fats, and proteins into glucose. The liver regulating the function of the pancreas is the phenomenon of wood controlling earth.

These Controlling Cycles apply to modern medicine. For example, current research into the treatment and cure of diabetes is focused only on the pancreas. However, type 2 (adult-onset) diabetes shows no problem with the cells in the islets of Langerhans, where insulin production occurs. This implies that the problem is not in the pancreas. If modern researchers were to turn their attention to the liver, which controls the pancreas, an effective treatment or cure would soon be discovered.

ESSENCE, SEX, AND THE BRAIN

The reproductive organs, brain, spinal cord, bone, and bone marrow all belong to the water element, and the kidneys supervise them. Especially the brain, spinal cord, and reproductive organs share similar characteristics, so mutual exchange of their constituents can occur. The kidneys store the Jing, the body's most essential substance, which throughout life can become either reproductive cells or cells that form the brain, spinal cord, and other parts of the nervous system. For this reason, enlightened masters, monks, and priests do not marry or engage in sexual relationships. When the reproductive cells and sexual energy deplete through sex, there is less substance that can become brain cells or nerve tissue. Without sex, the body utilizes essential substances to develop the brain and nerves.

After excessive sexual activity, the body fatigues, the head feels empty, and memory is poor. Nerve function dulls, and people may bump into things. In addition, there is an imbalance of the autonomic nervous system, which can manifest as night sweating or spontaneous sweating, hot flashes, or coughing while drinking water. These are the same signs and symptoms that occur during menopause because of a lack of female hormones that regulate the autonomic nervous system. Taking herbs that belong to the water element, or deer horn, an herb related to a deer's bone marrow, that nourish the human body's essence, can eliminate these problems.

Some Western doctors advise men to have frequent sex to increase stamina and sperm count. This recommendation, on the contrary, is the quickest way to speed up the aging process. As Jing, or essence, is energy that belongs to the water element, its insufficiency cannot restrain the fire to which sexual desire belongs. Thus, desire is easily aroused, not due to great stamina but to deficiency or false heat. Since the essence is energy that creates the next generation, the body replenishes it firsthand. But there is a limit to the body's reserve. When water is deficient, to produce water, overdevelopment in the organs that belong to the water element can occur. This action will break up the overall balance, resulting in an absolute energy shortage.

Excessive sexual activity is not a matter of great concern for men in their twenties, when their recovery function is good. But when men's recovery ability is not as good, they will age quicker. In addition, they can easily become sick because of a decline in physiological functioning.

MEDITATION AND THE BRAIN

In scientific terms, the abdominal breathing and meditative techniques performed by Tao-

ist masters, Buddhist monks, or yogis are for brain development. A human being's complex neural network is a compilation of the stimuli experienced by every organism that has ever lived or is currently alive. It began with the experiences of the first single-celled organism, which became more and more complex through evolution. This process is mirrored in the development of an embryo. As each embryo progresses through the process of "ontogeny recapitulating phylogeny," the neural network reorganizes in a way that centers around those neural circuitries activated by stimulation that human beings can receive.

The original human brain was a formation of neural networks that could sense the entire universe. These neural networks were created from every possible stimulus the universe offered.

However, only a small segment of the neural network is revived by stimulation that can be applied to a small social group in a restricted area of the Earth. As a result, it can only give commands that can address limited stimuli.

Humans can only hear sounds in the range of 20 to 20,000 hertz and only see light in the range of 4,000 to 7,000 angstroms because the brain's neural network is limited to perceiving only those ranges. However, if adequate nutrients and oxygen are supplied to the brain and an effort is made to resonate with every stimulation present in the universe, it would be possible to sense the entire universe and regenerate the original neural network able to communicate freely with the universe.

If human beings are created in the image of

God according to the Christian Bible, both the brain of God and the human brain should have the same potential. If we cultivate our brains, we can sense and move the entire universe as if it were a part of our body. This realization has far-reaching implications. For example, people would see that their enemies are actually part of themselves, and they would love and care for everyone else as they would their own bodies. If we concentrate our attention, we can understand the "feelings" of a stone in a far-off mountain range. Everything in the universe belongs to each of us, so taking other people's money and keeping it is like taking money from the left hand and placing it in the right.

Ancient masters of the East would advise people to slow down and deepen their breathing and sit calmly, stop the complicated thoughts of the world, and place themselves in the hands of the universe. Furthermore, they would say to avoid excessive sexual activity. This advice was given as a method for brain development, similar to the Zen meditation of Buddhism, yoga of India, and prayers and meditations of Christianity.

We can also interpret these brain development techniques in modern medical terms. The regulation of the blood flow to the brain is of great concern in treating patients with brain damage, so its mechanisms are well known in modern medicine. If breathing slows, the percentage of carbon dioxide in the blood initially increases. As a result, blood vessels relax so a larger quantity of blood can flow to the brain. Abdominal breathing puts additional pressure on the abdomen to redirect the blood meant for the abdominal cavity up to the brain. This pressure causes the brain's blood vessels to stay open despite an increased oxygen supply. Sitting in a cross-legged position further supports this process, putting pressure on the blood vessels of the legs where there is a great distribution of muscles.

Oxygen infuses into the blood through the alveoli of the lungs. Normal breathing does not inflate the alveoli 100 percent. But if you consciously inhale deeply, all the lungs' alveoli inflate, and an ample supply of oxygen will enter the blood. The brain cells will receive additional nutrients and oxygen through the arterial blood while sending out waste materials through venous blood. Consequently, the brain's function increases. Abdominal breathing supplies sufficient blood to the brain to receive everything necessary for its development.

Stopping mental and physical activities reduces unnecessary energy consumption and transforms energy into a substance. Essence usually spent making reproductive cells will become the structural material for the brain and spinal cord. Essence also forms bone marrow, from which arise red blood cells. An increase in red blood cells means more oxygen in the body. In the Taoist classics, this process is called "Transforming essence to augment the brain." The five-element theory describes it as the culmination of metal (lung) generating water (kidney essence) or accumulating carbon dioxide through abdominal breathing to produce essence.

The Yellow Emperor's Inner Classic, which first explained human physiology with the five-element theory, states that the kidneys store essence, the spirit resides in the heart, and the house of the spirit is the brain. This means that the spirit has two homes. During the day, the spirit is in the brain, and at night, it resides in the heart. So, according to Eastern medicine, the heart not only functions to pump blood through the body but also has a significant influence on certain mental faculties. Hence, the heart and the brain are often thought of in the same light (listen to your heart, bravehearted, evilhearted, lionhearted, loving heart, kindhearted, etc.). In the East, the mind is called Jing-Shen, meaning "essence-spirit." Through abdominal breathing, the essence of the kidneys transforms. The essence then becomes the brain needed to create the spirit; this spirit becomes one with the spirit of the universe.

The following diagram depicts the Qi transforming and materializing functions; the dual action of the human physiology, according to Tai Chi and the Generating Cycle of the five-element theory (fig. 18.1).

Several methods supply the brain with adequate oxygen and nutrients to facilitate its generation of nerve cells. These methods of cultivation will also relay all developmental experiences to the brain. One approach is attempting to listen to the sound of the universe or try to feel the universal energy through the skin (the Buddhist meditation of observation). Another is trying to see the light within the brain, a technique known as Wonsangbup (Original Imaging Method),[1] similar to the clairvoyant technique. A third method is reciting incanta-

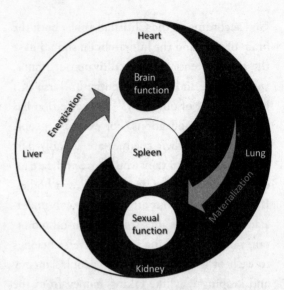

Figure 18.1 Tai Chi of the Five Organs. The pancreas is harmonized in yin and yang because it has ascending and descending functions. This is represented by the curved line drawn above and below it. The liver supports the Qi transformation function of the heart (wood generates fire), and the lungs help the materializing function of the kidneys (metal generates water). The white dot indicates the extreme of yin and symbolizes the Jing, or essence; the black dot indicates the extreme of yang and symbolizes the Shen, or spirit. The unification of Jing and Shen creates the conscious world. The Jing arises from the spinal cord and marrow, and the Shen arises from the brain.

tions or chants that contain a balance of all five elements to transform the human body into a resonant body balanced in yin-yang. This will, in turn, resonate with the frequency of the universe (Tantra). Practicing any of these meditative methods can bring about the complete development of the original neural network, making one able to sense the entire universe.

The Five Elements of Pathology and Treatment

According to Eastern medicine, disease occurs when the function of one or more organs is too strong or too weak. For instance, having either a weak or an overly strong heart function is considered a disease. When the heart is diseased, every tissue, organ, or system that belongs to the fire element will also become sick.

Sickness due to an overly strong heart does not imply that its physical pumping function is too strong. Instead, the strength of the heart is out of balance with the other elements, breaking the overall balance. The imbalance will manifest with signs and symptoms indicating excessive heat in the entities that belong to the fire element. Therefore, when the heart's function is stronger than the other organs, the fire element's corresponding entities will fall ill at the same time. They include the small intestine, tongue, blood, blood vessels, and spirit.

According to Eastern medicine, the small intestine is intimately connected to the heart and participates in water metabolism. If the fire element is overly exuberant, the urine may appear reddish, and there may be pain associated with urination. The tongue can become red and swollen and often develops ulcers, pain, and raised papillae. In addition, blood vessels can become easily damaged due to increased blood pressure from the heat in the blood. This can manifest as nosebleeds and stomach ulcers.

The spirit belongs to the fire element, so it likes what is cold and dislikes what is hot. When the fire element is in excess, the mind will become restless and anxious, and insomnia may develop. Excessive fire in the heart can present with hysterical and psychotic symptoms. In addition, if the heart's function is overly strong, it can cause lung disease due to the principle of fire controlling metal. For example, rheumatic fever can cause an insufficient closure of the bicuspid valve. In this situation, there will be a backward flow of blood from the left ventricle to the left atrium and a cessation of the blood flow through the pulmonary artery. This will cause blood stagnation in the lungs and result in lung disease. In this case, the heart is treated rather than the lungs.

Eastern medicine acknowledges three causes of disease: external factors, internal factors, and miscellaneous factors. External factors include wind, cold, summer heat, dampness, dryness, and fire. Though these imply inappropriate weather conditions, they are six types of earthly forces that influence human beings. Therefore, when classified according to the five elements, wind belongs to wood, cold belongs to water, dampness belongs to earth, dryness belongs to metal, and summer heat and fire belong to fire.

The human body is a mirror of the universe. The five elemental forces govern the body, presiding over the functions of the five internal organs. Likewise, the universe has five fundamental forces, which function and move according to the five elements. When these universal forces act directly on the human body, they transform into six types of energies. Thus, there is an additional fire element because of planet Earth's limited and unbalanced characteristics (the tilt of yin-yang).

The five elements of the universe are perfectly balanced. For example, because the fire element is one of the five elements, it controls one-fifth of the universal energy. However, in our solar system, the sun is ultimately more powerful than the other elements, so it has an overly strong function.

So to properly explain and order all phenomena on Earth, the masters and sages of the East extended the role of the fire element. They created two types of fire, which they labeled the "Monarch Fire" and the "Ministerial Fire." This changes the percentage of fire on Earth from one-fifth to two-sixths.

The Monarch Fire develops from yin and relates to summer heat, while the Ministerial Fire is yang fire, corresponding to the heat of late summer (as well as Indian summer). In the body, the function of the fire element is performed by the Ministerial Fire, while the Monarch Fire primarily deals with decision-making.

Although each bodily cell can develop an illness due to its deficiency or shortcoming, for the most part, the disease is due to surrounding influences. These influences affect the body differently depending on the strength or weakness of physiological functions. The body can fight off the surrounding influences if the immune system is strong. In the East, diseases of the human body are not seen from the body's viewpoint alone, because a single human body is a single cell of the universe. Therefore, the

movement of the universal forces was divided and grouped into five elements. The sages and masters then carefully studied their patterns and linked them to specific diseases.

When a disease develops, Western medicine looks for the cause of the disease by investigating the type of bacteria, virus, or substance that caused the toxicity or pathological transformation of the body. Western medicine also asks what antigen would cause an allergic reaction or whether a disease is due to senility or aging in a particular bodily region.

In reality, aside from discovering a few germ types, the ultimate cause of the disease is unknown, except in a few cases. For example, what is the principal cause of cancer? Most digestive disorders? Asthma? Alzheimer's disease? Heart disease? For the most part, the etiology of a disease is unknown. Even with the few diseases with a known cause, such as a common cold, the reason behind the illness and the factors that cause certain people to fall ill while others remain healthy are unknown. To understand the nature of a disease, it is important to know why, for example, a virus is prevalent at a specific time in a particular place.

The yin-yang and five-element theories explain why a particular virus is more prevalent in certain areas at certain times. There are five different forces in the universe. There is a yin force and a yang force in each of these five forces (table 18.1). Therefore, there are ten forces. Every year, each force, in turn, comes to a position where it can manifest its strength.

Yin and yang forces also exist in Earth's six types of forces. Therefore, there are twelve forces on Earth. To understand these forces more easily, masters of the past paired the forces with the natures of twelve different animals actively involved in the people's lives during those times (see chapter 2, "Tai Chi"). You might be familiar with these animals, as depicted on the place mats of many Chinese restaurants. They are the rat, cow, tiger, rabbit, dragon, snake, horse, sheep, monkey, chicken, dog, and boar (table 18.2). Every year one of these twelve forces takes its turn and dominates the energy of that year.

On Eastern calendars, the names of the forces governing the universe and the Earth for a particular year appear. For example, the name of the year 2000 is Geng (a celestial stem) Chen (a terrestrial branch). These names are also attached to each month, day, and time (every two hours). The yin-yang of the five elements in heaven (the universe) is called the ten celestial stems. The yin-yang of the six energies of Earth is called the twelve terrestrial branches. Together, they are the stems and branches.

If the stems and branches are written for this very hour, there would be four stems and

FIVE ELEMENTS	YANG	YIN
Wood	Yin = tiger	Mao = rabbit
Fire	Si = snake	Wu = horse
Earth	Chen = dragon Xu = dog	Chou = cow Wei = sheep
Metal	Shen = monkey	You = chicken
Water	Hai = boar	Zi = rat

Table 18.2 Twelve Terrestrial Branches (Six Energies of Earth)

branches according to the year, month, day, and time. The forces of the stems and branches for the year manifest all year round. But the stems and branches for the month, day, and time give influence according to the particular month, day, and time.

It is necessary to translate the stems and branches into yin-yang and the five elements and calculate their cycles of generation and control to determine the forces of the universe and the Earth that affect a person. These forces exert an effect that can change the body's physiological functioning.

For example, let's take a person of a Taeyangin constitution whose function of the wood element is too strong. Suppose the stems and branches for a given year are wood-fire, the month wood-wood, the day fire-fire, and the time wood-water. In that case, the function of the wood element will have a significant influence or effect on the person at that particular hour. This overactive wood function will create fire (wood generating fire), and the person will show signs of excessive heat in the body.

Remember that a Taeyangin constitution-

	YANG	YIN
Wood	Jia	Yi
Fire	Bing	Ding
Earth	Wu	Ji
Metal	Geng	Xin
Water	Ren	Gui

Table 18.1 Ten Celestial Stems (Five Elements of Heaven)

ally already has more yang and less yin. The wood and fire elements increase the yang even more. So the person's head, which is the most yang region, will throb and his or her brain will get abnormally excited, eventually leading to insanity. Meanwhile, the person's weak legs will become even weaker, potentially leading to paralysis. Of course, these are extreme situations; however, they are the mechanism by which diseases of both the mind and body manifest.

At the same time, let's suppose that this Taeyangin gets exposed to the virus that causes encephalitis. In the town where he lives, a swarm of mosquitoes carrying the encephalitis virus has bitten everyone living there several times. As a result, some people develop the disease while others do not. Each person's susceptibility toward the external influences created by the forces of the universe and the Earth determines who will get sick and who will not.

The brain belongs to the water element. But, as it is in the uppermost region of the body, and mental functioning is extremely quick, it belongs to fire within water. Mosquitoes, which spread the encephalitis virus, have quick movements, are light, and fly around. So they belong to the fire element. However, since mosquitoes transform from larvae (yin), they also belong to the water element. Therefore, mosquitoes can be said to be fire within water.

Meanwhile, viruses are less evolved and therefore belong to the water element. However, because they cause febrile disease, they belong to the fire element. So they are also fire within water.

According to the five-element theory, the brain, mosquitoes, and the encephalitis virus are closely knit together because they all have similar characteristics. Taeyangins and So-yangins, the yang body types, have an abundance of fire in their bodies and are much more susceptible to the encephalitis virus.

In contrast, Tae-eumins have a lot of yin energy and strong metal energy that can overcome wood energy (metal controlling wood). Therefore, they are less susceptible to infection by the encephalitis virus, and even if they were infected, the virus would quickly die in their bodies.

The times and peculiarities of the five elements differ in various regions of the Earth. For this reason, mosquitoes that carry encephalitis can be rampant in certain areas while not in others. Therefore, there must be a five-element analysis according to time, place, and constitution to understand the precise etiological and pathological mechanisms.

INTERNAL CAUSES OF ILLNESSES

The internal causes of illness involve injury to the internal organs because of an excess of the five fundamental emotions: anger, joy, overthinking, grief, and fear (or fright). For example, when a person suddenly becomes furious, the function of the wood element becomes excessive and can cause liver disease. In other words, the overactive energetic liver functioning will result in imbalance and disease. Likewise, the heart quickens when there is excessive joy, and blood vessels relax. This, too, can bring about an imbalance of the five elements, resulting in illness.

When a person overthinks, the parasympathetic nerves become excited, resulting in abdominal pain. The digestive system goes through peristalsis when the parasympathetic nerve is active. Too much stimulation will give rise to pain and spasms in the digestive tract. The pancreas also becomes excessively vigorous, causing the person to vomit or have diarrhea.

When a person is excessively sad, breathing slows down, bronchial tubes contract, and a stifling sensation in the chest develops. This brings about a decreased functioning of the lungs. With the inhibition of lung function, there is a decrease in the body's oxygen supply and an increase in the accumulation of carbon dioxide. So the lungs' metal gathering function becomes excessive.

Fear incites the parasympathetic nervous system (PNS), which causes contraction of the detrusor muscle, one of the four muscular layers surrounding the urinary bladder. With the contraction of this muscle and the simultaneous loss of the sphincter muscle control by the sympathetic nervous system, urination occurs. So if there is excessive fear, the kidneys' function becomes active, and a person will urinate frequently.

As previously mentioned, there are two stages to the cycle of yin and yang in the water element. One is the state before yin reaches its zenith, and the other is the beginning of yang. Fear is the emotion that appears before yin reaches its peak, and fright occurs at the beginning stage of yang.

The PNS maintains its peak of excitement with continued fear. Then if there is a sudden fright, the PNS activity stops, there is a loss of resistance to the sympathetic nerve, and the sympathetic nerves are immediately excited. This process is extreme yin converting into yang.

When an emotion explodes all at once, it causes a temporary excess phenomenon in the five-element function to which it belongs. However, when this state continues for a long time or repeats frequently, the five-element function that the emotion belongs to weakens.

This surplus phenomenon in the five-element function is an excess condition; it belongs to yang. In contrast, a weakened phenomenon is a deficient condition and belongs to yin. Deficient conditions arise from several sources. For example, an overactive organ that maintains overactivity for a long time will weaken and ultimately become deficient. Other factors that can weaken the body include constitutional factors, lifestyle behaviors, diet, stress, and so on. Acupuncture, herbal medicine, diet, meditation, and so forth can treat deficient and excess conditions. Supplementing or augmenting methods treat deficient states, while sedating or reducing techniques treat excess conditions.

STRESS (REDEFINED) ACCORDING TO EASTERN MEDICINE

According to Western medicine, stress is an elusive factor that creates havoc in people's systems. Although the symptoms of stress are measurable, the term "stress" is very ambiguous. Even psychiatrists have trouble clearly defining what the term implies. According to Eastern medicine, however, stress is categorized as the internal cause of disease. Regardless of the stressor, it is the person's reaction and the emotion elicited that ultimately cause imbalance and illness. The five-element theory systematically explains these causes.

Stress includes all of the following:

* immersion in thinking due to worry (yin of earth element);
* continuation of sadness/grief (yin of metal element);
* continuation of fear (yin of water element);
* fright/shock (yang of water element);
* annoyance before anger (yin of wood).

Stress implies a contracting or pressing force. When the word is used in a sentence, people are said to be "under stress," suggesting that stress has the upper hand and is bearing down on a person. So stress can be considered an outside force with a negative effect on a person. Alternately, it is the continuation of an emotion triggered by a stimulus contracting the expansion of life energy. Expansion is yang, and contraction is yin. Thus, stimuli that trigger yin types of emotions can be considered stress.

When a person is under stress, hormones such as adrenaline and cortisol secrete in various amounts. Unfortunately, modern experiments on stress do not define the types of stimuli that trigger a stress response, nor do they distinguish between the emotions that arise. Therefore, the various types of stimuli need to be analyzed according to the five-element theory, as should the triggered emotions, to diagnose and treat stress accurately. In addition, the investigation should focus on different stress hormones secreted according to the various stimuli and the fluctuating levels of each.

Stimuli initially relayed to the cerebral cortex first pass through the limbic system before receiving commands from the frontal lobe on handling any given stimulus. The limbic system is an area of the brain stem that governs emotions. Within the limbic system, especially in the amygdala, emotions are triggered based on records of similar stimuli previously dealt. Finally, the aroused emotions are rerecorded in the hippocampus. Careful differentiation of these emotions based on the five-element theory will give a complete picture of how the body deals with stress. Then an effective treatment protocol can develop for each individual.

Eastern medicine considers stress an internal cause of diseases and has emphasized it for the past five thousand years.

A Way to Treat Depression

Depression that results from prolonged grief is due to excessive metal function. It can be treated by bringing joy, the emotion of the fire element, employing the principle of fire controlling metal. Therefore, mobilizing all things that belong to the fire element is crucial. For example, depressed persons should receive as much sunlight, the largest fire available in nature, as possible. They should stay in a house or room that faces the south, bringing in the most sunlight, paint their house walls in bright colors, have brightly colored furniture, and set the thermostat higher. In addition, they should spend time with friends who are more yang-natured (i.e., Soyangins) and go hear live music that is yang-natured. They should sing and play fun games with their friends, watch comedy programs on TV or video, and play electronic games.

Depressed persons should drink ginseng or ginger tea and eat curry rice or other spicy foods. Furthermore, they should concentrate on doing some form of aerobic exercise every day to activate the dynamic activity of the heart. These will create a physiological functioning similar to fire. Finally, they should smell incense made from the flowers or bark of plants or trees grown in hot and dry lands.

Mobilizing things that simultaneously impact all senses will bring about the quickest effect. However, the stimulation must be continuous. In the case where fire is controlling metal, the son of metal, which is water, tries to take revenge for its mother. Water waits for the weakening of fire, and when it weakens, water gets stronger, causing the cycle of water controlling fire. This can bring back depression. To prevent this from occurring, eliminate sounds, colors, smells, and tastes that belong to the water element. In Eastern medicine, this treatment principle is "When there is a deficiency, tonify the mother; for an excess, sedate the son."

LAUGHTER AND ILLNESS

People say that laughter can cure any illness. However, according to the five-element theory, this is not true. For example, Soyangins, who are generally joyful and laugh constantly, can develop disease from a lack of substance (called deficiency of yin) because of excessive energy consumption from laughing. As a result, their lower backs and knees can easily develop problems from early degeneration. This originates from insufficient nutrients to the lower back and knees, the yin regions, because energy has only been consumed and not stored. Therefore, the diseases of Soyangins will become worse with laughter.

Fire of the heart will become exuberant with excessive laughter. When this happens, eliminating all things that belong to the fire element in order to weaken the heart directly is not a strong enough treatment and will not last long. It is more urgent to enhance the water element that controls fire. The person must become scared or frightened by watching a scary movie or reading a scary book. The house must remain dark and furnished with old, cozy furniture. They should listen to music with low tones and a slow tempo. They should try to accept things that are dirty and have a rotten smell to improve their health by nurturing their deficient water. In addition, they should eat foods that belong to the water element, such as barley, brown rice,[2] and pork.

To further weaken the heart, the earth element, the son of fire, should be sedated. When the earth element becomes weaker, its mother, the fire element, tries to support it to prevent its weakness. Thus the fire element, too, will weaken from its effort. Eastern medicine states that overthinking weakens digestive function, the earth element's energy. A person who has a good appetite and digestion thinks only of essential thoughts. That implies they think less. However, this is not always good because they can gain weight. Such a person needs to greatly increase self-reflection and think more meticulously to weaken the digestive function.

Such a habit will undermine the earth but reduce the intense fire in Soyangins. This results in the successful treatment of diseases caused by overjoy.

MISCELLANEOUS FACTORS

Miscellaneous factors that cause illness are those causes that are neither internal due to emotions nor external due to environmental factors in origin. These include excessive work, excessive sexual activity, physical injuries such as trauma from a car accident or sports activity, improper diet, insect or animal bites, and so on.

19

The Five Elements of Diagnosis

Eastern medicine employs four methods of diagnosis to determine illnesses and imbalances. They are observation (looking), auscultation (listening) and olfaction (smelling), inquiry (asking), and palpation (touching).

- *Observation* mainly involves looking at the patient's eyes, the hue or color of the skin, and examining the tongue body and coat. It also includes looking at the patient's overall body shape.
- *Auscultation* includes listening to the patient's voice, speech, cough, and breathing. *Olfaction* applies to the information gained by either smelling or asking the patient about the smell of their breath, body odor, urine, etc.
- *Palpation* includes checking the pulse, pressing on the abdomen, and inspecting areas of pain or discomfort.
- *Inquiry* involves asking questions regarding the patient's condition, the patient's and family's medical history, and their diets and lifestyles.

Various data are gathered with these methods so that the doctor may conclude which elements are strong or weak and make a proper diagnosis.

Observation

For the observational method, the primary inspection target is the light of the eyes. Intense light in the eyes indicates sufficient life energy (yang). But if the light is weak, the life energy is also weak. The next target is the face. If the color is bright, it is more yang; if dull, it is more yin. The paler color indicates weaker energy, while the darker color signifies the more excess condition. Various colors appearing on the face suggest imbalances of the corresponding elements. For example, the fire element is out of balance if it is red. A greenish complexion indicates an imbalance of wood energy. A yellowish complexion shows an imbalance of earth energy. A pale face signifies an imbalance of metal energy, and a dark complexion implies an imbalance of water energy. If there is a combination of two colors, deciphering the Generating and Controlling Cycles can help the practitioner ascertain a prognosis. In addition to the eyes and complexion, distinguishing the colors of the tongue, urine, sputum, and other secretions and excretions can reveal the strengths of individual elements.

Auscultation/Olfaction

Auscultation allows an understanding of the five elements' strengths and weaknesses through the sound of a voice. If the sound is angry, it indicates strong wood energy. Laughing denotes strong fire energy. If the speech is slow

with an ambiguous ending, it signifies strong earth energy. The sound of singing also belongs to the earth element. Crying sounds indicate strong metal energy, while moaning sounds indicate strong water energy. Besides these sounds, analyzing other bodily sounds, such as the sounds of coughing, heartbeat, and borborygmus (gurgling sounds in the intestine), can indicate that the organ is out of balance.

Olfaction involves smelling the patient's body odor, breath, secretions, and excretion. The nature of the disease is inferred by identifying different smells. If the odor is strong, the condition generally indicates heat, damp-heat, or excess. If the smell is mild or absent, the disorder is usually due to cold, dampness, or deficiency. Foul and sour smells indicate food retention.

The five element classification also applies to scents, as it does to sounds. The goatish odor, for example, is associated with the wood element, while the charred smell is related to the fire element. The earth element is connected with the fragrant scent, the metal element with the fishy smell, and the water element with the rotting stench.

Palpation

Palpation involves discovering an illness based on physical touch. For example, the disease is deemed a deficiency if the skin feels soft and lacks strength. But if the skin is solid and elastic, the disease is regarded as one of excess. The areas of palpation include the thorax and abdomen—the domain of internal organs—and the channels or meridians, which have an intimate relation to the organs' functions. An intricate pulse-taking method is also a significant part of the palpation.

The five-element principle of the universe (heaven) applies to organs within the thoracic and abdominal cavities, as they resemble the universe's functioning. On the other hand, the principles of the six energies of Earth apply to the areas outside the thoracic and abdominal cavities, since the acupuncture channels follow the principles of the Earth.

WHAT ARE ACUPUNCTURE CHANNELS?

Acupuncture channels separate the head, trunk, arms, and legs into different regions based on the principles of the five-element theory. There are four cardinal directions on Earth and four limbs on the body. The upper limbs are yang, whereas the lower limbs are yin. With the addition of the extra fire element (the Ministerial Fire), the five elements of the Earth become the six energies. Each of these energies has a yin and yang aspect, resulting in twelve branches (the terrestrial branches). Therefore, there are twelve channels in the body.

The Earth is a function or application of the universe, which is the essence or the foundation. Thus, the channels that correspond to the Earth are the energetic (functional) aspects of their respective internal organs, which correspond to the universe and sit in the thoracic and abdominal cavities.

The viscera are called Zang organs and be-

long to yin because they are solid (heart, lungs, kidneys, liver, and spleen/pancreas). On the other hand, the bowels are called Fu organs and belong to yang because they are soft and hollow. They include the small intestine, large intestine, urinary bladder, gall bladder, and stomach.

Since the Zang, or solid, organs are yin in nature, they connect to the inner side, which is the darker side of the limbs, head, and torso. These regions are more protected from harmful elements and get less sunlight. In contrast, the Fu, or hollow, organs are yang in nature, so they connect to the outer aspect, which is the brighter side, as they are more exposed. The functions of Zang organs within the thoracic cavity appear as channels on the arms' inner sides. In contrast, the function of those within the abdominal cavity appear on the inner sides of the legs.

The heart is the smaller of the two organs within the thoracic cavity and sits in the innermost aspect of the cavity. For these reasons, its function appears in the posterior (yin region) of the arms' inner (medial) sides. On the other hand, because the lungs are larger and lie in the outermost region, their function appears on the anterior of the arms' inner sides.

The five elements of the five organs did not correlate well with the six energies of the channels. So the ancient masters who discovered the meridian system assigned the sixth energetic function to the pericardium. The pericardium is the protective sac surrounding the heart, and its physical structure includes fat tissues and thick blood vessels. It corresponds to the Ministerial Fire. Due to its position between the heart and lungs, its function appears in the middle of the inner arms.

The principles that apply to the arms also apply to the legs. The functions of Zang organs within the abdominal cavity appear on the inner aspect of the legs. The liver is the largest organ in the abdominal cavity. As it sits in the front, its channel appears on the anterior part of the inner legs. Since the kidneys are the most yin organs, located in the posterior part of the body, their functions appear on the rear part of the inner legs. Meanwhile, the spleen sits in the middle, so its energies manifest in the middle part of the inner legs.

There are no hollow organs in the thoracic cavity. However, the hollow organs that pair with the viscera of the thoracic cavity also manifest on the arms. The small intestine is paired with the heart, the large intestine with the lungs, and the Triple Burner[1] with the pericardium. The functions of these organs manifest on the arms' exterior in the same positions (anterior, medial, and posterior) as their paired organs.

The back of the hands belongs to yang, whereas the palms belong to yin. On the palm, the area around the thumb's base is one area that reflects the lungs' function. It is called the "fish-belly" because of its shape. If a dark color appears in this region, the function has inclined toward yin. In modern pathological terms, there is an excessive accumulation of carbon dioxide in the blood vessels, and the function of the lungs has declined. Furthermore, the lungs are deficient and depleted in oxygen and nutrients if palpation of this region presents with very little elasticity. Understanding lung deficiency as the weakness of the metal function will allow knowledge of the five-element relationship.

Locating tender spots on the patient's arms, legs, or abdomen can indicate unbalanced elements. For example, suppose we palpate the area reflecting the liver's function. In that case, we can distinguish whether the person has a functional excess or deficiency of the wood element by whether or not the person likes the pressure. If the person likes the pressure, there is a deficiency, and the wood element is weak and needs additional stimulation. In contrast, if the pressure is painful or undesirable, there is a surplus of wood energy. This is an excess condition in which the body requires less stimulation.

Pressing the channel pathways can reveal the condition of the related organs. A diagnosis can also be made without considering the channels by palpating the abdomen. The abdomen then becomes Tai Chi (fig. 19.1).

The area halfway between the umbilicus and xiphoid process is the center of the abdomen and relates to the earth element. Palpating this region gives insight into the state of the earth element. The left side pertains to the wood element, and the right side pertains to the metal element. Below the umbilicus is the lower abdomen, related to the water element. Around the xiphoid process is the upper abdomen, which belongs to the fire element.

Simply stated, if the patient likes pressure in any of these areas, it indicates a functional weakness of the organ related to that area.

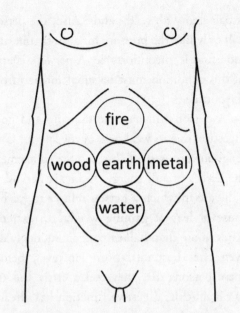

Figure 19.1 Five Elements of the Abdomen

If they dislike pressure, there is a functional overload.

The external regions of the body reflect the conditions of the internal organs. They also transmit external stimulation to them and can manipulate their function. For example, if the patient likes pressure on a particular area, mild acupuncture stimulation is done to invigorate the functioning of the organ connected to the acupuncture point. If the patient dislikes pressure, it implies that the organ has excess activity and does not want to function any faster. Applying intense acupuncture stimulation increases the organ's activity temporarily. But once the organ's activity reaches its peak, it will transform into the opposite situation and decrease. (This is the mutual transformation principle: yin or yang in the extreme will convert into its opposite).

ACUPUNCTURE AND EASTERN TREATMENTS

Acupuncture is a treatment based on stimulation. Stimulation is like spurring a horse to make it run faster and is an effective method for a robust horse. However, an old or weak horse will respond much more kindly to the lure of a carrot. The carrot is not for baiting the horse but to nourish it. If the weak and old horse is spurred or whipped, it will expend all of its energy and eventually collapse. It is in a state where its energy must be strengthened with a supply of nutrients so that it will have the power to run. All treatments based on palpation must adhere to this basic principle. The practitioner must consider whether the stimulation will activate the body to restart a stalled motor for a continued run or invigorate the movement temporarily, ultimately leading to exhaustion. The quantity of energy supplied to the organ determines the decision.

When a person can move vigorously after stimulation, the energy supply within the patient is adequate to accommodate the stimulation. But the energy supply is extremely inadequate when a person temporarily moves and then gives up trying to move altogether after stimulation. This situation requires an external energy supply. Food is helpful, but it distributes energy evenly to all the organs. Therefore, if one organ does not seem to receive energy from the food energy supply, a person should ingest herbs. Herbs can target specific organs and provide the necessary nutrients and energy to revive their functioning. These are called tonic herbs.

Ginseng, for instance, has a tremendous amount of the earth element, so its primary function is to help the spleen. However, since the earth element has an equal distribution of yin and yang and other elements, ginseng can eventually activate all the internal organs.

In animal experiments conducted by Soviet scholars, it was found that Siberian ginseng had an effect comparable to Korean ginseng, so it is in the spotlight as a health food. As Siberian ginseng has plenty of metal energy, it focuses the energy supply to the lungs. So if a person eats well and is otherwise healthy except for a lung weakness and feels good when pressed on the right side of the abdomen, it is good for that person to take Siberian ginseng.

The area below the xiphoid process is the domain of the heart. If a person refuses to let anyone touch it, the action of fire is too strong and the condition is fire controlling metal. The active fire reaches its peak by giving a strong acupuncture stimulation to the area, and the phase changes and returns to its normal state. The lungs will regain their strength.

Deficiencies and excesses of specific organs imply partially deficient and partially excessive states. There are situations in which the energy supply is overabundant or insufficient for all five yin organs. These are excess and deficient states of the whole system, where stimulation must be avoided entirely. In this situation, a person's entire abdomen will feel soft and he or she will like light, sustained pressure. But the patient will have an immediate negative response if the touching pressure intensifies or

is palpated with cold hands. Also, the person will only like the pressure for a short time and soon find it uncomfortable. A person's energy in this condition must be supplemented from the outside.

A person will have no appetite and poor digestion due to weakness of the spleen. Ginseng can be used in this case to supplement the body's overall energy. Anorexia nervosa is a disease in which a person refuses to eat because of fear of gaining weight. In extreme states, more than half of patients suddenly die even after hospitalization. However, before these persons die, they feel a crisis and try to eat, but the digestive function has already deteriorated, and they cannot eat. Ginseng, which protects against extreme deficiency, is effective in this case. In fact, ginseng is saving many patients with anorexia nervosa.

Eastern medical books discuss the role of acupuncture in sedating (weakening) excess conditions but not in tonifying (strengthening). However, there are acupuncture techniques explicitly for tonification. These techniques aim at the tonification of particular regions rather than treatments for the whole system. This is the distinction. These techniques focus on transferring energy from excessive areas to deficient areas to reestablish a balance in the system.

There are methods other than ingesting food and herbs that can supply energy to the body. For example, glucose can be injected intravenously, and heat can be applied to any bodily area where it is needed. As long as the whole body's energy is not completely exhausted, people with insufficient heat energy even like stimulation with extremely high temperatures; for example, very hot water. Older people, whose energy is declining, generally appreciate a hot bath much more than younger people full of energy. A method also exists to transmit energy through resonating high-energy frequencies to certain body parts. It is called Qigong and its practice of energy cultivation involves posture, breathing, gentle movements, and meditation. Used by masters in the East for many years, it is currently gaining popularity in the West.

There are three general treatment methods in Eastern medicine. They are acupuncture, moxibustion (heat therapy using moxa, which is made of mugwort leaves), and herbs. Traditionally, Eastern medical books state first to apply acupuncture, then moxibustion, then herbs. This implies that acupuncture should be used at the initial stage of a disease when the energy is not yet depleted. When the bodily energy has been depleted to a certain degree, to eliminate the disease, moxa can provide heat energy and mild stimulation to facilitate physiological activity without further consuming the body's energy. Once the energy is exhausted and the disease becomes chronic, tonic herbs should be used.

There are many categories of herbs. In contrast to tonic herbs, there is a category of herbs called "sedating herbs." These herbs *temporarily* strengthen the activity of one particular element. However, when the herbal effect declines, the activity of the element decreases. Since it was stimulated to work, its energy will also have weakened.

The diagnosis of a disease is not limited to the channels and abdomen. Because any part contains information about the whole body, regardless of the observed area, a diagnosis of excess or deficiency among any of the five elements can be made. Just as magnets contain both the north and south poles, no matter how small they are cut, any body part contains the five elements.

EAR AND HAND ACUPUNCTURE: MICROCOSM WITHIN MACROCOSM

A French doctor named Paul Nogier created a system of ear acupuncture based on the hypothesis that the ear resembles an upside-down fetus and represents the whole body. His theory states that bodily diseases can be diagnosed and treated using just the ears. Ear acupuncture is based on the Doctrine of Signatures ("birds of a feather flock together") rather than the five-element theory. The central, concave areas of the ear are called the cavum and cymba conchae and pertain to the torso of the body. The points found in these areas can diagnose and treat internal organs. The back of the ear relates to the back of the body. The lobes pertain to the head and face. The ridge connecting the lobes to the main body of the ear is called the antihelix, corresponding to the neck and spine. The antihelix divides into the upper and lower ridges called the superior and inferior antihelix crus. They relate to the hips, buttocks, legs, and feet.

In Korea, a system called Korean hand therapy was developed by a medical scholar named Tae-woo Yoo. This system transposes the internal organs onto the palms. The ends of the middle fingers pertain to the head, while the index and ring fingers relate to the arms. The thumb and little fingers become the legs, while the back of the hand corresponds to the back of the body (fig. 19.2).

The palm is said to reflect the condition of the internal organs. The center of the palm pertains to the earth element. On the right hand, the right side shows the state of the wood element, and the left side relates to the metal element. The region above earth and below the middle finger pertains to fire. The area below earth and above the wrist pertains to water. As in abdominal diagnosis, the balance of power between each element and its relative

excess and deficiency can be diagnosed by determining favorable and unfavorable pressure spots. Therefore, applying acupuncture directly to the place relays stimulation to the internal organs. Because this system can be learned quickly and has an immediate effect, it is popular worldwide.

These microsystems have merit and can guide a practitioner toward the area of imbalance. However, they represent a more tilted version of the five elements and are thus incomplete. The whole body gives a much more precise and realistic picture of the entire system's health. Therefore, it is more beneficial to analyze the whole body than any of its parts.

The universe is a balanced entity. It has equal proportions of all five elements, as does God. Human beings are said to be made in the image of God. Thus, human beings also contain all five elements, but since they are only a tiny part of a whole (universe), the proportion of each element differs. The proportions of the elements vary for each individual, depending upon the person's unique peculiarities, as no two are the same. One element always predominates, and one is always the weakest. Consequently, human beings are incomplete and unbalanced—selfish, commit sins, and develop diseases—unlike God.

Diagnosing the whole body just by observing the five elements of a hand is similar to analyzing the five elements' variance in humans and then projecting it to the whole (fig. 19.3). Since person A's environment differs from the whole universe, the five elements are similar

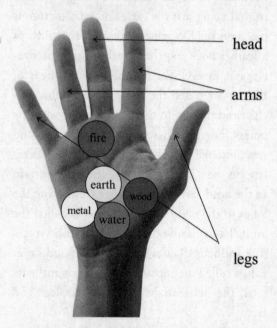

head

arms

fire

earth

wood

metal

water

legs

Figure 19.2 Korean Hand Acupuncture

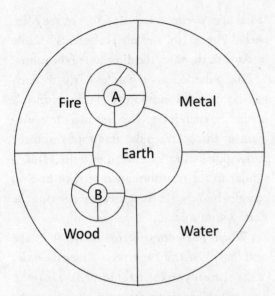

Figure 19.3 Human A: the force of fire is slightly stronger than earth, the perfect harmony of all five elements. Human B: the force of wood is somewhat stronger than earth. Although the shape of humans is identical to that of God, since they are only a part of the whole, variations in the five elements exist.

but different. Therefore, talking of the whole just by looking at the hand is the same as analyzing the five elements of a single liver cell and then discussing the variance of the entire body. Thus, the microcosms are reliable systems for diagnosis but incomplete.

PULSE DIAGNOSIS

Pulse diagnosis is the essential technique of palpation. Human physiology is very dynamic. No equipment was available to allow doctors to detect this movement in the past. Therefore,

Eastern doctors heavily emphasized the importance of the pulse, which directly relates to the state of the heartbeat. The heart is very active and influences the body, much as the sun does the Earth. In addition, the heart is sensitive to the actions of the other organs. Since the heart sends out necessary substances in the blood after receiving information regarding the situations occurring in each part of the body through the nerves, Eastern medicine compares the heart to the monarch.

Nevertheless, when Eastern medicine mentions the heart (fire), it does not refer to only the anatomical heart that pumps the blood. Instead, the main focus is on the Shen, or spirit (fire within water), the brain's activity, which becomes the monarch organ that governs and regulates all things in the body.

The conditions of each body part can be sensed through the neural network, allowing their reactions to appear in the form of a pulse. This can be clearly discerned in the region of the radial artery near the wrist. Careful observation of the pulse in this area can shed light on heart health and even the state of the brain. If you compare the act of pulse-taking to the internet, looking at the computer monitor is the act of pulse-taking. The heart is the hard drive of the internet server, while the heartbeat is the information sent to each terminal.

The act of pulse-taking is observing the information from every corner of the body, energetically recorded in a heartbeat. Just as you can clearly see the events that occur throughout every part of the world with the help of the internet, you can clearly see the information coming in from every part of the body by taking the pulse. However, the pulse signals arrive in analog mode. Therefore, we must classify the pulse (make it digital) by looking at the depth (deep or superficial), speed (fast or slow), strength (weak or strong), quality (slippery or choppy), and regularity (regular or missed beats), and so on. Analog signals switch to digital signals with the application of the binary system. And to change analog signals to digital signals, interpretation through the digital principles of the I Ching (yin and yang) is imperative. Such is the I Ching's role as an analog-digital converter. For the digital signal to appear on the monitor screen, it must be processed by a computer.

The heart's pulses are much more complicated than signals coming in through the internet, so interpreting with the human brain, the best available computer to date, is essential. Only then can each part of the body be looked at holistically. Unfortunately, the internet is incomplete, as it is only a tiny part of the information available on Earth. Furthermore, the uncertainty principle of quantum physics reminds us that at the smallest level, accuracy is an illusion. Therefore, the information about the universe and bodily information presented on the pulses' quality can only be inferred and must be handled statistically.

The pulse of the left radial artery reflects the condition of the water, wood, and Monarch Fire elements because it relates to the east, the direction of the sunrise. The pulse of the right radial artery reflects the condition of the Ministerial Fire, earth, and metal elements because it relates to the west, the direction of the sunset.

The pulse follows the order of the six energies (as depicted in figure 19.4). The principle of the six energies applies because the movement of the heart's pulse transforms into the radial pulse after entering the wrist. This is similar to the transformation of the universal energies into the six energies when entering the Earth's atmosphere.

When you compare this image with the next (figs. 19.4 and 19.5), you will see the order of the elements on the right hand has changed. The movement of the energies rises from the left and descends to the right. It begins with the water, continues with wood, Monarch Fire, Ministerial Fire, earth, and ends with metal. But the blood flows in the same upward direction for both the right and the left sides. Thus, the descending order of the six energies reverses with the Ministerial Fire at the bottom, earth in the middle, and metal at the top (as in figure 19.5).

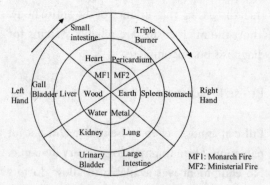

Figure 19.4 The Order of Circulation of Six Energies

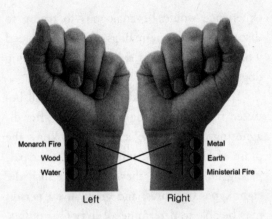

Figure 19.5 The Pulse Positions

and strength of a pulse. Each of these factors is classified according to yin and yang. When combined, these factors form the eight aspects of the pulse, which correspond to the eight trigrams of the I Ching. This can be drawn in a diagram as follows (fig. 19.6).

The pulse depth indicates the location where the pulse is felt and corresponds to the amplitude of the pulse wave. A superficial pulse is felt near the skin. A deep pulse is best felt near the bone. A superficial pulse indicates the disease of channels in the external regions of the limbs, trunk, or head. A deep pulse, in contrast, signifies a condition in the interior region—the body's internal organs.

In pulse diagnosis, as in the abdominal diagnosis, the balance of power between the five elements can be known by the sensation of strength or weakness upon pressing the regions corresponding to each element. There are three important factors to be considered when taking the pulse. They are the depth, speed,

The pulse speed represents the frequency of the heart or pulse beat. A slow pulse has a longer period between each beat, indicating a colder state in the body due to the decline of physiological functioning. In contrast, a rapid

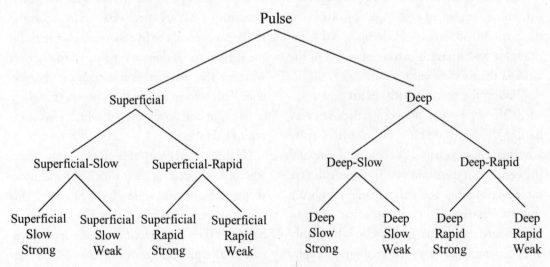

Figure 19.6 Diagram of the Pulse

pulse has a shorter period, suggesting a state of heat in the body due to the acceleration of physiological function.

The elasticity of the blood vessel determines the strength of the pulse. In a strong pulse, the inside of the blood vessel is full. As a result, the pulse feels long (a pulse that extends beyond three positions) and slippery (a pulse that feels like the slithering of a snake). In a weak pulse, the inside of the blood vessel feels empty, and the pulse has a short, rough feeling. A strong pulse indicates a bodily state with sufficient energy. In contrast, a weak pulse indicates insufficient energy for the body's needs.

Since the Zang (viscera) organs are yin and are more solid than the Fu (bowels/hollow) organs, their state is more evident in the deeper (yin) position. On the other hand, the Fu (hollow) organs are softer. Hence, palpation of the pulse at the superficial (yang) level better determines their conditions.

Eastern medical pulse-taking techniques determine the state of each organ by observing the position (superficial or deep), speed (slow or rapid), and strength (strong or weak) of the pulse at the six different regions.

Taking the pulse is both an art and a science. The differences between pulses are very hard to distinguish, as it is difficult to identify a normal pulse versus a pathological one and the variance in the positions. To make this task more challenging, the pulse changes with the seasons. Eastern medicine states that a person can understand the basics of pulse taking only after palpating at least ten thousand people. Attempting to interpret a pulse without ample experience would be analogous to trying to discern between many dogs of the same breed when having no prior experience in handling dogs.

The first step would be to distinguish between the yin and yang pulses. Then, after diagnosing many people, a person can know the pulse of Sasang (four pulses). Then after palpating more people, they can distinguish the eight types of pulses, and gradually, a person may be able to determine all sixty-four pulses. The ceaseless effort of every internal organ's movement will come up clearly in the head as if looking at a movie screen.

Inquiry (Asking)

Inquiry consists of asking the patient a series of questions to gather information for a proper diagnosis. For instance, if the patient complains of abdominal pain, the practitioner must first determine what region the pain is in according to the position of the five elements on the abdomen. Then the abdomen is palpated to discover whether the pressure is favorable or unfavorable. This information will show whether there is excess or deficiency and tell which element is out of balance.

If the patient complains of pain in the arms, legs, or head, determining which channel flows through the painful region is the first step. This will give insight into which element is out of balance. Then the practitioner can apply pressure to the painful area to determine the relative heat-cold and excess-deficiency conditions.

In the case of vomiting, it is important to ask several questions to the patient. They include whether vomiting occurs before (spleen/pancreas deficiency) or after (stomach excess) meals and whether the vomit is productive or dry. It is also important to ask whether there is projectile vomiting (heat) or if it is difficult to get out (cold). Another question is whether the patient gets irritated quickly and has a bitter taste in their mouth (wood controlling earth).

The questions asked during the inquiry should bring insight into where excess or deficiency occurs among the five elements. Once established, the answers can be applied to the mutual generating and controlling relationships of the five elements to understand the patient's condition further.

Knowing the foods the patient prefers and dislikes can give insight into the relative balance of the five elements in a person's body. For example, if a person claims to like beer, it will be helpful to determine whether he or she likes more bitter or sweeter-tasting beer. Also, if someone drinks coffee, ask if the person uses cream and sugar to help mask the bitter taste. A desire for bitter food or drink is the body's natural response to attempt to stop excessive physiological activity (water controlling fire). This situation indicates the exuberance of the fire element in the person's body.

People who like hot red peppers, mustard, or other hot, spicy foods are experiencing the body's natural desire to stop an excessive gathering function by eating foods with a pungent taste (fire controlling metal). It is, thus, indicative of an exuberant metal element.

If a person likes lemons, plums, or other sour foods and enjoys putting vinegar on food, it indicates an exuberance of the wood element. If a person likes sweet food, the earth function is weak. A person who likes very salty foods shows a functional excess in the water element.

20

The Five Elements of Herbs

Inferring the Effects of Herbs Based on the Five-Element Theory

There is an intimate relationship between human beings, nature, and the universe. A continuous, ongoing communication or mutual resonance exists between the macrocosm and its corresponding microcosm because the same five elements create them.

As parts of nature, plants or other substances used for herbs are also of the five elements (fig. 20.1). Thus, there is resonance between herbs and human beings. And this resonance allows us to infer the effects of the herbs and apply them to cure and prevent diseases and maintain health.

The stems of plants and tree trunks pertain to the wood element because they grow straight upward from their roots in the spring. The smaller branches and leaves relate to the fire element, as they spread out during the summer. Flowers also belong to the fire element because they are the brightest part of the plant. Fruits belong to the metal element, as they gather and lump together in the autumn. The seeds of the fruits, stored in the ground during the winter, pertain to the water element. The roots also belong to the water element because they are the plant's beginning and lowest portions hidden in the ground.

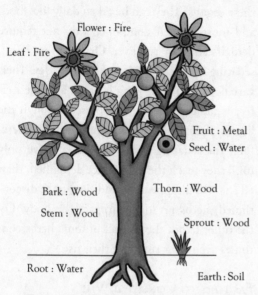

Figure 20.1 The Five Elements of a Tree

Finding the earth element in plants and trees is difficult. Since the earth is the center of the movement in the five-element system, it is more significant in the functioning of a system than in its form. However, the earth, as the soil, stores all of the nutrients and water vital to the plant's survival. It gives plants a solid hold to maintain their structure, assisting in nourishing their health by converting their fallen leaves and flowers into nutrients. In addition, the soil stores the plant's seeds so that they may reproduce. Because of this relationship, the earth (soil) is the earth element of plants. To choose a part of the plant representing the earth element, it would be the area

between the roots and the stem. If this stem base is plump, as in ginseng, it can augment the earth element of human beings.

The Inversion Principle

As mentioned in the yin-yang chapter (chapter 3) and throughout the book, the inversion principle also occurs with plants. If a plant's form or shape is yin, its function becomes yang. If it is yang, then its function becomes yin. The inversion principle also changes the nature of a plant's correspondence with the elements. In various aspects of the plant, the element corresponding to the form or structure has a controlling relationship with the element corresponding to the function.

For example, the shape of the roots relates to the water element. However, their function would be the earth element because the roots supply nutrients gathered from an external source to the rest of the plant. This action is similar to the function of the spleen. In this situation, water and earth are in a controlling relationship. The leaves, whose form pertains to the fire element, supervise the exchange of oxygen and carbon dioxide, much like the lungs in the human body. Therefore, their function corresponds to the metal element. This is the controlling relationship between fire and metal. This happens because the form and function change their yin and yang.

The animals' lungs receive oxygen but discharge carbon dioxide; it is the opposite for plants. Since animals are yang and plants are yin, their functions are complete opposites.

A plant's living function is not essential when we are using plants for food or medicine. Instead, the form or shape of the nonliving state is applied. Therefore, the five elements of plants follow their shape or form, not their function.

Tonification vs. Sedation Herbs

Eastern medicine classifies herbs into two major categories: tonifying and sedating. One major difference between Eastern and Western herbology is that most Western herbs "sedate" and treat disease by quickly reducing, weakening, and eliminating the causative factors. Sedating herbs are more potent and contain more toxins. They focus exclusively on the etiological factors and not on building the body's healing energy. On the other hand, tonics build the body's healing energy so that the body can naturally eliminate the etiological factors.

Herbs that tonify do not show their effects immediately. Western medicines are devised to have an immediate impact on the body. This is also why most Western medications have toxic side effects. There is no concept of tonics in modern Western medicine. A Western doctor will generally recommend bed rest if a patient comes in with a chronic disease and no effective treatment is available. Tonic herbs effectively treat chronic diseases in Eastern medicine, so it is no wonder people keep looking for herbal alternatives in the East.

Tonics are similar to food, with a slight variance in yin and yang. Thus, they tend toward certain organs (in the five-element system) and focus their action on nourishing one or two of these organs. They can be taken daily like food, and most of their components do not require detoxification by the liver. On the other hand, sedating herbs cannot be taken every day. Their variance of yin and yang is great, and their effect is rapid. They are also passed through the liver to detoxify their toxic components. Therefore, the sedating herbs will be effective only until they reach the liver. Once detoxified, their effects will disappear. In addition, once discontinued, herbs no longer impact the body. On the other hand, the impact of tonic herbs continues even after stopping their use.

FACTORS TO CONSIDER WHEN USING HERBS

Eastern herbology considers all of the following factors when deciphering the various effects of herbs. These effects were discovered more than five thousand years ago and emphasize the variety of characteristics that herbs have:

- part of the herb used
- method of preparation
- place and the time of cultivation and gathering
- taste
- temperature
- texture and shape
- target area (whether the herb acts on the upper or lower body or outer or inner part of the body)

- channel that the herb enters
- whether the herb tonifies or sedates
- cautions and contraindications

The Five Elements of Taste

Because the most important factor in inferring the effect of an herb is its taste, we will discuss the five-element analysis of taste in detail.

Sweet Taste

The sweet taste is the taste of the earth element. Like the earth, a sweet taste supplements the energy or substance of the body. In Eastern medicine, "tonification" describes supplementing the organs and tissues inside the body with energy or substance from outside. In contrast, "sedation" means energy or substance is extracted from the body through sweating, vomiting, bowel movements (diarrhea), or urination due to the effects of medicine or stimulation. It can also imply the consumption of energy or substance by stimulating activity.

Tonic herbs are primarily sweet but have a mixture of the four other tastes. The four tastes determine which bodily region can be tonified using that herb. For example, if an herb is sweet but has a slightly bitter taste, its tonic function will strengthen the water element. If an herb is sweet and slightly pungent, it will best tonify the wood element.

Examples of tonics with sweet tastes include honey, ginseng, Chinese angelica, elderberry, lotus seed, bee pollen, and maple syrup.

Bitter Taste

Though bitter herbs arise out of substances that belong to the fire element, like burnt foods, once they enter the body, they activate the function of the water element. The water element mimics the function of wintertime, when all activities are frozen. Thus, the bitter taste cools inflammation by the action of water controlling fire. It can even freeze water to reduce inflammation, edema and bleeding, and the oozing of suppuration.

Digestion and absorption of substances occur through the function of the fire element (digestive fire). So eating bitter herbs may give rise to digestive disturbances through the principle of water controlling fire. In fact, herbs with a bitter taste can easily cause abdominal pain, vomiting, or diarrhea. Bitter-tasting herbs include gentian, goldenseal, echinacea, and chicory.

Salty Taste

Salt comes from substances of the water element, like ocean water. However, once in the body, salt induces the activities of the fire element. The function of fire is like the function of summertime, when all activities are flourishing. The heart is in charge of supervising these summer activities of the body.

Whenever salt is ingested, less water is excreted from the body, and the blood volume increases, which leads to a stronger heartbeat. Congestive heart failure presents a weak heartbeat. It is treated in Western medicine with digitalis, a derivative of the foxglove plant. Digitalis retains sodium (Na), a component of salt, in the heart muscles for a long time. This, in turn, creates a stronger heartbeat, proving that salty tastes can strengthen the function of the fire element.

Animals are more active than plants, so they contain a lot more salt, the source of salty taste, and since meat is a more complex substance to digest than grains, it should be eaten together with salt, which has the action of fire for better digestion.

The metal element gathers energy to solidify it into a substance. Salty herbs counter this tendency by breaking down substances. This is the principle of fire controlling metal and is why salt is essential in the digestion of foods like legumes and meat, which are typically more difficult for the body to break down. It is also why slightly salty tomatoes complement dishes of legumes and meat.

Suppose a substance is primarily sweet but has a slightly bitter and slightly salty taste. In that case, it will be able to augment the fire within the water element, which is the Jing, or essence, that increases vitality. In general, herbs that tonify the essence and treat impotence are the ones that strengthen the fire within the water element in the body and have a sweet and slightly salty taste like that of tomatoes.

As salt is a mineral rather than a living entity, it has excessive fire. Thus, it contains toxins that can harm the body. To make salt more beneficial for the body, it can be cooked using bamboo to extract toxins and excessive fire elements. This will create a substance capable of supplementing the essence in human beings, particularly the elderly. Because it belongs to the water element, bamboo is used to weaken the excessive function of the fire element contained within salt (water controlling fire). Because there is almost no water in salt, heating it over a flame will incite its fire function to reach its extreme, after which the salt will explode and the volatile ingredient will diminish.

The salt is first put into a bamboo case and cooked over an open flame until it completely burns. It is then put into another case and cooked again. This process is repeated nine times. Because salt is the essence of seawater, the bamboo salt will tonify the essence of the body. This action is similar to replacing a car battery or reigniting the fire of life. By ingesting bamboo salt, a person can treat various geriatric illnesses and return to their youth. However, treating diseases is much more easily accomplished than returning to youth.

Although salt is effective in treating illness, it raises blood pressure due to increased blood volume and strengthening of the heartbeat by exuberant fire. It also impedes the function of the kidneys by the principle of fire controlling metal, which then cannot nourish water, creating edema.

PUNGENT TASTE

Metal objects have a pungent taste, but once in the body, the pungent taste has the function of the wood element. The function of the wood element is the function of springtime. It is the beginning of movement after a long winter slumber. It is the beginning of the transformation from substance to energy. Digestion is also a process of transforming matter into energy, so it also relates to the function of the wood element. Therefore, pungent herbs can aid digestion and are frequently used as spices in cooking.

The function of fire is the distribution of energy, while wood's function is the procurement and activation of energy. The energy supply does not come from outside; rather, it arises from the transformation of stored matter. The distribution of energy occurs with the support of the function of fire.

Herbs with pungent tastes, such as hot red peppers, black peppers, ginger, cloves, and cinnamon, support the digestive process of dissolving substances to create energy. They also invigorate physiological functioning and promote blood circulation. Indigestion, stomachache, vomiting, and diarrhea can be alleviated when the digestive function becomes vigorous. In addition, when blood circulation becomes vigorous, problems such as rheumatism, menstrual pain, and neuralgia, which typically worsen during cold or damp weather, disappear.

When energy forms from a substance, it permeates outward by creating a small hole in the fabric of the substance. The hole gradually increases in size as more energy erupts. The piercing or penetrating action required to produce the hole is a function of the wood element. The same principle applies to a blockage in the body, such as a cholesterol buildup in the capillaries. Ingesting herbs containing the wood element can break through the stagnation and transform the blockage into energy. The wood element can also open blocked bronchioles and induce sweating by piercing through clogged pores. Therefore, pungent herbs will invigorate blood circulation, pierce open blockages to lower cholesterol, stop asthma, expel phlegm, and promote sweating.

Interestingly, the wood element is also in charge of activating sexual energy from the Jing. Increased sexual stamina and improved circulation to the genitals can treat impotence or infertility. However, these pungent herbs must be cautiously used because they can significantly worsen a weak condition by expediting energy consumption.

Sour Taste

Unripe fruit is sour. Fruit ripens when a plant is beginning to gather energy. In the human body, the sour taste incites the function of the metal element, which is related to the autumnal energy. In autumn, energy gathers to materialize. As a result, animal activity dulls and plants stop growing to bear fruit.

When energetic activity is exuberant in the summer, sour foods taste good. Excess energy consumption harms one's health, so the body instinctively attempts to gather and store energy by craving sour foods. Vigorous work or exercise also consumes a great deal of energy. Afterward, the body craves water, nutrition, and drinks that have a slightly salty, sweet, and sour taste. The body craves the salt that it has lost by sweating.

The sweetness moderates the body's activities to slow things down while supplementing the loss of energy. The sour taste helps the body reabsorb the expended energy. Therefore, when the tastes of the earth (neutral), metal (yin), together with fire (yang) are combined, it makes the water taste better. This is the taste of popular sports drinks such as Gatorade.

The sour taste is functionally weak, so it is usually accompanied by or combined with astringent (puckering) tastes. Unripe raspberries are a typical example. Raspberries contain many seeds to strengthen the Jing. But to do so, a gathering of energy must occur with the sour and astringent tastes. Therefore, unripe raspberries are more effective for medicinal purposes than ripe ones.

Tonics in Eastern medicine that have only a sour taste without a basic sweet taste do not have a high value. This is because it is much more effective to supply energy from outside than to collect and store energy in the body. The sour taste primarily gathers the energies of the head, limbs, and exterior regions of the torso and concentrates them inside. So at this time, the peripheral energetic activity slows down. But in most cases, a strong fragrance supports the dynamic activity within the body cavity. Lemons, limes, grapefruits, bitter oranges, and citrons belong to this category.

Fruits

Fruits correspond to the metal element and will initially strengthen the lungs. The func-

tion of the lungs is to materialize energy, and fruits support this function. Children lacking in the metal element will generally prefer fruits to grains. Because children correspond to the wood element in this life stage, those that have an overly strong wood function in their constitution can readily develop diseases. These children will instinctively eat larger quantities of fruit to treat themselves.

The fruits of the vine have particularly strong metal functioning. They are unable to ascend straight upward because of their metal attributes. Therefore, grapes and hardy kiwi (*Actinidia arguta*) can supplement the function of the metal element lacking in the Taeyangin body type, whose function of the wood element is in surplus.

Tomatoes

Fruit belongs to the metal element and does not go well with meat. Spicy seasonings have the properties of wood or fire to promote digestion of meat, so they are eaten with meat, but fruits don't mix with meat. Only the tomato combines well with meat. Although the tomato belongs to the metal element, the outside and inside are red, and so it overcomes metal. Thus, it can promote digestion. It is also one of the saltiest fruits. Salty taste has a fire nature and can dissolve hard things. Therefore, adding more salt to tomatoes and heating them to make tomato ketchup is as good as a seasoning that dissolves meat.

At a sanatorium for cancer patients in France, tomatoes are the primary medicine for cancer treatment. No other foods are ingested, and it is said that many cancer patients have been cured. Cancer is a disease that often begins at age forty when the vital energy represented by fire starts to decline. Tomatoes, as a fruit, provide nutrition and have the nature of fire to ignite the fire of life and to soften hard things (cancer) with their salty taste, so that cancer can be cured.

Hawthorn Berries

Hawthorn berries are the small, red fruit of the hawthorn tree, with sweet and sour tastes. The sweet taste can tonify deficiencies, while the sour taste gathers energy. The leaves of the hawthorn tree have thorns, and the leaves pertain to the fire element. The strength of the fire element in a plant can be determined by observing whether the leaves are sharp or pointy (stronger function) or wide (weaker function). It is also determined by whether the texture of the leaves is stiff and dry (stronger function) or soft and moist (weaker function). The hawthorn berries strongly belong to the fire element since they have pointy leaves with thorns and red fruit. Nevertheless, fruit's sour and sweet taste slows and moderates their strong fire nature so humans can benefit.

Hawthorn berries can supplement the function of the heart and blood vessels, which belong to the fire element. Their effect is rather slow because of their sour taste but has a long-lasting impact. They effectively treat cardiac problems such as palpitations, angina, and tachycardia (rapid heartbeat). They are also ef-fective for lowering cholesterol and eliminating the plaque attached to the arterial walls.

Chili Peppers

Chili peppers have a pungent taste, but their leaves contain a lot of moisture, are very soft, and are eaten as a side dish in Korea. It is well known that chili peppers increase the heart rate, reduce cholesterol, and relieve neuralgia by stimulating blood circulation. In contrast to the hawthorn berries' sustained effect on the heart and blood vessels, these red peppers work much more rapidly. Due to their pungency, their effects are short-lived. Their effect is similar to whipping a horse to get it to run faster, whereas taking hawthorn berries is like feeding carrots to the horse.

Elderberries

Elderberries are dark. Since the water element (dark color) adds to the metal element (fruit), elderberries possess a powerful metal function. These berries are slightly toxic and should be cooked before you eat them. They are most effective in treating people with weak lung systems, like people with chronic asthma and the elderly. This type of person will present with a greater susceptibility to catching colds, and these colds will be more likely to turn into pneumonia. In addition, any cough that arrives with the cold will last for a long time as a lingering dry cough.

Elderberries add the water element to the lungs and nourish the lungs' fluids. In the case of a long-standing dry cough, they should be eaten for at least one week. Walnuts, pistachios, almonds, peanuts, and Job's tears can also treat chronic coughs. If these do not work, morphine can be taken. Morphine is the resin of the poppy fruit (opium). But due to its toxicity, a Western doctor will most likely prescribe codeine, which powerfully stops coughs and has few side effects. Nevertheless, codeine is a sedating medicine, so it should be combined with elderberries and various nuts to have a more prolonged effect. Such a strategy will strengthen the lungs and will thus have a preventative effect against common colds and flu.

Flowers

Flowers belong to the fire element because they have the yang characteristics of bright colors and strong smells. They are often near the top of a plant and blossom (spread out). Flowers generally affect the head, brain, eyes, and nose.

SAFFLOWER

Safflower, or *Carthamus*, is a red flower with sharp, thin petals. Therefore, it is fire within the fire element. It does, however, have a slightly rotten smell, possibly from rotten bug carcasses that combine with the flowers. It was previously mentioned that a rotten smell belongs to the water element. Thus, safflower effectively facilitates blood circulation (fire within water).

Drinking safflower decocted in wine can speedily alleviate bruising, swelling, and pain

when there is stagnant blood due to physical trauma. This potion is also suitable for menstrual pain and starting or restarting an absent menstrual cycle. The reason is that safflower breaks up weak capillaries due to a lack of oxygen to eliminate stagnant blood and create new capillaries. A word of caution, however, for those who have bleeding or blood clotting problems because of overly active blood circulation—do not take this herb!

When a child is about to be born, the capillaries in the mother's placenta wither and detach from the uterine wall. The placenta will also fall off the uterine wall with a certain degree of uterine contraction, which occurs in giving birth. Safflower can help the birthing process by activating uterine contractions to ease placental shedding. This herb should only be taken after the fortieth week and if there is no sign of contraction. It is contraindicated during any other time of the gestational stage of pregnancy because it can lead to miscarriage.

After childbirth, the darkened blood stuck in the uterus should bleed out when the placenta completely detaches and the uterus returns to its original position. However, the blood may not come out entirely, and the mother may experience pain similar to childbirth that tends to be much more severe at night. In this situation, a gynecologist will perform a D&C (dilation and curettage), which involves dilating the cervix and scraping the uterine wall to remove the blood.

A famous pizza parlor in Switzerland is known to induce labor. If a child arrives late, there are significant risks to both the mother and child. The infant will increasingly find it more and more difficult to receive proper nutrition because the placenta begins to wither. Many pregnant women visit this pizza parlor when they are due, to prevent this situation from occurring. The pizza recipe was a mystery for many years. Upon final disclosure, safflower was one of the ingredients.

Although the significant effect of safflower is to facilitate blood circulation in the body, like all flowers, it also affects the head. Therefore, its applications also include redness, pain, and swelling of the eyes or skin eruptions on the face.

LAVENDER AND JASMINE

The functional aspect of lavender and jasmine is not their tastes but rather their fragrances. Strong smells imply vigorous molecular activity and have the effect of increasing the energetic activities of the body. Because flowers are the most yang aspect of a plant, they work on the head, the most yang aspect of the body. Strong fragrances help facilitate the movement of blood to the brain.

An Eastern medical saying goes, "If it is open, there is no pain. If it is blocked, there is pain." When brain cells are overworked, they hunger for nutrition to feed their cravings. This will manifest as headaches. Once new blood, rich in oxygen, moves through the brain, the cells revive and the pain subsides. This is why headaches that come from excessive thinking can be relieved by simply going outside and breathing in the fresh air. Both lavender and jasmine have such an effect.

Lavender oil will prevent moths from damaging clothing or linens. Moths are less evolved, yin-natured creatures and consider fragrance, a yang-natured smell, to be poison. However, yin reaches its peak and transforms into yang in the evening. Thus moths run toward the fire and burn to death. Like lavender oil, those substances with a strong smell, such as naphthalene, smoke (food preservation method), ginger, garlic, clove, and camphor, all have antiseptic effects. They chase away or kill less evolved, yin-natured microorganisms or germs that like to live in dark and damp places.

Lavender oil improves symptoms of neuralgia, rheumatism, and sprains. Rubbing any fragrant oils on the body will more or less have the same effect. The reason is that the fragrances will vitalize the body's energetic activity and improve blood circulation. Peppermint, camphor, and eucalyptus oils have these effects and are the main ingredients in popular muscle rubs, such as Mentholatum and Bengay.

Cough drops also contain fragrance oils. Although coughs can be differentiated based on the five elements and the eight trigrams, they can divide simply into yin (deficiency) and yang (excess) types. A yang cough occurs when a person catches a cold and has a fever, headache, sore throat, and phlegm sounds while coughing. The treatment for yang coughs should not include elderberries, nuts, or codeine. Instead, those are for treating yin or deficiency-type coughs, which occur in chronic conditions. It is a cough with a weak sound that worsens upon exertion, with an absence of fever, and it occurs intermittently with little or no phlegm.

Improper use of elderberries, nuts, or codeine can make the cough last longer and be more severe. Take them only for yin cough.

Fragrant cough drops will kill germs with their fragrance and improve blood circulation so that headaches will disappear, congestion will subside, and inflammation will calm down. The fragrance also will stimulate the bronchioles to relax so that the sputum will come out more quickly. Simultaneously applying a muscle rub to the chest will double the effect of the oils. If chills are present, willow tree bark (the essential ingredient of aspirin) can also be taken.

Not all aromatic smells vitalize the energy of the body. According to the five elements, smell divides into five types but can generally also divide into yin and yang. People like yang aromas, such as lavender, jasmine, peppermint, eucalyptus, and camphor. However, there are also yin odors that people try to avoid. They include smells such as a rotting cadaver, rotten eggs, a garbage dumpster, or herbs such as patrinia, garden rue, and goldenseal. Yang aromas expand life energy, and yin odors make the life energy contract.

PATRINIA

As the name 敗醬草 (rotten soybean plant) suggests, this herb smells like rotten soybean paste. When harmful substances enter the body, humans suffer for two reasons. One is from toxic substances damaging the tissues, and the other is an inflammatory reaction (swelling, heat, redness, and pain) to expel the harmful substances. This is similar to how when war breaks out, soldiers suffer from enemy attacks from the front, and the people suffer under the burden of transporting supplies necessary for the soldiers at war.

An allergy is a case of suffering from over-reaction to a minor enemy invasion from the outside. Among the germs, some germs self-destruct, dying on their own at some point. In some cases, the body overreacts to these germs and self-destructs. In other, a beesting causes ana-phylaxis (a hyperallergic reaction), wherein swelling of the lungs causes death from suffocation.

The herbal medicine used to slow such hyper-inflammatory reactions is patrinia. This foul-smelling herb creates an excellent anti-inflammatory effect by contracting the vital activity of bodily defense. Foul odors are not only harmful to human physiological functions, but they also kill germs and weaken toxins. By freezing life energy, all living things are frozen. This herb has an excellent effect on various in-flammatory conditions, such as pleurisy, appendicitis, and boils.

RUE

Rue has an offensive odor. Many herb books site various inflammatory conditions that rue can treat. It is most effective, however, in the treatment of albinism. Albinism is a disease that results from an autoimmune response toward the melanin pigment (which causes skin color-ation). This disease will manifest in a decrease in melanin and skin whitening. The famous singer Michael Jackson suffered from this disease, for which there is no real cure. Nevertheless, there have been a few cases that have been cured with the use of rue.

Herbs with strong odors affect the body's exterior more than the interior. This means they affect the skin. Offensive smells belong to the water element. When the water element is exuberant, the skin will turn dark, the color of the water element. On the other hand, if the fire element is exuberant, the color of the melanin pigment will fade, leaving behind the color of the blood, and the skin will turn red. Rue causes the function of the water element to act on the skin so that the melanin pigment can recover its normal state.

Michael Jackson had large, intense eyes. He had broad shoulders and narrow hips. He was also extremely passionate (at least on stage). His manner of walking was so light that he seemed to be flying (e.g., the moonwalk). These are typical physical, mental, and behavioral manifestations of the Soyangin body type. This constitution has a weak water element and a strong fire element.

The Soyangin body types need to strengthen the body's systems that belong to the water element to correct their imbalances. This system includes the kidneys, brain, bone marrow, lower back, and legs. The hormone that stimulates the formation of the melanin pigment, called gamma-melanocyte-stimulating hormone, is secreted from the anterior lobe of the pituitary gland in the brain. Therefore, it may be possible to treat albinism by having persons with it ingest tonics that strengthen the function of their water element. This will, additionally, supplement their brains and skin.

Bee Pollen

There are certain herbal medicines in which only part of a flower is used. Bee pollen is one of them. Bee pollen is made by pollen dust that attaches to the legs of working bees while they travel from flower to flower. Because the pollen derives from the male gametes of plants, it corresponds to sperm. Bee pollen is not made from one single plant tilted in yin-yang. Instead, it is a mixture of multiple plants, making it much more balanced. Sex cells, unlike the other cells of the body, contain holistic information that is not tilted in yin and yang. The cells themselves, however, are tilted. But when they gather together, their variance of yin and yang is significantly reduced, much like a melting pot.

According to the I Ching principle, bee pollen is like a particle of yin created from the conversion of extreme yang within Tai Chi. Each bit of pollen contains the variation of the flower it was extracted from, but bee pollen is a conglomeration of multiple flowers, so it is balanced. Therefore, ingesting the pollen is like eating the earth element itself.

Bee pollen has been clinically proven to strengthen the immune system and increase overall bodily energy. Furthermore, laboratory analysis has determined that it contains 35 percent protein, 55 percent carbohydrates, 2 percent fatty acids, and 3 percent vitamins and minerals. Thus, according to the recommendations of modern nutritionists, bee pollen has the ideal proportion of protein, carbohydrates, and fats, along with rich contents of vitamins, minerals, trace elements, enzymes, and amino acids. Thus, the scientific analysis clearly demonstrates how bee pollen belongs to the earth element and contains balanced yin and yang components.

Any balanced food will strengthen the earth element. Earth is like a mother who does not like extreme things. Those substances with a great tilt of yin or yang are called poisons on Earth. Because the earth element is a mediating force, it can reverse the progression of toxins. As a detoxifying agent, bee pollen can counteract the side effects associated with radiation and chemical toxins.

The greater the variance or tilt of yin or yang a substance contains, the faster its effect will be. Therefore, bee pollen, which has a slight tilt, works slowly. It should be taken for several years to get a significant effect.

Feverfew

Both the flowers and leaves of feverfew are useful, but it is more effective to use only flowers for headaches. It is a type of chrysanthemum, which is a flower representing autumn. It has the clear and cool metal nature of autumn. Flowers belong to fire, and they enter the human head—the region of the fire element—and change the action of fire into metal. It is more effective if there is a slightly sweet taste that belongs to the earth to act as a mediator.

Migraine headaches have the nature of the wood element, and when one occurs on only one side of the head once a day in a paroxysm, like the wind, it can be treated with the principle of metal controlling wood. The action of wood that does not occur gradually but soars up from water to fire at once and acts quickly without roots is called wind.

A common cold is a disease belonging to the wind, and a cerebrovascular attack is a disease caused by the wind. A hypertensive headache, in which the blood rises to the top and makes the head seem full, with dizziness and ringing in the ears, is also a disease caused by the wind. Even a condition like vertigo, wherein a person feels as if he or she is swaying in the wind, is a disease caused by wind. Chrysanthemums or feverfew can treat these illnesses through the principle of metal controlling wood.

A good pillow can be made by boring several holes in a small wooden barrel so the fragrance can come out. Then fill it up with feverfew and wrap it with thin sponge. People who have headaches due to high blood pressure and are afraid of having a stroke can sleep on this pillow.

The use of a cylindrical pillow has an additional benefit. As a result of carrying a heavy head, upright walkers often suffer from cervical vertebral stenosis. Nerves that connect to the shoulders, arms, and hands originate in the cervical vertebrae. As we age, these nerves become inevitably compressed. This compression leads to frozen shoulder, tennis elbow, carpal tunnel syndrome, and finger arthritis. The cylindrical pillow relieves this narrowing by making the cervical spine into a C shape.

SAINT-JOHN'S-WORT

The medicinal aspect of Saint-John's-wort is the part of the plant above ground. If the plant is flowering, its effect will be more substantial, and if the leaves and the twigs around the flowers are used, it will have the most significant effect. These parts all belong to the fire element, and a sensitive person can feel a sudden rising up of heat simply by smelling the plant. The plant itself belongs to the fire element. Traditionally, this herb is gathered on Saint John's Day (June 24), when it contains the most remarkable function of the fire element.

This herb is used after soaking in olive oil. The oil will turn a reddish color, called the "Blood of Christ," indicating that the herb has the nature of the fire element. In many religions, blood signifies the heart and the spirit. The I Ching interprets the concept of spirit through the principle of Tai Chi. The transformation of extreme yang into yin is indicative of the spirit. The head is the most yang aspect of the body. Baptism takes that yang part and dips it in yin (water) to bring the body closer to God by rebirth through the Holy Spirit and water.

All herbs derived from flowers are effective for headaches and depression because flowers belong to the fire element. It has reached its extreme and is beginning to transform into the water element. However, suppose fire keeps rising without descending to be transformed into water (called mutual communication between water and fire). Then all of its energy stagnates in the head and causes headaches and depression.

Currently, Saint-John's-wort is used to treat depression. Depression can have more than one cause. If the fire element does not transform into water, it will cause headaches and depression. Additionally, if the metal element is too strong, the liver energy will stagnate, creating depression. Since this herb belongs to the fire element, it treats depression by the principle of fire controlling metal.

According to Western science, Saint-John's-wort contains hypericin, inhibiting neurotransmitters' breakdown. In other words, Saint-John's-wort sustains the function of monoamines such as epinephrine, endorphin, and serotonin, elevating a person's mood, increasing energy, and making the person more motivated. This is how Saint-John's-wort demonstrates its effect on depression, similar to Prozac or MAOIs (monoamine oxidase inhibitors).

Additionally, because Saint-John's-wort is the manifestation of the exuberant function of the fire element, supervised by the heart, it can improve blood circulation to treat various types of pain and inflammation, such as menstrual pain, sciatica, and arthritis. The type of inflammation Saint-John's-wort can treat is chronic inflammation without much heat, redness, or severe pain.

Eastern medicine recognizes two distinct types of inflammation: excess and deficient. An overabundance of energy causes an excess syndrome. Therefore, it needs to be treated by the action of the water element. A deficient syndrome, in contrast, occurs when there is a lack of energy. So it should be treated by the action of the fire element.

The excessive type of inflammation will present an abundance of the four cardinal inflammatory symptoms: heat, redness, swelling, and pain. The deficient type of inflammation will be much less severe, and the cardinal symptoms will be mild, yet there will still be tissue injury. The significance of this information is that when treating inflammatory conditions with Saint-John's-wort, it is essential to differentiate between the two types of inflammation. Using Saint-John's-wort to treat an excessive inflammatory condition can worsen the problem.

Saint-John's-wort has been reported to have the ability to cure cancer. According to the principle of the I Ching, this is possible because cancer develops when the fire of life is weak, and Saint-John's-wort can supplement that fire. It also has a strong antiviral effect, so it is used to treat herpes simplex and is currently under investigation as a possible treatment for AIDS. Viruses are the least evolved organisms on Earth and so belong to yin. Therefore, the fire energy of Saint-John's-wort can kill the virus and bring about a cure.

Leaves

Leaves belong to the fire element and therefore have the function of facilitating the total energetic activity. But they have less impact than flowers on reaching the head or the brain. Some leaves include barley grass, alfalfa sprouts, and eucalyptus. Others, such as gotu kola and ginkgo leaves, have an intense action on the head, while comfrey has a unique yin action of materialization, even though it is a leaf.

ROSEMARY, CHIVE, THYME, MARJORAM, AND CLOVE

These are commonly used as herbs or spices and help increase the palatability of food. In addition, these can strongly invigorate digestive functions and help facilitate the digestion of meat because they have the nature of the fire element.

The reason that cooked meat tastes better than uncooked meat is that cooked meat is easier to digest. If meat is cooked over a fire with spices and herbs, it smells and tastes better than raw, unseasoned meat. Using herbs and spices derived from fragrant leaves or twigs would be similar to mixing fire with fire.

Fragrance indicates significant molecular activity, with fragrant substances' molecules directly stimulating the nose. And because substances with vigorous molecular activity have greater energizing functions, they will invigorate the energizing function of the human body upon ingestion.

GOTU KOLA

Gotu kola is a slender, long, and creeping plant that commonly grows in swampy lands near the equator in India, Sri Lanka, Madagascar, South Africa, and so on. The characteristics of creeping and growing near water indicate that gotu kola is a plant that belongs to the water element.

Of the organs that belong to the water element (the kidneys, brain, bones, bone marrow, and genitals), the brain is situated in the highest region and is the most yang. The medicinal part of gotu kola is in its leaves, which belong to the fire element. Because the leaves are used, gotu kola can facilitate the energetic activity of the brain. In addition, the tips of the leaves have an even stronger effect on the brain.

In Ayurveda, the traditional medicine of India, gotu kola is considered one of the most spiritual and rejuvenating herbs. It is also said to help deepen the practice of meditation by developing and opening the crown chakra, the energy center situated in the center of the top of the head.

In general, the leaves of a plant that belong to the fire element will only promote the energetic activity of the yang regions of the body (the head, brain, skin, and immune system). But leaves of herbs that belong to the water element can supply nutrients of the water element to the yang regions of the body. The adrenal glands, like the brain, also belong to fire within water. So they are strengthened through the use of gotu kola.

Since the leaves rather than flowers are used, gotu kola vitalizes the brain's activity and stimulates the nerve cells throughout the whole body. Thus, it has an intimate relationship with the nerves and can strengthen the immune system, which is active in the more superficial part of the body.

Since gotu kola vitalizes the energy supply to the nervous system, including the brain, it can increase concentration and boost memory.

Moreover, as nourishment to the nerves improves, it helps a person relax. Therefore, gotu kola is well known as the "food for the brain" and is efficacious for children with ADD (attention deficit disorder).

Because of gotu kola's ability to supply energy and nutrients throughout the body, researchers have discovered the superior effect of gotu kola in the healing of the skin and other connective tissues, including lymph tissues, blood vessels, and mucous membranes.

The disorders of the blood vessels themselves are caused by poor materializing function. If the problem especially develops in the legs, which pertain to the water element, it is due to the malfunction of the water element. Thus, gotu kola is used for varicose veins, venous insufficiency, and phlebitis.

COMFREY

Comfrey has wide, large leaves and a yin nature. Its leaves correspond to the fire within yin. In addition, comfrey leaves have rough hairs on them. Hairs pertain to the function of the wood element in which energy tries to penetrate outward through a substance.

Herbs with yin natures promote the materializing function needed to vitalize cell production. Comfrey contains a chemical called allantoin, a cell multiplication agent that augments the healing of wounds. Comfrey can thus treat various skin disorders such as rashes and wounds. It is also beneficial for ulcers, which are wounds of the digestive tract. Moreover, it promotes the function of the lungs—the organ belonging to the metal element—and can treat various respiratory problems.

TEA (BLACK AND GREEN)

Tea leaves are small and pointy (fire). Younger leaves (wood) further strengthen the tea's fire nature (the principle of wood generating fire), which promotes the energetic activity needed to vitalize physiological activity in the body. Although tea vitalizes overall physiological activity, it primarily targets the brain, awakening the senses.

Tea can also improve blood circulation by delivering oxygen and nutrients to each cell, temporarily relieving fatigue, enhancing the desire to work, and eliciting feelings of courage. In addition, because younger tea leaves are generally used, the supply of oxygen and nutrients, particularly to the tips or ends of the body—the head, hands, and feet—is improved. As the oxygen and nutrient supply to the brain cells improves, the mind also becomes clearer.

The strength of the fire element in the tea trees, if acting on its own, would threaten the survival of the living plant. To balance the fire function, nature supplied the tea leaves with a substance called tannin, which belongs to the metal element. The tannin gives the tea its astringent taste, which gathers and slows the fire element's energy. Human beings drink tea to acquire its fire nature. But the tannin interferes with the augmentation of fire in the body, so the tea leaves are roasted (green tea) or steamed (black tea), thereby applying the principle of fire controlling metal. These cooking methods, while effective, are not complete, because some tannin remains in the tea. If there were no tannin, the human brain cells would receive too much stimulation from the tea leaves, and the effect would be similar to that of cocaine or marijuana.

Tea is not a food or a tonic. Although it contains a great deal of fire energy, that energy will stimulate the body's activities rather than supplement its energy. For this reason, sugar or honey is added to boost the body. Black tea (red) is especially good with sugar because it is the color of the fire element, which generates the earth (the sweet taste). Green tea, however, has the wood element in it due to its greenish tint, so it does not go well with sugar (wood controlling earth). In addition, the human body instinctively knows that the excessive fire of the tea can harm it. Therefore, the body craves a sour taste to gather the energy of fire, explaining why black tea (red) tastes better with lemon.

Green tea is made by briefly roasting the leaves over a fire instead of "sweating" or steaming them for a long time, as is the case for black tea. The leaves retain their original green color through the roasting process, which indicates that their yin nature is still present. Remember that substances are more yin in their raw state than after cooking. Thus, the effect of green tea in promoting energetic activity occurs for only a short time and then disappears, so a person will immediately feel settled and fall asleep. Green tea has been used for patient recovery from fatigue and headaches. It also acts as a tranquilizer or sleeping medication.

Nevertheless, green tea is not a tonic since it contains a toxin in the form of caffeine (actually theophylline, a milder form of caffeine). Its value was thus reduced to the lowest herbal grade in the toxin category by the masters who discovered the herbal effects according to the I Ching principles.

TOBACCO LEAVES

Tobacco leaves are broad, similar to comfrey leaves, and belong to the yin within the fire element. Tobacco has an odor or fragrance that may initially smell pleasant but, after a while, becomes offensive. Dogs do not like the smell of tobacco leaves. Goats, however, do like the scent and eat the leaves. There is a good reason for this.

Of the five elements on Earth, all elements except the earth have a yin-yang pair. The earth element has two of each (two yins and two yangs). The Eastern zodiac symbols assign each of the twelve elements to an animal. The sheep (of the same nature as the goat) belongs to the earth element and sits between the fire and metal elements. So the force that pertains to the sheep is in charge of transforming the fire element into the metal element.

Given the earth's balancing abilities, it would seem that the element would always be necessary. However, the activity can stop when there is a perfect balance of yin and yang. This is not a good situation for the element because it likes to receive stimulation that will facilitate its responsible work. Thus a goat (earth) wants to vitalize the function of transforming the fire element into the metal element by eating the tobacco leaves. In contrast, the dog, in charge of changing the metal element into the water element, does not like tobacco leaves because they do not share a common nature.

When humans who are relatively well-balanced in yin and yang eat tobacco leaves, there will initially be a dynamic action of the element fire due to the strong fragrance of the leaves. However, the energetic activity will soon slow down due to the function of the element metal of the wide tobacco leaves.

Tobacco leaves' function comes from the rapid fire nature of their smell, so they do not function properly when cooked. For this reason, they are smoked, allowing their fire components to immediately permeate the blood in the capillaries. This vitalizes the brain cells and speeds up brain activity. A person's ability to calculate and memorize improves, and they feel better emotionally. The blood circulation of the heart improves, and the capillaries expand so that each cell receives an adequate supply of oxygen and nutrients. Thus, a person's energy increases and fatigue is relieved. Even the digestive system's cells are stimulated to improve digestion, and the feeling of nausea that can arise from overeating meat will disappear. In the lungs, the bronchioles expand so that gas exchange is improved.

These effects, however, are temporary and only occur while the fire element is in charge. Shortly after, the metal element takes control to contract capillaries. As the supply of oxygen and nutrients to each cell decreases, the body and head feel heavy and tired. The activity of the digestive system slows down so that the feelings of nausea can reoccur. In the lungs, the bronchioles contract so that the chest feels congested, and the quantity of sputum increases. If a person smokes another cigarette, the fire element retakes charge, and the body returns to the state of fire controlling metal. The head and body will feel lighter because of the improved blood circulation. This is one of the main reasons why cigarettes are so addictive.

Aloe Vera

Aloe grows in the hot and dry desert. To survive such drastic weather, the function of the plant's metal element is greatly amplified. The metal's strong contracting nature, which arises to counter the environmental heat (fire) and the fire nature of leaves, gives the aloe thick leaves to prevent the moisture inside from evaporating. At the same time, ample liquid storage created by the metal function remains in the leaves' wide (yin) bodies. However, leaves belong to the fire element, and fire controls metal. So, while the force of fire within the aloe leaves is weak, its control of the metal element and its expanding force produce blunt thornlike protrusions that stick out from the surface of the leaves. The fire nature of these protrusions activates the function of the metal and water elements in the aloe plant. Therefore, the aloe leaves generally act on the human skin due to the fire element's dispersing nature.

The human skin belongs to the metal element system and can get damaged by fire from the environment or by a flare-up of the body's fire element. The clear aloe gel pertains to the water element and is excellent for treating skin injuries or burns. Its water can eliminate or control the fire, and its metal can help generate new skin. In Eastern medicine, the large intestine, like the skin, belongs to the system of the metal element. Therefore, constipation will likely develop when fire is added to enact the principle of fire controlling metal. The aloe gel can treat constipation by the water controlling the fire principle. The most effective type of aloe for constipation is the brown plant (a yin color), which has a bitter taste. It can also treat excessive types of ulcers that occur acutely.

Roots

Roots belong to the water element, and those with a bitter taste have an even stronger water function. Their actions are like the winter when the ground freezes and plant and animal activity dramatically slows down. Those animals with vigorous fire activity will survive, but microorganisms that have weak fire natures can quickly die. The bitter roots hinder all physiological activity.

Roots with a strong bitter taste, such as goldenseal, dandelion, gentian, and chicory, can treat various inflammations due to the excess function of the fire element, because water controls fire. Inflammation is a physiological reaction to eliminate germs. Therefore, if inflammation is hindered, germs can become even more active. However, the strong action of the water element can freeze the germs. Clinical studies have shown that germs cultivated in a laboratory will perish if they come in contact with these herbs. It is interesting to note that all antibiotics have a bitter taste because they contain the function of the water element.

GOLDENSEAL

Goldenseal is a small yellow root with a slightly offensive odor. A foul odor implies that the herb's energy spreads out well, but its action impedes physiological functions. Yellow roots (the earth element's color) have a much stronger disinfectant and detoxifying effect than black roots (the water element's color). The earth element is balanced, and the nature of germs, which are essentially classified as poisons or toxins, is tilted in one direction. Yellow roots also can regulate excessive water in the body by the principle of earth controlling water to decrease the swelling associated with inflammation. Other yellow roots with disinfectant qualities include skullcap, Phellodendron, gardenia, and rhubarb.

Many herbalists recognize goldenseal's ability to treat almost any disease because diseases generally arise from an inflammatory reaction to an invasion of some virus or bacteria. Thus, goldenseal is frequently used for the common colds and flu, sore throats, bronchitis, sinusitis, irritable bowel syndrome, colitis, gastritis, and intestinal parasites. In addition, it is used externally as an eyewash for eye disorders and

as a mouthwash for gum disease and canker sores. Moreover, it is used externally for various skin diseases, including athlete's foot.

It is imperative to remember that goldenseal should not be used for deficient types of inflammation, which are caused by decreased physiological functioning. Goldenseal is not a tonic to strengthen the immune system, so it cannot promote physiological functioning in some body areas like tonics do. When an increased susceptibility to germs due to a weakened state causes inflammation, goldenseal will exacerbate the disease or the problem rather than treating it. For inflammation such as this, herbs that are tonic roots with sweet and slightly pungent tastes, such as ginseng, garlic, or angelica root (Dang Gui), should be used.

DANDELION

Dandelion leaves are broad and very soft. In Korea, they are boiled in water to remove bitterness and eaten as greens. Rabbits like this grass very much. Rabbits have red eyes. When people drink too much, their eyes turn red. Marijuana can also cause red eyes. Its leaves are pointed like stars. Its flowers bloom during the summer solstice, and the flowers and leaves around the flowers have the strongest hallucinating action. The sharp leaves are fire, the summer solstice is fire, and the flowers are fire. So, naturally, it enters the brain, the fire of a person, and raises its function, causing the eyes, the fire sense organ, to turn red.

Dandelion would be bitter to a person with a harmonious yin and yang, but to a rabbit with red eyes, which belongs to wood among the five elements of the Earth, it will be sweet. To put out a rabbit's fire, it needs to consume bitterness, the taste of water element. Since the poison of marijuana is fire, it is possible that eating dandelion will remove its poison.

Dandelion, like goldenseal, can eliminate inflammation, a physiological activity like fire. However, while dandelion is more effective against liver inflammation, it invigorates the kidneys' function, and treats the inflammation of the kidneys. When a dandelion root is cut, white-colored juice comes out. This white juice corresponds to human blood. White is the color of the metal element and implies cleanliness. Hence, the dandelion enters the blood vessels and cools them. That is why its nickname is "blood cleanser."

In Western herbal books, it is said that having a bitter taste improves appetite and promotes digestion. This is a phrase to be very wary of. A bitter taste stimulates saliva and digestive juices. Still, it does not promote the secretion of digestive juices, like black pepper, ginger, or hot red pepper do. The bitter taste is indigestible, so the body secretes digestive fluids for proper digestion. That phrase applies to people who eat well because they are usually energetic and have a strong digestive system, such as Tae-eumins and Soyangins.

People who usually have low energy, who eat a small amount due to a weak digestive system and quickly get an upset stomach from slight overeating, are Soeumins. For them ingesting bitter herbs like goldenseal, dandelion,

and gentian is like instantly extinguishing a person's weak fire, similar to a candle swaying in the wind. Soeumins possess excess water and little fire. Therefore, such a person should ingest herbs that augment fire, such as ginseng, garlic, or ginger.

GENTIAN

Gentian flowers are purple. Since it is purple, when we subtract red, the fire color of flowers, blue, the color of water, remains. Gentian has few leaves, and its large stems rise straight up. It is a plant belonging to the wood element. With its bitter taste, it suppresses the fire of wood. Wood has an action of changing matter into energy, and when stressed, the energy cannot spread and stagnates in the liver. When the liver is stagnant, the pressure generates heat, which causes digestive problems as a phenomenon of wood controlling earth. As a result, a person becomes depressed with a bloated stomach, nausea, acid reflux, and a bitter taste in the mouth. Gentian will be effective for all inflammations that appear with these symptoms of wood controlling earth. It has an excellent effect on gastritis, colitis, cystitis, vaginitis, and urethritis.

The reproductive capacity of the genitals is under the jurisdiction of the water element, and the shape of the genitals is under wood, so gentian is very suitable for inflammation occurring in the genitals. However, since gentian is also a medicine for sedating excess syndrome, it cannot be used for inflammation of the deficient syndrome. Therefore, when Soeumins take this medicine, they get diarrhea and keep wanting to sleep because they have no energy.

CHICORY

Chicory is bitter, but it is not as strong as goldenseal or gentian. Its roots are soft and plump, having the shape of the earth element. When used as a coffee substitute, it is roasted over a fire to soften the properties of the water. Plants with a bitter taste harm the body by inhibiting physiological activity, so there is a sense of repulsion when one eats it in a raw state. However, these plants become more edible when the fire is added because they become more yang and do less harm to the body.

Since chicory has more earth nature than other bitter herbs, it can better treat inflammation of the digestive system represented by the spleen. Therefore, it is suitable for gastritis, colitis, irritable bowel syndrome, and cholecystitis. Furthermore, as it also belongs to water, it is suitable for arthritis or gout and is a mild laxative.

GINSENG

Ginseng is arguably the most balanced herb on Earth. It grows only in regions of the world balanced in yin and yang (half yin and half yang). In other words, it does not grow in places with too much sunlight or shade. Thus, ginseng is a root that contains the nature of the earth element. In addition, it is yellow, the color of the earth element.

Moreover, the plant has three (a yang number) branches spreading from the middle of the main stem, and each branch has a leaf divided into five (earth number) sections. Ginseng also bears red flowers and fruit, thus containing the nature of fire within the earth element. The root is used because the plant's energy is stored in its roots and not because the roots belong to the water element.

Ginseng has a sweet, slightly pungent, and bitter taste. The slightly bitter taste can settle the mind, while the somewhat pungent taste improves blood circulation. Its primary taste, sweet, strengthens the digestive system, the function of the earth element (represented by the spleen/pancreas). Once the digestive system becomes stronger, appetite increases and digestion and assimilation improve. In addition, proper assimilation of nutrients will allow the body's other organs to become stronger. Ginseng is the best herb to strengthen the entire body's health.

Nevertheless, even a good herb such as ginseng cannot treat all illnesses. For example, it will not be effective in treating the diseases of a person who has a strong spleen but weak kidneys (Soyangin). Nor can it treat a person whose function of the wood element is strong but has a weak metal element (Taeyangin). In addition, ginseng would not be suitable for a person with a weakness in the water element. Because ginseng strengthens the fire within the earth element, in the person with a weak water element, the fire will become stronger, and the water will dry out even more. And in a person with a weak metal element, the yang function will become stronger, while the metal function weakens even more.

Ginseng is a tonic that facilitates the body's physiological functions and can, therefore, worsen all acute inflammations. When ginseng is ingested, its effect does not only reach the body's cells but will also nourish any germs in the system. However, ginseng can have dramatic effects once a disease develops into a weak immune system or a chronic inflammatory condition in which there is almost no pain, redness, swelling, or heat. Therefore, people who frequently present with inflammation from germs and get no relief from antibiotics but instead develop digestive disturbances should take ginseng simultaneously with their antibiotics. The effects will be significant.

Since ginseng supplements the function of the earth element, it can treat disorders in which the body's homeostatic mechanisms are not functioning correctly. For example, ginseng can treat diabetes that repeats the high and low blood sugar cycle, an abnormality in the autonomic nervous system that replicates the cycle of high and low blood pressure, or an anomaly in hormonal secretion in which there is an alternation of chills and fever. Additionally, ginseng can treat irritable bowel syndrome (alternation of constipation and diarrhea) and various allergies.

Detoxification is also a function of the earth element. Therefore, ginseng can treat the side effects of chemotherapy, radiation, and withdrawal symptoms from drugs. Ginseng can also be used for patients before and after surgery. For instance, patients who cannot undergo surgery due to general weakness can be given ginseng for several weeks before the surgery date. This will improve their condition to the level at which surgery can be performed. Those experiencing delayed healing after surgery can also take ginseng to help speed up recovery.

Ginseng will be beneficial regardless of body type when one is in a highly weakened state. However, except for the Soeumin body type, the other constitutions will experience headaches, red eyes, irritability, and a stifling sensation in the chest at some point. Then, the administration of ginseng should be stopped immediately and exchanged with an herb more appropriate for the specific body type.

Chinese Angelica (Dang Gui)

Angelica leaves are soft and wide (yin). Its flowers are not very attractive and look like white racemes, gatherings of small flowers (yin). Like ginseng, the angelica root is plump with a sweet taste, which relates it to the earth element. Though angelica is an herb with a great deal of earth energy, it belongs to the wood element within the earth element. This is due to its fairly strong fragrance and slightly pungent taste. But the root contains a lot of moisture, which relates to the water element. Therefore, it can increase the blood supply and the body's water and improve circulation with the yang function of its fragrance and pungent taste.

With these functions, angelica helps to eliminate various symptoms, regardless of whether or not the red blood cell count is low. They include anemic symptoms such as dizziness, a pale face, numbness of limbs, and palpitations.

In men, ginseng can treat all symptoms of physical strain, including infection and inflammation. In women, angelica can treat anemic symptoms arising from excessive bleeding during menstruation or childbirth and all infections and inflammation that occur from them.

In Eastern medicine, a principle states that the doctor must first observe the signs of Qi deficiency due to overstrain to treat men's disorders effectively. And for the proper treatment of women's disorders, the doctor must first observe the signs of blood deficiency due to menstruation and childbirth. Men are yang and women are yin. Qi is yang, and blood is yin. So men will first present with conditions of Qi deficiency, and women will present with conditions that arise from blood deficiency. These issues must be addressed to treat any problem.

When the body's homeostatic mechanism (a function of the earth element) is normal, most infections and inflammations will be instinctively taken care of through cravings for foods that will have a medicinal effect. In men, however, when the energy lost by excessive physical labor or sexual activity is not quickly recovered, germs can easily invade the body and give rise to disease. In women, when the blood lost during menstruation and childbirth is not replenished, germs can easily invade the body and cause illness. Therefore, ginseng is the best herb for men to use to recover from

Qi deficiency, and angelica is the best herb for women to use to recover from blood loss. Ginseng and angelica are very effective for the early stages of deficient conditions. However, these herbs are no longer effective once a disease has progressed. At this point, the condition must be broken down into Sasang and the five elements, and the appropriate herbs must be applied.

A deficient pathogen enters the body when it is in a weakened state. In contrast, an excess pathogen gives rise to illness even though the body is strong. Tonics such as ginseng and angelica should be used for deficient pathogens, while sedating herbs such as goldenseal or gentian should be utilized for excess pathogens.

The majority of Western herbs are sedating herbs. When these herbs are not strong enough to treat an excess pathogen, antibiotics or anticancer medicines (or other Western pharmaceuticals) that are like toxins or poisons need to be used. These Western drugs have extreme variances of yin and yang. Surgery is essential to eliminate the diseased region if these medications are still insufficient. Afterward, tonic herbs should be used for recovery. Otherwise, tonics, in conjunction with sedating herbs, should be used.

Most commonly, diseases such as allergies, degenerative diseases, and cancer are due to deficient pathogens. Therefore, the proper time to treat them with ginseng and angelica may have passed. Thus, treating these conditions is possible only after deciphering the Sasang and the five elements of the patient's constitution and symptoms. Once done, the applicable tonics are mixed in a formula with the appropriate sedating herbs. These formulas are created according to the complex Eastern medical methods based on applying the I Ching principle.

In all, Chinese angelica has an excellent effect on all menstrual problems, including painful menstruation (dysmenorrhea), irregular menstruation (oligomenorrhea), a lack of menstruation (amenorrhea), PMS, uterine bleeding, and excess menstruation (menorrhagia). Angelica is also good for disorders of the reproductive system, such as problems of ovulation, vaginitis, and infertility. Moreover, angelica is effective for neuralgic or rheumatic pains that worsen during cold or damp weather. Nevertheless, angelica should only be used when accompanying anemic symptoms, such as dizziness, numbness in the limbs, and palpitations with weak and hollow pulses (indicating blood deficiency), are present.

GARLIC

Garlic is a root, yet it has a strong smell—not a fragrance, but an offensive odor (water)—which people tend to dislike. However, it contains a mixture of sweet and pungent tastes because it is a food. Though the garlic bulb does not have stems, it does have leaves that stick out sharply from the root, much like the leaves of an orchid. As stated before, the orchid is a plant that best represents the nature of the fire element, and plants that resemble the orchid also have attributes that correspond to the fire element. Garlic, therefore, has the nature of fire within water. In the body, the fire of the

water element corresponds to the functioning of the adrenal glands. Therefore, garlic has the effect of strengthening sexual vitality. In Korea, before the effect of garlic became widely known in the West, a medicine for vitality called Aronamin became popular; garlic was the main ingredient.

In Korea, the story of garlic is first mentioned in the mythology of the nation's founding. In China, the legendary Emperor Fuxi, the creator of the I Ching, and Emperor Huangdi, the Yellow Emperor, the father of Chinese culture, immensely enjoyed eating garlic. Likewise, Korean people are famous for eating during each meal a pickled cabbage called kimchi, in which there is a large quantity of chopped garlic.

When antibiotics were not widely available in the past, many Japanese people died of dysentery while many Koreans survived. To discover its reason, the Japanese researchers surveyed and found that garlic has a tremendous antibiotic effect. Thus, the bacteria that caused dysentery did not proliferate in the Koreans.

In the Tai Chi symbol, the fire (red or white color) within the water (blue or black) element is the single point of yang that arises from the extreme of yin. This is called Jing, or essence. Jing is in a state before energy transforms into matter and becomes the foundation for substance. Jing creates sex cells and becomes the energy during sexual activity. After the creation of sex cells, any remaining Jing transforms into other types of cells. When Jing is insufficient, the desire to work and the desire for sex diminishes. In turn, reproductive cell production decreases, leading to infertility. Consuming garlic can supply the material necessary to create Jing. Since Jing transforms into Qi and Qi, in turn, transforms into Shen, or spirit, Jing also becomes the source of energy corresponding to Qi and the raw material for the mind corresponding to Shen, or spirit.

A strong odor indicates that garlic supplies Jing, which can readily convert into energy. In addition, garlic, which activates physiological functioning, can also activate the immune system to have a disinfecting effect.

It seems as though garlic can treat just about any disease. However, garlic is a tonic herb that can worsen the acute inflammatory reaction of the excess syndrome. Although garlic can tonify, its fire energy is powerful. The Soyangin constitution has a constant energizing action in the body due to a deficiency of the water element. Therefore, if these persons take garlic, their activity will become more invigorated (though the effect will be less than if they ingested ginseng). As a root, garlic strengthens the water element through the tonification of the fire element within water. Thus, in the end, it consumes water more so than tonifying it.

When reading Western herb books, it is easy to assume that a single herb can cure every disease. However, a crucial thing to remember is that every herb or medicine has a tilt of yin-yang. And it is this tilt that counters the slant of the disease to slow or reverse the illness by restoring balance. If herbs are not properly applied, they can magnify or worsen any condition. In our universe, everything that

manifests has some degree of variation of yin or yang. Therefore, everything can be used as some form of medication and elicit some side effects. There is no panacea. Only God can cure all the diseases of this world.

GINGER

Ginger is exceptionally lumpy among the roots. It is common to see round spheres representing symbols of the universe and religion (circle, beads, and rosary). When an object is round, it is because of the strong centripetal force, which is the action of the earth element. Ginger has a good smell and spicy taste. Since ginger is a rhizome, it promotes the activity of earth, stimulating the digestive system with its pungent taste and smell.

Although ginger belongs to food, it cannot be eaten in large quantities nor frequently, like rice or wheat, and it is not a tonic due to its pungent taste and smell. Activation of the digestive system by the taste and smell of ginger is temporary, and the effect of ginger soon stops, so it does not satisfy the condition of tonic herbs. Stimulation of the digestive system eventually leads to a lack of energy in the digestive system. Therefore, ginger is considered a sedating herb, but as a food, it is not as severe as gentian or goldenseal.

Eating gentian or goldenseal with meat will burden digestion and worsen the taste. These bitter herbs harm rather than promote digestion. However, adding ginger when cooking meat improves the taste and sterilizes pathogens that multiply in meat. Ginger is good for nausea, such as morning sickness and car sickness.

When eating sashimi or sushi at a Japanese restaurant, the ginger and white part of green onions are served. Sashimi or sushi is not well digested because they are raw, and although invisible, germs can easily live on them. Eating ginger or green onion at this time improves digestion and kills germs. The smell and taste of ginger and green onions belong to yang, which promotes digestion and kills harmful bacteria that are yin-natured. Eating ginger during a common cold with chills and fever will lessen the symptoms.

Overthinking can weaken the digestive system. Ginger can prevent this. Because Confucius always thought a lot, he consumed sweets made of ginger and sugar constantly to maintain his digestive system.

Seeds

Like roots, seeds also belong to the water element. The water element of roots is like their nature of absorbing and sending nutrients upward. Therefore, roots have an ascending function. In contrast, the water element of seeds is like their nature of dropping to the ground and therefore has a descending function.

FENNEL, ANISE, DILL

Fennel, anise, and dill are plants that belong to the same family, even though their disease ap-plications are significantly different as noted in a wide variety of herb books. After analyzing the shape, smell, and taste of these plants and their seeds, it is easy to see that they have almost the same effect. All three seeds act on the lower abdomen, which is the region of the water element. In addition, they are all fragrant, so they facilitate the energetic activity of the body. The fragrance will also have an analgesic effect to penetrate obstructions that cause pain. Thus, they treat colic, pain, and spasms in the intestines.

Colic presents with a cold lower abdomen and dull achy pain in particular stomach areas. The cause of this problem may be in the intestines or, in many cases, the ovaries and fallopian tubes in women, and testicles, seminal ducts, or prostate glands in men. In such cases, there is chronic inflammation in these regions.

Children have a strong yang function but a weak yin function. Because this is true, the function of the lower abdomen (a yin region) is weak. Babies are very susceptible to colic and will cry for no apparent reason. Unless there is strangulation (compression or constriction) of the intestines or an intussusception (a part of an intestine slipping into another part just below it), seeds can be used as a possible treatment. If there is strangulation or intussusception of the intestines, but not severe, eating the seeds can treat it by increasing the peristalsis of the intestines. Colic arises due to a lack of Jing (essence). Fennel, anise, and dill have the effect of stopping pain and strengthening the

Jing. These three herbs are the most effective for treating colic.

Seeds correspond to sperm in men and help increase sperm count and improve sexual vitality. Taking them for an extended time can treat mild impotence. However, seeds are weaker than garlic or ginseng in strengthening sexual stamina.

The seeds of fennel, anise, and dill have a slightly pungent taste and fragrance, so they are sometimes used as spices. They also work well to ease nausea, promote digestion, and have a therapeutic effect on upper abdominal pain. Moreover, they can quell toothaches because teeth are considered a "surplus of bone" (bone belongs to the water element). And finally, as these seeds have descending energy and facilitate the kidneys and bladder functions, they have a diuretic effect.

BARLEY

Barely is the most challenging grain to digest and belongs to the water element. In Korea, barley is cheaper than rice. Some years ago, poor children's diets generally consisted of a small amount of rice with a lot of barley mixed in. In schools, it was easy to distinguish poor children from others. The poor children passed a lot of wind because barley is so hard to digest. However, barley is in the spotlight nowadays as a health food.

When a person eats barley, the stomach will remain full for quite some time while it is digesting. In addition, barley has a lower ratio of carbohydrates when compared to rice.

Moreover, it is a good source of fiber that will relieve constipation. These characteristics of barley attest to the fact that it has the consolidating energy of the water element.

Barley is the first grain to sprout at the end of winter. The green bud that penetrates through the consolidating power of barley carries a powerful function of the wood element. Because the barley sprout has the strong life force represented by the wood element, it can grow in the harshest environment. Roman gladiators valued the strength of barley sprouts' life force. They ate them in large quantities to develop their strength and stamina. The contemporary term for gladiators was "barley men."

The barley grain is suitable for the So-yangin body type because it contains a great deal of water energy. However, sprouted barley is ideal for the Tae-eumin body type, as it has a great amount of wood energy. Remember, Tae-eumins have a lot of trouble with their hearts and lungs, the organs responsible for spreading energy. They have a great amount of metal energy, which gathers energy and transforms it into matter. As Tae-eumins accumulate substances without dispersing them, they are generally overweight and have high cholesterol. Therefore, they are prone to arteriosclerosis, angina, myocardial infarction (heart attack), and cerebrovascular accidents (stroke). They can also readily develop diabetes because they are overweight.

The barley sprouting out of its shell is similar to oxygen, expanding a set of contracted lungs. This is the function of the wood element. On the other hand, carbon dioxide exiting the lungs as they contract is the function of the metal element. The following diagram demonstrates a simplification of this process (fig. 20.2).

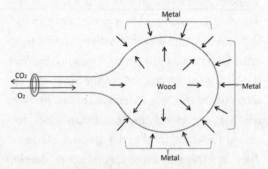

Figure 20.2 Diagram of Balloon Lung

Bronchial asthma, in which the bronchioles contract but do not adequately relax, frequently occurs in Tae-eumins because of their excessive metal energy. It would benefit the Tae-eumin constitution to eat a lot of barley sprouts to prevent and treat this disease. Alfalfa sprouts have almost the same function as barley sprouts.

LOTUS SEEDS

Lotus plants grow in ponds and have round, wide leaves. Thus, they are plants that belong to the water element. Lotuses' red blossoms resemble the human heart, which corresponds to the mind and spirit in Eastern medicine. A single lotus flower blossoming in a bluish pond represents the single point of yang created when yin reaches its extreme in the Tai Chi symbol. Buddhism reveres the lotus flower as "Buddha's mind."

In the East, lanterns in the shape of lotus flowers are hung around Buddhist temples to commemorate Buddha's birthday. This activity is similar to lighting candles and decorating with red ribbons and poinsettias during Christmas, when the water element is at its extreme. These all symbolize the I Ching principle known as "mutual communication between water and fire," and the "rebirth" professed by these religions.

For these reasons, it may seem that eating the lotus flower will give rise to Buddha's mind (compassionate, all-embracing, and most virtuous). Actually, the lotus flower does not have the element of fire within water. Instead, it only has fire. Acquiring the fire within the water element is possible by eating all the lotus plant's leaves, stems, and roots together. But unfortunately, this is hard to do. The seeds are the parts of the plant that have gathered all of the lotus's essence. So to ingest Buddha's mind that blossoms upward from the lotus plant, you can eat its seeds and let it blossom within your heart.

The lotus seeds have similar effects as gotu kola. Both herbs supply oxygen and nutrients to the brain to help with meditation and peace of mind. However, the energy supply will be of a shorter duration than that gained from the more substantive lotus seeds. This is because herbs that use energy have faster but short-lived effects. In contrast, herbs that use substances have slower and longer-lasting results.

Lotus seeds tonify when used without the germ. However, because the germ has a bitter taste, it also sedates heart fire. So, the cases in which the germ would be beneficial are those where the mind will not remain peaceful, like the mind of Buddha. Instead, as fire rises in mind, there will be greed and mental disturbance, like seawater in a turbulent storm. As a result, the face turns red, the tongue develops cracks and thorns, the mouth tastes bitter, and there is insomnia.

The lotus seed gathers and stores nutrients to help the lotus flower blossom. Therefore, it has a sweet taste and belongs to the earth element. Remember, the sweet taste mentioned here is not the taste of sugar but similar to that of rice or wheat. The seed alone is a tonic, but it sedates and hinders the tonification process when its germ is intact. Thus, removing the germ of lotus seed before its use is imperative.

Since lotus seeds belong to the earth element, they can strengthen the digestive system. Also, with their slight astringent taste, they can support the gathering function of the lungs to fortify them. Furthermore, the water nature of the lotus seeds can also strengthen the kidneys. Meanwhile, their red exterior signifies their ability to reinforce the heart.

Masters of the I Ching can pick up unknown seeds off the ground and identify their properties based on their shape, taste, smell, color, and texture, according to the theories of the I Ching, without ever seeing the plant. This is possible because there is a macrocosm within a microcosm.

The lotus seed can stop chronic diarrhea and cough by strengthening the digestive and respiratory systems. In addition, it can treat spermatorrhea and nocturnal emission, which are caused by the weakness of the heart and the weakness of the fire. Fortifying the weak heart can strengthen the heartbeat and prevent palpitations from a minor stimulus.

Bark/Peel

There are two different elements in bark. The bark of the outer layer belongs to the metal element, while the inner bark of the stem belongs to the wood element. Among the herbs whose bark is used, yohimbe and willow are the most famous. Generally, the internal-side-bark herbs are selected to utilize the wood function. Initially, energy becomes activated to manifest a dynamic physiological functioning, but energetic activity later slows down.

YOHIMBE

Yohimbe is a tree that grows in the tropical regions of Africa. It is a tree with the nature of the fire element. Using only the leaves or flowers (fire element) would make the physiological action even more vigorous. However, the effects would only act on the head or the heart, while the activity on the genitals, the lower region, would be weak. According to Eastern medicine, the function of the water element is to supply nourishment to the genitals. However, it is the function of the wood element to create an erection in the flaccid male genitalia.

The yohimbe bark has almost the same action as Viagra. Just as the initial intention for Viagra was to be a vasodilator to treat angina, yohimbe bark was used originally as a medicine to treat angina. Currently, the use of its extract is to treat functional impotence.

In scientific terms, the effective ingredient for treating impotence found within the yohimbe bark functions as the blocking agent for the alpha-2 adrenergic receptors. When the blood vessels that enter the penis are open, they fill with blood to create an erection. However, when the blood vessels constrict to close, blood entering the genital is reduced, and the penis becomes flaccid. The constriction of the blood vessels is due to the secretion of a neurotransmitter called α-2-adrenaline when excitation of the sympathetic nerve occurs. The yohimbe bark blocks this action to relax the blood vessels. When the blood vessels that supply blood to the genital region relax, much more blood enters the penis to create an erection, similar to how a balloon blows up when filled with air (fig. 20.3).

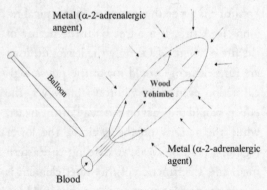

Figure 20.3 Yohimbe Bark: Wood generating Fire → Fire controlling Metal → dilation of blood vessels → erection

The wood function of yohimbe bark accelerates the number of heartbeats by the principle of wood generating fire. This action of yohimbe bark relaxes the blood vessels of the genital region and the whole body. Increasing blood volume raises blood pressure as well as body temperature. Nevertheless, these functions can manifest as the side effects of an overly vigorous fire, such as a racing heartbeat, irritability, restlessness, headache, dizziness, and so on.

WILLOW TREE BARK

The willow tree bark is famous for being the original plant to contain the active ingredient in aspirin. Willow and yohimbe are taken from the bark's inner aspects, maintaining the wood element's vital function. Thus, by the principle of wood generating fire, they have the identical function of invigorating the heartbeat and blood circulation to raise the body temperature. When the body temperature rises, sweating occurs. The difference between the two barks is that willow trees grow in places with a lot of water. Although its leaves are sharp and pointy, its small branches droop toward the ground, indicating its yin nature. Thus, the willow contains a lot of yin in its roots, leaves, and branches. Using the willow bark's inner side temporarily provides the wood element function, which soon transforms into yin.

Simultaneous occurrence of chills and fever does not indicate a significant rise in body temperature that dries up fluids. If energetic activity is made vigorous by wood and fire, a fever would increase slightly and then reach its extreme to transform into water. As sweat breaks, by the action of water, physiological functioning slows down and body temperature drops to a normal level. This is an explanation from the antipyretic (heat-clearing) viewpoint, but a reason in terms of strengthening the immune function is also possible.

When germs invade our bodies, the brain, which has received a report from the immune system, raises the body temperature to activate immune substances. If the body temperature rises at once, the immune system becomes activated without taking any medicine, and the invading germs die. Sweating occurs once, and the body temperature returns to a normal level.

However, if the body temperature does not rise suddenly at once, fever and chills will simultaneously occur. Ingesting the willow bark at this time makes the energetic activity become vigorous, the heartbeat increase, the blood circulation become active, and the body temperature rise. As proof of this rise in body temperature, sweating occurs. Subsequently, as the invading germs die due to the activation of the immune system, the energetic activity normalizes while body temperature drops. This is the effect of willow bark, as represented by the effect of aspirin.

The effect of willow bark is in activating the wood energy to invigorate blood circulation and not lowering the body temperature as if pouring water on fire. Aspirin will not reduce a normal body temperature. Its general use is for preventing embolisms that can cause heart attacks or strokes. It does so by accelerating the blood circulation to prevent the blood from clotting.

When aspirin is used at the initial stage of a germ invasion with simultaneous chills and fever, the body temperature will drop to a normal range and will not rise again. However, when aspirin is taken for fever alone, the body temperature will drop until the liver detoxifies the aspirin, then the body temperature will again rise. This is proof that the main effect of the willow bark (as represented by aspirin) is in activating the immune system due to the acceleration of blood circulation and ultimately not the lowering of body temperature. An interpretation generated through the I Ching principle gives a much more holistic view than the fragmentary interpretations of science.

Aspirin's analgesic and anti-inflammatory effects are due to the acceleration of the blood circulation accomplished by the properties of the willow bark. When blood circulation improves in a painful region, the immune system becomes activated and germs die. Additionally, the supply of oxygen and nutrients improves, allowing for faster recovery of the damaged area. The water function following the fire function allows for inflammation to subside.

Acetaminophen is effective in reducing fever and stopping pain. Aspirin, on the other hand, in addition to these functions, can reduce inflammation. Aspirin is an extract from a plant, while acetaminophen is a pure synthetic compound. Synthetic compounds have more potent effects, though their treatment scope is not as diverse. Tylenol also has strong side effects. Natural compounds, in contrast, have weaker effects, while their treatment scope is more varied, and they produce fewer side effects.

Though using willow bark instead of aspirin is a weaker treatment, it avoids the side effects of aspirin (in particular, the salicylic acid in aspirin), such as gastritis or ulcers. As the yin and yang are somewhat balanced in organisms, when an ingredient has an extreme action tilted in one direction, another component with an opposite activity is in place to neutralize the imbalance. Since salicylic acid is acidic, alkaline ingredients exist to balance it.

Resins and Sap

Myrrh and frankincense are plant resins historically used as medicines. Nowadays, they are no longer commonly used in Western herbology. But they frequently were in the past, and even the Christian Bible mentions them.

The Eastern masters astrologically predicted that a sage would be born in the Middle East and they came to Jerusalem on the day Christ was born. They brought gifts of gold, myrrh, and frankincense to the newborn. Gold was given in place of money, and the myrrh and frankincense were to eliminate the stagnant blood that developed after childbirth. Thus, these two herbs stop the pain and help heal the delivery wound faster. Eastern medicine frequently utilized myrrh and frankincense in such a way.

These Eastern masters who came to Jerusalem must have been masters of the I Ching. They used its principles to analyze the movement of the stars in the sky to predict future changes and to study the nature of matter for their use as medicine to treat disease.

Myrrh and frankincense are resins that derive from the bark. These resins correspond to the blood of humans. Both myrrh and frankincense are fragrant, and this fragrance vitalizes blood circulation. When the blood circulation is active, the stagnant blood disappears and pain is eliminated. Furthermore, by smoothly supplying more blood to the injured site, the substances necessary to recover are provided in ample amounts, expediting the recovery process. Resins help facilitate this action. For these reasons, myrrh and frankincense are frequently prescribed for postdelivery and traumatic injuries in the same way as safflower is.

MAPLE SYRUP

Maple syrup is derived from the maple tree in the springtime when the movement of the sap is active. As its taste is sweet, it is frequently boiled down and used as pancake syrup. Since it has no other tastes tilted toward any other element, it reinforces the earth element.

The leaves of the maple tree are in the shape of a star. Therefore, the sharp or pointy lobes of the leaves belong to the fire element. Still, since there are five of these pointed leaf lobes establishing harmony, they belong to the earth element. Therefore, they can be described as fire within earth.

As maple syrup is a sap, it corresponds to human blood. Furthermore, since it is active in the springtime and derived from the bark, it corresponds to the wood element. Putting all the information together, maple syrup fortifies the earth element to strengthen the digestive system, promoting food digestion and absorption. With the nutrients absorbed, a greater quantity of blood is created, and blood circulation becomes vigorous with the functions of wood and fire.

Since the nature of maple syrup is too mild (balanced in yin-yang) and the effect is too slow, it has less value as a medicine. So its use is not popular with Eastern medical doctors. However, it has been utilized to treat neuralgia in folk medicine. Neuralgia involves pain in multiple joints, such as the lower back and knees, which usually occurs in the elderly. There is increased pain with fatigue from movement and less pain with rest. The pain worsens when the weather is cold or cloudy, and is better with a hot bath, which increases blood circulation, and massage. In Western medicine, it belongs to the category of degenerative diseases. In Eastern medical terms, it is a deficient pain that improves with increased blood volume and circulation.

Neuralgia can heal, as long as it is not too severe, when one persistently takes maple syrup. Though maple syrup does not immediately affect pain due to deficiency, like Chinese angelica, it does not create digestive disturbance like Chinese angelica.

21

Attributes of the Eight Trigrams

Now that we have learned to read the al-
phabets of the I Ching, which are Tai
Chi, yin-yang, Sasang, and the five elements,
it is time to learn how to read the words, the
eight trigrams and sixty-four hexagrams. Let
us first divide the entire universe into eight
sections. When we further divide the yin and
yang of Sasang into two, there are two divisions per each yin and yang, and we will have
$4 \times 2 = 8$ trigrams.

The diagrams here (figs. 21.1 and 21.2) illustrate the trigrams' evolution, consisting of
three parallel lines from the Tai Chi, yin-yang,

and Sasang. Qian (Heaven) and Dui (Lake)
trigrams arise from Taiyang, while Li (Fire)
and Zhen (Thunder) arise from Shaoyang. Xun
(Wind) and Kan (Water) evolve from Shaoyin,
and Gen (Mountain) and Kun (Earth) evolve
from Taiyin.

The first diagram (fig. 21.1) simplifies the
understanding of the fractal structure of the
eight trigrams. It demonstrates the differentiation process from Tai Chi into the eight trigrams. The second diagram (fig. 21.2) depicts
the fractal structure of how the universe, humans, and the Earth exist.

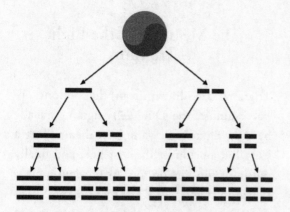

Figure 21.1 Differentiation of 8 Trigrams

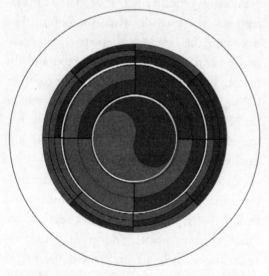

Figure 21.2 Fractal Arrangement of 8 Trigrams

The second diagram is in three layers. The innermost layer is the Tai Chi layer; the middle is the Sasang layer; and the outermost layer is the eight trigrams. The further you go out from the center, the more differentiation there is. This same differentiation process exists in human beings, the Earth, and the entire universe.

In human beings, the heart and kidneys sit in the torso corresponding to the center, so they have a yin-yang functioning similar to Tai Chi. The surrounding area that corresponds to Sasang is the form and function of all five Zang organs, including the heart and kidneys. The outer concentric circle corresponds to the eight trigrams, which include the heart, kidneys, and rest of the organs. It also includes channels that connect the front-back, left-right, above-below, and inside-outside of the body and the areas they nourish: the head, arms, legs, and trunk.

In the center of the Earth is a mixture of many substances in one single mass that is not easily differentiated, much like Tai Chi. On the next layer, matter is more differentiated than the center. The outer layer contains animals, plants, and minerals, and gaseous bodies.

In the center of the universe are innumerable small black and white holes. They have tiny universes attached to them, similar to how there are infinite numbers of Tai Chis within Tai Chi. There are black holes that swallow up various universes and white holes that spit them out, much like the activity of Tai Chi. And the layers of universes that follow them most likely will be in the form of Sasang and the eight trigrams. Each of these layers has increasingly differentiated matter. The concentric spirals of Newgrange and Mycenaean relics mentioned in chapter 14, "Trinity: Heaven, Earth, and Human Beings" also express this principle.

Though we do not know the entire universe, we can predict that its organization follows the I Ching principles. So far, none of the facts about the universe's organization we've discovered have crossed the boundary of I Ching's principles.

The shape of the universe appears much different than that of an atom. But this is only true when we view the universe with a microscopically fragmented, nonholistic standard. Observing the universe in a macroscopic and unified way with holistic standards demonstrates that their shapes are not much different. The big, empty spaces between stars are the same as the space within atoms formed by the distance between electrons and the nucleus. Stars and their satellites rotate and revolve almost the same way as nuclei and electrons do.

For five thousand years, the I Ching has been considered the top classic in the East. Its theories were accurate throughout history, except during a brief period when people believed the sun revolved around the flat Earth. Moreover, I Ching's principles are confirmed to be even more valid with every advancement in modern biology and physics.

As previously mentioned, Confucius read the I Ching so much that he had to replace its leather string three times. Still, he could not wholly understand its profound truth and lamented that the life of human beings is too short. Famous scientists, such as Leibniz, Einstein, and Niels Bohr, all deeply studied the I Ching. These men expressed the book's principles in terms such as the binary system, the law of complementarity, the theory of relativity, the unified field theory, and so on.

The Meaning of the Eight Trigrams

Trigrams are drawn from the bottom up. For example, the Dui (☱) trigram is made by drawing a single yang line, then adding a yang line on top of the first line, and finally putting a yin line on top. As previously mentioned in chapter 14, "Trinity," the three lines of a trigram represent the trinity principle of heaven (top line), earth (bottom line), and human beings (middle line). The top line can also represent the exterior, while the bottom line represents the interior. Alternatively, the center line is the interior, while the top and the bottom lines are the exteriors. In terms of time, the top line represents the future, the middle the present, and the bottom the past. Together, the eight trigrams represent all cosmic and earthly things and phenomena.

Each trigram correlates to various attributes that describe its nature. These attributes include body parts, family, jobs, seasons, animals, compass points, and so on. These correspondences help us understand the nature of each trigram and the hexagrams. We will discuss these attributes in detail later in this chapter.

There are two methods for reading a trigram. One approach is to look at the trigram's shape or form, much like a Chinese character. The second focuses on the function manifested by the forces of yin and yang, situated in the upper, middle, and lower positions (the heaven, human, and earth positions). The first method analyzes the *form* created by each line or mixture of all three lines. The second method analyzes the *function* manifested by a single core or nuclear line or by a cooperation of all three lines.

Thus far, we have explained the nature of yin-yang, but these forces also have structure. A shape with a hollow middle illustrates the form of yin (▬ ▬). The hollow indicates that the form can absorb and gather things inward. To the degree that it is hollow, its exterior is solid. Yin descends because things that absorb and gather are more efficient when situated at the bottom. Things that absorb are dark, to hide what is absorbed. Yin does not move because it is more efficient when it is still. In addition, the two short lines of the yin shape form a pair, and paired things do not like to move. For instance, married couples tend to enjoy a more settled life. Married couples are more attuned to dark places and consequently stay indoors, where it is darker. Being paired also leads to the preference for sitting low compared to standing up.

A line filled in the middle depicts the yang form (▬▬▬). Things filled inside are drawn to the outside and toward movement. Generally, it is better to ascend to go outside. Things filled inside also tend to be bright, their contents permeating outward little by little. The yang is a solitary shape, suggesting independence, the lack of a mate, and a constant movement to find this mate. Single persons frequently go out instead of sitting quietly at home. They also tend to wear conspicuous, brightly colored clothing and behave conspicuously.

I Ching was created during the legendary time of China. At that time, there were three forms of writing to record human thoughts. The first is the Chinese characters currently used. They are ideograms that express meanings with single or multiple radicals. The second is what is now the Korean alphabet that represents thoughts in speech and words and records sounds of speech by combining symbols that represent its basic elements. Consonants and vowels make up the initial, middle, and final sounds. The last is the unigrams, bigrams, trigrams, and hexagrams of the I Ching. These record thoughts of sages and enlightened beings, challenging to understand by average persons. The I Ching records the changing patterns of everything in the universe with continuous and broken lines representing yin and yang.

Since the changing patterns of everything in the universe are beyond the ordinary range of human thoughts, the Chinese characters or the Korean alphabet cannot express them all. Therefore, symbols such as the unigrams, bigrams, trigrams, and hexagrams are necessary. It is similar to how modern scientists use chemical and mathematical equations to document natural phenomena that ancient people could not witness or touch. However, there is a difference between the two.

Chemical and mathematical equations can only express or record certain parts of various natural phenomena. However, trigrams and hexagrams in the I Ching can express and document the totality because their original intent was to describe the changing pattern that applies to all phenomena in the universe.

Mobilizing all numbers is crucial to expressing everything that exists in the universe. Only by recording all the numbers can we express the totality of the universe. Though the numbers can describe the entirety of the universe, an average person's brain has a limit. When there is a mobilization of too many numbers, the entire universe cannot be clearly organized or understood in one's head. The hexagrams express the form or function of the entirety of existence in the universe by dividing them into sixty-four groups. Thus, it is difficult to define the parts in detail. But it is possible to describe the totality in general ways.

Among the three recording methods for thoughts, the Korean alphabet helps express the sounds. Still, it is difficult for them to articulate an idea or meaning. On the other hand, Chinese characters effectively express an idea or meaning, but it is challenging for them to articulate the sounds.

For example, if the Chinese character for the word "heart" (心) is pronounced, those who hear it would conjure various meanings. This is because everyone has a slightly different interpretation of the sound. But once a person writes the character, people can understand the exact intention and definition of the person who created it, aside from bringing up thoughts for the stored character of heart in their brain.

But a particular matter or function in daily life cannot be conceived by looking at a hexagram. The hexagrams are not a recording of every thought, nor do they reveal their meanings at once. Thus they are a highly inappropriate means for recording everyday affairs. Nevertheless, though it might not be useful in daily life, they are the most appropriate sym-bols for the quest for the truth, the ultimate purpose of all scholarship or academics.

Like the chemical equations or equations in higher mathematics that Einstein used to prove the theory of relativity, the hexagrams are a superior means for recording the truth. Though learning to read and understand them is more complicated than understanding those equations in higher mathematics, do not overlook them. So, again, those scholars who thirst in the quest for truth, such as Hegel, Einstein, Leibniz, and Niels Bohr, made an in-depth study of the I Ching.

The different interpretations of the trigrams occur because the trigrams are codes that represent all matter and phenomena in the universe. They are symbolic bodies that express the fundamental phases and changing systems of all existence. It boils down to differences in the interpretation of yin and yang, form and function. Another essential aspect of understanding the I Ching's totality involves studying two ancient maps, the Hado and the Nakseo, and the arrangements of the eight trigrams and the sixty-four hexagrams. To begin utilizing the principles of the I Ching in our lives, we must first be able to grasp these concepts. The following section presents in-depth discussions on applying the eight trigrams and the sixty-four hexagrams that arise from them.

Learning to Read the Eight Trigrams

When classifying something only with yin and yang, it is easy to conjure the idea of the complement when we mention its opposite. It is also easy to understand the overall relationship. But discerning the relationship of one to the whole becomes much more difficult when using the eight trigrams to classify information. Even at the level of the eight subdivisions, the idea of the whole becomes hazy. So when modern science dissects things into tiny, minute details, it does so at the expense of maintaining the integrity of the whole.

Each trigram retains specific virtues and meanings and symbolizes certain attributes.

The following is a table of trigram attributes (table 21.1).

The Dui (Lake) and Gen (Mountain) Trigrams

What image comes to mind when looking at the shape of the Dui trigram (fig. 21.3)? People of ancient times associated this trigram with the image of a lake, the top line being the exterior. Because the center is hollow, water can get in. Inside, there are two pieces of energy. A person who can envision surging, rippling

Trigram	Symbol	Energetics/ attributes	Season and nature	Family relation	Bodily region
Qian	heaven sky	creative powerful resolute	between autumn and winter cold frost	father	head mind/brain
Dui	lake sea pond	joyful fullness, pleasure	autumn rainy	youngest daughter	mouth hips
Li	fire sun	brilliance optimistic pomp passionate	midsummer sunny	middle daughter	eyes chest
Zhen	thunder lightning	arousing active exciting courageous	spring thunder earthquake	eldest son	foot legs
Xun	wind wood	gentle penetrating gradual movement changeability	between spring and summer windy	eldest daughter	arms

Kan	water moon	danger difficulty abysmal	midwinter rain snow	middle son	ears pelvic cavity
Gen	mountain	stillness stubborn calm	between winter and spring	youngest son	hand shoulders nose
Kun	earth	weak yielding dark nourishing	between summer and autumn	mother	belly/womb

Table 21.1 Trigram Attributes

waves has studied well. People who can visualize boiling water in a kettle or a fuel tank filled with gasoline show a talent to further develop modern science by applying concepts of the I Ching. However, it is difficult to know this trigram without looking at its counterpart.

The Gen trigram (fig. 21.4) is the yin-yang opposite of the Dui trigram. What comes to mind when looking at this trigram? In ancient times, people would have thought of a mountain because, generally, mountains are pointy at the top. However, the trigram has a flat exterior (the top line) and does not resemble a mountain. This is a dilemma, but there is an answer. The Dui trigram pertains to yang, while the Gen trigram pertains to yin. The reason is their position in Fuxi's or the Earlier Heaven arrangements of trigrams that we will cover in the next chapter.

Since the Dui trigram is situated next to the Qian trigram (south), it is yang. Therefore, its top line is the main force of the trigram. However, the Gen trigram pertains to yin since it is situated next to the Kun trigram (north). Because Gen is yin, the two bottom lines (yin) are its leading force. Therefore, with two yin lines strongly and steadily positioned at the bottom, the Gen trigram seems to have strong

Figure 21.3 Dui (Lake) Trigram

Figure 21.4 Gen (Mountain) Trigram

absorbing power. But it does not, because it is covered with a lid.

When a yang line situates on a foundation of strong yin lines, the middle part of the yang will sink in while the two outer pillars firmly support the yang line, demonstrating a mountain's quietness, firmness, and strength.

The shape of the Dui trigram is a pond or ocean positioned in a low place. Its primary function is to gather and pull in. On the other hand, Gen resembles a mountain situated in a high location and a nurturing home to plants and animals.

The Zhen (Thunder) and Xun (Wind) Trigrams

The upper and middle lines of the Zhen trigram are yin, and the bottom line is yang. Ancient people called this trigram Thunder (fig. 21.5).

Figure 21.5 Zhen (Thunder) Trigram

As with Dui trigram, the single line is the main force of the Zhen. When the sky is dark (the two top lines) and rain is imminent, bright light may temporarily split the sky when lightning strikes the ground (the yang line on the bottom). But the Zhen trigram is much more than just thunder and lightning. The trigram represents a seed starting to sprout, yet unsurfaced, or a snake about to emerge from brumation. This trigram could also resemble a rumbling volcano, leaking gas and lava just before it explodes. It is a phenomenon in which the fetus is wriggling in the womb. It is also a state in which the chick is about to break out of the egg. Moreover, the Zhen trigram represents pus seeping through a puncture in an abscess or boil.

A trigram represents the changing patterns commonly occurring in all things in the universe. If a trigram symbolized only one substance or phenomenon, it would be no different from a single Chinese character. Remember that each trigram represents one-eighth of all matter and phenomena in the universe. Therefore, the Zhen trigram must not be considered only as thunder and lightning.

While the form of the Zhen trigram is lightning, its function is movement. It is the movement of a wiggling yang line (bottom) trying to penetrate through two yin lines (top). It is the movement made by a bud, snake, lava, and pus trying to penetrate through the solid (yin) layer. In terms of physical phenomena, it is the movement of the first bubble when water is about to boil, or the activities of the bubbles as a soda or beer bottle is popped open.

The Xun trigram is the reciprocal of the Zhen. The single yin line becomes the main force, but because it is yin, it does not demonstrate a strong function. Yin, in general, has the function of pulling, gathering, and absorbing. The direction of such functions is downward. So if the top line is yin, as in the Dui trigram, it has a strong function but is relatively weak if the bottom line is yin. This is partly because descending yin does not have a long way to go when already at the bottom.

Sages related the form of the Xun trigram to the wind (fig. 21.6). The wind has no form and appears only in action. This action generally appears in the sky while moving horizontally above things. For example, if we look at the diagram of the Xun trigram, we will get an image of the wind blowing horizontally over buildings (yin), rocks (yin), mountains (yin), and water (yin).

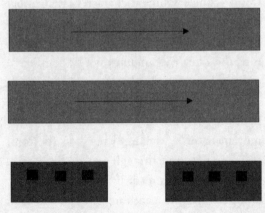

Figure 21.6 Xun (Wind) Trigram

In the Dui trigram, the yang lines were stored in a vessel (yin), pooled in a pond (yin), or stored in a fuel tank (yin). But in the Xun trigram, the yang lines have emerged from their containment and are in a dynamic state.

The single yang line in the bottom position of the Zhen trigram is wiggling to get out. Still, the two yang lines belonging to the Xun trigram have already broken free and are functioning actively.

We have said that the function of the Zhen trigram is movement. The function of the Xun trigram, too, is movement. However, their movements are in different directions. In the Zhen trigram, the yang line is trying to penetrate through and go up. Therefore, movement is in a vertical direction.

On the contrary, the Xun trigram's movement results from the dispersing yang energy already penetrated outward. Thus, its movement is in a horizontal direction. Moreover, the movement of yang is concentrated in one place in the Zhen trigram. In contrast, the Xun trigram is scattered.

Eastern medicine generally classifies external disease causes into six categories. One of these causes is "wind." The symptoms of diseases caused by wind occur suddenly and scatter throughout the body. For example, the common cold presents a generalized fever and muscle aches. A stroke induces a sudden loss of consciousness and multiple locations of paralysis in the body. Allergic dermatitis (hives, or urticaria), which forms rashes or inflammation sporadically on the skin, is also due to wind. These diseases correlate well with the Xun trigram when categorized under the eight trigrams.

Though surrounding yin restrains the

movement of the Zhen trigram, it is nevertheless a concentrated movement with a destructive force. On the contrary, the movement of the Xun trigram is without root. It has gone out of the boundary of yin's weak restraint (below) and lacks power, making it a weak destructive force. However, if this wind met another wind (yin) moving in the opposite direction, its strength would transform into a fiercely violent tornado.

All unrestrained movement belongs to the Xun trigram. In Korea, those who engage in illegitimate love affairs are said to be "playing with the wind." That is, they play the wanton because they are not having sex (yang) in their own houses (yin). Traditionally, women in the East who do not focus on domestic affairs but external social affairs are said to have wind inside them. This is the same movement as a helium balloon without a string (yin). Even vertical movements belong to the wind (the Xun trigram) without restraint.

A stock market or real estate boom is also called wind. The reason is that both quickly appear and disappear, like the wandering movement of the wind without fixation (yin) in one place. "Floating in the wind" refers to a singer or actor's popularity for a piece of work. Fame and popularity are transient, arriving swiftly, floating aimlessly, and then quickly disappearing, like the classic movie title *Gone with the Wind*. All of these movements pertain to the Xun trigram.

Movements made by a car or tank are horizontal. Yet they belong to the Zhen trigram because they occur within heaviness (two yin

lines). The marching of an army also belongs to Zhen because it is regulated and controlled. However, the movements made at a rally, demonstration, or in a crowd at an outdoor concert belong to the Xun trigram because they are unregulated. Getting angry at work because a superior has mistreated you but you cannot act belongs to Zhen because it is a regulated behavior. Acting on anger correlates to the Xun trigram. After ranting and raving, fretting and fuming, a woman crying (yin), a man sitting down due to weakness in his legs (yin), or even the act of drinking cold water (yin), are all ways to supplement the deficiency of yin in the Xun trigram.

Representing a pond and a mountain, the Dui and Gen trigrams both evoke images of stillness. In contrast, the Zhen and Xun trigrams arouse movement. Therefore, the Dui and Gen trigrams have quiet natures (yin) in opposition to Zhen's and Xun's dynamic natures (yang).

The Qian (Heaven) and Kun (Earth) Trigrams

Piling three yang lines forms the Qian trigram, one on top of another (fig. 21.7). Yang corresponds to all energy. It is bright, its place is at the top, and it has dynamic movements. In the environment surrounding human beings, yang is that which is the most brilliant, has the most active movements, and is situated above. The naked eye cannot see it, but this energy causes everything to happen. We call it heaven, and the Qian trigram symbolizes it.

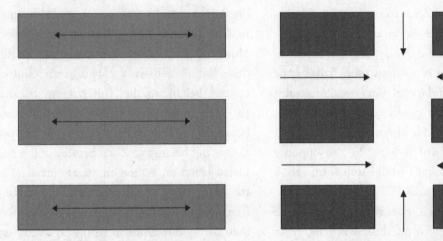

Figure 21.7 Qian (Heaven) Trigram

Figure 21.8 Kun (Earth) trigram

From the three horizontal lines of the Qian trigram, we can see the form of a sky in tiers above the horizon with parallel horizontal lines continuing without an end, never intersecting. The Qian trigram symbol clearly expresses the shape of heaven.

Piling three yin lines, one on top of another, shapes the Kun trigram (fig. 21.8). Yin corresponds to all matter in the universe. It is dark, its place is at the bottom, and it has either no movement or passive movements. In the environment surrounding human beings, yin is that which is the darkest, has slow movements, and is situated below. It is also the most conspicuous and solid. We call it Earth, and the Kun trigram thus symbolizes it.

We can see six blocks if we enlarge the three broken lines of the Kun trigram. They express the shape of hard, uneven, bumpy ground.

It was previously mentioned that the yang lines, unlike the yin lines, are not hollow in the middle and maintain a filled shape inside. That which is filled inside expands. If you can imagine a universe expanding from a white hole by looking at the three yang lines of the Qian trigram, you have studied this book very well. You can apply the principles of I Ching to the field you are engaged in.

In contrast, the yin lines, hollow in the middle, gather substances inward. If the three yang lines become hollow, a space is created in the middle. Try to bring up the image of a black hole sucking in the light and time, along with everything else in the universe.

If the Earth is Tai Chi, the Qian trigram is a positive pole (the South Pole), and the Kun trigram becomes a negative pole (the North Pole). A magnetic force emitted by the South Pole gets absorbed by the North Pole. At the same time, electricity begins to circulate perpendicular to the direction the magnetic force flows. Because the Li and Kan trigrams lie perpendicularly to the Qian and Kun trigrams (fig. 21.9), the Li and Kan trigrams become the positive and negative electrical potential. Coincidentally, the Korean national flag depicts these four trigrams.

Chemistry distinguishes acids and bases by their distribution of the hydrogen ion (H^+). Acids discharge ions, while bases absorb them. The Qian trigram relates to acids as it discharges protons (ionized hydrogen atoms, H^+), while the Kun refers to bases as it absorbs protons. Qian, made up of three yang lines, is a strong acid, whereas Kun, made up of three yin lines, is a strong base or alkaline.

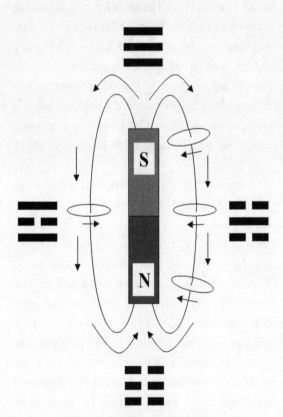

Figure 21.9 Magnetic Poles

In politics, the Qian trigram is the party in power, and the Kun trigram is the opposing party. In terms of space, Qian has three parallel lines in the upper, middle, and lower positions, justifying it as width. The Kun trigram, on the other hand, correlates with height, since it is like the stacking of a tower. Regarding human physiology, the Qian trigram corresponds to the life force, and the Kun is the pathogenic force. These forces apply to the universe's functioning, casting the force creating all things in nature as Qian and the force of destruction as Kun.

Let's consider the God of the Christian Bible as all-inclusive Tai Chi. Qian represents the angels, while Kun is indicative of the devil. Qian is the force of good, whereas Kun is the force of evil.

In the I Ching, the lines of the hexagrams have sequential numbers. They are not called first, second, or third; instead, the yang lines are labeled as the first 9, the second 9, and so forth. The yin lines, on the contrary, are marked as the first 6, the second 6, and so on. Readers are familiar with odd numbers being yang and even numbers being yin.

Although the first odd number is 1, it is ambiguous as the number of the whole. Thus, it is inappropriate to use the number 1 to name the lines that distinguish and symbolize matter. This is why the second odd number (3) is used instead. There are three lines in each trigram, so 3 becomes 9 ($3 \times 3 = 9$). In the end, the number 9 becomes the name for the yang lines. The first even number is 2, and since there are three lines in a trigram, 2 become 6 (2 × 3 = 6), and 6 becomes the yin lines' name. It is also the total number of blocks that form the Kun trigram.

According to the I Ching principles, the number 666 mentioned in the Christian Bible representing Satan expresses the Kun (Earth) trigram. The opposite of this in terms of the I Ching would be 999, which signifies heaven and the angels. The Qian trigram is the principle of creation, while the Kun is the principle of destruction. This destruction, however, is for the purpose of future creation. Destruction by Kun does not occur instantaneously. It is merely a guiding force. Instead, Zhen (thunder) and Xun (wind), two of the trigrams in charge of movement, are instantaneous and function to destroy things.

We can compare the destructive action of the Kun trigram to the autumn season, in which destruction occurs for the creation purpose. The withering of leaves and drying of branches prepares for the bearing of fruit to create new life when spring comes. Again, Kun oversees the autumn's destruction, while Qian is in charge of the spring's generative function.

Since Qian consists of three yang lines, its movement is dynamic. In human society, anything diligent or hardworking corresponds to the Qian trigram. In contrast, the Kun trigram corresponds to everything idle or lazy.

The nature of Qian is strong like a father, while Kun is soft like a mother. That which is strong expands energy outward, while soft consolidates energy inward. These are the external qualities of the Qian and Kun trigrams. Whereas metal corresponds to Qian, cotton corresponds to Kun. Similarly, an object that is solid and glittery corresponds to Qian, while soft and dull substances belong to Kun. So crystals and diamonds correspond to Qian, while charcoal corresponds to Kun. Though the same carbon molecules make up diamonds and charcoal, their natures oppose each other, as do the natures of Qian and Kun.

All things in nature are given life through the mutual exchange of heaven and earth. Similarly, the father (Qian) and mother (Kun) interact to create life. The six other trigrams arise from their relationship. The Heaven and Earth trigrams are the main force field of change in nature, similar to Earth's magnetic poles, as mentioned previously. The other trigrams are intermediary stages passed through during the transformation from Qian to Kun and back again and small independent forces that affect the change.

Because the Qian trigram is pure yang and the Kun trigram is pure yin, it is easy to distinguish what belongs to each trigram. Although generally thought to represent a father, the Qian trigram also represents any man. Similarly, the Kun is considered a mother but applies to any woman. If you think of both trigrams as a single stage of change, the Qian trigram is an older man, and the Kun trigram is an older woman. When the secretion of male and female hormones declines, a man becomes more feminine, and a woman becomes more masculine. In other words, they start to transform into their opposites.

The Li (Fire) and Kan (Water) Trigrams

The Li trigram consists of two yang lines in upper and lower positions with a yin line in the middle (fig. 21.10). The yang on the exterior is expanding outward while the yin on the interior, although weak, is holding back the expanding action of yang by absorbing it inward. The Li trigram brings up an image of fire with a higher temperature on the exterior and a lower temperature on the interior. This is evident because glass put through a flame will be stained dark with soot from the carbon at the center of the flame.

Figure 21.11 Kan (Water) Trigram

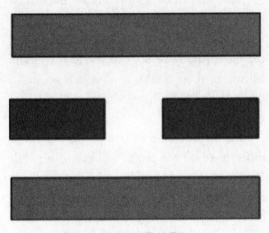

Figure 21.10 Li (Fire) Trigram

The Kan trigram (fig. 21.11) is the exact opposite of the Li trigram, with two exterior yin lines and one interior yang line. The two exterior yin lines gather energy inward, and the yang, although weak, awaits the opportunity to expand outward. When water drops onto a piece of oil paper, it retains the shape of a drop because it has surface tension. The creation of drops of water occurs by the phenomena of the yin's absorbing power on the exterior and the yang's expanding force in the interior. Water's transparent shine, even though two yin lines make up its exterior, is because of the single yang within.

Rivers and oceans are yin in nature because they are generally slow, gentle, dark, and quiet. They become active when other forces act upon them. Floods and tsunamis are due to the yang force of rain pouring from the sky or earthquakes on the ocean floor. This yang energy causes chaos in the stillness of yin. It activates the yang energy within the water so that its movements become rapid and destructive. This is the moment when Kan transforms into the Xun or Zhen trigrams.

The Li trigram represents all types of fire. The sun acts like a giant fire warming the Earth and belongs to the Li trigram. The sun has sunspots that correspond to yin. Though the universe is immense, the sun has the most significant influence on human beings. The Qian trigram is an element of force or foundation, and the Li trigram mainly does its work. Therefore, Li is responsible for carrying out the function of Qian.

In terms of industry, the electronic sector corresponds to fire due to its rapid growth and subjectivity to change. Light traveling along optic fibers or electricity flowing along copper wires corresponds to fire. At the center is a substance (yin) with dull movement, while the surface entertains light or electricity (yang), traveling rapidly. Both belong to the Li trigram.

Kan, a water symbol, relates to all things pertaining to water and its nature. Clouds, fog, and cloudy days are products of the Kan trigram because they are the gathering of small drops of water. Each drop is, in essence, Kan. Though the overall quality of water is soft, it has the yang nature of being light and moving freely. Both hide the sun (Li) but disappear when the sun shines brightly, demonstrating the polar relationship between the Li and Kan trigrams.

Oils and fats also correspond to the Kan trigram. The difference between the two occurs at room temperature, at which oil is a liquid and fat is solid. Oil can be thought of as the yang within Kan, while fat is the yin. Oil has the exact nature as water, virtually. It is soft and does not hold form and flow. It is the nature of yin to be more solid than yang. Until this point, we have stated that yang was soft and yin was hard. The theory does not seem to apply when we discuss water, which is repre-

sentative of yin. Yin-yang and Sasang are very inclusive, so they cannot always appropriately express certain matters. However, we can most appropriately express matter by dividing it into eight types.

The exterior of the Kan trigram is yin, and its interior is yang. The exterior expresses the coldness and tranquility of a gathering of water (like a pond, lake, etc.). The interior embodies the infinite potential energy and how the water roams without a particular shape. The interior and exterior describe the dual nature (yin-yang) of water. Overall, the water is yin but remains soft, as it contains a specific yang nature that remains dormant unless provoked.

Since oil can transform directly into fire, it has a more yang nature than water. But when we divide all things into the eight trigrams, the oil naturally belongs to the Kan trigram. Moreover, though fat is hard, it changes into a liquid with a bit of heat, relating it to the Kan trigram.

The nature of the Li and Kan trigrams differ in that Li is bright and beautiful while Kan is dark and unsightly. Aesthetic beauty, unhindered by reason, is vivid and magnificent, much like a fire, explaining the beauty of fire. Beauty, therefore, corresponds to the Li trigram. Though water is in no way unsightly, the yang of Kan is hidden inside alone, making it difficult to contend with the two yins. Thus yang is weak and cannot manifest its strength. This is the reason that water can easily be contaminated. Contaminated water is dark with a foul odor and is unsightly. So are urine and feces made by the function of the Kan trigram.

In contrast, the flame is always beautiful, whether old or new.

The Li trigram is tense, whereas the Kan trigram is relaxed. Like candlelight, the tip of the fire is gathered. It does not dissipate upon its creation and continues to exist because of its absorbing yin force within. In contrast, the exterior of water is loose, dispersed, and without form. The larger the quantity of water, the more intense the cooperation of the yang lines, which have dynamic activity and a powerful expanding force. A small amount of water holds its form because a small amount of yang cannot express itself outwardly. This is why the exterior of the Li trigram is taut and the exterior of Kan loose.

Things belonging to the Li trigram are tense, tending to have accuracy and order. In contrast, loose Kan expresses inaccuracy and disorder. For instance, electronic equipment is generally accurate, following technical orders by which it functions. Organisms that drink water, compared to electronic equipment, side with the Kan trigram. They are so irregular and disordered that the more they are studied, the more difficult they are to predict. As you can see, the accuracy and order of the Li trigram are more flexible than that of Gen, while the disorder of Kan is less than that of the Xun trigram.

Working belongs to the Li trigram, while resting belongs to the Kan trigram. Work corresponds to the two yang lines on the exterior of Li. In comparison, rest corresponds to the two yin exterior lines of Kan. Working diligently also corresponds to the Qian trigram, while continuously resting belongs to the Kun. The work and rest of the Qian and Kun trigrams are pure yang and pure yin, constituting no break. In contrast, the work and rest of the Li and Kan trigrams each have a break.

22

Arrangements and Applications of the Eight Trigrams

The legendary emperor Fuxi first created the eight trigrams after observing the Hado (Yellow River Map) about five thousand years ago. Then he arranged the eight trigrams in a systematic order, known as the "Earlier Heaven arrangement," based on the map.

King Yu, who established the Xia dynasty, discovered the Nakseo (River Lo Map) a thousand years later. Based on this map, King Wen, the founder of the Zhou dynasty, drew the "Later Heaven arrangement" of eight trigrams a thousand years after King Yu's discovery. These two arrangements of the eight trigrams

express the principles of the universe and serve as two of the essential principles of the I Ching.

King Wen arranged the sixty-four hexagrams according to the principles of the universe. Then he added his interpretations, known as "judgments," to each hexagram. Meanwhile, his son, the Duke of Zhou, added judgments to each line. About five hundred years later, after studying the works of Fuxi, of King Wen, and of the Duke of Zhou, Confucius appended his interpretations, called the "Ten Wings."

However, these historical facts should not be the primary concern of those studying the

I Ching. The implications of the arrangements of trigrams and hexagrams are far more important than where they came from or even how they developed.

Although words are essential, they are only a superficial aspect of the I Ching. Unfortunately, there is a tendency by scholars to focus on I Ching's lyrics instead of numerology or symbolism. The main reason for this tendency is that there are no clear explanations for the bigrams, trigrams, or hexagrams, so they are often neglected. However, fully mastering the I Ching takes a clear un-

derstanding of the images or symbols of these bigrams, trigrams, and hexagrams.

The Earlier Heaven arrangement, designed by Fuxi, is an arrangement of the I Ching trigrams that expresses the universe's design before the manifestation of the things we know today (fig. 22.1A). It is a map of a perfect universe. The Later Heaven arrangement, devised by King Wen, is an arrangement of the trigrams that depicts the principles of the universe as they exist today (fig. 22.1B).

If we diagram the Tao, the principle that

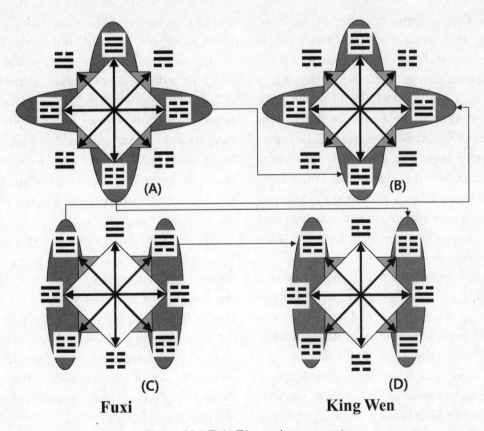

Fuxi

King Wen

Figure 22.1 Eight Trigram Arrangements

commonly applies to all things in the universe, Fuxi's arrangement emphasizes the form or structure, and King Wen's arrangement emphasizes the function. So if Hado (Yellow River Map) is yin, then Nakseo (River Lo Map) is yang. Fuxi's arrangement is the principle of the entire universe. In contrast, King Wen's arrangement is the principle that applies to the limited world of the Earth. Fuxi's arrangement is the change that occurs when yin and yang are in harmony. King Wen's arrangement is the change that occurs on Earth or with human beings, tilted because it is not the center of the universe.

Fuxi's arrangement is the principle of change that occurs when the Earth's axis is perpendicular. King Wen's arrangement is the principle of change when the Earth's axis is tilted 23.5 degrees. With the tilted axis, a tilt of yin-yang occurs on Earth that differs from the rest of the universe, resulting in more complicated changes than the rest. The complication arises from the inherent imbalance. Since Fuxi's arrangement applies to the changes in the entire universe and not to the changes that affect people's everyday lives, King Wen's arrangement was created.

Let's compare the four cardinal trigrams of Fuxi's arrangement (fig. 22.1A) with King Wen's (fig. 22.1B). The Li and Kan trigrams in King Wen's arrangement are in the positions of the Qian and Kun trigrams of Fuxi's arrangement. Fuxi's is an arrangement of the positions of the eight powers or influences of the universe, while King Wen's is an arrangement of the eight stages of change. Qian and Kun, or Heaven and Earth, represent the two central powers in the universe. But because they are the bodies of pure yin and pure yang, they do not have much functional value regarding stages of change. They can only assist the functioning of the other forces. They cannot independently function because there is no interplay between yin and yang, so they become stagnant. Therefore, King Wen's arrangement, expressing the principle of function, moves the Qian and Kun trigrams away from the cardinal positions into the four transitional positions that are less important in function.

In King Wen's interpretation, the Kan and Li trigrams are in the most critical functional positions—the north and south. These are the respective trigrams of water and fire, which have the greatest influence on the lives of Earth's inhabitants. The Li trigram has dynamic competitive activity between yin and yang, resulting from one yin line positioned in the center between two yang lines. It sits in the south, where movement is dynamic. Kan, the trigram of water, is located north where yin rules.

To mediate the transformation process from the Kan to the Li trigrams, King Wen placed the Zhen trigram, which symbolizes thunder and the revival of yang, in the east. Fuxi's arrangement places Li in the east, but the Zhen trigram is more dynamic. Also, in King Wen's arrangement, a trigram with a greater yin action must come into the west, so the Dui trigram, which represents a lake or sea, goes there. Remember that in contrast to the Zhen trigram, which signifies the wood or revival of yang energy, the Dui trigram represents metal or gathering energy.

The third arrangement (fig. 22.1C) shows that Fuxi places the Zhen and Dui trigrams in the northeast and southeast, respectively. King Wen sets these trigrams in the east and west, respectively. In King Wen's arrangement (fig. 22.1D), three trigrams in the transitional directions (Qian/Heaven, Kun/Earth, and Gen/Mountain) have little movement. (The Xun/Wind trigram is an exception.) The transitional directions are the positions that have dynamic movement. So when the Qian, Kun, and Gen trigrams are sitting here, they move dynamically. In King Wen's arrangement, the Xun and Gen trigrams, situated in the west (southwest and northwest, respectively) in Fuxi's arrangement, are now sitting in the transitional directions of the east, where movement is dynamic.

In Fuxi's arrangement, which is based on form, Zhen and Xun trigrams are arranged in opposition due to their compositional lines. But in King Wen's arrangement, which is based on function, they are juxtaposed and placed in the east and southeast. Likewise, the Qian and Kun trigrams oppose each other in Fuxi's arrangement. But they become neighbors in the northwest and southwest, where the movement is gathered into form in King Wen's arrangement.

In the past, the eight trigrams were applied to the disposition of troops during a war. Fuxi's arrangement is a diagram of the disposition of the troops during times of peace, while King Wen's is the disposition of the troops during war, as it is a diagram with more dynamic movement.

The yin-yang paired trigrams in Fuxi's arrangement are differently arranged in King Wen's arrangement. As the Qian and Kun trigrams are pure yin and yang, their movements are too dull. So just changing their positions from the cardinal to the transitional directions is not enough. Thus, their positions are inverted. The hexagram representing this inverted formation, in which Kun is on top and Qian on the bottom, is called Peace (Tai). The inversion of the position of Qian and Kun is good because they can mutually communicate. On the other hand, in the Stagnation (Pi) hexagram, the Qian trigram is situated at the top, while the Kun trigram is at the bottom. This is not good, because as yang rises and yin descends, there is a separation of yin and yang, thus resulting in an inauspicious omen.

King Wen's Arrangement and the Seasons

The arrangement of the eight trigrams, like the principles of Sasang, circulates as eight stages of function or change. This can be expressed in terms of seasons. In Fuxi's arrangement, Qian becomes Kun and then goes back and forth between the two trigrams. Fuxi's arrangement is convenient for expressing space, while King Wen's arrangement is convenient for expressing time. So, in terms of seasons, think of Kan as winter and Li as the summer in King Wen's arrangement. Then think about each stage of change (fig. 22.1B/D), moving from the bottom in a clockwise direction.

In the Kan trigram (☵), the yang line in the interior is trying to come out through the earth's surface in the Gen trigram (☶). This appears to be a seed stored deeply within the Kan trigram sprouting in the Gen trigram. Kan corresponds to the winter, and Gen corresponds to the intermediate stage between the winter and spring. The sprout is still within the ground in Gen. But it has already come out in Zhen (☳), which corresponds to the spring.

Though in terms of the trigram form, the sprout seems to grow more in the Gen trigram: the top yang line lacks strength and symbolizes the sprout that has not yet emerged from the ground. However, in the Zhen trigram, the yang line occupies the bottom position and has great strength. It expresses the sprout that has risen from the ground and grown to about one-third of its full size.

The Xun trigram's symbol expresses the yang that came out of the ground and gradually grew into an exuberantly dispersed state (☴). The Xun trigram is between spring and summer. It symbolizes how the leaves and branches of a tree are innumerably dispersed (upper two yang lines) above its big stem (lower yin line).

The upper and lower lines have already transformed into yang when we get to the Li trigram, corresponding to summer. It has reached the zenith of yang. If the meek yin were to transform into yang, the organism would instantaneously lose its life; an organism cannot exist as pure yin or yang.

For the seed (yang) within the Kan tri-

gram to sprout, it needs the help of the Qian trigram. Likewise, the support of the Kun trigram is required to protect the yin within the Li trigram to start a new life. These are the two most essential stages in the circulation of life led by the Qian (Heaven) and Kun (Earth) trigrams. That is why the Qian and Kun trigrams juxtapose with the Li and Kan trigrams.

The Dui trigram (☱) is situated in the middle stage of transformation from the Li to the Kan trigram. The Dui corresponds to the function of autumn. It is in a state where yang has been fully gathered through the hole of the yin line situated at the top. This symbolizes fruit that is hanging from a tree. There are seeds and nutrients (two yang lines) within the fruit for the next generation.

The Qian trigram consists of three yang lines, wherein the yang becomes completely full by adding an extra yang line to the Dui trigram. This force helps the sprouting action of the Kan trigram. It is in the middle of autumn and winter, the position where such force can adequately manifest.

The Kun trigram is a state of fullness of yin germinating from the Li trigram. It supports the function of storing the yang of the Dui trigram as matter. The position of Kun corresponds to the southwest, and it is the place that relates to the early autumn. It is an important position and a time when life will restart or stop. There must be a strong yin action (by the Kun trigram) to gather the strong force of the blazing fire of the Li trigram. This stage is the time and the position that triggers the so-called "mutual exchange of metal and fire." There could be dire consequences when the proper exchange of metal and fire does not occur.

For instance, for those cultivating the Tao, a seed of yang (called Dan or elixir) is sowed into a place called Danjun, or elixir field, which corresponds to the woman's uterus and is grown. But if the yang becomes excessive, it can engulf the person, and he or she may either be killed or fail in the endeavor to achieve enlightenment. This can happen at this stage of exchange between metal and fire. Therefore, it is a dangerous stage if the function of Kun, which is a strong yin function, is not adequately prepared.

In terms of social phenomena, revolution may occur at a point in time. Mass demonstrations, which have become vigorous in the Xun trigram stage, have reached their zenith. It is a point when protests can get suppressed through the strong opposing force, or the force of the new regime comes into play. But before this, there will be a bloody massacre at this stage. The plants finish their yearly life at this stage. The organisms that remain alive through such an ordeal will produce good seeds, and those that do not survive will get weeded out.

The Kun trigram supports the process of gathering energy into the mass from a superior position. In contrast, the Qian trigram helps transform substances into energy. In plants, the conversion into energy manifests as the phenomenon of sprouting. Sowing seeds without a careful selection will lead to a low sprout rate. It is the function of the Kun trigram to select the seed carefully. The Qian trigram's function is to give the germ power to penetrate outward through its shell. So the role of both Kun and Qian trigrams can raise germination percentage. The stages of the Kun and Qian trigrams' positions are most important. They determine whether an organism lives or dies. Therefore, they sit in the southwest (Kun) and northwest (Qian).

In Fuxi's arrangement, the lines of trigrams that face each other become opposite to maintain the polar relationship. As seen in the diagram (fig. 22.1B), in King Wen's arrangement, the Kan and Li trigrams that maintained opposite relations from the left and right are in upper and lower positions. Likewise, the Zhen and Dui trigrams in upper and lower places are now maintaining polar relations from the left and right. Meanwhile, the Xun and Gen trigrams on the right now maintain their upper-lower functional polar relationship from the left (fig. 22.1D). Finally, the Kun and Qian trigrams maintain a contrasting relationship from respective upper and lower positions on the right and have inverse lines.

Relationships Between the Eight Trigrams

In Fuxi's arrangement, the Dui, Gen, Zhen, and Xun trigrams are the "four transitional trigrams," and the Qian, Kun, Kan, and Li trigrams are the "four cardinal trigrams." As you can see from the diagram (fig. 22.2), the Dui trigram opposes the Gen trigram, while the Zhen opposes the Xun trigram. All four transitional trigrams oppose the four cardinal trigrams.

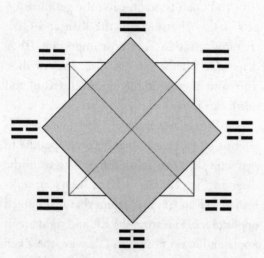

Figure 22.2: Arrangement of 8 Trigrams

The Qian, Kun, Kan, and Li trigrams lie in the four cardinal directions. Therefore, these trigrams form the force or the foundation of change. On the other hand, the Dui, Gen, Zhen, and Xun trigrams are between the four cardinal trigrams and are directly responsible for making changes. Thus, the Qian, Kun, Kan, and Li trigrams are yin, while the Dui, Gen, Zhen, and Xun trigrams are yang.

As you can see from the diagram, the Zhen trigram is in the intermediary stage between the Kun and Li trigrams, while the Dui trigram is in the intermediary stage between the Li and Qian trigrams. The Xun trigram is in the intermediary stage between the Qian and Kan trigrams, and the Gen trigram is in the intermediary stage between the Kan and Kun trigrams. Through such processes, the Qian trigram changes from top to bottom to become

the Kun, whereas the Kun trigram changes from bottom to top to become the Qian.

The Eight Trigrams and the Four Elements

In India, everything in the universe is considered to be composed of just four elements: earth, water, fire, and wind. These elements correspond to the Sasang, as previously mentioned in chapter 15. Both the Zhen and Xun trigrams correspond to the wind. The Qian and Kun trigrams belong to the earth element. The Kan and Dui trigrams belong to the water element. And lastly, the Li and Gen trigrams correspond to Fire. there is a tendency to interpret these elements only from a substantial point of view, as they are elements of substance. The secret is to look at them through functional lenses so they can easily match to a trigram.

Due to their moving nature, the Zhen and Xun trigrams symbolize the wind. The Qian trigram represents heaven or the sky, while the Kun trigram represents the earth. Still, both belong to the earth element because the stars in the sky are mainly composed of the same substances as the earth. Since the Kan trigram signifies water, it belongs to the water element. Similarly, the Dui trigram representing a pond, a lake, or an ocean is classified in the water group. The Li trigram, consisting of fire, relates to the fire element, as does the Gen trigram, retaining the form and function of shooting upward from the ground into the sky.

The characteristics of the eight trigrams can be more easily understood when we apply them to things we are familiar with. Therefore, the following sections will discuss family, jobs, the human body, and animals as they relate to the trigrams.

All in the Family

One method used in the East to facilitate the familiarity of the trigrams is applying their natures to the personality characteristics of family members. Families are like small societies, so understanding the nature of familial relationships in conjunction with the trigrams makes it relatively easy to associate them with other social relationships.

There is a particular method for associating the trigrams with the family. Qian is the father, and Kun is the mother. The other six trigrams have two lines within them that are identical and one that is the opposite. The single line determines whether the trigram represents a male or a female. If the single line is yin, the trigram represents a daughter in a family with two sons. If the single line is yang, the trigram represents a son in a family with two daughters. The location of the single line indicates the respective relationships between the siblings. The lines in the bigrams, trigrams, or hexagrams are always drawn from the bottom up. The bottom line represents the foundation or beginning. It corresponds to the eldest son or daughter, the middle line to the middle child, and the top line to the youngest.

The Dui trigram represents the youngest daughter in a family with two older brothers. This girl never lacks attention and affection, so she comes to desire these traits. They have given her a quiet self-confidence that later turns to pride as she gets older. The two yang lines hidden in the Dui trigram represent this pride. The youngest daughter always has people around to help with her tasks, allowing her to become dependent and setting a precedent for her to accept help and guidance willingly. The Dui trigram's nature is to gather things necessary for survival from the environment. Similarly, the youngest daughter has a charm that pulls in all of the love and affection around her.

The Dui trigram also relates to any young woman under twenty who is not yet an adult. It is the charm of young women's beauty (yang) as well as their modesty (yin) and shyness (yin) that appeal to men.

These traits apply to family members and to running a small business. Classifying employees into eight groups makes it easy to understand each employee's aptitudes, and entrusting work according to their aptitude increases efficiency. Among them, a person who is not necessarily a woman but has strong self-esteem, like the Dui trigram, and attracts a lot of attention from people around them and does not reveal themselves can be classified as a Dui trigram.

The top line of the Gen trigram is yang, relating to the youngest son in a family with two older daughters. This boy is considered precious, so his older sisters dote on him, making him more in tune with female concerns.

He is calm and stable, much like a mountain. He will tend to be less competitive and will, instead, derive pleasure from building things and working with his hands. He will become very steady and detail-oriented.

Socially, Gen relates to any young male under the age of twenty. Young men put great effort into showing off what they have (a yang exterior). However, they are not at a time in their lives when they have the power or strength to back up their claims. The idiom "All bark and no bite" describes them well. It takes a long time for two yin lines to convert into yang.

The Zhen trigram is compared to the eldest son. This is the eldest son of a family with two younger sisters. To take care of his younger sisters, the son must act diligently and responsibly. In preparation for his role as a father, the eldest son learns and undertakes the responsibilities and actions of a father and watches out for his sisters. His actions are well received by others around him.

The Xun trigram represents the eldest daughter in a family with two younger brothers who act out of control due to the activation of their strong latent energy. Thus, she has to gently guide their actions and behaviors to ensure they head in the right direction. This is usually the role of the mother, so the eldest daughter learns her role early. Yet she makes many mistakes in playing the mother and lacks the strength necessary to guide her family properly.

The Li trigram represents the middle daughter, and the Kan trigram represents the middle son. The middle daughter receives a lot of love from her older and younger brothers. Her older brother's adventurous behavior becomes restrained due to his affection for his sister. At the same time, she encourages the timid conduct of her younger brother. She is unlike the oldest sister, who must sacrifice herself for her two younger brothers, nor is she like the youngest daughter, who only receives love but does not need to perform her role as a daughter.

The middle son encourages his older and younger sisters. The older sister is diligently active and paves the way for her younger brother. The shyness she is born with is reduced due to receiving her brother's vitality. The middle son sets an example for his younger sister through dynamic activity and activates her stagnant energy. However, the activity of both sisters is innately passive since they are women. The middle son is unlike the oldest son, who has great strength and is very active. Nor is he like the youngest son, who constantly attempts to show off.

The Eight Trigrams and Jobs

Qin Shi Huang was the first to unify mainland China. Every book except those essential for daily life was burned during his dictatorship. People's political and ideological maturity frightened him. Specifically, philosophical, religious, and political books were burned, but he did not burn I Ching, even though it belongs to the same category. In that period, I

Ching was thought to be a book on divination, and divination books were essential to daily life. Divination was used when sending troops to war, and it was also used when determining other important matters of the state. A common habit in the lives of the people was fortune-telling.

It is true that I Ching can clearly provide a theoretical foundation for protesting against the ruler's dictatorship. Still, its disguise as a divination book is the main reason it wasn't burned. Following the creation of I Ching, as explanations of hexagrams and hexagram lines were added in writing, it took on the form of a divination book. The experts of I Ching who added explanations did so based on their prediction that Qin Shi Huang would burn all books.

As I Ching enters the modern age, Easterners lose interest because superstitious divination no longer interests them. Now I Ching does not appear to be burning, but it is disappearing. The advantages of the past have become disadvantages in the present.

As we learn I Ching, we are taught that experts of I Ching do not perform divination. Using I Ching for fortune-telling is due to a lack of understanding of I Ching's principles. The explanations of I Ching's hexagrams and their lines scarcely encompass the natural properties or phenomena of myriad things in the universe. Rather, they mostly focus on the auspiciousness or inauspiciousness of various activities in social life. The hexagrams of I Ching were deciphered using the historical background mentioned in the *Classic of History* (Shujing), the oldest Confucian classic.

Even today, scholars studying I Ching in Korea, China, and Japan cling to its words, so no book explaining I Ching in natural scientific terms has been published. However, several fragmentary writings applying the principles of I Ching to science exist. Regrettably, scientists do not study I Ching deeply enough.

The nature of the eight trigrams becomes less complicated to understand and more self-evident when we associate them with things we already know. The previous section on the family has illustrated certain aspects of the characteristics of the trigrams. Another way we can associate the eight trigrams with our lives is in terms of our jobs or career paths.

There are many records concerning the classification of the eight trigrams regarding jobs or professions. By studying these records, you can become familiar with the characteristics of the eight trigrams. From the following, you will see that occupations pertaining to the Kan and Gen trigrams coincide, and jobs relating to the Li and Xun trigrams are similar. In King Wen's arrangement of the trigrams, these pairs are juxtaposed and thus possess similar functions. Since the function is of primary importance in social activities, King Wen's arrangement of trigrams applies most appropriately to work.

THE QIAN TRIGRAM

The Qian trigram symbolizes the energy of the sovereign. It corresponds to all leaders, regardless of their fields. In terms of Sasang body types, Qian pertains to the Taeyangin constitution. Because Taeyangins are pure yang, they do not accept the advice given to them by others, allowing them to become dictators and despots easily. Napoleon and Hitler epitomized these dictatorial traits.

The three yang lines of the Qian trigram show that it possesses great energy. This means that persons of the Qian trigram are very resolute and diligent. There must be at least one yin line for wealth to be accumulated. As there are no yin lines in this trigram, Qian people are disinterested in money, so they are incorruptible. Yin is also needed to enable one to receive advice. As no yin exists, Qian people easily become dictators.

Yang energy represents life rather than death, and life is creation. As the Qian trigram is pure yang, it most closely approximates the function of God as sovereign and creator. Thus, if God were ever to live among everyday people in human society, He would definitely hold the job pertaining to the Qian trigram. Remember, though, that God is Tai Chi and, as such, is inclusive of all eight trigrams.

Highly creative artists belong to the Qian trigram, including Van Gogh, Picasso, and Beethoven. These men each possessed superior artistic talent and a unique vision. However, the pure yang of the Qian trigram did not fare well with the passive currents of their time, so their lives were not without turmoil. What's more, for people of this nature, their progressive yang perspective is incomprehensible to those around them simply because they tend to be "ahead of their time." Thus, most artists of the Qian trigram produce work that only

becomes appreciated decades or even centuries after their deaths.

Brilliant inventors and scientists also belong to the Qian trigram. Tesla, Edison, Einstein, Leibniz, Niels Bohr, and Stephen Hawking are among those who fall under this category. As with Qian artists, Qian scientists are generally not recognized or appreciated during their lifetimes. Like Copernicus, Joan of Arc, or Galileo, those who sacrifice themselves for the truth are also typical of Qian energy. Being pure yang, they have a passion for their beliefs or causes that will outweigh the value they put on their lives or the suffering.

THE KUN TRIGRAM

Three yin lines form the Kun trigram. It corresponds to earth, the lowest position, and the abdomen of the human body. Yin by nature is slow, dark, unsightly, and low and pertains more to matter than to the mind. As far as Sasang body types are concerned, people of the Taeeumin constitution belong to the Kun trigram.

Small business owners perhaps best represent the Kun trigram. Such people always pay attention to the abundance of practical materials and do not concern themselves with such impractical matters as fame or honor. As long as they can accumulate wealth, they are happy. Even the loss of self-respect is a small price to pay.

Since the Kun trigram corresponds to earth, it is in the lowest position and can draw anything and everything into itself. In the same way, the Earth's gravity pulls in all things around it. Furthermore, the Earth supports all things in nature and nurtures them as a mother would her children. Those who correspond to this trigram take on several "earthly" characteristics. They tend to have plenty of tolerance and understanding toward others. They also may take on jobs closely associated with land or property. For example, real estate brokerage or the leasing buildings (property management) are jobs typically belonging to people of the Kun trigram.

Those of the Kun trigram are not very competitive and thus always seem to have composure and can comfort those around them. But since yin is associated with slowness, laziness tends to be the vice of Kun people. Therefore, they may become extremely lazy when they are working impractical jobs (jobs with no monetary reward). Still, they can be diligent and persistent when working for money.

THE LI TRIGRAM

The Li trigram has a yang exterior with a yin interior and corresponds to fire. The Li trigram is best represented by the fiery Soyangin constitution as far as body types are concerned.

Jobs that require flare, splendor, rapid movement, and general popularity belong to this trigram. Such jobs include singers, actors/actresses, radio/TV announcers, and reporters. To succeed in these jobs, a person has to be beautiful and sumptuous like a flame, able to flow with the latest trends and present him- or herself in the best way possible. Furthermore, since the interior of the Li trigram is yin, those that belong to this trigram must be able to gather the attention or interest of people to be successful.

A job suitable for Soyangin with their fire-like personality, quick movement, and constant need to show themselves off belongs to the Li trigram. Salespeople who must demonstrate their products' value ideally belong to this trigram. Jobs in communications or the computer field requiring the ability to handle sudden changes and assess up-to-the-minute information also pertain to the Li trigram.

THE KAN TRIGRAM

The exterior of the Kan trigram is yin, but the interior is yang. It corresponds to water and the Soeumin constitution. Jobs that require a slow pace, attention to detail, calmness, composure, and few mistakes correspond to the Kan trigram. Such jobs include clergypersons, teachers (primarily elementary, middle, and high school), accountants, bank tellers, repairers, crafts people, and mechanics. To be successful in these jobs, individuals must maintain a water-like calmness to minimize mistakes. These jobs are the complete opposite of jobs of the Li trigram, which require flamboyant, attention-grabbing behaviors.

Although risk-taking may guarantee success for jobs of the Li trigram, they tend to lead to failure in the precision-oriented Kan jobs. Also, employment of the Li trigram often demands that a person travel to many different places. In contrast, jobs that belong to the Kan trigram require settling down in one place and pondering deeply. Li trigram jobs, in other words, tend to be like brilliant fireworks, while Kan jobs tend to be more ordinary.

The Zhen Trigram

There are two yin lines on top and one yang line on the bottom in the Zhen trigram. It captures the image of a single yang line trying to ascend and symbolizes thunder and lightning. As the Zhen trigram represents the beginning of new works, jobs that lead to discovering or creating new things belong to the Zhen trigram. Similar to the Qian trigram, inventors and explorers are typical Zhen occupations. In a corporate setting, the planning department corresponds to the Zhen trigram.

Similarly, various fields' idea people or think tanks also correspond to Zhen. So are the missionaries who try to convert people into different religions or revolutionaries who try to establish new societies. People who hold jobs belonging to the Zhen trigram must develop novel ideas and initiate new actions to be successful.

The Zhen trigram is a penetrating force. It is a pattern associated with bravery or courage. Jobs requiring great bravery, such as soldiers, especially commandos or raiders, belong to this trigram. For similar reasons, gangsters are of the Zhen trigram.

The Dui Trigram

The Dui trigram has one yin line on top and two yang lines on the bottom. It represents a still pond containing much potential energy. Seasonally, it corresponds to autumn with its gathering energy. People of great financial power belong to this trigram, as do those who have retired with a significant sum of money. The Dui trigram has a gathering nature, so service trades such as those in hotels or restaurants belong to it. Real estate investors or mine owners also belong to this category.

People of financial power appear self-satisfied because their money corresponds to energy. Thus, they can afford to keep their exteriors plain and simple (remember that the top line is yin). They do not need other people to recognize them, so they don't pay so much attention to their external appearances. In contrast, young people who lack knowledge or possessions in the "real world" (yin interior) dye their hair a bright color like red, wear ripped clothing, and wear chains (yang exterior) to compensate for what they lack.

The jobs that pertain to the Zhen trigram require ceaseless effort to discover new things. In contrast, jobs related to the Dui trigram necessitate staying put and quiet and quelling rash and thoughtless action so that the water in the dish (Dui trigram) will not spill out.

The Xun Trigram

In the Xun trigram, two yang lines are on top and one yin line is on the bottom. This symbolizes wind, ceaselessly moving here, there, and everywhere. Jobs that belong to the Xun trigram include trading businesses that require frequent location changes, wholesalers who must distribute goods, overseas workers, and employees who must make frequent business trips. Other jobs include photographers, sailors, drivers, and anyone involved in the transportation or shipping businesses.

People who feel stifled or stuffy working in one place for a long time can find success in Xun trigram jobs. However, they must pay a heavy price, for those who succeed in Xun trigram jobs tend to have difficulty maintaining good family relationships. To maintain a family, a person needs to sit tight in one place. However, a person of the Xun trigram or who has a Xun-type job will feel stifled by family life and will long to escape from the confines of the home.

The talents of singers and actors require splendor and beautiful attributes. Thus, these jobs belong to the Li trigram; however, since the popularity they pursue changes rapidly like the wind, they also belong to the Xun trigram.

Because the movement of the Xun trigram is rootless, it is hard to predict its course. Thus, people who have Xun-type jobs must not be content to simply ride high on the wind; they should prepare for the time when the wind does not blow.

The Gen Trigram

The Gen trigram has one yang line on top and two yin lines on the bottom. It symbolizes a mountain. It also indicates a strong and firm organization, a country, or a corporation. It is a trigram that represents minor changes with underlying stability. Jobs that involve few changes and are, for the most part, stable pertain to the Gen trigram. Thus, rank-and-file officials, postal workers, company clerks, and bureaucrats belong to this trigram. Moreover, as the Gen trigram pertains to the hand, jobs that involve heavy use of the hand belong to it. Thus, industrial-art object makers, assembly workers, dentists, and orthopedic surgeons belong to this trigram.

Remember that knowing the meaning behind each trigram does not equate to a complete understanding of the eight trigrams. It is more important to be able to apply them to all aspects of daily life and work. For example, when the trigrams are applied to your profession, they will illuminate your relationship to the outside world and other aspects of your life. When one element is singled out, not only can we determine where that element belongs among the totality of your specialty, but also which point it occupies within the entire universe. This can be illustrated by placing a dot on the coordinate system of the universe. Not knowing where the nature of your work belongs in relation to the universe is like navigating the ocean without a compass or map. Working day and night without such knowledge may bring undesired results, like a ship crashing into many pieces.

However, you cannot exact your vocation's location in the universe's spectrum like a mathematical calculation. Besides those specializing in quantum physics, many try to put an accurate dot on things using mathematical calculations. The uncertainty principle reminds us that we can only approximate what we think we know. In knowing the probability, the principle of the I Ching is applied. First, we divide the position of the whole into two (yin-yang) and confirm which section the dot goes into. After establishing this, we divide the section again (Sasang), and make another confirmation. Then, we divide that section into two (eight trigrams). When confirmed, the position becomes accurate to one-eighth among the total. This is the probability based on the eight trigrams. When divided into sixty-four hexagrams (which will be further expanded later), we can know the element's position more accurately.

Universally, this principle holds true everywhere. When applied, it is possible to mark a single point on the coordinate system of the entire universe. Again remember that having only addition-and-subtraction knowledge does not always guarantee an accurate calculation. It is necessary to solve innumerable practice questions to make a precise calculation. In the same way, knowing the eight trigrams does not necessarily result in their proper application. Practices of classifying numerous things into the eight trigrams must be ongoing.

The Eight Trigrams and the Human Body

The eight trigrams can be associated with the physical shape or the human body's physio-logical processes (fig. 22.3). Many scholars of the I Ching use this classification method, illuminating specific characteristics of the symbols representing each of the eight trigrams. In addition to the ancient classifications, we have added additional information based on modern Western physiology.

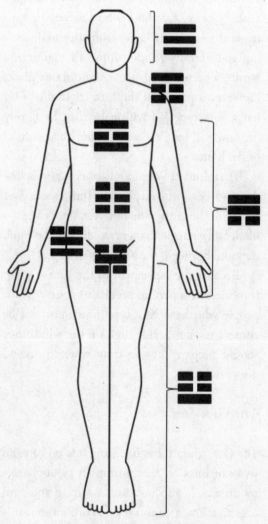

Figure 22.3 Trigrams of a Body

THE PHYSICAL BODY AND THE EIGHT TRIGRAMS

QIAN (HEAVEN) AND KUN (EARTH)

The Qian trigram corresponds to the human head, and the Kun trigram corresponds to the human torso. The head can divide into three major compartments: the frontal lobe, the parietal lobe, and the occipital lobe. Each of these sections is round, which relates to yang. So the formation of the head is related to the gathering of three yangs, or the Qian trigram (fig. 22.4). The trunk also has three major divisions: the thoracic cavity, the abdominal cavity, and the pelvic cavity. As their name implies, these areas are hollow, so they resemble the three yin lines of the Kun trigram.

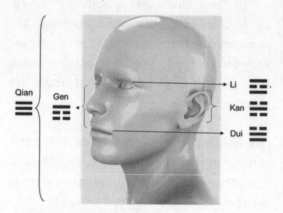

Figure 22.4 Trigrams of a Head and Face

LI (FIRE) AND KAN (WATER)

The eyes resemble the Li trigram (fig. 22.4). At the center is the pupil, which is dark (yin) and surrounded by the sclera (the white part of the eye). Because the sclera is lighter, it is representative of yang. The eyes are as bright and beautiful as a fire. The eyes of animals shine brightly at night. Thus, the eyes belong to the Li trigram because they share their nature.

The ears resemble the Kan trigram (fig. 22.5). Careful observation of the ears will reveal that they sink into the head, and so they are yin. The protruding circular part is yang. The exterior part of this protruding part is again sunken inward, and so it is yin. This is in the shape of the Kan trigram. Overall, the ear seems to be a figure with a potent absorbing function, as it is an orifice sunk deeply into the head. Since the Kan trigram has a solid, absorbing function, it coincides with the function of the ear.

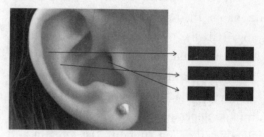

Figure 22.5 Ear and Kan (Water) Trigram

DUI (LAKE) AND GEN (MOUNTAIN)

The Dui trigram is associated with the mouth or women's genitals. The mouth is sunken inward like the shape of the Dui trigram (fig. 22.6), and so are women's genitals. The mouth gathers food that eventually becomes the energy needed to create new cells in the body. Likewise, a woman's genitals gather in the male genitalia (or the essence called Jing) to produce cells for the next generation, thus represented by two lower yang lines.

The nose resembles the Gen trigram (fig. 22.7). The tip of the nose protrudes like a mountain. This is the yang line on the top. The nostrils are sunken inward, and so represent the two lower yin lines.

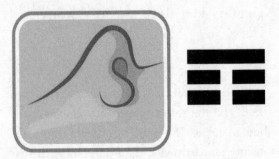

Figure 22.7 Nose and Gen (Mountain) Trigram

Figure 22.6 Mouth and Dui (Lake) Trigram

The Gen trigram can also correspond to the hand. The top line of the Gen trigram is yang. It is the principal line of the trigram, and its function pertains to the hands. They are attached to the top (end) of the arms and have dynamic activity (yang), while the forearm and upper arm are less mobile (yin). This resembles the Gen trigram. The forearm and upper arm correspond to two lower yin lines, which are the foundation for the dynamic activity of the hands.

Xun (Wind) and Zhen (Thunder)

The upper limbs can also correspond to the Xun trigram. The upper arm has three aspects: the hands, forearms, and upper arms. When a person raises their arms above the head, they resemble the Xun trigram. The hands are the most dynamic and active, corresponding to yang. The forearms are also relatively active and are also yang. The upper arms are restricted in their movements by their attachment to the body, so they are yin.

The carpal bones of the hands are restricted in their movements, so they are yin. However, the metacarpals and fingers are free to move about and relate to yang. Therefore, we can also see the image of the Xun trigram just in the hands.

The lower limbs consist of the feet, which are relatively unrestricted; the calves, which are more restricted; and the thighs, which are attached to the trunk. The feet relate to yang, and the calves and thighs are yin. This resembles the shape of the Zhen trigram.

The classification thus far is based on the traditional method used by the I Ching scholars. However, in addition to that category, there is another way to view the eight trigrams.

When viewed from the functional aspect of the body, the head and trunk can divide into four sections. This is similar to the division mentioned in the Sasang chapter. The four cardinal trigrams are assigned to the head and body because their sluggish movements mirror one another. The head relates to the Qian trigram, the chest correlates to the Li trigram, the abdomen corresponds to the Kun trigram, and the pelvic cavity relates to the Kan trigram. The four transitional trigrams are assigned to the arms, legs, shoulders, and hips, as they have dynamic natures.

Since the head regulates the whole body, it corresponds to the Qian trigram representing heaven. The organs within the abdominal cavity digest and absorb food to nurture every part of the body. The belly resembles the earth in such a way and corresponds to the Kun trigram.

The chest is the place where passion and other emotions are felt. It is also the center for the circulatory functions of the heart and lungs. It is like the sun supplying energy to all things in nature and corresponds to the Li trigram. The pelvic cavity is in charge of reproductive functions. It is the location of the kidney system, the bladder, and reproductive organs. Therefore, it corresponds to the Kan trigram.

The shoulders correspond to the Gen trigram. Because the arms are freer to move about, they are yang. In relation to the arms, the trunk and the legs are less mobile and are yin. Thus, the arms and hands represent the top yang line, while the trunk and legs represent the two lower yin lines.

The Dui trigram relates to the buttocks. The top yin line is represented by the trunk, which is immobile, while the two yang lines on the bottom correlate to the legs and feet, which are more active than the trunk.

The upper limbs correspond to Xun, and the lower limbs correspond to Zhen.

HUMAN PHYSIOLOGY AND THE EIGHT TRIGRAMS

QIAN (HEAVEN) AND KUN (EARTH)

The Qian trigram corresponds to the head, and the Kun trigram corresponds to the belly. Human beings resemble heaven and earth. According to I Ching theory, the universe (heaven) is round, and so is the human head.

The Qian trigram is also similar to the cranial nervous system. To sense the shape of heaven, the brain branches out through the eyes (light energy of heaven) and ears (sound energy of heaven). To sense the earth, the brain branches out through the nose (smell molecules of the earth) and mouth (taste molecules of the earth). To sense various body parts, the brain branches out through the nerves in the body. This resembles the unrelenting yang energy of the Qian trigram spreading out in all directions.

After sensing heaven, earth, and body, the brain gives various commands that regulate the entire body to stay tuned to the energies of heaven and the earth's substances. In this way, the brain resembles the universe (heaven), which regulates all things in nature, including human beings. Therefore, the head corresponds to the Qian trigram.

Though the belly is round, it feels flat. Similarly, the Earth is round, but it, too, has the appearance from our perspective of being flat. The Earth is called "Mother Earth" because it protects and nourishes everything, much like a mother takes care of her children.

The Kun trigram also resembles the uterus

(fig. 22.8). The primary function of the uterus is to produce a child. To do this, it must absorb blood through the arteries in its upper region, eggs through the fallopian tubes on both sides, and sperm through the vagina in its lower part. The Kun trigram also takes in from the top, middle, and bottom. Don't the three orifices of the uterus's triangular structure resemble the Kun trigram's three lines?

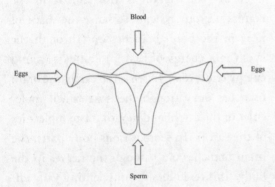

Figure 22.8 Uterus

There are two centers in the human body. Firstly, there is the brain that senses the body and gives commands accordingly. The other is the torso, the pivotal point of the head and four limbs. The torso, which houses the spine, regulates the whole body. It accomplishes this by being the reflex center for limb stimuli and the autonomic innervation center. It also controls the supply of nutrients and oxygen to the head and limbs.

As the mind's center, the brain corresponds to the Qian trigram, while the trunk corresponds to the Kun trigram as the body's center. These two centers vary in nature and are simply two centers of influence or forces like the North and South Poles, as mentioned earlier. They do not directly carry out the work of the physiological functions. The heart and the kidneys are the ones that actually execute the physiological processes. Since the heart is in charge of the blood (red, fire), it belongs to the Li trigram, while the kidneys are in charge of water and so belong to the Kan trigram.

LI (FIRE) AND KAN (WATER)

In Eastern medicine, the brain, marrow, bone, and kidneys are tissues, organs, and systems belonging to the water element. This organization takes into consideration the Kan trigram of the I Ching. Kidneys are emblematic of systems that belong to the water element. The arteries and veins that connect the kidneys to the heart give them their bean shapes. If the kidneys did not connect to the heart, they would have a spherical shape, similar to a drop of water, due to their contracting force (figure 22.9). Even the glomerulus, the smallest unit of the kidney, is made up of capillaries tangled up into the shape of a ball because of the kidneys' compressing force.

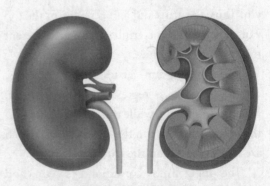

Figure 22.9 Kidneys

Bone and marrow can be seen as one entity. The exterior of the bone is yin, as it is hard; inside, it is full of fat, so it contains a yang nature. Therefore, bone is associated with the Kan trigram. On the other hand, the brain is a type of marrow consisting primarily of fat and surrounded by the skull. Therefore, the brain and marrow, mainly composed of fat, correspond to the Kan trigram, along with the head, as it is hard on the outside (the outer yin lines) and soft on the inside (the center yang line).

A thick fatty layer surrounds the kidneys, similar to the packaging of fragile merchandise in Styrofoam. The fat, in this case, is like "bubble wrap" around the kidneys. Fat protects the kidneys, but the kidneys also play a great role in fat metabolism. When a person is young, the function of the kidneys keeps fat outside at the exterior. As energy decreases with age, fat accumulates in the kidneys' glomeruli. This, in turn, causes arteriosclerosis in the renal arteries. Also, marrow is infiltrated by fat when the production of red or white blood cells is slow. Such information indicates that *The Yellow Emperor's Inner Classic,* which also happens to be the first to associate kidneys and marrow with the water element, had some early clue about the relationship between those organs and tissues with fat.

The heart and blood vessels belong to the fire element because both pertain to blood, red in color and strong in movement. However, blood's essential nature is water, yin on the inside and yang on the outside, clearly showing its correspondence to the Li trigram.

The heart, surrounded by a thick muscular layer, beats constantly and pumps blood. Its shape correlates well with the Li trigram. It has been previously stated that life is ultimately the ascending water and descending fire, the interaction between heart and kidneys. In other words, life is the interaction between Li and Kan trigrams.

ZHEN (THUNDER) AND DUI (LAKE)

The liver and lungs are the communicative devices that allow the influences of the heart and kidneys to reach one another. The liver has a function that corresponds to spring, and like the spring, it is in charge of the ascending functions in the body. More simply stated, the liver controls transforming matter into energy in the body. Thus, it corresponds to the Zhen trigram, which converts the universe's substance into energy on a grander scale. The lungs function in the opposite direction. They conform to autumn and are in charge of the descending function of the body. They control energy transformation into matter, just like the Dui trigram. The Dui trigram absorbs energy and compiles it until it is matter again.

GEN (MOUNTAIN) AND XUN (WIND)

The kidneys function similarly to the wintertime, when storing energy as matter occurs. When matter is ready to transform into energy once again, the springtime function of the liver activates the process. However, converting the substance into energy is difficult, so the liver needs assistance. A system in the body called Mingmen (the Gate of Life) in Eastern medicine corresponds to the adrenal glands. The adrenals help the kidneys function by secreting hormones that facilitate the liver processes. The function of the adrenals relates to the Gen trigram. This function is like the top yang line in the Gen trigram.

We have previously discussed the Ministerial Fire that helps the Monarch Fire of the heart. The Ministerial Fire assists the kidneys in the lower region through Mingmen, which corresponds to the adrenals and supports the heart in the upper area through the pericardium. The pericardium is the protective sac surrounding the heart in Western anatomy. In Eastern medicine, the pericardium's function is the sum of the pericardium and the thyroid gland. The supply of energy, nutrients, and oxygen to the body's cells is only possible when proper thyroid hormone secretion occurs. This function of the thyroid and pericardium is the function of the Xun trigram. These functions can be put into a diagram (fig. 22.10).

This diagram illustrates the trigrams in terms of their relationship to the human body. The Qian and the Kun trigrams function as the polar force that gives the body its form and function. The workhorses are the trigrams that correspond to the six types of energy. Qian influences the energy transformation function of the Mingmen, liver, heart, and pericardium, while Kun influences the materializing function of the lungs and kidneys.

Just as yin and yang change according to perspective, the trigram arrangement also changes according to whether the trigrams describe the body's functional or structural aspects.

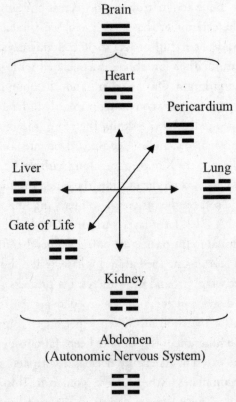

Figure 22.10 Organs and Trigrams

Animals and the Eight Trigrams

Since the eight trigrams have universal applicability, we can better understand this concept through their relationship with animals. Each trigram corresponds to a specific animal according to its characteristics and nature. For example, because the horse is sinewy in shape, has rapid movements, and is highly diligent, it can be associated with the Qian trigram. In addition, the horse frequently dislikes bending down or sitting still, which is also a trait that correlates with Qian. On the other hand, a cow is very docile and slow and prefers stillness to action. Its characteristics convey a stable nature that closely associates it with the Kun trigram.

The six remaining trigrams also correspond to certain animals. Pheasants and tropical birds belong to the Li trigram. Birds are widely considered beautiful creatures. Because of their dynamic activity and capability of flight, they capture the fire nature of the Li trigram. Reptiles, such as turtles and alligators, belong to the Kan trigram and are more negatively viewed as hideous creatures when compared to the beauty of birds. For the most part, reptiles are sluggish creatures, and the water usually surrounds their natural habitats. For these reasons, reptiles correspond to the Kan trigram. However, certain mammals with a yin nature, such as the pig or rat, also relate to the Kan trigram.

Although belonging to different trigrams, the offspring of both birds and reptiles hatch out of hard-shelled eggs. The eggs are the products of Kan, which represents reproduction. They also manifest the Kan shape of a tough exterior (shell) and a mobile interior. Thus, though the Kan and Li trigrams are in a polar relationship, they are classified under the same category of a form-function relationship, compared to other trigrams. Therefore, the commonality of laying eggs exists between reptiles and birds.

Sheep are very soft and docile (yin) and correspond to the Dui trigram. While the exterior of the sheep relates it to yin, the strong goatish smell of lamb meat correlates to yang. Any substance with a strong smell indicates dynamic molecular activity. In the case of sheep, the goatish smell belongs to the wood element, which is also a yang element. Another characteristic of sheep that indicates their strong inner yang nature is the hardness of their stools and their lack of moisture. Thus, sheep correspond to the Dui trigram by having two interior yang lines and one exterior yin line.

The Gen trigram, meanwhile, can be compared to the dog. Though many types of dogs with diverse natures exist, dogs are courageous on average. They can form packs and attack animals larger than or equal to their size. This represents the yang nature of dogs. In general, carnivorous animals are yang, while herbivorous animals are yin. Dogs have the carnivorous nature of being fierce, aggressive, and agile. However, they also maintain an herbivorous nature by eating foods from plant sources and being very docile and loyal to their owners. Moreover, unlike many other carnivores, the dog mates for a long time, owing to the more fundamental nature of yin.

Though not a real animal in today's beliefs, the dragon belongs to the Zhen trigram. Legend states that dragons have dwelled in a water world unknown to humans for centuries, and a sole king of dragons governs them. In legend, the goal of the dragon is to make an ascent into heaven. Only then can it become a deity and live forever. But before a dragon can make its ascension, it must wait for one hundred years without being seen by humans.

Two yin lines in the Zhen trigram represent the underwater realm, while a single yang line on the bottom represents the wiggling dragon hiding in the water. The metaphoric action of the dragon rising from the water and ascending to the heavens represents the latent function in the Zhen trigram.

A person cultivating oneself by gathering the life force into the Danjun (uterus in women) to be enlightened (pure yang state not hidden by yin) is similar to the dragon. Likewise, an examinee who has studied medicine or law since childhood to pass board exams is analogous to the dragon. A king praying to heaven for the wants and wishes of his people during monarchical days is also comparable to the dragon. All of these are perfect examples of the Zhen trigram.

Lastly, the Xun trigram is associated with none other than the rooster. Though small in size, a crowing rooster can be quite loud. This animal is easily excited and can be ferociously arrogant, making him fearless in fights and oblivious to the safety of his own body. Such overreaction displayed by the rooster is a definite characteristic of the Xun trigram.

FOUR MYSTICAL ANIMALS

There are drawings of four mystical animals in the tombs of ancient Korean kings. In the south, the position of the Li trigram, according to King Wen's arrangement of trigrams, is a drawing of the phoenix (fig. 22.11), the firebird. Like the Li trigram, it burns brightly and has dynamic movements. In the north, the position of the Kan trigram, is a drawing of an animal called Hyun Mu (fig. 22.12), which

Figure 22.11 Phoenix, National Museum of Korea

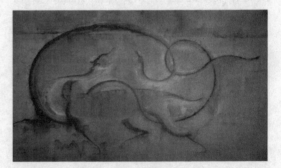

Figure 22.12 Hyun Mu or Turtle, National Museum of Korea

has a turtle's body and a snake's head. The turtle, slow in movement, expresses the laziness of the Kan trigram. This laziness, however, is balanced by Hyun Mu's snake head, symbolizing sharpness and high intelligence. The brain is formed when yin reaches its extreme, constituting Hyun Mu's intellect. A lesson can be learned from this animal. Suppose a person is in a negative yin situation but is devoted to his or her work. In that case, the results will be favorable, balanced like the yin and yang of the turtle's body (yin) and snake's head (yang).

In the eastern position is a dragon drawing (fig. 22.13), while in the west, there is the white tiger (fig. 22.14). Again, according to King Wen's arrangement of trigrams, these animals correspond to the Zhen and Dui trigrams. The dragon corresponds to the wood springtime energy and represents the yang energy of propulsion, generation, and resoluteness. The tiger is generally reserved (yin) until it pounces upon its prey, the direction of his jump focused on a downward motion (yin). No matter where the tiger is or the shape of its condition, it always manifests an air of bloodthirstiness

Figure 22.13 Dragon, National Museum of Korea

Figure 22.14 White Tiger, National Museum of Korea

or fierce spirit. Such is the energy of the metal element, which stops the energy of generation and growth and corresponds with autumn.

Together, the phoenix, the Hyun Mu, the dragon, and the tiger represent the energetics of the four directions, or the Earth's four corners. In fact, these animals represent the four directional forces of nature and are frequently mentioned when discussing Feng Shui, the art of placement discussed previously in the Sasang chapter.

The Eight Trigrams of the Natural Environment

The following is Fuxi's placement of the eight trigrams labeled with the substances representing each of them (fig. 22.15):

Figure 22.15 Natural Environment and Trigrams

There are eight natural environmental factors influencing human beings. First, heaven on top gives sunlight and oxygen, and the earth at the bottom provides water and nutrients. The Li trigram, symbolizing fire, is in charge of the sunlight of heaven (the sun), and the Xun trigram, symbolizing wind, is in control of oxygen. The Kan trigram supervises the water of the Earth. Finally, the Gen trigram, which denotes the mountain, pertains to rice and other grainfields and is the supervisor of nutrients.

The Earth consists of high (mountains) and low (lakes) ground, with water flowing between them. In heaven, lightning (thunder) operates from above to below, and wind moves from below to above. The fire sits between wind and lightning.

On Earth, mountains create water, and lakes gather it, while in heaven, lightning generates fire. The wind assists it in burning vigorously. So in heaven, lightning and wind exist in polar relationships to activate and operate the fire necessary for human beings. Likewise, on Earth, the polar components of mountains and lakes activate and manage the water needed for humans. The following diagram schematically demonstrates these relations (fig. 22.16).

In Fuxi's sequence of the eight trigrams (fig. 22.1), the order of the trigrams comes down from the top (south) to the fourth Zhen trigram (northeast). Then, it suddenly returns to the top again, to the fifth Xun trigram (southwest). This change in order is because the Zhen and the Xun are two trigrams responsible for movement and change.

Six types of energies, excluding heaven and

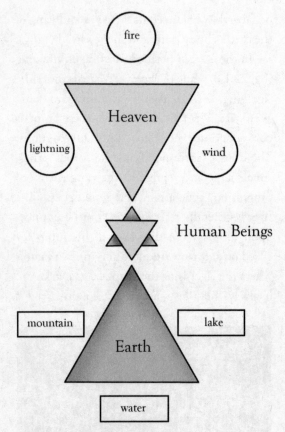

Figure 22.16 Environmental Factors and Human Beings

earth, directly influence humans (fig. 22.17). These are the six energies that divide into three yin and three yang: Shaoyin (lesser yin) Monarch Fire corresponds to the fire trigram, and Shaoyang (lesser yang) Ministerial Fire corresponds to the thunder/lightning trigram. Jueyin (declining yin) wind-wood corresponds to the wind trigram, and Taiyang (greater yang) cold-water corresponds to the water trigram. Yangming (bright yang) dry-metal corresponds to the mountain trigram, and Taiyin (greater yin) damp-earth corresponds to the

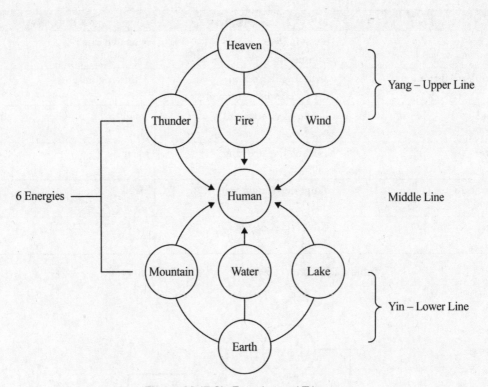

Figure 22.17 Six Energies and Trigrams

lake trigram. Eastern medicine, which views the human body as a microcosm, describes the meridians that connect the internal organs and the bodily surface with the six energies (see diagram A3.17 in Appendix 3 for details).

The correlation between these energies, the five elements, and the eight trigrams is shown in table 22.1.

Figure 22.18 vertically depicts humans and the environmental forces that impact them. There is fire above and water below the humans. Fire represents yang, and water represents yin. The humans in the middle of yin and yang correspond to the earth element. The earth below human beings sits lower than the water, containing wood, metal, mountains, and lakes. Above humans is heaven, which includes wind and lightning. Together, they make up the five elements and form the eight trigrams. The diagram elucidates the relationship between the eight trigrams, the five elements, Sasang, and the yin-yang.

As mentioned earlier, the function of the universe, human physiology, and Tai Chi is the "ascending of water and descending of fire." The "ascending of water" is attributed to the mountain and lake, constituents of the Earth. Meanwhile, the "descending of fire" is attributed to the wind and lightning, constituents of heaven.

TRIGRAMS	SIX ENERGIES	FIVE ELEMENTS
Fire	Shaoyin (lesser yin) summer heat	Monarch Fire
Thunder/lightning	Shaoyang (lesser yang) fire (late/Indian summer)	Ministerial Fire
Wind	Jueyin (declining yin) wind	wood
Water	Taiyang (greater yang) cold	water
Mountain	Yangming (bright yang) dry	metal
Lake	Taiyin (greater yin) damp	earth

Table 22.1 Trigrams, Six Energies, and Five Elements

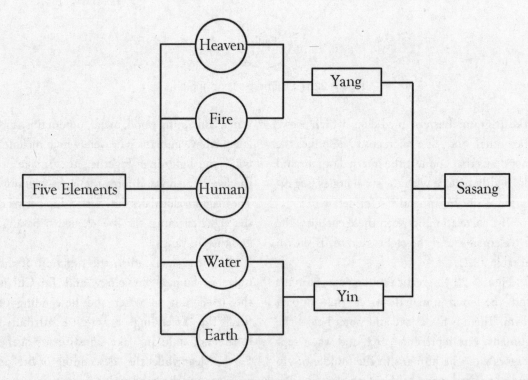

Figure 22.18 The Relationship between the Eight Trigrams, the Five Elements, Sasang, and the Yin-Yang

Though wind and lightning have the shared function of moving the things of nature, the wind shifts and lifts things from the ground up (thereby dispersing) toward heaven. In contrast, thunder/lightning destroys things from heaven toward earth. These elements are in charge of transforming all things in nature that are generally still and function to create new things.

The mountain and lake share the same function of bringing all things in nature to a stop. The mountain's function is ascending from the earth to heaven (below to above) to stop the water's horizontal movement (gently flowing river). Meanwhile, the function of the lake sweeps down from heaven to the earth to prevent the movement of animals and the water's vertical movement (valley water flowing from high places). As a result, animals and plants are nourished by the water.

Eight Trigrams of Music

Chapter 11, "Yin and Yang of Music," described how music was used to govern people and for self-cultivation. Through the resonance of wave frequency, music can correct imbalances of yin and yang in both commoners and people practicing spiritual discipline, all consisting of vibrating subatomic particles.

Musical instruments tilted toward yang tones can balance people of a yin disposition who lack yang energy. The opposite holds true for instruments inclined toward yin tones. When people resonate with music balanced in yin-yang, their yin-yang becomes harmonized. As a result, they become more complete and perfect human beings without greed, selfishness, or wickedness.

Since humans originally possess the entire universe pattern, they constantly prefer to balance their yin and yang. Thus, they instinctively want to hear music balanced in yin and yang. But their inclinations fluctuate according to the era, so preferences can tilt slightly toward yin or yang. Nevertheless, the fundamental nature of wanting to harmonize their yin and yang does not change. Therefore, for the kings in power, understanding the inclination of yin and yang in people and the ability to regulate the central tone (Hwangjong, or Golden Bell tone) was a critical issue.

When people listen to music harmonized in yin-yang and sing or dance to it, their minds become joyful. The kings will not need to educate and enact laws or imprison those who violate the law. The king merely has to set the central tone of the Golden Bell correctly, and people just need to make music according to its central note and dance or move to it. Then the yin and yang of their bodies and minds will become balanced, and their minds will become like that of God, who loves the entire universe. Will there be any need for laws and regulations when everyone is enlightened and can live and work in a perfectly balanced state? There will be no need for laws, only the knowledge of Yulryeo. Therefore, in the past, when the monarchy was the main form of government in the East, the standard of peaceful reign was thought to be when people were not consciously aware of the king's existence and only sang and danced.

SOURCE OF SOUND	DIRECTION	SEASON	INSTRUMENT
Stone	northwest	autumn–winter	ringing-stone (磬)
Metal	west	autumn	bell (鍾)
Silk	south	summer	lute (琴) or zither (瑟)
Bamboo	east	spring	flute (笛) and pipe (管)
Wood	southeast	spring-summer	tiger-box (敔)
Skin (leather)	north	winter	drum (鼓)
Gourd (dipper)	northeast	winter-spring	reed-organ (笙)
Earth	southwest	summer-autumn	globular flute (壎)

Table 22.2 The Sound Sources of Eight Traditional Instruments

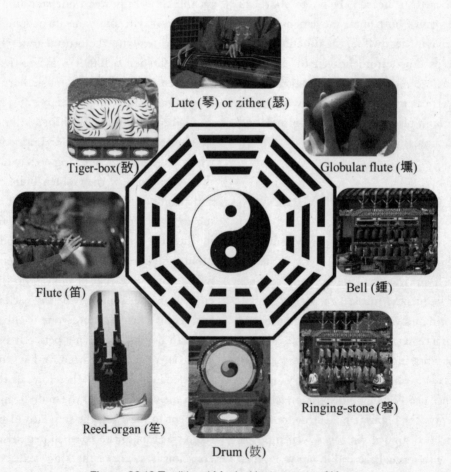

Lute (琴) or zither (瑟)

Tiger-box (敔)

Globular flute (壎)

Flute (笛)

Bell (鍾)

Reed-organ (笙)

Ringing-stone (磬)

Drum (鼓)

Figure 22.19 Traditional Musical Instruments of Korea

Jongmyo Ritual

Since the kings of the past emphasized music, the music for religious ceremonies at the shrine of royal ancestors, known as Jongmyo, played a vital role. The music can directly affect the souls of the deceased (ancestral monarchs) by entertaining them through the harmonious melodies balanced in yin-yang.

The nature of the sound produced by musical instruments used in Jongmyo can be distinguished and placed in each of the eight directions (eight trigrams) (fig. 22.19). Thus, the nature of the music of these instruments can be known by observing their placements in literature, such as in the following table from Joseph Needham's *Science and Civilisation in China* (table 22.2).[1]

There are annual rituals in Jongmyo, where sixty-four officials dance to the court music of the Eastern orchestra (fig. 22.20). If the I Ching shows the changing pattern of the universe with sixty-four hexagrams, the dance of the Jongmyo ritual shows the different movements of the sixty-four hexagrams as human motions.

Figure 22.20 Jongmyo Ritual

23

Interpretations of the Sixty-Four Hexagrams

Interpreting the sixty-four hexagrams is difficult because there are many different perspectives from which one can view them. Therefore, the following interpretations focus on the energetic nature of the hexagrams rather than the actual words of the text found in most translations of the I Ching. These energetic interpretations serve as a guide for everyone to discover the most appropriate understanding for them.

However, it is important to understand the basics of the I Ching outlined in this book before attempting personal interpretations. With-

out the fundamentals, one can easily be misled. Therefore, begin with an understanding of Tao and Tai Chi, then move on to yin-yang, Sasang, the five elements, and the eight trigrams, and finally attempt interpretations and analyses of the sixty-four hexagrams. Since each hexagram comprises two trigrams, you must thoroughly understand their shape and energetic nature. Otherwise, you won't be able to move on to interpreting the hexagrams.

Each hexagram has a number according to the sequence attributed to King Wen. So the numbers with each hexagram represent this sequence. Next to each hexagram is a description of its form or shape and energetic aspects, defined by one or two words. These words are concise descriptions of the hexagrams' true nature. However, they should not be the sole basis of consideration when interpreting. Remember that there can be multiple interpretations, so concentrate on the energetic images and symbols.

It is possible to illustrate the sixty-four hexagram arrangement either in a circular or square format (figs. 23.1 and 23.2). As explained at the beginning of chapter 21, the circular arrangement of the hexagrams is in a fractal structure. But it also denotes the binary arithmetic codes, as does the hexagram arrangement expressed in a square format with black and white squares representing yin and yang.

The great Song dynasty Confucian Shao Yong (1011–1077 CE) created the arrange-

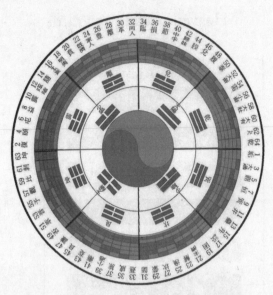

Figure 23.1 Circular Arrangement of Hexagrams

ments of hexagrams based on binary arithmetic. He named it the Fuxi arrangement to differentiate it from the King Wen arrangement.

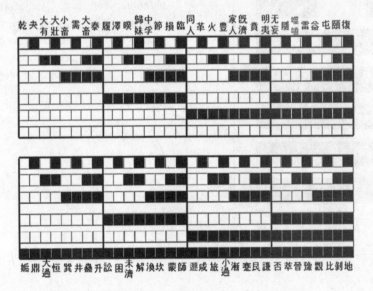

Figure 23.2 Square Arrangement of Hexagrams

Heaven (Qian) Trigrams

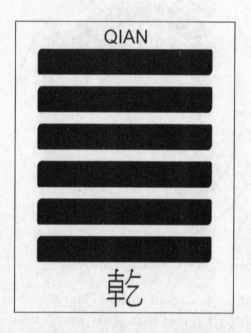

(1) Qian/Heaven (Supreme Power)
The Qian hexagram represents heaven, a great mass of energy of only yang lines. Thus, its force of expansion is powerful. Its image is identical to the exploding function of the white hole. It is also the purest, brightest, healthiest, and most indefatigable of all energies, as it consists only of yang.

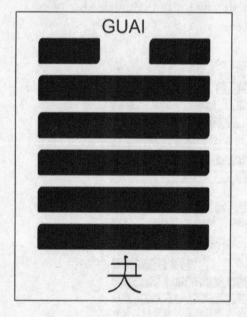

(43) Resolution (Explosion)
In explaining the hexagrams, the I Ching emphasizes the yang lines. This hexagram is an image in which the five yang lines beneath a single exterior yin line try to escape its control and explode. Positive and virtuous forces (yang) resolutely eliminate negative, evil, and inferior forces (yin).

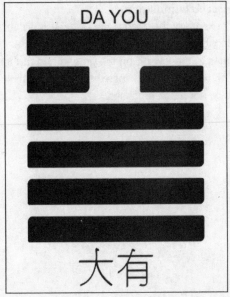

DA YOU

大有

(14) Great Existence/Possession

This hexagram displays the sun above heaven. This indicates that the sun is in a great position from where it can demonstrate its ability and exert its influence. It radiates heat and light. Hence, it is deemed to have great possession, abundance, and prosperity. The fifth line represents the king line, which is generally the ruling line of a hexagram. Because this is a yin line surrounded by five yang lines, there is plenty of yang energy for the yin line to draw from.

Nevertheless, unlike yin substances, yang energy cannot be maintained for long periods. That is why this hexagram is not related to having great monetary wealth. Remember, yin is associated with matter, money, and similar concrete objects.

DA ZHUANG

大壯

(34) Great Power (Bravery)

This hexagram symbolizes thunder over heaven and how the sound of thunder high up in the sky demonstrates its power. The yang lines (energy) completely fill beneath the king (fifth line). Yang energy is gradually expanding and developing upward to replace the yin energy. Thunder's attribute is courage stemming from its movement and penetrating force. Heaven's attribute of resoluteness derives from its powerful exploding function. Therefore, the hexagram is indicative of great power and bravery.

(9) Lesser Accumulation

In this hexagram, the wind is above heaven. When the wind blows, erosion occurs, and debris accumulates in the low pit on the ground and at the bases of mountains. But since the wind blows high in the sky, not much amasses.

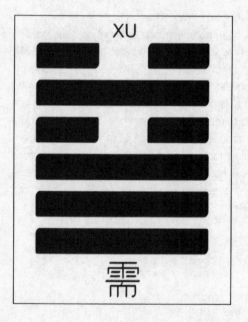

(5) Demand (Waiting)

Water is in the heavens, representing rain sprinkling evenly to supply the water needed (demanded) by myriad things in nature. Another interpretation is that even though there is a strong spirit and function (Heaven trigram), since there is grave danger (Water trigram) ahead, it would be best to wait before making a move.

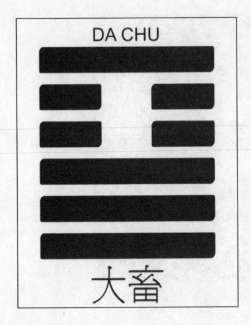

(26) Greater Accumulation

This hexagram displays a mountain above heaven. Mountains are very large and have a great accumulating force, as their attribute is restraining and stockpiling. Additionally, a mountain above heaven can represent the reserve of noble virtue (yang).

(11) Peace (Prosperity/Tranquility)

The earth above heaven represents a state where the communication between heaven (yang) and earth (yin) is harmonious. Everything runs smoothly, and the mind is at peace when this occurs. The figures of two mystical animals on a royal porcelain plate (fig. 23.3) succinctly demonstrate the energetics of this hexagram. It shows ascending of a dragon (yang) and descending of a phoenix (yin), which symbolizes a well-governed universe and country.

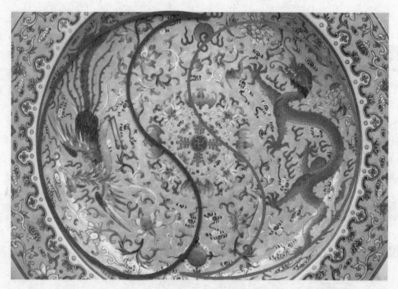

Figure 23.3 A Royal Porcelain Plate, National Palace Museum, Taipei, Republic of China (Taiwan)

Lake (Dui) Trigrams

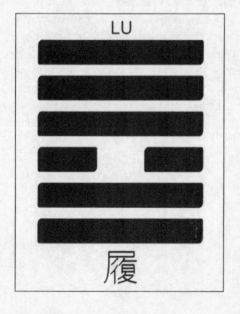

LU

履

(10) Covering
Heaven above a lake. A Lake trigram pulls things inward, gathering and storing yang from the environment. There is a sufficient supply of yang to be collected, as heaven, the epitome of yang, hovers over the lake.

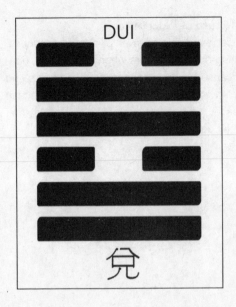

(58) Dui/Lake

This is the pairing of the Dui trigram, which represents a lake. Since the Dui trigram has the nature of gathering things inward, doubling it implies that a greater number of things can be amassed and that the force of gathering is twice as strong.

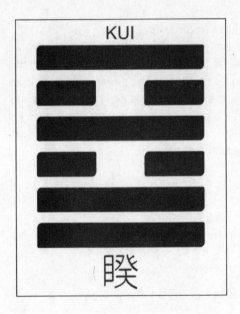

(38) Misalignment (Estrangment)

This is the sun above the sea. It is an image of an arrow that left its bow, or a rocket that just blasted into space. It can also signify separation (fire ascending upward and a lake descending downward). Here, the yang energy (Li trigram) accumulated in the waters of a lake or sea (Dui trigram) has separated and risen to the surface.

(54) Return of Elder Sister
This displays lightning over a lake or an ocean. Lightning primarily occurs when there is rain, generally caused by the vaporization of the lake's and ocean's water. So lightning over the lake or ocean implies the return to a place of origin, like a married daughter coming home for a visit.

(61) Utmost Sincerity
There are two yang lines above and below with two yin lines in the center. It resembles an egg, with the yolk in the middle (yin) and the white on the outside (yang). It is an image of a hen incubating an egg. When the proper time arrives, the chick emerges. So, like a hen hatching an egg, one must have sincerity, faith, and caution.

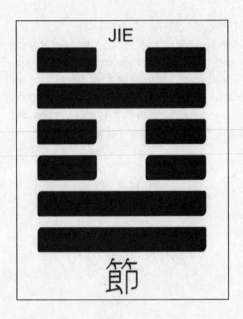

(60) Regulation

Water is above a lake. The hexagram symbolizes how water, contained within the limited boundary of a lake, gets its shape and, by extension, relays the image of regulation. Water must not overflow nor dry out and must be pure and fresh, so fish and plants can live.

(41) Deficiency (Decrease)

This denotes a mountain above a lake. The mountain and the lake antagonize one another, so if they are together, there is loss. The lines of each trigram are opposite, expressing the opposing nature of yin and yang. The energy of the mountain ascends, while that of a lake draws inward.

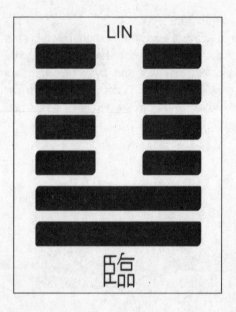

LIN

臨

(19) Approach (Draw Near)

The earth above a lake symbolizes the level of water rising and gradually approaching the earth's surface. The strong yang lines of the lower trigram are progressively increasing, like the water permeating the ground underneath to fill the lower trigram, and are drawing near the upper trigram.

Fire (Li) Trigrams

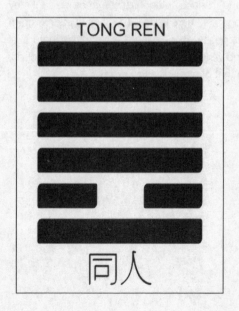

TONG REN

同人

(13) Camaraderie

The sun is beneath heaven. The sun and heaven share similar natures, as they are yang and have ascending attributes. Fire moving upward to heaven conveys an image of genuine friendliness toward one another.

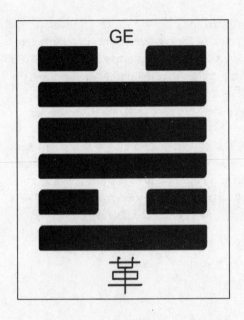

(49) Revolution

This portrays the sun beneath a lake. When the sun rises, the darkness disappears, representing the dawning of a revolution. Also, water and fire oppose one another, indicating conflict and an image of a revolution. This hexagram has the youngest daughter (Dui) on top of a middle daughter (Li) in conflict. Thus their incompatibility is like a revolution.

(30) Li/Fire (Separation)

The doubling of fire. It is beautiful and is in dynamic motion. Things that are in dynamic motion will eventually separate.

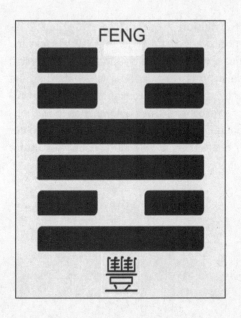

(55) Abundance

This indicates fire beneath lightning. Lightning creates fire, but fire (sun) already exists around it. So there is a gathering of the yin fire (lightning) and the yang fire (the sun). A combination of the two produces a state of abundance and affluence.

In Korea, when visiting a friend who has recently moved, a box of matches is brought as a housewarming gift. The yang energy of the match is said to repel all yin energies (evil spirits, germs, etc.). It also suggests earning money quickly like a raging fire. Fire symbolizes abundance.

(37) People in the Home

Wind blowing over the fire. In King Wen's arrangement, the wind, a constituent of heaven, supervises the function of a fire. Both wind and fire act on the upper region, heaven, so they are like people of the same house.

(63) Already Accomplished

This shows water over the fire. The original nature of water is to descend, while fire ascends. In this hexagram, water is situated above and fire below, signifying water descending and fire rising. It is a state in which changes are smoothly proceeding in accordance with the universe's purpose. Therefore, it was named "Already Accomplished."

(22) Decoration (Elegance)

This illustrates a mountain over a fire. Flames illuminate the immense grandeur of the mountain's majestic contours. The fire beneath the mountain also symbolizes the expanding and ascending of fire. The fire will certainly spread over the mountain.

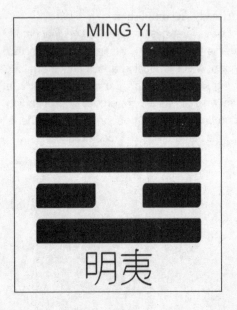

(36) Bright Dongyi Tribe

This portrays the sun underneath the earth. China's legendary Dongyi tribe left relics of the Yin (Shang) dynasty. Around the time that explanations for the hexagrams were added to the I Ching, the current mainstream people of China (Han tribe) cast the Dongyi aside. The Dongyi tribe is the sun holding its breath underneath the earth. However, in the future, the Dongyi tribe will rise like the yin-yang principle of night transforming into day.

Thunder (Zhen) Trigrams

(25) Absence of Foolishness

This symbolizes lightning below heaven. These two forces compete against one another. Heaven is immense and powerful (three yang lines), while lightning (one yang line), in its attempt to show off its power, is being foolish. It is like a group of gangsters (lightning) trying to take on the US Marines (Heaven trigram) or a child showing off their math skills to a graduate student.

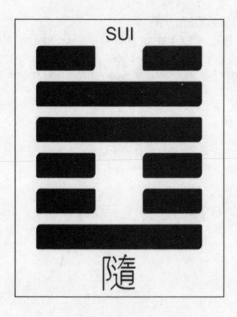

SUI

隨

(17) Following

This is thunder below a lake. One function of the lake is to gather rain or water. Thunder occurs when there is rain. The rain is created by the evaporation of water from the lake. So here, the thunder is following the lake that serves as the source of the rain.

SHI KE

噬嗑

(21) Clicking of Teeth

The Li trigram, yang fire, is situated above the Zhen trigram, yin fire. They work well together. It is like the cooperative movement of the upper and lower teeth.

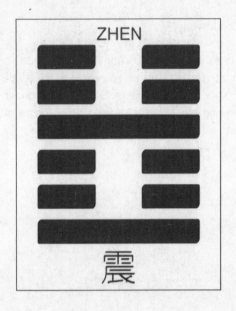

(51) Zhen/Thunder

This is a doubling of the Thunder trigram. It represents those things that closely resemble thunder: strong earthquakes, explosions, rocket launches, car crashes, etc.

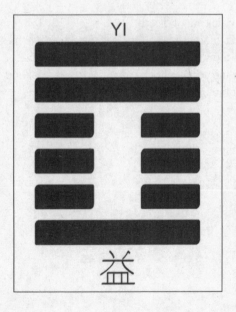

(42) Increase

This shows thunder beneath the wind. It is a cloudy day, the wind is blowing, and there is thunder. Rain is almost inevitable. When these elements are combined, their potential to make rain greatly increases.

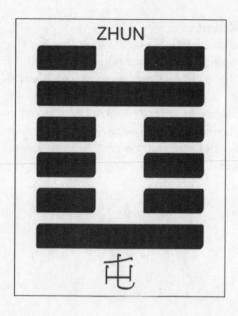

(3) Encampment

This stands for thunder within the water. It is like a baby (yang) waiting to break out of the amniotic fluid (yin) in its mother's womb. Thunder encamps in the water, hiding its firepower and preparing for a battle.

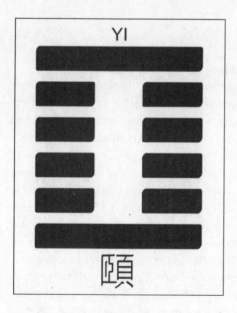

(27) Mandible (Nourishment)

This portrays a mountain over thunder. Because only the first and the sixth lines are yang, with four yin lines between them, it resembles the mandible (chin). This hexagram symbolizes a mandible with uniformly arranged upper and lower teeth. Moving the mandible enables us to take in nutrients to nourish ourselves physically, but we must also nurture ourselves mentally.

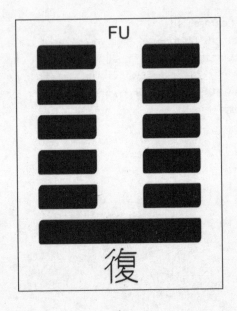

FU

復

(24) Return

This characterizes the earth above thunder. The yang energy is in the beginning stage of recovery from the pure yin Earth hexagram. As it is the thunder beneath the earth, it has to wait before it can manifest its strength. Extreme yin converts to yang. So negative, dark, decaying forces (yin) have reached their limit, and now positive, light, regenerative forces (yang) are returning.

Wind (Xun) Trigrams

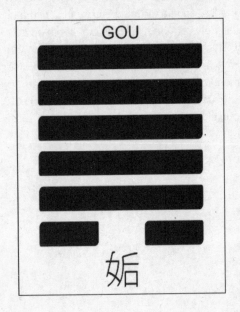

GOU

姤

(44) Meeting (Getting Married)

Wind beneath heaven. In ancient Eastern times, married life was torturous for women. Transportation was not good, so they could rarely visit their relatives. There was also no means of communication (like the telephone, text, or email we have today), so getting married meant isolation. Moreover, most marriages were prearranged, and women were betrothed to men without seeing or meeting them. During these times, when a woman married, she entered the lowest position on the family ladder. She was overwhelmed by new faces and an unfamiliar environment (represented by a single yin line underneath five yang lines). Everything she did was critically scrutinized. To understand this hexagram, try imagining how painful and frightening such an experience would be.

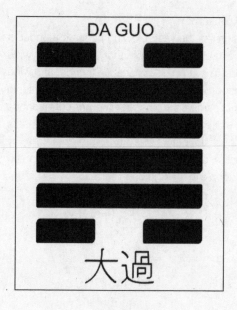

(28) A Great Mistake/Excess

This shows the wind blowing beneath a lake. Wind beneath a lake has no purpose and thus no value at all. It cannot stir up waves to circulate the water. This is the portrayal of a great mistake. Additionally, there is an excess of yang lines (four) in relation to the yin lines (two), hence the name.

(50) The Cauldron

This is the wind blowing below a fire. A cauldron is designed to have wind blow under it to fan the fire heating it. Also, it is an image of cooking wherein wood generates and nurtures fire. It is an auspicious state in which everything is going well.

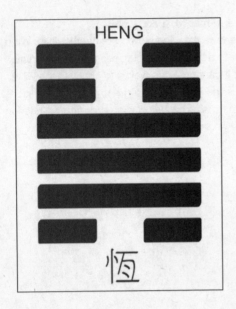

(32) Constancy

This signifies the wind blowing beneath thunder. It is an established principle that thunder and wind go hand in hand. This is because thunder and wind are responsible for all changes and movements. In terms of family, the Thunder trigram corresponds to the eldest son, while the Wind trigram represents the eldest daughter. This hexagram, therefore, by extension, signifies the enduring marriage of an elderly couple in their golden years.

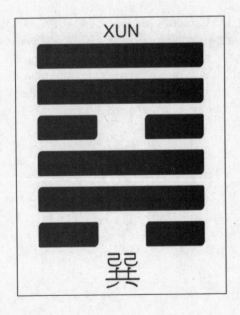

(57) Xun/Wind

This is the doubling of the Wind trigram. The nature of the other seven hexagrams in this Xun category is similar to the wind. However, because of the doubling, this hexagram represents an almost identical state to the wind. Therefore, it can epitomize extremely powerful winds such as a tornadoes, hurricanes, or typhoons.

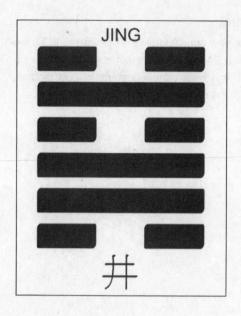

(48) Wellspring

This illustrates wind beneath the water. The wind is the dynamic force that pumps water upward. Spring water gushes forth due to this dynamic force. A further developed state of spring water is a well. In ancient times, a well was made to protect spring water from contamination.

(18) Decay (Worm-Eaten)

This stands for the wind blowing beneath a mountain. The mountain eroding little by little resembles a leaf slowly being eaten by a bug. Both Mountain and Wind trigrams have yin lines underneath the yang. Yin is confined by yang, resulting in stagnation and eventual decay.

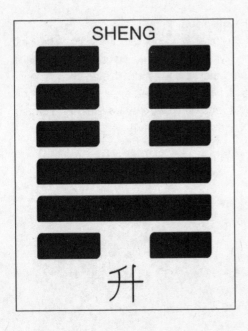

SHENG

升

(46) Rising

This is wind beneath the earth, which naturally rises upward. Since the Xun trigram represents a tree or wood, this hexagram represents a bud ready to sprout and rise above the ground.

Water (Kan) Trigrams

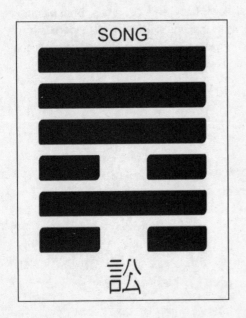

SONG

訟

(6) Conflict (Contention)

This characterizes water beneath heaven. It is the state in which the sky is full of clouds, and they interfere with the function of heaven. This is like contending with heaven, disturbing and pestering it to prevent it from performing its duty.

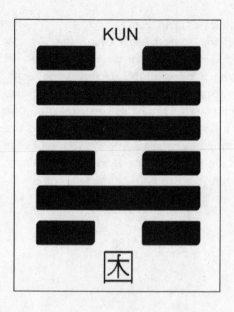

(47) Adversary (Exhaustion)

This is water beneath a lake. It is a state in which there is very little water in a lake. Usually, the water level should be near the top of the lake, but here, the water leaks underneath the ground into a stream and is drying up. This is a problematic situation, signified by the wood energy confined within a box (困).

(64) Before Completion (Unsettled)

This signifies water under fire. When fire rises and water descends, it is a terminal state in which there is no longer any circulation. Such a state is regulated by the God of the universe, the king of a country, a monk or priest who is in tune with the Tao, or any doctor who treats illnesses. They are all situated in the center and belong to the earth element.

The fifth line from the bottom is the center of the upper trigram and corresponds to a king or emperor. For the health of a nation, it should be yang. The second line from the bottom is the center of the lower trigram and corresponds to a feudal lord. In the relationship between an emperor and a lord, the lord should be a subservient yin line. But in this hexagram, the position of the emperor is yin, and the feudal lord is yang, concluding that there is no control.

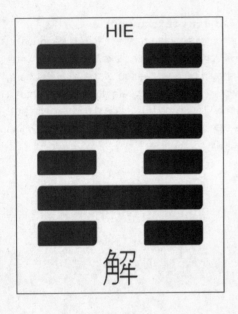

HIE

解

HUAN

渙

(40) Release (Deliverance)

This characterizes thunder over water. Thunder emerging from the water serves the function of releasing or liberating. Thunder represents springtime, while water signifies wintertime. Animals emerge from hibernation as plants ramp up their activity. Another way to view this hexagram is that everything can be released when you first loosen things with water and shake them up with thunder.

(59) Dispersion (Exchanging)

This is the wind blowing over water. The wind acts to stir and mix water, exchanging. It is also an image of a warm spring breeze melting frozen winter ice. Like the winter, bodily Qi energy can stagnate like frozen ice (water element). But the penetrating energy of wind (wood element) disperses the stagnation.

(29) Kan/Water

This is a doubling of water. Unlike the Dui trigram, which represents stilled water, this is a flowing body of water, such as a stream, river, flood, fountain, etc. Also, as Kan symbolizes an abyss and a body of water, it relates to darkness, danger, and difficulty. These are amplified to a greater degree in this hexagram.

(4) Youthful Folly (Darkness)

A mountain is on top of the water. The water had just escaped from the mountain. It's ignorant and has a long way to go to unite with the ocean. It is also an island, isolated, with uneducated or uncultured people.

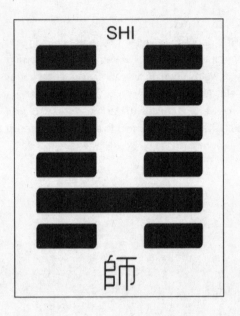

(7) Teacher

This depicts water beneath the earth and its purity. Purity is a moral quality that all teachers should have. There is only one yang line in this hexagram. It is the centerline of the lower trigram, so it must guide and enlighten all the yin lines that are not yet pure, similar to the job a teacher must perform.

Mountain (Gen) Trigrams

(33) Retreat (Steering Pigs)

This shows a mountain beneath heaven. Its image is that of a mountain rising higher toward heaven. The two yin lines at the bottom are progressing upward. In addition to "Retreat," this hexagram is also named "Steering Pigs." Though slow, like the pigs that do not walk in a straight line, the mountain continues to move toward heaven. In this situation, a person does not want to leave, yet he or she must. From the yang perspective, it is not a desirable situation, because yin symbolizes death and destruction. But the person must face this reality and speedily take appropriate measures to cope with it.

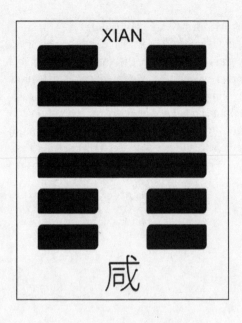

(31) Attraction (Totality)

This shows a lake above a mountain. The Gen trigram can symbolize the male genitals, whereas the Dui trigram can symbolize the female genitals. This hexagram manifests as a state in which the male and female genitals have joined together. The hexagram consists of both yin and yang, so it is Tai Chi, the totality.

(56) Traveling

This characterizes fire above a mountain. Fire has great power when it develops in the lowlands. However, it has difficulty spreading out if it grows in the highlands. Also, a burning flame blown away by the wind to various places is like someone who is traveling or roaming around, unable to settle.

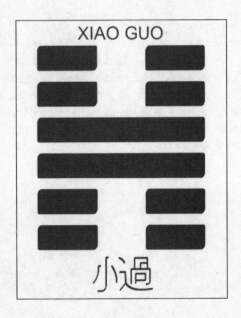

XIAO GUO

小過

(62) A Minor Mistake (Blunder)

Lightning is above a mountain. Since the lightning striking the mountain is constantly happening, it is small and insignificant. Yin represents small, trivial things or a petty individual. In contrast, yang signifies something large, significant, or a great person of virtue. A Great Mistake/Excess (Hexagram 28) has four yang and two yin lines. This hexagram has four yin and two yang lines, hence the name.

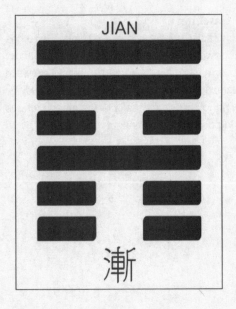

JIAN

漸

(53) Gradual Progress

The wind is blowing over a mountain. Its force gradually gets stronger as it rises toward the top of the mountain.

(39) Obstacle (Limping)

Water is above a mountain. Water does not remain still at the top of a mountain, nor does it flow down in one direction. Instead, it lumbers, similar to a person with a limp. There is danger (water) and stoppage (mountain)—double trouble. This hexagram portrays a state when work is not progressing smoothly.

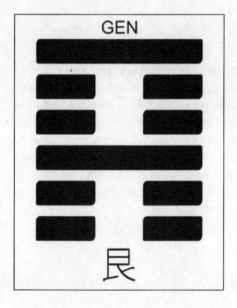

(52) Gen/Mountain

This is the doubling of the mountain, constituting a stifling state. There is a strong blockage or stoppage because of the two mountains. Like the Great Wall of China, the mountains act as a screen, partition, or insulation.

(15) Humility (Moderation)

This stands for a mountain beneath the earth. In nature, mountains loom high above the earth. However, this hexagram depicts the mountain under the earth, signifying humility and modesty.

Earth (Kun) Trigrams

(12) Stagnation (Obstruction)

Heaven sits above the earth. Although they are in their respective places, their movements are obstructed. This is because the nature of yang (heaven) is to ascend, while that of yin (earth) is to descend. Because they are going in different ways, no communication is possible, resulting in stagnation. It is not good to be in a situation like this while transformation or change occurs.

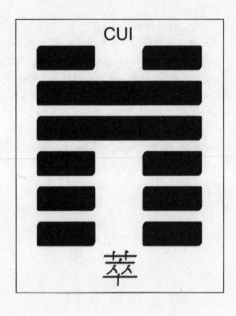

(45) Gathering

This portrays a lake over the earth. The lake's water provides sufficient moisture to produce an abundance of densely grown grasses. Also, the rain that falls will eventually seek lower ground and gather, whether in a pond, a lake, a river, or an ocean.

(35) Progress (Advance)

This is depicted as the rising sun. Peeking around the bend, it continues to advance into the day, gradually increasing its power. In King Wen's arrangement, the Li trigram sits in the south (yang), where there is a dynamic activity of progress and advancement (yang). The Jin dynasties of China and Japan (the "Land of the Rising Sun") derived their names from this hexagram.

(16) Prediction (Enthusiasm)

Thunder above the earth. Thunder is in a position to manifest its greatest strength so that one can predict its locus beforehand. Thus this hexagram urges the awareness of such places to avoid damage. The sound of thunder represents the dynamic energy of yang. As it dominantly resounds over earth, it nurtures all things. Like music, it stirs enthusiasm and delight in all things.

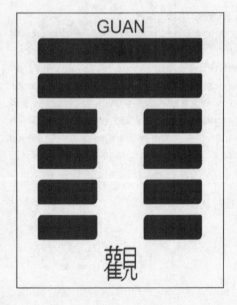

(20) Observation

Wind above the earth. The wind blowing over the earth does so without a fixed destination. This is similar to traveling.

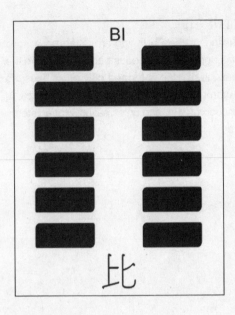

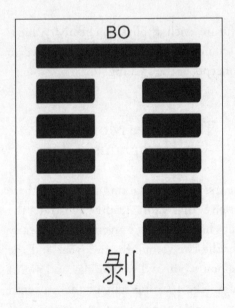

(8) Comparison

Water above the earth. Water flows from high to low. It knows by comparison which is the more natural location for it to be in. This hexagram reveals that it is important to weigh all options before deciding. The fifth line from the bottom is the seat of a king. It is preferable if the yang sits in its place. If the second line below is yin, it is even better since yin and yang become harmonized. But too many yin lines surround the king. The king must rule them well by comparing their yin-yang variances and giving them appropriate duties.

(23) Peeling Off (Splitting Apart)

Mountain over the earth. In this hexagram, the force of yin is filling up from the bottom so that there is only one yang in the sixth line. It is a situation in which yang is being peeled off or stripped away. It is the end of the road for the dictator who has only fostered "yes men."

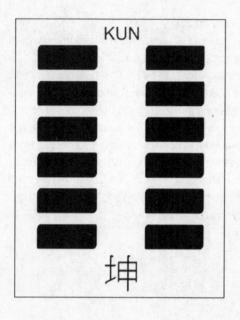

(2) Kun/Earth

A doubling of the Earth trigram. Stars in a solid state (as opposed to gaseous bodies) belong to the Kun hexagram. Kun is formed only of yin lines, so it has extreme absorption power. The black hole is the function of Kun, and universal gravitation stems from it.

The names and words of the hexagrams of the I Ching are interpretations based on Confucianism. Even before Confucius, ethical and moral interpretations were added to the hexagrams of I Ching, which eventually transformed into the Confucian classic.

The hexagrams, however, can be renamed according to interpretations from the viewpoint of the natural sciences or the various interpretations of different religions. The study of the I Ching emphasizes the symbolism of the bigrams, trigrams, and hexagrams that can lead to reinterpretations befitting any individual's specialty or interest. The interpretations in this book should give some insight into all the symbols in the I Ching. We expect that there will be new interpretations according to the various specialties of people in the near future, such as physics, chemistry, medicine, computer science, and so on, added to the concepts of the I Ching.

The Twelve Monarch Hexagrams

Of the sixty-four hexagrams of I Ching, there are twelve that most readily illustrate the flow of change in the universe. They clearly signify the twelve months in a year and the twelve hours (yin and yang of day and night) in a day. The I Ching tells of the universal laws applicable to the form and function of all things, so it contains a collection of hexagrams that appropriately symbolize all matter and phenomena.

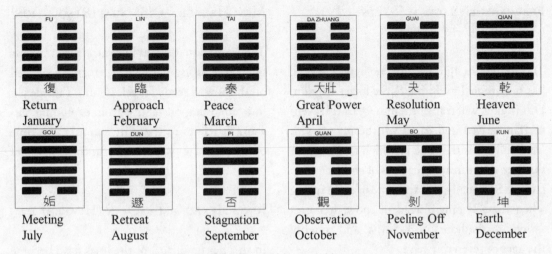

Figure 23.4 The 12 Monarch Hexagrams

The movements of the stars initiate all of the changes on Earth. There are six segments to these movements and twelve hexagrams representing them. Because of their importance, they are called the Monarch Hexagrams (figs. 23.4 and 23.5).

JANUARY: HEXAGRAM 24, FU (RETURN)

This hexagram was named Return, which implies the revival of yang. It represents the rising of yang after the winter solstice, when the days gradually become longer. It symbolizes the beginning of change when yin has reached its extreme. This hexagram corresponds to the time when the weather begins to get warmer with the passing of winter, even though a person might not feel it. It can be compared to the time when a car is just beginning to move forward or to a state when the source of electricity has just entered a machine. Compared to human life, it is the stage from birth to about age seven. It corresponds to the daily time of 1–3 A.M.

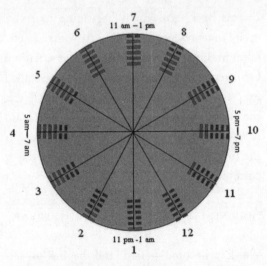

Figure 23.5 Monarch Hexagrams and Time

FEBRUARY: HEXAGRAM 19, LIN (APPROACH)

This hexagram signifies the state in which yang has now rooted itself. Soon, the lower trigram, Dui (Lake), will transform into Qian (Heaven) so that heaven and earth will be juxtaposed. Medically, it is the time in which the frequent illnesses that threaten the lives of children have passed. Seasonally, it is the time of early spring when there is rain instead of snow. It corresponds to the hours of 3–5 A.M. and roughly the ages of seven to twelve.

MARCH: HEXAGRAM 11, TAI (PEACE)

This hexagram corresponds to the spring equinox, when the length of day and night are equal. In it, yang has taken over half the hexagram, and yin and yang are balanced. It thus symbolizes peace and tranquility. It relates to the dynamic activity of puberty. It corresponds to the hours of 5–7 A.M., the time of the sunrise.

APRIL: HEXAGRAM 34, DA ZHUANG (GREAT POWER)

In this hexagram, there are four yang lines and two yin. Yang is the source of energy, so its spirit is mighty. It corresponds to late spring and the time of life after age twenty-one. It corresponds to the hours of 7–9 A.M. April is known as the month of boiling blood. During this month, especially in Korea, many events wherein young people bravely resisted dictatorships (two yin lines at the top) transpired.

MAY: HEXAGRAM 43, GUAI (RESOLUTION)

This hexagram displays five yang lines and only one yin. It is a state in which an arrow, nocked on the bow, is ready for release. But the one yin line remaining prevents it from exploding outward. It relates to the early summer, the time of life after age twenty-eight, and the hours of 9–11 A.M.

JUNE: HEXAGRAM 1, QIAN (HEAVEN)

In this hexagram, all of the lines have become yang. It represents the summer solstice, when days are at their longest. It is the state of extreme yang. In life, it is the period after age thirty-five, and in a day, the hours correlate to around midday.

JULY: HEXAGRAM 44, GOU (MEETING)

In this hexagram, yin is beginning to revive itself. It represents a newlywed woman's state upon finding herself in an unfamiliar situation. Or it represents when stock prices have stalled for the first time since they were soaring. Here, the yin line represents aging, and the hexagram represents the beginning of old age. In life, it is the time around age forty-two, and in a day it corresponds to the hours of 1–3 P.M.

AUGUST: HEXAGRAM 33, DUN (RETREAT)

Yin has become paired and begins to settle down. According to Eastern medicine, a woman's life progresses in cycles of seven years.

According to this hexagram, it is the time around forty-nine years old ($7 \times 7 = 49$), when aging has settled in. In women, it signifies the beginning of menopause—the drying up of heavenly dew. In a day, it corresponds to the time between 3 and 5 P.M.

SEPTEMBER: HEXAGRAM 12, PI (STAGNATION)

This hexagram has three yang lines on top and three yin lines at the bottom, forming a balance. However, there is no exchange between yin and yang because yang is on top and yin is on the bottom. That is why this hexagram is called Stagnation. It corresponds to the autumnal equinox, when the length of day and night are equal. In life, it corresponds to the age of fifty-six (7×8), the time in which the aging process deepens. In a day, it corresponds to the time between 5 and 7 P.M., in the evening before night.

OCTOBER: HEXAGRAM 20, GUAN (OBSERVATION)

There are now two yang lines and four yin lines. Though yang still occupies the position of the king, it has no real power. It can only watch the growing influence of yin as the general trend shifts toward yin, and yang is barely able to maintain its existence. It is the season of late autumn, the time when frost forms. It corresponds to age sixty-three (7×9), the arrival of old age. In a day, it corresponds to the time between 7 and 9 P.M.

NOVEMBER: HEXAGRAM 23, BO (PEELING OFF)

There is only one yang line in this hexagram, which will soon peel off. Even the throne has been taken away by the enemy's forces. The sixth line indicates a retired king, while the fifth indicates the emperor. So here, the king no longer holds power, and instead, the former king is being formally treated. It is the season of early winter when the first snow falls. It corresponds to the age of seventy (7×10), the time to prepare for the closing of a life. It also relates to the hours between 9 and 11 P.M., the time of deepening night.

DECEMBER: HEXAGRAM 2, KUN (EARTH)

This hexagram has now completely changed into yin. It corresponds to the winter solstice, when daylight is at its shortest. In the cycle of life, it represents death after breathing has already stopped. It relates to the hours just around midnight.

The Principles of I Ching Discovered by Science

The Necessity of Studying the I Ching

In the West, the perspective of the natural environment has changed over time. Until the discovery of the theory of relativity and quantum physics, and before the New Age and New Science movements, the West sought materialistic truth based on the ideals of rationalism. The truths of Newtonian physics presided over these viewpoints and worked their way into other schools of thought.

During Newton's time, the mechanics of science attempted to explain all phenomena through a few physical laws commonly found in nature. According to these laws, the actual conditions inferred were found true. Consistent application of scientific theories developed from those physical laws impacted people's daily lives. Consequently, people have wondered in amazement at the accuracy and greatness of science.

Around the same time, the East developed a different viewpoint than Western physics. As Western imperialism invaded the East, this viewpoint lost its credence. As a result, many Easterners began to discard their Eastern views in the name of material civilization. Instead, they accepted the perspective of science led by Newtonian mechanics, which had formed the basis of Western scientific culture.

The I Ching (yin-yang and the five-element theory), the basis for understanding the natural environment, was eliminated from public education in the East. Western science became the only science taught in public schools. Despite the I Ching's brief mention in universities educating students in Eastern studies, it was no longer widely taught or as popular in comparison to the edification of Western science.

As science advanced, we discovered that Newtonian mechanics did not apply to the microcosmic world of the quantum. It also was not entirely helpful in explaining the macrocosmic world. In addition, Heisenberg's uncertainty principle illuminated flaws in the already failing Newtonian mechanical view. Finally, as new developments in quantum physics came onto the scene, it led to the realization that the perspective of quantum physics is the same as that of the I Ching in the East. For instance, in the landmark book *The Tao of Physics,* physicist Fritjof Capra draws a parallel between Eastern philosophy (and the I Ching) and quantum physics. Gary Zukav also illuminates the similarities between Eastern philosophy and modern physics in his book *The Dancing Wu Li Masters.*

As the paradigm shifted to quantum physics, professionals in various fields who presided over the academic education of the world began reorganizing their studies. Previously, their studies followed the paradigm of traditional physics. However, due to quantum physics' successes, education rapidly began to move in that direction.

Some of these professionals also started to gain interest in the I Ching, the essence of Eastern philosophy. Basic sciences, such as physics, chemistry, and biology, have quickly implemented new paradigms to organize their studies. The applied sciences, such as engineering and medicine, have recently incorporated the quantum paradigm. Such changes have brought about the New Age and New Science movements. Moreover, the NIH (National Institutes of Health) has begun to accept alternative medicine, including traditional Eastern medicine, as a viable form of health care. In 2001, the NIH allotted $120 million in research funding to study alternative medicine.

The interests of physics and Eastern ascetics are the same. Both fields are searching for the common patterns of the universe. To find this pattern, physicists sometimes forgo all food and drink, like the fasting done by many Eastern ascetics undergoing spiritual training.

Eastern ascetics consider discovering the common pattern of the universe their main topic of interest and assiduously devote their spiritual discipline to it. The only real difference between these two groups—physicists and Eastern ascetics—lies in the expression of the findings. The pattern is expressed in mathematical formulas for physicists, while in codes known as yin-yang and the five elements for ascetics.

The I Ching is a book that illustrates the pattern of the universe called Tao in digital codes developed by enlightened Eastern masters. Therefore, there is no reason why it would not be discovered by the watchful eyes of Western physicists or mathematicians searching for the truth in the same subject matter.

In the seventeenth century, Gottfried Wilhelm Leibniz discovered the binary system and ignited the current digital revolution. He was shocked that the binary system was already used five thousand years before in the East. Niels Bohr, the father of quantum physics, discovered the atomic model that consists of protons (+) and electrons (−). His theory of complementarity accurately reflects the yin-yang theory of the I Ching. He revered the

I Ching and wore the symbol of Tai Chi on his coat of arms when he received his knighthood in 1947.

Einstein broke away from the perspective of Newtonian science and created the theory of relativity. This theory recognizes matter in terms of yin and yang or the relative perspective of complementary opposites. Matter (yin) can always transform into energy (yang), and energy can always coalesce and transform into matter. Such is the mutual transformation of the yin-yang theory expressed in the famous equation $E=mc^2$. The significance of this theory in modern science cannot be overstated. After all, it did lead to the creation of the atomic bomb.

The I Ching is like a minefield of ideas. The more one contemplates the I Ching, the more ideas will come to light. Those Western scholars who have an eye to see the future are studying the I Ching. There are more than 120 books on the subject of the I Ching in English. The more recent books written on the I Ching are by scientists who have discovered ultramodern scientific findings, such as fractal structure and DNA codes, all within the text.

Although the I Ching comes from the East, there are only a few Easterners who truly understand what it attempts to express. The reason may be that the recent modernization of education has not provided real opportunities for traditional I Ching education. Or perhaps the reason is the difficulty of finding the profound meaning of I Ching from the analysis of the I Ching written in the Chinese language used at the time of the Zhou dynasty.

Eastern custom teaches that any book titled "Ching" is a text written by a supremely enlightened being or god. The I Ching is among the most revered and prestigious classics in all Eastern philosophy. However, the value of the I Ching differs from other classics because I Ching is expressed in codes rather than words.

The I Ching is not merely a book that illustrates the changing patterns of things or phenomena commonly seen around us. Instead, it describes the common pattern that applies equally to both the worlds of quanta and microorganisms that may live on a star billions of light-years away. This common pattern is known as the Tao, and the I Ching is the only book that illustrates the Tao in digital codes known as yin and yang.

There are limitations to words that people use. Words are symbols or codes we associate with common matter or phenomena in our environment. So they are not appropriate (optimally or aptly) in expressing the common pattern of all things in the universe. We cannot truly express something we have never seen, felt, or imagined using our current language. Also, as things change over time, you can lose their true meanings if you fix them with words.

For instance, if you say roses were beautiful ten days ago, today the roses may have withered and died. Additionally, depending on the era, region, and mental tendencies of the person reading the words, words can have vastly differing meanings. That is why Lao-tzu has said that "the Tao that can be called Tao is not the real Tao." The I Ching used a polar code (yin and yang) rather than words with limitations to accurately transmit the Tao. Later, King Wen of the Zhou dynasty and Confucius added explanations in comments to the codes (hexagrams), and the I Ching eventually became one of the Confucian classics.

Unfortunately, many scholars found the pattern of the I Ching code difficult. As a result, they wasted much time interpreting Confucian verses, thereby neglecting the discovery of the Tao within the I Ching. In contrast, the Western scientists who diligently spent countless hours in contemplation in the quest for the truth discovered many insights from the I Ching without clinging to the ancient verses.

Among the three Eastern nations that have studied the I Ching, there are remarkably many Tai Chi symbols that express the pattern of I Ching in a single picture in Korea. Tai Chi is drawn at each gate of village schools to educate people about I Ching, the highest level among the Four Books and Three Classics.[1] Tai Chi, a symbol of God and the universe, is at the Hongsalmun (red arrow gate) and Jongmyo (ancestral shrine), where worship of previous kings as gods takes place (see figs. 14.21 and 14.27 in chapter 14 for illustrations). Yulryeo, a study of sound-wave frequency, is the interpretation of music according to I Ching. The drum, which generates waves closest to the human body, bears a Tai Chi symbol (see fig. 15.13 in chapter 15). Because I Ching was the study Koreans respected the most, the trigrams and Tai Chi, symbols of I Ching, were drawn

Figure A1.1 The Korean National Flag

on the national flag as the emblem of the Korean people (fig. A1.1).

Therefore, Koreans frequently encounter architecture, music, art, customs, and games their ancestors made with the creative patterns in I Ching. Its patterns are ingrained in their bodies, even if they do not clearly understand I Ching.

Legend has it that Emperor Fuxi created the bigrams, trigrams, and hexagrams of the I Ching after contemplating the Hado (Yellow River Map) bestowed by heaven.

I Ching states that Fuxi is from the Zhen direction. Zhen is one of the eight trigrams and refers to the eastern part of the Yellow River basin in China. The famous Chinese book *Huainanzi* (Master Huainan) portrays Fuxi as a deity of the East who ruled over the Jieshi Mountain[2] and its eastern side, present-day Korea and Japan. And in the book *Mencius,*[3] it is written that Emperor Shun[4] was of the Dongyi, or Eastern Yi, tribe and that King Wen of the Zhou dynasty, who wrote I Ching, was of the Xiyi, or Western Yi, tribe. So it implies that King Wen is of Yi people, not Han, of China.

One of the sixty-four hexagrams of I Ching is Bright Dongyi Tribe (Hexagram 36). It combines the Kun trigram, which represents the earth, and the Li trigram, which signifies a fire or the sun, a great fire. It has an image of the sun that lies over the horizon momentarily before rising, and it tells of the bright future of the Yi people. It would be a problematic statement if King Wen were Han Chinese. As such, I Ching is a book that contains the basic ideas of Korean ancestors who were part of the Dongyi tribe. Therefore, it is more intimate and remains in the culture for a long time.

Legend also has it that the upper body of Fuxi was that of a human being, while his lower body was in the form of a snake. Inferring from the scientific nature of the I Ching, it may just be possible that Fuxi was an extraterrestrial. Though Fuxi created the hexagrams, there were various other arrangements of the I Ching hexagrams. One is called Lianshan Yi, invented by Shennong, later in the Xia dynasty. The other is Guicang Yi, created by the Yellow Emperor, or later in the Yin dynasty.

Because they were made according to the trend of thought and the environment of different periods, they were different interpretations, making the I Ching more readily applicable to daily life. The current I Ching is named Zhou Yi because it is that of the Zhou dynasty. However, since it is ancient, it isn't easy to understand or apply.

Therefore, it is necessary to create a scientific interpretation and application of the I Ching using modern scientific language. Only in this way can we truly integrate the findings of modern science with Eastern philosophy. Scientists such as Niels Bohr and Albert Einstein, who extensively studied I Ching, led modern science. Accordingly, I Ching's perspective will likely guide and enlighten all future sciences.

Modern Science Within the I Ching

CODE THEORY

A coding system is a method of designating a particular matter or phenomenon by selecting one code in a system of symbols with a uniform rule. This system is superior to a method of attaching names through words, such as John or Cindy, because matter or phenomena linked with codes are simpler to understand in terms of their mutual relationships. Thus, their changes can easily be known and managed.

The best-known coding systems are barcodes and genetic codes. Attaching codes to the merchandise in a marketplace can facilitate inputting their information to a computer. Once the information is inputted to the computer, monitoring incoming and outgoing inventory can be done at a glance. In addition, it is easy to understand critical information, such as what items are selling well or needed for reordering.

The West did not recognize these codes' importance until the advent of computers. There was only the occasional use of codes as secret passwords or ciphers, despite their advantages.

In contrast, the sages of the East recognized the importance of codes very early on. These codes were applied to the principles of the I Ching five thousand years ago.

The diagram here (fig. A1.2) is two hexagrams converted from a barcode. Barcoding is a system in which red laser light is shone onto a series of dark and light spaces that either absorb (yin, 0) or reflect (yang, 1) the laser light, thereby sending a signal back to a computer that can read the program. The light is absorbed by the bars and reflected by the empty spaces. Because barcodes and hexagrams are digital codes of binary systems that interpret information similarly, they can convert directly into one another. So, for example, when the two digital codes, the numbers 0 and 1, are read as yin and yang, the barcodes can translate directly into hexagrams.

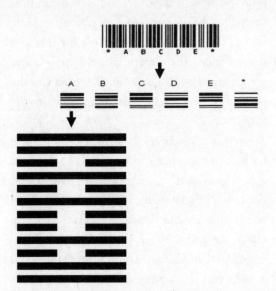

Figure A1.2 Yin–Yang of Barcodes

I Ching observes particulars of all matter and phenomena from multiple angles and determines their yin and yang. This is expressed in monograms, bigrams, trigrams, and hexagrams, symbolizing yin and yang. So then, as all changes are within the book, the conditions, circumstances, and situations of change can be known at a glance.

GENETIC CODES

Purine and pyrimidine are organic compounds that determine the genetic makeup of all organisms. They divide into four bases or nucleotides: adenine, guanine, cytosine, and thymine. Adenine and guanine derive from purine, while cytosine and thymine derive from pyrimidine. The arrangement of these four bases creates and determines the characteristics of all varieties of plants and animals.

The I Ching uses a similar mechanism to define all the components of the universe. It first divides all things into yin and yang. Then yin subdivides again into Taiyin (yin within yin) and Shaoyin (yang within yin). At the same time, yang divides into Taiyang (yang within yang) and Shaoyang (yin within yang) (fig. A1.3). This example illustrates the similarity between the five-thousand-year-old code of the I Ching and the recently uncovered genetic code.

There is a strong correlation between the structure of DNA and the symbolic images found in the I Ching. Each strand of DNA's double-helix configuration contains an arrangement of four bases. These four bases

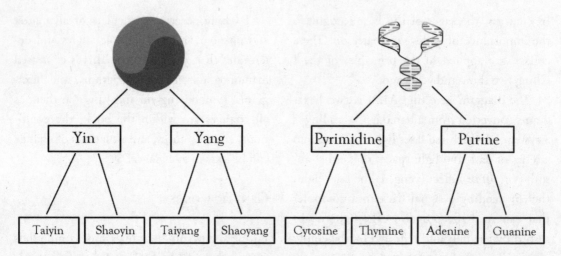

Figure A1.3 DNA and I Ching

correspond to I Ching's Sasang or Four Symbols —Taiyang, Shaoyang, Taiyin, and Shaoyin. When the bases divide in two, we see the separation of yin and yang. The pairing of DNA corresponds to the eight trigrams, composed of four pairs of yin and yang. A vertical view of DNA shows a spiral ladderlike structure. It is a helical structure that, when it is viewed from the top, resembles the Tai Chi symbol.

The similarity between codons and the I Ching is too precise to be a coincidence. Codons are the fundamental building blocks of all organic matter. They are thought of as the language of our genetic text, as their sequence determines amino acids' sequencing and the resultant proteins' structure. Enzymes created from these proteins dictate the characteristics of every organism.

Codons are sequences of three pairs of nu-

cleotides. Each paired nucleotide has one of four possible forms. Thus, there are 4^3 ($4 \times 4 \times 4$) or sixty-four possible codons. Here we see the connection to the I Ching. Codons, which make up all organisms, have sixty-four possible varieties. The I Ching uses sixty-four hexagrams to describe all cosmic matter. It would be difficult to view this as a coincidence. The genetic and I Ching codes are identical coding systems illuminating the principles of creating all organisms in the universe.

A recent discovery is a royal tomb dating back to the second century BCE in Turpan, a city located in China's western region and the center of communication on the Silk Road connecting ancient China to Central Asia. On top of the coffin was a silk cloth with a drawing of Fuxi and his wife Nuwa (fig. A1.4). Fuxi was the emperor who governed the eastern part

Figure A1.4 Fuxi and Nuwa, Shandong Museum, City of Jinan, Shandong, China

of China five thousand years ago and the first person to create the trigrams of the I Ching. His wife Nuwa, according to legend, made people by blowing air into clay formed in the shape of human beings.

According to legend and the depiction on the cloth, both Fuxi and Nuwa had upper bodies in human form and lower bodies in the form of snakes. Fuxi was regarded as the first male, and in the picture he holds a square, thought to be needed to create all things, while Nuwa, the first female, has a protractor. The lower bodies of the couple are intertwined. Surrounding them are many stars, while on the upper and lower centers are two wheels. Many similar drawings, either on cloth or stone, are frequently excavated in China.

Though this drawing does not have a single word, it suggests many things. Fuxi symbolizes yang, while Nuwa symbolizes yin. The intertwined lower bodies symbolize the union of yin and yang, or Tai Chi. The surrounding stars, the square (yang), and the protractor (yin) imply that they created all things in the universe according to Tai Chi and yin-yang principles. Though the wheels' meaning is unclear, they may be representative of the sun and moon and their orbits or the circular arrangement of I Ching's hexagrams.

From this picture, it seems that Fuxi, who created the trigrams and hexagrams as the code of all things in creation, was aware of the genetic code. Fuxi and Nuwa's intertwined bodies are similar to how the two polynucleotide chains that make up the DNA of human cells are intertwined to form a double helix (fig. A1.5). Was Fuxi conscious of DNA when he created the I Ching?

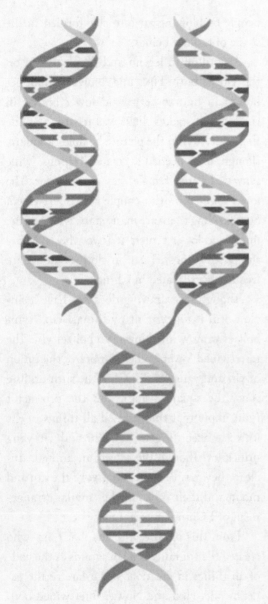

Figure A1.5 DNA Strand

Digital Theory

Stimulations such as sound, light, smell, taste, and touch sensed in the real world are con-

verted into digital signals through the analog–digital converting function before sending them to the brain. Before being recognized by our brains, the real world is continuous and not broken down into segments. The continuous, real world is called the analog world. In contrast, the segmented world, identified through the cognitive function of the nervous system, including the brain, is called the digital world.

A digital clock expresses time in numbers, while an analog clock expresses time with hands. In addition, the digital clock shows a fraction of time in decimal points, thus showing time in segments. In contrast, the analog clock does not show fractions of time; therefore, there is a continuation of time.

Musicians can listen to a single sound and decipher where that note belongs on the musical scale. When that sound is transferred and recorded onto a music score, it is segmented according to the musical scale. Still, there is an innumerable number of notes between any two notes on the music score. The sound is not disconnected but instead connected in a gentle curve.

A classic record album records sound by carving a plastic disc with sound vibration. The needle of a stereo system creates the sound by reproducing the exact vibration. A compact disc records a sound by segmenting the sound vibration in a short and uniform time frame. It then records each segment's average tone (fig. A1.6). Since the compact disc produces a clear tone in a mode that the human brain can easily recognize, the distinction of the sound is distinctively clear.

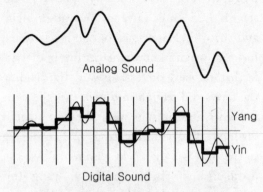

Analog Sound

Yang

Yin

Digital Sound

Figure A1.6 Analog and Digital Sounds

A traditional record disc is an analog apparatus, while a compact disc is digital. The digital apparatus can be expressed in numbers based on the binary system. Instead of using the decimal system, the binary system can replace the "yes" and "no" so that the significance of each number or gathering of digits becomes clear. Digital measurements in the analog world used the decimal system in the past. But when Leibniz created the binary system in 1679, the invention of digital apparatuses, including computers, was made possible.

The binary system clearly distinguishes each concept as "yes" or "no." Since recognizing a matter or a command uses only two concepts, the recognition pattern is simple. Thus, such recognition of a matter or a command can be mechanized into switches. The switches in the many overlapped stages/levels can turn on or off at each stage/level. The multiple combinations represent one situation. This combination of switches in one state enables a machine to recognize or record a certain matter or a stage of function, leading to the creation of a computer. The brain function, which only humans had, was now being performed by computers that could continue to work at high speeds and nonstop, day and night. This revolutionized the information industry, previously maintained only by human brains.

Gottfried Wilhelm Leibniz's development of the binary system in the seventeenth century introduced the Western world to a digital system that used binary codes. In the East, however, a digital coding system was in place five thousand years ago within the pages of the I Ching. The digital coding system is the most accurate way to express the variation of any system. In addition, when information about a system enters a computer, its overall tendencies and characteristics are much more evident because of its digital expression. Such is the reason I Ching employs the digital coding system.

The main theories of I Ching were transmitted to the West during the Tang dynasty (618–907 CE), during a time of active cultural exchange between the East and West. There was also a transmission of the methods of cultivating elixirs, Taoist self-cultivation techniques, which later developed into alchemy. This is evident from the mysterious alchemical picture in the book *Museum Hermeticum,* published in 1625 in Frankfurt, Germany (refer to fig. 14.14 for the diagram).

Leibniz even wrote a book that compares the parallels between the binary system and the I Ching. The binary system is simpler than the decimal system. So it can more clearly distinguish one thing from another and is easily translated into the on-and-off switches utilized in computers. It was, after all, the development of the binary system that led to the discovery and ultimate success of computers.

SENSE ORGANS

Inside the ear are three rings of the semicircular canal that senses the position of our bodies. The rings are arranged according to x, y, and z coordinates and measure the differing information from the front and back, left and right, and top and bottom.

We can know in which direction our bodies are tilting through this sensory system. First is the distinction between yin and yang. We can know whether our bodies are tilted up or down, front or back, or left or right. The next stage is the Sasang (Taiyang, Shaoyang, Taiyin, and Shaoyin). Here, when our bodies are tilted forward, we can know whether our bodies are farther forward or less forward by dividing the forward direction into two. It is the same for other directions as well. The next stage is distinguishing yin and yang in each Sasang so that if it is Taiyin (yin within yin), we can distinguish yin-yin-yin and yin-yin-yang. This corresponds to the eight trigrams. Thus, our nerves, brain, and sensory organs' functional principles are all digital. In other words, they function according to yin and yang. The x, y, and z coordinates convey three trigram lines, and each line represents yin or yang (fig. A1.7).

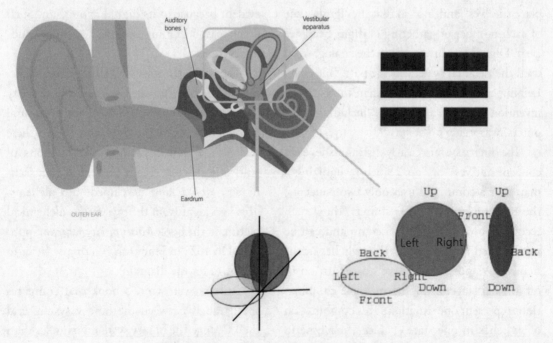

Figure A1.7 Hearing and Kan (Water) Trigram

The digital sound is clear. It splits into yes or no, yin or yang. Although the digital sound is not continuous and real like the analog sound, it sounds clearer to our ears, as our nerves operate digitally. The digital cognitive mode of our sensory organs is most appropriate for our physiological makeup. In recognizing all things, the mode of recognition according to yin and yang is a simple way to identify the whole.

When we see a particular object, its information is crossed three times before reaching the visual cortex in the brain. First, the object's left and right sides cross as they pass through the eye's lens, so that the object's left side goes to the retina's right side to form an image, and its right side goes to the left side to create an image. The comparison of the left and right by both eyes gives information on the front-back of the object.

The image is then converted into a digital signal and transmitted through the nerve. The image formed next to the nose of both eyes intersects at the optic chiasm—left goes to the right, and right goes to the left. The images created outside of both eyes are conveyed directly without crossing.

The images formed next to the nose cross to transmit the information seen from both eyes to one side of the brain. Signals crossed at the optic chiasm intersect again at the geniculate body of the thalamus. They are then transmitted after crossing up and down. In this way, the information is exchanged between the top and bottom.

Ultimately, the signal of an object detected by one side of the brain results from transmitting information on its eight facets ($2 \times 2 \times 2$) like in the I Ching: up-down, left-right, and front-back. It is shown in the following diagram (fig. A1.8). It is identical to observing a particular object or the changes in the universe from eight aspects with the eight trigrams of the I Ching.

I CHING AND THE BINARY SYSTEM

Books that relate the history of computers generally credit the digital theory that is the foundation of computer systems to Gottfried Leibniz, often referred to as the Father of the Digital Revolution. A diagram (fig. A1.9) was originally sent to Leibniz on April 2, 1703, by his friend Joachim Bouvet, a French missionary in China. This diagram illustrates the sixty-four hexagrams of the I Ching in a circular (active, or yang, arrangement) and a square (passive, or yin, arrangement) pattern. It originally comes from the book *Zhouyi Benyi* (周易本義), *The True Meaning of I Ching* by Zhu Xi, the famous neo-Confucian of the Song dynasty (960–1279 CE). After receiving this diagram, Leibniz was shocked to discover that the binary system had existed in the East for five thousand years. From then on, Leibniz devoted himself to I Ching's study and visited China several times. He added the numbers and letters to the diagram.

The following picture (fig. A1.10) illustrates Leibniz's binary system, and the picture (fig. A1.11) after that shows the sixty-four

BINOCULAR VISION

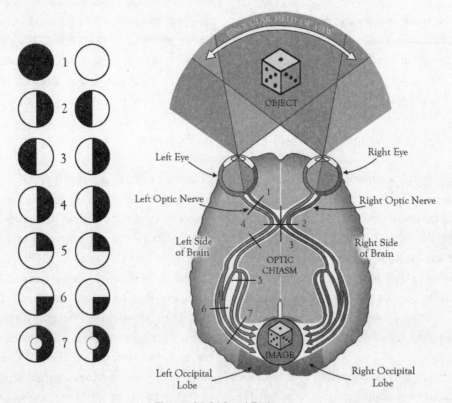

Figure A1.8 Visual Pathway

hexagrams of the I Ching. There is not much difference between the two illustrations. The image on the left merely uses the numbers 0 and 1 rather than the symbols of yin and yang.

In the next image (fig. A1.12), the upper illustration is the digital code of I Ching, while the lower is the principle underlying the creation of computer chips. The upper one is the digital code of a polar binary system called yin and yang, demonstrating the processes of dif-

ferentiation and unification, the common pattern of all things in the universe. The lower one is the on-and-off switch and shows a three-byte computer chip.

Imagine a switch above the yin, or broken, line. When the yin line is connected, the switch turns on, and if disconnected, the switch turns off. This corresponds to 1 and 0 of digital codes. Observe in the lower illustration of digital computer codes that there are three stages/levels. In the bottom layer, three

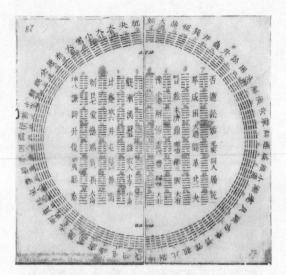

Figure A1.9 A diagram of 64 I Ching hexagrams sent to Gottfried Wilhelm Leibniz by Joachim Bouvet, a French missionary in China, on April 2, 1703. Leibniz added the Arabic numerals, while Bouvet added the Greek letters.

switches are stacked, showing a three-byte computer chip that can store memory for eight different situations.

This illustration demonstrates the core principle of computers, which use a binary system rather than the vaguer decimal system. The trigrams of the I Ching also utilize the binary system as an effective way to define the many objects in nature. Because there are only two possible situations, on or off, combining these switches is the most accurate way to represent any object or function. This method of differentiation serves as the basis for all computer design.

With digital codes, differences in matter or phenomena can be distinguished and mechanized clearly, and unnecessary information omitted. For example, a cartoonist

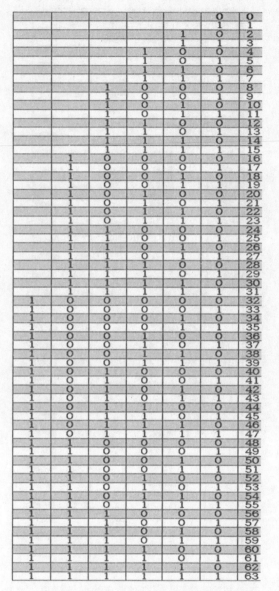

Figure A1.10 Binary System of Leibniz

					0	0
					1	1
				1	0	2
				1	1	3
			1	0	0	4
			1	0	1	5
			1	1	0	6
			1	1	1	7
		1	0	0	0	8
		1	0	0	1	9
		1	0	1	0	10
		1	0	1	1	11
		1	1	0	0	12
		1	1	0	1	13
		1	1	1	0	14
		1	1	1	1	15
	1	0	0	0	0	16
	1	0	0	0	1	17
	1	0	0	1	0	18
	1	0	0	1	1	19
	1	0	1	0	0	20
	1	0	1	0	1	21
	1	0	1	1	0	22
	1	0	1	1	1	23
	1	1	0	0	0	24
	1	1	0	0	1	25
	1	1	0	1	0	26
	1	1	0	1	1	27
	1	1	1	0	0	28
	1	1	1	0	1	29
	1	1	1	1	0	30
	1	1	1	1	1	31
1	0	0	0	0	0	32
1	0	0	0	0	1	33
1	0	0	0	1	0	34
1	0	0	0	1	1	35
1	0	0	1	0	0	36
1	0	0	1	0	1	37
1	0	0	1	1	0	38
1	0	0	1	1	1	39
1	0	1	0	0	0	40
1	0	1	0	0	1	41
1	0	1	0	1	0	42
1	0	1	0	1	1	43
1	0	1	1	0	0	44
1	0	1	1	0	1	45
1	0	1	1	1	0	46
1	0	1	1	1	1	47
1	1	0	0	0	0	48
1	1	0	0	0	1	49
1	1	0	0	1	0	50
1	1	0	0	1	1	51
1	1	0	1	0	0	52
1	1	0	1	0	1	53
1	1	0	1	1	0	54
1	1	0	1	1	1	55
1	1	1	0	0	0	56
1	1	1	0	0	1	57
1	1	1	0	1	0	58
1	1	1	0	1	1	59
1	1	1	1	0	0	60
1	1	1	1	0	1	61
1	1	1	1	1	0	62
1	1	1	1	1	1	63

selects the peculiar characteristic of a person and expresses it with a few lines when drawing a portrait. Similarly, the digital codes of I Ching are a few lines drawn by selecting the peculiar characteristic of the universe. This has

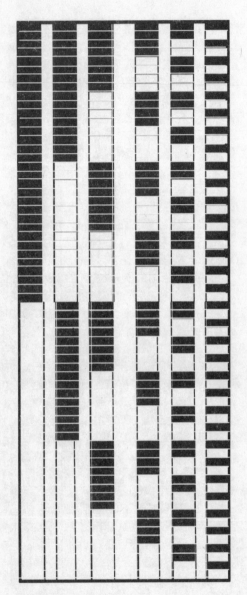

Figure A1.11 64 Hexagrams of I Ching

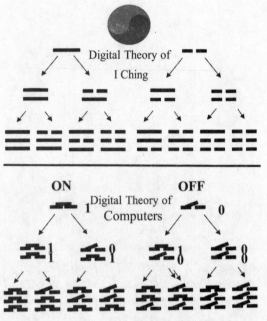

Digital Theory of I Ching

ON   OFF

1   Digital Theory of Computers   0

Figure A1.12 Digital Theory of I Ching and Computers

Quantum Mechanics

Traditional or Newtonian physics can clearly explain the world of matter we can see. Still, it is insufficient to explain the phenomena in stars billions of light-years away from us, the phenomena occurring inside atoms, or even the wonders of life. Quantum physics, on the other hand, can easily explain those phenomena that are unexplainable by traditional physics. It is interesting to note that the concepts used in quantum physics resemble those used in the I Ching, such as Tai Chi, yin-yang, and Sasang.

The smallest unit of matter in quantum physics is a quantum, the basic component of light, protons, and electrons. Every quantum has the dual nature of particle and wave. In a

the advantage of condensing the vast world of analog. For example, a single compact disc can store information from all the books in a bookcase, while the I Ching distillates the changes of everything in the universe into a single book.

Figure A1.13 Coat of arms of Niels Bohr (the father of quantum physics) with the motto *contraria sunt complementa* ("opposites are complementary") and the collar of the Danish Order of the Elephant

peatedly. It eventually becomes all cells that each hold the information of the entire body in its DNA, and these cells gather to form a human body. Similarly, the collection of all quanta, with differing natures of yin and yang according to the variance of force in their particle and wave nature, creates the universe.

The universe, too, according to the differentiation mode of the I Ching, began from Wu Chi (the Great Void). It is the stage at which there is no distinction between energy and matter. Next, it becomes Tai Chi, the stage where the difference between energy and matter first appears. The phase that follows is the yin and yang, a complete differentiation into energy and matter. Then comes Sasang, or the Four Symbols. They are greater (Shaoyin) or less (Taiyin) materialization of energy, and greater (Shaoyang) or less (Taiyang) energization of matter.

As this differentiation process repeats, innumerable quantum numbers are created and gathered together to form the universe. Each quantum has a duality of yin-yang or wave-particle duality and holds the whole pattern, just like the cells of our bodies.

Among the people who established the basics of quantum physics, Einstein and Niels Bohr published and validated many theories that closely resemble the yin-yang and Sasang theories of the I Ching. Niels Bohr's coat of arms on his formal dress when he received his knighthood in 1947 was the symbol of Tai Chi (fig. A1.13). He created the atomic model consisting of protons and electrons.

macroscopic way, the universe divides into energy that corresponds to yang, and matter that corresponds to yin. Similarly, a quantum, the smallest unit that forms matter, has the nature of a wave that corresponds to yang and a particle that corresponds to yin.

A single cell called a zygote differentiates into two, then four, and then into eight, sixteen, thirty-two, sixty-four, and so forth re-

In the I Ching, Tai Chi is simultaneously the all-encompassing totality and all its parts. Yin and yang form Tai Chi, similar to the atomic model, consisting of the proton (yang) and the electron (yin).

Bohr's reverence for the principles of the I Ching was apparent in his decision to wear the Tai Chi symbol when advancing into knighthood. He is also known for creating the theory of complementarity, which states that opposites are complementary, reflecting the mutual dependence principle of yin and yang formulated in the I Ching. Bohr also declared that the "great truth is a statement whose opposite is also a great truth." The great truth he speaks of corresponds to Tai Chi, which encompasses yin and yang.

Since Leibniz discovered the I Ching and wondered at its profoundness, many Western scientists have been covertly studying the principles of the I Ching. Einstein was no exception. Before the theory of relativity, scientists could not divide nature into matter and energy and recognize their mutual relationship. Einstein may have first identified the fundamental principle of the I Ching, which states that yin constantly changes into yang and yang to yin, before he created $E=mc^2$. This famous formula describes a situation in which energy constantly changes into matter and matter into energy (fig. A1.14). The amount of energy created when matter disintegrates equals its mass times the square of the speed of light. Oppenheimer subsequently created the atomic bomb based on this theory.

In Western science, innumerable principles

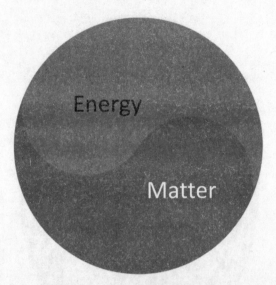

Figure A1.14 Theory of Relativity: $E = mc^2$

exist in physics, chemistry, biology, and so on that cannot relate to one another. As a result, it is nearly impossible to find out each entity's detailed laws. Quantum physics, which looks at the law in an integrated way, identifies four forces (gravity, electromagnetic force, and strong and weak nuclear forces) in the universe that transform and move matter.

In the East, the Li-Qi (organizing principle and vital energy) theory concretely applies the yin-yang theory of I Ching to the principle of creation of all things in the universe. When the Qi gathers, it becomes a form; when the form disperses, it becomes Qi.

Eastern philosophy states that one Qi or single source creates the universe, and according to the force of Li, it gathers or disperses. Based on this gathering and dispersing of Qi, all things in the universe maintain their distinctive forms, and they change according to the intrinsic movement of Qi. This is identical to the appearance and disappearance of various ocean waves created according to the wind. The ocean water is the one Qi, and the wind is the Li. The four forces of quantum physics correspond to the Li.

Among the four forces, the electromagnetic force and gravity mainly function in the macroscopic world. In contrast, the strong and weak nuclear forces primarily act in the microscopic or atomic world. As previously mentioned in chapter 15, "Sasang," the electromagnetic force that spreads out instantly corresponds to the Taiyang, while the gravity, which has centripetal force, corresponds to the Taiyin. The strong nuclear force, which bonds the neutron and proton inside the nucleus of an atom, corresponds to the Shaoyin, while the weak nuclear force that causes the collapse of the nucleus corresponds to the Shaoyang.

The sphere of influence created by the four universal forces is called a field. Each force acts according to individually differing principles. In the I Ching, however, a single unified theory applies to all things in the universe. Einstein attempted in his later years to create a unified field theory that tied together the four forces. The unified field theory is identical to the unified theory of Tai Chi in the I Ching, which Einstein attempted to handle more profoundly.

Nevertheless, Einstein was not able to achieve his objective. Currently, many physicists are continuing to research this theory. Still, authors believe that the I Ching theory will ultimately be proven as the unified field theory.

FRACTAL PATTERNS WITHIN THE I CHING

The chaos theory introduced the scientific and artistic communities to the intrinsic patterns of nature and labeled these patterns fractals. This picture (fig. A1.15) is a computer-generated image of a fractal pattern. Every aspect of our universe follows this same fractal pattern and can be systematically broken down into smaller and smaller concentric pieces. Observing this picture carefully, you will see that there are continuations of smaller nautiluses around a giant nautilus. The small image in the upper right-hand corner is a condensed version of the whole picture. A nautilus that is the same size as the condensed version from the entire image can be found: if you carefully observe the smaller nautiluses, you will see a continuation of even smaller nautiluses, although they are vague. When parts endlessly repeat the pattern of the whole, it is called a fractal.

Figure A1.15 A Fractal Pattern

The word "fractal" means separating into parts. It was first used in 1975 by Benoit B. Mandelbrot, who later became a professor of mathematics at Yale. Many scientists agree with the theory that everything in nature possesses such a pattern. Thus it is spotlighted as the pattern that expresses the principle of the universe.

In the times of Newton, it was believed that knowing a few fundamental laws and a few elements that belonged to them enabled a person to know everything in the universe. Also, the universe was believed to be the gathering of various parts that neatly fit together, like a watch or an automobile with four wheels, one engine, two pumps, and so on. Thus the universe and all its creations were believed to be a gathering of many constituent components.

However, with the observation of the microcosmic world of quanta, scientists are now saying the universe is complete chaos without a uniform principle. Einstein himself said, "God does not play dice," expressing his skepticism in the unpredictability of quantum physics. But then by making an even closer examination, scientists discovered fractal patterns. Within the chaos of the entire universe, there exists a fractal pattern, wherein the part repeats the pattern of the whole.

It is possible to divide the universe, its stars, and their constituents into distinct elements using fractal patterns. The various components that make up the Earth, a component of the universe, include minerals, plants, and animals (of which human beings are a part). Within a human being, tissues form the internal organs. Tissues, in turn, are created by cells, and a nucleus is among the components that make up a cell. Within the nucleus, there are DNA molecules. This differentiation continues into many different dimensions, yet within each dimension exists a common pattern linking the smallest portion to the largest aspect. Each division contains the information of the entire structure. Because of this consistency in differentiation, the part represents the whole. The computer-generated image (fig. A1.15) succinctly demonstrates such a fractal pattern of the universe.

There is nothing in this universe not made up of fractal patterns. By watering a garden and observing the ground configuration where the water flows, there are grasses, a mound, a brook, and a pond. By extension, there are trees, a mountain, a river, and an ocean. A single grain of sand repeats the pattern of a rock, and a rock repeats the pattern of a mountain.

Structures have different names but have identical structural patterns according to which position the magnifying glass of one's mind is applied. Whether viewed from a map, a plane, a mountain along the shoreline, or a sandy coastal plain, the coastline appears identical from every angle. Moreover, when the coastline created by sand and seawater is viewed through a magnifying glass, or pulverized sand with a single drop of seawater is viewed under a microscope, the curvy patterns of the coastline are all identical. This is because the part repeats the pattern of the whole.

A drop of water or a snowflake has a pattern of life-form. An inanimate object that most closely resembles the earliest life-form is water. Water on a planet suggests the possibility of life, and the earliest life-form is believed to have been born from water. Thus, there is an intimate relationship between water and a life-form. The classics of the East record, "The heaven first created the water." Therefore, the water has a particular fractal pattern. It is even more so for the structure of snow crystals, which are solid states of water, like the living organisms that appear solid (fig. A1.16).

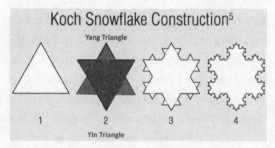

Figure A1.16 The Fractal Geometry in a Snow Crystal

The second figure in this diagram is that of the Star of David. It is the pattern drawn onto the flag as the national symbol of Israel. It corresponds to the Tai Chi symbol of the I Ching. The upright triangle is yang, and the upside-down triangle is yin. When the upright and upside-down triangles continually overlap at the six tips of the star, they become snow crystals with a fractal pattern. Though the actual shape is slightly different, the patterns of the snow crystals are in this shape. It is the most settled and well-created shape. A single snowflake is the fractal pattern of an innumerable number of Stars of David (Tai Chi) gathered to create a large Star of David (Tai Chi).

Human beings, the most evolved (the lord of all creation) among all the organisms on Earth, also have a fractal pattern (see fig. 14.9 in chapter 14). The fractal pattern appears in humans and in all things in the universe. But among them, human beings most closely resemble God, or the totality, and thus possess even more fractal-like patterns. For example, the human body has three sections: the head, torso, and legs. Each segment is further subdivided into three. The human head comprises the cranium, maxilla, and mandible.

The torso consists of three segments: the thoracic, abdominal, and pelvic cavities. The spine also comprises the cervical, thoracic, and lumbar vertebrae. The arms divide into the upper arm, forearm, and hand, and the legs consist of the thigh, calf, and foot. Finally, the fingers and toes repeat the pattern of the arms and legs and separate into three segments. In each of these parts, we can see the structure of threes. This pattern continues perpetually and indefinitely down to the cells, molecules, atoms, and quanta.

According to the fractal theory, the whole becomes affected when a part is influenced. There is a resonance among each part and each dimension. For example, in hand acupuncture, needling a point in the middle of the palm can treat abdominal pain. This is because the needle stimulation influences the abdomen, as acupuncture is also based on the fractal principle. This same principle applies to ear acupuncture, in which the ear resembles the upside-down fetus, or applies to traditional whole-body acupuncture, in which needles are placed along the channels or meridians at the skin surface to treat disorders of internal organs. Again, this is using the fractal theory.

A stimulus given to the small nautilus influences the large nautilus, and an impact reaching the small dimension spreads to all the other dimensions. Though the dimensions are different, stimulating yin or yang regions of the ears or hands can treat yin (e.g., kidneys) or yang (e.g., heart) organs of the body, corresponding to the whole.

With the advancement of treatments based on the fractal principle, a single human cell can be taken out of a body and treated to improve the function of the entire body. Though such a treatment method is still in the experimental stage, it can be utilized to correct the DNA when there is an inherent abnormality in the gene. Viruses are organisms that only have genes. That is, they only possess the common pattern of the organism. When the viruses enter the body, they plant their genes into those of humans. Then humans produce viruses.

The experiment involves selecting the cold virus, implanting the gene that is missing from a patient with a genetic disease into the virus, and infecting the patient with that virus. Then the few cells of the patient infected with the virus will replicate and restore the missing gene. Not only will the patient's genetic disease, which wholly comprises individual cells, be cured, but the patient will also have a normal child. Since humans consist of fractal structures, a single cell contains the fractal pattern of the whole body. Therefore, each cell has the DNA information necessary to reproduce all bodily systems. This is the reason cloning is possible.

The following pictures (figs. A1.17A and A1.17B) can conjure images of many things. The one on the left is an actual tree, and the one on the right is a tree fractal pattern drawn by inputting a fractal numerical formula into a computer. It demonstrates an infinitely dividing tree and its stems and branches. It is a whole pattern with the iterating shape of a single stem separating into two, then each two separating into other twos. The entire bronchial tube, or bronchus, of a lung has such a pattern of differentiation, and so too do the four limbs that divide into two categories from the human trunk. The two upper limbs differentiate from the torso. Each limb further differentiates into the radius and ulna below the elbow. After the wrist joint, they divide into a bundle of two- or three-jointed fingers. Thus the differentiation of limbs shows a similar pattern to this figure. Like plants and animals, blood vessels and nerves also display a fractal pattern.

Figure A1.17 A tree (left, A) and a computer-generated tree fractal pattern (right, B)

The pattern in the next image (fig. A1.18) is another computer-generated fractal pattern resembling bracken or fern brake. A single leaf has a twig pattern, and the pattern of a twig has a stem pattern.

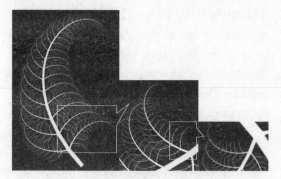

Figure A1.18 A Leaf Fractal Pattern

Though the above figures are patterns with the mathematical rule, an actual natural product such as broccoli (fig. A1.19) is usually three-dimensional and slightly irregular. However, recognizing such a pattern allows an understanding of the whole by simplifying the chaotic world.

Figure A1.19 Fractal Pattern of Broccoli

Sages of the past who created the I Ching five thousand years ago recognized such patterns in nature. Thus, they made the universe's model through the digital coding system of yin and yang, which is more advanced than the fractal theory.

The following picture is a diagram that illustrates the fundamental structure of the I Ching in a single circle (fig. A1.20). First, there is Tai Chi (yin and yang), the most significant dimension, and four bigrams known as Sasang in the next dimension, then eight trigrams, followed by sixty-four hexagrams, creating concentric circles in order. Each concentric circle expresses the different stages of differentiation with differing implications.

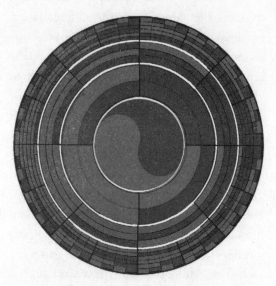

Figure A1.20 Fractal Structure of the I Ching

The circle in the middle is Tai Chi, which divides into yin and yang. The whole universe can be divided and seen within these two groups. The subsequent division is called Sasang, formed by two lines (each line symbolizing yin or yang) at the bottom and the top. The bottom line in this bigram is the *foundation,* and the top line is the *manifestation.* Again, the whole universe can be divided and seen within these four groups.

If the Sasang is observed with the bottom lines as the foundation, it consists of two yin bigrams and two yang bigrams. The top lines representing manifestation have differing yin and yang in the two bigrams that share the same yin or yang bottom lines. Viewed holistically, the sum of the Sasang dimension is ultimately yin and yang, thus the pattern of Tai Chi.

Following the Sasang dimension are eight trigrams that arose from the differentiation of the four bigrams. These eight trigrams represent the entire universe divided into eight groups. Each trigram is composed of three yin or yang lines laid out horizontally, one on top of another, each holding a top, middle, or bottom position. The bottom, or foundational lines, contain four yin and four yang lines. The center lines of the four trigrams with bottom yin lines consist of two yin and two yang lines. Following this differentiation pattern, the top lines of the two trigrams with base and middle yin lines consist of one yin and one yang line each. This exhibits the patterns of Tai Chi that differentiate into yin and yang in the dimension of the eight trigrams.

Within the eight trigrams are Tai Chi, yin-yang, and Sasang. If a concentric circle is a single dimension, a pattern arises by repeatedly dividing yin and yang elements. In the same way, the sixty-four hexagrams (the outermost layer) repeat this pattern, dividing yin and yang into six stages. Therefore, the I Ching represents a fractal theory and uses the yin and yang symbols to represent infinitely repeating dimensions of universal fractal patterns. It illustrates the structure and movement of everything in the universe with only six phases.

When the ordered model of the universe of Newtonian mechanics crumbled merely by the uncertainty principle, and the universe was found to be in chaos, the modern fractal theory came into the limelight. A regular pattern was discovered in which the part has a similar structure to the whole by repeating the whole pattern. Unfortunately, however, there has been no further advancement in its theory since its discovery. The I Ching, however, clearly presents what that common pattern is.

That pattern has polar elements with ceaseless transformation between them, which appears as the function of matter. The common pattern is called Tai Chi, expressed as a diagram with circulating yin and yang. As Tai Chi expresses constant circulation, it includes space and time factors. Two polar elements exist in space yet mutually transform into one another according to time.

It also expresses the change in the force between the two elements, the yin and yang, constantly occurring between the movement and stillness of the circulation. Therefore, I Ching is a highly evolved theory explaining the structure of the form, like the fractal pattern and the fractal pattern of the function of all things in the universe changing according to time.

Actually, scientists who study fractal theory have not attempted to express the structure of the entire universe as a fractal pattern. Though they vaguely understand the universe as a fractal pattern, even fifty years after the first presentation of the theory, the fractal theory is still incomplete, and its application is immature. The I Ching has the fractal pattern as its fundamental structure while containing many more advanced theories.

I Ching is a theory that has been utilized in many fields aside from natural science, such as politics, economics, ethics, social sciences, and mental and spiritual cultivation methods, including Tai Chi, Qigong, Zen, and other forms of meditation. Therefore, its application is unrestricted. It is unhindered in its explanation of the entirety of the universe or the structure and function of quanta, considered the smallest forms in the universe.

The Holographic Theory

A hologram is a picture with a three-dimensional image created with laser light. A single laser beam, passing through a semitransparent mirror, splits into two laser beams to create a hologram. One beam, called the "reference beam," passes through a diffusing lens and reflects off a mirror onto an unexposed photographic plate. Meanwhile, the second beam, known as the "object or working beam," undergoes the same process but illuminates the object to be photographed before being recorded on the photographic plate. The two beams create an interference pattern that produces the hologram before falling onto the photographic plate. Under ordinary incoherent light, such as incandescent light, the hologram only reveals a smoky haze without a trace of the filmed object.[6] However, the three-dimensional image of the object appears when viewed with coherent laser light (fig. A1.21).

In terms of yin and yang, a hologram is an image created by the interference pattern (Tai Chi) with a reference beam (yin) and object or working beam (yang). Because the hologram is an image created by the union of information from mutually differing yin and yang perspectives, it possesses three-dimensional images. The image created by the interference pattern between yin and yang beams creates an image of Tai Chi. In the Tai Chi image, a part repeats the pattern of the whole, creating a fractal image. No matter how small it is cut, such a holographic film can recreate the whole image because a piece always contains the information of the whole. Only the vividness diminishes.

In our bodies, we can see the holographic principle taking place. Even when the parts of the brain responsible for hearing or seeing are damaged, we can still hear and see because the brain records incoming information in a holographic manner. A single cell containing the data of the whole body in its DNA uses the same storing method as the hologram.

When reading a unigram, a bigram, a trigram, or a hexagram, knowing only that one part will limit or render it impossible to

Laser

Diffusing Lens

Diffusing Lens

Object or
Working Beam

Interference
Pattern

Object

Mirror

Reference Beam

Holographic
Film Plate

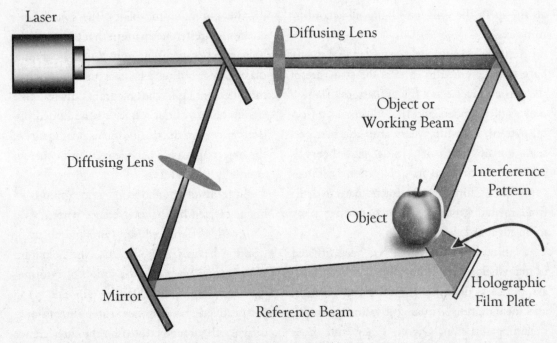

Figure A1.21 Creation of a Hologram

understand. The others in the same dimension must be known. When looking at the yin line, the yang line must be understood. When reading a Shaoyang bigram, Taiyang, Shaoyin, and Taiyin bigrams horizontally arranged from it must be studied. Vertically, its parent, as well as its children, must be grasped. This is the same for the eight trigrams and the sixty-four hexagrams.

One hexagram contains six yin or yang lines or any combination of them. The bottom line becomes yin and yang, the second line (bottom two lines) forms Sasang, and the third (bottom three lines) creates eight trigrams. There are sixteen, thirty-two, and sixty-four hexagrams from the fourth line onward. A vertical and horizontal structure of a single unigram, bi-

gram, trigram, and hexagram all contain spatial and temporal information of the whole. Yet each represents a different nature. For instance, a single hexagram, as a Tai Chi and 1/64 of a holographic film, shows the holographic image of the entire universe while showing 1/64 of its differing aspect.

A Question on the Creator of the I Ching

According to the legend, Fuxi first created eight trigrams after observing the Hado, or Yellow River Map, drawn on the back of the dragon horse that sprang out of the Yellow River. Meanwhile, Shennong, the second legendary emperor, created the sixty-four hexagrams. (The more popular belief is that King Wen made the sixty-four hexagrams.) The "Great Treatise" of I Ching states that people built houses and invented farming tools after studying the trigrams and hexagrams. As seen in an earlier drawing (fig. A1.4), Fuxi had the upper body of a human and the lower body of a snake. Shennong is famous for writing *Shennong's Herbal,* the first book from the East on pharmacology, after discovering the effects of herbs by personally tasting all the herbs himself. He is said to have had horns on his head and clear glass-like skin. He tasted more than one hundred herbs daily, and by looking through his transparent skin, he knew where the herbs entered and what actions they had in his body. His antidote to ingesting poisonous herbs was to quickly grab the horns on his head, which detoxified poisons. According to one version of the legend, he once consumed an extremely toxic herb and died because he could not grab the horns in time.

Many drawings in ancient books and stone tablets or mural paintings in tombs from credible sources show in diverse ways how Fuxi had the lower body of a snake and Shennong had the head of a cow. However, the astounding scientific principles behind the I Ching, Fuxi's and Shennong's original creations, make us think they may have been aliens. Their half-man, half-animal forms also make us conceive of them as aliens. If people built houses and invented farming equipment by observing trigrams and hexagrams during the times of Fuxi and Shennong, it can be assumed that they created and utilized computers by discovering the digital principles from the trigrams and hexagrams.

Inferring from this information, there is considerable credibility in assuming that Fuxi and Shennong were aliens. Two pictures validate this assumption.

The top image (in fig. A1.22) is an engraving on a pillar inside an ancient Egyptian temple near the pyramids. The picture below it is an enlarged version of the same, in which many flying objects appear. To the left and below the flying objects is the Xun trigram. This trigram represents wind. Because the eight trigrams represent all things in the universe, flying objects that float on the wind correspond to the Xun trigram. Thus, ancient Egyptians used the Xun trigram to explain flying objects.

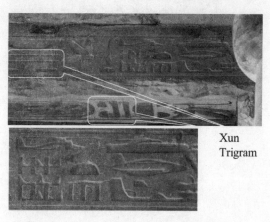

Xun
Trigram

Figure A1.22 I Ching in an Egyptian Temple

From the perspective of the I Ching, pyramids are structures that embody the principle of the numbers 2 (4) and 3. The pyramids are fractal structures because when transversely cut, the result is always a smaller pyramid. We can presume that ancient Egyptians applied the principle of the I Ching to their buildings. Ancient Egyptians were not primitive people, as they could build the pyramids, apply the science of the trigrams, and knew about or used flying objects. It may be possible that their civilization was composed of alien visitors, because they knew the I Ching, indicative of modern science, and flew on flying objects.

The next two images (fig. A1.23) show the prototype ideograph of modern Chinese characters inscribed on bones and tortoise shells from the Yin (Shang) dynasty. The ideograph on the left represents heaven, drawn as a person wearing a helmet. Perhaps people of that time believed an alien visitor was a God sent from heaven. The ideograph on the right means "light," or "bright." It is in the form of a kneeling alien with large ears and a funnel-shaped head, resembling Mr. Spock from the TV show *Star Trek*. It may depict an alien wearing a metal space suit to pro-

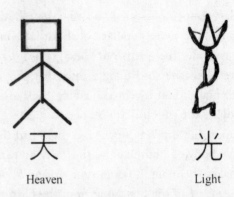

Heaven   Light

Figure A1.23 Oracle Bone Script from the Yin Dynasty

tect his body while passing through the Earth's atmosphere. It could also be an alien whose body is filled with energy and thus shines brightly. Apparently, the creators of the ideograph equated this bright light with aliens. Observation of both ideographs may also lead one to believe that the characters who drew them were aliens or imparted knowledge of alien civilizations.

I Ching in Daily Life

This appendix applies the principles behind the I Ching to unravel the mysteries behind the pyramids of ancient Egypt, the Catholic rosary, the Holy Place, the game of Go, and the Korean game of Yut, among others. By applying the I Ching theory to various aspects of people's cultures and religions, we can derive a clear and simple understanding of their purpose. Furthermore, these interpretations elucidate, educate, and help us better understand the I Ching principles.

The I Ching and the Pyramids

Every philosophy and religion on Earth uses symbols to represent the most important things in people's beliefs. For example, Christianity has a cross, Judaism uses the Star of David, Native Americans worship many different

things in nature, and the East employs Tai Chi. A culture's symbol represents its heart and soul, a force that unites all ideologies. This force is God, Tao, or the principle of the universe.

Numbers join symbols to express the form and function of all things. Therefore, numbers are inherent in the construction of the I Ching. The numbers 2 (yin) and 3 (yang), representing earth (yin) and heaven (yang), essentially manifest the I Ching's principle, for every statement expressed in it indicates the relationship of its numbers. For example, the hexagrams configure from numbers 2 and 3 ($2 \times 3 = 6$). Two can be represented geometrically as a square, while 3 is a triangle or circle ($\pi = 3.14$).

The environmental movement of the West was in response to the fear of ecological destruction. There is little acknowledgment of the importance of living in harmony with natural laws, except in the light of the potential cession of human existence. Native American cultures attempt to teach, through traditions and customs, the vital necessity of recognizing the interconnectedness of humans to the Earth. Still, for the most part, the pace of American life is too rapid to take notice of its impact. Like the Native American cultures, Eastern cultures show great concern for the environment because of the potential threat of ecological destruction. Additionally, they understand that living by natural laws is the most healthy and productive way to live.

Theories such as Feng Shui (literally windwater), based on the I Ching principles, involve the environment and are difficult to understand. However, by issuing guidelines to harmonize surrounding energies, they seek to help people live in harmony with their environments. A few examples include the proper placement of the furniture in a house, the best location to build a home, or even the best place to bury family members.

Whether it is a house for the living or a grave for the dead, the best location is an area where the yang influence of heaven and the yin influence of earth are in balance. The Feng Shui theory teaches that burying the dead in balanced graves brings comfort to their souls (see Hexagram 11: Peace). Positive Qi is formed and resonates with all of their descendants, who contain the same type of Qi so that the descendants' yin and yang become harmonized. This harmony will eliminate all of the shortcomings of the deceased's descendants and ultimately deliver excellent health, power, and prosperity.

Builders of pyramids may not have had these same ideas in mind when they constructed them (figs. A2.1, A2.2, A2.3, and A2.4), but one thing is clear; they intended to bring comfort to the deceased.

We can infer that the pyramids symbolize heaven and earth, and analyzing them according to the principles of the I Ching better clarifies their purpose.

Regardless of East or West, past or present, a horizontal line is representative of the earth, and a vertical line is representative of

Figure A2.1 Pyramids of Egypt

Figure A2.2 Pyramid of Chichen Itza, Yucatan, Mexico

Figure A2.3 Pyramid of King Cyrus of Babylon

Figure A2.4 Pyramid in Seoul, Korea

will always result in a smaller pyramid. Similarly, in each stage of the division of Tai Chi into Sasang, the eight trigrams, and the sixty-four hexagrams, there exists yin and yang. This symbolizes how a part contains the whole.

The front view of a pyramid is a triangle. A single tip at the top (number 1) represents heaven, and two tips at the bottom (number 2) represent the earth. The three tips of the complete triangle represent human beings, or all things in nature that arise through the union of heaven and earth.

A bird's-eye view of a pyramid has its tip in the center (figs. A2.5 and A2.6). The four corners surrounding the center are Sasang, and the combination of the four corners and the center equals the five elements. The four corners in these figures become the four cardinal and four transitional trigrams, and they become the eight trigrams.

heaven. Therefore, the pyramid's tip symbolizes heaven, while the base represents earth.

The tip also symbolizes the chaos before the differentiation of all things in the universe or Tai Chi. Just as Tai Chi contains sixty-four hexagrams, a pyramid, a microcosm of the universe, is condensed within its tip.

A horizontal cut anywhere on the pyramid

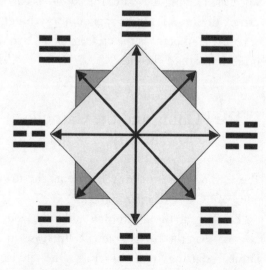

Figure A2.5 Pyramids and Fuxi's Arrangement

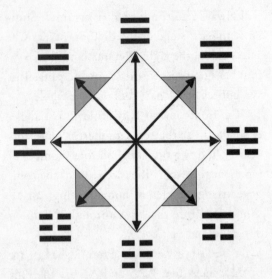

Figure A2.6 Pyramids and King Wen's Arrangement

Figure A2.7 Catholic Rosary

Interpretations of the Hado and Nakseo diagrams resulted in the creation of the I Ching theories. Examining the generative principles of the pyramid's design from various angles shows that they are identical to I Ching's views. Since the I Ching illustrates the common pattern of all things, its ideas apply to everything in nature, and perhaps the creators of the pyramids knew these theories.

The I Ching and the Catholic Rosary

The Catholic rosary clearly represents the totality of I Ching theories (fig. A2.7).

Looking at the illustration carefully, you can see that the beads gradually increase in number starting from the cross. The single bead represents Tai Chi and totality. Uniting a horizontal line symbolizing the earth, yin, and a vertical line representing heaven, yang, makes a cross. The intersection of yin and yang is also Tai Chi, God, or the universe. The four protruding regions of the cross are Sasang and, together with the center (the earth element), are the five elements. The whole cross itself is Tai Chi, God, and the universe.

Beads are used to express such principles in terms of time differentiation. They are symbols, each like a star in the sky, creating time. The first bead following the cross represents Tai Chi, and the three beads after it symbolize heaven, humanity, and earth, representing the universe. However, the Catholic Church perceives them as the Holy Trinity of the Father, the Son, and the Holy Ghost. The Father is the God of heaven, the Son is the spirit of humanity, and the Holy Ghost is the spirit of the earth.

Five individual beads represent the five elements. Ten beads are strung in a row, separated by one of the five single beads to express the five elements within the five elements. Five groups of ten represent the ten celestial stems or the five generating numbers (yang) and the five completing numbers (yin) of the Hado and Nakseo diagrams. The Hado and Nakseo principles could be the basis for creating the rosary, like the pyramids and the I Ching.

In Christianity, a cross (fig. A2.8) symbolizes Christ's crucifixion, but its meaning may have deeper connotations. Many Christian missionaries have visited China since the sixteenth century, and some have studied the I Ching extensively. However, it is possible that the I Ching, considered the highest book of knowledge by Eastern scholars, was transmitted to the West through the Silk Road before the Christian missionaries arrived in the sixteenth century. Transmission may have occurred around Christ's birth, when the Three Kings of the East visited him.

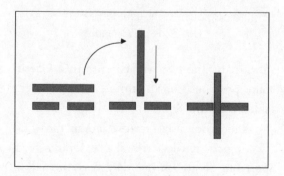

Figure A2.8 A Creation of a Cross

In terms of the I Ching, the cross represents the meeting of yin and yang (as in fig. A2.8). The yang lines better express their dynamic nature when drawn vertically. And in this situation, yin and yang meet one another naturally. Therefore, a cross forms when yang is placed in the space of yin. The hole in yin represents its gathering nature. While the bigrams, trigrams, and hexagrams of the I Ching merely denote the external form, the cross is an excellent symbol that expresses both the properties and the functions of yin and yang.

The I Ching and the Holy Place

People who visit the East can easily see many shrines or sanctuaries where the worshipping of ancestral tablets of great names in history takes place. They are ancient yet well maintained, and many have become famous tourist attractions.

There are recordings of such a place in the Old Testament of the Christian Bible. It is called the Holy Place, or tabernacle, wherein lies God's dwelling place or throne. Jewish people built a Holy Place according to God's command in the middle of the town of the twelve tribes of Israel during the Old Testament period. An outer court (fig. A2.9) with many pillars and delicate white linen curtains surrounds the Holy Place (fig. A2.10), a rectangular enclosure partitioned into two chambers by a veil.

Figure A2.9 Bird's-eye View of the Holy Place

Figure A2.11 The Covenant Box

Figure A2.10 The Holy Place

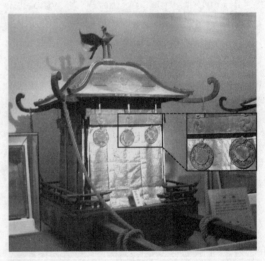

Figure A2.12 Omikoshi, a Portable Shinto Shrine, Usa Shrine, Usa, Japan

Of the two sections, the one that lies deeper is called the Holy of Holies and contains the Ark of the Covenant (fig. A2.11). Inside the box are two stone tablets with the Ten Commandments inscribed on them, held together with the pot of manna, flaky seeds of white color, and the sprouted rod of Aaron. There is God's throne on the top of the box, and on top of the throne is the divine glory or light, called Shekinah. The two winged creatures, Cherubim, positioned on the throne's left and right sides, cover the light.

Rabbis from Israel traveled around the world looking for ten lost tribes. The Omikoshi, a portable Shinto shrine they encountered in Japan, was a huge surprise—they did not expect to see something so holy in a city shrine instead of deep in a remote mountain cave (fig. A2.12). In many ways, it resembles the Ark of the Covenant. Despite their distance and time gap, they are very similar. An unusual feature of Omikoshi is that three trinity symbols are drawn outside.

By taking a bird's-eye view of the Holy Place, we can see the principle of the I Ching. The Holy Place situated in the center corresponds to Tai Chi. The Holy Place divides into two sections, while Tai Chi divides into yin and yang.

Since the Holy Place is a rectangular enclosure (four sides), it corresponds to the Sasang. The twelve tribes of Israel encamped outside the Holy Place. We previously mentioned that twelve Monarch Hexagrams are the most important of the sixty-four hexagrams. Therefore, the twelve tribes correspond to the twelve Monarch Hexagrams and the twelve zodiac animals, which are twelve types of energies derived from dividing six terrestrial energies into yin and yang. There are twelve disciples, twelve spring wells, and twelve pillars in the Bible.

Thus, there is a great significance to the number 12. According to the principles of the I Ching, 12 also implies two situations, yin or yang, that create each of the six lines ($6 \times 2 = 12$). Like the sixty-four hexagrams, the number 12 represents everything in the universe with differing shapes. Therefore, it has something in common with God's creation of the universe in six days.

God's throne in the Holy of the Holies is like the single point that manifests when the yang becomes extreme in the Tai Chi diagram. In Eastern medicine, it is like the brain situated in the upper region of the body, even though it belongs to the kidney system (water element). Since the whole is always in part, there are five element correspondences in the Holy of the Holies.

For example, the inside of the courtyard tent is a flat, plane arrangement. However, the Holy of the Holies is a three-dimensional array with upper and lower aspects. If the courtyard's layout is a horizontal plane, then the Holy of the Holies' interior is a vertical plane. Thus, it reminds us again of the meaning of the cross.

The Covenant Box can be interpreted according to the five elements. God's throne becomes the earth element. The Shekinah becomes the fire element, and the two stone tablets inside the box correspond to the metal element. The rod of Aaron corresponds to the wood element, and manna corresponds to the water element. The rod of Aaron was placed inside the Covenant Box to commemorate God's miracle that made the rod, a dead piece of wood, sprout, and also to show the beginning of life, which is that of the wood element among the five elements.

The two stone tablets with the Ten Commandments inscribed on them contain information about the whole. We previously stated that one simple sentence, "Three-heaven and two-earth," sums up the principle of the I Ching; the numbers 2 (yin) and 3 (yang), representing earth (yin) and heaven (yang), essentially manifest the I Ching's principle, for every statement expressed in it indicates their relationship. A general assumption would be that two stone tablets with the inscription of the Ten Commandments would be equally divided with five commandments on each tablet. But in actuality, one tablet has six commandments and the other has four.

The eight trigrams and the five-element theory of the I Ching were created by observing the forms of Hado and Nakseo, the two maps bestowed by heaven. There is a similar meaning in the Ten Commandments to Hado and Nakseo. The two stone tablets imply yin and yang (heaven and earth). The six commandments point to the number of heaven as three yin and three yang. The four commandments denote the number of earth as two yin and two yang. In other words, they imply "three-heaven and two-earth" of the I Ching.

Manna corresponds to the water element that nourishes life. The three items—two stone tablets, the rod of Aaron, and a pot of manna—are the substances of earth and stored inside the box in the shape of a regular hexahedron (cube). The regular hexahedron has special significance as it is the three-dimensional space of the x, y, and z coordinate systems. The eight trigrams can also be arranged three-dimensionally.

In the center of the box is the symbolic throne of God. On top of it is the Shekinah, which relates to the fire element. We previously mentioned that God corresponds to the earth element in the center with yin and yang in perfect harmony. In such a way, the five elements organize three-dimensionally in the Holy of the Holies.

The wood used for the Ark of the Covenant and the structure of the Tabernacle is acacia. Interestingly, a tree called Goemok (槐木) in Korea is believed to be the tree of God. This tree belongs to the same family as acacia (Fabaceae). Shrines, Buddhist temples, and palaces where Sam-Taegeuk, the trinity symbol, is present always plant Goemok in their courtyards (fig. A2.13). It is also the material used for the seal that prints the amulets. Goemok is a member of the Sophora genus and has the nicknames "Chinese scholar tree" or "Japanese pagoda tree." There are many myths associated with it. One such myth is its ability to chase away evil spirits.

The name of the wife of Fuxi, the creator of I Ching, has the same pronunciation as Jehovah (God) in Korea (Yeowa). Moreover, Jehovah instructs the people of Israel to weave the entrance curtains of the Tabernacle with red, blue, and purple threads. Similarly, Korean shrines have a Sam-Taegeuk drawn on their doors. Blue is yin, red is yang, and purple is a mixture of blue and red, signifying the middle.

Figure A2.13 Goemok Tree at the Jinwi Confucian Temple and School, Pyeongtaek, Korea

In the courtyard before the Holy Place, priests perform sacrificial rites at the Burnt Offering Altar (fig. A2.9). Behind the fire burning vigorously at the altar is a laver, a large bronze basin filled with clear water. The rites are identical to placing water drawn from the well at dawn in a cup with candlelight on the altar and praying. Such a ritual enacts the cyclical principle of the universe and symbolizes the "ascending of water and descending of fire" required for humans to be reborn.

Since the Hado and Nakseo, which became the basis for the I Ching, were bestowed by heaven, the I Ching is a creation of God to awaken humanity.

The I Ching and the Game of Go

Go is a military strategy game played using black and white stones. It also consists of a board with nineteen horizontal lines and nineteen vertical lines combined to form 361 crossing points where the stones can sit. The game's object is to trap the opponent and acquire as much territory as possible by the end of the game.

Legend states that Emperor Shun created Go during the golden age of antiquity in China. He was known to be one of the most successful emperors. As he was a remarkably effective ruler who governed his people well, Confucius revered him. The story goes that Emperor Shun created the game to improve the intelligence of his son, who was not very smart.

Although its popularity has only recently reached the West, Eastern countries like China, Japan, and Korea have enjoyed the game for centuries. Because this game is known to improve IQ, it has become quite popular in Korean academics. There is even a TV channel entirely devoted to games of Go. In Japan, tournaments are held for Go "professionals" from various countries to compete for enormous sums of prize money.

Like martial arts, Go consists of different levels, recognizing a person's expertise in the game. As people improve, they are tested to certify them of a certain rank. When two players compete, the lower-level player is allowed to place several stones before the beginning of the game onto nine darkened dots on the board. It is more advantageous to do so, similar to a handicap in golf.

The object of Go is to surround the opponent's stones and take them "prisoner" while acquiring as much territory (crossing points) as possible. When there is no longer room to place the stones, the game has ended, and both sides must tally the number of prisoners and crossing points each person has. The empty spaces of the opponent's collective territory are filled with your captive stones. If you fill up your opponent's territory with your prisoners and your opponent cannot fill up yours, you win. But if your and your opponent's territories are replete, then the number of remaining prisoners decides who wins. The way to figure out the final score is to count one prisoner or territory as one point, meaning that you can win by a single point.

Despite a passion for the game, few people know the Go board's real meaning. Many assume that the board was made by roughly observing the stars in the sky. As you can see on the board (fig. A2.14), there are eighteen vertical and horizontal spaces (blocks) on the board. The button-shaped stones are placed on the points of intersection made by the horizontal and vertical lines. There are 361 (19 × 19) possible locations for the stones, including the nine points on the board.

Even dedicated players of the game may have difficulty deciphering the underlying meaning behind the placement and number of dots and lines. The only way to solve this mystery is by applying the I Ching principle. But for the most part, people simply enjoy playing Go without much thought to the placement and number of dots and lines. Those few who attempt to understand have trouble compre-

hending the game unless they possess a thorough knowledge of the fundamental principles of the I Ching.

If we draw four lines that create six spaces in between, as with the lines of hexagrams, the board divides perfectly into nine sections. This is identical to the diagram of Nakseo (River Lo Map). Since this game has many abrupt changes, the Nakseo diagram applies well. By numbering these sections, the board transforms into the Nakseo diagram (fig. A2.15). The sum of the numbers in opposing compartments is 10, and the number in the center is the balance of the two numbers, 5. The sum total of any three numbers in a row, vertical, horizontal, or diagonal, is 15.

Nakseo served as the foundation for King Wen's arrangement of the eight trigrams, which expresses function and movement. The eight trigrams, placed in the eight directions, surround the center (fig. A2.16). The nine

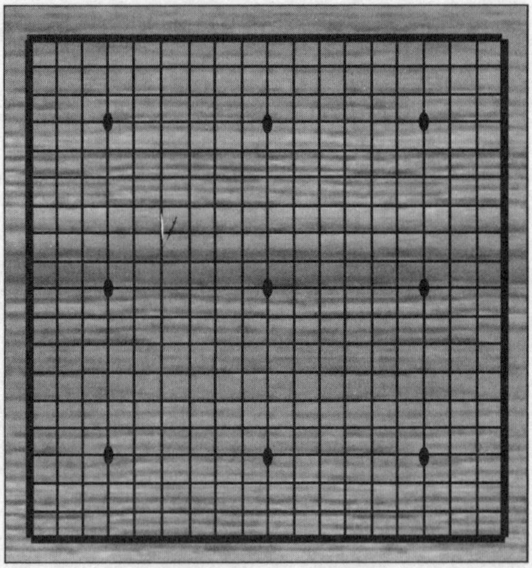

Figure A2.14 Go Board

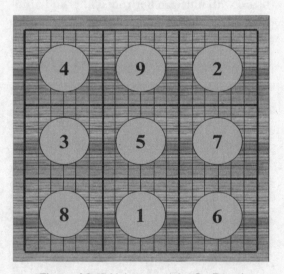

Figure A2.15 Nakseo and the Go Board

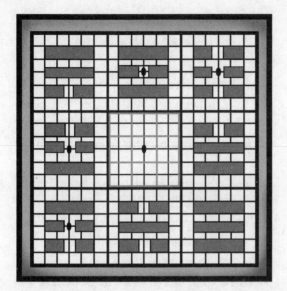

Figure A2.16 King Wen's Arrangement of Trigrams

compartments are called the nine palaces. Because of the various changes that can occur in them, as in the Generating and Controlling Cycles of the five-element theory, the nine palaces are useful in multiple fields, including astronomy, geography, divination, politics, and military strategy. It is also the basis for Feng Shui or the art of geomancy.

The central compartment is called the "central palace" and corresponds to the earth element. It is a position of balance of yin and yang. It is also the position of God that corresponds to the center of a cross. As it is the central location representing the earth element and Tai Chi, it contains within it the information of the whole. Each compartment can be further divided by four lines, creating another nine palaces.

The most central point on the Go board is called the "celestial source," which implies heaven's foundation. It is the source of all the

Go board's information and represents the entire universe. Corresponding to the tip of a pyramid, it is also Tai Chi (fig. A2.17). Except for the central celestial-source point, all other crossing points have a yin-yang pair in the upper-lower, left-right, and diagonal lines. This is because it is where yin and yang are in harmony. If this point is taken out, there are 360 points where Go stones can sit. This corresponds to the 365 days of a year. The total number of lines in the hexagrams of the I Ching is 384 (64 × 64). However, the Qian, Kun, Kan, and Li hexagrams are abstractions and do not exist in any concrete fashion, so they are not counted. By subtracting 24 lines (4 hexagrams × 6 lines each) from 384 lines, we arrive at 360. Therefore, the total number of places to put the stones corresponds to the individual lines of the sixty hexagrams.

Both players in the game start with a container of either black or white stones, and the game alternates back and forth. This is, in essence, the same as drawing the individual yin and yang lines in the I Ching. The players' alternate placing of the stones is in accord with I Ching's principle, "Tao is the alternation of

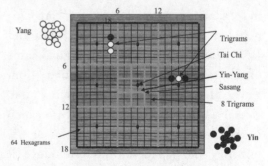

Figure A2.17 I Ching and the Go Board

yin and yang." The world is a constant interplay of and competition between yin and yang, good and evil. Therefore, the game of Go simulates the reign of the world of Tao or God by alternately placing a black stone and a white stone.

Koreans call Go "Baduk." It is a word derived from "batduk," the embankment around a field. The banks are built on the fields or paddies to demarcate one's land from another person's. Batduk, seen from the top of the mountain, is like a Go board (fig. A2.18).

Figure A2.18 Batduk

The Chinese call it "Weiqi," but the Chinese characters "weiqi" (圍棋) or "qi" (碁) do not indicate a field bank. Again, as mentioned in *Mencius*, Emperor Shun was not Han Chinese but of the Dongyi tribe of Korea and Japan. Thus, it appears that the original name of this game is Baduk, and it originates from Korea. If Baduk was imported from China, Koreans would have named it "Gi," which is the Korean pronunciation of 棋 or 碁, just like the Japanese who pronounce it "go" (碁).

The I Ching and the Game of Yut (Four-Stick Game)

Yut, a four-stick game, is popular in Korea. In the Korean language, the number 6 is called "yuk," "yeohseot," or "yeot," and this is how the name of this game originates. In this game, four sticks are created by vertically cutting two wooden rods into equal parts. Players throw these sticks like dice to play.

There are two sides to each piece of wood. The rounded side is yang, while the flat side is yin. When a player throws the four pieces together, they create five situations. For example, three yang and one yin are called Do (pig), two yang and two yin are called Gae (dog), one yang and three yin are called Geol (sheep), four yin are called Yut (cow), and four yang are called Mo (horse).

The purpose of this game is for its players to learn yin-yang, mathematics, computations, and the I Ching. Thus, the Yut game was played not only as a game but as a tool to select sixty-four hexagrams of the I Ching.

If you observe carefully, the game board of Yut (fig. A2.19) also has the pyramid's principle of creation in the same way as the Hado (Yellow River Map). They are both model structures that demonstrate the principles of the I Ching.

Dori Dori, Jjakjakoong, Jeom Jeom, and Gonji Gonji

In the past, the king of Korea and his subjects were the masters of I Ching. The civil-service

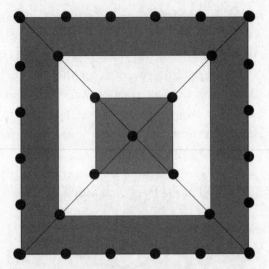

Figure A2.19 Yut Game Board

examination even consisted of writing a poem with nothing but the title given that day. An appointment to an official position depended on the scoring of how well the poem applied and expressed the Tao, the cosmic principle of all things in the universe that I Ching expounds. Among the officials that passed, brilliant ones in charge of education made educational games for children to naturally educate them on the cosmic principles of change.

When a baby can hold his head with the strength of his neck, grown-ups say "Dori Dori," and the baby turns his head left and right. Though babies can't speak, they know that adults like how they react to the word "Dori Dori." "Dori" (道理) means the principle of Tao or the emergence of Tao (道來).

A passage in *The Yellow Emperor's Inner Classic* states that the universe is round, and the head, modeled after the universe, is also round. The head symbolizes the universe. It

teaches that the turning of the head and "the emergence of Tao" coincide. This game aims to promote the development of the part of the brain that controls the muscles. Still, such a name was attached to give it a philosophical meaning.

After learning the Dori Dori, the next thing is to perform Jjakjakoong, Jjakjakoong, which means "to make a thumping sound by matching pairs." If the grown-ups repeat "Jjakjakoong, Jjakjakoong," the baby claps his or her hands and delights in it. It signifies the harmony of yin and yang. In addition, the clapping motion promotes brain development by moving the muscles of the arm, which are more differentiated than the neck but less delicate than the fingers.

When learning these two movements, the baby can distinguish between Dori Dori and Jjakjakoong. Knowing how to discern the two implies knowing how to differentiate yin and yang, fostering the brain's judgment function.

Once the baby can do the above two movements, he learns Jeom Jeom, a motion in which both fists are clenched and opened. It is a movement to develop the finer controlling function of the brain by exercising the more differentiated muscles of the fingers. When the head, corresponding to the universe, first starts to turn, it is the action of the spring (Dori Dori). Next is the summer's action, in which the baby delights in clapping hands loudly (Jjakjakoong Jjakjakoong). After these two movements comes Jeom Jeom, a movement symbolizing the function of autumn. It wraps the energy dispersed during the summer and gathers it into matter.

After Jeom Jeom, the baby learns Gonji Gonji, a movement in which the palm of the left hand is opened, and the right hand's index finger repeatedly touches the left palm. Gonji is a word made up of two Chinese characters: Gon (坤) refers to Kun, or Earth trigram, and Ji (地) means earth. "Ji" can also imply "to reach" (至), and "Gonji" can denote "to reach the earth." Therefore, it signifies that the Tao, or Way, of heaven reaches the earth. Gonji Gonji is a very subtle movement. Only one finger of the right hand (yang) is stretched to repeatedly touch the left palm (yin) (symbolizing flat land). This movement is only possible once the baby's fine neural network has formed. Repeating this movement allows for the development of a stable neural network without errors.

An exhibit at a Japanese fair featured a robot that turned a toy top while walking on a blade. It was made possible by moving the electrical circuits corresponding to the robot's brain back and forth whenever it lost its center and fell on the blade. An accurate neural network formation occurs when the baby repeats the minute finger movements he or she recognizes. Gonji Gonji plays a significant role in brain development. Still, it also teaches the winter function of storing the gathered energy of autumn deep underground.

The I Ching and Tai Chi Throughout Many Civilizations

A Mycenaean civilization's relic of the sixteenth century BCE, a bronze sword, depicts three mutually connected concentric spirals on its gold hilt (fig. A2.20). The three concentric spiral patterns make up the whole in all directions. A similar pattern appears in another relic of the Mycenaean civilization excavated near the tomb of Agamemnon in Greece (fig. A2.21). Here, concentric circles form a fractal pattern connected by triangles and hexagons.

The pottery from the seventeenth century BCE stored in the Heraklion Museum, Crete,

Figure A2.20 National Archaeological Museum of Athens, Greece

Figure A2.21 National Archaeological Museum of Athens, Greece

Greece, shows concentric spirals that rotate in opposite directions wrapping around each other (fig. A2.22). Relics of the Minoan civilization around Santorini and Crete exhibit this typical pattern. These concentric spirals represent the essence and beginning of the change of all things. Perhaps their makers might not have known it. Still, they express the center of change in everything in the universe by depicting the galaxy and the solar system.

There is a Sam-Taegeuk pattern on the pillar of the entrance door to the Korean palace library (fig. A2.23). Like any other Tai Chi, it also expresses the essence of cosmic change. Both East and West define the crux of cosmic transformation with concentric patterns. They represent the change that starts at the center and spreads outward to the periphery. These are all patterns used by the king, which also connotes that he should correctly grasp the core of change as the center of the people.

Figure A2.23 The entrance to the Royal Library in Secret Gardens, Seoul, Korea

However, there is a difference between Eastern and Western concentric patterns. Concentric spirals in the West are continuous, with open edges. On the other hand, concentric circles in the East have closed outer boundaries. The pattern of concentric circles or spirals is a model that explains the change in the universe—the Western concentric spiral is an open model. In contrast, the Eastern concentric circle is a closed model. For the East, it implies limited differentiation, beginning with yin-yang, Sasang, eight trigrams, and ending at sixty-four hexagrams. For the West, it alludes to incessant differentiation to infinity.

Such is the difference between Eastern and Western studies. The first introduction of Western studies to the East was labeled a science (科學). 科 means "to analyze or divide," and 學 means "to study." It implies that Western studies deal with cosmic changes in a very detailed way. It seems that the difference in the method of learning and the paradigm of East and West stems from the difference in symbols representing the core of cosmic change.

Figure A2.22 Heraklion Museum, Crete, Greece

The Celestial Code Classic

一
始無始
一析三極無
盡本天一一地一
二人一三一積十鉅無
匱化三天二三地二三人二
三大三合六生七八九運三四成
環五七一妙衍萬往萬來用變不動本
本心本太陽昂明人中天地一一終無終一

The Celestial Code Classic written in a pyramidal format. The total number of characters is $3 \times 3 \times 3 \times 3 = 81$. Like the pyramid, it expresses the harmony of the numbers three and four.

One is the beginning; out of the Void, One begins.[1]

One divides into the Three Poles, but its foundation remains boundless.

Arising from One, Heaven represents One, Earth represents Two, and Humanity represents Three.

One accumulates and culminates into Ten but still remains limitless, with Three directing all changes.

In the second division, Heaven, Earth, and Humanity all embrace Three.

The great Three unite into Six, giving rise to Seven, Eight, and Nine.

Everything moves according to Three and Four, leading to the cycles of Five and Seven.

One expands in mysterious ways, emerging and disappearing in perpetual cycles; their functions change but not their basis.

The Mind is the ultimate foundation, held high and illuminating like the sun.

In Humanity, Heaven and Earth unite as One.

One is the end; in the Void One ends.

The Celestial Code Classic and I Ching

No evidence suggests that Dangun's[2] teachings form the basis of the Celestial Code Classic. However, from an I Ching perspective, we can presume that it is older than the I Ching and was composed by an enlightened being. The reason is that the Celestial Code Classic is a basic introduction to the principles of numbers, while the I Ching is a detailed discussion of the subject. Nevertheless, the I Ching and its foundation, the Hado (Yellow River Map) and Nakseo (River Lo Map), share this common theme of using numbers and codes with the Celestial Code Classic. Therefore, understanding one will lead to understanding the other. We can, therefore, determine its validity and order of writing.

A current archaeological consensus is that China's Yellow River civilization did not originate with the Han people but rather with a group living farther east, called the Dongyi. Following the Dongyi's full-fledged expulsion from the Yellow River region during the Han Dynasty (206 BCE–220 CE), Korean authorities began fabricating history to suit their needs.

As Korea's power declined daily, its ruling class, who believed in fabricated histories, assimilated into China's Han civilization. But some lived beyond the reach of nation-state power. Namely, the Rang family, who later became the Samurai in Japan, descended from the Hwarang, an ascetic group practicing primitive Taoism from the Dangun era.

Their folk culture based on the principles of the Celestial Code Classic still remains to this day.

Koreans traditionally built a Dangote[3] in the mountain behind their villages to enshrine the Sangdangshin,[4] the deity corresponding to the heavenly god. In the middle of the town, they also enshrined the Hadangshin,[5] corresponding to the god of the earth—whose likeness is embedded in Sotdaes[6] (fig. A3.1), totem poles (fig. A3.1), menhirs, and pagodas. Figures A3.2, A3.3, and A3.4 are other objects influenced by Sotdae.

Figure A3.1 In the middle of the photo is a Sotdae. The bird on the top acts as a messenger between the gods and the villagers, crossing the realm of the gods. Next to them are male and female totem poles (Jangseung). The male Jangseung, yang, is the god who rules the world, and the female Jangseung, yin, is the god who controls the underground.

Figure A3.2 Canadian Indian totem poles. Their shapes are a combination of Jangseung and Sotdae.

Figure A3.3 The spire of Matthias Cathedral, located in the Holy Trinity Square, Budapest, Hungary. The bird on the cross is a messenger, like Sotdae. It is usually a symbol of the Holy Spirit. The original Hungarian tribe, the Magyar, seem to remember Sotdae.

People lived between these shrines. As such, the village embodied the triad pattern of the universe, the elemental principle behind the Celestial Code Classic.

The Shinju Danji,[7] equivalent to the heavenly god, was enshrined in the attic of each household. The Tuhju,[8] corresponding to the earth god, was enshrined in the Jangdokdae[9] and the kitchen. People lived between these enshrinements at home. Such an arrangement is also a fractal pattern that embodies three, the pattern of the whole in parts.

Creating and residing within such an environment was thought to prevent a collision with the universe. Unlike with chaos theory's butterfly effect, people's words, actions, and thoughts would not return to haunt them.[10] To further enhance the well-being of the people and village, shamans performed rites for the Hadang-shin, and they wore a garment of three primary colors and danced with tridents (fig. A3.5).

The Celestial Code Classic Is an Amulet and Incantation

The Celestial Code Classic is the sutra that forms the basis of Dangun ideology. Hwanung,[11] the son of Hwanin, the Heavenly Emperor (God), came down to Shindansu,[12] a spiritual tree of life in Mount Taebaek.[13] He brought three amulets, known as the Chunbuin, or heavenly seals, consisting of the sword, the bell, and the mirror.

Figure A3.4 Mainz Cathedral in Germany. Notre Dame Cathedral in France also has a bird on its cross. It seems that the religious beliefs of the Huns, who believed in Tengri Khan, combined with Christianity.

Figure A3.5 Shaman's Garment and Trident, National Museum of Japanese History, Sakura City, Japan

An amulet is similar to a Mapae (a horse requisition tablet) given to a secret royal emissary. It signifies that the king has delegated the power to command the troops to an official dispatched to a particular area on a special mission.

When paper was unavailable in the past, clay plates engraved with letters or symbols or jade stamps were used instead. Then they were split in half. The king kept one, and an official on a mission received the other. The matching of two sides proved the amulet's authenticity, a process called Buhop, or the "matching of the seal." Today, the tradition no longer exists, but the custom of using amulets to command spirits in the name of the Jade Emperor remains.

Ge Hong (283–343 CE), a scholar and alchemist, wrote a famous book of Taoist self-cultivation called *Baopuzi* (抱朴子), One Who Embraces Simplicity. In the book, there is a story of the Yellow Emperor (2707–2598 BCE), the father of the Art of Immortals (also known as Huang-Lao Art, named after Huangdi, the Yellow Emperor, and Lao-tzu, the founder of Taoism). While passing by Chinggu,[14] he met a teacher named Zabu. The Yellow Emperor learned *Sanhuang Neiwen* (三皇內文), The Inner Teachings of Three Emperors, from him and gained the ability to govern all spirits. A classic of the Dongyi, *The Inner Teachings of Three*

Emperors can be thought of as an amulet capable of controlling spirits. It could also be the Celestial Code Classic brought by Hwanung.

Historically, Chinese civilization began under the Yellow Emperor. Interestingly, his teacher, Zabu, was of the Dongyi, and he studied the Dongyi classic, as mentioned by *Baopuzi*. The Celestial Code Classic is a sacred sutra that commissioned God's authority. It also corresponds to the principle of heaven. It is the most profound teaching transmitted from the times of Hwanung to modern times. Chi-won Choi (857–900 CE), a poet and philosopher of the unified Shilla dynasty, initially recorded it.

More interesting is the fact that the Celestial Code Classic is a type of amulet and incantation. It is composed of words and speeches that communicate with the spiritual world. It is a collection of powerful energetic waves that create ripples in the universe, like an Amazon butterfly that can bring a storm to New York City with the flick of its wings.

As mentioned in the chaos theory, it corresponds to the initial variable that creates significant changes. While the Amazon butterfly creates a wave with yin-yang variance by flapping its wings, the Celestial Code Classic creates a balanced wave. Initially, the universe is a single entity. Nevertheless, when differentiated according to the yin and yang, an amulet can directly create undulations in the material (yin) or the spiritual world (yang: readers' minds or the Universal Mind), influencing the entire universe.

Unlike other amulets, the Celestial Code Classic does not influence only a single spirit with multifarious variations in yin-yang. Instead, it can move an entire pantheon of gods that represents the totality of the universe and is therefore balanced in yin-yang. Its content emphasizes yin-yang harmony to generate harmonized yin-yang waves in its readers.

The Core Number of the Celestial Code Classic Is 3

To obtain a center, one must know both poles or extremes. These poles are yin and yang. When expressed in numbers, they are 1, 2, and 3. As a number representing the middle of yin and yang, the number 3 is significant. Even the Celestial Code Classic, which expresses the common pattern of the universe with merely eighty-one (9 × 9) words, places tremendous emphasis on the number 3. It freely repeats the number eight times.

It is possible to consider Korea's culture and civilization as number 3. There are countless places to discover it, from words and speech to tools and architecture. As it goes without saying, the spiritual world directly related to Dangun expresses the number 3 in the form of three spirits (Hwanin, Hwanung, Dangun) and three truths (original nature, life, and essence). There are also the Three Treasures (Jing, Qi, Shen), three gates of a Taoist temple, a three-legged cauldron, bowing thrice, a trident, three carved birds on Sotdae, and a trident-shaped golden crown of the Shilla dynasty.

Moreover, the number 3 appears in the primitive Tao classics, such as *Samil Shingo* (Teachings of God on Three and One). It also appears in the Taoist terminologies in *Daozang* (道藏), denoting Taoist Canon, consisting of fourteen hundred texts, comparable to the *Palman Daejanggyeong* (Tripiṭaka Koreana). The composition of *Daozang* consists of almost all 3s or multiples of 3.

Koreans commonly use the number 3 as a byword for numbers. Examples include:

- "Even three mal (unit of measurement: about 9.5 kilograms) of beads must be pierced to be precious."
- "Even if the beard grows three feet, you must eat to be a yangban (aristocrat/scholarly official)."
- "Scissors, rock, and paper three times."
- "Dong Bang-sak lived three thousand gapja."[15]
- "Even a three-year-old child knows."
- "It is threefold in the eyes (vivid or attractive)."

The number 3 is also present in the structure of Hangul, the Korean alphabet. A letter consists of three tones: the initial, middle, and final. The most basic vowels are the horizontal line, "eu," corresponding to yin; the vertical line, "ee," corresponding to yang; and "alaea" (dot), which corresponds to the middle. The horizontal line, "eu," becomes an "oh" sound when combined with "alaea" above. When "alaea" is combined below, the yin sound, "woo," is produced. And together with the middle sound, "eu," they form a system of three (fig. A3.6).

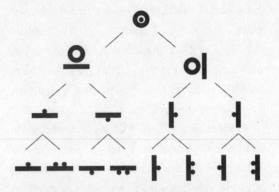

Figure A3.6 The System of Three in the Structure of Hangul, the Korean Alphabet

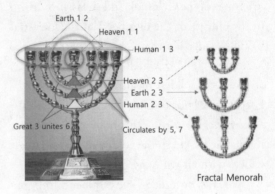

Figure A3.7 Menorah

In addition, there are countless other structures made of the number 3 besides those listed in chapter 14, "Trinity: Heaven, Earth, and Human Beings." For example, a menorah, a candelabra in the Holy of Holies, also has a structure of the number three (fig. A3.7).

The Celestial Code Classic Is the Doctrine of Mean

According to the Celestial Code Classic, the number 3, which expresses the *middle,* is the number of human beings born between heaven and earth. Therefore, it is the middle of heaven and earth and the middle of the yin and yang. Even for the I Ching, which studies the yin and yang, the ultimate goal is to attain the center, or the golden mean.

Confucius loved the I Ching. As repeatedly mentioned, he read the book so much that on three different occasions, the leather binding tore. He also desired to live in his hometown of Jiuyi (九夷). Confucius also acquired the golden mean by either directly receiving the teachings of the Celestial Code Classic or living in the culture of the number 3 of the Celestial Code Classic. He therefore got the nickname "Zhongni" (仲尼), which means "one who has attained the golden mean as a human being." Fortunately, he and his disciples wrote *The Doctrine of the Mean*. This book made it easier for people to obtain the golden mean and use it widely without studying the I Ching.

Koreans, devoted to the number 3, the core number of the Celestial Code Classic, commonly use three-letter words, such as 역 (pronounced as "Yuk," made up of ㅇ + ㅕ + ㄱ) and 학 (pronounced as "Hak," made up of ㅎ + ㅏ + ㄱ). In addition, Koreans traditionally have an excellent sense of sound.

For Confucius, directly administering the waves of the golden mean balanced in yin-yang to people's bodies was more important than explaining its significance. Therefore, he organized the *Classic of Poetry* by combining music with his knowledge of Yulryeo and Hwangjong, the Golden Bell.

Koreans have music that has gained a golden mean due to the influence of the Celestial Code Classic. Still, Han Chinese music, which uses words skewed toward the yin (Shang, corresponding to the metal element among the five tones), is high-pitched. Because the amplitude and the width are narrow, the song and performance tend to be monotonous. People who have watched the Peking Opera, a traditional Chinese opera, will understand the monotony of their vibrational world compared to the Korean *pansori*. The reason is that pansori does not lose its mid tone amid the ever-changing sound variations. The Chinese culture has lost even Confucius's ceremonies. And it is said that the musicians who led the traditional Korean imperial ritual music went to China to teach them. Clearly, the Celestial Code Classic places a great deal of emphasis on the golden mean (Hwangjong).

Along with Emperor Yao,[16] Emperor Shun, a Dongyi national, was the sage most revered by Confucius. Emperor Yao handed his throne to Emperor Shun, and although there are no written records, he must also be Dongyi. If Emperor Yao were of Han Chinese, he could not hand over the throne to Emperor Shun, a foreigner, based only on his virtue. Even in the United States, a country of immigrants, a person who is not born in the country cannot become president.

When Emperor Yao handed the throne over to Emperor Shun, he said, "Honor the essence and one, and sincerely grasp the golden mean" (維精維一, 允執厥中). These eight Chinese characters succinctly express the core idea of the eighty-one characters of the Celestial Code

Classic. It defined the essence, the foundation of the human body, and the number 1, the foundation of the universe. Furthermore, it revealed the golden mean, which everyone should practice.

The Korean Sangsuhak (a study of symbols/images and numbers, mentioned in chapter 14) practitioners demonstrate Emperor Yao's expression and the meaning of the Celestial Code Classic with yarrow (fig. A3.8) or bone sticks. These sticks are essential for calculating the image number to derive a hexagram.

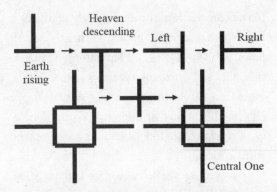

Figure A3.9 Expressing the Structure of the Universe and the Golden Mean with Yarrow Sticks

Figure A3.8 Yarrow Sticks

The following figure (fig. A3.9) forms the basis of the Chinese character "middle" (中) and the character "number" (數). The radical "female" (女) (fig. A3.10) in "number" (數) expresses disordered sticks, suggesting that the universe is chaotic, similar to the disordered sticks. Nevertheless, the "number" (數) character represents an orderly and centered universe.

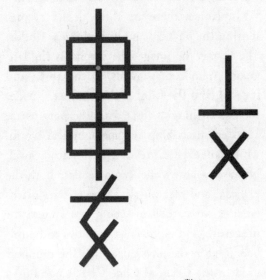

Figure A3.10 Character "Number (數)" made with Yarrow Sticks, Expressing "Center (中)," the Basis of the Universe

The Celestial Code Classic Is Basic Mathematics

The Celestial Code Classic is the foundation of mathematics. It corresponds to Tai Chi in the pyramid system of the I Ching. It is equivalent to the constitution, the parent body of all laws. Eastern mathematics books, such as *Choubei Suanjing* (籌備算经), Preparatory Calculation Classic, *Jiuzhang Suanzhu* (九章算術), Nine Chapter Arithmetic, and *Huangji Jingshi* (皇極經世), Book of Supreme World Ordering Principles, are like law books based on the constitution.

By naming visible forms, we can verbalize them. Still, only Sang, which is a system of codes, or numbers, can depict the Qi of the wave world in patterns before the creation of forms.

In Korea, there are three devices representing the physical and metaphysical worlds. The first is the image, the second is the language (phonetic symbols, ideograms, and speech), and the third is the number. Images such as I Ching's trigrams and hexagrams are a system describing the metaphysical world, while language expresses the physical world. Numbers, meanwhile, can articulate both the physical and metaphysical worlds. The mathematics we learned in school is a system for measuring and expressing quantities and numbers used in the physical world. The numbers used in the Celestial Code Classic pertain to their use in the metaphysical world.

There is a concept in Eastern philosophy known as the "void," where energy exists without any form. Each stage of how energy materializes from the void requires an appropriate term. A system of number patterns appropriately describes the first stage of materialization (differentiation). A system of image patterns, such as trigrams of I Ching, describes the state before visible form. If a visible form already ex-

ists, a language system can accurately express it. Numbers, images, and language are not different from each other. They can translate to other systems at any time. Only their suitability for use is different. The material world is not inexpressible with numbers, nor is the world of Qi indescribable with words. It is a complicated matter because it can easily lead to misunderstanding.

Here, the number system is not the system for counting and calculating things we learned while receiving a Western-style education. Instead, it is a system of numbers for expressing patterns occurring in the world of Qi before the physical form. However, it is not entirely different from the mathematics we learned. For example, the number system mentioned in the Celestial Code Classic has a dimension close to the vertex of the pyramid fractal structure of numbers. The mathematics learned in school is the operation of numbers near the pyramid's ground base.

The images representing the world before materialization are symbols such as the hexagonal star of the Israeli flag, the swastika of Buddhism, the various symbols of chemistry (e.g., C, O, H), and the trigrams and hexagrams of I Ching. They are all expressions of images that do not exist in the real world. The hexagonal stars and swastikas lack a system in a consistent pattern, but the symbols of the I Ching do not. This system is not incapable of expressing the world of matter.

Compared to the number system of the Celestial Code Classic, the symbol system of the I Ching is more advanced. The Celestial

Code Classic uses numbers up to 10, while I Ching uses sixty-four hexagrams and 384 hexagram lines. The use of large numbers, however, may not always be beneficial. While there are countless forms of language and Western-style mathematics using more digits than words, they are unsuitable for expressing Qi or mind.

The Celestial Code Classic defines each number from 0 to 10 by utilizing time (beginning and end), space (heaven, earth, and humanity), and space-time (foundation, mind, and middle). With properties of numbers, it reveals the attributes and mutual relationships, as well as their compositional and functional principles of the "heart," the core of human beings; the "sun," the center of our solar system; and the "foundation," the essence of the unified universe. In other words, with eighty-one characters, it expresses the common pattern of the formation and function of the universe. The Celestial Code Classic speaks of the Tao using intimate numbers that we can count with our fingers.

Numbers and Korean Language and Heritage

The terms from the image-number school are so pervasive in Korean that it is difficult to speak without numbers. There are so many phrases about numbers that it can be seen as the language of enlightened masters. Everything from "whether or not one has an ability or possibility," "playing tricks," "luck," "high skills," "making mistakes," to knowing one's lot—all involve the word "number" (數) in their use.

It is easy to see how enlightened the Korean ancestors were in the principles of numbers by their commonly used words, which are mathematical terms of the masters. They used mathematical terms naturally in everyday life because mathematical scripture, such as the Celestial Code Classic, was the nation's most important scripture. Hence, it can be seen from these words that there were applications of complex mathematical principles in real life. If we unravel the Celestial Code Classic according to the significance of the numbers, it is as follows:

In the beginning, the corporeal universe, 1, arises out of 0, a mass of energy without form. This single universe divides into 3, becoming heaven, earth, and humanity. In the first stage of creation (Qi phase), the creation of heaven occurred with an attribute of 1 (yang). The earth was created second with the characteristic of 2 (yin). Humanity was created third and possesses the quality of 3 (yin-yang harmony), the sum of 1 and 2. Though they divide into 3, they are not separate from each other. Due to their original nature of 1, even in the second stage (Sang or image stage—the stage between Qi and form), there are 3 that correspond to heaven, earth, and humanity (yang, yin, and the middle of yin-yang—ultimately Tai Chi) within heaven, earth, and humanity.

In the third stage (the stage of the form), the creation of humanity and all things corresponding to 3 arises by the sum of the great number 3—heaven, earth, and human beings. Here, the fundamental numbers of heaven and earth are combined. When the great number 3 of heaven and earth adds up, it becomes 6, the number of all things when I am in a state of freedom from all ideas and thoughts without any desires.

When my heart inclines toward heaven, 1, the first number of heaven, adds up to become 7. When my mind tilts toward the earth, 2, the first number of earth, adds up to become 8. But 3, the first number of harmonious human beings, combines to make 9, so all things have the attribute of 9.

All things with the attribute of 9 operate in units of 3 or 4, and 5 or 7 become cycles. For example, in the heaven (3) - earth (2) structures, added together, they become 5, and in the cold (3) - heat (4)[17] function, it is the cycle of 7. These are changes in which the number 1 mysteriously expands, emerges, and disappears in myriad forms. But the 1, the basis of the universe, does not waver (added or subtracted).

Its foundation is the mind for humans and the sun for the earth. Therefore, the mind should be held high toward the sky and illuminated like the sun so humanity can be one with the entire universe as the middle ground between heaven and earth (fig. A3.11).

This 1 disappears in form, but not forever, as it begins again as one.

Figure A3.11 Shinto Shrine, Dazaifu Tenmangu, Fukuoka, Kyushu, Japan. In Japanese shrines, prayers are held over a mirror instead of an image of God. In Japanese, God is kami, and the mirror is also kami. The mirror symbolizes the sun as well as the heart. So the king wore a mirror on his chest. This is an act that symbolizes the true nature of the heart. In comparison, if the solar system were a human body, the sun would be the heart.

Eastern symbols and numbers express the collective pattern of each dimension of the fractal system of the universe. The Celestial Code Classic and the I Ching state the same thing with differing terminologies. For example, the Tai Chi of the I Ching is number 1 in the Celestial Code Classic. The Wu Chi is the void, yin is the earth, yang is heaven, and humans are in the middle of harmony between yin and yang. Just as the I Ching speaks of fractal patterns, so does the Celestial Code Classic.

The Celestial Code Classic Is Geometry

A basic number can represent a primary figure. For example, 1 can describe a one-dimensional point or a line segment where points have gathered; 2 can illustrate a two-dimensional surface; and 3 can epitomize a three-dimensional space. Since two-dimensional surfaces and three-dimensional space consist of a set of points, we can consider them as points (1).

Of all the numbers, 1 is the first to appear after 0. Heaven refers to the universe, corresponding to 1, because it was the first to be created. Since everything starts from a point, it can be called 1. Therefore, 1 can be configured as a point, and heaven represents a point among all things in the universe.

The next number created after 1 is 2, and it is the first number paired with 1. Without considering the numbers greater than 2, we cannot think of 2 without 1, so 1 is included within 2. Earth, the second largest among all things in the universe, created after the universe and paired with it, corresponds to the number 2. The number 2 represents a plane formed by two or more line segments generated by points.

The number after 2 is 3, and 3 cannot exist alone without the concept of 1 and 2. So 3 includes 1 and 2. Space is created based on points and planes. So 3 manifests as space; humans fall under this among all things in the universe. From a human perspective, the three major elements of the universe are heaven, earth, and human beings. Sequentially arranged, heaven is 1, the earth is 2, and humanity is 3.

The Tao Te Ching states that 3 creates all things in the universe. As 3 is the number of myriad things, it is appropriate to consider it the number of humanity because humans best represent all things between heaven and earth. Thus, instead of using only the character ren (人), which means "human," the character gan (間), meaning "between heaven and earth," is added to represent humans truly. Therefore, calling a person a "ren gan" rather than just "ren" connotes the meaning of the number 3, which includes humans and all things of the universe.

The Celestial Code Classic is commonly known as the principle of the circle (圓), the square (方), and the triangle (角). Modifying and combining the primary figures of circles, squares, and triangles can represent the form of any object, just as numbers countable with fingers can express the universe. Thus, numbers and basic shapes are interchangeable.

For example, 1 is a less differentiated state and is a shape that expands or contracts, so it is a circle. The number 2 is a shape with two line segments opposing each other, so it is a rectangle. Finally, 3 is a shape that simultaneously has opposition, contraction, and expansion and becomes a triangle. Thus, the Celestial Code Classic considers heaven as a circle, the earth as a square, and humans as a triangle. Since we can draw heaven, the earth, and the human forms in such a way, it is something even children can instinctively understand.

Furthermore, the phrase "circular heaven and square earth," commonly used in Eastern classics, is derived from the Celestial Code Classic.

A pyramid is the most harmonious combination of a circle, square, and triangle, best expressing the principles of the universe mentioned in the Celestial Code Classic. The tomb of King Jangsu[18] and about ten thousand stone mound tombs in its vicinity from the Goguryeo dynasty[19] are all in the shape of pyramids and embody the principle of the Celestial Code Classic (fig. A3.12).

On the pyramid, the top vertex is 1, the heaven; the square in the horizontal section is 2, the earth; and the triangle in the vertical segment is 3, humanity. The Celestial Code Classic expresses this as "Arising from One, Heaven represents One, Earth represents Two, and Humanity represents Three."

Three pyramids manifest when we horizontally divide a pyramid into thirds ("In the second division, Heaven, Earth, and Humanity all embrace Three."). The basic pattern of the

Figure A3.12 The Tomb of King Jangsu, Tonghua, Jilin, China

universe consists of circles, squares, and triangles before the emergence of forms. It is evident from the pyramid figure that the same patterns are inherent in the heavens, the earth, and humanity after the emergence of forms.

The core principle of the Celestial Code Classic is also expressed in the decorative treasure sword excavated near the tomb of King Michu of Shilla[20] (fig. A3.13). On the sword are three distinct trinity symbols, each representing heaven, earth, and humanity. In each trinity symbol, heaven, earth, and humanity are there. Thus, these trinity symbols represent the trinity within each of heaven, earth, and humanity in the second stage of differentiation. They express the statement, "In the second division, Heaven, Earth, and Humanity all embrace Three."

Around the border of the trinity symbol, twenty-eight marbles on the top and bottom represent the twenty-eight constellations in the sky. Therefore, there are seven constellations in four directions—east, west, north, and south—forming seven cycles. This is "Everything moves according to Three and Four, leading to the cycles of Five and Seven." Finally, there are nine beads to the right and left, indicating the number of heaven, earth, and humanity of three Sam-Taegeuks.

The shape of the golden crown from the Shilla Cheonmachong (Heaven Horse Tomb), a tumulus located in Gyeongju, Korea, also shows the basic principle of the Celestial Code Classic (fig. A3.14). Three branches extend upward around a circular tube worn on the head, and two bead lines descend below. The circular tube represents heaven, the two rows of

Figure A3.13 Decorative Treasure Sword Found Near the Tomb of King Michu, National Museum of Korea, Seoul, Korea

Figure A3.14 Golden Crown from the Shilla Cheonmachong, National Museum of Korea, Seoul, Korea

beads that descend represent the soft ground, and the three branches that shoot up represent humans. The one branch in the middle and two on each side represent the trinity principle within humans. The lateral branch divides into two in the shape of an antler. This signifies the earth among humans. Human branches add up to three (center, left, and right) or five (center, two on each side). The middle branch represents heaven among humans and is made up of three, showing three nodes in the shape of a mountain. They display the fractal structure of I Ching and the Celestial Code Classic.

"Leading to the cycles of Five and Seven" is one of the passages in the Celestial Code Classic that is difficult to understand when viewed in mathematical terms. But when viewed as figures, it is easy to comprehend.

The stars in the sky are brighter and bigger than the sun. Thus, one could assume it would be brighter and hotter on a multistar night. But why isn't that the case? One scholar said the stars are appropriately distanced and arranged in a fractal form, as shown in the following diagram (fig. A3.15). If you look at this from a flat plane, you will see five points (left diagram), and if you look at it three-dimensionally, you will see seven points (right diagram). These are the points in the circle formed by the movement of the triangle (3) and the square (4). So if you connect the seven dots, it becomes the Big Dipper, believed to be an object governing the universe in Korean folk beliefs.

The diagram on the left is the primary figure of the Celestial Code Classic. The center dot represents 1, the two points on the top/bottom and left/right represent 2, and three points, including the center, represent 3. The middle dot is usually called an Are. It is an egg in animals, and in plants, it is a seed. Together, they are called Seeare (seed-egg). The egg of the mind is called Ul (soul).

The center dot can either expand and develop into an outer triangle, square, or circle or constrict and degenerate into a point. Humans repeat life and death (the process of creating seeds by gathering all human information), and the universe repeats expansion and contraction. The diagrams show this process. The Celestial Code Classic describes expansion as "One expands in mysterious ways, emerging and dis-

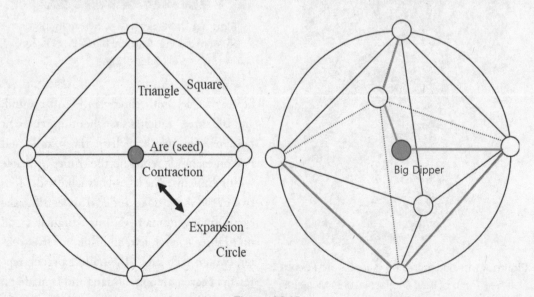

Figure A3.15

appearing in perpetual cycles." The repetition of life and death, expansion and contraction is expressed as "one beginning and one ending."

Changes Made by the Fundamental Numbers 1, 2, and 3

The first part of the Celestial Code Classic defines the formation of the universe and the primary numbers. Then, from the middle part, the text elaborates on how the numbers function and operate relative to the physical universe. Among them, there is a statement, "Everything moves according to Three [yang number] and Four [yin number], leading to the cycles of Five and Seven."

Still, it is not a familiar concept in the I Ching or other image-number books. So it is challenging to understand. But a careful examination of what is happening in the real world around us shows that this statement holds very well. In particular, even the experts of I Ching did not know the background of the creative principle of the twelve meridians that suddenly appeared in *The Yellow Emperor's Inner Classic*.

1. A SYSTEM FORMED BY THREE (YANG) AND FOUR (YIN):

- I Ching hexagrams: vertically (yang) in ternary (three, six), horizontally (yin) in binary (two, four)
- Pyramid: vertically (yang) in the triangle, horizontally (yin) in the square
- Yutpan (fig. A3.16): a three-point structure in four directions

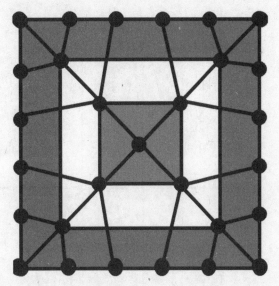

Figure A3.16 Yutpan: Three-point Structure in Four Directions

- Dongyi's architecture (pyramid structure): a three-story, rectangular building
- The basic structure of DNA: a codon with three paired bases, four types of bases
- Human figure: four-segment vertebrae spinal column (cervical, thoracic, lumbar, sacral) and three-segmented torso (chest, upper abdomen, lower abdomen)
- Each of the four fingers consists of three joints. The fortune tellers count these twelve joints with their thumbs to calculate the ten celestial stems and twelve terrestrial branches—heaven and earth operating segments.
- The basic structure of twelve meridians (fig. A3.17): three cycles of four meridians
  - Hand Taiyin (Greater Yin) Lung channel → Hand Yangming (Bright Yang) Large

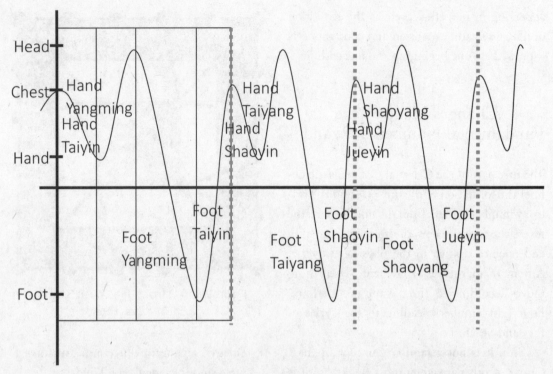

Figure A3.17 Operation of the Numbers 3 and 4 in Acupuncture Meridians

Intestine channel → Foot Yangming (Bright Yang) Stomach channel → Foot Taiyin (Greater Yin) Spleen channel

o Hand Shaoyin (Lesser Yin) Heart channel → Hand Taiyang (Greater Yang) Small Intestine channel → Foot Taiyang (Greater Yang) Bladder channel → Foot Shaoyin (Lesser Yin) Kidney channel

o Hand Jueyin (Declining Yin) Pericardium channel → Hand Shaoyang (Lesser Yang) Triple Burner channel → Foot Shaoyang (Lesser Yang) Gall Bladder channel → Foot Jueyin (Declining Yin) Liver channel

♦ The fundamental structure of space: three axes (x, y, z) and four cross-sectional areas

♦ The general shape of a house: triangular-shaped roof, rectangular walls

♦ The fundamental structure of a year: four seasons made up of three months

♦ The fundamental structure of twelve terrestrial branches: pig/rat/cow—water element; tiger/rabbit/dragon—wood element; snake/horse/sheep—fire element; and monkey/chicken/dog—metal element

♦ A common denominator of time is three and four: twelve months, twenty-four solar terms, twenty-four hours, sixty minutes, sixty seconds

2. THE CIRCULATORY SYSTEM ESTABLISHED BY FIVE AND SEVEN:

Those that go around to make a circular pattern have a cycle of five or seven. The Celestial Code Classic calls it "leading to the cycles of Five and Seven."

- In the twenty-four solar terms (seasonal days), each term consists of three "hou" (weather cycles). Since one solar term is fifteen days, one hou is five days. Also, two cycles of three cold and four warm[21] is one solar term. So three cycles of five days make one solar term.
- One month has twenty-eight days in the lunar calendar, and four cycles of seven days are a month.
- In the sky, there is the sun, the moon, and the five planets of Mars, Mercury, Jupiter, Venus, and Saturn, which preside over changes in the universe (known as governing by seven). The week is modeled after this cycle of change.
- In the Northern Hemisphere sky, there are twenty-eight stars, seven stars each on four sides, centered on the North Star. Seven constellations change in one season. Four cycles of seven-star units equal one year.
- The seven stars of the Big Dipper, a basic pattern of twenty-eight constellations, were incorporated into the Buddhist shrine consecrated to the Big Dipper as an object of the Korean people's faith.
- Fifty-two cycles of a week (seven days) becomes one year.
- The human head exchanges Qi with the universe through seven orifices, and the heart expresses seven emotions through seven arteries and veins (two superior and inferior vena cava, two pulmonary arteries, aorta, and two pulmonary veins).
- The five transportative energies are the cycle of the universe, and the five elements are the cycle of all things.
- Humans have two hands with five fingers each, and two feet with five toes each.
- There are five Zang or solid organs in the body and five transporting points on the meridians that circulate Qi in the body's interior and exterior.

The Celestial Code Classic as a Self-Cultivation Method

The critical point of the Celestial Code Classic is that one must unite with the universe within oneself by upholding and illuminating the mind, the essence of the universe, since humanity is equated with heaven. To the Tibetans who worshipped the god Tengri, this was the realization of the Great Self. To the Jewish people, who could be the descendants of Fuxi's wife, Nuwa (Yeowa in Korean), humans were created in the image of God. They were taught to believe in themselves as God, have a generous mind (big heart) like God, and love the entire universe as your body. (I am in the Father, and the Father is in me [John 14:11]).

The Celestial Code Classic validates the appropriateness of such teachings through the concept of numbers. It unfolds the logic in the following way:

Everything began from 1, implying that everything started from the void. So this 1 divides into 3 poles, but it does not deviate from its foundation.

1 divides into 3. At the beginning (1), it differentiates into heaven with the nature of 1 (the whole and yang in regards to 2). Next, it divides into the earth with the nature of 2 (yin). Finally, it divides into humans with the nature of 3 between heaven and earth. Since humans were made by dividing 1, like heaven and earth, they are equal to heaven.

Even if 1 increases to 10, it does not stop increasing as if it is in a crate but increases further, with the pattern changing in units of 3.

Heaven embodies the nature of 3, the pattern of the whole, which is secondary differentiation from 1. Earth and humans also have the nature of 3. Thus, heaven and the earth, represented by 3 and 1, also exist in humans.

The great 3 of heaven and earth add up to 6. Adding 1 (heaven—yang) of humans to this results in 7; 2 (earth—yin) results in 8; and 3 (human—middle) results in 9. According to the yin-yang inclinations of the human mind, heaven, earth, and all things vary in their appearances.

Constituents with the properties of 3 and 4 operate alternately to form a cycle of 5 or 7. But this, too, is just 1 functioning in a different form.

Myriad substances and phenomena constantly emerge and disappear. Yet this is simply a change in their usage, not their foundation, just as trees' leaves emerge in spring and wither in fall, while their roots remain the same.

That foundation is the mind and, like the sun of this world, becomes the root of all changes. Therefore, it should be held high up to the heavens and illuminated like the sun, to unite with 1, the foundation of the universe within humans.

The 1 within that mind also ends, and the 1 that ends is the void. At once, it will begin again as 1.

Without an in-depth study of the Celestial Code Classic, many questions can arise regarding the meaning of the binary system of I Ching and the number of hexagrams made up of two three-lined trigrams. It is not possible to achieve a proper understanding of Eastern studies without knowledge of the I Ching. Likewise, a study of the I Ching cannot be complete without reading the Celestial Code Classic.

Master Tae-hoon Kwon and Master Jae-hyung Lee

Dr. David S. Lee studied extensively with two masters in Korea, Master Tae-hoon Kwon and Master Jae-hyung Lee. What follows is an account of his experience with both of them.

Master Tae-hoon Kwon

Before the reign of Emperor Qin Shi Huang, Chinese people believed that the "Three Immortals" lived east of the Bohai Gulf on the east coast of China. There is a reference to this in the ancient book *Shanhajing* (山海經), *Classic of Mountains and Seas.* The Yellow Emperor, the founder of Chinese civilization, wrote *The Yellow Emperor's Inner Classic.* Ge Hong (283–343 CE), an alchemist and scholar, wrote *Baopuzi, One Who Embraces Simplicity.* It is a Chinese classic featuring inner alchemy and the accomplishments of Taoist masters. In the

book, he explains that the Yellow Emperor studied Tao under the guidance of an Immortal of Baektusan, or "White-Head Mountain."

The Chinese people call White-Head Mountain Changbaishan, meaning "ever-white mountain," and worship it just as much as Koreans do. The Korean anthem begins with the word "Paektusan" or "White-Head Mountain," so it's easy to see Koreans' reverence for it.

Master Kwon inherited the Tao tradition of the immortals of White-Head Mountain. It was the time when Dr. Lee went to college. Though the term "Qi" appears in *The Yellow Emperor's Inner Classic,* he had difficulty feeling it. Consequently, he sought many masters to learn to "feel" this Qi through Tao cultivation. Then one day, while gathering the Qi into the Danjun to refine it, Dr. Lee could not regulate the fire generated from the Qi and fell ill. As a result, he went to Master Kwon for the first time to treat his illness. At the time,

Master Kwon was more than eighty years old. Yet, despite his age, he had no wrinkles on his face, and with his long white hair and beard, he resembled a Taoist immortal.

Master Kwon taught Dr. Lee several breathing methods and a concentration technique called Wonsangbup (Original Imaging Method),[1] similar to the clairvoyant technique. He also instructed Dr. Lee on how to make herbal medicine that would help increase the body's power by twofold, fourfold, or tenfold.

Wonsangbup involves sitting quietly and mentally focusing on the depths of the forehead, commonly referred to as the third eye, and mentally writing the text summarizing the essence of I Ching. For beginners, the first stroke they draw usually disappears when they try to write the next. It is no easy task to hold the first stroke in mind without it vanishing while engraving the next letter in its entirety. By the time one can complete the writing of the complete text like a tombstone inscription, the letters disappear. Instead, something similar to a movie screen appears in their place. This screen is similar to a Western fortune teller's crystal ball, so whatever one wants can be seen like a movie screen.

Depending on one's level of training, the screen's resolution level varies. For instance, if the person has been training diligently, it will be as clear as a high-resolution computer screen. Once he or she attains a certain degree of mastery, it is easier to see current events, slightly more challenging to see past events, and extremely difficult to see future events. The difficulty lies in how much of a time difference there is to the present moment.

Master Kwon frequently spoke of the legendary stories dating back some four thousand years. He relayed the stories in such detail and spoke so realistically that all the students joked he must be watching it play on the screen in his head. Master Kwon also told of past-life stories. In his immediate past life, he was a woman who was an oracle and lived in China. Master Kwon visited the town he saw on the mental screen as a young man. He disclosed who he was—a descendant of the house. The oldest person there asked, "Which room did you live in? Bring the brush you used often and write. What were your daily habits?" and so on. When he replied based on what he saw on the screen, the oldest person said, "You were my grandmother," and then gathered family members to bow to pay their respects.

Master Kwon also told a fascinating story about his experience before Korea's liberation from Japan in 1945. When he was young, Korea was the subject of Japanese occupation. Japanese invasions of Southeast Asia were in full swing. Interested in how far Japan would expand its territory and when it would come to its demise, Master Kwon could see it clearly on the screen. So he marked what he saw on the map but did not give it much meaning. Later he was arrested for financially supporting the independence movement. A Japanese detective who searched his house happened to find the map. Upon learning that the map was identical to their secret map, they added the charge of espionage, and he was tortured and sentenced to life in prison. He was finally released when Japan lost the war.

When he focused on why Japan collapsed, he saw two planes fly in and drop bombs. A mushroom cloud appeared immediately. When he tried to figure out what the bomb was, the person who made the atomic bomb came out and explained it to him in Korean. His explanation was so simple that Master Kwon was able to understand it. He also said that if Master Kwon had a good understanding of nuclear physics, he could teach him how to make an atomic bomb in no time.

These abilities are merely a technique called clairvoyance and do not indicate the Tao's full attainment. Magic is an aspect of God's power utilized by humans. When a person formally cultivates the Tao, he or she will acquire this ability incidentally, but if the person trains for it exclusively, it is as dangerous as a child holding a sword. Master Kwon repeatedly warned his students against this technique's selfish and evil use and its dire consequences.

Master Kwon first learned breathing techniques from his mother. When he first learned to read books, his mother said he should have a clear mind and taught him proper breathing. Then one day, while reading a book, Master Kwon saw the book's last page. After that, he could memorize a book's entire content from that day forward as if he were taking photographs of it. After that, he rapidly committed to his memory more than ten thousand books.

Whenever Master Kwon told the story about the miracles performed by his seniors, he described them in such a clear and vivid manner that it was as though the event had just occurred. The words spoken were not those of an eighty-two-year-old. The accomplishments of Master Kwon's seniors were as remarkable as if they came out of a Chinese kung fu movie. Unlike a worn-out old cliché, they were fascinating real-life stories of extraordinary supernatural powers never seen in books or movies.

Chukjibeop, the magic art of shortening spaces, usually describes a rapid walking technique. To reduce wind resistance, one turns the body sideways so that the shoulder is facing forward. Both arms simultaneously rise and fall as one walks to deepen breathing and maximize lung function. Stance is lowered by deep bending of the knees and pushing off strongly with the feet. If you actually try to walk in such a position, you will experience that it is more efficient than running. Master Kwon said that one time the Japanese cavalry chased after Korean independent fighters who marched with Chukjibeop, and they had to give up their chase, defeated in the act.

The consumption of certain substances enhances the training process. For instance, mica increases lung capacity, and the blood of the chicken raised consuming copper and iron increases strength in the legs. In addition, these methods allow red blood cells to carry even more oxygen and nutrients in terms of physiology.

The medicines that increase strength twofold, fourfold, or tenfold are minerals. However, since many of these minerals are toxic, it is first necessary to remove their toxicity before forging the desired elements to make them safe for consumption.

The stories of Korean ascetics told by Master Kwon were more interesting than the Chinese martial arts novels or movies. The future of Korea seen through the Original Imaging Method was so inspiring that Dr. Lee asked him to make the stories into a book. But Master Kwon refused by saying that it was not the right time. Subsequently, he permitted a writer to chronicle his story while many students were busy with their school studies and could not visit him frequently. As a result, the story became a novel and bestseller, setting off a boom in studying internal alchemy in Korea.

Although Master Kwon did not directly teach I Ching to his students, its theories overflowed in his words and actions. So the students naturally learned I Ching. Although Dr. Lee could not be at Master Kwon's bedside at his passing, he never felt that Master Kwon really left. He can still see his master anytime he desires, though not as clearly as he would like, through the old TV screen given to him by Master Kwon.

After his passing, Dr. Lee went to White-Head Mountain, thinking perhaps Master Kwon's disciples or students still lived there. Fortunately, Master Kwon's guidance enabled him to find a person. When he was young, the man was a border patrol officer at White-Head Mountain. He recounted his story with Master Kwon.

One day, he was dispatched into the forest to investigate reports of an old man illegally hunting bears. When he arrived at the scene, he saw a man picking pine nuts off the top of pine trees, jumping from one to another like a squirrel. Once he came down, the old man recognized the patrol officer as a Korean and told him to come to visit him at his home, showing him where it was on a military map. He detected that the old man was not ordinary and soon paid him a visit and subsequently became his student. The old man was a senior student who had studied under the same teacher as Master Kwon, and the Tao he learned was the same as that of the Yellow Emperor, who learned from the teacher Zabu while traveling to Qinggu.

The former patrol officer explained that the old man loved drinking wine. However, the wine he stored in a crock pot was always full, no matter how much he drank. Whenever a pub in a nearby town poured the wine, it was immediately transported to his pot. From the mountain, if he wanted to eat sushi, he was able to catch a fish from the sea two hundred kilometers away. Before the old man's passing away at 103 years of age, the patrol officer entered a treasure warehouse within White-Head Mountain with the old man and flew in a flying saucer. They could visit Korea freely, even though he wasn't allowed to visit Korea at that time as a Chinese citizen. They traveled to various areas of Korea under the Japanese reign.

Inside the flying saucer, there was no mechanical or actuating system. Instead, it functioned according to the riders' minds. The flying saucer merely provided physical protection for their bodies. Since the radar could not detect the flying saucer, they were free to fly anywhere they wanted.

Master Kwon helped tremendously in writing this book. Before leaving for the United

States to study science, Dr. Lee could not visit Master Kwon. One day before his departure, Dr. Lee visited Fifth Street in Jongro, Seoul, where many Eastern medical clinics lined the road, to purchase supplies. It was around dusk when he suddenly spotted Master Kwon walking toward him. Dr. Lee tried to approach him and say goodbye, but his feet didn't move, and he could not speak. Then, while Dr. Lee was in a state of surprise, Master Kwon quickly disappeared. Dr. Lee believes that perhaps Master Kwon knew he would not see him while alive, so he briefly showed himself one last time. Still, Master Kwon would provide ideas whenever Dr. Lee deeply pondered a problem, even after that time. For example, when Dr. Lee faced an unsolvable problem and utilized the Original Imaging Method, Master Kwon would appear and provide the needed answer. At other times, Master Kwon would place the required material into Dr. Lee's hands even before he knew he needed it.

Master Jae-hyung Lee

During the Japanese reign over Korea, Master Lee was to graduate as the valedictorian of an elite high school in Japan. However, the day before graduation, the principal called Master Lee into his office and said that the high school could not have a Korean graduate with the highest honors. In addition, the principal told him that if he conceded and took second place, he would be permitted to study abroad in the United States. Master Lee took the offer and left to study in the United States. He subsequently received a doctorate in law and lectured at Sorbonne University in France.

While he was leading a busy life as a very competent prosecutor after returning to Korea, a blind acquaintance from Master Lee's hometown came to recommend that "Someone as smart as you must learn Eastern studies." Master Lee replied, "Eastern studies has plunged into the world of fiction and is not practical learning. So there is no need to study it." But the blind person insisted, "If I chant a spell and move a rock from that mountain and drop it here in this yard, would you believe that Eastern studies are practical?" To that, Master Lee immediately replied, "Yes."

The blind man uttered the incantation, and the rock virtually dropped right in front of Master Lee's foot. He then pleaded with the blind man to become the man's student. However, the blind man said he learned from Master Lee's uncle, so he should study directly from him.

Afterward, Master Lee dug two caves in the mountain behind his house, one for a library and the other to dwell in. To find rare books unavailable in Korea, he even went through every nook and corner of a rural village in China in search of them.

When Dr. Lee first met Master Lee, his physical features did not impress him. He was small in stature and not handsome by any standard. Yet Dr. Lee knew from how his eyes glistened that he was not an ordinary person. According to people around him, Master Lee's head contained tens of thousands of ancient

Chinese texts. When he lectured, he'd always write Chinese characters on the board and explain them, and the content was always extremely interesting.

Master Lee's lectures on Eastern medicine were the highest level of knowledge that Dr. Lee had ever heard, even though Dr. Lee had studied various Eastern medical classics. He was always impressed when listening to Master Lee's lectures. Dr. Lee could only comprehend less than 50 percent of what Master Lee taught. Nonetheless, what he understood was always new. Furthermore, there was no way of knowing the source of his materials.

Dr. Lee had researched all annotations on the Suwen (Simple Questions), a part of *The Yellow Emperor's Inner Classic*. But Master Lee's lectures on the topic were remarkably profound compared to the successive generation of exegetists. Moreover, he explained in diverse ways—for instance, understanding each phrase through the literal interpretation method, or as a part of the Taoist cultivation method, or breaking down or disassembling each character into radical elements and interpreting through I Ching—known as the Paza method.

A large portion of the Suwen is on the subject of the Five Transportative Energies and Six Climatic Energies. It is a complicated subject matter as its content is mathematical and astronomical. The annotations by the generations of exegetists are very confusing, but Master Lee's interpretation was unambiguous. Dr. Lee has seen annotations by renowned scholars of China

and Japan on *The Yellow Emperor's Inner Classic*. But the difference was similar to comparing a PhD scholar with an elementary student. Dr. Lee began his studies with Master Lee later than other disciples. The other disciples said the teacher's secret came from the library next door. But no one had ever been inside the library, and there was even a student who waited for Master Lee's death to gain access.

Since Master Lee studied law, he was utterly unfamiliar with natural science. However, the more Dr. Lee delved into Eastern studies, the more he realized he had to know science to better understand them. Around this time, Dr. Lee realized that numerous things could be discovered by reading books alone without a teacher. So he informed Master Lee he would study Western medicine in America. Master Lee was sad to see him go, but he said Dr. Lee should still proceed.

Dr. Lee still remembers the way Master Lee gave a lecture. While chain-smoking cigarettes soaked and dried in a special medicine he developed, he mentioned he needed to smoke as a contrary treatment to stay healthy since the body's physiology reverses in the cave. Still fresh in Dr. Lee's memory was every Thursday when Master Lee took out a wrinkled suit from the closet in the den, paired it with a fedora hat, and went down the mountain using a cane. It was to give a law lecture at the University of Maryland branch school inside the US military barracks.

Master Lee is said to have succeeded in the left-wing practice of Tao cultivation in Korea.

In Tao cultivation, there are right-wing and left-wing schools. The right-wing method mainly consists of breathing techniques and meditation cultivation to achieve enlightenment. In contrast, the left-wing practice primarily consists of cultivation using incantation, charms, and I Ching numerology.

Master Lee always carried a ghost with him. When there was something he didn't know, he would ask the ghost questions. Sometimes they had a very intense discussion about learning, and then other times, they fought and despised each other.

Master Lee's disciples, feeling pity that he had to live without a stove inside the cave in cold weather, installed a briquette-burning Korean floor system. Master Lee accepted the offer despite not liking it, out of fear that the disciples would catch a cold while learning in the crypt.

Soon after, Master Lee suffered a stroke, attributed to the ghost attacking him after being severely reprimanded for misconduct. The ghost apologized and wrote an herbal prescription as Master Lee lay in bed due to the stroke. Unfortunately, he refused to take the formula, as it didn't conform to the traditional Eastern medical theory. However, after the ghost strongly recommended it, Master Lee eventually took the medicine and was healed. It was a miraculous recovery.

There was a student who closely observed and served Master Lee. One morning when it snowed heavily, Dr. Lee visited Master Lee at his cave to see how he was doing. Unfortunately, he had already left at midnight for a family memorial service held in Mount Taebaek, some 130 kilometers away from Seoul. Nevertheless, despite the heavy blizzard, he went there because it was a gathering of all family members. The student told Dr. Lee he was afraid that Master Lee, using the Distance Shortening Technique, might fall and injure himself upon his arrival in the mountains.

Dr. Lee once worked as an Eastern medical doctor at a mining town deep in the mountains. There was a valley where only shamans lived. After much difficulty, he acquired a book that described various magical or witchcraft techniques, such as carrying a child ghost, taking out precious goods from a drawing on paper, incantations, and many others. When he showed the book to Master Lee, he smiled and said that as a young man, he had tried all the techniques and that they worked. He once drew a door to the warehouse, opened it, and took out a good. It was taboo to enter the door, but when he did, he was in someone's warehouse. However, Master Lee warned Dr. Lee not to focus on magic and witchcraft, as they would impede his progress in Tao cultivation.

One time, Dr. Lee returned to Korea but could not obtain a reentry visa to the United States and had to wait one year. Witnessing this, fellow disciples asked Master Lee if he could go to the United States without a visa using the Distance Shortening Technique. He said it was possible not with the Distance Shortening Technique but by the "Throw of Gods." However, he told Dr. Lee that he could not go there because it was too far away, and he had to go to Hawaii first and then to the US mainland. Master Lee calculated with his fingers a state beyond time-space called Kongmang, or "Void," where no force, including gravity, can affect humans. It seems that Master Lee expressed calculating the proper opening time to the fourth-dimension gate mentioned in the science fiction movies and novels, like *Doctor Strange* and *A Wrinkle in Time*, and entering it to travel to the United States as the "Throw of Gods."

Select Bibliography

English

Bentov, Itzhak. *Stalking the Wild Pendulum*. Rochester, NY: Destiny Books, 1988.

Capra, Fritjof. *Tao of Physics*. Boston: Shambhala Publications, 1975.

Deng, Liangyue et al. *Chinese Acupuncture and Moxibustion*. Beijing: Foreign Languages Press, 1987.

Fung, Yu-lan. *A Short History of Chinese Philosophy*. New York: Free Press, 1966.

Garvy, John W., Jr. *Yin and Yang: Two Hands Clapping*. Newtonville, MA: Wellbeing Books, 1985.

Hawking, Stephen. *A Brief History of Time*. New York: Bantam Books, 1990.

Huang, Alfred. *The Complete I Ching*. Rochester, NY: Inner Traditions, 1998.

Liu, Jilin. *Chinese Dietary Therapy*. New York: Churchill Livingstone, 1995.

Lu, Henry C. *Chinese System of Food Cures*. New York: Sterling Publishing, 1986.

Palmer, Martin. *Yin & Yang: Understanding the Chinese Philosophy of Opposites and How to Apply It to Your Everyday Life*. London: Piatkus Books, 1997.

Pitchfold, Paul. *Healing with Whole Foods*. Berkeley, CA: North Atlantic Books, 1993.

Robertson, Robin. *Beginner's Guide to Jungian Psychology*. York Beach, ME: Nicolas-Hays, 1992.

Taylor, Jill Bolte. *My Stroke of Insight*. London: Penguin Books, 2006.

Tierra, Michael. *The Way of Herbs*. New York: Pocket Books, 1998.

Walter, Katya. *Tao of Chaos*. Boston: Element Books, 1996.

Wilhelm, Richard. *I Ching. Third Edition,* Princeton, NJ: Princeton University Press, 1990.

Wong, Eva. *Taoism: An Essential Guide*. Boston: Shambhala Publications, 1997.

Zukav, Gary. *The Dancing Wu Li Masters*. New York: HarperCollins, 2009.

Korean

Choi, Wan-sik. *I Ching*. Seoul: Hyewon Publishing, 1998.

Chun, Chang-sun, and Yoon-hyung Uh. *What Is Yin and Yang?* Seoul: Seki Publishing, 1994.

———, *What Are Five Elements?* Seoul: Seki Publishing, 1994.

Han, Kyu-sung. *Discourse on the Principles of I Ching*. Seoul: Eastern Culture Publishing, 1989.

Kim, Hong-kyung. *Self-Healing*. Seoul: Shikmoolchoojang Publications, 2000.

Shin, Jae-yong. *Strengthen Sexual Energies in Men*. Seoul: Doongji Publications, 1994.

Notes

Introduction

1. Actually, *Journey to the West* is one of the top literary works of all time in China and one of the three most important books of Taoism.

1. Tao

1. Burton Watson, *The Complete Works of Chuang Tzu* (New York: Columbia University Press, 1968), 240–41.
2. Katya Walter, *Tao of Chaos* (Boston: Element Books, 1996), 147.

4. Yin and Yang of Human Beings

1. Eastern physiognomy discovers a person's nature and destiny by analyzing the shape of eyes, ears, nose, and mouth as well as the whole face, according to the principles of the I Ching. It is similar to Western palm reading (palmistry).

5. Yin and Yang of Sex

1. John W. Garvy, *Yin and Yang: Two Hands Clapping*, vol. 2 (Newtonville: Wellbeing Books, 1985), 8.

2. Ibid.
3. Considered one of the top three traditional sex manuals in the world, along with *Kama Sutra* and *The Perfumed Garden*.

6. Yin and Yang of the Brain

1. Jill Bolte Taylor, *My Stroke of Insight* (London: Penguin Books, 2006).

11. Yin and Yang of Music

1. Don Campbell, *The Mozart Effect* (New York: Avon Books, 1997), 82–83.
2. Ibid., 14.

14. Trinity: Heaven, Earth, and Human Beings

1. Robin Robertson, *Beginner's Guide to Jungian Psychology* (York Beach, ME: Nicolas-Hays, 1992), 17.
2. Ibid., 38.
3. The founder of ancient Korea in the year 2333 BCE and god-king. He is known around the world as Tengri Khan.

16. Sasang Medicine

1. Stephen Hawking, *A Brief History of Time* (New York: Bantam Books, 1990), 59.

2. The Four Books are *The Great Learning, The Doctrine of the Mean, The Analects,* and *Mencius.*

17. The Five-Element Theory

1. NMR spectroscopy: Every atom, with its varying axis, spins independently. Due to such differing spins, different atoms possess different magnetic natures. Their central axes align when a strong magnetic field is applied. Once given a high-frequency radio wave that resonates with hydrogen atoms that are uniformly aligned, their central axes tilt 90 degrees. Then they slowly return to their original positions while emitting energy. Each atom has a different return speed according to what it bonds to in its surroundings and its surrounding state. A wave can be determined by measuring the energy released as each atom returns to its original axis over time. The molecular structure can be determined once this wave is analyzed. A cross-sectional image of an object can be obtained by dividing the image into 64 × 64 pixels and then showing the light intensity for each pixel. This is called MRI (magnetic resonance imaging). When this analysis is related to the five elements instead of determining the chemical structure, its five-element relationship will be discovered.

2. Nine palaces: just as adding the earth element to Sasang makes the five elements, adding the central palace to the eight trigrams creates nine palaces.

18. The Five Zang Organs and the Five Elements

1. The original image is not the image seen from my own point of view, but the image seen from the perspective of the Holy Spirit of the universe. We have said that if there is a yin, there is a corresponding yang. If there is a cosmic form (yin), there is a nervous system (yang) that controls the universe. This nervous system is connected to my nervous system. The Original Imaging Method involves viewing the original image from the perspective of the universal nervous system without seeing it directly. If you practice the Wonsangbup, you can see images that transcend time and space. You can see the image you want through the cosmic vision of the universal nervous system, just like searching the internet in one universe.

2. Though all types of rice belong to the earth element, brown rice is most tilted to the water element due to its darker color.

19. The Five Elements of Diagnosis

1. Together with Mingmen, or the Gate of Life, the Triple Burner is one of the internal organs that only exist functionally and is without form. In the operation of life, it is a general term for the function of transformation and transportation, digestion and assimilation, and elimination.

22. Arrangements and Applications of the Eight Trigrams

1. Needham, Joseph, *Science and Civilisation in China,* vol. 4 (Cambridge: Cambridge University Press, 1962) 155.

Appendix 1

1. The Four Books are *The Great Learning, The Doctrine of the Mean, The Analects,* and *Mencius.* The Three Classics are *Classic of Poetry, Book of Documents,* and I Ching.

2. Located about three hundred kilometers east of Beijing, China.

3. Mencius, *Mencius,* Book 4, Li Lau, part 2 (New York: Dover Publications, Inc., 1970) p. 316. Mencius (372–289 BCE) was a great Chinese philosopher, who inherited and expanded Confucius's philosophy.

4. Emperor Shun (d. 2184 BCE) was a legendary sage-ruler of ancient China.

5. Swedish mathematician Helge von Koch introduced the Koch snowflake construction in 1904. In a zig-zag pattern, four equal-length segments replace each line segment of an equilateral triangle. Self-replicating and infinitely complex shapes result from this iterative process. Von Koch's work significantly contributed to fractal geometry advancement.

6. Incoherent light emits diffuse light waves with differing frequency, wavelength, and phase. Coherent light, in contrast, typically has light waves of the same frequency, wavelength, and consistent phase relationship.

Appendix 3

1. Translation by the author.

2. The founder of ancient Korea in the year 2333 BCE and god-king. He is known around the world as Tengri Khan.

3. A shrine to the village deity.

4. Translated as the "Upper Shrine Deity," this deity also corresponds to the Tengri Khan and the mountain spirit in Korean shamanism.

5. Translated as "Lower Shrine Deity."

6. Large wooden poles built at the village entrance or on the roadside to pray to the village deity for the well-being, good harvest, and prosperity of the village.

7. An ancestral spirit jar.

8. The house-lot spirit.

9. The platform for crocks of sauces and condiments.

10. Living in a harmonious environment will neutralize karmic actions.

11. Regent Supreme of the Divine, who is the father of Dangun.

12. A sandalwood tree.

13. It is now called Baekdusan, or White-Head Mountain, located at the border between China and Korea.

14. Near White-Head Mountain.

15. A legendary figure who lived 180 millennia by eating the peaches at the stream of the goddess of immortality, Seo Wang-mu.

16. Emperor Yao (2324–2255 BCE) was a legendary sage-ruler of ancient China.

17. A weather phenomenon that occurs in northern China and Korea during winter, in which there is a seven-day cycle of change—three days of cold and four days of heat.

18. Jangsu of Goguryeo (394–491 CE), the twentieth monarch, is renowned for his elaborate tombs.

19. Goguryeo (37 BCE–668 CE) was one of the greatest powers in East Asia, and one of the Three Kingdoms of Korea, along with Baekje (18 BCE–660 CE) and Shilla (57 BCE–935 CE).

20. King Michu (264–284 CE) is the thirteenth king of the Shilla dynasty.

21. See footnote 17.

Appendix 4

1. See footnote 1 in Chapter 18.

Illustrations and Photo Credits

Introduction

Fig. 1: Wikimedia Commons
Fig. 2: author

1. Tao

Fig. 5: author
Fig. 6: author
Fig. 1.1: Shutterstock.com
Fig. 1.2: author

2. Tai Chi

Fig. 2.1: author
Fig. 2.2: author
Fig. 2.3: author
Fig. 2.4: Animals: Shutterstock.com;
Tai Chi symbols: author
Fig. 2.4: author

3. The Basic Principles of Yin and Yang

Fig. 3.1: Pixabay

4. Yin and Yang of Human Beings

Fig. 4.1: author

5. Yin and Yang of Sex

Fig. 5.1: author
Fig. 5.2: author

6. Yin and Yang of the Brain

Fig. 6.1: Tai Chi: author; brain: Shutterstock.com
Fig. 6.2: Homunculus: Shutterstock.com; Tai Chi: author

7. Yin and Yang of Food and Diet

Fig. 7.1: author
Fig. 7.2: Shutterstock.com

9. Yin and Yang of the Economy

Fig. 9.1: Courtesy of Sammy Silberstein

10. Yin and Yang of Perspective

Fig. 10.1: author

11. Yin and Yang of Music

Fig. 11.1: Keitma@123RF.com
Fig. 11.2: author
Fig. 11.3: author
Fig. 11.5: author

12. Yin and Yang of Wave

Fig. 12.1: Courtesy of Sammy Silberstein
Fig. 12.2: Courtesy of Soo-an Kim

13. Yin and Yang of the Universe

Fig. 13.1: Courtesy of Sammy Silberstein
Fig. 13.2: 123RF
Fig. 13.3: Courtesy of Soo-an Kim
Fig. 13.4: The photograph of Earth (fig. 13.4) in chapter 13 is used with permission of Clipart.com © 2010 Jupiterimages Corporation. Dotted lines with arrows courtesy of Sammy Silberstein
Fig. 13.5: Courtesy of Soo-an Kim
Fig. 13.6: Courtesy of Soo-an Kim
Fig. 13.7: Courtesy of Soo-an Kim
Fig. 13.8: Courtesy of Soo-an Kim

14. Trinity: Heaven, Earth, and Human Beings

Fig. 14.1: author
Fig. 14.2: A: author; B: Pixabay
Fig. 14.3: author
Fig. 14.4: author
Fig. 14.5: Shutterstock.com
Fig. 14.6: Shutterstock.com
Fig. 14.7: Shutterstock.com
Fig. 14.8: Shutterstock.com
Fig. 14.9: author
Fig. 14.10: author
Fig. 14.11: author
Fig. 14.12: Candle: Shutterstock.com; background: author
Fig. 14.13: author
Fig. 14.14: Cosmological View of Alchemists, used with permission of Bridgeman Images
Fig. 14.15: author
Fig. 14.16: author
Fig. 14.17: author
Fig. 14.18: author
Fig. 14.19: author
Fig. 14.20: author
Fig. 14.21: author
Fig. 14.22: author
Fig. 14.23: author
Fig. 14.24: author
Fig. 14.25: author
Fig. 14.26: 123RF
Fig. 14.27: author
Fig. 14.28: Shutterstock.com
Fig. 14.29: author
Fig. 14.30: author
Fig. 14.31: author
Fig. 14.32: author
Fig. 14.33: author
Fig. 14.34: Pixabay
Fig. 14.35: author
Fig. 14.36: author
Fig. 14.37: Shutterstock.com
Fig. 14.38: author
Fig. 14.39: author
Fig. 14.40: author
Fig. 14.41: author
Fig. 14.42: author
Fig. 14.43: author

15. Sasang—The Four Symbols

Fig. 15.1: author
Fig. 15.2: author
Fig. 15.3: author
Fig. 15.4: author
Fig. 15.5: author
Fig. 15.6: author
Fig. 15.7: author
Fig. 15.8: author
Fig. 15.9: author
Fig. 15.10: author
Fig. 15.11: author
Fig. 15.12: author
Fig. 15.13: Shutterstock.com
Fig. 15.14: author
Fig. 15.15: author
Fig. 15.16: Shutterstock.com
Fig. 15.17: author
Fig. 15.18: author
Fig. 15.19: Shutterstock.com
Fig. 15.20: Shutterstock.com
Fig. 15.21: Shutterstock.com
Fig. 15.22: author
Fig. 15.23: author
Fig. 15.24: 123RF
Fig. 15.25: author
Fig. 15.26: author
Fig. 15.27: author
Fig. 15.28: author
Fig. 15.29: 123RF

16. Sasang Medicine

Fig. 16.1: author
Fig. 16.2: Courtesy of Soo-an Kim
Fig. 16.3: Courtesy of Soo-an Kim
Fig. 16.4: Courtesy of Soo-an Kim

Fig. 16.5: Courtesy of Soo-an Kim
Fig. 16.6: Courtesy of Soo-an Kim
Fig. 16.7: author
Fig. 16.8: author
Fig. 16.9: author
Fig. 16.10: author
Fig. 16.11: author

17. The Five-Element Theory

Fig. 122: author
Fig. 17.1: author
Fig. 17.2: author
Fig. 17.3: author
Fig. 17.4: author
Fig. 17.5: Shutterstock.com
Fig. 17.6: Pixabay
Fig. 17.7: Shutterstock.com
Fig. 17.8: author
Fig. 17.9: author
Fig. 17.10: Pixabay
Fig. 17.11: author
Fig. 17.12: author
Fig. 17.13: author
Fig. 17.14: author
Fig. 17.15: author
Fig. 17.16: author
Fig. 17.17: author
Fig. 17.18: author
Fig. 17.19: author
Fig. 17.20: author
Fig. 17.21: author
Fig. 17.22: author
Fig. 17.23: author
Fig. 17.24: author

18. The Five Organs and the Five Elements

Fig. 18.1: Pixabay

19. The Five Elements of Diagnosis

Fig. 19.1: Pixabay
Fig. 19.2: Pixabay
Fig. 19.3: author
Fig. 19.4: author
Fig. 19.5: Pixabay
Fig. 19.6: author

20. The Five Elements of Herbs

Fig. 20.1: author
Fig. 20.2: author
Fig. 20.3: author

21. Attributes of the Eight Trigrams

Fig. 21.1: author
Fig. 21.2: Courtesy of Jae-ho Kim
Fig. 159: author
Fig. 160: author
Fig. 161: author
Fig. 21.3: Pond: Shutterstock.com;
    trigram: author
Fig. 21.4: author
Fig. 21.5: author
Fig. 21.6: author
Fig. 21.7: author
Fig. 21.8: author
Fig. 21.9: author

Fig. 21.10: author
Fig. 21.11: author

22. Arrangements and Applications of the Eight Trigrams

Fig. 22.1: author
Fig. 172: author
Fig. 173: author
Fig. 174: author
Fig. 175: author
Fig. 176: author
Fig. 22.2: author
Fig. 22.3: Shutterstock.com
Fig. 22.4: Shutterstock.com
Fig. 22.5: Shutterstock.com
Fig. 22.6: Shutterstock.com
Fig. 22.7: Shutterstock.com
Fig. 22.8: Courtesy of Soo-an
    Kim
Fig. 22.9: Shutterstock.com
Fig. 22.10: author
Fig. 22.11: author
Fig. 22.12: author
Fig. 22.13: author
Fig. 22.14: author
Fig. 22.15: author
Fig. 22.16: author
Fig. 22.17: author
Fig. 22.18: author
Fig. 22.19: Shutterstock.com
Fig. 22.20: Shutterstock.com

23. Interpretations of the Sixty-Four Hexagrams

Fig. 23.1: author
Fig. 23.2: author

Fig. 198: Shutterstock.com
Fig. 199: Shutterstock.com
Fig. 200: Shutterstock.com
Fig. 201: Shutterstock.com
Fig. 202: Shutterstock.com
Fig. 203: Shutterstock.com
Fig. 204: Shutterstock.com
Fig. 205: Shutterstock.com
Fig. 23.3 author
Fig. 207: Shutterstock.com
Fig. 208: Shutterstock.com
Fig. 209: Shutterstock.com
Fig. 210: Shutterstock.com
Fig. 211: Shutterstock.com
Fig. 212: Shutterstock.com
Fig. 213: Shutterstock.com
Fig. 214: Shutterstock.com
Fig. 215: Shutterstock.com
Fig. 216: Shutterstock.com
Fig. 217: Shutterstock.com
Fig. 218: Shutterstock.com
Fig. 219: Shutterstock.com
Fig. 220: Shutterstock.com
Fig. 221: Shutterstock.com
Fig. 222: Shutterstock.com
Fig. 223: Shutterstock.com
Fig. 224: Shutterstock.com
Fig. 225: Shutterstock.com
Fig. 226: Shutterstock.com
Fig. 227: Shutterstock.com
Fig. 228: Shutterstock.com
Fig. 229: Shutterstock.com
Fig. 230: Shutterstock.com
Fig. 231: Shutterstock.com
Fig. 232: Shutterstock.com
Fig. 233: Shutterstock.com
Fig. 234: Shutterstock.com
Fig. 235: Shutterstock.com
Fig. 236: Shutterstock.com
Fig. 237: Shutterstock.com

Fig. 238: Shutterstock.com
Fig. 239: Shutterstock.com
Fig. 240: Shutterstock.com
Fig. 241: Shutterstock.com
Fig. 242: Shutterstock.com
Fig. 243: Shutterstock.com
Fig. 244: Shutterstock.com
Fig. 245: Shutterstock.com
Fig. 246: Shutterstock.com
Fig. 247: Shutterstock.com
Fig. 248: Shutterstock.com
Fig. 249: Shutterstock.com
Fig. 250: Shutterstock.com
Fig. 251: Shutterstock.com
Fig. 252: Shutterstock.com
Fig. 253: Shutterstock.com
Fig. 254: Shutterstock.com
Fig. 255: Shutterstock.com
Fig. 256: Shutterstock.com
Fig. 257: Shutterstock.com
Fig. 258: Shutterstock.com
Fig. 259: Shutterstock.com
Fig. 260: Shutterstock.com
Fig. 261: Shutterstock.com
Fig. 262: Shutterstock.com
Fig. 23.4: Shutterstock.com
Fig. 23.5: author

Appendix 1. The Principles of I Ching Discovered by Science

Fig. A1.1: Pixabay
Fig. A1.2: author
Fig. A1.3: Left: author; right: Shutterstock.com
Fig. A1.4: author
Fig. A1.5: Shutterstock.com
Fig. A1.6: author

Fig. A1.7: Ear: Shutterstock.com
Fig. A1.8: Right diagram of vision: Shutterstock.com; left: author
Fig. A1.9: Wikimedia Commons
Fig. A1.10: author
Fig. A1.11: author
Fig. A1.12: author
Fig. A1.13: Wikimedia Commons
Fig. A1.14: author
Fig. A1.15: Shutterstock.com
Fig. A1.16: Shutterstock.com
Fig. A1.17: Left: author; right: Pixabay
Fig. A1.18: Shutterstock.com
Fig. A1.19: Pixabay
Fig. A1.20: Courtesy of Jae-ho Kim
Fig. A1.21: author
Fig. A1.22: Adobe Stock
Fig. A1.23: author

Appendix 2. I Ching in Daily Life

Fig. A2.1: 123RF
Fig. A2.2: 123RF
Fig. A2.3: Shutterstock.com
Fig. A2.4: Shutterstock.com
Fig. A2.5: author
Fig. A2.6: author
Fig. A2.7: author
Fig. A2.8: author
Fig. A2.9: Shutterstock.com
Fig. A2.10: Shutterstock.com
Fig. A2.11: 123RF
Fig. A2.12: author
Fig. A2.13: author
Fig. A2.14: author
Fig. A2.15: author

Fig. A2.16: author
Fig. A2.17: author
Fig. A2.18: Shutterstock.com
Fig. A2.19: author
Fig. A2.20: author
Fig. A2.21: author
Fig. A2.22: author
Fig. A2.23: author

Appendix 3. The Celestial Code Classic

Fig. A3.1: author
Fig. A3.2: Shutterstock.com
Fig. A3.3: Pixabay
Fig. A3.4: author
Fig. A3.5: author
Fig. A3.6: author
Fig. A3.7: author
Fig. A3.8: Shutterstock.com

Fig. A3.9: author
Fig. A3.10: author
Fig. A3.11: author
Fig. A3.12: author
Fig. A3.13: Shutterstock.com
Fig. A3.14: author
Fig. A3.15: author
Fig. A3.16: author
Fig. A3.17: author
Fig. A3.18: author

Acknowledgments

We would like to express our sincere gratitude to the following people whose contributions of time, energy, guidance, and support have made this book possible.

First and foremost, we would like to thank Dan Strutzel, our agent, for his invaluable support, guidance, and professionalism.

We are further indebted to the following people at St. Martin's Essentials for their continued support and valued recognition of our work. Joel Fotinos, the founder, vice president, and editorial director, enthusiastically and graciously offered to publish this text. Kate Davis, the copy editor, edited with exceptional clarity, insight, and judiciousness. Emily Anderson, the editorial assistant, cared for and assisted us compassionately.

Dr. David Lee would like to thank his teachers, Master Tae-hoon Kwon and Jae-hyung Lee, for their profound and wise teachings in Tao, medicine, and martial arts. Finally, he would like to thank his dear wife, Jinah, for her unwavering love and support.

Joseph K. Kim would like to thank the following people:

Naomi Gelperin Richman for her clear insight and meticulous editing of the entire manuscript.

Robin Schiesser, for her keen observations, careful proofreading, and thorough editing of the yin-yang chapters.

Seth Gold, Kim Moraes, Jonathan Gelperin, and his niece, Christine Chung, for reading, commenting on, and editing the yin-yang chapters of this book.

Alexia Miller, Amy G. Lederman, and his nephew, Christopher Kim, for their reading and editing of appendices.

Mr. Soo-an Kim, a freelance artist, for his help with many of the drawings accompanying the text in the Yin-Yang and Sasang chapters.

Mr. Sammy Silberstein, a graphic designer,

for many diagrams and drawings in the Yin-Yang chapters of the book.

His teacher, Professor Jae-yong Shin, for his inspiration, wisdom, and encouragement.

Lastly, his wife, Anne, and daughter, Clara, for their love and ongoing support.

About the Authors

Dr. David S. Lee, MD, OMD, PhD

Since his teenage years, Dr. David S. Lee has been deeply intrigued by Eastern philosophy, religion, and mysticism. Since then, he has studied the disciplines of Tao, meditation, and martial arts from many teachers. He is one of the chief disciples of both Master Tae-hoon Kwon and Master Jae-hyung Lee, two of the most celebrated and revered Taoist masters of Korea.

Dr. Lee began his study of Eastern medicine with a profound desire to apply his insights and experiences for the betterment of humanity. After receiving advanced degrees in Korea, he moved to the United States. He taught at several acupuncture colleges in the subjects of acupuncture, herbal medicine, Qi Gong, and Tai Chi. Feeling a need to link the perspective of traditional Eastern medicine to those of modern medicine, Dr. Lee earned his Doctor of Medicine (MD) degree.

Dr. Lee has served as a professor at the prestigious Kyung Hee University in Seoul, Korea, and conducted research at the University of California at Irvine and the Kwang Ju Institute of Science and Technology in Korea. He is the author of *Japan, the Country of Korean Immigrants* (in Korean) and *The Science and Tao of I Ching* (the Korean version of this book, co-authored with Joseph K. Kim). Currently, Dr. Lee maintains a private practice in Seoul, Korea.

Joseph K. Kim, LAc, OMD, PhD

As a third-generation Eastern medicine practitioner, Joseph K. Kim has been enthralled by the I Ching and Eastern philosophy since his teens. He served as a Chairman for the Department of Oriental Medicine at Emperor's College of Traditional Oriental Medicine in Santa Monica, California. In addition, he is a former acupuncture researcher at the University of California at Irvine, where he studied the effects of acupuncture on brain activity, as revealed by a functional MRI.

Kim has written and translated four books: *Oriental Medicine: A Modern Interpretation, An*

Introduction to Sasang Constitutional Medicine, Compass of Health: Using the Art of Sasang Medicine to Maximize Your Health, and *The Science and Tao of I Ching* (the Korean version of this book, co-authored with Dr. David S. Lee). A longtime Taoist arts practitioner, including Qi Gong and Tai Chi, Kim served as the team doctor for the 1988 United States Tae Kwon Do team (ITF). He maintains a private practice in Encino, California.

Index